1992

FIFTH EDITION

TELEVISION PRODUCTION

DISCIPLINES & TECHNIQUES

FIFTH EDITION

TELEVISION PRODUCTION

DISCIPLINES & TECHNIQUES

Thomas D. Burrows
California State University
Northridge

Donald N. Wood
California State University
Northridge

Lynne Schafer Gross
University of California
Los Angeles

 Wm. C. Brown Publishers

Book Team

Editor *Stan Stoga*
Developmental Editor *Jane F. Lambert*
Production Editor *Jane Matthews*
Designer *Eric Engelby*
Art Editor *Mary E. Swift*
Photo Editor *Laura Fuller*
Visuals Processor *Andrêa Lopez-Meyer*

Wm. C. Brown Publishers

President *G. Franklin Lewis*
Vice President, Publisher *Thomas E. Doran*
Vice President, Operations and Production *Beverly Kolz*
National Sales Manager *Virginia S. Moffat*
Group Sales Manager *Eric Ziegler*
Executive Editor *Edgar J. Laube*
Director of Marketing *Kathy Law Laube*
Marketing Manager *Carla J. Aspelmeier*
Managing Editor, Production *Colleen A. Yonda*
Manager of Visuals and Design *Faye M. Schilling*
Production Editorial Manager *Julie A. Kennedy*
Production Editorial Manager *Ann Fuerste*
Publishing Services Manager *Karen J. Slaght*

WCB Group

President and Chief Executive Officer *Mark C. Falb*
Chairman of the Board *Wm. C. Brown*

Cover photos: front: © Cosimo Scianna/The Image Bank; back: © Jon Love/The Image Bank

Copyeditor: Marla Irion

Copyright © 1978, 1982, 1986, 1989, 1992 by Wm. C. Brown Publishers. All rights reserved

Library of Congress Catalog Card Number: 90-85804

ISBN 0-697-12917-9

Printed in the United States of America by Wm. C. Brown Publishers, 2460 Kerper Boulevard, Dubuque, IA 52001

10 9 8 7 6 5 4 3 2 1

To our many students who have helped make teaching the most rewarding of all professions.

About the Authors

Thomas D. Burrows is a professor in the Radio-TV-Film Department at California State University, Northridge, in Los Angeles. He entered the teaching profession after a considerable career in the broadcast industry. Starting as a disc jockey in his hometown of Tucson, he worked his way up to a position with ABC, Los Angeles, serving as the director of the KABC-TV evening news program and of the nationally syndicated rock music show, *Shivaree*. Subsequently, Professor Burrows was with KCET-TV in Los Angeles where he received the Christopher, Emmy, and Peabody awards as producer of the PBS series *The Advocates*. As a consultant to ABC Sports in 1984, he set up a special training program that resulted in the employment of a number of students during the televised coverage of the Olympic Games. He holds a Master of Arts degree from the School of Journalism at the University of Southern California.

Donald N. Wood, professor of Radio-TV-Film, has been teaching at California State University, Northridge, since 1970. He has also taught at San Diego State University, The University of Michigan, and Westminster College (Pennsylvania). Dr. Wood's professional background has been largely in educational broadcasting. He was program coordinator for National Educational Television, area coordinator for the Midwest Program on Airborne Television Instruction, and director of ETV for the Hawaii State Department of Education, during which time he was executive producer of more than eight hundred television productions. Dr. Wood is the co-author of the textbook *Educational Telecommunications* and author of *Mass Media and the Individual* and *Designing the Effective Message*. He has his M.A. and Ph.D. degrees from The University of Michigan.

Lynne Schafer Gross teaches television production and theory at UCLA—in addition to her worldwide consulting assignments ranging from Malaysia to Africa to the Soviet Union. She was formerly professor and vice-chair of the Department of Communications at California State University, Fullerton, and has taught at several other colleges. She has served as Director of Programming for Valley Cable TV and has produced a number of television series for Los Angeles area TV stations. She has been very active in both the Academy of Television Arts and Sciences, serving as a governor and head of several committees, and in the Broadcast Education Association, serving as a board member and convention program chair. Her publication record includes nine books and over fifty articles. Her M.A. is from California State University, Long Beach, and her Ed.D. from UCLA.

About the Authors

Contents

Contents

Preface

As we complete the fifth edition of this text, it is an eye-opening experience to look back over the earlier editions in terms of technological changes during the past fifteen years or so. In the mid-1970s, the earliest computer-generated graphics were to be found only at the larger stations, networks, and production houses. We were only beginning to realize the potential of electronic field production—utilizing single-camera shooting techniques and postproduction editing facilities.

No one could begin to forecast the impact that would be made by CCD cameras, stereo audio, component recording, camcorders, digital technologies, relatively inexpensive computer-graphics programs, and so forth. In succeeding editions of the book, these revolutionary hardware developments and corresponding production adaptations have been treated with increasing detail as these technologies made their way into university-level production courses.

Most of us who have been teaching video production during the past decade have also been heavily involved in the struggle to obtain needed new equipment for our courses. For many of us, the process has been slow and disheartening. The battle to update our teaching equipment to anything that comes close to state-of-the-art facilities is a continuing frustration. Looking ahead, the move into sophisticated computer-graphics operations, expanded field production and editing applications, and the whole new world of digital equipment will be even more difficult.

At the same time, we are reminded over and over again—with each curriculum review, each industry advisory report, and every other pedagogical introspection—that we can never teach our production students everything they need to know about every piece of new equipment; the hardware will be outdated within a few months or couple years after they graduate. We can best teach equipment utilization by stressing principles of function and signal flow—by emphasizing fundamental concepts and disciplines of self-reliance so that our alumni can teach themselves how to operate the next generation of electronic magic boxes. We can best prepare them for the next three or four decades of video production by teaching them the fundamental concepts of how to use pictures and sounds to create good programs.

With these realities in mind, we have endeavored to present equipment function and operation in the most practical terms possible. It is important that students gain a basic understanding of the operation of all studio components. It is even more important that students comprehend how the use of each unit fits into the larger scheme of the video production sequence.

Our audio mixer, switcher, and other equipment examples have been updated, but—as in earlier editions—they have been selected because they are typical of the facilities that are being used at many of our teaching institutions.

In chapters 2 and 3, the audio mixing console we use as an example is the Yamaha MR-1642. Its sixteen input channels make it an ideal piece of equipment for professional applications in medium-sized studios. It has the added virtue of being designed to handle the special needs of stereo audio pre-record sessions. In chapter 7, we have used the Grass Valley Group 100 model as our primary example for the switcher. It is found in many industrial production facilities, and it also fits the needs of most university-level teaching situations.

As in previous editions, the equipment examples we use are provided as a way of helping students understand those underlying principles that are generic to all switchers, audio consoles, graphics programs, video recorders, and the rest of those other wonders of the electronic media. As professors of video production, we realize that we can't attempt to teach our students how to walk in off the street and sit down at any of the equipment at NBC Bur-

bank. What we do teach, and what is ultimately of utmost value, is a combination of attitudes and disciplines, analytical techniques, and operational skills that will serve our students well when they *do* get to NBC Burbank or to that top video production house in Mason City, Iowa.

As the dedication implies, we continue to revise this book as a *teaching text*—not as a reference book, not as a theoretical discussion, not as a catalog. We have included the technical information that we feel is essential for the beginning student to know, but we have not tried to produce an engineering manual. We have touched upon the basic elements of directing, but without undue emphasis that would detract from the basic production material.

In short, this text is designed to teach the first-year student what he or she needs to know about audio, lighting, cameras and lenses, the switcher, recording and editing, sets and graphics, on-camera talent, crew positions, and directing—both for studio production and for single-camera field production.

Therefore, in this edition, we continue to be concerned not only with the *techniques* of TV production (operating equipment and performing basic crew assignments) but also with the *disciplines* of TV production—those intangible professional attitudes and behaviors involving responsibility, self-control, initiative, judgment, respect, and similar attributes. We hope the reader will bear with us if we continue to return to this theme—but it is true that success in any aspect of the broadcasting field is going to depend more upon one's internalized set of attitudes than upon specific learned skills and techniques.

As in earlier editions, the text places essential information relating to equipment function and production crew organization within a sequence that is most suitable for broadcast laboratory instruction. We feel strongly that production proficiency (both the techniques and disciplines) can ultimately be gained only through continued involvement in a production operation. Students must have the opportunity to understand the creative process by working at all of the various positions within the crew structure. They must, however, be allowed to come to grips with the complexity of the ongoing production sequence by means of a series of planned gradual steps, each building upon previously mastered concepts and skills.

The two chapters on audio have been retained at the beginning of the book in order to present the student with an early model of the concepts of equipment function and crew organization. It is felt that this sequence of information—with an emphasis upon the audio signal flow—will facilitate a better understanding of comparable elements when they are presented later within the integrated audio and video operation.

We realize that many instructors will wish to structure their course units in a manner different from our suggested order. Some may wish to study cameras before audio—or place lighting considerations after basic camera structure and lens design. Others may want to discuss crew positions or basic directing skills earlier than our text does. To this end, we have tried to make each chapter as independent as possible—using appropriate cross-referencing of material. In keeping with this flexibility, extensive cross-referencing has been included with the new material so that instructors may be free to work out their own individual sequence of the presentation of material.

We have retained, at the end of each chapter, suggested training exercises or class projects. It is strongly recommended that these exercises and projects be carried out—to the extent possible in various facilities—in order to reinforce and adapt the material presented in each chapter. These exercises have been designed to resemble, as nearly as possible, the production realities of the primary types of programming and are structured to permit individualized input by both student and instructor. Production project scripts and materials are provided in appendix D on perforated pages so they can be revised and used apart from the text in studio exercises.

Having received positive feedback on the *Instructor's Manual* that accompanied the fourth edition, we have again included the handbook with this new edition. And we again solicit feedback from our colleagues who are using the manual and would like to contribute to its effectiveness.

We have had the advice and help of many colleagues and students in putting this text together. Although we cannot hope to single out everybody who has assisted or influenced us in the writing of the text, we should like to thank specifically those who have made major contributions to this revision of the text. In addition to those who have been acknowledged in earlier editions, we especially want to express our appreciation to Mike McDonald of Yamaha and Craig Shadburn of the Grass Valley Group, both of whom have given generously of their time and technical explanations and graphic resources. We again thank Professor Augie Grant (University of Texas at Austin) for the material in the color plates and related information in chapter 5. We extend our continued gratitude to Wayne Parsons, technical director of *Entertainment Tonight,* and his graphics colleagues at Paramount Studios—Ron Clark and Harry Sherman. We are indebted to Ralph Sariego, vice-president of TV production at Universal Studios and several of his associates—Carl Large, Rick Bigby, and Steve Spencer. And we thank many of our fellow professors—especially Jay Roper (NBC News west coast director) for his repeated formal and informal contributions.

Despite the support and assistance from our colleagues and students, there undoubtedly are errors to be found. For these, we assume full responsibility.

Except for those otherwise credited, all photographs used in the text were taken by the authors.

Introduction to TV Production

●●●●●●●●●●●●●●●●●

Electronic camera television production is a fascinating, demanding, and rewarding enterprise—whether done in a studio or on a remote location. There is not only the obvious intoxication of glamour and activity but also the quiet exhilaration of being part of a very captivating and important process of modern communications technology.

Although this text may appear to be concerned primarily with developing proficiency in the technical aspects of television production—the *techniques* of operating the TV tools and the *disciplines* of functioning in a television team—another primary purpose should be kept in mind. The most important goal of a college-level production course should simply be that of creating an understanding of the video production process—regardless of one's ultimate vocational objectives.

The realities of television employment are such that, while some members of the class may follow a career in production-based positions, others will find employment in office-based jobs such as operations, programming, sales, or management. However, studio production training will also provide a basis for these categories of employment. Management decisions constantly revolve around what is done in the studio or, of more importance, how efficiently it is done. Sales representatives, scriptwriters, advertising executives, and general managers must all have a grasp of the production techniques presented in this book.

1.1 Techniques and Disciplines

Successful television is dependent upon the premise that every member of the production unit has, over a period of time, developed a set of individual *techniques* and *disciplines* in order to cope with the complexities of various types of programs. Although these two terms do not necessarily refer to mutually exclusive categories, they do describe somewhat differing aspects of the total production sequence.

For their use within the broadcast context, the following definitions of these terms will be utilized.

Techniques refer to specific skills unique to the performance of any single position within the television crew structure. A technique reflects a degree of formal (or possibly informal) training related to production equipment, electronic or otherwise. An audio engineer's ability to select and position microphones for correct balance would be considered a technique. Such a definition, however, does not preclude the possibility of interaction with other crew members. A director's method of using cameras is thought of as a matter of individual initiative and specialized talent—founded upon a few basic techniques and principles of television communication.

At the beginning, it may be easiest for students of TV production to think of techniques as being those particular skills used in operating various pieces of equipment—knowledge of which buttons to push, how far certain knobs should be twisted, and where to connect a given plug, for example.

Disciplines comprise a complete series of procedures that are shared by and relate to the entire production unit. The use of proper voice procedure on the intercom network is a specific example. The thorough preparation and planning necessary before starting out on a remote EFP (electronic field production) recording involves considerable discipline. The interaction of the stage manager, the stage crew, the camera operators, and the performers in a studio involves a whole range of disciplines for efficient operation. Disciplines imply a consistency of individual action as well as a consideration for others in the same team effort.

One of the most crucial elements of TV production discipline is that of *responsibility*—dependability, a conscientious effort always to do one's best. In the complex chain of the television crew, there can be no weak link. In any given production situation, the efforts of dozens of persons may be coordinated in an intricate pattern. If one person fails to carry out his or her specific function at the right moment, many precious minutes—or hours—of costly production time can be wasted.

Production discipline also implies many other intangible values and skills. An attitude of *respect* must be acquired, respect for equipment as well as for other members of the production crew. A balanced sense of *initiative* and *self-control* must be concurrently developed—knowing when to jump in with a suggestion or action and when to remain quiet and stick to your own job. Learning how to deal with your own anxiety—how to remain *calm* when the production elements start to fall apart—is another important aspect of developing a sense of television discipline.

To use a simple analogy, when learning to drive a car, most people quickly master the separate *techniques* of turning, braking, accelerating, and shifting gears. The manner in which we combine these skills, make instant judgments, and coordinate timing to make a left turn in heavy traffic requires the additional element of *discipline*.

As a television production student you therefore must be concerned not only with the *techniques* of knowing precisely how to use all of the equipment but also with the development of your own sense of production *discipline* so that others will be able to depend upon you with confidence. In fact, one of the most revealing tests of your production capabilities is to answer this simple question: Do other people want you on their production team? Unless you can answer *yes* with confidence to

Figure 1–1
What kind of student are
you? What is your attitude?
What do you hope to get
out of this course?

that query, you probably will want to rethink your studio attitudes, your sense of professional discipline and dedication, and your academic and professional goals.

1.2 Development of a Professional Attitude

In talking about abstract concepts such as *discipline* and the development of something called *professional attitude,* it may be helpful to think about them from two different perspectives—first, personal goals and self-image, and second, attitudes toward others.

Attitude and Self-Image

To begin with, you need to ask yourself something about your personal goals. *What are your professional aims?* What do you hope to do in broadcasting or film? Do you have specific occupational goals? Are you broadly concerned

with doing something socially constructive with media? In any case, what role will education or specific training play in attaining those goals? Then ask yourself *what your immediate learning goals are.* What do you hope to get out of this class? What are you doing to ensure that this will be a constructive experience?

In answering queries such as these, you can come closer to defining a personal value system and a sense of direction. These, in turn, lead to a sharpening of your own sense of professional development and the need for internal discipline. This should help you begin to see specific goal-oriented tasks that revolve around the educational system. You are better able to recognize the need to learn. (See figure 1–1.)

You should be able to think in terms of educational course work beyond your immediate TV production class. What other related academic work do you need? Journalism?

Business communications? Political science? Public relations? Management? Communication history? Government regulations? Message design? English? And what academic course work is needed in the liberal arts that will help give you a perspective on humankind and your place in contemporary society—an understanding of the *role* of modern telecommunications? Philosophy? History? Foreign cultures? Psychology? The arts? Environmental sciences? You cannot be a successful communicator unless you know something of the content you have to communicate—and unless you understand the environment of the communication process.

When asked what kind of broadcasting student they would like to hire, many top television executives and network officers reply, "Give me students who are intelligent, sensitive, aware of social issues, alert, concerned with human relations, adaptable, and able to solve problems, and I'll teach them the tools and techniques of the business in a few weeks on the job."

In this specific production course, you should begin to realize the need to learn how to understand the telecommunications process and how to use the tools of the communication enterprise. You will start to develop a sense of studio discipline that grows out of an appreciation of the total process of TV production.

One specific discipline mentioned in section 1.1 is the *balance between initiative and self-control*. There are numerous times on any television production when some little thing appears to be wrong. The lighting director is not adding enough back light. The director is ready to take the wrong shot. The stage manager looks as if he or she were going to walk in front of the camera. What do you do in each of these situations? Do you speak up or remain silent? Do you know enough about the total situation to understand what is really happening? Only with enough studio experience and a knowledge of all equipment and all positions can you determine when you should take the initiative to avert a problem and when you should remain in your place.

Another kind of production self-discipline concerns the problem of *dealing with your own anxieties*. In any television production, various crew members are going to experience differing degrees of anxiety. First, you must accept the fact that some anxiety—some amount of nervousness—is good; it keeps you on your toes. People would not be able to turn in a peak performance if they were not a little bit edgy and apprehensive. Second, you will derive some solace from the fact that you are not alone. Every topflight director has gone through the same process, and everyone in your class is experiencing the same sensation to some extent. Third, you should realize that anxiety is born of insecurity—ignorance of specific equipment or procedures. If you are uneasy about a particular assignment or function, make certain you find out what you can about it. Face your shortcomings and fill in your gaps. For example, review the special effects **bank** (or bus) of the switcher, or ask your instructor to go over the master control room patching again. With knowledge and experience comes confidence.

Recognize also that everyone else is demonstrating some degree of tension and near-panic during the stress of early production. In the heat of studio operations, people will often act and react with a sense of urgency and impatience that borders on abrasiveness. Accept this as uncharacteristic behavior and try not to take any criticism or sharp comments personally.

Attitudes toward Others

As you cultivate more confidence and build a positive self-attitude, you will also be able to develop a better sense of production discipline and an affirmative attitude toward the entire crew effort.

You must recognize the fact that studio television production is emphatically a *team effort*. There is no room in the production process for the lazy or the goldbrick (if you eventually want to succeed in the field). Neither is there room for the braggart or the ego-tripper (even if your uncle owns the station).

A strong sense of discipline and a professional attitude will result in a concern about the success of the program itself. If you are truly interested in the field, then you are, by definition, a *communicator*. In addition, if you are concerned with the communication process, then you want to see the communicative act—the creation of the television message—succeed. You *care* about contributing to a successful communication experience. If the communicative act, the television production, should not succeed, then you care—as a student of the process—to learn why it did not work. You analyze the problems and dissect the mistakes so that you can be part of a successful effort on the next production. If you do not deeply care about seeing the communication process work, then perhaps you should not pursue studies in this field.

As you develop your sense of professional concern, you will also increase your professional responsibility toward others and toward the production. You will want to make certain that your dependability cannot be questioned. When you are assigned a job, it will be done. When you are supposed to be somewhere (including the start of a lab production), you will be there on time—or earlier.

Another important attribute of studio discipline is *respect*—respect for equipment and respect for other individuals, both **talent** and crew. As explained in the following chapters of this text, by gaining an understanding of the way most equipment works, you will begin to develop some appreciation and sense of *respect for the equipment*. The tools you are working with are not toys; they are not to be mistreated and played with. No professional handles a piece of equipment just to play with it. The tool is there to do a specific job, and that is what it is used for. Remember that the purchase and maintenance and repair of all equipment is limited by a very strict budget—whether in a plush network, a small studio, a noncommercial station, or a university training facility. Once a piece of equipment is broken, two things happen: (1) the studio, or some small part of the studio operation, is out of commission for some period of time; (2) someone, somehow, must pay for the repair of the equipment.

You also show your respect for the equipment and studio by adhering to the established studio policies and regulations. Most studios will have certain operating policies concerning safety rules; supervision of use of facilities; prohibition of eating, drinking, and smoking in certain areas; storage of materials; and so forth. Make certain you are aware of the specific regulations in the studio where you are working—and follow them.

Respect for individuals is manifest in several ways. Most of the people you are working with in a training situation are learners—as you are. They deserve the same respect and patient treatment to which you are entitled. Unless you feel you are so superior to your colleagues that you are above evaluation, you have no right to treat others with disrespect. You show your respect—to crew members and performers alike—by being patient and understanding, by offering assistance when appropriate, and by being genuinely appreciative and congratulatory when a good job is done.

There are several occasions when assistance is appropriate. Two specific instances are in setting up a production and in **striking**—or cleaning up—after a program is recorded. While a show is being set up, some crew members may have relatively little to do—camera operators, recording engineers, projectionists, technical directors, and the like. (Some of these crew members may have specific jobs assigned to them.) People who are free during the early stages of studio preparation should make themselves available to the lighting and staging director or directors to assist in the initial setup.

The same thing is true after the production is completed. Everyone has his or her own area to strike (camera operators coiling cables, audio engineer putting away microphones and cables), but some positions (for example, those of technical director, recording engineers) may be free sooner than others. Whenever these crew members have finished cleaning up their positions, they should assist in the general strike. It is everyone's job to see that the studio and all equipment are restored to their original condition—ready for the next production crew or class. (In unionized shops, of course, one should not cross union jurisdictions to assist someone else. Camera engineers do not handle stage props, and so forth.)

Whether and when to offer assistance often become a gray area. Do you move to "save" a fellow student if he or she is about to commit some obvious blunder? (This is related to finding a balance between initiative and self-control.) Do you, as technical director, follow the director's command when he or she tells you to punch up the wrong camera? Do you, as a floor assistant, obey the stage manager when he or she tells you to move a prop while the camera shooting it is on the air? In a professional, real-world situation you would probably be correct to hold off on executing the given instruction; you would try to save the person giving the instruction by quickly and considerately pointing out the apparent error. In a learning situation, however, you may not be doing the person a favor by saving him or her too frequently. If a director repeatedly makes the same kind of mistake by giving the wrong command and crew members repeatedly save the director by not following the command, are they really helping the di-

rector to learn? Or are they just helping reinforce a bad habit? The lab production is, after all, the place to learn by making mistakes—and seeing the results of those mistakes.

There are many similar gray areas where there is no fast and simple correct response. It is the challenge and excitement of these uncertainties that make television production the stimulating field it is. It is the quick-thinking professional who, because of training and experience and sense of personal discipline, is able to make the right decisions.

1.3 Production Operations

At the outset it will be realized, of course, that there are several different levels of television production. Some TV productions are staged in mammoth studios with millions of dollars' worth of equipment and crews consisting of dozens of people. On the other hand, many worthwhile productions are undertaken in tiny, makeshift quarters with a few hundred dollars' worth of equipment and a crew of two or three—or even one. In between these two extremes are most of the typical situations you are likely to encounter.

Broadcast Categories

The most complex kind of studio productions are likely to be found at *network levels*—both commercial and noncommercial. Figure 1–2 shows typical network productions. (It should be stressed that noncommercial public television operations can—and often do—surpass commercial television productions in terms of program complexities, size of crews, glamour and excitement, and vital production challenges.) Productions at a network level will usually be well budgeted and housed in a large modern facility.

At the *station level* of production, there is a wide variety of origination complex-

Figure 1–2
Major network studio productions can involve a crew of several dozen engineers, technicians, and production positions. Syndication markets including cable TV have provided new programming formats and job opportunities. (Photos courtesy of KCET, Los Angeles [*top*]; and *Entertainment Tonight,* [*bottom*])

Figure 1–3

Even a small-station production will involve a crew of a dozen or so audio, camera, lighting, staging, and other production operators and technicians.

ities. Some commercial network-owned-and-operated stations and some of the major public TV stations will have production facilities that rival the network operations. At the other end of the station spectrum, many smaller stations will have woefully inadequate facilities—cramped studio or studios, small production crews, and older equipment patched together to meet minimal Federal Communications Commission (FCC) broadcast standards. (See figure 1–3.)

Another level of professional operations includes *independent production centers*. There are many different kinds of facilities that are not directly connected with a broadcast outlet. Some are major studios producing commercials or independent programs for network-level distribution. Some are smaller outfits that produce a wide variety of commercial and noncommercial programming. Many independent companies turn out programming without any studio facilities or production crews of their own; they pull a package together and then go out and rent a studio and hire a crew to do the actual production. Most of the major network entertainment series, for example, are produced by independent production centers—ranging from large Hollywood film studios (Universal, Columbia, Paramount) to major independent television producers (Spelling-Goldberg, Dick Clark, MTM) to specialized packagers (Goodson-Todman, Proctor & Gamble, Children's Television Workshop).

Nonbroadcast Telecommunications

A growing and increasingly important area of production operations is found in nonbroadcast areas. These afford many professional opportunities—with some fields outlined in the following discussion expanding at a rate of 30 to 40 percent a year. For example, over one billion dollars is spent annually on noncommercial programming for industry, government, schools, and religious groups.

Figure 1–4
Many closed-circuit audiovisual television installations for schools, corporate video setups, and medical training centers will need a production crew of only two or three persons.

The term *corporate video* (or *industrial TV* or *private video*) encompasses all types of telecommunications used for various business and industrial applications—sales training, corporate public relations, employee staff development, administrative and management communication, and consumer relations. When integrated with computers, laser discs, fiber-optics distribution systems, and satellites, these uses result in some of the most advanced applications of the television medium.

One of the biggest fields of all is *government media*. Local, state, and federal agencies are involved in a myriad of telecommunications projects. The federal government, for example, is probably the world's largest television and film producer. Military applications, including the Armed Services Radio and Television Network, account for worldwide operations—as does the State Department's Voice of America and its worldwide satellite operation, *Worldnet*.

Possibly the most rapidly expanding area is in the field of *medical and health services*.

More than 80 percent of the 7,000 hospitals in the country use television and related media for patient education, in-service training (staff development), and/or public and community relations.

Another burgeoning field is in *religious productions*. Although many of the established denominations have long made use of free public-service time offered by commercial broadcasters (*Directions, It Is Written, Christophers*), the greatest use is with the evangelical or charismatic groups. At least five such church bodies operate their own satellite networks. The Christian Broadcasting Network in Norfolk, Virginia, claims to have some of the most advanced TV studios in the world.

School-level productions are another category to be considered. Thousands of schools, ranging from preschools to medical schools at universities, have television production facilities for various instructional and demonstration purposes. A typical media-center studio is illustrated in figure 1–4. Again, the quality of production facilities ranges from converted broom closets to massive **closed-circuit (CCTV)** installations that rival anything seen at the network level. Most college and university facilities used for teaching TV production are probably equipped on a level comparable to that of a local station—barely adequate to do the job, never extensive enough to do everything desired.

A final major area to be considered is *cable TV production*. Although closely related to broadcast distribution in terms of quality and audience, cable TV represents another whole ancillary field. There are approximately 30,000 persons employed in the cable industry—mainly in sales, management, and distribution. However, another completely new field has emerged around the cable production companies—outfits such as Home Box Office, Showtime, Cable News Network, Black Entertainment Television, the Entertainment and Sports Programming Network (ESPN), and dozens of others. Supplying programming to the cable systems via satellites, these companies—none of which existed prior to 1975—account for a rapidly expanding production market.

An idea of the significance and magnitude of all of these various nonbroadcast production operations can be gleaned by simply looking at respective employment figures. According to United States Department of Labor statistics, in 1990 there were well over 200,000 people employed in broadcast operations, including both stations and networks. By contrast, it is estimated that close to 300,000 people were employed in all of the nonbroadcast areas just discussed (cable, corporate, government and military, medical, religious, and school projects).

Small-Format Television

Although most of us tend to think of television in terms of the professional levels we have discussed previously—and, indeed, most production courses and textbooks are geared toward

this type of production—we should also be aware of an increasingly important phenomenon known as **small-format television** (sometimes referred to simply as "video"). This term generally refers to nonbroadcast television designed for limited circulation, as well as to cable production and low-power (LPTV) station operations. Many of the topics in this book—such as principles of audio, lighting, theory of camera operation, VTR recording and editing, single-camera production, and pictorial design—apply to small-format television as well as to professional uses.

During the past several years, we have seen a communications evolution (the term *communications revolution* is too much overworked) in the development of smaller, inexpensive television gear. For a few hundred dollars it is now possible to obtain a small, nonbroadcast, hand-held **camcorder**—which includes an industrial-quality camera, a built-in microphone, and a video recorder (either of several ½-inch or 8mm formats) all built into one lightweight unit. With this basic equipment, a two- or three-person crew—or even a one-person operation—is in the small-format television business. (See figure 1–5.)

Small-format television operations are undertaken for a variety of reasons. Most of them could probably be divided into three basic areas: personal recording, community communicators, and video art. *Personal recording* includes several approaches and purposes. Basically, it is concerned with those video uses that are never intended to be seen by a large number of viewers. It may be thought of in part as an extension of home movies—recording family reunions, weddings, baby's first steps, birthday parties, last wills and testaments, and so forth. It may also include more serious purposes, such as self-evaluation improvement programs, recording marriage counseling sessions, psychiatric training programs, or recording and analyzing an individual's golf backswing. What all of these personal re-

Introduction to TV Production

cording applications have in common is that the product is never intended for distribution or viewing beyond a very small handful of participants.

The area of *community communicators,* however, gets into a little more ambitious use of the small-format medium. Concerned individuals use what is sometimes called "guerrilla television" or "underground video" in order to try to tell a story or get a message across. Equipped with portable cameras or camcorders, private citizens record an event, a social happening, or a neighborhood problem—often dealing with consumer affairs, ethnic problems, or environmental concerns. Using school closed-circuit systems, community cable TV systems with public access channels, and portable video players at

community meetings, community communicators try to reach as large an audience as possible, to offer an alternative to establishment-type channels dominated by government bureaucracy and conventional economic enterprises.

Another whole category of video usage might be labeled *video art.* This is the intriguing use of video equipment to create artistic images and sounds perhaps entirely unrelated to actual reality. In video art, the artist/producer is concerned solely with the artistic elements of composition—balance, mood, tone, intensity, shading, color, pacing, sounds, harmony, texture. The artists may be concerned solely with the creation for its own aesthetic sake, or they may want to try to reach as large an audience as possible through any

Figure 1–6
Many types of video-art techniques can be achieved even with the simplest kind of monochrome facilities.

of the community channels. This usage of television may, of course, also be carried into the studio, as illustrated in figure 1–6. Using the variety of professional equipment available for electronic controls, video manipulation, special effects, and signal distortion, the creator has moved far beyond small-format television.

1.4 Production Approaches

One other distinction should be made at this point. This is a distinction that somewhat parallels our discussion of professional and small-format television, although it applies primarily to major professional situations. Students of television production today should be acutely aware of the contrast between *multiple-camera production* and *single-camera production.*

Multiple-Camera Production

Until a few years ago, any discussion of television production dealt almost entirely with **multiple-camera production,** which was concerned primarily with multiple-camera *studio*

production. All TV production was presumed to occur in a "real-time" situation—in which a 30-minute program actually took thirty consecutive minutes of production time—with two or more cameras covering the action, and all editing decisions instantaneously executed as the director switched from one camera to another during the half hour.

Usually this took place in the TV studio, although location or *remote* productions such as political events or sporting contests could be covered wherever the action was taking place. The underlying principle of all multiple-camera productions remained the same, however: several cameras would cover the production from different angles and with different perspectives, with all **editing** (camera switching) being executed while the program was in progress.

During the first decade of popular television, up to the mid-1950s, this meant that all production was done *live*—it was actually happening while the viewers watched. Regardless of the rehearsal time involved, once the program was on the air live—whether a drama, musical program, variety show, or

Introduction to TV Production

wrestling match—the audience watched it at the exact time it was taking place. If the set fell down or the costumes ripped, the viewers saw it all. Although there are relatively few live productions on television today, those production personnel involved in live telecasts—whether a local parade, the news, the Olympics, or a national political event—would readily agree that this is still the most exciting, nerve-racking, and challenging area of television programming. The 1976 debate between Jimmy Carter and Gerald Ford when the audio line went dead for twenty-eight minutes is a good example.

In the mid-1950s, **videotape** recording came into existence making it possible actually to record a program—in its entirety—on videotape and play it back at a later time. It was no longer necessary to present everything live as it happened. It was possible to schedule productions at more convenient times and to go back and re-record a program that had a bad production problem. The era of **live-on-tape production** was created. Most programs—variety shows, talk shows, game shows—were still produced in their entirety, but were then recorded for later playback. Many multiple-camera productions, of course, are still produced in this manner today.

In the late 1960s and early 1970s, *electronic editing* facilities became more and more sophisticated. It was now possible to record programs in segments and then piece them together in a **postproduction editing** process. Variety programs were one of the first genre to take advantage of this process. Segments with guest stars could be shot out of sequence; production numbers with costume and scenery changes could be interrupted while the changes were made; programs could be shot in different locations and edited together later. A 60-minute variety-musical program might take all day to record. A 90-minute extravaganza special might take days or even weeks to record and edit together.

The principle, however, was still one of multiple-camera recording. Several cameras would be shooting each segment, with instantaneous editing decisions being made at the switcher; and the individual segments would be put together later. This process was carried into dramatic formats also with daytime serials (which have always been produced using video, nonfilm techniques) and some situation comedies (which started using multiple-camera video techniques and postproduction editing in the early 1970s).

Finally in the late 1970s, there evolved the ultimate adaptation of multiple-camera production—using separate videotape recorders to record each camera independently and simultaneously during the continuous performance. This *multiple-camera recording* process allows the director to concentrate on acting and camera work—without having to make instantaneous editing decisions. Then at some time well after the production recording, the director can sit down with the four or five videotapes of the program and use sophisticated computer-based postproduction editing equipment to put the program together—picking and choosing among the four or five camera angles available at any given moment in the action.

Many major network-level productions now regularly use this technique. Although there are increased production costs incurred by the use of three or four extra video recorders and postproduction editing facilities, producers generally feel that the slick-paced, more polished final program is worth the slight increase in production price. (This multiple-camera recording process was pioneered in the 1950s, using multiple film cameras to record continuous action in the shooting of *I Love Lucy*.) By the late 1980s, some of the more ambitious 3- to 10-minute music videos were using such elaborate multicamera and postproduction editing techniques that they were costing as much as an hour-long variety show did just a decade earlier.

Single-Camera Production

By the mid-1970s, however, it was evident that an entirely new television production process was evolving—**single-camera production.** With computer-based editing facilities, it was now possible to put together a very polished studio or location production using only a single electronic television camera. Actually, this evolution had two parallel movements.

On the one hand, single-camera production techniques came about as an attempt to emulate filmic techniques in recording *dramatic* programs. Motion picture films have almost always used a single-film camera in the making of dramatic pictures. This method represented the maximum control a director could have over the production elements. Each shot could be carefully staged; lighting could be arranged individually; microphone placement could be worked out for a single camera; actors could be positioned precisely. This was an exactitude of control that was never attainable when shooting with multiple television cameras in a continuously running scene. The first experimentation with prime-time, full-length single-camera recording of television drama started in the early 1970s. As editing devices have become more sophisticated, both commercial and noncommercial dramatic programs have made use of this production approach.

As a counterpart to the dramatic uses of single-camera production, *journalistic* applications evolved even faster. With the development of small, hand-held broadcast-quality video cameras in the 1970s, a new era of **electronic news gathering** (ENG) was ushered in. (Professional single-camera ENG techniques are not to be confused with small-format video, described in section 1.3.) Rapid coverage of news had always been hampered by film cameras because of the delay in processing the film. With the advent of small video cameras and portable recorders, however, news footage could be recorded on videotape, immediately edited as needed, and put on the air without delay. Thus, for both dramatic programs and journalistic purposes, the concept of single-camera video production came into its own in the mid-1970s.

By 1980, many other broadcast applications of single-camera *electronic field production* (EFP) were in common usage for local commercials, documentaries, promos, magazine-format productions, location interviews, talk-show segments, videos, and so forth. And as the equipment became even lighter and less expensive, other nonbroadcast video programming turned to ENG/EFP techniques; corporate video, medical uses, training materials, government productions, schooling applications, and cable TV were all moving out of the studio and into the field—adopting filmic techniques for video programs.

1.5 A Quick Survey of the Tools and Working Areas

Before getting into any of the specifics of television techniques and disciplines, it may be helpful to have a quick overview of the various elements of TV production. What are the tools you will be using? Where are they usually used? And, generally, how are they used?

Although this book is not to be concerned with the creative processes of writing and producing, it should nevertheless be stressed that the first tool used in any TV production is the *typewriter* or *computer/word processor;* the first working area, the office or den. First and foremost, television is a medium of communication. The tools exist so that people can attempt to communicate with one another, so that they can send messages from one point to another. Without that message—without that attempt to communicate—the glamour of television is reduced to a meaningless pile of glittering gibberish. In the words of Edward R. Murrow, "All you have is a lot of wires and lights in a box."

Introduction to TV Production

Figure 1–7
The graphics workstation is where all electronic artwork is generated.

Once the program is conceived, once the message is designed and the script is written, you still are not ready to move into the arena of the television studio. Several other working areas come to your attention first. Are there sets to be built? Start in the *scene shop.* Are there costumes to be obtained? Are there props or furniture to be used? Rummage through the *storage area* or visit commercial rental agencies for that Louis XIV chair or the coonskin cap. Are there graphics to be designed? Get your order into the *graphic artist's studio* or *computer-graphics workstation* (figure 1–7).

Many different kinds of TV productions will demand some type of simulated studio rehearsal before you can get into the actual facilities. If there are dramatic scenes to be rehearsed or complicated pieces of stage busi-

ness to be worked out, reserve the *rehearsal hall,* find an empty studio, or use masking tape to mark off the area in the cafeteria.

The television **studio** (figure 1–8) is, of course, the main center of activity that almost everyone associates with TV production. Whether a converted classroom, a remodeled warehouse, or a million-dollar facility, the studio is where everything is brought together—and the action is frenzied. One of the first things you will notice upon entering a studio for the first time is probably the *permanent sets*—the news set, the kitchen for the homemakers' program, the discussion set for the noontime talk show.

There probably also is a cyclorama or other wall covering stretched out over two or three of the studio walls. Look overhead and

Figure 1–8
The studio—with its lights, cameras, and sets—represents the hub of all production action.

you will see one of the key elements of any production—the tools of *television lighting*. The lighting instruments themselves, the spotlights and scoops, are probably hung on some sort of grid or **catwalk** suspended from the high ceiling of the studio. Many different types of lighting are used in various studios. Possibly over in a corner will be the lighting control center, a patching system, and a dimmer board; these elements may be located in a control room.

Probably the most important tools in the production situation are those electronic pickup devices that can translate the pictures and sounds into electric impulses, which can then be handled electronically as separate elements of the television signal—the **camera** and the

microphone. The cameras are the most obvious of these devices, stashed away in one corner of the studio. In a basic studio setup, there will probably be two or three small cameras mounted on simple tripods. In a large studio, there may be four or five professional color cameras mounted on pedestals, with at least one mounted atop a large crane or boom.

The microphones are more inconspicuous. Stored out of sight until time to set up for the production, they are then connected to cables and plugged into studio inputs located around the studio walls. One microphone might be attached to a **boom** or **giraffe** where it can be suspended above a performer's head and manipulated by an operator holding on to the other end of the boom arm. Some microphones are mounted on stands for the announcer or newscasters. Many are designed as **lavalieres** to be worn around the neck; others can simply be carried by the performers.

Many productions, of course, do not take place in the studio. They may be **remote** recordings (or **live** broadcasts) from a concert hall, political convention, council chamber, sports arena, main street, or playing field. In fact, with today's lightweight camcorders, portable equipment, and satellite **uplinks,** one of the "working areas" of television production happens to be anyplace on the planet where something interesting is going on.

Once outside the studio, problems are considerably complicated. Extraneous noises cannot be controlled; lighting is inconsistent; background distractions cannot be eliminated. If outdoors, audio problems may be compounded by wind and crowd noises; lighting conditions may suddenly change; the weather may be unpredictable; equipment may fail many miles from the repair shop; local demonstrators may suddenly decide they want to be on television. If indoors at a nonstudio location, the artificial lighting may have to be supplemented by portable television lighting. Such is the fun and challenge of location productions.

Back in the production center, the next working area to examine is the control rooms. There may be several different kinds of control areas associated with the TV studio. The first of these may be the **audio booth,** or audio **control room,** as shown in figure 1–9. This is where all of the sound elements are mixed and handled. The microphone inputs from the studio are terminated in the audio booth, usually in a **patch board.** Then the microphones can be mixed through a master audio board or console. Other audio elements can be added here also—record turntables, audio recorders, sound from a video recorder, and so forth. The composite sound output can then be either re-

corded or sent to a master control room where it is mixed with the video signal and recorded onto videotape—or transmitted live.

In the **video control room** or studio booth (figure 1–10), you will find the comparable video mixing elements. Together with a bewildering array of television monitors of varying sizes and functions, the most important tool you will see is the **TV switcher.** This is the piece of equipment that selects and mixes television signals from various cameras and other sources (in much the same way the audio control board handles the sound sources) and comes up with the final composite picture that is the visual half of the entire production. The studio control room may also contain the lighting controls and dimmer board if they are not located on the studio floor. In many production setups, the **character generator** may also be found in the video control booth. This allows the director and technical director to have immediate physical control over the electronic visuals.

The next stop on a quick tour would probably be the **master control room.** (See figure 1–11.) Located a short distance from the studio and control booths, the master control room is the "hangout" for the engineers. The **videotape recorders** are located here, as well as the time-base corrector (TBC), electronic monitoring equipment, processing amplifiers, and so forth. Depending upon the scope of the operation, this might be quite an imposing array of machines. Finally, and most important, the master control room usually is the center for all camera-control functions—the generator for the synchronizing pulse that drives all cameras and the individual electronic controls for each camera.

In any modern production operation, another major facility is the **editing room** or rooms. Possibly located close to the master control room (but, ideally, not part of it) may be one or more small semiprivate cubicles

Figure 1–9
Two audio control rooms: *top,* many audio booths are arranged so that the audio operator has a view of the studio floor; *bottom,* in other audio control rooms, the audio operator will watch all program action on monitors. (*Bottom* photo courtesy of KABC-TV, Los Angeles)

Introduction to TV Production

Figure 1–10
Two video control rooms: *top,* the technical director would sit at the switcher at the left; the director, associate director, and production assistant, would be on the right of the lighting board—the large monitor is the program line and the smaller monitors are for cameras, videotape playbacks, remote pickups, special effects previewing, and so forth; *bottom,* the technical director punches the buttons on the switcher to put the selected camera on the air. (*Top* photo courtesy of KTLA, Los Angeles; *bottom* photo courtesy of KABC-TV, Los Angeles)

Introduction to TV Production

Figure 1–11
In many large stations and production centers, the master engineering facilities may be located either in a centralized master control room or in a number of specialized centers. These are two areas in the engineering complex of a large independent station. *Top,* the master switching area with its comprehensive monitoring facilities for all studios and cameras, videotape players, remote feeds, satellite pickups, and auxiliary lines. *Bottom,* one crucial engineering area holds monitoring equipment; seldom-used 35mm film chain; and videotape recorders for studio recording playback, duplicating editing, and transmission purposes. (Photos courtesy of KTLA, Los Angeles)

Introduction to TV Production

Figure 1–12
This remote unit, converted from a large motor home, contains a complete control room and engineering facilities for a major production. (Photo courtesy of Learning Resources, California State University, Long Beach; Bob Freligh, photographer)

with complete electronic editing facilities—playback and record video recorders and editing controllers. In a large production center, you will find an impressive array of several editing suites.

If the production area is a remote location—outside of the studio—the corresponding control rooms also have to be taken outside of the main production center. The audio control, video control, and master control functions are all placed in some sort of van, truck, trailer, or motor home (as shown in figure 1–12), which can be readily moved from one location to another. Depending upon the scope of the production, all of the control functions may be handled in one small van, or they may have to be housed (in the case of some major sporting events) in several portable buildings that are set up on location several days in advance of the production.

If our quick tour of tools and working spaces were of an actual station, the final working area—but one with which we will not be concerned in this book—would be the **transmitter** itself. Usually located on some high ground several miles from the studio operations and connected by a microwave link, the transmitter—along with any associated satellite facilities—is the final engineering tool in the complex link that sends out the sounds and pictures of the television portion of the communication message.

1.6 Producing and Directing

Although most of the emphasis of this book is on the specific production skills concerned with individual positions and pieces of equipment, it is also necessary to introduce the concepts of producing and directing. Keep in mind that in many class productions (as in much of noncommercial TV and low-budget professional video) one may function in both of these positions simultaneously—serving in a hyphenated producer-director capacity. The functions of these two positions can, however, still be differentiated.

The **producer** is the one key person who is responsible for pulling the total production together. He or she is ultimately in charge. From the communication standpoint, the producer determines the communication need, analyzes the potential audience, designs the television message, oversees the general construction and transmission of the message, and is the recipient (target) of viewer feedback and evaluation.

In practice, the producer is in charge of the entire program-making process: conceiving the program, hiring the scriptwriters and other talent, setting up the budgets, dealing with all union and guild problems, taking care of all copyright and other clearance details, looking over the program director's shoulder during the actual production, worrying about legal problems such as libel, handling details of packaging, and selling the finished product.

In television, budgets and responsibilities are usually broken down into **above-the-line** and **below-the-line** costs. Above-the-line costs include creative and performing personnel such as the producer, associate producer(s), director, art director, writers, musicians, actors, and other performers. The producer is directly in charge of all these related functions, working closely with all personnel involved.

Below-the-line costs include all production and engineering standard costs such as those for associate director, stage manager, floor assistants, camera operators, technical director, lighting and staging crews, audio engineer, and other engineering positions. Although the producer is broadly in charge of the operation, it is the director who is in direct charge of the production positions, working with them on a close supervisory level.

One way of differentiating between the roles of the producer and the director is to think of the producer as the person who is in charge of pulling all of the elements of the program together prior to getting it into the studio. The director is in charge of everything once the production is at the studio stage—setting up the visual and graphic elements, deciding on the fine points of creative presentations, blocking all action, arranging for technical and production support positions, conducting rehearsals, handling the talent, directing the actual production, and following up on post-production editing and other concerns.

Generally, the **director** will be the one most closely associated with the creative decisions involved in the final look and feel of the production—how the microphones are placed and used, how the action is blocked, how the cameras are placed, what actual shots get on the air, the overall artistic design of the visual elements, the timing and editing of the production, and so forth. It is sometimes helpful to think of the director in terms of three different competencies—planner, creative artist, and executor.

As *planner,* the director must be fully aware of all the demands and disciplines of the television medium. He or she must be dedicated to a meticulous preparation of myriad details prior to actual studio production. He or she must be concerned, in conjunction with the producer, with the ordering and reserving of all studio facilities and equipment needed, planning for graphics and special film, requisitioning props and scenery, arranging for crew and engineering personnel. The director must carefully lay out the basic scenic and graphic elements with the art director, lighting and staging personnel, and so forth. He or she must accurately prepare a marked working script and instructions for all other key crew positions—planning all shots and camera transitions well before production time. In short, the director must thoroughly prepare every aspect of the production during the time available before actually getting into the studio.

Introduction to TV Production

The director must also function as the *chief creative person* involved in the production. (Depending upon the nature of the production and the inclinations of the personalities involved, the producer may actually retain overall creative control.) The director designs the basic creative feel for the production—working with the art director, musicians, actors, lighting and staging designers, and so on. The director plans the basic audio and visual impression of the program. How will cameras be used? What kind of shots will get on the air? What about the pacing and timing of the program? All of these creative decisions are up to the director.

Finally, the director must function as the actual *executor* of the program. Sitting in the control chair and calling the shots during the program, he or she must be calm and cool, authoritative without being irritating, gentle without losing control, responsive without being excessively nervous. Possession of these qualities can be the final test of how well an individual can function under pressure. Remember that the rest of the crew will likely respond to the tone and attitude of the director. If the director is nervous and overtly anxious, the entire crew will react with anxiety; if the director manifests a cool and controlled attitude, all production personnel will react with more assurance and confidence.

Different directors will possess abilities—as planner, as creative artist, and as executor—in varying ratios. Some are excellent methodical planners without being creative; some are creative but tend to fall apart under pressure; some are outstanding at calling shots in the director's chair but hate to do the paperwork prior to production. Needless to say, the successful director is the person who can combine all three abilities to the fullest extent. In chapters 13, 14, and 15, we will look at the role of the director in greater detail.

Summary

Television production is a complex and confusing enterprise. Each individual member of the television team must master and demonstrate an exacting combination of *techniques* and *disciplines*—knowing technically how to use all of the TV equipment and being able to interact with all other team members and production elements to produce a successful television program.

This is true whether you are involved with *broadcast operations* (at the network, station, or independent producer level), *nonbroadcast telecommunications* (corporate video, government media, medical TV, religious productions, schooling applications, or cable TV), or *small-format television* (personal recording, community communication, or creating video art).

Similar techniques and disciplines must be mastered whether you are involved with *multiple-camera* live production (in the studio and on location) or if you are working with *single-camera* filmic procedures (for either dramatic or journalistic purposes).

In any kind of TV production situation, you must be concerned with a wide variety of working areas and tools of the medium—the typewriter or computer, studio facilities, sets, props and costumes, graphics workstation, lighting instruments, cameras and microphones, audio and video mixing areas, editing equipment, and various engineering and control facilities. Students in beginning TV production must also be familiar with the jobs of the producer and director. As producer, you must assume ultimate responsibility for the entire program—from its initial conception to final audience feedback. As director, you are responsible for the specific elements of production—pre-production planning, creative use of the medium, and control room execution of the production. Each position entails its own set of techniques and disciplines.

In chapter 2, we start looking at the specific production elements that make up the sound and picture of the television message. It is often tempting to start first with the video process—the cameras and associated equipment. We prefer, however, to begin with the audio operation for two reasons. First, the audio part of the production is frequently slighted in the treatment of the larger and more complicated aspects of picture production; by beginning with audio, we will give it the emphasis it deserves. Second, there are several functional similarities between audio and video signal production and manipulation; by studying the audio operation first, it is easier to grasp the bigger and more complex picture of the video side of the program in subsequent chapters.

1.7 Training Exercise

Write a brief (500-word) essay setting forth your own personal professional goals in the broadcasting/film field. What do you hope to be able to accomplish in the area? What specifically do you feel you will get from this course that will help you to achieve your goals? Can you get any more out of the course? How?

The Audio System: Signal Flow and Technical Control

• • • • • • • • • • • • • • • • • • •

2

The task of understanding and ultimately operating television equipment becomes much easier if the individual components are seen in terms of the *functions* each piece of equipment is designed to perform. Each item has been developed to ensure that the crew and eventually the director will have the ability to control, with split-second accuracy, the flow of the numerous audio and video signals available during a production situation.

The **audio** system is an excellent place to start the process of comprehending the basics of television engineering structure. Once audio is understood, the same principles can easily be applied to video. Each audio component has a somewhat analogous counterpart in the video system.

2.1 Technical and Creative Functions of Audio

In many elements that comprise audio and video production, we will see that there coexists both a *technical function* and a *creative function.* It is necessary to meet certain requirements simply to get adequate sound and picture produced (technical function); it is then possible to manipulate these elements for certain aesthetic effects (creative function).

In the audio system, we will initially be concerned with the basic *technical requirements* needed to faithfully reproduce original sound for broadcast or recording purposes. We will be involved with controlling signal flow, understanding microphone construction and proper usage, mixing other prerecorded audio sources, and so forth. For the beginning audio operator, the most important job is simply to be able to pick up and reproduce faithfully the actual sound that is being produced as the audio portion of the TV production. Here the operator is seeking clean, clear sound at adequate balanced levels.

The *creative side* of audio production may have as its goal a specific *mood* or *emotional setting,* achieved through the use of carefully selected sound effects or even music. At the same time another goal could be an *illusion of reality* achieved by purely technical devices, such as a special filter that can create the distinctive voice quality of a telephone conversation. An opposite effect, that of *enhancing* particular sound frequencies to produce what sounds like a "natural" voice quality, is quite a common practice in the broadcasting and recording industries. Several of these elements are discussed in this and the next chapter: **mixing** and **shaping** the audio signal (section 2.2); microphone selection and usage, including such considerations as acoustical differences, mike distance, sound balance, audio perspective (sections 3.2 and 3.3); and adding other audio sources (section 3.4).

A more detailed discussion of the creative side of audio production, however, is beyond the scope of this book. It involves such specialized topics as musical balance and instrumental characteristics, performing and acting techniques, and advanced engineering concepts. The emphasis in these two chapters will be primarily upon faithful technical reproduction of conventional television sound and the basic elements of creative control.

2.2 The Seven Basic Control Functions

Each piece of equipment in the studio or control booth can perform one or more of seven basic control functions. If you look carefully at your own audio booth and adjoining studio, you will find that audio facilities are generally designed to move, modify, or otherwise control a signal in these seven ways: (1) *transducing,* or converting sound waves into electrical energy and back again; (2) *channeling,* or routing the signals, sending them wherever

necessary; (3) *mixing* two or more sound sources; (4) *amplifying* the signal strength; (5) *shaping* the sound by enhancing or in some other way changing the quality of the tone; (6) *recording* and *playing back* material ranging from inserts to the completed production output; and (7) *monitoring* individual signals as well as combined program feeds by visual and aural means.

In looking over this list, many examples of these functions will probably come to mind from your experience in operating a home entertainment center with recorder and playback capabilities. As you apply the previously mentioned characteristics to your unit, you will begin to see that some components perform more than one function. For example, the speaker that transduces a signal into listenable sound is also obviously a *monitor.* The bass and treble controls that *shape* the final output of the unit do so by allowing for separate levels of *amplification.*

Keep in mind that the terminology used to define the various components and their functions may vary somewhat with time and location. There is, however, a basic structure of functional design common to all audio control rooms. Understanding the essential elements of this structure in your own facility is the prerequisite that is necessary to successful operation of the equipment in a production situation.

2.2.1 Transducing

The entire process by which sound (voices, music) is converted into a broadcast signal (electrical information) is referred to as *transducing.* Figure 2–1 shows in simplified form how the transducing elements—the microphone components that actually change sound waves into electrical energy—perform this function in a dynamic microphone.

The tone production of a human voice or musical instrument creates pressure waves in

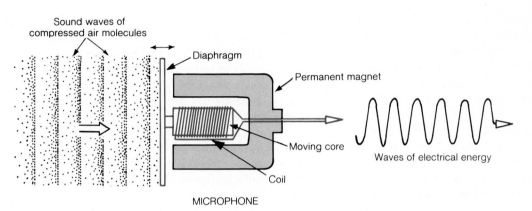

Sound waves of compressed air molecules

Diaphragm

Permanent magnet

Moving core

Coil

Waves of electrical energy

MICROPHONE

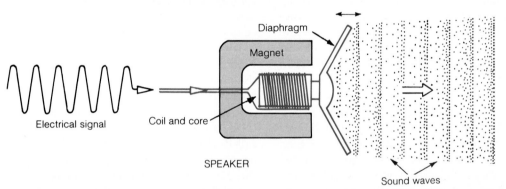

Diaphragm

Magnet

Electrical signal

Coil and core

Sound waves

SPEAKER

Figure 2–1
Transducing element of a dynamic microphone and corresponding speaker elements.

When sound waves from a voice or musical instrument strike the diaphragm of the microphone, the waves of compressed air molecules cause the attached coil to vibrate. As the coil moves back and forth within the magnetic field of the permanent magnet, a small fluctuating electric current is produced. This minute current, which will be amplified many times, carries the same information as the original sound waves. At the receiving end, when this minute electrical signal reaches the speaker coil it produces fluctuations in the magnetic field that then cause the diaphragm of the speaker to vibrate, creating sound waves that reproduce the original sound picked up by the microphone.

the molecules of the air. If these waves are produced at a constant rate of 440 cycles per second, the result is the musical tone of A above middle C.[1]

These waves fall upon and vibrate the **diaphragm** of the microphone and cause the attached coil to vibrate around a part of the permanent magnet. When this coil moves within the resulting magnetic field, an electric current is produced. This signal is now in its new electronic form but retains the original **frequency** pattern of 440 oscillations per

1. The term *cycles per second* (cps) is used as the basic unit of measure for sound pressure waves and, in the past, for electromagnetic waves. In recent years, engineering terminology has for the most part replaced the term *cycles per second* with the term *Hertz* (abbreviated Hz) in honor of Heinrich Hertz, who first demonstrated the existence of electromagnetic waves.

second.[2] (A more detailed explanation of wave theory is contained in appendix A.)

The electronic waveform at this stage is said to be an **analog** of the original sound pressure wave, in that the electronic wave retains those essential elements of wave frequency, length, and amplitude that characterized the original sound pressure waves.

With the newer **digital** recording processes—used for compact discs (CDs), digital audio tape recording (DAT), and digital compact cassettes (DCCs)—the audio signal goes through an additional encoding/decoding stage. Using computer technology, the structure of the waveform is further converted into groups of off-on digital pulses. (See the discussion of "digital effects" in section 7.5.) In this digital form, the signal is almost immune from nonsignal *noise* and can therefore reproduce a much higher quality of sound.

It must be noted that digital audio and digital video will, for a number of years, be primarily limited to in-studio production and postproduction work (such as editing and graphics) and direct recordings for sale to the public (CDs and DAT recordings). To broadcast or cablecast a digital video signal would take a channel capacity in excess of what is available at the present. However, broadcast engineers and FCC (Federal Communications Commission) regulators alike are beginning to investigate various strategies for moving into digital radio broadcasting—including the possibility of a direct satellite digital service.

The transduced microphone signal previously described is amplified at several stages in its journey through the audio control room and is then sent to the transmitter. At this point it is **modulated** for broadcast. This is a process by which the signal is superimposed onto the *carrier frequency* specifically assigned to the radio station and amplified more than a million times for transmission. This is still, of course, an electronic signal. The broadcast *carrier wave* makes no change in the molecules of the air through which it passes. Such a signal can travel millions of miles into space. Figure 2–2 illustrates in simplified form how this modulation phase is but a part of the total broadcasting sequence.[3]

At the receiver, an analogous procedure takes place—only in reverse order. This is called *demodulation.* The relatively weak broadcast audio signal is first removed from the carrier wave (the actual demodulation process), amplified, then sent to the speaker of the TV set or radio receiver. The speaker is a *transducer* something like a microphone with the elements—a coil and a magnet—placed in reverse order. The electrical (audio) signal sets the diaphragm in motion, which pushes against the air molecules, creating the sound pressure waves at a rate of 440 cycles per second; you hear the original tone of A above middle C.

The cartridge in the pickup arm at the turntable also is a transducer that deserves to be included within this general category. In a way, it is a type of microphone that transforms the vibrations picked up by the needle into an electronic energy form.

---

2. Actually, the A 440 cps frequency in our example is only the fundamental tone. It is by far the most prominent of many tones that are simultaneously produced when a voice or an instrument is sounded. The other tones, which are much softer in volume and occur at higher frequencies, are called "overtones" or "harmonics." Their presence and relative volume are what produce the distinctive quality of any individual voice or instrument. To reproduce any single complete tone accurately, all of these resultant frequencies must be picked up and simultaneously transduced into the electrical signal. A more complete explanation of the overtone series is presented in appendix B.

3. For a simplified explanation of how a carrier wave is theoretically modulated, both by amplitude modulation (AM) and by frequency modulation (FM), see appendix A.

The Audio System: Signal Flow and Technical Control

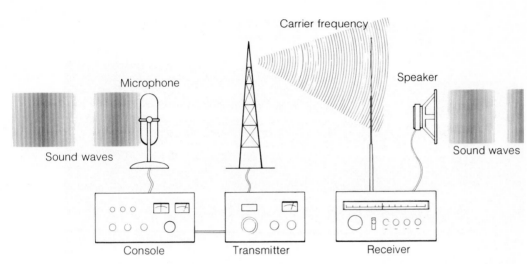

Figure 2–2
Modulation and
demodulation in the
broadcasting sequence.

The original sound waves are transduced into an electrical current that, at the transmitter, is modulated or superimposed over the assigned carrier frequency of the broadcasting station. (By this point, the original signal has been amplified over a million times.) This carrier wave is the specific broadcasting frequency assigned by the Federal Communications Commission—either part of the television channel, or, in the case of radio, a sep- arate part of the electromagnetic spectrum (see appendix A); for example, 690 kiloHertz ("six-ninety on your radio dial"). The TV or radio set then receives this carrier frequency, demodulates (or strips off) the superimposed electrical signal, which is the program information, and the speaker transduces the electrical energy back into sound waves that the ear can perceive.

2.2.2 Channeling

The term *channel* is used as a verb when it refers to the procedure of moving signals from one place to another and as a noun when it describes the actual pathway the signal follows through cables and other control equipment from its source to its final destination. Much of the channeling takes place within the **audio control board** or **console** in the audio booth. Other avenues of channeling are the cables and external lines that connect the console with the studio inputs, audio recorders and other players, master control room, transmitter, and so forth. The routing device that makes possible the connection of these various sources and destinations is the **patch bay** (see figure 2–3).

Audio Signal Flow   The concept of *signal flow* is critical in understanding several different aspects of television production. It is introduced here as it applies to audio signal flow or audio channeling. It applies also in subsequent chapters to the concepts of video signal flow, and lighting patching, and even to the construction of computer graphics.

This audio channeling procedure must be grasped within a conceptual framework and not just as a memorized list of patches made, switches moved, and pots opened. Understanding each step of the audio signal flow in its proper sequence is not only the most efficient and foolproof way to achieve your desired audio objectives, but it is also the only way to effectively troubleshoot audio problems.

Figure 2–3
Typical audio patch bay.

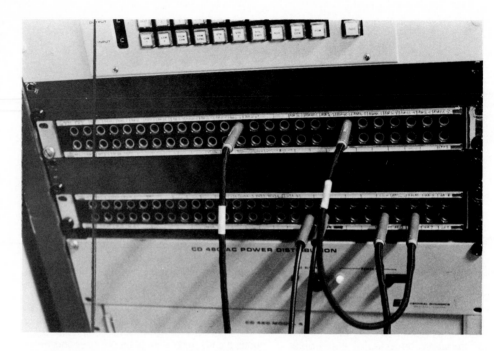

Figures 2–4 and 2–5 together lay out a simplified schematic diagram of a representative audio signal flow. Although equipment design and terminology of our model will differ somewhat from the equipment with which you will be working, the same basic principles and sequence of channeling steps should easily be adapted to your situation.

Our model is designed to show a representative route that a monaural signal would take from its source, through a connecting **patch bay,** and into one of a number of **input channels** within the **audio console.** There the signal continues on through one of several **group masters** (also known as *submasters*) to a final fader controlling **program line output.** Figure 2–6 shows how the console engineer would envision this **sequence of signal flow** from an operational standpoint.

The signal coming in on a line from a studio mike temporarily terminates its flow at the patch bay at a round-holed receptacle called an **output.** (See figures 2–3 and 2–4.) In addition to a number of other mike outputs, the patch bay will contain outputs for components such as cart (cartridge) machines and CD players as well as for audiotape and videotape machines. Just below the output receptacles, there is another row of receptacles that are the *connection points* to however many **input channels** the board is capable of handling. In figure 2–4 we show "mic 1 output" being connected down and over to "input channel 4" by means of a **patch cord.**

Normalled Connections   We could have patched mike 1 into input channel 5 or into any of the other available input channels depending upon our *audio setup plan.* However, had we wanted to use input channel 3 (just below the output), we would not have needed to use a patch cord to make the connection into that input channel. Notice the dotted line running from mike 1 to input channel 3 (and the

The Audio System: Signal Flow and Technical Control

similar dotted lines for the other corresponding vertical pairs). It denotes that in our model patch bay, as on most equipment, a permanent hard-wired connection already exists between these two points. This is called a **normalled** connection because it is *normally* in place. It saves time as the operator does not have to make a patch for the input of equipment constantly in use, such as audiotape and videotape recorders and certain basic studio microphones. All normalled connections are designed so that the existing connection is broken (separated) any time a patch cord is placed in either the input or output receptacle. It should be noted that many operators will prefer to use a patched connection in order to have the left-to-right sequence of faders on the console resemble the left-to-right position of mikes in the studio.

With our patch between "mic 1 out" and "input channel 4," we have moved our signal into the **audio board** itself (see figure 2–5). Due to the fact that at this point we are only concerned with the concept of *signal flow,* the input channels depicted have been simplified to show only **gain** and **fader** controls for the main feed, along with one gain control used for an **auxiliary send** feed. This *send* feature is a special audio feed that allows an anchor person in the studio to hear a videotape sound track or mixed program output through an earphone during a live news production or some other similar operation. We have also included another very important routing switch known as a **group assign switch** for each channel. This channeling control allows any of the input channels to be fed into either or both of the two **group master faders** (also known as *submasters*), discussed later. One or both of these selected groups of audio inputs then moves on to a final master fader for control of the volume

of **program line out.** If the board were designed for stereo, the input channels, group faders, and master faders would work in pairs—along with some special controls (**pan**) to handle the left and right channels of stereo sound.

The capacity of an audio console is often increased by the use of a **routing switcher,** which can feed two or more inputs into any one input channel. While not included in our simplified depiction, it would be placed just "downstream" of the patch bay—that is, immediately after the signal comes out of the patch bay. Its value is based upon the concept that while some productions will feature a heavy use of prerecorded feeds, such as videotapes or cart and cassette inserts, others will have an emphasis on the use of studio microphones. With the routing switcher, the operator has a choice of *either* a mike *or* a recorded signal being fed into a channel, with the ability to switch quickly between the two sources without repatching.

It is important that one gets the **input** and **output** concept clearly in mind. As a signal moves through any system, it is repeatedly going *into, through,* and *out of* a series of controls and other components. The *output* of one component becomes the *input* into the next. A thorough knowledge of the *sequence of signal flow* within any system is the key to being able to set up and test audio in any production situation. When trouble occurs, a point-by-point sequential check is the most efficient way to find the button that was not pressed or the fader that was not opened. Another important thing to keep in mind is that no matter how complex an audio system's design may be, it is still only an extension of the basic operational design outlined in figures 2–4, 2–5 and 2–6.

2.2.3 Mixing

Only a few short decades ago, the main function of most audio consoles was simply that of serving as a mixer of six to ten sound inputs. Each input source was controlled by its own volume control, and the combination was fed into a *mixing bus* that was, in effect, the *program-out* feed. This older design has been largely replaced by the concept of separate *input channels* as shown in figure 2–5. As we see, a number of controls have been placed on one channel module based upon the needs of the operating engineer. It may help to think in terms of a signal flow that starts at the top of the module and continues down to the bottom with the volume control of the fader. This is an oversimplification, not totally accurate, but

it will help us for the moment in our general understanding of component function.

The basic concept of *mixing* the output of this one input channel with the output of a number of similar channels should not be too difficult to understand. Working from a script or information from the director, the audio operator is aware that one channel's sound is to predominate (for example, voice over background music and sound effects).

Because of the usual fluctuations of volume level in the sound effects, the music, and the speaker's voice, the audio operator makes a continuing series of volume control adjustments with the *potentiometer* or *fader* (see figure 2–7). Thus, the operator is able to maintain a proper *balance* among the three separate sound sources, always making sure

Figure 2–4
Diagram of a simplified patch bay.

This diagram shows the configuration of a simplified patch bay. The top row of receptacles are source outputs. The lower row are input receptacles leading to numbered input channels at the audio console. Hard-wired (normalled) connections are indicated by a dotted line. A sample signal pathway is shown in red.

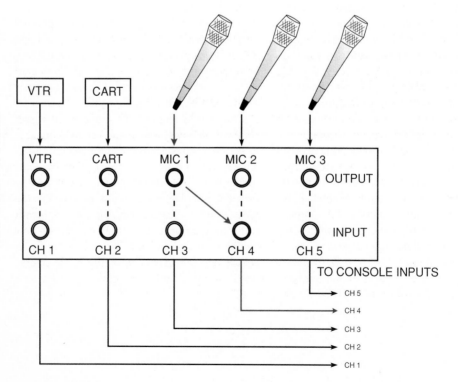

The Audio System: Signal Flow and Technical Control

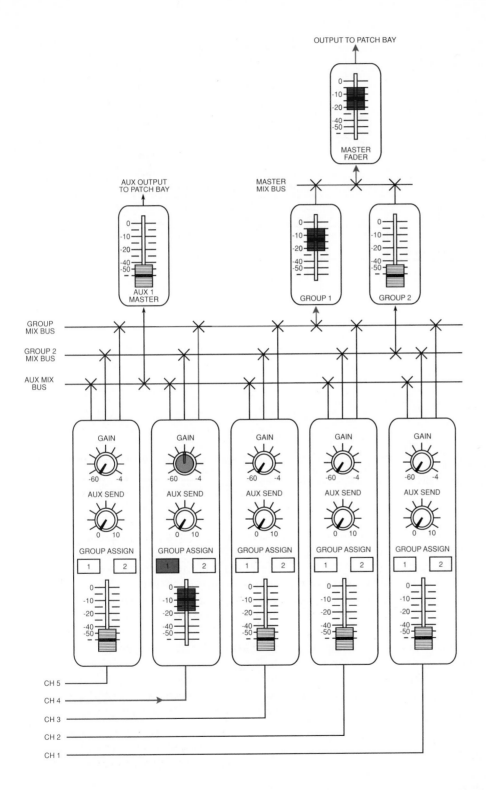

OUTPUT TO PATCH BAY

MASTER FADER

AUX OUTPUT TO PATCH BAY

MASTER MIX BUS

AUX 1 MASTER

GROUP 1

GROUP 2

GROUP MIX BUS

GROUP 2 MIX BUS

AUX MIX BUS

GAIN
-60   -4
AUX SEND
0   10
GROUP ASSIGN
1   2

GAIN
-60   -4
AUX SEND
0   10
GROUP ASSIGN
1   2

GAIN
-60   -4
AUX SEND
0   10
GROUP ASSIGN
1   2

GAIN
-60   -4
AUX SEND
0   10
GROUP ASSIGN
1   2

GAIN
-60   -4
AUX SEND
0   10
GROUP ASSIGN
1   2

CH 5
CH 4
CH 3
CH 2
CH 1

Figure 2–5
Signal flow through an input channel.

This indicates the continuation of the signal flow through an input channel, out to a group fader, and on to the master fader for final volume control.

Figure 2–6
Audio signal flow model.

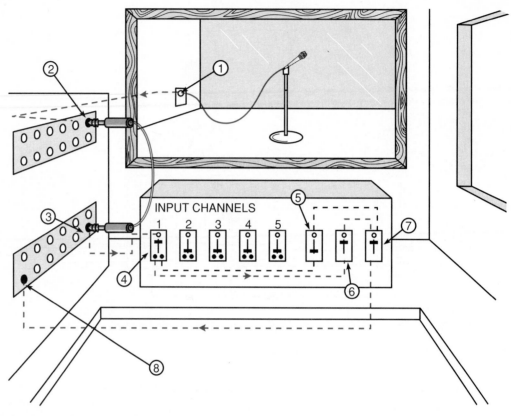

INPUT CHANNELS

1. Studio microphone wall receptacle input. *2.* Patch bay output from studio. *3.* Patch bay input to console. *4.* Input channel #1. *5 and 6.* Group master faders. *7.* Master fader for program output. *8.* Program-out patch bay receptacle.

that the voice predominates. This process is known as *riding gain.*

Another look at figures 2–4 and 2–5 indicates that there is a further stage to this mixing process. Consider that in our simplified model console, studio mike 2 and studio mike 3 have been designated to cover the small orchestra and studio mike 1 is for the announcer. Using the *group assign switch* on each of the input channels, the operator can separate control of the musical and the speaking elements of the program by sending mike 1 to the group 1 master fader and mikes 2 and 3 to the group 2 master fader. Now multiply this simple example and envision twenty-four or even forty-eight *input channels* controlled by eight to sixteen *group masters* in the sort of multiple combinations of microphones that would allow for separate group masters controlling percussion, brass, woodwind, and string sections. It is easy to see how important this concept of *submastering* specified groups of inputs becomes in the mixing process.

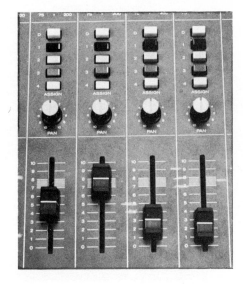

Figure 2–7
Potentiometers/faders: *left,* older audio consoles used rotary potentiometers (or ''pots'') to control the signal level or volume; *right,* newer boards use slide-faders. This board has channel-select ''assign'' switches (which enable the operator to select different output channels for each fader or input channel) and a rotary ''pan'' knob (which allows the operator to balance two stereo channels).

2.2.4 Amplifying

The electronic signals that come into our audio console are in the form of moving waves of negatively charged electrons within the molecules of a wire. Generally speaking, the console is designed to handle these inputs at two different strengths. Signals that come out of an already amplified audio source or videotape machine are at what is called **line level.** This is much more powerful than the weak signal generated by the sound waves of your voice hitting the magnet and coil of a dynamic microphone (see figure 2–1). This **mike level** feed is further divided into two subtypes, **low-impedance** (Lo-Z) level and **high-impedance** (Hi-Z) level. The term *impedance* refers to a measured amount of resistance on a line and is a part of the way in which all signal strength is measured (see section 3.1). Studio micro-

phones, including those with batteries, use long low-impedance cables. The microphones on many portable audio recorders use short high-impedance cables.

Contemporary audio consoles cope with these various input levels by having a number of small amplifiers (**preamps**) at key points in the console—as well as a number of strategically placed devices called **pads,** whose function is to absorb or reduce signal strength.

To explain how this works, we need to take a careful look at an input channel in a professional-level audio console. Let us look at the Yamaha MR 1642 Mixing Console (see figure 2–8). It is the sort of unit that would be ideal in an industrial video studio or an educational institution doing broadcast-quality production and class instruction. It is a stereo board with sixteen input channels making it ideal for small-format ''live-to-tape'' produc-

Figure 2–8
Modern audio boards
feature numerous input
channels and a variety of
channel controls and
routing switches: *top*,
Yamaha MR 1642 Audio
Mixing Console; *bottom*,
Pacific Recorder STX
Board. (*Top* photo courtesy
of Yamaha; *bottom* photo
courtesy of Pacific
Recorder)

The Audio System: Signal Flow and Technical Control

tions. It also has a number of features that would make it useful for the teaching of multitrack music-recording techniques.

Starting at the top of the input channel shown in figure 2–9, we have examples of the controls that deal with varying levels of input. *Control #1* is a **tape switch** that works in conjunction with *control #2,* a **pad switch.** These switches are needed because, on the back of the audio console, each input channel has four different input receptacles. Each is a different type of receptacle, allowing the channel to be matched with signals from microphones of differing impedance or from line level equipment such as videotape, cart, and CD machines.

In effect, these multiple inputs increase the capability of the board by expanding the capacity of each channel. For example, an input channel can be used for a microphone during the first part of a program and then switch to a videotape feed later when needed. By pressing *control #1,* the tape switch, the videotape signal is brought into the input channel at line level, which is usually forty decibels stronger than microphone level. There are, however, other signal inputs such as amplified guitars and electronic keyboard instruments that have varying strengths. In this situation, *control #2,* the pad switch, is used to reduce the strength of those signals by twenty decibels. These inputs are then further adjusted by the use of *control #3,* the gain control, which can adjust levels within a range of forty decibels. (Shown as −20 decibels to −60 decibels.)

If a microphone (with the usual low-impedance level feed) is being fed into the input channel, then neither the tape nor pad switches need be utilized. Once the proper settings are established, *control #12,* the **channel**

fader at the bottom of the input channel, is used to maintain consistent sound levels. The *control #4,* the **clip LED** (light-emitting diode) **indicator,** is a monitor that will be discussed in section 2.2.7.

2.2.5 Shaping

The function of *shaping*—of altering the tonal characteristics of the sound—is to a great extent a creative function. As previously described, amplification, for instance, exemplifies one aspect of shaping the quality of a sound. But there are many more specialized things that can be done to affect the quality of a sound signal. In both a technical and a creative sense, much of the technique and discipline of a trained audio engineer results in the ability to electrically reproduce the same quality and dimension as existed in an original sound pressure wave—replicating the natural sound as we would hear it without electronic intervention. A related goal is that of creating an enhanced version of that original sound so that it sounds like the tone the listener *expects* to hear in a given program situation. The problem in turning natural sound into electronically reproduced sound is that much of what shapes the quality of the sound is strongly affected by the physical conditions of the recording location as well as by the microphones and other audio equipment utilized.

Appendix B partially explains how the presence and relative loudness of fundamental and overtone frequencies give every tone its distinctive quality. A trumpet has a different

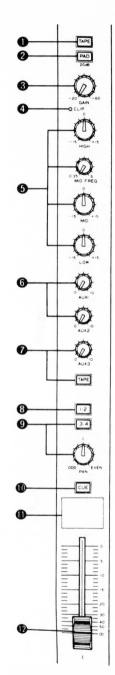

Figure 2–9
Schematic drawing of an input channel for the Yamaha 1642.

sound from a flute because its overtone pattern (as can be seen on an oscilloscope) is very different from that of a flute. The sound of a trumpet as produced in a studio is further affected by such things as soundproofing on the walls, cloth material in a cyclorama, or even furniture. These various textures will cause some of the overtones or harmonics to be absorbed or reflected in varying degrees. This process alters the quality of the sound after it leaves the horn.

The electronic components of the audio system further shape the tone of the original sound—for example, the ability of the microphone to capture and reproduce most of the frequencies being fed into it. Mikes vary greatly in their designed capacity to capture overtones at varying distances and levels of loudness. Microphones should always be used for the purpose for which they were intended. The rugged all-purpose mike designed for an outdoor public-address system will not be able to reproduce the subtleties of musical tones required in a recording studio. (See sections 3.1 and 3.3.)

It is apparent that signals coming into an audio system may produce an effect somewhat different from what was originally intended. The Yamaha MR 1642 we are using as our example has audio components that are designed to help solve these problems by shaping the electronic signal. The four knobs of the #5 control, the **three-band equalizer,** are used primarily to *strengthen* any of those overtone frequencies that make a trumpet sound like a trumpet. Going one step further, these same controls can *reinforce* additional frequencies to create an even more mellow trumpet than originally existed. The controls function in three separate frequency ranges—*high, medium,* and *low.* If, for some of the reasons just mentioned, our trumpet sound is deficient

in the higher level overtone frequencies, we can use these controls to **equalize** the incoming frequencies to reproduce something that is very close to the quality of the original tone. Since the midband of frequencies is the one most important for both voice and instrumental sound reproduction, there is a fourth control knob that allows the operator to "*sweep*" across this range to continually enhance the tone with selected frequencies.

Although not a standard part of this Yamaha mixing console, there are some additional components that are sometimes added to existing equipment for special purposes. A **limiter** might be used to cut off levels when they reach a volume that is too strong for equipment to handle without creating distortion. An **audio compressor** can be used to compress the distance between the lowest and highest volume levels—in effect, raising the lowest levels to bring them up close to the loudest levels the system can handle.[4] **Echo** and other **reverberation** devices (see section 3.4), often used for musical programs or certain dramatic effects, also fall into this shaping classification.

2.2.6 Recording and Playing Back

While the functions of audio recording and playing back differ greatly in the way they are used during a production, there is a definite

4. The compressor is what is often used on commercials to bring the sound up to a consistently high volume. When listeners complain about loud commercials, what they are actually experiencing is a consistently high-level signal. The loudest parts of the commercial are no louder than any other audio track; but unlike other audio segments, the "compressed" commercial has no valleys—the volume relentlessly holds at the same intensity.

The Audio System: Signal Flow and Technical Control

relationship between the process of recording an audio segment (or a full program) and the playing back of prerecorded segments during a production. The equipment and the setup procedures may be the same, but the operational disciplines can be quite different. The essential factor involved in playing back an audio segment during multiple-camera video production is time—being ready and knowing how to react quickly to operational cues from the director. Section 2.3 discusses some specific audio playback sources (videotape, audiotape, cart machines, records, and CD players), and section 3.4 details some particular techniques and cueing procedures.

The audio portion of most television programs is recorded directly onto the videotape. One of the audio engineer's most important tasks is to make sure that the output of his or her audio console is properly connected to the videotape recorder (often by patching from the audio board to the master control room). The audio operator must constantly be aware of the total signal flow pattern.

The other top priority of the audio engineer, during any recording session, is simply "getting the sound right." Is the mike quality appropriate? Is there proper balance between voice and music? Does the audio perspective match the picture? Is the stereo balance right? (See section 3.3.) The neophyte audio operator may simply make sure the patches are all set and then open the pots and assume the job is done. Nothing could be further from the actual truth. Painstaking attention to detail is crucial throughout the entire recording process. Quality control during production is the ongoing responsibility of the operating engineer. The *discipline* of the good audio person involves continual attentiveness and monitoring—which leads us to our final equipment function.

2.2.7 Monitoring

For an operator to perform the functions necessary to signal flow and control, the audio engineer must have the benefit of some sort of simultaneous information **feedback** of that signal or combination of signals. It takes several components to perform that function adequately. The most obvious of such equipment is the **speaker** in the audio booth, which plays what is being fed out over the program line. In a live broadcast situation, there is usually also a separate **air monitor** to check the transmitted signal.

One must also have the ability to monitor separately any single sound source from among the ten, twenty, or even more channels that are being mixed for transmission or recording. This is done by means of a preview or *cue channel*. Each input channel and each group master channel will have a **cue button** (figure 2–9, *control #10*), which when pressed will send that channel's output into a common line. At this point the signal becomes a part of a totally separate sound system with its own amplification, gain control, and speaker. The operator can select either one single mike or a group master for audition purposes while the full orchestra is playing.

The **volume unit (VU) meter** (figure 2–10) provides another essential informational feedback. In spite of the marvelous structure of the human ear, it is not able to discern differences in volume accurately enough to be able to exert the sort of precise control needed for amplified electronic signals. From an operational standpoint, this could cause some serious problems.

Within the interacting processes of mixing, shaping, and amplifying, there is a point of amplitude at which the electronic equipment ceases to function properly. At this point—which is theoretically 100 percent of

Figure 2–10
VU meter.

On most professional VU meters, the top scale indicates the decibel reading and the bottom scale
is a "percentage preference" scale, with "100"
corresponding to the ideal maximum reading.

the signal strength that can be handled by the
equipment—the ability of the components to
process the electronic wave patterns begins to
break down. The result is a distortion of the
signal.

On audio consoles comparable to the
Yamaha MR 1642, there is a VU meter for
each group master channel as well as one for
the final program feed. For stereo applications, both left and right group and master
faders would have VU meters. Some sophisticated boards will have a VU meter for each
input channel.

On most newer equipment, the VU meter
readout utilizes a **decibel** (db) scale. Slightly
to the right of the top of the arc, there is a zero
point. The zero does not signify a lack of
volume; rather, it indicates a point where the
signal is at its *optimum* level. All differences
in signal strength are measured from this point
either in **plus decibels** (to the right) or **minus
decibels** (to the left). As you can see in figure
2–10, the range of measurement goes down as

far as minus twenty decibels and only up to
two or three decibels on the plus side. (On some
older audio control boards, you will have two
superimposed scales, one with numbers running roughly from zero to 120, having the zero
decibel point coinciding with the "100" point
on the lower scale—the "100" indicating a
theoretical optimum recording level of 100
percent.)

A *decibel* is not a measurement of an absolute unit such as an ounce or a foot. Instead,
the decibel scale is an indication of *differences*
in signal strength as measured from an established level or "0" point. This point of cali-
bration is determined by several measurements
that include the amount of electrical energy
applied to the signal (amplitude), the resistance to the flow of current in a wire (impedance), and other factors. It should be noted that
the decibel is used to measure sound pressure
waves (for example, the noise in an industrial
factory or the loudness of a jet airplane taking
off) as well as electromagnetic wave energy.

As with several other subjects covered in
this text (camera operation, editing equipment, computer graphics, and so forth), it is
not necessary for students to try to comprehend the engineering concepts in depth; it is
sufficient that you concentrate upon the basics
of operational use. As long as you understand
what the equipment can do—how you should
use it properly, how you can get the desired
results you want—you do not have to master
the theoretical physics involved. With that
disclaimer, we will delve into the world of
decibel readings.

For example, let us compare the volume
strength of a "0" *(optimum)* level and a much
lower volume level at the −20 position on the
VU meter. At the lower (−20) level, the signal
is only *one-tenth as strong* as it would be at
the "0" level. Put another way, each time signal
strength is multiplied by ten, twenty decibels
have been added to the measurement. In most
operational applications, the audio operator

The Audio System: Signal Flow and Technical Control

adjusts the fader knobs to keep the needle positioned between a point around minus two or three decibels and the optimum "0" point. There is a constant fluctuation of the needle that reflects the ongoing variations in program volume. Ideally the needle is made to **peak** (reach the highpoint of its swing) at the "0" position. This process of using the fader to keep a relatively constant volume level is called **riding gain.** It is a primary discipline or skill developed by all successful board operators.

During the preproduction setup period of any complicated program, audio inputs from many sources must be prechecked and adjusted so that they provide a uniform level of sound volume. The audio operator *sets mike levels* by getting a volume check from all persons using a microphone (section 3.3). The proper technique is to first set the fader at the zero (optimum) position and then adjust the gain knob to get the VU meter to peak at "0." Similarly, all prerecorded audio sources such as CDs, carts, records, and videotapes must be checked for their signal levels. This is done to achieve a consistent level from all sources—a concept known as *unity gain.* In a similar process, most audio consoles can electronically generate a zero-decibel (0 db) audio tone, which is used to calibrate the console feed with video recorders or transmitter equipment.

One small but important type of monitor is to be found in figure 2–9 at *control #4.* It is the **clip LED** (light-emitting diode) **indicator,** which—by continuously flashing—tells the operator that the gain control has been properly set. If it is constantly on or off, levels should be checked.

We previously briefly mentioned the *auxiliary send* feature (section 2.2.2), which is located at the midpoint of the input channel shown in figure 2–9. One of its main purposes is that of providing on-the-air talent with an audio monitor for selected feeds. The volume knob *control #6* shown in figure 2–9 could be used to provide studio talent with either instructions from the director on the intercom or program sound from a field reporter. *Control #7* would be used to send the news anchor sound from a videotape insert.

There are two final controls that complete the structure of our example input channel. *Controls #8 and #9* are the *group assign switches,* which send the output of the input channel to the group master faders. As seen in figure 2–9, they are in a stereo configuration and would work in conjunction with the **pan** control located just below them.

And there you have, in a very simplified form, an insider's guide to the audio control room. If this beginning knowledge makes you feel less of a stranger within the confines of the audio booth, it is probably because it is in reality only an expanded version of the amplifiers, tuners, cassette recorders, turntables, compact disc players, cables, and speakers that form the components of our home stereo systems.

2.3 Sources of TV Audio

The previous discussion of the seven basic control functions and audio signal flow represents a typical, somewhat simplified model, based primarily upon the microphone as the audio source. Actually, the audio operator should think in terms of two different categories of audio sources—the *microphone* and other *prerecorded sources.* Each broad grouping has its own techniques and disciplines that must be mastered and practiced.

Microphones

The microphone comes in a wide variety of types and sizes, designed for a multitude of specialized purposes. They vary as to *frequency response;* some will pick up low frequencies well, while others respond best to higher frequencies. They differ as to *pickup pattern;* some will pick up everything around them (omnidirectional), whereas the performer has to stand directly in front of other microphones (unidirectional) to be heard well. They will vary in the technical construction of their *transducing elements*—the way they actually transform sound waves into electrical energy. As a result, some are more rugged than others. Microphones vary in *physical design,* to be used in different ways; some are to be placed in mike stands, some are hand held, others are worn around the neck or attached to special boom stands.

These different distinctions and differences are discussed in chapter 3. By becoming familiar with the different microphone classifications and characteristics, the audio operator will be able to select the most appropriate microphone for each application. Which microphones should be used for talk shows? Drama? Musical productions? What kinds of mikes are best suited for outdoor (location) productions? Which microphones are used for picking up sound from a great distance? What if you want a microphone that can be concealed or hidden? These are just some of the considerations that an audio operator has to be ready to think about.

Prerecorded Sound Sources

The basic audio signal flow concept also applies to sound from sources other than the microphone—although the patch starts somewhere other than in the TV studio. The origination of the prerecorded sound may be in the master control or telecine room, or even in the audio booth itself; however, the same basic principles of signal flow apply.

For the most part, the audio operator could probably think of prerecorded sound as coming from one of five basic sources: videotape, audiotape, cartridges, records, and CD players. Although other variations (such as **film** or **audiocassettes**) may occasionally be encoun-

tered, these five basic origination media represent the common nonmicrophone sources of television audio.

Even though some professional studios still have sound film facilities, very little film is "rolled in" to live or videotaped programs in most of today's production operations. Generally, the film is transferred to videotape ahead of production time—in order to assure color control and to simplify the actual production situation. Commercials, even though shot originally on film, are transferred to videotape for broadcasting.

Videotape Audio Tracks   Many types of productions will have videotape inserts, in which a short, previously recorded videotape segment is incorporated into the body of another television production. The insert videotape recorder or recorders will usually be located in master control or someplace other than the audio booth. Someone other than the audio operator, usually the video engineer, will be responsible for threading up the videotape playback machine and patching the audio line into the audio control room. The primary concern of the audio person will simply be correct operation of the console, getting cues precisely, and riding gain.

Audiotape Playback   On the other hand, operation of any audiotape recorder is usually completely in the hands of the audio engineer. The typical audio control room will have one or more audiotape recorders (see figure 2–11). The audio engineer will be in charge of making certain the tape is correctly threaded and patched or connected to the audio console. (Often the audiotape recorder will be normalled or permanently wired into the audio console. See section 2.2.2.)

Audiotape frequently is the most convenient medium to use for prerecording longer segments of program inserts—background music, sound effects, or announcements—and

Figure 2–11
Production model
audiotape recorder.

for premixing several sound sources. For example, if the production calls for an audio segment that has an off-camera announcer, background music, and a sound effect, it is easier—and much safer—to prerecord that segment rather than to try to mix those several elements during the actual television production.

When audiotape is used in a production, the audio operator must watch out for several important factors. First, make certain that the booth audiotape machine can play back audiotape at the correct speed. Several different tape speeds can be used for recording audiotape. (Generally, the faster the tape speed, the higher the fidelity of the recording—because more tape is used in the recording, more overtones can be recorded.) In most cases, the booth audio machine will be able to play back at least two tape speeds; make sure

you have selected the correct speed for your recording. Occasionally you may find, however, that the originating machine recorded the audiotape at a speed other than what the booth audiotape recorder can handle.

Second, the track configuration must be checked. Although most audiotape is one-fourth inch, various recording configurations use the tape differently. It is possible to have full-track recording (rarely used today), half-track recording (wherein only half a track is used in each direction or both tracks are used for stereophonic recording in the same direction), and quarter-track (or four-track) recording (most commonly used for stereo recording). (See figure 2–12.)

Finally, the audio operator must check to make certain that the supply reel (usually on the left side of the machine) and the take-up reel (which receives the audiotape, usually on

Figure 2–12
Audiotape track
configurations.

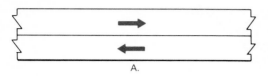

A. Half-track monaural. In monophonic recording, only half of the audiotape track is used for information as the tape is played in one direction. When the tape reels are reversed (the take-up reel being threaded up as the supply reel) and the tape is played in the other direction, the other half of the track is used.

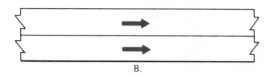

B. Half-track stereo. Both tracks are used when the tape is played in one direction. One half-track contains the information for the left channel, and the other half-track is the right channel recording. In this configuration, the tape cannot be reversed and played back in the opposite direction.

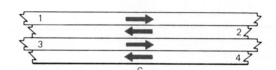

C. Quarter-track (four-track stereo). In this more common stereo configuration, tracks 1 and 3 are used for left-channel and right-channel information when played in one direction. Tracks 2 and 4 are used for the two stereo channels when the tape is reversed and played back in the opposite direction.

Figure 2–13
Audio cartridge player
designed to access nine
different carts on three
different channels.

the right side of the recorder) are the same size. Tape reels come in several diameters, and if the two reels are different sizes, there is a greater possibility of breaking the tape or spinning the tape off the reel when in either the fast-forward or rewind mode.

Audio Cartridges Until the advent of the compact disc, the audio cartridge unit, or *cart machine,* had been the workhorse of most audio control rooms. Figure 2–13 shows a typical three-channel cart machine. Since there

are no variations in tape speed, track configuration, and reel size, the use of the cartridge is uncomplicated. Also, because the cartridge automatically rewinds itself and is self-cueing, it is very simple to operate. For these reasons, cart machines have established themselves as an integral part of most audio operations.

Vinyl Records The long-playing record has been a fixture in audio booths for over four decades. It is still used as a source of pre-recorded audio—primarily for musical selec-

The Audio System: Signal Flow and Technical Control

Figure 2–14
The CD (compact disc) player has become a standard audio playback unit in most radio and TV stations because of its crisp digital sound and its ease of cueing. (Photos courtesy of KLOS–FM) (*Top*): The Sony CDS-3000 control unit allows split-second cueing of the CD, as well as separate monitoring capabilities, sophisticated programming, and a standby mode. (*Bottom*): Station KLOS uses a bank of three units and controllers to enable the operator to play back one CD, have a second unit cued up in the standby mode, while previewing a third CD.

tions and sound effects. Most audio control rooms will have one or two record turntables, capable of playing both the 12-inch 33⅓ rpm (revolutions per minute) long-playing records and the smaller 45 rpm records for single musical selections. Like the cart machine, the audiotape recorder, and the CD player, the record turntable(s) will often be normalled into a preselected channel on the audio board.

Compact Discs   The CD player has found a secure spot in most modern audio booths. (See figure 2–14.) Complete libraries of sound effects and stock musical selections have been released on CDs. The advantages of CDs, of course, are well-known. Because the audio is recorded in a digital format (see section 2.2.1), the sound is as crisp as can be transmitted; the CD represents a higher fidelity format than any of the other audio sources discussed in this chapter.

There are several other advantages of the CD medium. The physical disc itself is as indestructible as any recording medium yet devised; it will stand up to considerable abuse and virtually unlimited playings. Also, the computer-based encoding and read-out system facilitates easy cueing and virtually instantaneous on-air playback. The digital controls allow you to automatically cue up any of dozens of tracks within a couple of seconds. Finally, you can leave the machine in the *pause* mode (unlike audiotape or records) for extended periods with no wear and tear on the disc—because there is no physical contact with any moving parts.

In chapter 3 (section 3.4), we will discuss other aspects of operating these various audio sources—loading and threading audiotape, cueing up records and audiotape, production uses of the CD, special effects (such as echoes and cross-fading), riding gain, and using the television program monitor for audio cues.

Summary

As an introduction to the audio system, we have been concerned more with *technical* functions than with *creative* functions. The seven *basic control functions* are transducing or modulation (and demodulation), channeling, mixing, amplifying, shaping, recording (and playing back), and monitoring.

These control functions were traced through the *audio signal flow* pattern—typically from studio microphone input, through the patch bay, into the audio console, through an input channel, through the volume control or potentiometer/fader, into a submaster channel, through the master potentiometer, out of the board through the line out, and back to the program-out position on the patch bay.

This basic audio signal flow applies generally to any sound source—either a *microphone* or various *prerecorded sound sources* (videotape audio track, audiotape, audio cartridge, record, or CD player).

In the next chapter we will look more specifically at the microphone and consider some basic creative aspects of audio control.

2.4 Training Exercises

1. Make an outline of the equipment found in your own audio facility using the seven control functions presented in this chapter.
2. Draw a sketch of both the audio patch panel and the audio console in your own facility. This will help you become familiar with the equipment and save considerable time when you operate it later.
3. Use the sketch along with the signal flow model in figures 2–4, 2–5, and 2–6 to trace a signal flow sequence through the equipment of your own audio facility.
4. Compile a list of terms from this chapter that are somewhat unfamiliar. Write out an extended working definition relating to your own facilities. This is an excellent discipline to maintain with every chapter.

The Audio System: Signal Flow and Technical Control

Audio Equipment and Creative Production Techniques

● ● ● ● ● ● ● ● ● ● ● ● ● ● ● ● ● ● ●

3

As stated in chapter 2, the function of a microphone is that of translating the pressure waves that we can hear as music or voices (sound energy) into an electronic wave pattern (electrical energy). Most of what is broadcast, music or otherwise, is an incredible combination of fundamental and overtone frequencies. Imagine, if you will, a hundred-piece symphony orchestra, each instrument of which is producing at any given point in time a fundamental tone and ten or more related **overtone** frequencies—or **harmonics**—that fall within the range of the human ear. (See appendix B.) A relatively small number of well-placed microphones can do an amazing job of capturing sound. The problem faced in the design of a microphone is that of the accuracy or **fidelity**—the ability to pick up and modulate as many frequencies as possible.

3.1 The Microphone: Function and Construction

In order to be able to appreciate what kinds of microphones are best suited for specific jobs, it is necessary to take a quick look at the phenomenon of audio **frequency range.**

Frequency Range

The optimum range of human hearing—from the lowest rumbles to the highest overtones—lies between twenty **Hertz (Hz),** or **cycles per second,** and 20,000 cycles per second (Hz). Hearing ability, however, may vary greatly with the individual as a result of inherited characteristics or ear damage.

AM radio, FM stations, and television sound vary in ability to transmit a wide portion of the frequency range. AM transmission is somewhat limited in the broadcasting of music because its upper frequency limit is only 7,500 Hertz. High-fidelity sound is achieved

Figure 3–1
Omnidirectional
microphone pickup pattern.

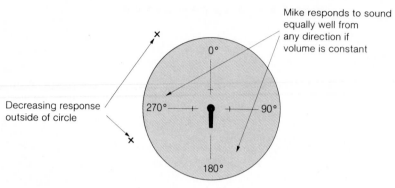

The omnidirectional microphone picks up sound
equally well from all directions.

on FM radio as a result of its ability to broadcast up to 15,000 Hertz. The audio portion of the television signal is also received as FM sound with the same theoretical upper limit of 15,000 Hertz. Up until the mid-1980s, however, the average home TV set was not equipped to take advantage of the higher frequencies, and as a result, broadcasters have been slow to utilize this potential.

There are two related qualities to look for in the performance of a microphone: first, its *frequency response*—the microphone must be able to respond to a wide range of fundamental and overtone frequencies—second, its ability to transduce those frequencies in the same proportion as they occur in the original sound pressure waves. It is the overtones that give a voice or musical instrument its own distinctive quality of tone. (See appendix B.) A mike's design may vary according to its mode of use, but basically what you pay for is the range and fidelity of sound reproduction.

Microphone Pickup Patterns

Another important criterion in selecting a microphone is its *pickup pattern*—the area within which the microphone can accurately pick up

sound. Some microphones respond well to sound coming from only one direction; others can adequately pick up sound from all directions. In addition to information concerning the upper and lower limits of frequency response, most microphone manufacturers provide a pickup pattern for each model. It is an attempt to express pictorially the limits of a microphone's response pattern at stated decibel volume levels.

Such information has valuable applications for the trained audio engineer in determining its use. For the production student, the response pattern can be used more simply as an aid in determining the directional qualities of a mike. Such two-dimensional visualization is called a *polar pattern* because it shows the limits of accurate mike response as would be seen from above. The actual response pattern is in reality a three-dimensional sphere of varying shape.

Figure 3–1 shows an **omnidirectional** (equal from all directions) response pattern. These microphones are also referred to as **nondirectional**. A mike with such a pattern would respond equally well to a sound source placed at any point within the circle (that is, sphere)—providing the size of the circle is not so large as to exceed the effective range of the microphone. The quality of the audio pickup is determined by the distance of the source to the microphone—not by the *direction* of the source from the mike. In other words, the effective range of a microphone can be expressed only in relation to a decibel volume level. (Obviously, the microphones in the illustrations have not been drawn to scale with respect to the size of the response pattern.)

Figure 3–2 illustrates a heart-shaped, or **cardioid,** response pattern. Such a pattern is considered being mainly from one direction, or **unidirectional.** Outside of the pattern area, some of the small **amplitudes** (lower volume) that constitute the sound source will not be picked up as well as others, if at all. The lesser amplitudes of overtone frequencies, for example, could be those that might be partly lost. The result is an **off-mike** distortion of the original sound.

Figure 3–3 illustrates a pear-shaped, *highly directional* pickup pattern. Specialized long-distance, or **shotgun,** mikes operate with this sort of pattern structure. To further increase their sensitivity, they are sometimes used in conjunction with a parabolic dish, which can collect and concentrate a relatively distant audio source and reflect this focused audio beam directly into the microphone.

Standard radio production formats popularized the *bidirectional* microphone pickup pattern. These mikes picked up the sound equally well from either side of the instrument. This was a desired feature in radio drama and interviews because the speakers and actors could stand on either side of the microphone, facing each other while speaking. Obviously, there is little use for this feature in television production.

Proximity Effect Certain microphones have a tendency to boost the bass frequencies when placed close to a sound source. Cardioid and bidirectional mikes are the most suscep-

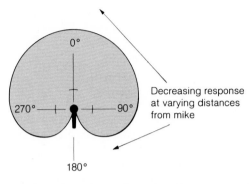

Figure 3–2
Unidirectional microphone pickup pattern.

The cardioid, or heart-shaped, pattern represents a microphone that picks up sound primarily from one direction.

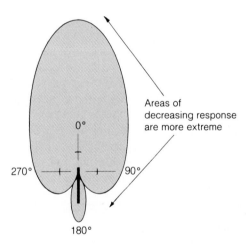

Figure 3–3
Highly directional microphone pickup pattern.

The highly directional microphone is designed to pick up sound, in a narrow response pattern, from relatively long distances.

tible to this **proximity effect.** This phenomenon emphasizes the "boominess" of an audio source and increases the volume of bass sounds—for example, a male voice appears closer to the microphone than a female voice even though they are both the same distance from the mike.

Most microphones are equipped with a *bass roll-off,* which reduces the proximity effect. Another possible solution to the effect is simply to increase the distance between the bass sound and the microphone. (Omnidirectional mikes are not troubled by the proximity effect.)

Microphone Construction: Transducing Elements

In addition to classification by pickup pattern, the audio operator should be familiar with the basic categories of microphone construction. Depending upon the purposes for which a microphone is to be used, there are several criteria that should determine selection of a mike for a particular job—*durability and ruggedness, frequency response, fidelity, physical use* (stationary or movable), *location* (in a studio or outdoors), and *cost*. There are several ways that the actual transducing element of a microphone can be built; these different categories meet different criteria.

The **moving coil** or **dynamic microphone** (see figure 2–1) generally is the most rugged and dependable.[1] It is sturdy and can stand more abuse than other commonly used microphones. It is especially useful for remote and outdoor locations. The moving coil or diaphragm stands up well to moderate shocks and sudden variations in the intensity of sound, and it can be used close to the sound source, which is especially valuable in noisy locations where the announcer or singer must work very close to the mike. The frequency response is good, but not as sensitive as other types listed in the following discussion. The dynamic microphone, in its many variations and models, is probably the workhorse of the television industry today.

1. Technically speaking, both the *moving coil* and *ribbon* microphones are "dynamic" mikes because they transduce energy electromagnetically—that is, by some sort of a dynamically vibrating element (either a moving coil or a ribbon) causing changes within an electromagnetic field. However, traditionally, the moving coil microphone has been referred to as a "dynamic" mike. We shall follow this conventional usage.

The **ribbon microphone** (also called velocity mike), by contrast, was the standard of radio production for many years. Its transducing element is a thin strip of metal foil. The mike is generally larger, less mobile, and considerably more delicate than the dynamic microphone. The quality and frequency response are very good, however, and it is an excellent mike for both voice and musical pickup, especially in the lower frequency range.

The **condenser microphone** (whose transducer is a variable *capacitor* activated by sound pressure waves) is also a high-quality, fragile instrument with a very wide frequency range. Because the capacitor generates a very low-level signal, it needs a preamplifier; this requires a battery power source either within the mike itself or very near to it, which can be inconvenient at times. The excellent fidelity and wide frequency response, however, make this microphone popular for musical pickup wherever stationary mike placement is possible (for example, for an orchestral string section but not for a rock singer's hand mike). It is considered a superior microphone in professional recording studios. It is also generally the most expensive. (See figure 3–4.)

Other types of transducing elements are used for specialized purposes, but none have the quality needed for broadcast usage. The less expensive *ceramic* and *crystal* elements, which translate vibrations from the diaphragm into electrical currents, have neither the fidelity nor the ruggedness needed for professional use. Granular *carbon* transducers are one of the earliest types of microphones. They are still used in telephones but have few other professional applications.

Impedance Levels

In our discussion of the audio console amplifying function (section 2.2.4), reference was made to differing impedance levels. **Imped-**

Audio Equipment and Creative Production Techniques

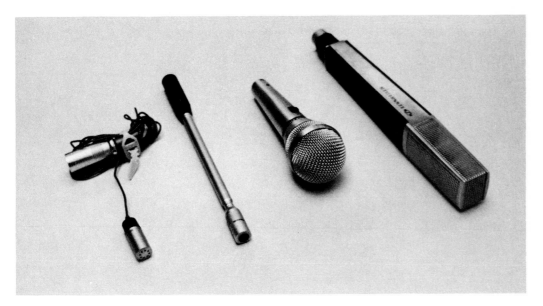

Figure 3–4
Representative studio microphones: *from left to right*, the Sony ECM–16 and the SuperScope EC–12B mikes are both condenser microphones; the larger Electro-Voice 671A and Sennheiser MD 441-U are dynamic mikes.

ance refers to resistance to the flow of an audio signal in the microphone cable. Professional studio microphones are always of the *low-impedance* type. Because there is less resistance to signal flow in the mike cable, the signal can be carried a great distance to the audio console, where it is amplified. Low-impedance cables are less susceptible to hum, static, or other forms of outside electrical interference. Professional ½-inch and ¾-inch video recorders are also designed to work with low-impedance mikes and lines.

However, most amateur and some industrial-level video recorders call for *high-impedance* mikes. These produce a stronger electrical signal than low-impedance microphones, but the signal deteriorates rapidly because of the higher resistance; therefore, relatively short cable lengths must be used with high-impedance mikes. Care should be taken not to mismatch high-impedance and low-impedance microphones, cables, and inputs. Unless a transformer is used, sound distortion will result.

3.2 Microphone Usage Categories

No single, all-purpose microphone has ever been designed. The most expensive microphone would have limitations in some situations. Instead, manufacturers provide a wide variety, each of which may combine a number of qualities suited to differing needs. A tremendous amount of time could be spent classifying the large variety of instruments available. However, it is not necessary for the television student to memorize a long list of microphones and their characteristics. It is of more immediate value if the student clearly understands some general usage classifications under which most mikes can be listed.

Some writers and practitioners have tried to classify microphones into the categories of *on-camera* and *off-camera*—those that are designed to be seen by the audience and those that are to be kept from view. Others have made the distinction between *stationary*

Figure 3–5
Many hand microphones such as the EV 671A can also be used as stand mikes.

and *mobile* microphones—depending upon whether or not the mikes are to be moved during the production. Rather than try to rely upon these categories, which often are not very functional distinctions in production, we would like to suggest the following three broad practical categories:

1. Hand and/or stand mikes
2. Limited-movement mikes
3. Attached personal mikes

These categories are obviously artificial designations—devised for learning purposes only. (For instance, you will never find a section of a microphone cabinet labeled "limited-movement mikes.") These classifications, however, should help you in thinking about the different ways in which microphones can be positioned and used—keeping in mind the positive qualities and limiting factors of each grouping. Also, note that these are not mutually exclusive categories; there is obvious overlap. Many mikes could fit into two of the groups.

Hand and/or Stand Mikes

Probably the most versatile group of mikes are those medium-sized, elongated instruments designed to work best at a range of six inches to three feet from a speaker or musical performer. Although a few require a fixed mount, most are structured to fit into a holder on a desk (for a news program or panel show) or in a floor mike stand (for a performer). The same microphone is used as a hand-held mike for, say, an on-location news event or for spontaneous interviews with members of an audience. This category overlaps both the stationary and mobile distinctions, for instance, in the case of a performer who begins a number by using a mike stand (stationary) and then removes the mike from the holder and concludes the number using it as a hand mike (mobile). (See figure 3–5.)

Resistance to the rugged handling of, say, a rock music performer is an important quality for such a mike. Most microphones in this category are *dynamic* mikes utilizing the coil and

Audio Equipment and Creative Production Techniques

magnet transducer. Many such instruments have a **pop filter** that minimizes the plosive effect of *T*'s, *K*'s, and *P*'s. Such a mike is all the more useful if it is designed to function in the outdoor conditions of news and sports remotes. These mikes require a fairly wide angle of sound acceptance and are usually either omnidirectional or cardioid in their pickup pattern.

Limited-Movement Mikes

This category encompasses several different kinds of microphone applications from stationary, fixed-position uses to a considerable amount of movement on large **perambulator booms.** Generally, microphones in this category are larger than those that are intended to be hand held. Almost always, mikes in this grouping are not intended for use on camera—they are seldom seen by the audience. As off-camera mikes, they are required to have good pickup qualities at relatively moderate to long distances. Some hand mikes, however, are designed to function adequately as omnidirectional boom mikes.

The label of "boom mike" can cover a wide variety of applications. The big boom, or *perambulator dolly* (see figure 3–6), is a large, three-wheeled movable platform that holds the boom operator and has a long counter-weighted boom arm that can be extended and tilted while the microphone itself can be rotated in almost a full circle. It is a large, cumbersome piece of equipment requiring two operators—one dolly pusher and one mike manipulator—and is effective only in spacious studios. They are used in pairs, for example, to cover the dramatic action in soap operas or to cover guests on a talk show, such as *The Tonight Show.*

A smaller boom, similar to that in figure 3–7, is the *giraffe*—a counterweighted boom arm supported by a tripod on casters that can be operated by one person. Although not as flexible as the big boom, the giraffe can be moved easier and takes up much less floor space. Even though it is thought of as a movable boom, the giraffe is often stationed in a fixed position for an entire production.

Finally, you may consider the use of the **fishpole**—literally a small, lightweight pole to which the microphone is attached. The operator hand holds the pole in order to get the best audio position for any given scene. Although extremely flexible, the operation of this device can be quickly tiring, and it is prone to cause mistakes because of the inexactness in operation (causing boom shadows, dropping it into a picture, accidentally hitting scenery, and so forth).

The fishpole is of most value on remote (location) single-camera shoots. First, it often is not practical to haul a boom mike—or even a giraffe—to many EFP locations. Second, on a single-camera production, the mike operator only needs to hold the fishpole in position for a few seconds (or a minute or two at the most) for a given shot.

Additionally, there is today a group of larger and more versatile instruments, all of which have excellent omnidirectional frequency response for instrumental or voice pickup.

The **PZM** (pressure-zone microphone), for example, is a condenser-type mike that consists essentially of a thin pickup plate. It is designed to lie flat on a large table or to be mounted on a large sheet of plexiglass; it can also be ceiling mounted. It uses the sound vibrations as transferred through the mounting medium (tabletop or plexiglass) to establish an "acoustic boundary," which eliminates phasing problems and tends to balance the sound levels of voices that are at different distances from the mike. Thus, it can be useful for picking up audience reactions, large choral groups, speakers around a large conference table, and so forth.

When sound must be picked up from unusually long distances (fifteen to twenty feet), there are several highly directional specialized

Figure 3–6
Two large studio perambulator booms used to cover a drama. (Photo courtesy of KCET, Los Angeles)

Figure 3–7
A giraffe, or tripod, microphone boom.

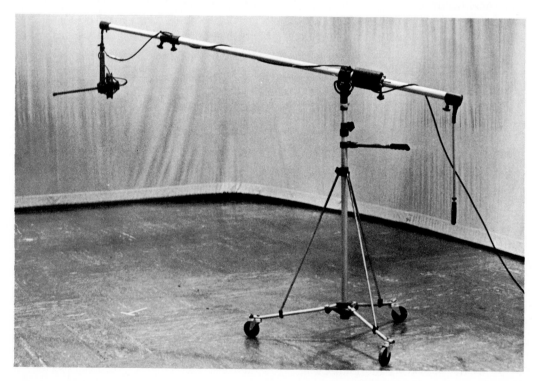

Audio Equipment and Creative Production Techniques

instruments that are used. Older versions of the so-called **shotgun** mikes have a frequency range that is adequate for speech or the related sound perspective of a sporting event, but not for instrumental music. Recent developments with the condenser shotgun, however, have resulted in a long-range microphone with excellent frequency response.

A special category of the fixed-position microphone would be the **hanging mike.** In certain situations (usually a drama) where it is impossible to mike a speaker in any other manner, it is possible to suspend an overhead microphone—hanging it from the catwalk or lighting grid. As a rule, a dynamic microphone with a cardioid pattern would be used. Most audio directors would rely on a hanging mike only as a last resort because there are several disadvantages: the sound source is often fairly far from the microphone; the actor or speaker may be slightly out of position and no adjustment can be made to reposition the mike; the speaker is usually projecting—at best—at right angles to the microphone; the mike is picking up the sound as reverberations off the studio floor, emphasizing any studio floor noises such as shoes and cables dragging. The result is most often a distant, off-mike quality with considerable ambient noise.

Attached Personal Mikes

Television created the necessity for an unobtrusive instrument that could move with the performer. The *lavaliere* microphone (worn around the neck) and the *lapel mike* are the result. Most of the earlier lavaliere models were effective omnidirectional mikes although they were limited to the frequency range of the human voice. Later models filter out unwanted noise caused by clothing rubbing against the mike. The more recent lapel models have a frequency response more than adequate for instrumental pickup.

Since earlier models tended to be somewhat bulky and obvious, many performers tried to hide the lavaliere under a tie or inside a blouse with a resulting muffled audio quality. Later models are so compact (no larger than a small thimble) they can be worn on top of clothing unobtrusively, with better audio pickup resulting. (See figure 3–8.)

The problems caused by mike cords have resulted in the development of the RF (radio frequency) **wireless microphone.** A miniature transmitter—either a part of the mike itself or in a concealed pack—sends an FM signal to a portable receiver that can be placed as far as several hundred feet from the performer. Although these systems have obvious advantages for television production, a propensity for dead spots in the transmission pattern and some limitations in frequency range have been the major limitations to their use. Recent progress with sophisticated receivers, however, has eliminated many of the problems. Ambitiously staged productions and musical videos have made the wireless mike almost indispensable in contemporary programming. Their advancing reliability and miniaturization make them increasingly popular for talk shows, remote productions, musical numbers, audience-participation segments, and so forth.

3.3 Using the Microphone

The proper procedures for microphone utilization are largely a matter of common-sense application of a few simple principles. With this section, we begin to get specifically into the area of the creative functions of audio production. Most successful audio/microphone usage is just an extension of three basic considerations: (1) selection of the correct microphone; (2) microphone placement; and (3) balance and perspective. A considerable amount of experience should also be included in this list.

Figure 3–8
The Sony ECM–30
illustrates how small the
lapel mikes have become.

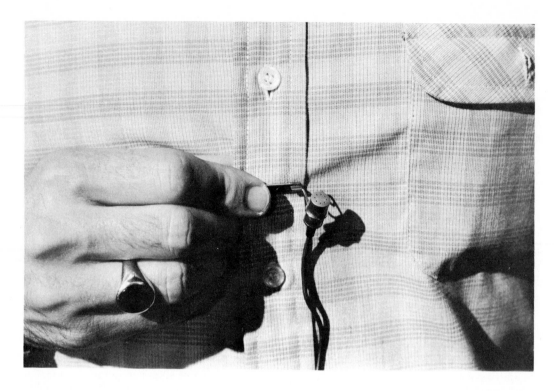

Microphone Selection

In many small stations and university studios, the question of microphone selection may be purely academic. If you have nothing more than a few basic dynamic cardioid microphones, that is what you will use. In most larger situations, however, the audio engineer will have a choice of several different kinds of mikes for any particular production.

When selecting the proper microphone, first define the audio job to be done. Let's take, for example, the task of picking up a well-tuned concert grand piano. Mikes should be selected on the basis of their known positive and negative qualities. Voice-frequency-range lavalieres and older long-distance shotgun mikes are not going to pick up all of the true tonal quality of the piano. Any of several full-frequency ribbon or condenser stand mikes placed either inside or underneath the instrument can do this satisfactorily. These same mikes placed with the piano outside of the pickup pattern would be equally unsatisfactory.

If you are concerned with recording a pop vocal personality, you must take into consideration whether or not the singer is likely to want to use a microphone as part of the performance—as a hand prop. If the singer does, you would want to use a fairly rugged dynamic mike. If, however, the production calls for an off-camera boom mike, then a full-frequency condenser microphone might be used, especially if fidelity to the musical quality is uppermost.

When producing a news program or panel discussion, the full-frequency range of a condenser or ribbon mike is not necessary. Depending upon the "look" of the production, you may decide on either a dynamic desk mike (desk mikes are often subject to considerable table pounding and verbal abuse) or lavalieres.

Suppose you are to handle a remote assignment covering a parade or sporting event. You would probably want a rugged, relatively insensitive unidirectional dynamic mike for the narrator/announcer (to allow him or her to work closely to the mike, cutting out as much background noise as possible) coupled with a highly directional shotgun mike to pick up selected crowd or parade sounds as desired. The first task, however, is always the same: define the job to be done in terms of frequency response needed, appropriate pickup pattern, physical abuse the microphone will likely be subjected to, and so forth.

In selecting microphones correctly for a particular audio pickup, one must be aware of two critical considerations. One is *aesthetic* and the other is *acoustical*. In a dramatic production, the mike should not be seen as part of the picture. Usually, directional long-distance pickup mikes mounted on movable booms are used. In some cases, wireless RF (radio frequency) equipment may be utilized. On the other hand, if you are working in a news, public affairs, or sports situation, the use of a hand mike is accepted by the audience—as is an occasional camera shot that reveals an operator holding a shotgun mike mounted in a parabolic dish.

Sometimes one must compromise between aesthetic and acoustical needs. In the telecast of a symphony performance, for instance, the quality of sound is very important. A number of mikes must be placed relatively close to the musicians to assure proper balance and timbre. This is especially true of string and woodwind instruments. An unobtrusive, sensitive microphone placed on a small stand would generally be accepted by the audience.

Microphone Placement

The earlier sections of this chapter have introduced several concepts relating to the selection of the proper microphone for a specific audio task: pickup pattern, frequency response, sensitivity, ruggedness, mounting considerations, and so forth. During this audio setup process, the engineer must also be considering the exact placement of each mike. A microphone that works well at one location may be inadequate in a slightly different position. One must, to use an old adage, "consider the source."

Sound, especially the higher frequencies, diminishes in loudness (amplitude) very rapidly as it passes through the air. This loss directly relates to the amount of energy it takes to propel the pressure wave through the molecules of the air. The rate of drop-off is scientifically described by the *Inverse Square Law*. Although this text is not the proper place to attempt to describe all of the principles of physics involved, the operating concept is easily understood: *as microphone-to-source distance is doubled, the loudness is reduced to one-fourth.*

Therefore, if you have an audio source (voice) giving you a constant level of sound one foot from a microphone, and then you move the mike back to a distance of two feet, the loudness of the sound hitting the microphone will be only one-quarter as loud as it was when the mike was one foot from the source. Similarly, if you again double your distance and place the microphone four feet from the source, you will reduce your loudness level to one-quarter of what it was at two feet (or one-sixteenth of what it was at one foot).

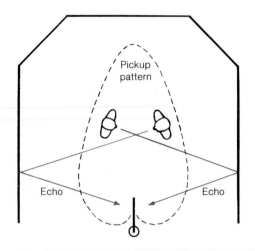

Figure 3–9
Incorrect placement of
directional mike between
two performers.

Although the two actors are standing "in the pattern" of the directional mike, their voices will be picked up with a hollow "off-mike" quality because they are not facing toward the mike; they are directing their voices away from the microphone.

Putting this principle into simple operational terms, suppose you have done a microphone level check (measuring a performer's voice loudness prior to going on the air in order to determine where to set your pot level) with a person who is seated one foot away from a desk mike. (See section 3.5.) Once the program starts, however, if that person then decides to lean back just one foot to be more comfortable, you have lost close to 75 percent of that person's volume! On the other hand, if you have a performer working ten feet from a long-distance directional microphone, and that person moves one foot backward, there will not be much of a noticeable difference (the performer has only increased his or her distance by one-tenth).

You must remember, however, that each microphone has its own pickup pattern involving distance and sensitivity, and outside of that pattern, the quality of sound will rapidly deteriorate.

Acoustical considerations for microphone placement can be thought of in terms of two interacting factors: *audio direction* and *microphone distance*. Audio direction refers to having the source (voice or musical instrument) squarely in the path of the directional pickup of the mike—with the audio source aimed directly at the microphone. If the audio source is not in the directional path of the microphone, or "on the beam," the resulting pickup will be off-mike. This results in a hollow, distant effect similar to being too far away from the microphone.

The audio operator must be constantly aware of *microphone-to-source* distance as it relates to *sound-power wave distortion*. If, for example, two actors are playing a dramatic scene, they will face each other more than toward the "audience" area. The audio operator must work closely with the director to determine the various speaking positions of the actors as they move about the set. An all-too-common error in this situation is to place a one-directional mike in the "audience" area in an attempt to pick up both voices. (See figure 3–9.)

At first glance, the actors would seem to be within the pickup pattern of the directional mike. One must keep in mind, however, that each sound source has a *projection* pattern, which is somewhat similar to the pickup pattern of a microphone. With the human voice, the shape of the mouth and lips tend to focus the strongest pressure waves in a relatively narrow channel as represented in figure 3–10.

When mikes are placed at a side angle (forty-five or more degrees to the direction of the direct sound pressure waves) the result is a considerable drop-off in audio level and in "presence." If you attempt to turn up the amplification at the pot to compensate for this loss, you will also begin to hear the reflected echo sound waves coming back from the set and walls of the studio. The result is an "off-mike" distortion of the original sound. While these reflected echoes are always a part of any sound pickup—contributing to the effect of natural room "presence"—they should be heard only in their natural proportion to the primary sound waves.

The proper placement of microphones for a two-person conversation is shown in figure 3–11. Using two mikes, the audio operator must position one mike directly in the path of each voice to pick up the best and most direct voice quality. If the two persons move about the set during the conversation, the perambulator dolly is necessary—the boom arm is extendable and the angle of the mike can be changed to keep the proper distance and mike direction in relation to the actors.

Determining the correct distance from source to microphone is a fairly simple and obvious matter and, at the same time, a highly complex study. Depending upon the type of microphone and the audio quality desired, the optimum speaking distance may be anywhere from a few inches to several feet. A typical shotgun directional mike might give fairly good audio pickup as far away as ten or fifteen feet. Because of the pickup patterns, speakers should generally work closer to an omnidirectional mike than to a unidirectional mike. Under good studio conditions, with a normal speaking voice, the announcer or talent should work about a foot away from an omnidirectional mike and up to two feet away from a cardioid mike. These are only rough rules, of course, and much depends upon such factors as studio conditions, specific microphone characteristics, and vocal qualities.

Balance and Perspective

In establishing the overall sound quality, the audio director must also give consideration to the subjective factors of how various sources balance each other and sound in perspective to

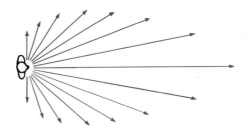

Figure 3–10
Sound pressure waves decrease rapidly in intensity except those projected straight forward.

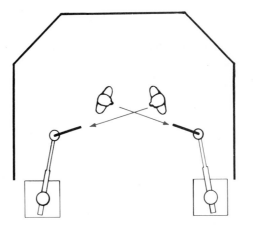

Figure 3–11
Correct placement of directional mikes.

In order to achieve optimum audio pickup from two actors facing each other, it is necessary to use two directional microphones; a separate mike is placed directly in the vocal path of each actor.

each other. No frequency response chart or VU meter can replace the human ear in determining the final sound of a program.

Getting the right proportion of volume levels from different sources is necessary. Are the musical instruments balanced? Is there too much piano for the vocal group? Are all of the panelists speaking at the same apparent level? Can a proper balance be achieved simply by adjusting volume levels with the faders, or should microphone placement be altered?

This last question gets into the area of audio **perspective**—an especially important concept in dramatic audio. Actors should appear to have an audio **presence,** or proximity that matches their video distance. The tighter a shot (the closer a character appears to camera), the closer a person should sound; as a character gets farther from camera, the more distant his or her voice should become. Thus, as two characters move in relation to each other on the screen, their audio perspective should change also. As a person walks out of a scene, his or her voice should appear to get further off-mike; as a person looms larger on the screen, we should get the feeling of more presence. An extreme close-up shot often calls for an exaggerated audio intimacy—a stream-of-consciousness technique suggesting a stage whisper or an aside to the audience.

This audio presence cannot be achieved simply by adjusting volume levels with the pots. Microphones have to move in relation to the actors. Either the actors walk farther away from the microphones (to achieve audio distance), or the mikes, on booms or fishpoles, have to be moved away from the actors. Care must be taken to ensure that video distance and audio presence do not unintentionally contradict each other. Many an amateur dramatic effect has been ruined by using a hidden microphone concealed near a doorway in the rear of a set; the player bids an emotional adieu only to have his or her audio presence increase as he or she walks away from the camera.

A related problem is that of "apparent loudness." The human ear is not equally sensitive to all frequencies. The loudness of a sound will affect how well we hear relative high and low frequencies. At low volume, the ear is less sensitive to low pitches. And at high volume, the high and low frequencies sound too loud in relationship to the mid-range pitches. Therefore, the audio engineer must pay particular attention to the relative volume of high and low frequencies—boosting the level of quiet low-pitch sources and balancing mid-range frequencies at high volumes.

Phasing and Stereo Considerations

Television audio is taking on new dimensions with the advent of **stereophonic sound** or *MTS* (multichannel television sound). By early 1987, more than a quarter of all TV stations were already broadcasting in stereo. Production for stereo programming involves a couple additional considerations—stereo microphone placement and phasing.

Stereo Mike Placement   In its simplest configuration, stereo audio pickup requires two microphones—one for the left channel and one for the right channel. But there is nothing simple about sticking two mikes on the set and achieving decent stereo audio. Proper microphone placement is a very critical element in creating realistic stereophonic sound. There are three basic approaches you should be familiar with.

The simplest setup would be the **spaced microphones** (or "split-pair" mikes). In this configuration, two mikes are placed parallel to each other facing into the set—roughly analogous to the placement of your stereo speakers at home. The pickup pattern is usually directional. Distance between the mikes can be a problem in this setup. When the mikes are more than about three feet apart, the stereo image becomes distorted; sounds in the center become louder than those on the right or left. If the mikes are more than ten feet apart, the sounds in the center become lost; an audio source that is moving slowly across the stage will suddenly appear to skip or bounce between the left and right channels. And serious phasing problems can occur if the mikes are not carefully positioned. This configuration often requires a third mike in the center. (See figure 3–12, top.)

Audio Equipment and Creative Production Techniques

A second, and usually more effective, technique is the **X-Y** (or "crossed-pairs") mike placement. This is what is known as a *coincident* miking technique. This involves placing two cardioid microphones like crossed swords, forming (as seen from above) a perfect X and Y axis (figure 3–12, center). The angle actually can be anywhere from 60 to 120 degrees, depending on the specific production requirements—the wider the angle, the greater the apparent stereo separation.

A third configuration, also a *coincident* pattern, is the **M-S** or "mid-side" miking. This involves three microphones arranged somewhat like an inverted "T" forming two 90-degree angles (figure 3–12, bottom). This is a more technically sophisticated setup in that it requires a transformer matrix or mixer. The matrix decoder can then combine the middle mike (M) with the two side mikes (S) separately to form the two complementary stereo channels. Although it involves more electronic juggling, the result can be very effective because the audio engineer can easily manipulate spatial perspectives and stereo effects without having to physically move either microphones or audio sources.

Phasing As described in chapter 2, electrical sound energy can be thought of as traveling in waves. (See figure 2–1.) In many situations—but especially so in stereo production—electrical waves from a given studio source (e.g., an actor's voice) will arrive at the patch bay/audio console/recorder/transmitter via more than one channel (two or more open microphones in the studio). Technically, **phasing** is a measure of how close the signals from the two microphones are to being in perfect synchronization.

If the two signals arrive at the mixing bus at precisely the same instant, they are said to

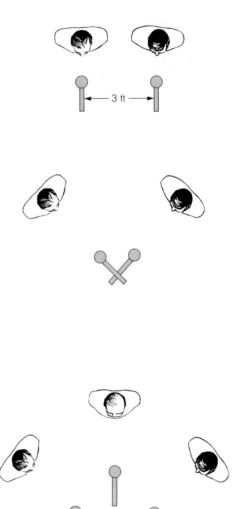

Figure 3–12
Three basic stereo microphone patterns.

Top, the "split-pair" setup works best if the microphones are about three feet apart.
Middle, the X-Y or "crossed pairs" setup is a coincident pattern, meaning that sounds from both directions reach both microphones at the same time (coincidently), avoiding potential phasing problems.
Bottom, the M-S ("mid-side") setup, another coincident pattern, involves an auxiliary transformer matrix to balance the center mike with the two side mikes.

Figure 3–13
Sine waves demonstrating phasing problems in a multiple-microphone setup.

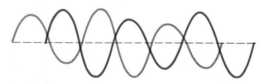

Top, two different sine waves (one black and one color) representing left and right stereo signals in phase.
Middle, two signals (sine waves) that are slightly out of phase; this would result in a "beating" effect with the perceived volume rapidly fluctuating up and down.
Bottom, when the two sine waves are 180 degrees out of phase, the signals completely cancel each other out, and there is no sound at all.

be "in phase." Quite often they will be slightly out of phase—that is, the signal from one microphone will reach the mixing bus a split second before the signal from the second microphone (because the source of the sound, the actor's voice, is a little farther away from one mike than from the other). If the two signals

are completely out of phase 180 degrees, the positive *sine wave* from one source will be peaking at the same instant that the negative wave from the other signal is hitting bottom.[2] As a result, the two signal components cancel each other out and the effect is silence—no signal at all (figure 3–13).

Thus, it can be seen that phasing is a crucial consideration when working with stereo production. The main problem comes when the left and right channel stereo signals are combined for monaural reception—which is quite frequently the case. If the signals are out of phase, the monaural sound will range from an annoying *beating* as the signals reinforce and weaken each other (with a resulting rapid fluctuation in volume) to actual silence if the signals are 180 degrees out of phase.

In order to guard against such phasing problems, there are a couple of things you can do. First, of the three stereo microphone setups described previously, consider using the latter two configurations (the X-Y pattern and the M-S pattern). These are so-called coincident patterns because the microphrones are placed right next to each other; thus, all audio sources reach each microphone simultaneously and the signals are transmitted to the mixing bus *coincidentally,* thereby guaranteeing that they arrive in phase.

Secondly, if you must use a variation of the *split-pair* or "spaced" microphones, follow the **3–to–1 rule.** Make sure that the microphones are at least three times as far apart from each other as each microphone is from its sound source. Thus, if each mike is one foot from a reporter, make sure that the micro-

---

2. The sine wave is the periodic oscillation representing the electronic signal. The wave is graphically pictured as having a positive phase (when the wave is above the horizontal reference line representing the exact assigned frequency) and a negative phase (when the wave is below the horizontal reference point).

phones are three feet from each other. The reason for this is that each microphone will be picking up both voices, and—since one voice is closer to microphone A than it is to microphone B—mike B will pick up the voice a split second later than mike A; therefore, as the two signals are sent to the audio booth, the signal from microphone A will get there a split second earlier, and the two signals will be out of phase. However, if the mikes are spaced three times as far apart as they are placed from the sources, the delayed signal will be weak enough (remember the Inverse Square Law explained under "Microphone Placement") that the out-of-phase signal will be negligible.

Phasing can often be a problem with conventional monaural production also. The same out-of-phase situation can occur any time more than one mike is picking a given source. Therefore, the same 3–to–1 rule should be applied in any studio situation whenever you have several speakers miked separately.

3.4 Adding Other Audio Sources

Up to this point we have been concerned entirely with the microphone as the source of television audio. We now turn our attention to other sources of prerecorded sound (as outlined in section 2.3).

Patching Audio Sources

All prerecorded audio sources generally come from one or two locations—either the audio control room or the telecine (the master control room). Those playback machines located in the audio booth—CD player, audiotape recorder, record turntables, cartridge player—either will be normalled (permanently wired) into the audio console or will be patched through the audio patch bay in the booth. Those audio sources coming from the telecine

or master control—videotape players, film projectors (if used at all)—will probably be fed into the audio booth through some sort of external patching arrangement.

In many studio operations, the master control room has a patch bay similar to the one in the audio booth, except that the master control room patch bay has inputs not for microphones but for audio outputs from videotape recorders and film projectors. These audio outputs (and there often are two audio tracks per videotape recorder) can be fed to each other and to other terminals in master control and/or they can be connected to **tie lines.** The tie lines are used to connect the master control room with other key locations, such as a transmitter or the audio control room.

It is these tie lines that are used for sending audio signals from the audio booth to master control (for example, the program audio from "line 1 out") where the audio can then be recorded on videotape recorders or sent out to the transmitter via further patching. Similar tie lines are used for sending various audio signals (for example, from film projectors and VTR machines) from master control to the studio audio booth for mixing into program audio.

Once the prerecorded audio sources are patched or normalled into the console, they then follow the signal flow as explained in section 2.2.2. The correct input selector switch for each source must be flipped on, the channel selector (pot on-off) key must be set, and the pot or fader is then used to control the volume. Like microphone levels, the volume level or gain of prerecorded audio should be adjusted to peak at close to zero db (or "100") on the VU meter. Riding gain on prerecorded audio *should* be somewhat easier than riding gain on live microphones, because the prerecorded audio has already gone through a mixing and recording process and should be set at a fairly constant level.

Figure 3–14
Cueing a record.

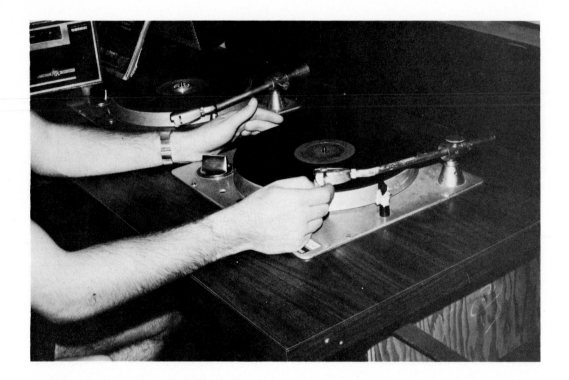

Cueing Procedures

A crucial aspect of using prerecorded audio of any type is getting the sound **cued up** to exactly the right starting point so that the correct sound is available precisely when the director calls for it. Except for the audio cartridge, which cues itself automatically, and the CD player, which can easily be cued up digitally, the audio operator is going to have to get the sound cued up at the correct spot.

Using the Turntable For purposes of a detailed explanation, it would probably be most worthwhile to look at the specific procedures involved in cueing up a phonograph record. Although the layout of audio booths—the re-

lationship of audio console and turntables—varies considerably, the following steps can be adapted to any situation.

1. Place the potentiometer in the **cue,** or **audition, position.** With a knob-type pot, this will be all the way to the left. With a slide-fader, this will be all the way to the bottom of the scale. This particular pot is now connected only to the cue audio system, which has its own speaker.

2. With the turntable power off, place the needle in the outside groove of the record (see figure 3–14). Lightly place your fingertips on the inside label of the record. Turn the record clockwise

until the first tone is heard. (Most turntables are equipped with a felt pad that allows the record and the felt to move independently of the turntable surface.)

3. Stop the record at the first tone, now move it in a counterclockwise direction one-quarter of a revolution and stop. If the record is not backed up in this manner, it will **wow** as it comes up to speed when it is put on the air.

4. With your free hand, immediately take the fader (pot) out of the cue position, being careful to leave it at the "0" volume-level position. (More than one TV audio operator or beginning disk jockey has been blissfully unaware that the record he or she thinks is on the air is being heard only on the cue speaker.)

5. Just prior to playing, gently lay your fingers on the record. (With the slightest jolt, the needle will jump out of the groove.) Use your other hand to switch on the turntable power. This is called *slip cue,* because the turntable is now up to playing speed while the record is being held in readiness.

6. At the proper command, the record is released and the pot is brought up to the desired level. This is called "sweeping the pot." The one-quarter turn now allows the felt to grip the turntable and bring the record up to playing speed. One danger with this method is that you may hit the wrong level when you are opening the pot. An alternative method is to preset the pot to the proper level (determined earlier when you are obtaining levels for all audio inputs and recorded

sound) and simply open the key when you release the record; the danger here is that if you misjudge the timing of the opening of the key, you have an abrupt audio miscue. With either method, the timing of the operator is very critical. If the pot is already opened when the record is released, we will hear scratches prior to the first tone. If the operator is a fraction of a second late in opening the pot, the first tones will be *upcut.* This means that the beginning of the record either will not be heard at all or will be played at a very low level.

7. As soon as the record starts, you should immediately glance at the VU meter to see if any further adjustments in level are necessary. It is a good idea—prior to the actual production—to check the level of the opening section of any record to be used during a production situation. This *cannot* be done when cueing a record because the VU meter does not monitor any signal on the cue system.

If your turntable is equipped with a non-slip rubber mat, the record must be started from a dead-stop position. In this case, a half revolution is suggested in order to bring the turntable up to playing speed to prevent a wow.

Master Control Sources   In working with videotape and film projection, the audio operator is probably not involved with loading the playback machine nor concerned about the cueing process at all. This is usually handled by an engineer in master control or the projection-film chain area. The playback engineer will have the VTR machine or film pro-

Figure 3–15
Stereo audiotape recorder.
This recorder has four
heads: an erase head, a
record head, and two
playback heads,
depending upon the track
configuration desired.

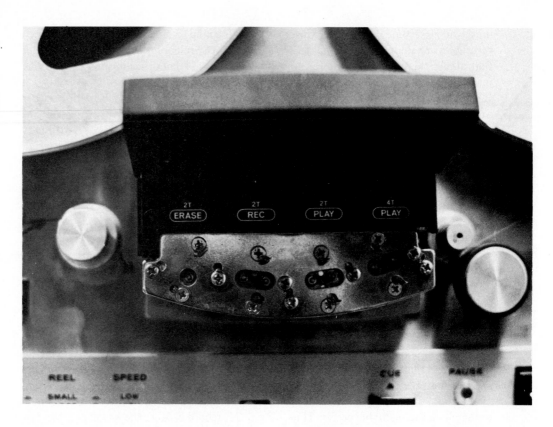

jector threaded and cued up according to the film or videotape leader or footage counter. This procedure indicates exactly how far ahead of the desired sound and picture the machine is set. The primary job of the audio operator is simply to check his or her signal flow (input channel settings) and be ready to bring up the volume when directed to do so.

In most studio situations, the audio booth will be equipped with a TV line monitor. This enables the audio operator to see the actual TV program as it is being put together. Thus, the operator can get a visual cue for the videotape and film inserts—which reinforces the direct cue from the director—and time his or her audio starts accordingly.

Audiotape Cueing   In working with audiotape, however, the audio engineer has the responsibility for threading and cueing.

Threading the audiotape recorder is a simple process, as long as one carefully follows the threading diagram. Always check to be certain that the audiotape has not been incorrectly wound on the reel, that the magnetic side of the tape (usually dull) is threaded so that it comes in contact with the playback head of the recorder, and that the base (usually the shiny side) is facing away from the heads.[3] The audio recorder has three or four heads arranged in a row—the erase head, the record head, and one or two playback heads. (See figure 3–15.)

In cueing up the audiotape, the principle is the same as for cueing records. Once the first tone is heard (with the pot set in the cue position), the supply and take-up reels should si-

3. On most *video*tape, the oxide or magnetic side of the tape is the shiny side.

Audio Equipment and Creative Production Techniques

multaneously be turned backwards by hand so that the first tone is about two inches from the playback head. For tape recordings at 3¾ ips (inches per second), it need only be about one inch; for 15-ips recordings, it should be closer to four inches.

Production Use of the CD Player　The process of cueing and using a CD player is so operationally sensible that you can easily master the necessary techniques with a few minutes of practice. The operator is able to move almost instantly from the beginning of one numbered cut to another, fast forward, reverse to any point in the selection, and then place the unit in *pause* for an instant startup.

The significant thing to remember about this technology is that when the unit is in *pause* or any of the *shuttle* modes, there is absolutely no wear on the disc itself. The light waves of the laser beam that scans the disc in no way parallel the physical contact made by a phonograph needle on a vinyl record or by the recording head on an audiotape or videotape. The laser beam consists of tightly focused rays of light that cannot damage the information stored in the disc; the laser beam in no way can wear away the disc itself.

While many teaching facilities simply utilize inexpensive consumer CD players, the professional broadcasting models that are now available offer a great array of search, pause, and cueing options along with many dubbing and editing features. (See figure 2–14.)

Mixing and Other Techniques

When two or more sound sources are mixed together—microphones and prerecorded sources or some of each—the audio operator must rely upon his or her ear to be sure that the balance is correct. Recorded music may vary considerably in volume within the space of twenty or thirty seconds of playing time. For this reason, the operator must be careful not to let a sudden increase in the volume of background music distract from what is being said. Unless otherwise occupied with cueing records or tapes, most audio engineers keep their hands right on the pots or faders in order to ride gain, constantly adjusting to even small changes in the input level.

Occasionally the audio mixing can be rather complex. Sometimes several microphones will have to be *potted down* (faded out) simultaneously while a prerecorded announcer on audiotape is started. This can be accomplished on a dual-channel board if one of the channels has been converted (or can be switched) to a submaster; then the several microphones can be put on the submaster by means of the channel selector switch and controlled with one submaster pot.

At other times, there may be constant balancing and readjustment of several sound sources—say, background music on a tape, sound effects on a turntable, and two different microphones. Dramatic continuity may call for a **cross-fade** or **segue** between different musical selections. A cross-fade is a transition whereby one sound (musical record) is faded out while another is faded in, thereby effecting a temporary overlap of the two musical selections. A segue is similar except that the first sound is completely faded out before the second one is brought in. Both of these procedures call for the simultaneous control of two different turntables or other sources.

Continuous sound effects can be achieved with audiotape by **looping.** With a **reel-to-reel** player, a single tape loop can be spliced together and played continuously, which will give several seconds of a background sound. With an audio cartridge player, by removing the stop-cue the entire cart loop will keep repeating.

Occasionally the audio operator may have to make some fast switching for special effects. A **filter** is often used to simulate a telephone conversation, for example. If the picture changes in the middle of one person's dialogue on the telephone (that is, if we are looking at John talking on the telephone and then the picture changes to Susan listening to John), we must instantaneously have a corresponding change in audio in order to maintain the proper sound perspective. Watching the TV line monitor, the audio operator must make certain that we perceive the filter effect (to simulate the other end of the telephone conversation) when the picture changes from the speaker to a reaction shot of the listener.

Finally, mention should be made of **echo effects.** Even without fancy reverberation chambers and special devices, a simple echo effect can be achieved in most control booths with just one audiotape recorder. It is necessary only to patch and connect the tape recorder for simultaneous recording and playback. That is, the *line out* from the console must be patched into the *audiotape in* as well as the *audiotape out* being fed back into the console. Then by introducing an independent audio source, say a microphone from the studio, this source is recorded on the record head of the tape recorder and, as it passes over the playback head a split second later, fed back into the console. It can then be mixed—through the pot controlling the audiotape playback—with the original sound coming directly from the studio microphone. The result is the original sound, followed a split second later by a recorded version of the same sound. Depending upon the level of the audiotape playback pot, this effect can range from a very slight echo suggestive of a large hall or cave to some very bizarre futuristic electronic distortions. When using this procedure, however, the operator must be careful to ride the gain on the master pot very closely; as the reverberation is increased, the feedback effect greatly amplifies the master level very rapidly.

3.5 Production Techniques

We are now approaching the point where you should be ready for your first production exercise. It may be helpful at this juncture to emphasize the difference between single-camera film techniques and the immediacy of a continuing process inherent in a multiple-camera TV production (see section 1.4); this distinction generally shapes the nature of television production and determines the roles of the crew members.

Television and Film Production

Conventionally, live studio television seeks to achieve the nonstop production of entire programs or at least complete segments of programs. Film technique, especially as used in dramatic motion pictures, involves the shooting of multiple takes of short 10- to 20-second segments. These are usually shot totally out of story sequence. Much of the art of filmmaking lies in the later painstaking editing process. In live television, the director is doing all of the editing as the program progresses. What you see (on the line monitor) is what you get. With advances in technology, however, the two processes are gradually coming to resemble each other more and more. Various TV sports and public affairs programming borrow heavily from the film genre for its videotape editing techniques. The simultaneous use of three film cameras employed on several MTM productions is like live television, although there is a later editing process.

Television's primary virtue is that it is able to capture the reality of a continuing performance or event in real time, not a stop-and-go re-creation of time. In the arts, this is an important ingredient of the creative process, especially for the performer. It is also essential

Audio Equipment and Creative Production Techniques

to sports, news, and some public affairs programming.

Television's ability to function within the "real-time" continuum, however, places considerable demands upon all of the crew members. Before beginning our initial class production exercise, we should mention the intercommunication network, the elements of vocal command procedures, and some audio setup procedures.

The Intercom Network

The system by which all production elements are brought together at the precise moment they are needed in a program is the intercommunication network, or **intercom network.** Also known as the **P.L.** (private line), this is, in essence, a closed-circuit audio network that connects all primary production and engineering personnel by standard telephone **headsets** that have an earpiece and a small microphone or mouthpiece. Thus, the director can talk to the **stage manager** or **floor director**[4] without the conversation being picked up by any microphones; the technical director can talk to camera operators; the audio engineer can give commands to the boom operator; the associate director can check with the video recording engineer; and so forth.

Of course, with everyone trying to communicate with everyone else, the system would result in absolute and continual chaos—without a measure of discipline and self-restraint by all involved. Ordinarily the director predominates, and the system is at his

or her disposal at all times; when the line is clear—or when the director specifically assigns the P.L. to some high-priority function—the appropriate crew members have access to the system. In some large systems, separate P.L. networks may be set up for engineering and production personnel. Thus, the video engineer and technical director can carry on a conversation without interfering with the director and floor crew.

A double headset system might also be used by the audio personnel. This enables the audio director and boom operator(s) to hear the P.L. with one earpiece and to monitor the program audio with the other earpiece. This is invaluable for a boom operator who is following a fast-moving piece of dialogue among three people; for instance, he or she can directly monitor the balance and perspective being picked up while manipulating and adjusting the boom position.

The **studio address (S.A.),** or **studio talk-back** system, is another link in the production crew intercommunication network. The S.A. talkback microphone in the control room (and there may be a parallel system out of the audio booth) enables the director to activate a special studio speaker so that he or she can talk to everybody in the studio, regardless of whether or not they have on P.L. headsets. (The S.A. speaker automatically cuts out the regular program microphone input to guard against any unintentional feedback, which could damage the audio system. Needless to say, the studio talkback should not be used while microphones are activated during a program.) Part of the discipline of the television director is knowing when to use the S.A. (to communicate efficiently and quickly with the whole crew and all talent simultaneously) and when to rely on the floor manager (to interpret and carry out direct orders and implied threats).

4. The terms "stage manager," "floor manager," and "floor director" are used interchangeably in this text. Used in different parts of the country, by different kinds of production centers, they all refer to the chief crew member on the floor—the director's surrogate for the studio stage.

Figure 3–16
Time frame for a simple audio production.

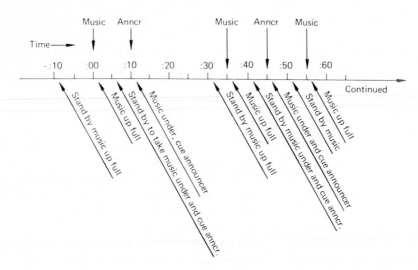

This time chart shows the commands to be given in a simple commercial announcement. This should apply to the preparation and first minute of the Class Audio Production Project in appendix D–1.

The commercial starts at ":00" with music; the announcer reads the first copy starting at ":10" (10 seconds); music comes up full at ":35"; the second announcer starts at ":45"; music comes up full at ":55"; and so forth.

The total intercommunication system is further extended—to the performing talent during the production—by the hand and arm signals of the floor manager. This is the pantomime system by which different directions can be given to persons while they are on camera without having to vocalize any commands and thereby possibly unintentionally getting these directions picked up as part of the program audio. (See appendix C for illustration of basic hand and arm signals.)

Vocal Command Procedures

At this stage, you also need to be aware of the vocal commands that are used to direct the entire production. Over the years, television production has evolved a system that separates commands into two phases—preparation and execution. The *commands of execution* are those cues that directly affect what goes out over the line monitor. "Take camera one" and "Cue the announcer" call for an immediate action at a precise point in time. For a crew member or performer to be able to respond with this immediate action, however, he or she must be given adequate preparation time to be mentally ready and/or physically prepared to perform some action or operate the equipment. For this reason, all commands of execution must be preceded at some point by a related *command of preparation*. Figure 3–16 shows how the commands fit into the time frame of the production sequence for a simple audio exercise. (The commands and timing indicated in figure 3–16 are designed to be used with the commercial/production exercise in appendix D-1.)

Audio Equipment and Creative Production Techniques

The term **standby** (announcer, music, record, and so forth) is probably the most functional preparatory command for our present needs. It should alert the audio operator—and all other personnel—to listen carefully for the next command. *Cue* is quite often used to begin a command of execution. Sometimes just the term *music* or *announcer* can be used as the command of execution. Complete voice command procedure for a total television production is, of necessity, somewhat more complicated than what we have presented here; other commands will be discussed in conjunction with the explanation of video switching procedures (section 7.5).

Audio Setup Procedures

Finally, prior to the initial class audio production exercise, we should outline some basic steps in an audio setup. During any production setup, the audio assistants will follow the audio engineer's instructions as to which studio inputs to use and where to set up the mikes. This is an important introduction to the concept of position responsibility within the chain of command. By the same token, it is the director who has the ultimate responsibility for the operation.

The person in charge of audio should first go through the entire signal flow process mentally before giving any instructions. If a mike does not work, it is he or she who must initiate a step-by-step signal flow checkout.

To gain the most from any training exercise, it is suggested that all patches and mike cords be unplugged and redone with new input numbers as each new director takes over.

Once the mikes are all working, the audio operator should get a **level** from each of the performers. Different person's voices vary considerably in strength. Using the VU meter, the audio operator can find an optimum position on the potentiometer for each voice. This is an average or middle position between the highest and lowest movements of the needle. The highest points or peaks should only occasionally exceed the 100 percent modulation position of the meter—the "0" point.

Summary

As part of the *technical* requirements for audio production, it is important to know something about *microphone construction*—frequency response, pickup patterns, construction of transducing elements (dynamic, ribbon, condenser, and other types), and impedance levels. These factors determine the way different microphones can be physically handled—as hand or stand mikes, limited-movement mikes, and attached personal mikes.

Getting into *creative* considerations, the audio director must be concerned with the way microphones are utilized—*selection* and *placement* of the mikes, and *audio balance* and *perspective*. Moving into *stereo* production adds additional problems of balance and *phasing*.

In adding other prerecorded sound sources, the audio operator must also be familiar with *patching* from different areas, *cueing* techniques for various media, and *mixing* procedures. In preparation for our first audio production exercise, the audio operator must also understand the basic television production procedures, the *intercom network,* the *vocal commands,* and the *audio setup* operations.

In the next chapter, we turn from audio to video considerations as we look first at lighting requirements and techniques.

3.6 Training Exercises and Class Audio Project

Class Exercises

1. Prepare a list of all of the microphones that are available for use in your own facility. Using the manufacturer's specifications, if available, describe the specific design qualities for each, as well as any limitations that should be noted.
2. Go through a live demonstration for each mike, showing the pickup pattern and range of frequency response. Listen carefully for the distinctive differences in sound quality occurring in each of the basic types of instruments.

Class Audio Production Project (appendix D-1)

This audio production exercise is in the form of a radio commercial. It is designed to develop the techniques and disciplines needed to set up microphones and mix two announcers with music. Although one mike could be adequate, it is suggested that two stand or desk mikes be used for the exercise. This use will provide more practice in setup, patching, and operational techniques. The mikes should be placed at least three feet apart and side by side so that both announcers can see the stage manager's signals. The announcers should work about twelve to eighteen inches from each mike.

First of all, let us consider the production elements that must fit together in a precise sequence for the initial portion of the commercial script. You must first establish the music, which is then faded under (at low volume below the announcer's voice, but still audible) for the announcer who speaks for twenty-five seconds. The music is then brought up again for ten seconds, then under again as the second announcer speaks for twenty seconds. The music is brought up again, and you have completed the first part of the commercial. Figure 3–16 illustrates the production time frame.

It looks simple, and it really is, just as long as the two announcers and the audio engineer are able to coordinate their actions. For this we need some sort of director. In most smaller audio operations, the audio engineer serves this function. As preparation for later, more complicated television production exercises, it is suggested that a separate person act as director.

Audio Equipment and Creative Production Techniques

TV Lighting Equipment and Techniques

4

Television production consists basically of two elements—audio and video. Chapters 2 and 3 dealt with audio. Chapters 5 through 10 deal specifically with different aspects of the television picture. (The rest of the book is concerned with putting it all together.) Before we can look at how cameras and lenses work, however, it is necessary to spend some time looking at that physical phenomenon that makes all vision possible—light! Without light there would be no video. And without good lighting, there would not be good video.

4.1 Types of Light: Incident and Reflected

Light comes to us in two somewhat different forms. There is light that comes directly from a source such as the sun, a light bulb, or a candle. This is called **incident light,** and as important as it is, it tells us little beyond the fact that we are looking at a light source.

Our ability to see is the result of a second kind of light that has been reflected from and, as a result, altered by the surface of a material substance. This **reflected light** transmits information to us regarding our environment; the brain has been conditioned to respond to this information as perceived by the eye.

As children, we constantly reinforced our developing visual sense by touching the objects in our immediate environment. We were, in effect, programming our computer-like so that we could "believe our eyes." Looking out on the world, we see a series of flat planes and curved surfaces occurring at various angles. The reflected light from these diverse surfaces comes to our eyes in differing intensities—depending upon the position of the incident light sources. Our brain learns to translate these variations of light and shadow into the concept of shape and texture.

Take as an example the instructor's desk in a classroom. The dimensions of the top of the desk are defined for us by the uniform intensity of the light reflected from all points of its surface. The light reflected from the side of the desk is of a different intensity, possibly somewhat of a shadow; this tells us that these side surfaces are at a different angle from the top and indeed are the sides of the desk. Other features, such as the drawer handles and the legs, are defined by the shadows that the light source "molds" around them.

Reflected light also tells us much about the *texture* of a surface. The even, shiny quality of light reflected from the desktop denotes a hard, uniform surface. Cloth is much more light absorbent. We can perceive the texture of a heavy cloth material by the many tiny shadows created by the design of the weave.

Illumination for video production, as we shall see, is an art that involves the proper use of lighting equipment to control the light that is reflected *from* the subject *to* the camera. It is the way we shape and control this reflected light that determines what the TV camera perceives as a picture.

4.2 Lighting Objectives: Basic Illumination

When the lighting director (L.D.) sets out to design the lighting plan (section 4.6) for any type of video production, he or she must think in terms of two interacting concerns. On the one hand, there are important considerations that grow out of the *artistic* or *creative needs* of the program. These will be examined in section 4.3. On the other hand, the L.D. knows that the creative aspects of lighting must exist within the larger context of *general illumination,* which is necessary to meet the technical needs of the camera system. These two categories—basic illumination and artistic concerns—correspond to the basic technical and creative functions as introduced in section 2.1.

The term most often used to refer to this general or primary illumination is **base light.** The first consideration of base light is simply to make sure that there is sufficient illumination so that the cameras can operate. Like the human eye, unless there is a minimum amount of light, the camera cannot "see." However, modern cameras can function with a relatively small amount of light. Therefore, our main concerns with base light are achieving a consistency of brightness and maintaining color quality on all cameras on all shots.

Base light should not be thought of as a separate planning entity. It is, rather, the sum total of specialized and general lighting used throughout the set. A specialized artistic effect light falling on a performer may also illuminate parts of the set and thereby contribute to the total base light effect. To accomplish an even base light, the L.D. must take into consideration two technical aspects of the lighting conditions (whether artificial or natural sunlight)—*intensity* (contrast ratio) and *color quality* (color temperature).

Contrast Ratio

The first of these factors has to do with the complexities of the video camera pickup tube or CCD chip (see section 5.2) and the way it reacts to differing degrees of brightness within a single picture. For example, in an evenly lit living room scene on a wide shot, the colors are correctly balanced and the detail of the picture is clear. Now, as we introduce into this shot a person wearing a white raincoat who fills the left-hand quarter of the frame, several rather drastic things happen—as a result of the camera's *automatic gain control* (AGC), which maintains an overall brightness level and reacts to the introduction of the very bright area by decreasing the intensity of the rest of

TV Lighting Equipment and Techniques

the picture. Without any changes in either the lighting or the camera controls, the right-hand three-quarters of the picture will suddenly become much darker. The colors will have a somewhat muddy tone, with the details of the set obscured. The raincoat will be an out-of-focus blur, and the person's face a dark spot. Stated in simple terms, the acceptable range of contrast between the brightest and the darkest elements of the picture has been greatly exceeded. The light level that was previously sufficient for a picture has been "compressed" by the introduction of an over-powering amount of light.

The human eye can accept a *contrast range* or ratio of up to one hundred to one. A somewhat conservative but safe figure for television would be nearer to thirty to one—or even twenty to one. This means that the brightest elements within a picture should not be more than twenty or thirty times as bright as the darkest elements.

When elements reflect greatly varying amounts of light (such as the raincoat and the person's face in our example), the problem is even more critical. It is then referred to as a **contrast ratio** between the two elements. As a rule, lighting directors should try to avoid a contrast ratio more than about twenty to one. The picture generally will look better if an extreme ratio is avoided.

While the relative size and degree of brightness of the raincoat in our example are somewhat extreme, the basic principle of contrast range and contrast ratio is an important one to observe when lighting any set or, more important, the people within that set.

There is a very common error that often occurs as students are learning lighting techniques. The faces in the picture may seem too dark, so to solve the problem, more and more light is added to the set, which falls upon the face and on the background. The problem usually is that there is already too much light

Figure 4–1
Light meter scale.

Although construction may vary from model to model, most light meters register light falling on the meter in terms of footcandles (ftc).

being reflected from a light-colored background in relation to the light reflected from the face. As more light hits the background, the camera's AGC is going to compensate and allow less light to enter the camera; thus, the face will still be dark—maybe even darker. The problem is compounded if there is too much back light hitting the hair and shoulders (section 4.5).

Light Meter   The human eye is much less sensitive in detecting differences of light intensity than a video camera. The relatively narrow range of what is acceptable to the camera as an adequate light level is difficult to judge with the unaided eye. For this reason, all lighting for television should be done with the aid of a **light meter.** Using the **footcandle** (ftc) as a unit of measurement, the meter visually indicates the intensity of light coming from the direction in which the meter is pointed (figure 4–1).[1]

1. One footcandle is the amount of light that would fall upon a surface placed at a distance of one foot from an established theoretical source approximating the brightness of one candle.

Figure 4–2
Incident and reflected light readings.

Incident
light reading

Reflected
light reading

An incident light meter "reads" in footcandles the
actual amount of light coming from the light source.
A reflected light reading indicates the amount of
light reflected back from the surface of the subject
being lit.

The intensity of television lighting can be measured in two different ways. We can find out how much *incident* light is falling upon a subject by holding the meter very near the subject and pointing it toward the light source. This incident light measure tells us how much light arrives at a given point. Equally important is the *reflected* light reading, which tells us how much light is reflected from the various surfaces of the subject into the camera lens. For this reflected light reading, point the meter directly at the subject from the perspective of the camera. The meter should be held close to the subject, but care must be taken to avoid blocking the light source. Obviously these two methods of measuring light (incident and reflected) will result in two greatly varying read-

ings (figure 4–2). These two different types of readings are used for different purposes.

For the most part, the light meter is used to measure incident light as it comes from the source. The L.D. first adjusts the strength of individual lighting instruments and then uses the meter from different points in the set to find *hot spots* where overlapping projection patterns have caused the intensity to exceed the average level. These readings, however, do not tell the whole story.

Depending upon the texture and color of a surface, only a percentage of the original source light is reflected into the camera. A light green knitted dress might reflect 30 to 40 percent of the illumination falling upon it, whereas a black knitted dress might reflect less than 10

TV Lighting Equipment and Techniques

percent. A white vinyl jacket, on the other hand, might reflect well over 90 percent. Different elements of the set also may have large variations in reflected light bounced back to the camera. These reflected "hot spots" coming from the set or the performers must be measured by reflected light readings with the meter pointed toward the subjects at close range. (See color plate D.)

It is these reflected light readings that can tell the L.D. when the contrast ratio for a given camera has been exceeded. For example, if the brightest spot the camera is aiming at is 600 footcandles and the darkest spot in the picture is twenty footcandles, this is a ratio of thirty to one; the camera probably will not handle that too well. If, on the other hand, the brightest spot is 450 footcandles and the darkest is thirty footcandles, you have a contrast ratio of fifteen to one; this is more acceptable. If the contrast range is too great, either the bright hot spots must be toned down or the darker areas must have more light. Because reflected light readings are only a small percentage of the power of the original light source, the L.D. may wish to use a second, more specialized meter with a magnified scale so that the variations are more visually apparent.

In summary, it should be noted that the overall level of base light can best be determined by a direct incident light meter reading. On the other hand, the contrast ratio can be determined only by a comparison of reflected light readings from the brightest and darkest elements in the picture. Divide the brightest reflected light reading by the darkest reading and you have your contrast ratio.

Color Temperature

One other factor must be taken into consideration when working with base light for color television. This is the phenomenon of color temperature. You have probably noticed that different light sources may have slightly different color tints. A fluorescent bulb gives off more of a bluish light compared to the reddish light given off by an incandescent tungsten bulb. When working with monochrome cameras, the color temperature of different light sources has little effect on the picture quality. In color television, however, the pickup tube is very sensitive to the color temperature of various kinds of light sources.

The color temperature of light is actually measured on a scale known as the Kelvin scale; different light sources are calibrated in degrees Kelvin (K). The redder the light source is, the lower the Kelvin temperature; the bluer a source, the higher the Kelvin temperature. A color temperature between 3,000 degrees Kelvin and 3,200 degrees Kelvin is considered to be the ideal white light for color television—about the range of incandescent bulbs. Most color television lighting is designed to fall within the range of 3,000 degrees Kelvin to 3,400 degrees Kelvin.

If a light with an ideal Kelvin temperature (perhaps 3,200 degrees Kelvin) is used on a dimmer, however, its color temperature will decrease as the lighting instrument is supplied with less and less voltage. (See section 4.6.) Thus, a light may give off a perfect white light when operated at full intensity; but when the light is brought down on the dimmer, the subject being lit gradually takes on a reddish tint. This color distortion is not readily perceived by the naked eye, but the color camera is very sensitive to any drop in color temperature over a couple of hundred degrees Kelvin. This is a common error that beginning lighting directors make. Once you have determined that a specific lighting instrument is the correct color temperature (most lighting sources designed for color television are rated at 3,200 degrees Kelvin), make certain you do not lower the voltage of the light by using it on a dimmer (section 4.6) at a setting lower than "8" on a 10-point scale.

Shooting in an outdoor setting where sunlight becomes a major source of illumination necessitates an added awareness of Kelvin temperature. Depending upon haze and cloud conditions, outdoor color temperature readings can range anywhere from 4,500 degrees Kelvin to 12,000 degrees Kelvin. In these situations, video cameras must be adjusted for the abundance of bluish light by changing the built-in color temperature filter (section 5.4) and/or by resetting the white balance (section 5.5). One of the main problems with outdoor shooting occurs as the sun moves across the sky or as weather conditions change. Scenes shot during different parts of the day will have differing color values and may not edit well together.

4.3 Lighting Objectives: Creative Purposes

As a creative or an artistic factor in video production, lighting can be said to have four main purposes: (1) to define the shape and texture of physical form and, by extension, to create a sense of depth and perspective within the elements of the set or location; (2) to imitate the quality of light characteristic of a situation or setting in reality; (3) to establish and enhance the psychological mood of a performance or setting; and (4) to focus attention upon a single performer or aspect of the production and thereby separate that subject from any feeling of relationship with setting or location.

While this last concept usually has a specialized application, the other three purposes should be thought of as principles that can be simultaneously applied within a given production situation. The same light that gives shape to a person's features can also provide mood and, at the same time, relate to the setting itself (for example, a beam of sunlight coming through a window and falling on the heroine's face). At first glance, it might seem that some of these purposes apply only to dramatic productions. This is not necessarily true. These principles apply to all types of programs, from game shows to live news remote transmissions.

Perspective, Shape, and Texture

When a light source is placed right next to a camera, the light waves reflected back into the lens will be of a generally uniform quality. This effect is *flat lighting* because the illumination has "filled" the hollows and curves that are the distinguishing features of the subject. When the light source is moved so that the beam comes from a different angle, the resulting shadows "etch" the features so that the eye can perceive depth and texture. The camera system functions best when there is an exaggeration of contrasting light values within the video picture. The art of creating the illusion of depth on a flat video tube is largely a matter of accentuating the illumination patterns that we utilize in the normal process of vision.

The experienced lighting director knows it is the manipulation of shadows, rather than bright spots, that can most effectively add form and texture to any object. Light coming from the side or rear of an object will throw shadows in certain shape-defining ways. Extreme side lighting (at right angles to the camera position) will emphasize textural quality by exaggerating shadows, making any object look much rougher than it would otherwise appear.

The heightened sense of perspective that is necessary to the video picture is simply an application of this basic concept in the context of the entire set. Performers and foreground objects can be separated from the background when the angle and intensity of the light beam are adjusted to create a slight "highlight" effect (section 4.5).

Reality

Light operates on our conditioned responses in other equally important ways. We all have tuned in to the middle of a television play and watched a series of close-up shots. Usually, either consciously or unconsciously, we are aware of being indoors or outdoors and of the time of day by the quality of light on the actor's face. It is probably outdoors and near noontime if the light is relatively bright and there are definite shadows under the eyebrows, nose, and chin of the actor. The scene may have been shot inside a studio, but the *imitation of reality* is a product of the lighting.

Other specific shadow and lighting effects suggest certain kinds of realistic situations. Shadows of venetian blinds or prison bars cast on the rear wall of a set help to suggest a particular locale. Other **off-camera** lighting effects help to pinpoint a setting: a low-angle flickering light indicates a campfire or fireplace; a continually flashing red light indicates the presence of an emergency vehicle. Other effects help to carry forth the dramatic narrative: a shaft of light coming from under a door of a room previously unoccupied indicates the presence of an intruder; a flashlight probing around a darkened room helps reveal evidence of a burglary.

Mood

Similarly, the psychological *mood* of a performance or production can be reinforced by the quality of light and its abundance or absence. Comedy is bright; **high-key lighting** is used, which gives an intense overall illumination with a fully lit background. Situation comedies, game shows, and big musical numbers in a variety program rely on this kind of lighting to establish a light-hearted mood.

Conversely, tragedy or fear are communicated when the area surrounding an actor is dark or dimly lit. **Low-key lighting** refers to selective illumination that highlights only the necessary elements of a picture: usually the background is dark, extreme lighting angles may be used, and only part of the picture is disclosed. Again, specific dramatic moods may be reinforced by special effects: a flashing neon sign outside a sparsely furnished hotel room suggests a seedy part of town; lightning flashes create an eerie mood; lighting from a low angle tends to give a character a sinister, unnatural appearance (figure 4–3).

Focus of Attention

When a high contrast exists between the light on a subject and the light falling on the background area, the eye is drawn to the subject. The most obvious example is the use of a *follow spot* on a performer in a musical or variety show. Another variation of this technique is **limbo lighting,** whereby the subject is placed "in limbo" against a softly lit cyclorama or some other nondescriptive, neutral background (section 10.2).

Another way of achieving focus of attention is with **cameo lighting**—the performer is lit, but the background is completely dark (figure 4–4). A **silhouette** effect—with the performers kept in darkness but outlined against a brightly lit background—may be desired for a dance routine or other special situation (figure 4–5). A single shaft of light may be used to accent a contestant in a suspenseful climax of a game show. The host of a documentary may be accented with a strong back or side light. Subtle lighting highlights may be used in many other dramatic and nondramatic settings in order to control focus of attention.

So, above and beyond the necessity of using enough base light for basic illumination, the lighting director must also plan creative lighting in order to add shape and texture and perspective, heighten the illusion of reality, create and enhance a specific mood, and focus attention.

Figure 4–3
Sinister lighting effect.

Lighting from unusual angles or sources can give
unnatural or symbolic effects; for example, lighting
from a low angle usually results in a foreboding,
sinister appearance.

Figure 4–4
Typical cameo lighting:
figure against a dark
background.

TV Lighting Equipment and Techniques

Figure 4–5
Representative silhouette
lighting: dark figures
against a light background.

4.4 Types of Lighting Instruments

A visit to a commercial supplier of theatrical and television lighting equipment can be a dazzling experience in every sense of the word. There are hundreds of highly specialized pieces of equipment either on display or in the catalogs. One sees a range of instruments designed for the largest studio set as well as the newest lightweight portable gear for EFP and ENG uses. In section 4.5 we will examine the basic studio lighting techniques as a way of establishing a foundation for all video illumination. These principles will be adapted to small-format and EFP production in section 15.8.

Our understanding of lighting technique is made easier by the fact that most lighting instruments fall into one of two basic categories—the controlled-beam **spotlight** and the diffused-beam **floodlight.** (Many lighting professionals use the term *hardlight* to refer to spotlights, distinguishing it from the "soft" light of a floodlight.)

Controlled-Beam Spotlights

The classic controlled-beam spotlight illustrated in figure 4–6 is the workhorse of studio lighting. The spotlight is used wherever a highly directional beam of light that can be shaped and focused is desired. Its chief characteristic is the ability to throw a spot of light on any particular area or performer. It is commonly referred to as a **Fresnel** (pronounced without the *s*) although each manufacturer will have a different name for it.[2] Figure 4–7 shows the characteristic structure of the Fresnel lens.

2. The lens generally used in the instrument has a series of raised concentric rings on the outer face that help to dissipate the tremendous heat buildup in the enclosed structure. Augustin-Jean Fresnel was a nineteenth-century scientist who did important research into the nature of light.

Figure 4–6
Focusing mechanism of
the Fresnel spotlight.

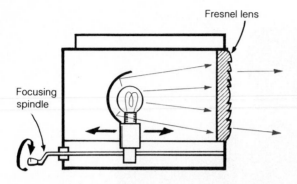

By turning the focusing handle or spindle, the bulb-reflector unit can be moved toward the lens or back to the rear of the housing. When in the forward position, the spotlight beam is "spread" to cover a relatively wide area. When moved to the rear of the housing, the beam is more narrowly focused, or "pinned," on a smaller area.

Figure 4–7
Design of the Fresnel lens.

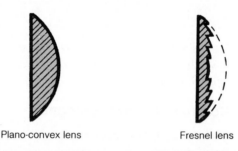

Plano-convex lens   Fresnel lens

The plano-convex lens and the Fresnel lens have the same surface curvature, enabling them to share identical focusing characteristics. However, by using a succession of concentric ring-shaped steps—with the surface curvature of each concentric ring being congruent with the same relative surface of the plano-convex lens—the weight and bulk of the Fresnel lens is substantially reduced, which also cuts down on the heat buildup.

In addition to the distinctive lens structure, the other distinguishing feature of the spotlight is the movable assembly that allows the illuminating unit (bulb and reflector) to be

---

3. The focusing mechanism described here (and pictured in figure 4–6) is moved forward or backward by turning a crank or focusing spindle. Other spotlights accomplish this by means of a focusing ring or ring focus or (on smaller quartz instruments) by a horizontal focusing lever.

moved back and forth between the rear and the front of the instrument.[3] With the bulb in the rear "pinned" position, the light rays are focused in a narrow beam of high intensity—spreading no more than, perhaps, ten degrees. As the bulb is moved forward in the housing, the beam becomes "spread" and its intensity is diminished. In the full-forward spread position, the beam forms approximately a 60-degree angle.

The models most generally in use range from 500 watts to 10,000 watts. In a 2,000-watt instrument (commonly called a "junior"), a spotted (pinned) light will produce an intensity of 600 footcandles when measured at a distance of twenty-five feet. In the fully flooded (spread) position, the intensity of the same instrument drops to roughly sixty footcandles—but the light now covers an area six times larger in diameter. Fresnel spots are also classified by the diameter of the lenses. The most common studio sizes are the 6-inch, 8-inch, 10-inch, and 12-inch models.

Some newer lights are designed to be fully adjustable from the floor with a long pole. The 2,000-watt, 8-inch instrument in figure 4–8 has knobs located on either side of the yoke and on the lower assembly that can be engaged by a connector on the end of a matching pole. The light can be spotted and flooded, adjusted up and down, and moved sideways back and forth without having the crew member climb a ladder.

The **ellipsoidal,** or **leko,** spotlight diagramed in figure 4–9 gains its name from its fixed reflecting mirror at the back of the unit. By means of its tube shape and focused lens (either Fresnel or **plano-convex**), it projects an intense directional beam that is well-defined at its edge point.

The beam can be further shaped by movable metal shutters (also known as *cutters*) located inside the lamp housing, behind the lens.

TV Lighting Equipment and Techniques

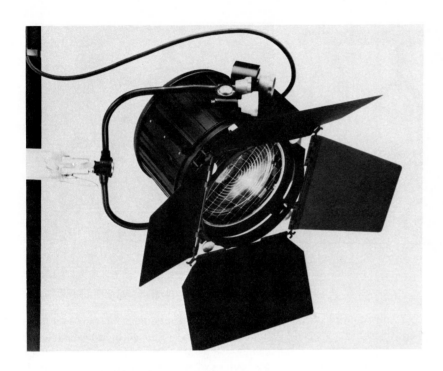

Figure 4–8
Fresnel spotlight. (Photo
courtesy of Strand
Lighting)

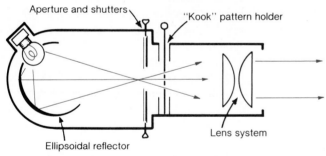

Aperture and shutters   "Kook" pattern holder

Ellipsoidal reflector   Lens system

Figure 4–9
Lens system of the
ellipsoidal spotlight.

Light rays are reflected from the ellipsoidal reflector and focused through the aperture. At this point the shutters can be partially closed to shape or narrow the beam of light. Special cucalorus patterns may also be inserted at this point to project hard-edged shadows. The beam is then further focused through the lens system and projected as a sharp directional beam with a well-defined edge.

At this point—where all the reflected rays of light are in sharp focus—there is also a place to insert a patterned metal design cutout. The shadow of this **cucalorus** or **cookie** or **kook** is then projected to add visual interest to large, plain background surfaces. Some common kook patterns include prison bars, arabesques and Moorish motifs (figure 4–10), venetian blinds, crosses, squares and other geometric designs, cloud patterns, and so forth.

Because it throws a very harsh beam, the ellipsoidal spot is rarely used as the basic in-

Figure 4–10
Ellipsoidal spotlight. *Left,*
ellipsoidal spotlight (photo
courtesy of Strand
Lighting); *right,* example of
a shadow pattern cast by a
"cookie" inserted in a leko
(ellipsoidal) spotlight.

strument in lighting a person or an object for television. It is to be used strictly as a special effects light.

There are several other varieties of fixed-beam spotlights. One popular type is much like an auto headlight with the lens, bulb, and reflector built together as a single unit. This *internal reflector* spotlight is common as a portable source of light, or as a *clip light*—it often is used to fill in and highlight areas that are otherwise not adequately lighted.

Another type of portable spotlight is the *external reflector* model—a highly efficient quartz lamp in a small housing with no lens. Although not as controllable and precise as a Fresnel spot, this model is lightweight, is easily moved (often with a clip-on attachment or a lightweight tripod), and is more than adequate for most remote lighting assignments.

Floodlights

When we examine the specific techniques of lighting (section 4.5), we see that the effects of the focused-beam spotlight are balanced by the use of a somewhat lesser amount of softer

light from a different angle. The purpose of this light source is to soften and thereby control the shadows that are created by the angle of the focused spotlight. When a number of floodlights are used in a set, the effect is a soft, diffused light that eases the harshness of the shadows.

To help achieve the shadowless effect of a large source area, the floodlight does not use a lens; it will probably have a diffusing reflector, which has the effect of spreading out the source; it may use a soft-light bulb with no exposed filament at all; and it may use a **scrim**—a soft, spun-glass filter or other translucent piece of material in a rigid frame—attached to the front of the instrument (see section 4.6).

The classic model for a floodlight is the one-half hollow globe structure known as a **scoop** (figure 4–11). Its large reflecting area is made of a light-diffusing material that spreads the illumination in a nonfocused scattered pattern. Floodlights built in a rectangular shape are known as **pans** or **broads** (figure 4–12). Some of these have controls that allow for an adjustment of the degree of spread. Their square shape makes possible the additional use

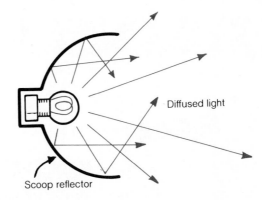

Figure 4-11
The basic scoop. Scoops are designed for both incandescent bulbs and for quartz lighting. Popular sizes for most television studio applications are the 14-inch and 16-inch diameters (photo courtesy of Strand Lighting). Drawing indicates the diffused pattern of the reflected light rays.

Diffused light

Scoop reflector

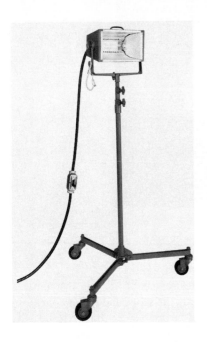

Figure 4-12
The *pan* shape of the reflector or the *broad* beam provided is the source of the name that describes the lighting instrument. *Left,* pan mounted on a floor stand (photo courtesy of Mole Richardson); *right,* ColorTran 1-K broad with barn doors.

of blocking devices known as **barn doors.** (See section 4.6.) A 2,000-watt floodlight will have a pattern of illumination that is more than twice the area of a 2,000-watt Fresnel spotlight in the maximum spread position.

When a series of pans are constructed in a continuous side-by-side row, they are called **strip lights.** They are most often used—frequently with colored **gels**—in lighting the background **cyclorama** (**cyc,** pronounced

"sike") or other large set surfaces (see figure 4–13). Each individual lamp will typically be from 500 to 1,000 watts.

For larger studio productions, huge multi-bulb instruments such as that pictured in figure 4–14 may be used. Such an 8,000-watt "super-softlight" may either be mounted on a floor stand or hung from a lighting grid (section 4.6). The eight 1,000-watt bulbs can be separately controlled in order to produce a variety of in-

Figure 4–13
Strip lights.

Figure 4–14
Super-softlights. *Left,* in this 8-K *super-softlight,* there is no direct light from the eight 1,000-watt quartz bulbs; all light is reflected by the large curved surface (photo courtesy of Mole Richardson). *Right,* the Lowel Softlight 1500 has two bulbs that bounce light off the canvas reflector impregnated with foil for a diffused light.

tensity levels. The bulbs are positioned so that only diffused light is sent out from the large reflector.

Today, most spotlights and floodlights are designed to use the **quartz** bulb (also referred to as a *globe* or *bottle*). The term "quartz" is applied to a variety of quartz-iodine, tungsten-halogen, and similar illumination sources that have largely replaced the incandescent bulb. Its advantages are that it is smaller, is longer lasting, is more efficient (producing more illumination per watt), and does not darken with carbon deposits as it gets

older. It does, however, tend to lose some of its Kelvin temperature as it ages—producing a slightly yellowish light.

This brief review of lighting instruments barely suggests the scope and variety of equipment that is available. In the past decade, leading manufacturers have developed a whole new generation of highly efficient, lightweight, and portable lighting systems. This section has been presented to provide a practical background for an understanding of the principles on which all stage, film, and television lighting is based.

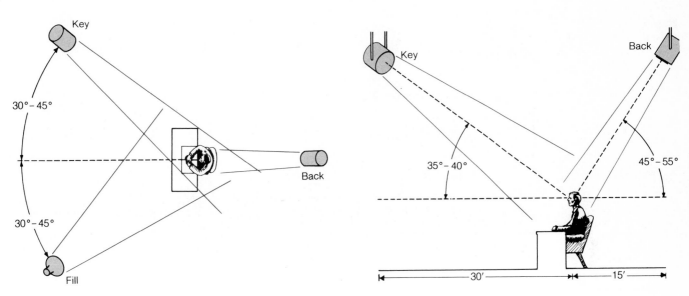

The key light and the fill light should normally be placed approximately 30 to 45 degrees from a line drawn straight in front of the talent (with the fill being more directly in front of the talent). The back light should theoretically be directly behind the talent, at a steeper angle than the two front lights.

Figure 4–15
Three-point lighting.

4.5 Fundamental Lighting Concepts

As noted in section 4.3, creative lighting is largely a matter of careful control of the effects of both light and shadow.

Three-Point Lighting

The specific techniques through which these effects are accomplished can be easily understood by examining the classic lighting setup borrowed from motion pictures. It is known as *three-point lighting* because it involves the use of three different light sources—the **key light,** the **fill light,** and the **back light.** Each has a separate effect upon the subject being lit as the three lights differ in relative angle or direction (or apparent source), level of intensity, and degree to which they are either focused or diffused. Taken together, the cumulative effect is that of a balanced and an aesthetic unity— what Rembrandt called a "golden triangle" of light. Figure 4–15 illustrates how the three sources are used in a typical situation. This three-point lighting arrangement not only provides the *base light* but also meets the *creative purposes* of form and texture, reality, mood, and focus of attention.

It is important to keep in mind that our three-point lighting model is an ideal, based upon a concept that was developed for film production whereby a *single* camera shoots the subject or subjects from one angle only. Each

Figure 4–16
Angles of incidence and reflection.

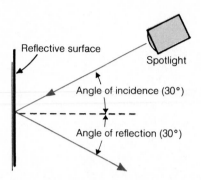

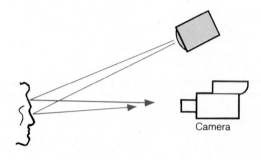

Basic laws of optics tell us that the angle at which the rays of light hit a flat reflective surface (angle of incidence) will equal the angle at which the reflected rays (angle of reflection) bounce away from the surface. Therefore, if the reflective surface (talent's shiny forehead or gleaming nose) is normally

sloped, the reflected light from the spotlight may well be bounced back directly into the camera lens causing an unwanted highlight or glare. Close coordination between the lighting director and makeup personnel is necessary to avoid this problem.

shot could be separately set up and lit. The ways in which this underlying concept is modified to apply to multiple-camera continuous-action video production are discussed throughout the rest of this section. (Single-camera EFP video production, of course, can come closer to the filmic model of separate setups with balanced three-point lighting carefully plotted for each shot; see section 15.8.)

Key Light   The primary, most important illumination in any lighting plan is the *key* light. It is the apparent source of the light hitting the talent and provides the majority of the light that is reflected into the camera lens. (See figure 4–17.) Almost invariably, a spotlight is used for the key light; its strength and directional beam emphasize the contrast of light and shadow, defining the shape and texture of the subject. It is the use of the key light that brings out the features of the face and illuminates the eye itself.

While more extreme angles can be used to produce special dramatic effects, the optimum result is achieved by placing the key off to one

side of the face of the subject, coming in at an angle between thirty and thirty-five degrees. (If the key light is placed directly in front of the talent, the result is a flat, washed-out appearance with no shadows, no sculpting or molding of the face.) The height of the key will depend to some extent upon the facial contours of the talent. It should be placed high enough to produce a slight shadow under the chin and nose, yet it must be low enough to get the light directly into the eye socket itself. (If the talent has deep-set eyes and the key light is at too steep an angle, the result is simply two dark shadows under the eyebrows.) A good rule of thumb is that the key should normally be placed at a 35- to 40-degree angle above the vision line of the subject.

In setting all lights—but especially the key—you must consider carefully the angle of the light hitting the subject as it relates to the intensity of the light being reflected back into the camera lens. In terms of the basic laws of optics, *the angle of incidence equals the angle of reflection*; or, reflected light bounces off a flat surface at the same angle as the incoming light hits the surface.

Figure 4–17
Subject with key light only.

If you have a light source projecting a beam perfectly perpendicular to a flat surface, that beam would reflect directly back upon itself. However, if you raise the light source so as to create a 30-degree angle above the perpendicular, as in figure 4–16, the reflected beam will bounce back downward at a corresponding angle of thirty degrees. If the subject being lit has a rough texture or an uneven surface, the reflected light will be diffused and this angle is not important. However, if you are lighting a smooth and relatively polished surface (such as vinyl or even oily skin), this angle can become very critical.

Applying this principle to the way light is reflected from the face of a subject, you can see how the relatively smooth (and sometimes oily) surfaces of the forehead and nose can create shiny, highly reflective, "hot" spots as light is bounced back directly into the camera lens. This same effect may occur many times over within a large set with its various angles and planes. Similarly, productions using studio graphics or photographs mounted on cards may have trouble with reflected glare—unless a dull matte surface is used or the cards are properly angled to reflect the light away from the camera lens.

Fill Light   In order to "fill in" on the dark side of the face or object being lit, some sort of *fill* light is needed. It should come in at an angle on the side opposite from the key. Ordinarily a floodlight (such as a scoop or broad) would be used, although a spotlight in its *flooded* position can often be effective. In any case, a soft diffused light is desired. (See figures 4–18 and 4–19.) It is used simply to soften the shadows and give some illumination to the otherwise dark side of the talent. Fill light should not be as strong nor as directional as key light; it should not compete in creating shadows or countering the shaping qualities of the key.

In much color television production, a great amount of fill light is used to achieve a consistently even *wash* of illumination over the entire set. In this application, the fill light comes close to serving the same purpose as base light. (See section 4.2.)

Figure 4–18
Subject with fill light only.
Note the spill on the
background cyc.

Figure 4–19
Subject with balanced key
and fill lighting.

Back Light   As the name implies, *back* light comes from behind and above the subject. A spotlight is virtually always used so that the light can be directed and focused like the key. The back light falls upon and, as a result, accentuates such features as hair, shoulders, and top surfaces of set elements. (See figures 4–20 and 4–21.) This highlighting effect sep-arates the talent from the background, adding to the illusion of depth within the total picture. Without adequate back light, the subject appears flat and tends to blend in with the background, as in figure 4–17.

Back-light requirements will vary with the color of the subject, the background, and the desired effect. Hair color and texture are es-

TV Lighting Equipment and Techniques

Figure 4–20
Subject with back light
only.

Figure 4–21
Subject with balanced
three-point lighting (key, fill,
and back light).

pecially crucial. For example, blondes require relatively little back light. Their natural hair color separates them from the background. Also, tightly curled hair generally needs extra back light because it does not reflect light well.

Auxiliary Light Sources

There are several other terms that refer to more specialized types of lighting. Two of these are actually variations of key and back light.

A *side light* is a key that hits the subject on the side of the face—usually at eye level. A **kicker** is basically a back light that works at an angle (about forty-five degrees from dead center) instead of directly behind the subject.

One of the most important additional sources of illumination is the **set light** or **background light** (not to be confused with the *back* light). This is the major source of lighting for the cyclorama or background set behind the performers. In addition to helping fill in the overall picture (basic illumination), background lighting can give form and texture to the setting, provide a sense of reality, or suggest mood (creative functions). Set lighting can tell the audience whether it is an indoor or outdoor locale, daytime or evening. Specific locations can be suggested by certain kinds of window effects or cookie patterns in the ellipsoidal spot (venetian blinds, prison bars). Mood can be reinforced with high-key or low-key lighting. Colored gels on a plain cyclorama can help establish mood on a color production.

In one function or another, most types of lighting instruments can be appropriately used for background lighting. Floodlights (scoops or strip lights) are often used for general illumination of a cyclorama or flat space. Spotlights can be used to highlight certain areas or present dramatic lighting effects (for example, strong diagonal slashes of light or selected low-key elements). And, of course, the ellipsoidal spot can be used with a variety of cucalorus patterns for various shadow effects. (See figures 4–10 and 10–22.)

Other special lighting effects depend upon careful background lighting. A good *silhouette* demands an evenly lit background, balanced from top to bottom as well as from side to side. A good *cameo* effect, on the other hand, requires a complete lack of any light hitting the background; front lighting must be carefully controlled to make certain that no spill is reflected onto the set behind the talent.

The background lighting must also be balanced with the three-point subject lighting to ensure that no undesired semi-silhouette effect is attained. As mentioned in section 4.2, if the background is too strongly lit, the faces of people in front of the background will tend to go dark by comparison.

Actually, in any moderately complicated lighting setup, the illumination is coming from many directions and angles. In addition, the subjects—the persons being lit—will be moving within the set. The concept of key,

back, and fill lights should be used as a guide, not as a rigid set of rules. Auxiliary lighting and special effects will be added as needed for certain creative purposes. The important consideration is that the lighting director be totally in control of the *direction, intensity, quality* (harsh shadows or diffused), and *color* (if applicable) of light falling upon performers and set.

Multiple-Camera Lighting

As previously mentioned, the concept of three-point lighting was developed for the motion picture single-camera technique—always concerned with lighting from the viewpoint of the camera. With this approach, every shot has its own lighting setup. When the subject and camera are moved, the lighting is changed. Detailed care can be taken to sculpt the face and other features of the subject with the key light, blended with back and fill lights.

With television's multiple-camera formats and continuous-action productions, lighting directors found it difficult to adhere to the pure disciplines of classic three-point lighting. In a game show or variety program, for example—shot from three or four cameras (and possibly even more angles)—the participants and performers move unpredictably all over the set. The solution to this situation is to create a base light *wash* throughout the entire set. The result is a "flat" but practical lighting job.

Some situation comedies shot with electronic multiple-camera techniques have had substantial success in overlaying the concept of three-point lighting within a flat-lit set. Working together, the TV director and lighting director can select points within the scene where the actors will remain in place for a period of time; in these spots careful three-point lighting can be used for close-ups. When portions of the scene contain physical move-

TV Lighting Equipment and Techniques

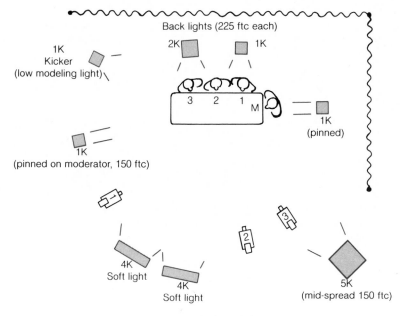

Figure 4–22
"Plan A" lighting plot.

Back lights (225 ftc each)

1K
Kicker
(low modeling light)

2K   1K

3 2 1 M

1K
(pinned)

1K
(pinned on moderator, 150 ftc)

4K
Soft light

4K
Soft light

5K
(mid-spread 150 ftc)

Modified three-point lighting plan designed for participants primarily addressing the audience.

ment, the action is picked up by the cameras on wider shots (section 6.2)—so the flat lighting will not matter as much. Close-ups are kept to a minimum in the areas lit by flat lighting. It is a compromise, but it works fairly well.

Daytime serials ("the soaps") that crank out an hour a day of multiple-camera production are hard pressed to do much in the way of delicate lighting; but using the previous technique, they do manage to achieve an overall satisfactory lighting effect. Since productions of all types operate within tight budget limitations, lighting directors never have all of the time and crew they need to do a perfect job. They simply do the best they can with what resources they have. But in all video production, three-point lighting—with its potential for texture, depth, modeling, perspective, and focus—remains the standard against which all lighting work is measured.

Different Production Approaches   As a way of examining some of the problems of multiple-camera lighting—as well as their solutions—let us look at the example of a four-person discussion program such as the one suggested by the "Frame of Reference" script in appendix D-3. The participants are seated in an L shape with the host on the camera right side. This arrangement allows the host to keep eye contact with the three guests while leading the discussion.

If the nature of the format is such that the three guests will tend to speak straight out to an audience area behind the camera 2 location, and the host will often address the viewers by means of camera 1, then we can use the "Plan A" lighting plot as shown in figure 4–22. In this plan, we will be using a modified three-point lighting setup.

If, however, our program is such that the guests for the most part turn to each other and

Figure 4–23
"Plan B" lighting plot.

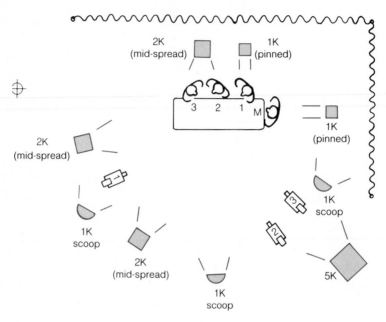

Cross-key lighting may be appropriate when participants are involved in considerable give-and-take head-turning discussion.

to the host during the course of the discussion, then the "Plan B" lighting arrangement (figure 4–23) would be more appropriate—utilizing a *cross-key* lighting technique.

Three-Point Lighting   In the "Plan A" plot, the key light is provided by the 5-kilowatt Fresnel-type spotlight, which is spread so that it covers all four participants. Its angle will create slight shadows on the faces of the three guests. It should be tilted so that its light also falls on the cyclorama in the background. Fill light is provided by the two 4-kilowatt *soft-lights* (see figure 4–14) from the camera left side.

One possible problem may occur when guests one and two occasionally turn to their right to speak to guest three (on the camera left side)—they would have only fill light on their faces from the angle of camera 1. This problem can be solved by placing a spotlight

kicker from over their right shoulders to provide a "modeling" light effect. To do its job properly, this controlled beam light should be hung as low as possible, but not so low that the head of one guest will cast a shadow on the side of another guest's face.

The host is covered by a pinned spot from a slightly different angle from the camera 1 shooting perspective. This gives the host's face some shape and definition. The host's fill light comes from the two *softlights*.

The back lights are located as indicated on the lighting plot (figure 4–22). Their intensity should be adjusted to take into account the relative back light needed by blondes and brunettes—as well as light or dark clothing around the shoulder area. Light falling on the cyclorama must be checked to be sure that its quality is even behind all camera shots. Problems can be solved by placing additional scoops or broads to fill any dark spots on the cyc.

TV Lighting Equipment and Techniques

Cross-Key Lighting   On the other hand, if the discussion program is expected to be such that most of the conversation will take place with participants facing each other, move camera 3 (and possibly camera 2) farther to the right so that most camera shots will not be profiles of the people speaking. The participants, especially guests one and two, need to be lit from two divergent camera angles because they will be facing both to their right and to their left at different times. One solution to the situation is *cross-key* lighting as illustrated in figure 4–23. Most lighting directors consider this "Plan B" approach a compromise at best.

Cross-key lighting can usually be accomplished with spread spots from four different positions. Some additional fill light should be used to soften the keys and to make sure that the cyc is evenly lit. There still may be unflattering shadows on both sides of the noses (resulting from the relatively harsh controlled-beam spotlights hitting the subjects from opposite directions). This effect is known as a *butterfly.*

There is a variation of *wash* lighting that can solve the butterfly problem. You simply fill the entire set from all angles with illumination from a number of floodlights and *softlights.* There are no harsh shadows remaining. You have solved the "butterfly" problem, but the trade-off is that you now have no modeling or sculpting—all of the faces are completely flat. An adequate lighting job, however, has been accomplished in a relatively short period of time—a compromise at best. Good, strong back light is especially important with this type of wash lighting.

Balanced Lighting by Ratio

The first thing a lighting director must do in creating a three-point lighting pattern is to decide on the relative strengths of each of the source lights. There are some basic guidelines that lighting directors use in making their pre-

The following lighting ratio figures are only rough guidelines and should be adjusted for skin tone, clothing, and set materials.

Light	Footcandles	Relative Strength
Key	150 ftc.	Reference point of 1
Fill	75 ftc.	½ of key
Back	225-300 ftc.	1½ to 2 times key
Background	75-115 ftc.	½ to ¾ of key

liminary plans. Figure 4–24 shows an average ratio of key, back, and fill lights that can be applied in most basic lighting situations. The footcandle figures represent incident meter readings that would be made at the point where light strikes the subject.

The key light, being the primary light source, is given the reference point of *one.* Other light sources are then adjusted in relation to the strength of the key. The back light is typically up to *one and one-half* the strength of the key; the fill is roughly *one-half* of the strength of the key.

Such ratios are only guidelines, of course. Once the lights are turned on, the lighting director can then check the shot through the camera monitor and get a better picture of the reflective qualities of the subject and the rest of the set. The final lighting decisions have to be based upon many factors, such as the color and shading of the object being lit, the texture and shade of the background, the illusion of reality, and the desired mood. Particular care must be taken with skin tone and hair. Too much light on the hair and shoulders can cause the face to look relatively darker than it naturally is. If any picture elements appear out of balance, they should be checked by reflected light meter readings.

Of the three fundamental light sources, the back light is the most difficult to measure

Figure 4–24
Ratio of key, back, fill, and set lights.

and to work with. Achieving the desired effect of highlighting the hair, shoulders, and so forth, calls for considerable intensity. Because of the steep angle of the typical back light, much of this intensity does not reflect into the camera. The direct incident meter reading, therefore, will seem quite high in relation to the effect on the picture. Because it is usually much closer to the subject than the key light, the wattage needed in the back-light lamps will often be less than that used for the key lights.

The light falling upon the background, which usually has its own independent sources, also consists of some contribution (*spill*) by both the key and fill lights. For this reason, it is sometimes difficult to predict background light level accurately in the initial plan. The reflective quality of background materials varies considerably. The same amount of incident footcandles falling upon a light-colored cyclorama and upon dark wood paneling will produce considerably different amounts of light reflected into the camera.

As we have stated, during the process of lighting setup, the basic lighting balance is achieved by means of incident light reading. When the performers are in place, there must be a final adjustment process that should utilize a more accurate set of reflected light readings. The footcandle readings will, of course, be on a much lower scale, but the same basic ratio will apply. Again, however, the final suitability of a picture should never rest with an arbitrary ratio and a light meter. Ultimately it comes down to how the picture looks on the monitor to the director and the lighting director.

Economy of Lighting

Frugality in the use of lighting instruments is an important consideration. Good lighting technique is often as much a matter of knowing when to take out or dim lights as it is of knowing how to add lights to a set. The modeling and texturing effects of a few well-placed key lights are easily wiped out by adding too many lights from too many directions. As newer cameras are developed that require less light for basic illumination, it is possible to be more artistic and creative in the use of selective lighting—as long as you maintain the even base light needed for color production.

Another important consideration is the manipulation and control of unwanted shadows. Although facial and textural shadows are desired for modeling and dimension, many kinds of shadows are undesirable and distracting. An obvious example is the shadow of a microphone boom on the set behind the performers. Other examples are the shadows often cast by other performers, by large props, or sometimes by the camera itself.

Many a beginning lighting person has tried to counteract these unwanted shadows by adding more light to the shaded area—trying to "burn out" the shadow. In essence, what this does is throw the overall lighting intensity out of balance, producing hot spots for the camera. The correct solution is to eliminate the shadow—either by moving or repositioning the object casting the shadow (such as raising the boom arm) or by moving or controlling the light source (for example, by lighting from another angle or by masking off part of the light with barn doors as outlined in section 4.6).

4.6 Studio Lighting Procedures

Having looked at some of the basic television lighting requirements and concepts, we are ready to consider the actual techniques and procedures involved in lighting a television setting. Several of these aspects also involve

TV Lighting Equipment and Techniques

practice and discipline in the execution of specific lighting functions—for example, in the precise preparation and use of lighting plans and plots and in careful observance of all safety precautions.

Mounting Lighting Instruments

Our first concern should be with the way the lights are actually mounted or supported. How are they to be positioned and held in place? Basically, there are two ways—by *hanging* them from above or by mounting them on a *floor stand.*

Hanging Mounts   Most television studios are equipped with some **lighting grid** for mounting lights above the staging areas. This facility gets the lighting instruments up at about the right height for most applications and leaves the studio floor uncluttered for camera and talent movement, microphone placement, and various set elements. Most studios have some sort of pipe grid or batten system upon which the lights are actually suspended. The pipe grid is a rigid permanent arrangement of pipes a foot or two beneath the studio ceiling; the lights are fixed directly to the pipes by any one of several kinds of hanging devices. The counterweighted batten system, on the other hand, allows the battens to be raised or lowered by some sort of counterweight system so that lights can easily be worked on from the studio floor.

After lights are hung in the right position, final adjustments (**trimming**) have to be made at the operating height, even on a counterweighted batten. Some of these might be accomplished with a *light pole,* which can be inserted into the ring-focus mechanism on some spotlights to adjust the spot-flood position of the bulb-reflector unit. Some larger studios will have a *catwalk,* which allows

lighting operators to move around on a permanent scaffolding to reach most of the lights from above. In most studios, however, some sort of special movable *lighting ladder* is used that allows lighting personnel to climb up to any instrument for final adjustments and focusing. Two types of studio ladders are pictured in figure 4–25.

Lighting instruments may actually be connected to the grid or batten with a variety of fastening devices. Many are simply placed into position with a **C-clamp,** which connects the light firmly to the grid but allows for no vertical adjustment of the instrument (see figure 4–26). A *sliding rod* and a **telescope hanger** are two arrangements whereby a light can be attached to the bottom of a long rod that can be positioned at varying heights on the grid or batten. The **pantograph** is a scissors-like spring-counterbalanced hanger that allows lights to be pulled down or pushed up quickly and easily to any level. This is the most convenient arrangement for rapid adjustments and easy positioning of lighting instruments.

Floor Stands   In many kinds of studio arrangements, the suspended lights often have to be supplemented by lights mounted on floor stands. Although too many floor stands tend to clutter the studio floor and get in the way of other production elements, they do represent a certain degree of flexibility and simplicity of setup. Sometimes there are positions where it is simply impossible to get a light except on a floor stand.

Floor stands usually are mounted on tripods with casters that facilitate easy movement and quick repositioning. They come in a variety of weights and sizes capable of handling many different kinds of lighting instruments. Of course, for location productions (wherever supplemental lighting is needed), the portable floor stand is indispensable.

Figure 4–25
Two types of lighting
ladders: *left*, ladder with
four free-wheeling casters
must be steadied by an
assistant on the floor; *right*,
the ladder with a tricycle
steering arrangement and
a lockable wheel can be
operated by one person.

TV Lighting Equipment and Techniques

Lighting Control

The video camera system is extremely sensitive. Optimum performance is possible only when illumination is kept within certain carefully prescribed limits. The lighting director must work within four separate yet interrelated parameters in order to achieve the artistic and technical purposes of lighting:

1. The level of intensity
2. The degree of focus or diffusion
3. The shape of the projected beam
4. The color quality

After the initial setup is completed, the lighting director, working with the director and video control operator, makes a continuing series of adjustments throughout the rehearsal period and prior to the final take. There are a number of mechanical and electronic controls that are utilized during this process.

Intensity   We have already described the way in which the beam from a Fresnel-type lamp can be spread in order to lessen its intensity and at the same time cover a much wider area. It must be remembered that the fully spread beam has only a small fraction of the intensity of the strength of a pinned beam.

Inverse Square Law   Whether a beam is focused or diffused, there is another factor that has important implications in terms of intensity. Although it is not easily apparent to the naked eye, variations in the distance between a source light and the subject create large differences in intensity.

The same *Inverse Square Law,* which in section 3.3 warned us how critical microphone-to-speaker distances can be, also applies to illumination. As with sound, the strength of a light source is reduced to one-quarter of its original strength as the source-to-subject distance is doubled. (And the strength is multiplied by four as the distance

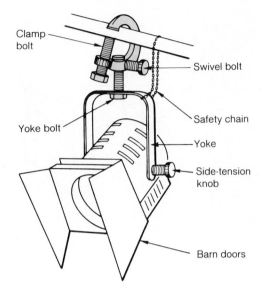

Figure 4–26
C-clamp.

Clamp bolt

Swivel bolt

Yoke bolt

Safety chain

Yoke

Side-tension knob

Barn doors

The C-clamp holding this Fresnel spotlight to a pipe grid has four adjusting screws or bolts.

is cut in half.) As shown in figure 4–27, a light that produces 1,600 footcandles at a distance of ten feet is reduced to only 400 footcandles at twenty feet.

In terms of a practical field production example, let us assume a *clip-on* spotlight attached to a camera working twenty feet from a subject produces a reading of forty footcandles. (Note that this is one-tenth of the reading illustrated in figure 4–27.) Should the subject move to within ten feet of the camera, cutting the distance in half, the reading would now be 160 footcandles. The illumination has been increased four times! This substantial increase would call for a large change of the *f*-stop setting—as well as an adjustment in the *white balance* of the camera. (See sections 5.5 and 15.9.)

On the other hand, in a studio situation where we are working with much stronger illumination and with the talent at greater distances from the lights, a change of ten feet in the source-to-subject distance should be noted

Figure 4–27
Inverse Square Law
applied to television
lighting.

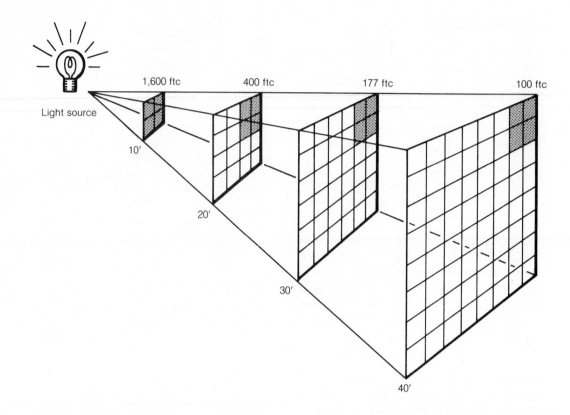

but is not critical. Again using the ratios presented in figure 4–27, we can use the example of an actor performing at distances of thirty to forty feet from a light source. In this case, the range between 177 and 100 footcandles would probably call only for a minor change in the *f*-stop setting—if one were needed at all.

Therefore, as a general rule, the closer the lights are to the talent, the more critical the lighting and camera adjustments are going to be with every little movement the talent makes.

The Dimmer Board   Located some distance from the actual lighting instruments— either in a corner of the studio or in some control room—is the patching and control equipment, which in any kind of sizable studio operation is centered around the dimmer board. Although dimmers vary tremendously in construction and operation, they all func-

tion on the same general principle: by controlling the amount of power that flows to the lighting instrument, the lamp gives off more or less light. Two types of dimmer boards are shown in figure 4–28.

Patching and dimming equipment is, in many ways, analogous to the patch panel and console in the audio control booth. Apart from the creative considerations, we are concerned with power flow instead of signal flow. There is a basic routing system for getting power to a light.

This equipment varies greatly from one studio to another in both sophistication and capacity. Therefore, it would serve little purpose to attempt to describe all of the possible techniques of a patching operation that would follow the many individual designs. This is best learned from the specific construction of the equipment in your own studio. As a frame of

TV Lighting Equipment and Techniques

Figure 4-28
Two types of dimmer board installations. (*Top* photo courtesy of KCET, Los Angeles)

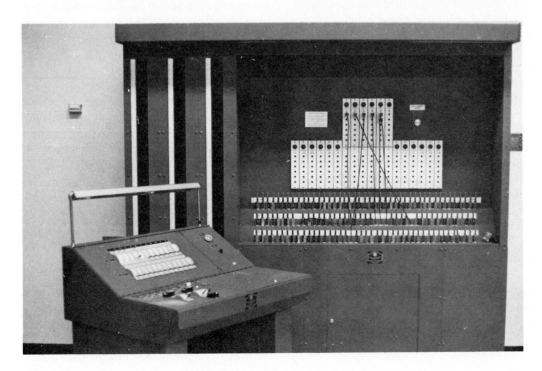

Figure 4-29
Lighting scrims: *top,* half
scrim; *bottom,* full scrim.
(Photos courtesy of Mole
Richardson)

reference to that process, it may help to consider some fundamental functions common to all lighting control equipment.

When a light on a grid has been connected to the nearby numbered line or grid outlet, the electrical power to turn on that light is available from two different sources in most studio setups—either a nondimmer circuit or a dimmer circuit. If no intensity control over the lamp is needed, a patch is made from the grid outlet or *load circuit* to a numbered nondimmer circuit and turned on at the switch or circuit breaker. This connection is normally referred to as a *hot patch*. If intensity control is called for, the patch is made from the load circuit into the dimmer board for a controlled power source. Here the circuitry may vary according to the design of the board.

In most boards, multiple units of lights can be connected into a single dimmer circuit. There is, of course, a definite limit to the amount of power that can be fed to any one circuit. This limit must be ascertained and always observed.

As mentioned in section 4.2, when there is a reduction in the amount of current being supplied to a bulb filament, there is a corresponding lowering of the Kelvin color temperature of the light. Care must be exercised so that key and fill lights are not dimmed into the yellow or red ranges. Because back lights do their job of separation without reflecting as much light directly into the lens, they can be dimmed into the yellow range without as much apparent effect.

Selection of Instruments   Our final note on intensity is one that should seem obvious; however, it is one that is all too often forgotten in the pressure of production activity. The lighting director must choose the *correct* instruments and the correct *number* of instruments to do the job at hand. Frequently, lighting crew personnel will spend time trying to adjust a 2 KW (2,000-watt) spotlight when a 1 KW or even a 500-watt unit might be more suitable. Similarly, the use of too many instruments can enormously complicate the process of achieving proper light levels. Or you might be trying to spread one spotlight too thin when you really need separate instruments to cover the areas to be lighted.

Focus and Diffusion   There are several ways by which diffused light is created and controlled in order to keep it in its proper perspective in relation to the focused key light. The primary control factor is that of adjusting intensity through some of the methods described previously. Placement is also very important. The best diffused light is achieved by using several instruments placed at differing angles.

There are also several devices that are important to the lighting director's toolbox. The most commonly used pieces of equipment for these purposes are either attached to the front of the instrument or mounted in front of it.

A *scrim* is a wire mesh shaped to fit the front of the lighting instrument. (See figure

TV Lighting Equipment and Techniques

4–29.) It works by scattering the beam and cutting back on intensity. Scrims are used to soften a spread Fresnel light. To further soften scoops, pans, and broads, a clothlike opaque filter made out of spun and pressed fiberglass is used. Available in three thicknesses, it greatly cuts down on the intensity and projects a soft, almost shadowless light.

When shooting outdoors, using the sun as a key light, a *foil reflector* is often used to provide a relatively diffused fill light. (See figures 4–30 and 15–22.) It can also be used to provide a key light with the sun serving as the back light.

Shape   If lighting directors had to work with only the large raw beam projected by most instruments, their work would be difficult indeed. Fortunately, there are a number of shaping devices that are used to modify and block parts of the beam.

One of the main difficulties is that of controlling the overlap of multiple light sources that produce high-intensity hot spots. The most common solution to this problem is achieved through the use of *barn door* shutters, which are attached to the front of a spotlight. (See figures 4–8 and 4–26.) Used in pairs or sets of four, these hinged plates can provide an adjustable edge to the beam. By moving the shutters, both the height and width of the projected light can be limited. Most assemblies can be rotated to provide maximum adjustment. In a leko or ellipsoidal lamp, the movable shutters are inside the instrument (adjusted with outside handles) in order to provide an even greater definition to the projected pattern. (See figure 4–9.)

There are times when the lighting director needs to create a small area of reduced intensity *within* a projected beam. For this a *flag* or *gobo* is used. Flags are rectangles of varying size made either of metal or of frames covered with black cloth. They can be hung from the lighting grid or mounted on a floor

Figure 4–30
Foil reflector. The two-sided reflector is an invaluable part of all outdoor location shooting. The partitioned foil-leaf side (shown) produces a soft diffused light. A smooth silver-paper surface on the other side produces a brighter, more intense light. (Photo courtesy of Mole Richardson)

stand in a position to block out the light to a specific area. (See figure 4–31.) One use, for example, is to cast a slight shadow on the forehead and top of the head of a person with thinning hair who otherwise might appear almost bald under bright lights on a close-up shot.

Occasionally, an added amount of light must be pinpointed at a particular area of the set. If barn doors cannot project quite as precise a pattern as needed, a *top hat* or *stovepipe* can be used to do the job. Inserted in the same frame designed to hold the barn doors, the top hat, which ranges in size from four inches to a foot, can reduce the spotlight's beam to a smaller, clearly defined circle without increasing the intensity of the spot. Even portable lighting kits for EFP remote shoots will have holders for barn doors and other shaping devices. (See figure 4–32.)

TV Lighting Equipment and Techniques

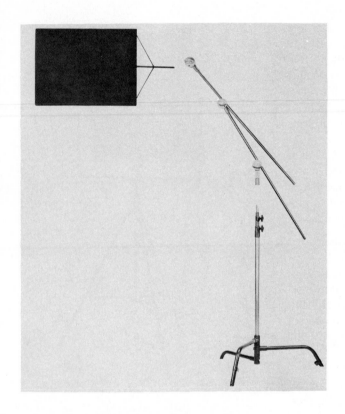

Figure 4–31
Flag. Flags are used to block the light on specific areas of the performer or set. With their stands and extension arms, they provide an important final control over illumination. (Photo courtesy of Mole Richardson)

Figure 4–32
ARRILITE 650/4 portable lighting kit. This package contains four 650-watt instruments and stands that are especially designed to fit into a lightweight container for convenient portability. The lamps can be easily pinned or spread in order to serve as either key or fill illumination. (Photo courtesy of Arriflex Corporation)

The *cucalorus* (or the kook or the cookie, as it is often called) is a cutout design that when placed in front of a spot projects a pattern upon a cyclorama or large set surface. Ellipsoidal spotlights are designed so that smaller metal kooks can be inserted into the instrument housing by means of a "dipstick." (See figure 4–9.)

Color   There are occasions when a set or other production location is simply too dull and drab for attractive pictures with sufficient color contrast. It may be that more "warmth" from red-brown earth tones is needed. Or possibly the "cool" effect of green and blue is desired. To solve this problem, variously colored *gels* are used to add color to the setting and occa-

TV Lighting Equipment and Techniques

sionally to the performers' clothes and flesh tones. The gel is a thin transparent celluloid material, available in a wide variety of colors. The gels can be cut to fit a specially designed holder that slides into the same frame that is intended to hold the barn doors on a spotlight. (See figure 4–33.)

In using gels, the lighting director must work carefully with both the video control operator and the makeup artist. The effect of projecting three or four different colors onto a set can be subtle but must be carefully controlled. Since the camera system tends to pick up and accentuate red, you should be especially cautious with its use. And because most normal makeup is in the reddish range, too much light through a red gel will greatly exaggerate flesh tones. (See section 11.5.) Light from a green gel, on the other hand, has an unflattering effect on most persons—especially on those with darker complexions.

One of the most effective applications for gels is that of using them with strip lights to color a cyclorama. A wide variety of color combinations and effects are possible. A continually changing dawn effect, for example, can be created with the background shifting from a deep violet through various reds and pinks to a light blue during the shooting of a scene.

Safety Precautions and Disciplines

Safety is the responsibility of everybody connected with a television production. Any unsafe situation can be avoided by using common sense and observing basic precautions. Part of the *discipline* of television production is the habit and attitude of *thinking safety*. Every crew member, whether or not part of the lighting team, should be disciplined to think always in terms of avoiding or correcting hazardous conditions.

Figure 4–33
Gel holder on a scoop. Frames that hold a gel filter in place are designed for all types of floods and spotlights. (Photo courtesy of Mole Richardson)

Think Overhead   Are all lights, mounts, and other equipment securely fastened? When heavy equipment is moved or repositioned overhead, is everybody warned and the area below the equipment cleared out?

Think Electrical   Is all equipment turned off before moving or inspecting it? Is the circuit turned off before you attempt to plug in an instrument?

Think Hardware   Has the item of equipment been thoroughly checked out and is it ready for use? Has everything been connected? Tightened? Tested?

Whenever a lighting assistant is moving or trimming lights, there should be at least one person steadying the ladder from below. The person on the ladder should always carry a wrench (secured by a band or tie around the wrist to prevent dropping it on persons or equipment below) to tighten any lamps that have become loose from excessive turning. When making any adjustment on any lighting instrument, the safety cable or cord should always remain fastened, securing the light to the pipe or grid.

Figure 4–34
When adjusting hot lights make sure you always wear asbestos gloves. (Photo courtesy of Dina Fisher)

When changing the direction of a light, always loosen the thumb screw (swivel bolt) first. Do not mistake it for the bolt holding the lamp hanger to the clamp—loosening that bolt will detach the lamp from the lighting grid.[4]

When moving a light (clamp, hanger, and housing) always make certain that there are no people or equipment below the area in which you are working. Be certain the power to the lamp is off. Just because no light is being emitted does not mean that there is no power coming to the cord. Damaged lights, burned-out bulbs, and short circuits are all potential dangers. Again, be sure that the power is off

at the lamp's new location before plugging it into the grid outlet or load circuit. When moving an instrument from one location to another, the safety cable is always the last item to be unfastened, and it is the first thing to be hooked up when the instrument is repositioned.

When moving or focusing lights, do not look directly into a light. A light that measures 200 footcandles at thirty feet may approach 100,000 footcandles at the source. Studio lights are bright enough to permanently damage or even blind the naked eye.

A 2,000-watt lamp creates a dangerous amount of heat. After being on for only a few minutes, most studio lamps are hot enough to cause serious burns. Most studio lamps have handles—use them! Lighting technicians should also be furnished with heavy-duty asbestos gloves (figure 4–34). Use them! Special caution must be used when adjusting barn

4. The most common type of lamp hanger is the C-clamp. (See figure 4–26.) There is a bolt that holds it to the lighting grid and a bolt that holds the light holder to the C-clamp. This bolt (Y-bolt, yolk bolt) should *never* be loosened. To turn a light, there is usually a thumb screw in the side of the clamp. Make note of this when studying lighting in your own studio.

TV Lighting Equipment and Techniques

doors, as they are directly in the path of the light source at only a few inches and absorb a large amount of heat.

Before moving a lamp, whether a large studio model or a small portable light, let the lamp stand for ten to fifteen minutes. This will help the lamp cool, help prolong the life of the filament, and also lessen the possibility of lamp explosion or burnout from the shock of moving.

Make sure you never touch the surface of a quartz bulb with your bare fingers (even when the bulb is cold). Always use gloves or some other cloth between your hand and the globe. Quartz lamps generate tremendous amounts of heat, and even a small amount of finger oil or acid on the face of the globe will interact chemically to weaken the glass envelope and hasten discoloration.

Preproduction Planning

One final note about production *discipline* from the standpoint of lighting procedures. In lighting—as in every aspect of television production—it is imperative that as many details as possible be taken care of before walking into the studio for the production setup and rehearsal. Every minute counts in the studio. You cannot afford to start your planning once you reach the studio.

The lighting director must use a lighting plan or **light plot.** This plan will be worked out well in advance of the actual studio setup time. It will include a schematic layout of the primary staging areas and the lighting requirements for each one. It should indicate each lighting instrument to be used and the intensity ratios among the various instruments. Often there is space for additional notes. Here the director will indicate which lights are to be placed together on dimmer circuits or what kinds of lighting effects will actually be used on the air. Figure 4–35 represents a sample

lighting plan for a simple talk show. Study also the examples used in figures 4–22 and 4–23.

In many production situations, the lighting director will also prepare a more detailed set of working instructions—a work sheet that lists, for each instrument to be used, the description of the light (spot, scoop); its size (500 watts, 2 KW [kilowatts]); the staging area it is to cover; its function (key, kicker); the grid outlet or load circuit it is to be plugged into; the dimmer or nondim circuit it will be patched to; and so forth. Again, the detailed preparation at this point will later save valuable minutes of studio setup and rehearsal time. The disciplined production person knows the importance of thorough **preproduction planning.**

Summary

As with audio considerations, lighting directors must be concerned with both technical (*basic illumination*) needs and creative purposes. In addition to establishing the correct amount of *base light* (usually determined by an *incident light* meter reading), the L.D. must also work within an acceptable *contrast ratio* (established by *reflected light* meter readings) and maintain the correct *color temperature* (3,000 to 3,400 degrees Kelvin).

The creative lighting objectives include perspective and molding *shape* and *texture,* establishing a feeling of *reality* (or non-reality), creating a *mood* or emotional setting, and *focusing attention.* All of these functions are accomplished with *spotlights* that have a highly directional focused beam and/or with *floodlights* that give off a nondirectional diffused light.

Lighting a typical subject involves standard *three-point* lighting (key light, fill light, and back light). *Auxiliary sources* such as a side light (or a kicker) or background light may

Figure 4–35
Sample studio lighting plot.

Producer/Director:_____

Production Title:_____

Lighting Setup: (Date)_____ (Time)_____

Air/Recording: _____ _____

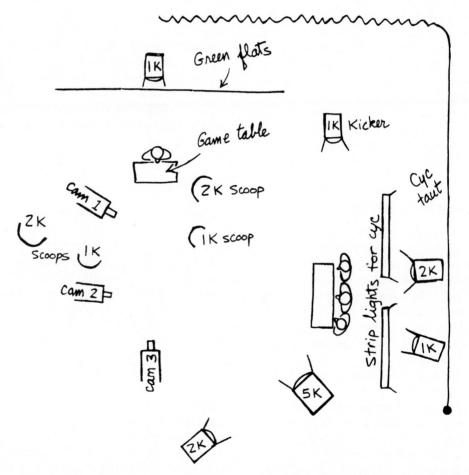

The director of the television production would fill out a light plot on a form similar to this. Although the symbols are not to scale, these instructions indicate generally how the director envisions the production from the lighting standpoint: where the talent will be, how the numbered cameras will be positioned, and basically what lighting instruments would be used. The lighting director could then take this lighting plan and devise a more detailed lighting worksheet for the lighting crew to follow.

TV Lighting Equipment and Techniques

also be incorporated. When working with *multiple-camera lighting,* certain modifications and compromises in the ideal three-point lighting concept have to be accepted—such as *cross-key* lighting.

As a starting point, lighting directors sometimes use a *basic ratio,* with the back light strongest, then the key light, and the fill being the weakest source. Complete studio lighting procedures also include knowledge of various *mounting devices* and, most importantly, various approaches to *lighting control* (intensity, focus and diffusion, shaping the beam, and color control). Finally, we must be concerned with essential *safety precautions* and the discipline of thorough *preproduction planning.*

All of the lighting considerations, of course, are but a means of creating the picture that will be picked up by the camera and its lens system. Camera/lens structure and camera operations are discussed in the next two chapters.

4.7 Training Exercises

Illustrate, on camera, the modeling effects of light upon the structure of the face by means of the following demonstrations.

1. From a straight-on position in line with the camera, direct a key light only upon a subject's face from angles of sixty, forty-five, and thirty degrees from the horizontal. Note the generally uncomplimentary effect of shadows under the eyebrows, nose, and chin at the steeper angles.

2. Set the key at a 30- to 35-degree vertical angle, straight on to the subject's face. Start with the camera position exactly in line with the direction of the light. Then have the subject slowly turn his or her face to the right. Have the camera make an arcing movement in the same direction, keeping a full-front face shot. Stop both of these movements at regular intervals, observing how the shadows created by the various lighting angles model the shape of the face. Note how the lines of the subject's forehead, nose, cheek, and so forth, are much more definite than with straight-on front lighting.

3. Set up a basic key, back, and fill light structure. Alternately take out and then put back one or even two of these basic light sources. This is most effective when the lights are on dimmers and the process is done gradually. Experiment with the various footcandle ratios among the three light sources by means of the dimmer control.

4. With the basic key, back, and fill setup, use different subjects so that the variations created by hair, skin color, and clothes can be noted.

5. Using a mirror and a flashlight for a light source, experiment with the optical principles equating the angle of reflection with the angle of incidence. Hold the flashlight at eye level and shine it directly into the mirror. Raise the flashlight above your head, point the beam downward, and note where the reflected beam hits you on your body. How do the reflected angles change as you vary the angle at which the flashlight beam hits the mirror?

Camera Structure and Lens Design

5

•••••••••••••••••••

With this chapter, we begin a look at the video system. It is a complex chain that includes lenses, cameras (and their mounts), camera control units and a synchronizing generator, monitoring equipment, a switcher, possibly an editor, usually a video recorder, and (ultimately) a transmitter. The next five chapters will be concerned with various components in this system.

5.1 Video Signal Flow and Control Functions

Just as we discussed the audio system in terms of audio signal flow, so also would it be helpful to think in terms of the **video signal flow** for the picture part of the television production. The same seven basic control functions introduced in section 2.2 can be applied to the video system. Figure 5–1 illustrates in simplified form the basic units in the video signal flow.

The first step, *transducing,* is accomplished by the camera itself. The camera, like the microphone, is a **transducer** that receives physical energy (light waves) and transforms it into electrical energy (video signals) that is suitable for electronic distribution. Although considerably more complex than the microphone, the camera performs this same basic function.

The video signal is then *channeled* directly or indirectly into the video switcher. Although no patch bay is as obvious as that in the audio system, cameras nevertheless can be patched or connected to different inputs in the switcher or to other points in the master control room.

The switcher (chapter 7), like the audio console, is the heart of the video signal flow. Here is where all video *mixing* occurs. Camera pictures can be selected and combined in a variety of ways.

Figure 5–1
Diagram of the video signal
flow.

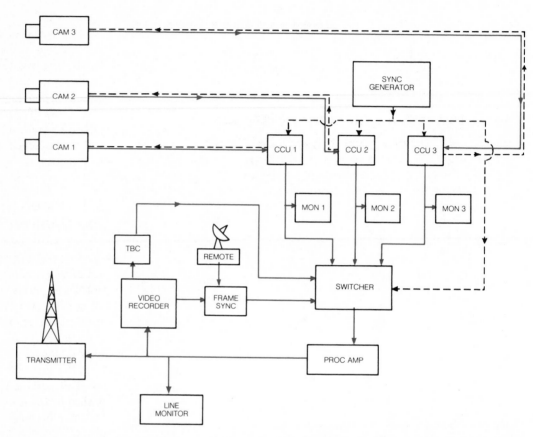

A portion of the synchronizing ("sync") pulse (dotted line) is sent out from the sync generator to each camera control unit (CCU) and on to each camera—keeping all cameras in perfect synchronization. The complete sync pulse is also sent to the switcher. Simultaneously, the picture information (solid line) flows from each camera to the CCU, where the video signal can be shaped and altered. The composite signal (picture plus sync pulse) is then channeled into the switcher, with the picture information also being displayed on the video monitor for each camera. (In the diagram, from the CCU on through the rest of the system the solid line represents the composite signal—

picture plus sync pulse; the dotted line is omitted for the sake of simplicity.)

From the switcher, the composite signal can be sent, through a process amplifier, on to the line monitor, to a video recorder, and/or to the transmitter. A video recorder also can be used, of course, as a picture source—sending its recorded program material through the time-base corrector (TBC) and on to the switcher or to the transmitter. Remote sources (satellite feeds, microwave links) also can serve as inputs to the switcher, flowing through the frame synchronizer that conforms the sync pulse with the other composite signals.

The *amplification* of the video signal occurs at several different points in the total system. Whenever the signal is distributed any significant distance through the various camera cables, *distribution amplifiers* are used to boost the signal periodically. Our simplified

diagram (figure 5–1) does not attempt to show all of the points where distribution amplifiers are placed throughout the system.

Some amount of video *shaping* can also occur at the switcher. This function, however, is controlled primarily through the **camera**

Additive Color

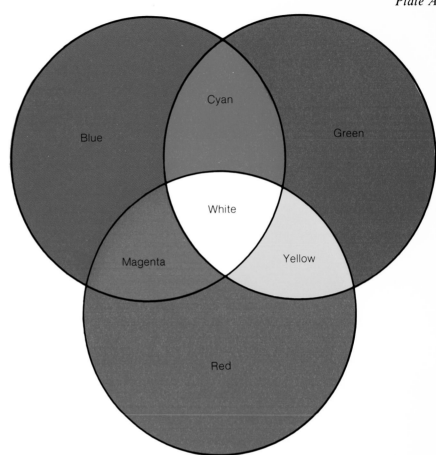

Additive Color

Where any two of the three primary colors (red, green, blue) overlap, they form a secondary color—cyan (green-blue), magenta (blue-red), or yellow (red-green). Combinations of varying intensities of the three primary colors can produce all possible hues. All three primary colors in a balanced proportion produced white.

Saturation

Low   Med.   High

High

Brightness

Med.

Low

Red

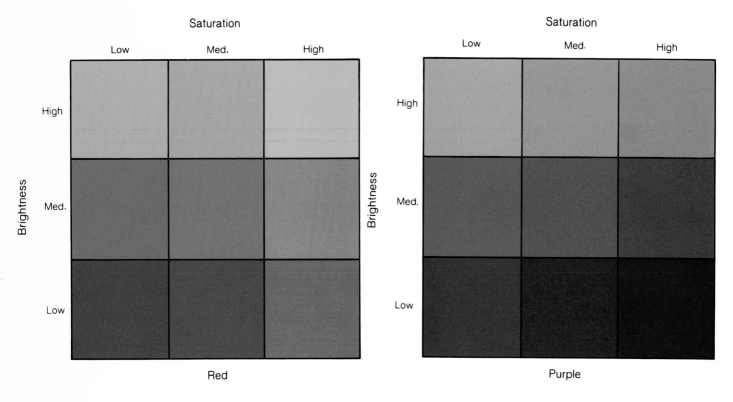

Saturation

Low   Med.   High

High

Brightness

Med.

Low

Purple

The Properties of Color: Hue, Brightness, and Saturation

These three boxes illustrate the different combinations of colors possible by varying the saturation and brightness of a single hue. This is especially important in working with character generators and electronic graphics. As the number of choices you have in hue, brightness, and saturation increases, the number of possible colors increases. For example, a character generator that can produce 100 different hues at twenty different brightness levels and twenty different saturation levels has a total "palette" of 40,000 colors!

Saturation

Low   Med.   High

High

Brightness

Med.

Low

Green

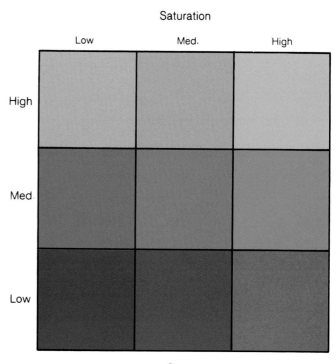

Plate C

Which Monitor Is Adjusted Correctly?

The monitor looks as if it is adjusted correctly, but the vectorscope to the right shows that this color signal is out of adjustment. (The points on the green display are outside of the boxes etched on the overlay.) The phase of the color signal should first be adjusted (by a competent technician or engineer) and then the monitor should be adjusted so that it will reproduce the color signal *faithfully*.

In this case the vectorscope shows that the signal is accurate, therefore the monitor is out of adjustment. This usually happens when the monitor is adjusted by someone trying to make a bad signal look better. The picture on the monitor should be corrected by a competent technician or engineer.

Typical Video Problems

The pictures on the right illustrate a number of video problems that should be watched for in every production. The top picture is getting too much light, as indicated by the "blooming" of the white shirt. This can be corrected by adjusting the lighting or adjusting the iris on the camera. While the white shirt makes the problem worse, it is also visible in the white patches on both faces. The middle picture shows the opposite problem—the scene is too dark. This may be due to improper lighting or incorrect iris setting on the camera, but it could also be caused by a low "pedestal" (black level) setting on the camera. (When the pedestal is too low, darker areas lose all detail and look completely black.) The bottom picture has color problems that could be due to (1) a camera that was not correctly "white-balanced," (2) a playback of a tape that is "out of phase" with the switcher, or (3) an improper monitor adjustment. To correct the picture, first check the white balance (for a camera) or the phase—using color bars and a vectorscope (for a tape machine). As a last resort, have a technician use a properly calibrated reference signal to adjust the monitor. Remember—do not adjust a monitor just because it does not look right!

control unit (CCU). What most people think of as the camera is actually only part of a much larger unit known as the **camera chain.** Most of the equipment necessary for the control and shaping of the video signal is not located at the camera itself but at a separate point under the supervision of the video control operator. (On newer and simpler cameras—variations of the vidicon—controls are preset and do not need continual adjusting or attention.)

Various types of video recorders (chapter 8) are used for **recording** and **playback** of the television signal. Usually, the signals recorded by the video recorder include both the video and audio information for the entire TV production.

As with amplification, *monitoring* takes place at several different points within the system. In any regular studio production, the camera operators will have a camera monitor to enable them to see what they are picking up with their cameras. The most conspicuous display of TV monitors is in the control room, where the director has a monitor for every camera and other video source being used in a particular program. In the simplest of studio operations, this involves three or four monitors. In ambitious network productions, dozens of monitors may be used in a single control room. In the master control room, an array of specialized monitors and scopes are used for technical monitoring. (See the following section.)

Control Components

The video signal is much more complex than the audio signal. It takes roughly 600 times as much "information" to produce a video signal as to produce sound to cover the same period of time. Consequently, the picture is vulnerable to a number of disruptive influences within the system itself. There must be several specialized components that monitor, adjust, refine, and stabilize the picture throughout the

video signal flow. Discussion of these sophisticated pieces of equipment is introduced here in order to provide a reference point for the remainder of this chapter—although some aspects of their technical nature will not be covered in detail until later chapters.

Sync Generator   In order to coordinate the functioning of all components in the video system, the **synchronizing generator** creates a series of timing pulses that lock together all elements of the video signal at every stage of production, switching, recording, editing, transmission, and reception. This sync pulse has often been called a system of *electronic sprocket holes* that keeps everything coordinated in a lock-step pattern. This timing pulse is based upon the basic 60-cycle alternating current used in the United States and in many other countries using the NTSC television system.[1]

Proc Amp   It is the job of the **process amplifier** to take the *composite video signal* from the switcher—color, brightness, and synchronizing information—and then stabilize the levels, amplify the signal, and remove unwanted elements or *noise.*

TBC   Video signals from videotape recorders will often have synchronizing pulses that have been slightly altered or have deteriorated during the recording and playback process. The **time-base corrector** takes these signals, encodes them into a digital form, and then reconstructs an enhanced synchronizing signal for playback and editing purposes. (See section 7.5.)

1. In 1941 the United States adopted the recommendations of the National Television System Committee (NTSC), which defined the basic 525–line, 30–frame format described in this chapter. This NTSC system—still the standard for North and South America and Japan—is one of three different formats used by various countries throughout the world.

Figure 5–2
Waveform monitor.

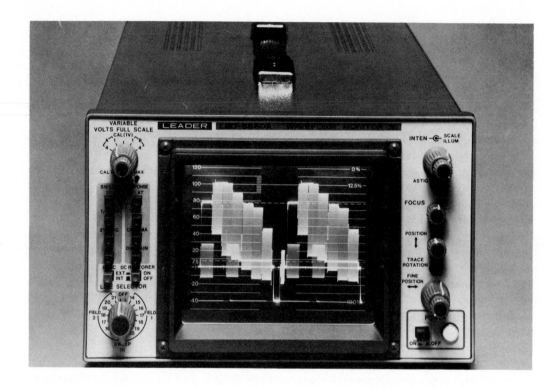

Frame Synchronizer   A relatively recent and sophisticated piece of equipment, the **frame synchronizer** (and "field synchronizer") takes video sources from outside of the studio control or video recorders, compares their sync pulses with studio sync, and adjusts the differences between the two. The signals are put through a digitalized phase prior to output. Satellite and other out-of-studio feeds can thereby be coordinated through the studio switcher.

Color Bar Generator   One other control element to be mentioned here is the **color bars.** The color bar generator sends a standardized pattern of vertical colored bars through the switcher. This is used to calibrate the color values and adjustments on all cameras, video recorders, and monitors. The color bars are also

recorded at the beginning of a video recording so that the playback machine can be matched to the color levels set at the time of the recording. (See color plate C.)

Oscilloscopes

Just as the VU meter provides a visual indication of an audio signal, two special types of visual monitors called *oscilloscopes* provide information about video signals. Essentially, oscilloscopes are cathode-ray tubes that depict changes in electrical information by means of visual displays.

The **waveform monitor** (figure 5–2) indicates the strength of the video signal, allowing the technician to compare and adjust the brightest and darkest elements in a picture. The **vectorscope** (figure 5–3) provides information about the part of the video signal car-

Camera Structure and Lens Design

Figure 5–3
Vectorscope.

rying color information, showing the individual levels for the three primary colors and the three complementary colors—red, green, blue, yellow, cyan, and magenta (see section 5.2).

At first, it might seem rather simple to find out how bright the picture is and what colors are present in the signal by merely looking at a color monitor. However, monitors may be misadjusted. Using television monitors to evaluate the video signal is comparable to using an audio speaker to judge an audio signal. (If the sound level does not appear loud enough, some persons might just erroneously crank up the volume of the speaker, rather than properly adjust the audio level at the console; in reality they have not increased the audio signal one bit.)

In fact, one of the most common mistakes made by novices is that when they see a pic-

ture that is too bright or one in which the color is slightly off, they adjust the monitor. This does not change the video signal at all. Instead of correcting for a bad signal, the misadjustment of the monitor will make the correct video signal (when it appears on the monitor) look worse.

While the audio speaker and video monitor can provide some valuable (but limited) information, the strength and quality of audio and video signals must be measured by the VU meter and oscilloscopes (waveform monitor and vectorscope), respectively.

To evaluate a video signal, you should first look at the picture on the waveform monitor. Since this measures the strength of the video signal—the luminance—the highest point on the waveform display indicates the brightest part of the television picture. If the display

Camera Structure and Lens Design

registers above the "100" mark, the signal may be too strong and will become distorted. This level can be decreased by adjusting the iris of the camera lens or by decreasing the CCU *video gain*—the strength of the video signal coming out of the camera.

It is also important to pay attention to the lowest part of the waveform display. This represents the brightness of the dark areas of the picture. The strength of the signal in this range is controlled by adjusting the part of the video signal called the *pedestal*. Adjustment of the pedestal level is more difficult than adjusting the gain; but it is important to make sure that the dark areas of the screen are dark enough—without losing detail.

The vectorscope provides a different type of readout—indicating the balance of colors present in the video signal. Reading the vectorscope like a clock face, red signals are displayed just to the left of the 12 o'clock position; blue signals are displayed at the 4 o'clock position; and green is displayed at the 7 o'clock spot. (See color plate C.) Complementary colors—magenta, cyan, and yellow—are displayed in between these three positions. *Saturation* (section 5.2) is indicated by displays closer to the outside of the scope area; the lower the saturation, the closer to the center of the monitor the glowing color dot will be.

The waveform monitor is generally more valuable for making on-the-air adjustments during a production. However, the vectorscope is invaluable during setup and whenever more than one source is being used at the same time—for example, integrating a videotape machine into a live production. Since the part of the video signal carrying the color information or *chrominance* is separated from the brightness or *luminance* (see section 5.2), it can become out of phase (i.e., all colors will be a little bit off). Before beginning any production, the phasing can be checked with the vectorscope by using the internal color bar generators in most cameras.

5.2 The Color Video System

At the center of the entire television operation is the camera. Throughout virtually the entire history of television technology, the heart of the camera has been the *pickup tube*—that miraculous variation of the cathode-ray tube that can transform (transduce) frequencies of visual light (as reflected from a solid object) into electrical signals. In recent years, however, an offshoot of the computer chip, the *charge-coupled device* (**CCD**), has replaced the pickup tube in most professional cameras as well as in consumer models.

At the receiving end of the television system—the home TV set—the cathode-ray tube (kinescope tube) is still the primary element in the *display* of all video pictures. However, many major companies have definite plans to develop liquid crystal display (LCD) screens, which will revolutionize the reception technology just as the CCD has transformed the production side of the system.

Three Attributes of Video Color

Most professional cameras have three CCD image sensors or three pickup tubes. (Single-component cameras will be covered in the following discussion.) Because all video utilizes an *additive color* process, all shades and tones are the result of combining the three *primary video colors—red, green, and blue.*

To do its job, the camera must first separate incoming light into these three primary colors by means of a **beam splitter,** made up of a glass prism and reflective mirrors. The three tubes or CCD chips are identical in structure. They are labeled red, green, or blue only because the beam splitter separates the three colors and directs just one designated color to each pickup device.

To understand how the color system works, we must look at three specific sensations or attributes that contribute to our perception of

Camera Structure and Lens Design

images. There is first of all the color itself (**hue**); then we must consider the purity or intensity of that color (**saturation**); and finally we need to examine the concept of luminance or lightness (**brightness**). All three of these factors interact to contribute to the phenomenon of video color. (See also the discussion of these variables in section 10.1.)

Hue   The concept of "hue" refers to what we normally would think of as the actual tint or *color* base itself—red, yellow, green, and so forth. Color plate B (bottom) lays out the three **primary colors** (red, green, and blue) and shows how any two of the primary colors can be combined (in the overlapping areas) to produce the three additional **complementary colors**—*cyan* (a turquoise formed from blue and green), *magenta* (blending red and blue), and *yellow* (the combination of red and green).

These primary and complementary colors are the basic pure hues seen when a prism breaks up white light into its constituent wavelengths (every hue has its distinctive frequency and wavelength)[2] or when we marvel at a rainbow (which essentially is millions of droplets of water acting as tiny prisms to create the vivid primary and complementary colors—ranging from violet to red).

We have known for centuries that a prism separates white light into its spectrum of component colors. Similarly, when light waves of all three primary colors—*at their full brightness*—are added together in the correct proportion (59 percent green, 30 percent red, and 11 percent blue), the resulting effect is *white*. However, as the brightness is diminished, the white fades to varying shades of gray; the less bright the image, the darker the gray.

2. As indicated in appendix A, red, the lowest visible color in the electromagnetic spectrum, has a wavelength of 6,500 angstroms (each angstrom is one ten-millionth of a millimeter). Violet is the shortest wavelength we can see, with a wavelength as short as 4,000 angstroms.

Therefore, white is not the absence of color; it is the presence of all colors! If you have trouble accepting this physiological phenomenon on faith, prove it to yourself. With a strong magnifying glass, take a close look at a white portion of any picture on your own color TV set. What you perceive from a distance as "white" is actually composed of very intense red, green, and blue stripes or dots surrounded by black borders! Similarly, a careful look at white beach sand will reveal a wide range of colored grains.

As the proportions are varied between any two or all three colors, an enormous range of hues becomes possible. (Computer-graphics programs can discriminate among millions of individual colors.) For example, when red and green are added together, a range of pure hues from red to orange to yellow to green can be created. As the third primary color, blue, is added, you can achieve a wide variety of browns, tans, mahoganies, beiges, ochers, maroons, sepias, and so forth.

Saturation   The intensity or vividness of a color is described in terms of its "saturation." Basically, this indicates the *purity* of a color. A heavily saturated color is one pure hue—it has no other hues blended in with it. A vivid pure green, for instance, is more heavily saturated than a grayish olive green. The pure green consists of no hues other than green, while the olive green is diluted with red and blue.

In effect—since all three colors blended in the right proportion results in white (or gray, if the colors are not at their brightest)—we can say that we have added white (or gray) to the color to make it less saturated.

Therefore, as a color becomes less saturated, it moves closer to the gray scale—anywhere from white to black. As we add red and blue to the saturated green, it becomes a grayish olive—as we add more red and blue to the olive, we eventually arrive at some shade of gray. And if the colors we have blended together are all at their full brightness (as explained in the following discussion), we will have white. White (or gray) is the absence of saturation—no hue predominates.

On color plate B, the greens in the right-hand vertical column of the green quadrant are all highly saturated—ranging from dark green at the bottom to pastel green at the top. The grayish greens in the center column are less saturated; and the greens in the left-hand column approach unsaturated grays.

Brightness   If we think of saturation as a scale ranging from gray to a pure color, think of "brightness" as a scale ranging from dark to light. In painting with opaque colors, *brightness* (lightness) or *value* refers to how much white is present in any given hue. In television terms, however, brightness or *luminance* can better be thought of as the strength or intensity of the electrical signal. Think of it as the opposite of "dimness."

Even though a fully saturated pure green (as previously described) might appear quite vivid on a TV screen and a grayish olive green might look quite dull, the two colors could well have the same brightness value or luminance level on a gray scale.

If we look at a pure (that is, heavily saturated) green color in a television picture, it can be bright or dark depending upon how much electrical signal it is sending out. Its brightness is diminished as the strength of the green signal is decreased. No red or blue is added to the picture (which would decrease its saturation), but the green signal itself is simply diminished—which decreases its brightness or luminance (but not its saturation).

Let us look again at the green quadrant in color plate B. The bottom row of greens, ranging from dark gray on the left to a pure dark green on the right, represents a low level of brightness or luminance. As we move up each column, the colors become *lighter* or brighter. In the upper right-hand corner of the green sample, we now have a light or pastel green. It is the same saturation as the lower right-hand corner, but it is brighter.

The camera's ability to reproduce the correct attributes of hue, saturation, and brightness depends upon the light that is reflected from the subject matter and is focused through the lens onto the image-sensing CCD chips or tubes. The camera can only respond to color in terms of the varying amounts of light energy that are created by this reflective process.

In a television picture, one way that brightness or luminance is affected, of course, is by lighting. If we have a grayish blue chair in a set (low in saturation because its "blueness" has been diminished by adding considerable red and green to give it some "grayness"), it can be either bright or dark, depending upon how much light falls upon it—and is therefore reflected into the camera. This blue-gray chair, which is low in saturation (not brilliantly colored), may be relatively high in brightness if it is well lit. On the other hand, a brilliant pure blue chair (heavily saturated, with little red or green in it) may be dark (low in brightness) if not in a lighted area.

Luminance and Chrominance Signals

In examining how the color video picture is put together, we now need to understand something about the concepts of *luminance* and *chrominance* signals. The sensations of hue, saturation, and brightness are meaningful only as they can be translated into electronic information to be sent out in a video signal.

Keep in mind that the camera receives an image through a lens and then focuses it upon a pickup device (either a CCD chip or a camera tube). In the case of the three-chip (or three-tube) camera, separate red, green, and blue images are filtered out (by means of the

Camera Structure and Lens Design

beam splitter) and directed to their respective chips or tubes. Each CCD chip is therefore sensing the brightness of its designated color.

This image capture (using a three-chip camera as our example) can best be examined by looking at the previous explanation of the grayish-blue chair. Because of the beam splitter, the blue CCD chip will pick up the primary image of the chair. The video signal will vary as the light and dark areas of the chair are registered. This is the **luminance** signal, and as it reacts to the differing levels of brightness in the picture, it is, in effect, defining the shape of the chair.

The luminance factor, therefore, is a function of an image's brightness as reflected into the camera from the subject of the picture source. This must not be confused with an increase in the **video gain**—which is a matter of adding brightness to an entire picture by amplifying the video signal.

The contrast of brightness and shadow in any television picture is what gives it the illusion of depth and structure. This is the function of the luminance signal—which has often been described as the "skeleton" upon which the more subtle aspects of hue and saturation are imposed. In monochrome television, the luminance signal was the black-and-white picture, which was all that was transmitted. In earlier color TV systems, the luminance information was generated from a fourth (black-and-white) tube in the camera as a separate signal that was sent along with the color information. In today's color systems, luminance and chrominance (color information) are combined in different ways (as explained in the following discussion).

At the same time that the luminance is being picked up by the CCD chips, each chip is also reacting to the saturation or *chroma* of the chair—whether it is a grayish blue or a bright blue—as the beam splitter directs various hues to the three chips. The grayer or less saturated the color is, the more that some of

the picture information will be picked up by the red and green chips. It is this blending of the saturation of each of the three primary hues that provides the basis for the **chrominance** signal.

In effect, you can think of the chrominance signal as the combination of hue and saturation, while the luminance signal captures the brightness of the image.

In many video systems, the luminance and chrominance signals are combined (along with other scanning control information) as they leave the camera. This is referred to as a **composite** video signal. In some newer formats, however—such as Betacam and S-VHS—the luminance and chrominance data are recorded as two separate signals. This type of system, a **component** rather than a composite signal, results in better resolution and detail.

Strictly speaking, what the camera system does is to *separate* the colors. No mixing of the several colors takes place in the camera chain. In fact, the colors—the luminance and chrominance signals—remain distinct entities (even when combined within the composite video signal) throughout the entire switching, recording, editing, transmitting, and receiving process. Your TV set at home even displays separate pinpoints of distinct primary hues as the individual red, green, and blue phosphor dots, strips, or bars are illuminated. It is only when these microscopic pinpoints are interpreted by our brain that the sensation of "color" is perceived.

Camera Image-Sensing Technologies

The **image-orthicon (I-O)** tube was the first practical camera tube developed. For many years, models such as the venerable TK-41 (figure 5–4) were the standard of the professional industry. During the 1960s, the **vidicon** tube was developed and, because of its operating advantages (it was more rugged, had a

better contrast ratio, and was more stable from
an engineering standpoint), it soon found its
way into most applications formerly reserved
for I-O cameras.[3] Over the past thirty years,
the vidicon design was constantly improved,
and sophisticated versions such as the
Plumbicon[4] and the **Saticon**[5] evolved, which
resulted in better picture detail at much lower
light levels (down below fifty footcandles).

As the charge-coupled device (CCD) has
replaced the camera pickup tube in the 1990s,

we have seen an extension of the same semi-
conductor technology that earlier gave us the
transistor radio, the modern computer, and a
number of other electronic wonders. The CCD
consists of a number of tiny *photodiodes,* each
of which can generate a small electrical current that is proportional to the intensity of the
light falling upon it. When the photodiode is
combined with a *transistor* (with its important
storage and discharge capabilities), the result
is a microscopic pinpoint called a **CCD image
sensor.** Each of these specks is also termed a
pixel and, as such, corresponds to the light-
producing pixels or phosphor dots of the video
receiver (kinescope) tube in your TV set at
home. As with all NTSC video systems, there
are 525 horizontal rows of pixels from top to
bottom (a few of these do not carry picture information), and each of these rows contains at
least 450 pixels (see figure 5–6). This adds up

---

3. The first pickup tube developed was actually
the **iconoscope** tube developed in the 1920s. It was
never put into extensive use, however, as it was very
insensitive to light, requiring large amounts of
illumination to give a decent picture.

4. *Plumbicon* is a registered trademark of N. V.
Philips.

5. *Saticon* is a trademark of Hitachi.

Camera Structure and Lens Design

Figure 5–5
The CCD–1 was the RCA prototype CCD camera (no longer in production). The model is holding one of the three chip-like silicon-based charge-coupled devices that have replaced the camera pickup tubes in the foreground. (Photo courtesy of RCA)

to over 250,000 points of light sensitivity on the camera chip—and a corresponding number of pixels on the TV receiver tube.

CCD technology has produced lighter, more compact cameras. Figure 5–5 shows the size of the CCD chip compared to the tube it replaces. In spite of its thumbnail size, the CCD performs the same basic job that the cathode-ray camera pickup tube does—but more dependably, with increasingly better resolution, and with several other advantages. Among the CCD features are the elimination of both *image lag* (the smearing or streaking of white areas of the picture when the camera is moved across the scene) and *burn-in* (a type of "image retention" where the tube remembers the image of a picture it has been focused on and superimposes a negative image of that scene over succeeding shots). Another major advantage of the CCD camera is its ruggedness and durability. Experience has shown that the chip simply does not wear out under normal use.

In cameras having three CCD image sensors, the image-detection technology may differ from the three-tube camera, but the end product is much the same as with tube cameras. A beam splitter must first separate the red, green, and blue light so that each hue can be sent to its respective CCD chip.

There are, however, many excellent industrial and consumer-level cameras that use only one CCD image sensor to produce a color picture. Rather than divide the incoming light with a beam splitter, one approach to the single-CCD camera uses a checkerboard pattern of red, green, and blue *color filter elements* placed just in front of the CCD chip of pixels, as shown in figure 5–6. There is an individual filter for each pixel, but notice that

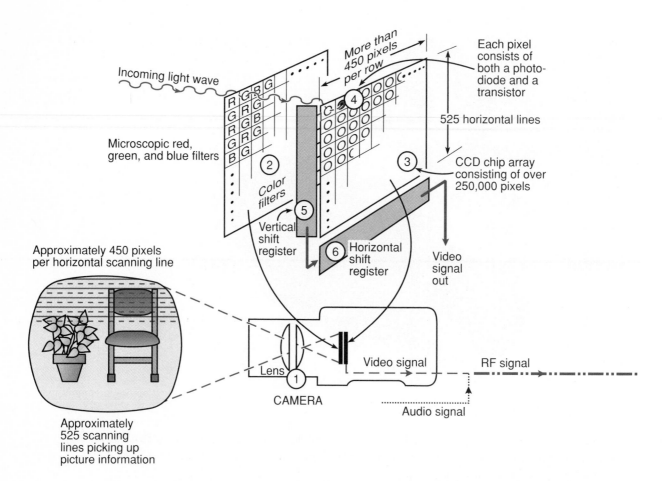

Incoming light wave

More than 450 pixels per row

Each pixel consists of both a photo-diode and a transistor

525 horizontal lines

Microscopic red, green, and blue filters

CCD chip array consisting of over 250,000 pixels

② Color filters

⑤ Vertical shift register

⑥ Horizontal shift register

Video signal out

Approximately 450 pixels per horizontal scanning line

Lens ①

CAMERA

Video signal

RF signal

Audio signal

Approximately 525 scanning lines picking up picture information

Figure 5-6

(*Left Page*) Cameras with only a single CCD chip can produce a three-color image by utilizing color filters placed between the lens and the chip. After the incoming image travels through the lens (1), it passes through a color filter consisting of a checkerboard pattern of red, green, and blue filter elements (2). One common arrangement uses green filters for half of the pixel elements because green is also used for the luminance signal. The filtered color images are then focused on the two-dimensional image-sensing CCD chip located immediately behind the filter (3); therefore, there is a tiny red, green, or blue filter in front of each pixel on the chip. The precise alignment of these microscopic filters and corresponding pixels is crucial for a clear picture. Each pixel (4) consists of a photodiode (which generates an infinitesimal electric current in proportion to the amount of light hitting it) and a transistor (which stores the current for a tiny fraction of a second). When a trigger impulse is generated by the vertical shift

register (5) (sixty times every second), the stored charge in each photodiode is transmitted along each row in sequence to the horizontal shift register (6). The information in the horizontal shift register then is shifted out and becomes one scan line of the video signal. This video information, along with the horizontal and vertical sync pulses, is combined with the audio signal and is ready for transmission or recording. (*Right Page*) At the receiving end, the picture and audio information are stripped from the carrier wave (demodulated), and the blue, red, and green information is sent to three electron guns (7) in the rear of the kinescope or picture tube. Each color gun shoots out an electron beam, which varies in intensity corresponding to the strength of the electric signal initially created by the CCD photodiode. This electron beam is directed back and forth (and up and down) by a ring of deflection coil magnets (8) controlled by the same sync pulse that triggered the vertical and horizontal shift registers in the camera.

Camera Structure and Lens Design

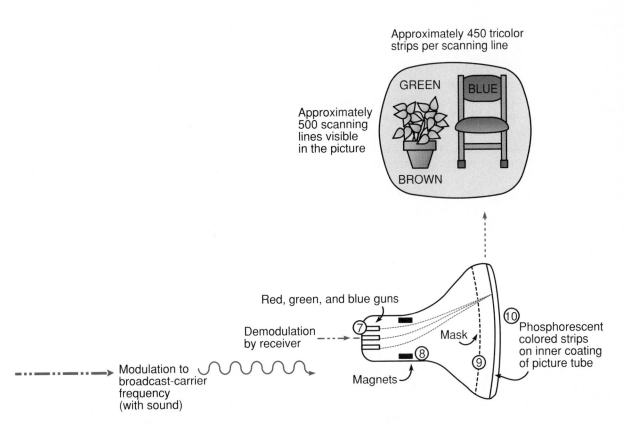

Approximately 450 tricolor strips per scanning line

GREEN   BLUE

Approximately 500 scanning lines visible in the picture

BROWN

Red, green, and blue guns

Demodulation by receiver

Modulation to broadcast-carrier frequency (with sound)

⑦

⑧

Magnets

Mask

⑨

⑩ Phosphorescent colored strips on inner coating of picture tube

HOME RECEIVER TUBE

Thus, the scanning beam re-creates the picture information for each color in the same pattern and at the same intensity as the signal from the camera. Each electron beam is precisely aimed through a mask (9) that directs the stream of electrons at the face of the tube with pinpoint accuracy. The electrons bombard the tiny

phosphorescent strips or pixels on the inside of the tube—usually arranged in vertical bars or strips of the three primary colors (10)—making each one glow with an intensity that corresponds to the original picture signal. As the various red, green, and blue pixels are combined in varying intensities, the original image is re-created at the rate of sixty fields every second.

there are as many green pixels as there are red and blue pixels combined. The reason for this is that the green signal is also used to produce the luminance information. Even though both the luminance and chrominance information can be integrated this way, the resulting picture is generally not as rich or detailed as the three-chip cameras.

The Scanning Process   As the lens focuses the incoming picture on the 250,000 image-sensing pixels, a picture mosaic is created. The brightness and color information from each individual pixel are transformed into a minute electrical charge, depending upon the amount of light falling on the pixel. This infinitesimal electrical charge is passed on in an

Camera Structure and Lens Design

incredibly precise and rapid sequential pattern—in a manner that somewhat resembles the way the beam of electrons scans the image target in a pickup tube.[6]

This sequence of picture information is gathered by *vertical and horizontal shift registers* at the left side and bottom of the CCD chip. After the picture/electrical information from the first line is scanned from left to right, the current is momentarily turned off by a **blanking pulse** and pulled back to the left side of the chip by the **horizontal synchronization pulse.** Then the information on the *third* horizontal line of pixels is scanned. Sequentially, the process is repeated as all of the *odd-numbered* lines on the CCD chip are scanned. It takes one-sixtieth of a second to scan all of the odd-numbered lines (1–3–5–7 . . . 521–523–525). This top-to-bottom half picture is termed a **field.** Because only half of the lines have been scanned (picking up information from only half of the pixels on the chip), this field represents only half of the total video picture.

Now a **vertical synchronization pulse** repositions the vertical and horizontal shift registers to start the scanning process all over again. This time, the *even-numbered* lines on the CCD chip are scanned to produce another "half-picture" field. These two fields—the odd-numbered lines and the even-numbered lines—make up the total picture that is referred to as a **frame.** Thus, there are thirty full frames per second. The basic pattern of this scanning process is similar to that of your eyes reading across a line of type on a page and then

jumping back to the left side of the page and starting on the next lower line—525 lines per page, thirty pages per second!

It is the transistor part of the pixel, with its ability to store and then quickly move small electronic signals, that lets the vertical and horizontal shift registers gather the total signal of the 250,000 pixels—thirty times per second. From this are generated the chrominance and luminance signals as well as the vertical and horizontal sync pulses so important to picture stability. All of this electrical information is amplified and in other ways modulated within the camera to produce either the composite or component video signal. The resulting electrical message is the electronic signal that has just begun its long and complicated path.

The Receiver Picture Tube   Just as the radio speaker resembles the microphone (the speaker's components are in reverse order of the microphone's signal flow), so is the TV set's picture tube the mirrored analog of the older technology of the camera pickup tube. By extension of the same analogy, it can be said that the display tubes of the future will probably relate more to the CCD and LED (light-emitting diode) technologies.

As the camera is picking up the picture—and during the subsequent channeling, mixing, shaping, amplifying, and monitoring of the picture—the signal remains in a "pure" line *video* format. Switchers, studio monitors, recorders, and editors all process this line level signal. However, for the picture to be transmitted, the audio signal must be added, and then the video and audio information must be converted to a **radio frequency (RF)** signal. It is this RF signal that can then be modulated onto a **carrier wave** that can be broadcast on a radio frequency in the electromagnetic spectrum.

The first task of the home TV set is to strip off the audio signal; next it has to demodulate the picture information. Then the red, green,

---

6. In the tube-type camera, the light image falling on the face of the pickup tube charges individual pixels on a "target" located at the front of the tube. The electrical charge on these pixels is then "read" by a beam of electrons that are being shot from an electron gun at the rear of the tube. This beam is pulled back and forth and up and down the face of the tube by magnets. As the beam *scans* back and forth across the pickup tube, it creates the electrical current that becomes the video signal.

Camera Structure and Lens Design

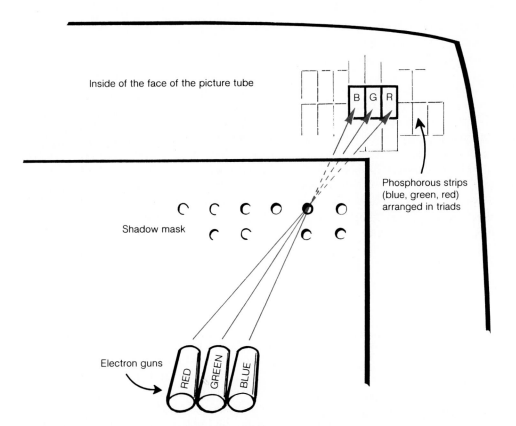

Inside of the face of the picture tube

B G R

Phosphorous strips
(blue, green, red)
arranged in triads

Shadow mask

Electron guns

RED GREEN BLUE

Figure 5–7
Shadow mask for color
receiver.

Most color receivers utilize a shadow mask, a thin metal sheet perforated by tiny holes. These carefully aligned dots or slots ensure that as each of the three electron beams is pulled across the face of the tube in its scanning pattern, it will hit only those phosphor strips colored to correspond with its designated electron gun in the rear of the tube.

and blue guns in the receiver or **kinescope** tube each shoot out a stream of electrons. This electron beam, like the scanning beam in the older camera pickup tubes, is controlled by a ring of magnets that deflects and controls the beam to reproduce the left-to-right and top-to-bottom scanning pattern initiated in the camera.

In most TV sets, the electron beams pass through a **masking plate** that focuses the electrons as they strike the designated phosphor pixels on the inside glass of the picture tube. (See figure 5–7.) This inner coating can be either in the form of triad groups of red, green, and blue dots or in the form of tiny vertical phosphorescent strips of the same colors.

It is the control information on the synchronizing pulse (including the horizontal and vertical blanking intervals) that guarantees a synchronized scanning rate of sixty fields (thirty frames) per second—the TV receiver tube electron beams reproduce the video picture essentially as it was originally picked up by the camera tube.

Like the image picked up by the camera, the picture displayed on the receiver screen never exists as a completed frame, even for an infinitesimal fraction of a second. The TV frame does not have a discrete existence the way a frame of motion picture film does. What we have is the linear tracing of a point of light

Camera Structure and Lens Design

moving at an incredible rate of speed. At any given microsecond, one "half-picture" field is always at some stage of the continual scanning process.

But because of the phenomenon of *persistence of vision* ("visual lag"), the brain perceives this incredibly rapid series of light flashes as a moving picture. The human eye tends to retain images for a split second after the image has been removed. If about fifteen or more separate images per second are flashed before the eye, human perception will cause them to blend together, thus creating the illusion of motion. This persistence of vision is what makes simulated moving pictures possible—on celluloid film as well as on the face of a television tube.

5.3   Lens Characteristics

In conjunction with the CCD image sensor (or pickup tube), the single most important element in the whole pictorial process probably is the lens. As illustrated in figure 5–6, it is the lens that focuses the picture upon the face of the beam splitter (or directly onto the CCD chip in single-chip cameras). A good lens can help the cheapest camera produce a sharp, clear picture. An inferior lens can turn the best professional camera into blurred trash.

Shortly after its introduction in the early 1960s, the **zoom lens** became standard equipment on virtually all studio television cameras. For most types of video production, this will likely remain true in the future. Indeed, most television production students will probably never see a **fixed-focal-length lens** on a television camera. The zoom lens, however, because of its numerous lens elements, can never be as optically perfect as a fixed-focal-length lens designed for a specified magnification.

The introduction of **high-definition television (HDTV)** may well set the stage for a return to limited applications of the fixed-focal-

length lens. Those who have seen an HDTV demonstration, with its incredibly sharp picture resolution, cannot help but be impressed with its potential for both theatrical and industrial applications (see figure 5–8).[7] In order to take advantage of the HDTV high picture quality, it may be practical to utilize the better optical characteristics of the fixed-focal-length lens. (One Sony HDTV camera comes equipped to accept a variety of fixed lenses, ranging in focal length from 11.5mm to 56mm.) This possibility may lend some added importance to our preliminary study of lens function in which the fixed-focal-length lens will serve as our model.

The characteristics of **focal length, focus, *f*-stop,** and **depth of field** are all simpler to grasp with a non-zoom fixed-length lens. It is much easier to comprehend the concept of a **long lens** compression of a picture or **wide-angle lens** giving a greater depth of field if one visualizes the actual length and angle of the lens. In fact, any serious still photographer who has worked with fixed-focal-length lenses will find it much easier to understand what a zoom lens can do—and why—than the photographer who started out with only a zoom lens.

Therefore, this section will deal with lens characteristics using the fixed-focal-length lens as a reference point. Section 5.4 will deal specifically with the zoom lens.

Focal Length

The *focal length* of a lens is measured from the optical center point of the lens (when it is focused at infinity) to a point where the image

---

7. In the past few years, many national and international bodies have held numerous conferences to demonstrate and debate various types of HDTV formats. The engineers and bureaucrats have yet to decide on a specific global standard. All proposed systems use a wide-screen format and a scanning system around 1,100 lines. Compared to the NTSC 525–line system, the HDTV picture is astonishingly crisp and lifelike.

Camera Structure and Lens Design

is in focus. This focus point will be either the film in a film camera (movie or still camera) or the surface of the pickup tube in an electronic camera (see figure 5–9). Focal length is measured in either millimeters or inches (25.4 millimeters is equal to one inch). The lenses used for 35mm film cameras are the same lenses that were used on most of the earlier professional image-orthicon cameras and, therefore, provide a convenient reference point. Lenses used on earlier large vidicon cameras, on the other hand, are comparable to those used with 16mm film cameras.

Lenses of differing lengths are used so that more or less of a scene can be included in the picture. *The longer a lens is, the narrower its viewing angle will be, the less you will be able to get in the picture,* and therefore, *the larger individual subjects will be.* Conversely, a short focal-length lens will give you a wider viewing angle, thereby allowing you to get more in the picture, but individual subjects will appear smaller than normal.[8]

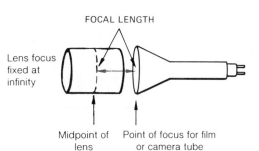

FOCAL LENGTH

Lens focus fixed at infinity

Midpoint of lens

Point of focus for film or camera tube

Figure 5–9
Measurement of lens focal length.

With the lens focus adjustment set at infinity (on adjustable lenses), the focal length is measured from the center of the lens to the point where the subject image is in focus on the surface of the pickup tube.

8. Because the face of the camera CCD chip or pickup tube is not processing *all* of the picture information passed through the lens, which is a circular scene, there is an apparent difference between the horizontal and vertical angles perceived by the camera. The electronically scanned picture is four units wide and three units high. The perceived angles, therefore, have the same four to three ratio. A 1-inch focal length vidicon lens, for example, will have a horizontal angle of about twenty-seven degrees and a vertical angle of approximately twenty degrees. For most planning purposes, the horizontal angle is the most commonly used.

Figure 5–10
Law of lenses.

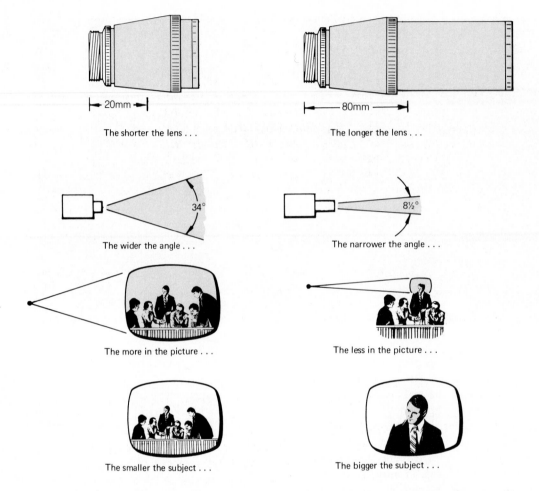

20mm

The shorter the lens . . .

80mm

The longer the lens . . .

34°

The wider the angle . . .

8½°

The narrower the angle . . .

The more in the picture . . .

The less in the picture . . .

The smaller the subject . . .

The bigger the subject . . .

This *law of lenses* is illustrated in figure 5–10. Long lenses, therefore, can be used to obtain closer views of objects. A long **telephoto** lens can get a relatively close-up view of an object from a great distance. On the other hand, a **short** (or wide-angle) **lens** will tend to increase distance and make things look farther away than they are. This fact can lead to distortion of distance.

A long lens (or a long-lens setting on a zoom lens) will *compress* distance. Two objects that are far apart from each other and at a great distance from the camera will be brought closer to the camera with a long lens

and, consequently, will seemingly be brought closer to each other. A common example is the baseball shot of the pitcher and batter as seen with an exceptionally long telephoto lens from center field. Although the pitcher and batter are about sixty feet apart, the camera is perhaps 400 feet away. Thus, the two players are brought much closer to the camera, and consequently, the distance between them is apparently compressed; on the home screen they may look as if they are only ten or fifteen feet apart.

On the other hand, a wide-angle lens (or a short-lens setting on a zoom lens) will *ex-*

Camera Structure and Lens Design

Two subjects viewed simultaneously through different sized lenses. The monitor on the left shows them as seen by a narrow-angle lens; note how close they appear to be. The right-hand monitor

shows the same subjects as seen through a wide-angle lens; note how the short lens exaggerates the distance. The woman and man are actually about seven feet apart.

Figure 5–11
Comparison of long and short lenses.

Figure 5–12
Standard vidicon studio lenses.

Lens Length	Viewpoint
10 mm	Extreme wide angle
25 mm	Wide angle
40 mm	Normal
100 mm	Narrow angle
200 mm	Extreme narrow angle (telephoto)

aggerate distance for exactly the opposite reason. The shorter the lens, the farther apart objects appear to be spread. Small studios can be made to look immense by use of a wide-angle lens. The apparent force of a punch thrown at the camera will be greatly exaggerated with a wide-angle lens. If the person throwing the punch is only four feet from the camera, and the punch brings the person's fist three feet closer to the camera (so that the fist stops one foot short of the lens), the person's arm has covered a great amount of viewing space by moving only three feet—the distance is exaggerated. Figure 5–11 illustrates how two lenses—one **narrow-angle** and one **wide-angle**—will vary the apparent distance between two persons.

Figure 5–12 lists the relative viewing angles of common sizes of larger vidicon lenses (or settings on a zoom lens) compared to the normal perception of the human eye. Although there may be some changes in lens structure as a result of CCD technology, the chart is still basically valid in that it shows the relationship of viewing angle to lens size.

Focusing Characteristics

Many fixed-focal-length lenses will have two adjustable rings. One will be the *f*-stop, or aperture opening, and the other will be the focusing ring. This focusing ring, which is common to all who have worked in still photography, can be adjusted anywhere from a few inches to infinity.

With zoom lenses, as we shall discuss in section 5.4, the focusing mechanism is complicated because of the number of lens elements that have to be rearranged within the housing of the zoom lens. Most contemporary TV cameras, including consumer camcorders, have zoom lenses where the focus automatically adjusts with the action of the zoom lens. This adjustment is usually accomplished on professional studio cameras by remote control from the rear of the camera—often on the **pan handle.**

The f-Stop Aperture

As we mentioned when discussing lighting and contrast range (section 4.2), the television camera has a relatively narrow range of light tolerance as compared with the human eye. All camera lenses, therefore, have an adjustable **diaphragm** (or *iris*) that can open or close the *aperture.* This lens opening is strictly to control the amount of light, within acceptable limits, falling upon the surface of the CCD chip or pickup tube; in no way can it affect the size of the picture the lens will pick up. (The size of the picture is strictly a function of the lens diameter and its relationship to the focal length of the lens.)

Modern cameras with zoom lenses usually have this iris control designed to function automatically. It is important, however, that students understand the following principles in order to understand how manual operation of the *f*-stop can affect the picture quality. As will be explained, there are many production situations where the camera operator will want to override the automatic iris control and adjust the iris manually.

The size of the **aperture,** or lens opening, is given an *f*-stop number. Because the formula that determines the *f*-stops results in a fraction, *the lower the* f-*stop number the larger the lens aperture,* and *the higher the* f-*stop number the smaller the lens aperture.* Just re-

member that the fraction ¼ is larger than ⅛; similarly *f*-4 is a larger opening than *f*-8.

For instance, *f*-22 is typically the smallest aperture found on most television lenses. The widest opening usually may be anywhere from *f*-1.4 to *f*-3.5, depending upon the structure of the lens. (Longer lenses generally cannot "open up" as far as shorter lenses; they cannot let in as much light. More light therefore is needed when using long lenses.)

The most obvious application of *f*-stop adjustments is to enable the production technicians to adjust to varying light sources. If you are working under very poor lighting conditions, it might be advisable to open up to *f*-2 or even *f*-1.4. On the other hand, if you are working under extremely bright conditions (perhaps outdoors on a sunny day), you might want to "stop down" to *f*-11 or *f*-16.

Depending upon whether one is moving up or down the graded scale of *f*-stops, the amount of light permitted to enter the lens is either doubled or cut in half with each *full* f-*stop change.* On most lenses, each marked change equals one full *f*-stop; for example, from *f*-2.8 to *f*-4 is a full stop. When the *f*-number is doubled (e.g., from *f*-4 to *f*-8), you have stopped down two full *f*-stops.

Let's take, for example, a given amount of light entering a camera with the lens set at *f*-16. By opening up to *f*-11, you have increased the aperture by one full stop. The opening is made twice as large, and you now have twice as much light entering through the lens as you did when the lens was set at *f*-16. Conversely, stopping down from *f*-5.6 to *f*-11 is two full *f*-stops, and you have cut the amount of light entering the lens down to a quarter of what it was at *f*-5.6. (See figure 5–13.)

One word of warning about *f*-stop adjustments should be stated at this point. Generally speaking, the camera operator should not routinely think of the *f*-stop as a means to compensate for bad lighting. The *f*-stops, together with the various electronic camera controls,

Camera Structure and Lens Design

should be set by the studio technician or video engineer and then left alone. Bad lighting or uneven lighting should be handled by correcting the lighting, not by tampering with the camera adjustments.

Although most modern cameras have an automatic iris control that continually adjusts the aperture opening to the lighting conditions, you will not always want to rely on this feature. If it is necessary to control the *f*-stop manually (for specific darkened or purposely overexposed effects), this "auto setting" must first be defeated (turned off). For instance, if you are recording on a remote shoot inside someone's kitchen and the talent walks past a bright window, your automatic iris will reflexively stop down to compensate for the sudden bright light hitting the lens. However, this throws your talent into a dark silhouette. It may be that you would rather keep the subject exposed properly and let the exterior of the window be overexposed. Therefore, you will have to turn off the auto iris. (See section 15.8.)

Depth of Field

One final consideration at this point is the depth of field of a lens on a particular shot. Depth of field refers to *the distance between the nearest point at which objects are in focus and the farthest point at which objects are in focus.* In a typical shot, objects close to the camera will be out of focus and objects too far away may be out of focus; the middle ground where objects are in focus is referred to as the depth of field.

Three different factors interrelate to determine the depth of field: *the f-stop* (the smaller the lens opening the greater the depth of field); *the distance from the subject to the camera* (the greater the camera-to-subject distance the greater the depth of field); and *the focal length of the lens* (the shorter the lens the greater the depth of field). Figure 5–14 illustrates these three variables.

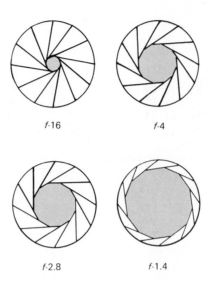

f-16

f-4

f-2.8

f-1.4

Figure 5–13
Diagrams of various *f*-stop openings.

Each marked position on the lens represents one full *f*-stop, e.g., from *f*-2.8 to *f*-4. Therefore, opening up the lens from *f*-4 to *f*-2.8 (one full stop) doubles the amount of light entering the lens. From *f*-2.8 to *f*-1.4 is two full stops; therefore, *f*-1.4 allows four times as much light to enter the lens as does *f*-2.8. And note that going from *f*-4 to *f*-16 is a jump of four *f*-stops; therefore, *f*-4 allows sixteen times as much light to enter the lens as does *f*-16.

Of these three factors, however, the only one that really gives you much flexibility is the *f*-stop. The camera-to-subject distance and the lens focal length are both related to the size of the picture. You cannot alter either of these two variables without drastically changing your picture. In other words, if you have a given medium shot that you do not want to change and you want to increase your depth of field, you cannot increase your camera-to-subject distance (by moving the camera back) or you cannot decrease your lens focal length (by changing to a shorter lens) without changing your picture to a long shot. The only option left, therefore, is to stop down to a smaller lens opening; to compensate for that factor, you will need to add more light to the scene.

Occasionally, production students begin with the conception that the ideal lighting sit-

Figure 5–14
Depth of field.

The depth of field of a lens can be increased by altering any one of three different variables:

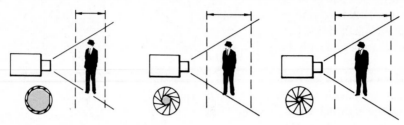

(a) by decreasing the lens aperture;

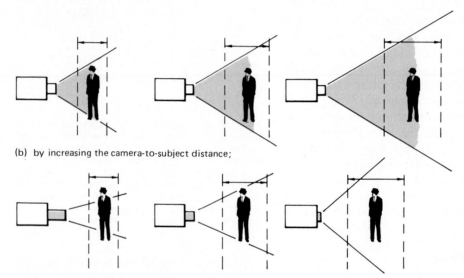

(b) by increasing the camera-to-subject distance;

(c) by decreasing the lens focal length.

The depth of field of a lens can be increased by altering any one of three different variables: (a) by decreasing the lens aperture, (b) by increasing the camera-to-subject distance, (c) by decreasing the lens focal length.

uation is one in which the lens can be stopped down to the smallest possible opening—thereby attaining the greatest depth of field (area of focus) possible. This, however, may not always be a desirable aim. First of all, for aesthetic reasons, the director may not want the background in focus, as it may detract from the foreground action of the performers. Or the opposite may be true: the director may want the foreground to be out of focus (for example, he or she may be shooting through some defocused leaves of a tree) in order to concen-

trate on the action in the background. This is referred to as **selective focus**—when either the foreground or background is deliberately kept out of sharp focus.

In order to achieve these effects, it is necessary to have a shallow depth of field—a wide-open aperture. This, of course, necessitates low-level lighting. Depending upon the exact lighting conditions, the camera operator may have to defeat the "auto setting" of the automatic diaphragm.

Camera Structure and Lens Design

Figure 5–15
Canon J55X 9B IE
"SUPER" field zoom lens.
This 55-to-1 zoom lens is
the largest field production
zoom lens in professional
use today. When it is
zoomed in, its picture is
fifty-five times larger than
when it is zoomed out. It
has a zoom range
extending the unit from a
9mm lens to an effective
500mm lens. With its 2X
extender, it doubles that
range—from 18mm to
1,000mm. Weighing over
thirty-seven pounds, it is
almost twenty-two inches
long, roughly ten inches
high, and ten inches wide.
It is used extensively for
sporting events and similar
productions. (Photo
courtesy of Canon)

Occasionally, for dramatic effect, the director may want the camera operator to **pull focus** to shift a shallow depth of field from a foreground object to the background, or vice versa. This also can be accomplished only with a wide-open aperture. For example, the director may want to open on a tight close-up shot of a half-empty glass close to the camera with the background out of focus; the camera operator could then change the focus (without otherwise altering the shot at all) to focus on the figure lying on the sofa while the foreground glass goes blurry.

Other factors may also necessitate a deliberate shallow depth of field. Perhaps the dramatic setting calls for low-key lighting, which means you have to operate with the lens aperture opened up. Another consideration is simply that of creature comfort; high-key lighting—solely for the sake of working with a greater depth of field—may not be worth the toll it takes on the performers working under the more intense lighting for a prolonged period.

5.4 The Zoom Lens

The development of the *zoom* lens allowed camera operators and directors to achieve rapid and continuous adjustment of the focal length of the lens—and consequently to control precisely the size and framing of shots. It has changed the way in which directors approach visual continuity. In addition to giving the director and camera operator a wider range of lens lengths that are immediately available, the zoom lens also facilitates very smooth on-the-air movement. Figure 5–15 illustrates a large modern zoom lens used for out-of-studio productions.

This **variable-focal-length** zoom lens is essentially an arrangement of gears and optical elements that allow the operator to shift the lens elements—moving them back and forth in relation to each other. This achieves varying focal lengths by changing the theoretical center point of the lens. While zoom lenses will vary greatly with price and manufacturer, those

Camera Structure and Lens Design

Figure 5–16
Range of a zoom lens.

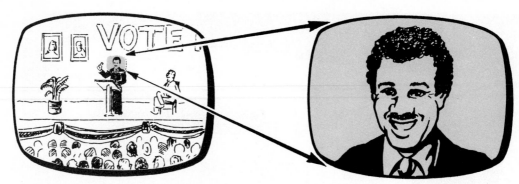

These two views represent the extreme focal lengths of a 10-to-1 zoom lens: *left,* zoomed ''out'' to the shortest focal length (widest angle); *right,* zoomed ''in'' to the longest focal length (narrowest angle).

lenses designed for professional and industrial levels all share some of the same basic characteristics.

Lens Ratio   For most production situations, a ten-to-one magnification ratio is common. On a typical lens this would result in focal lengths ranging from, maybe, 10.5mm at the wide-angle position to 105mm at the *zoomed in* high-magnification or "long-lens" position. Figure 5–16 provides some indication of the range of shots available with a ten-to-one ratio lens. Smaller vidicon cameras might be equipped with just a six-to-one zoom lens, giving them the limited flexibility of, say, a 12.5mm-to-75mm range. For sporting events and other outdoor public events programming, zoom ratios of thirty-to-one and greater are not uncommon. The 55-to-one range of the Canon J55X (figure 5–15) is the greatest ratio of any field zoom lens commonly used.

Movement Control   Virtually all zoom lenses will have some sort of motor-driven zoom mechanism. Less expensive models may have only one or two rates of speed. This does not give you much artistic control over the effect you may want to achieve. Therefore, professional lenses will usually have *variable-speed* controls. Generally, professional zoom lenses also will provide an optional manual zoom control lever for those times when only the human touch will suffice. It should be noted, however, that serious damage will result if the manual lever is engaged while the power zoom control is in operation.

It is this ability to obtain smooth on-the-air zoom movement that gives the director production flexibility when using zoom lenses. It is possible gradually (or quickly) to **tighten up** a shot, going smoothly and slickly from a **long shot** to a **medium shot** to a **close-up.** This simulated movement is much safer and easier to handle than trying to move the camera physically. In addition, there are many occasions—especially on remote location productions—where it is simply not possible to move the camera. The movement of a zoom is not the same as the movement of **dollying,** however, and this distinction can make a subconscious difference in the reaction of the audience. (This area is discussed in section 6.1.)

Camera Structure and Lens Design

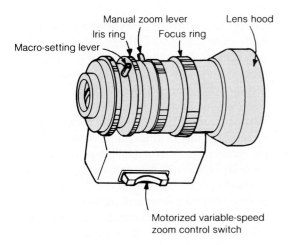

Manual zoom lever

Iris ring   Focus ring   Lens hood

Macro-setting lever

Motorized variable-speed
zoom control switch

In addition to the motorized variable-speed zoom control switch, adjustments on the lens include the macro-lens setting, the iris (*f*-stop) setting, the manual zoom lever, and the focus ring.

Figure 5–17
Diagram of a typical zoom lens.

Focusing   On all zoom lenses, the focus control is the slip ring located farthest toward the front of the lens. This ring is usually adjusted by remote control when cameras are set up for studio use. Staying in focus can be a problem with zoom lenses. As cameras are moved to different positions on the studio floor, there are constantly changing distance relationships between the camera and the various subjects. Each change necessitates checking to be sure that the lens is set for a "zoomed in" close-up shot—before it is needed. If it is not set, the operator coming from an in-focus wide shot may zoom into an out-of-focus close-up.

To preset your focus, zoom in all the way to the tightest shot you can get and adjust the lens focus. Now, zoom back slowly and check to make sure the subject is in reasonable focus throughout the entire length of the zoom. If not, the only slight adjustment you can make is with the zoom lens focus.

As long as you have a few seconds and you are sure that the talent is not going to move or the director is not suddenly going to ask you to get a shot of something at some other distance from the camera, you should be able to get the zoom focus preset. But problems do occur—especially when you quickly have to get the unexpected shot you were not prepared for.

Macro Lens   This special adjustment has become a standard focusing feature of most of the newer lens units (figure 5–17). In the **macro** position, one can take extreme close-ups of printed material or small objects at distances of two inches or less from the lens. The procedure will vary with individual equipment, but the rather sensitive process of such delicate focusing is usually handled by adjusting the manual zoom lever and not the focus ring.

Iris   As outlined in section 5.3, the iris (*f*-stop) position has an important relationship to picture focus. If incorrectly set, it can also greatly affect the quality of color in the pic-

Camera Structure and Lens Design

ture. In a studio situation where light values are fairly constant, settings will stay within a narrow range. Operating instructions for each camera will usually provide optimum **lux** or *footcandle* levels as related to an *f*-stop setting.[9] For example, on many lenses an *f*-4 setting would be proper for a 200-ftc reading.

Also, as mentioned previously, on many lenses there is an automatic iris control that reacts to incoming light and continually adjusts the *f*-stop as light values change. Some manufacturers provide a *temporary automatic* feature that allows the lens to hold any *f*-stop position set by the automatic sensor.

One reason for overriding this automatic diaphragm setting is to achieve a *selective focus effect* with a shallow depth of field. This is because the auto setting simply reacts to light; it cannot comprehend any desired artistic effect. Another reason for overriding the automatic setting is to select the features that you want correctly exposed when there are both extreme bright and dark elements in a picture. If you are shooting someone against a bright blue sky, the auto setting is going to adjust to the vast expanse of the light sky, and you are going to get the person in silhouette—which is fine if that is the effect you want. However, if you want to see the features on the person's face, then you are going to have to manually open up the *f*-stop (to a lower *f*-number) to correctly expose the relatively dark face—and thereby deliberately overexpose the bright sky.

On the other hand, when shooting outdoors, light values can often change drastically—as camera angles are changed, as shadows appear, as sun and cloud patterns interplay. Under these conditions, the automatic iris can make the production much easier.

9. The ''lux'' measurement is based upon an amount of candlelight falling upon an object from the distance of one meter. While not completely accurate, footcandle readings are often multiplied by ten to get a rough *lux* measurement (e.g., 40 ftc = 400 lux).

Color Temperature Conversion Filters

Professional cameras designed for both studio and field production usually have a built-in filter system to compensate for Kelvin temperature differences between indoor and outdoor lighting. Located just in front of the beam splitter (section 5.2), this filter component is an integral part of the optical system within the camera. As an example of how this works, the Sony DXC 1820 has a rotating disc of four filters (figure 5–18) for different lighting conditions: (1) iodine lamp and sunrise and sunset; (2) bright outdoor; (3) cloudy or rainy; and (4) white fluorescent. It is interesting that sunrise and sunset have the same color temperature as artificial quartz-iodine light. This has to do with the angle of the light rays and the filtering effect of the atmosphere at those two times of day.

One should also carefully follow the instruction book that comes with each camera, as some filters will screen out more total light than others. For instance, in the DXC 1820, outdoor positions 2 and 3 allow one-half as much light to get through to the target as setting 1. This means that *f*-stop settings for indoor or outdoor shooting must be carefully adjusted with the filter position in mind.

5.5 Operator Control Adjustments

Teaching institutions that have professional or industrial-level cameras possess sophisticated items of equipment having a number of controls that make possible high-quality pictures. On the other hand, misuse of those controls will greatly diminish picture quality and even cause permanent damage. Each class should establish a definite policy as to which controls on the camera (or CCU) are for student adjustment and which are to be handled only by the instructor or trained staff personnel.

Camera Structure and Lens Design

Figure 5–18
Sony DXC 1820 camera.
Note the settings for the
built-in filter disc.

Those controls relating to zoom operation described earlier would normally fall within the realm of student control. Such controls should be checked for correct settings as part of camera setup. On the camera itself, however, there are several controls that, although they may not be designated for student operation, should nevertheless be understood so that settings can be checked for proper positions and levels prior to camera operation.

White Balance   This is a control that establishes the correct color balance to produce a pure white. In a studio situation where all illumination is produced by lights having a consistent 3,200 degrees Kelvin temperature, it is possible to do most production work with the **white balance** switch at the factory-established *preset* position. If, however, a camera is to be used for field production where Kelvin temperatures are constantly changing, the white balance procedure must be understood and utilized.

The alternate white balance switch position on most cameras is labeled *auto,* which simply means that the camera will automatically accomplish the necessary adjustment process. In this mode, with a white card filling the lens image, the camera color system senses any excess of either red or blue light and within a few seconds adjusts accordingly. The white card serves as a neutral reference point so that the camera can judge the balance between red and blue in the light source(s). On some cameras there are additional fine-control adjustments that permit the operator to subtly tint with additional amounts of red or blue without having to go through the entire balancing procedure.

To get the proper adjustment for flesh tones, the white card must be placed exactly where the subject's face will be for the shot.

Camera Structure and Lens Design

In field work where a change in the camera-to-subject angle may introduce a new light source, a new balance adjustment may be necessary. Also when shooting on location, lighting conditions will change throughout the day (the sun changes color when it descends; cloud covers vary), and occasional adjustments to the white balance will need to be made.

Video Output Level Selector   Many cameras have an **automatic gain control (AGC)** that automatically adjusts video levels to compensate for differing light conditions. However, other cameras have a **video output** control that allows the operator to adjust to some degree for low light levels. The "0 db" position is established by the manufacturer as the standard level of video output for the camera under prescribed lighting conditions. The term *decibel* (db) has been borrowed and slightly altered from its audio derivation; but as with audio, each 6-db increase means that the amplified signal is doubled. This control should never be thought of as a way to make a badly lit picture good. All it can do is make the bad picture look a little brighter.

Viewfinder Visual Indicators and Controls
On some cameras the **tally light,** which tells both the operator and the talent/subject that the camera is feeding the switcher, will also light up to indicate that the white balance adjustment in the camera has been completed. On those cameras designed for field use, there may be several **warning lights** that indicate *low battery power, insufficient lighting,* or *abnormally high setting of the gain control knob,* which is causing excessive drain on the battery.

It should also be noted that the **brightness** and **contrast** controls are only for the viewfinder adjustment; *they do not have any effect on the video output of the camera.* Operators who are unaware of this basic fact can be a menace to any proper camera setup procedure. Such uninformed operators may take one look at their incorrectly adjusted viewfinder picture and—assuming the camera settings are wrong—begin to mess up a perfectly good camera output by changing the *f*-stop, filter setting, and gain controls. The viewfinder controls—like the camera controls themselves—should be adjusted only while the operator is in headset contact with the person (usually the instructor or technical director) who is in charge of camera setup in the video control center.

Other Controls   Some cameras have several additional control units that—while not necessarily complicated—are best suited to an individualized-study approach. Such items as the **fade time control,** the **negative/positive selector,** and the **phase control selector** all have clearly marked "0" or neutral positions. The beginning student should be made aware of these *off* positions in order to be able to confirm their negative status during the process of learning camera operations.

Modern video cameras have incorporated numerous other internal monitoring systems, feedback circuits, and computer-based controls. Figure 5–19 shows the electronic complexity of the inner workings of the contemporary camera. An awareness of the fragile nature of these circuit boards should help the novice camera operator appreciate the need to treat these instruments with care.

Summary

As with audio techniques and lighting considerations, a discussion of camera characteristics and operations could also be broken down into technical aspects and creative concerns. The sections dealing with the camera image-sensing devices (CCD chip or pickup tube), the

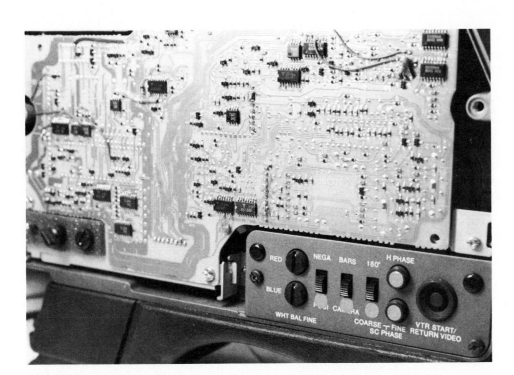

Figure 5–19
The circuit board of a modern camera gives some insight as to its electronic complexity.

receiver picture tube, the lens characteristics, and the zoom lens have been concerned largely with *technical matters.*

The *video signal flow* can be seen as parallel to the audio signal flow. The same functions apply to both audio and video control: transducing, channeling, mixing, amplifying, shaping, recording (and playback), and monitoring. Additional sophisticated *control components* are added to the video system—sync generator, proc amp, time-base corrector, frame synchronizer, waveform monitor, vectorscope, and color bars.

The color video system is concerned with accurately rendering three color components—*hue, saturation,* and *brightness.* The transducing function is identified largely with the *CCD* chip. The three principles that led to the development of the television system are *persistence of vision, electrochemical conversion,* and *scanning.*

The three-chip color camera splits the incoming light into the three primary colors of red, green, and blue—each one being channeled to its own image sensor creating both a *luminance* and *chrominance* signal. The *receiver picture tube,* which can be thought of as a mirrored version of the old camera pickup tube, also has clear similarities to the newer CCD technology in that it is driven by the same synchronization pulse that keeps all elements of the production-distribution-reception system locked together.

Mechanical and optical considerations of the fixed-focal-length lens include consideration of the *focal length, focusing characteristics,* f-*stop lens aperture,* and *depth of field.* While the zoom lens has several advantages pertaining to *flexibility in selecting focal length* and facilitating *smooth movement,* it also has some potential drawbacks relating to focusing characteristics. Operating considerations of the zoom lens include *lens ratio, movement control, focusing, macro-lens setting, iris control,* and *color temperature filters.*

There are several other camera controls that students should be familiar with, although they would not necessarily be authorized to make such adjustments without explicit approval and supervision: *white balance, video output level,* and *viewfinder picture adjustments,* among others.

5.6 Training Exercises

In order to familiarize yourself with the cameras and focusing characteristics of the lenses in your own studio, work through the following projects.

1. Draw a schematic diagram of the video signal flow in your studio and control rooms. Physically locate components such as the sync generator, camera control units, proc amps, and time-base corrector. Draw in their positions in relation to cameras, monitors, switcher, recorders, and so forth.

2. With a trained staff engineer on the P.L. intercom at the camera control unit, show how the camera picture on the studio monitor is affected when CCU controls such as automatic black level, chroma, and video gain are maladjusted. Experiment with camera-located controls such as the iris setting, filters, and focus. Run through the white balance procedure. Then deliberately change the color in the light source; show that picture on the monitor; then run the white balance procedure again and show the corrected results.

3. Experiment with varying depth-of-field conditions and different focal-length lens settings. Position and adequately light two classmates about ten feet apart in an almost straight line with the camera—similar to figure 5–11. Using a long-lens setting (zoomed in all the way), how close can you move in toward them and keep them both in focus? Try the same with a wide-angle lens setting (zoomed back all the way). Keeping the foreground subject the same relative distance from the camera, how do the size and camera-to-subject distance of the background person change as you vary the focal length? Keeping the focal-length setting constant, vary the light levels and *f*-stops accordingly. How close can you get with the lens opened wide (low-key lighting)? How close can you get with a smaller aperture (high-key lighting)?

4. Demonstrate the zoom ratio of the cameras in your studio—using measured horizontal distances on a wall or against the cyclorama. Using the macro-lens setting, determine how small a portion of a printed page you can use to fill the camera shot. Note critical focus problems. How much depth of field do you have?

Camera Structure and Lens Design

Camera Operations and Production Techniques

● ● ● ● ● ● ● ● ● ● ● ● ● ● ● ● ● ● ●

Camera work is the result of the interaction of four elements of movement, functioning either in combination or singly: the angle and magnification changes made possible within the *lens* itself; changes in the *direction* a camera can be pointed or aimed; *elevation* changes achieved through the utilization of the **camera mount;** and changes of *camera position* accomplished by the movement of the mount itself.

The first two of these movements (zoom lens movement and camera panning/tilting) are possible with all types of camera setups—in the studio or on-location productions. The last two types of movement (camera-elevation and camera-mount movement) depend upon the type of camera mount involved. And as a basic generalization, these camera movements are usually accomplished easier in the studio than in the field—unless expensive field cranes or vehicle-mounted cameras are involved.

6.1 Camera Movement

The first of these four elements—the angle and magnification characteristics of the lens—was introduced in the last chapter.

Movement of the Zoom Lens

The development of high-quality zoom lenses considerably changed the shooting patterns used on all types of television programs. Prior to this, directors and camera operators had to be well versed with what eight or so basic fixed lenses could produce in terms of angle, magnification, and other optical qualities. Some directors were noted for plotting angle and distance for each shot with a military precision. The result was often excellent television. Unfortunately, this process meant that much of a camera's usable airtime was lost in simply getting to and from specific locations and in rotating the turret to the correct lens.

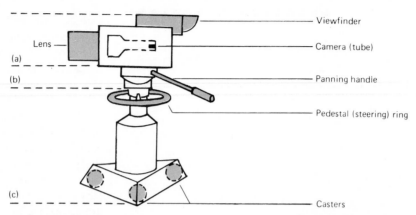

Figure 6–1
Three basic parts of the camera.

Lens

(a)

(b)

(c)

Viewfinder

Camera (tube)

Panning handle

Pedestal (steering) ring

Casters

(a) **Camera Head** includes the camera tube and electronics, the viewfinder for the camera operator, and the lens.

(b) **Camera Mounting Head** with the panning handle that controls pan and tilt movements.

(c) **Camera Mount** pictured is a "studio pedestal" with the steering ring and enclosed casters.

With the zoom lens, of course, much of this lost time has been regained. The camera operator always has the lens in position, and it is relatively easy to adjust the variable-focal-length zoom control (on the air as necessary) to obtain the exact viewing angle desired. With this ease of operation, however, also comes the tendency to get lazy and careless.

In the hands of a director and/or camera operator who is inexperienced, indolent, or both, the use of a zoom lens often results in dull, unimaginative camera work. It is easy to fall into the trap of assuming that it is always possible to get a decent shot from any camera position at any time. Good camera work, however, requires that the director and camera operator always plot out each shot as carefully as possible, whether using a lens turret or a zoom lens. A large part of successful camera production *discipline* is related to this careful preplanning process. When truly creative people are involved, the zoom lens provides a versatility that amply compensates for the few limitations of the instrument.

The beginning camera operator soon begins to feel familiar with the production terminology. When the lens is *zoomed in,* the angle of the shot is made narrower and the degree of magnification is increased. The effect is that the viewer is *pulled in* to the subject. The reverse is true when the lens is *zoomed out.* The viewer is *taken out* from the subject.

An important consideration with any zoom movement is that of making sure that the lens focus is preset. The correct procedure for presetting the zoom lens (so that the subject is in focus from long shot to close-up) varies with the individual camera design, the ratio of the zoom range (i.e., the relationship of the widest angle to the narrowest angle), the distance from the camera to the subject, and whether the camera is monochrome or color. General instructions were mentioned in section 5.4; specific directions are usually included as part of a camera's performance specifications.

Camera Operations and Production Techniques

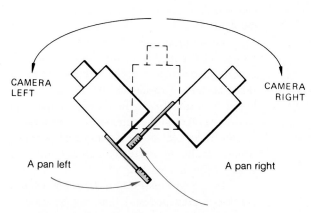

Figure 6–2
Camera panning.

CAMERA
LEFT

CAMERA
RIGHT

A pan left

A pan right

In order to pan the camera in a given direction, the panning handle must be moved in the opposite direction. Thus, in order to execute a "pan left," the camera operator has to move the panning handle to the right.

Camera-Head Movement

The second type of camera-lens movement—changes in the direction a camera can be pointed or aimed—is accomplished by the use of the **camera mounting head,** or **panning head.** This pan head is used to attach the camera itself (with its system of lenses and the camera viewfinder) to the camera mounting or support. Thus, there are essentially three basic parts to the complete studio camera setup—the camera head; the mounting or panning head; and the camera mounting. (See figure 6–1.)

The camera mounting head allows two kinds of movement: **panning,** which is a horizontal movement of the camera by rotating the camera mounting head; and **tilting,** which is a vertical movement of the camera by pivoting up and down.

There are two types of camera mounting heads that are most often used in professional studio operations. The *cradle head* balances the camera on a rocker mechanism that assures a fairly good balance of the camera during most panning and tilting moves. The

cam head uses two cams, one placed on either side of the head, to provide even better balance than the cradle head, while enabling the camera a greater range of movement in tilting.

It should be noted that all instructions for a change in camera direction are given in terms of the camera operator looking toward the performance area. A new picture subject is identified as being *camera right* or *camera left* of the operator. Thus a *pan right* or *pan left* is a horizontal move of the lens of the camera in that same direction. (See figure 6–2.)

For vertical movements, *tilt up* and *tilt down* are used to denote a change of shot framing in those respective directions. Although some directors may use the word *pan* to refer to a vertical movement, this usage can result in some momentary confusion on a busy intercom line and is not recommended. (See figure 6–3.)

Camera Mounts

Of the four types of camera and lens movements mentioned in the introductory paragraph of this chapter, the last two—camera

Figure 6–3
Camera tilting.

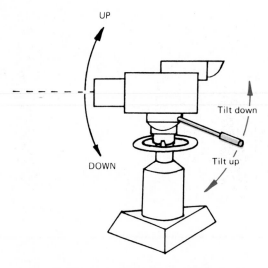

In tilting the camera up or down, only the camera head is pivoted. The camera mounting head (panning head) is not physically moved up or down with the camera mount.

Figure 6–4
Camera mounted on an adjustable tripod.

elevation and camera position—are both dependent upon the camera mount.

The simplest and least expensive camera mount is the **tripod**. This three-legged stand is usually fastened to a dolly base consisting of three casters. The casters either can be allowed to rotate freely, facilitating quick and easy movement of the camera in all directions, or can be locked into a nonmovable position, which results in a steady camera unit for straight-line movement.

The tripod illustrated in figure 6–4 has a crank-operated pedestal that can be used to raise and lower the camera—although not smoothly enough to be used on the air. Most tripods, however, have no elevation adjustment other than the laborious process of mechanically adjusting the spread of the tripod legs. Thus, there is no real way to achieve any elevation repositioning during an actual production. The tripod, however, is lightweight, and most models are readily collapsible. This makes the tripod a desirable camera mount for most remote productions.

A much more flexible type of camera mount is the *pedestal*. The simplest version is the lightweight *field-studio* pedestal. There are a couple varieties of this mount, which is basically a cross between a tripod and the heavier counterweighted studio pedestal. The field-studio pedestal, with its three larger casters, can be maneuvered like a tripod. Its distinctive feature is the central pedestal that can be raised or lowered, usually by a hand crank. Although this method of camera elevation is not normally smooth enough to use on the air, it does allow for relatively quick elevation positioning of the camera between shots.

The *counterweighted studio pedestal* is a much more flexible and maneuverable studio mount. (See figure 6–5.) It has two main features: a thick central pedestal that contains the

Camera Operations and Production Techniques

counterweight (or compressed-air) system that enables the camera operator to raise or lower the camera smoothly on the air; and a steering ring that can control all three casters in a synchronized manner so that smooth on-the-air camera movements across the studio floor can be achieved. This ease and steadiness in camera movement have made the studio pedestal a popular workhorse in many studio situations.

Inherited from the film industry, the **studio crane** is the largest and most flexible type of camera mount. Although camera cranes come in a variety of sizes, they all have two elements in common: everything (including a seat for the camera operator) is mounted on a large four-wheeled crane base; and the camera itself is mounted on a boom arm, or tongue, that can be moved vertically or laterally without moving the crane base. Even though the studio crane provides the ultimate in smooth and flexible camera movement—for instance, the camera can be elevated from floor level to more than ten feet high with the larger cranes—it does have the drawbacks of being relatively large and bulky and of requiring more than one camera operator. For these reasons, studio cranes are seldom seen in medium-sized studio operations.

For more ambitious and expensive location productions, the crane has been adapted for a variety of outdoor applications. From single-camera dramatic programs to multiple-camera remotes such as Olympic coverage, the field crane plays a major role. Figure 6–6 illustrates two typical uses—a studio crane adapted for outdoor usage mounted on tracks for smooth travel movement, and an extended boom crane mounted on a truck for mobility. Other specialized mounts include everything from blimp installations to camera platforms built on vehicles for car chases.

Figure 6–5
Camera on a compressed-air pedestal mount.

Camera-Mount Movements

There are several different ways in which the entire camera and its mounting can be moved about the studio floor. One of the most obvious is moving closer to or farther away from the subject; this is referred to as **dollying** the camera. With a lens turret of several fixed-length lenses, the physical movement toward or away from a subject was an important movement option for the director. It was the only way to get closer to or farther away from the subject without changing lenses. (See figure 6–7.)

For the most part, the zoom lens has eliminated the need to rely extensively upon the *dolly in* and *dolly out* movements. There is a subtle difference between the types of move-

Left, crane adapted for field use, designed to be pulled along special tracks for trucking movements; *right,* special truck-mounted crane for following Olympic bicycling events. (Photos courtesy of ABC Sports)

Figure 6–6
Crane-mounted cameras
for Olympic coverage.

Figure 6–7
Camera dollying.

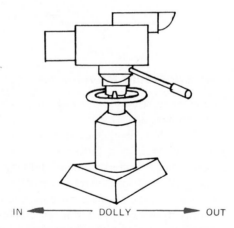

IN ◄———— DOLLY ————► OUT

In a dolly movement, the camera is simply moved closer to or farther from the subject.

ment, however, and a dolly is still preferred to the zoom for certain effects. The dolly movement physically moves the viewer past foreground objects, changing the relationship of various objects in the picture; the viewer's angle of vision remains the same, but physical elements are changed. With the zoom, on the

other hand (as illustrated in figure 6–8), the viewer's physical relationship with all objects in the picture is not altered; however, the viewer's angle of vision is narrowed down to exclude unwanted material—thus a sense of concentration is achieved without physically moving the viewer.

Lateral movement of the camera and its mount is known as **trucking.** A change of picture is accomplished as the camera *trucks right* or *trucks left* because the camera moves sideways without panning to the right or left. (See figure 6–9.)

In the field, dollying and trucking movements normally cannot be attempted unless special tracks have been laid down to facilitate smooth level movement. Usually, such movements are set up only for ambitious productions—expensive dramatic programs, major sporting events, and so forth.

It should be noted that both trucking and dollying movements are difficult to accomplish with a long focal-length lens or with a zoom lens that is zoomed in to a narrow angle. The

Camera Operations and Production Techniques

Figure 6-8
Comparison of dollying in and zooming in.

Dollying In: *top,* as the camera dollies past the foreground objects (or persons), the viewer is physically transported closer to the primary subject. The viewing angle is not changed; therefore, the viewer arrives at the subject with a relatively wide-angle view that exaggerates the distance between foreground and background objects. Note how the prisoner's head becomes larger in proportion to the background objects—the pine trees and the gallows are relatively unchanged while the cactus is completely lost behind the prisoner's head. The camera obviously is very close to the prisoner.

Zooming In: *bottom,* as the camera zooms in to the primary subject, the viewing angle is narrowed down to exclude the foreground objects (persons). However, since the resulting picture has a relatively narrow viewing angle, the distance between foreground and background objects is compressed, resulting in less depth in the picture. Also, the relationship among the picture objects remains unchanged. Note how the association among the pine trees, the noose, the prisoner, and the cactus has remained the same. They have all increased in size to the same extent, resulting in a "flattened" perspective. Obviously the camera has not moved.

slightest unsteadiness during the camera movement is exaggerated because the long lens, while magnifying the subject, is also magnifying the shaky camera movement. To a lesser extent, the same problem is apparent with panning and tilting movements. Generally, *the longer the lens, the more difficult any kind of camera-head or camera-mount movement is going to be.*

A valuable camera movement is the **arc,** which is a combination truck and pan. As the camera circles, or arcs, to one side of the sub-

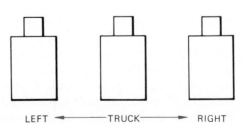

Figure 6-9
Camera trucking.

In a trucking movement, the camera and mount are moved laterally without any adjustment of the camera mounting head.

Figure 6–10
Camera arcing.

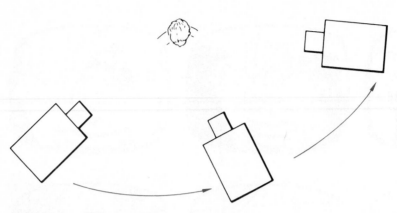

As the camera arcs to the right, the camera operator also has to pan left in order to keep the subject centered in the picture.

ject, the camera head is rotated so that it always points at the subject. The resulting picture maintains the same subject and the same-sized shot, but the perspective or shooting angle changes as the camera movement is executed. (See figure 6–10.)

While the tripod mount does not allow for any on-the-air adjustment in the elevation of the camera, most studio camera pedestals are designed to facilitate a smooth change in camera height. In this case, the word "pedestal" is used as a command verb as the camera operator is asked to *pedestal up* or *pedestal down*. While such elevation changes may be limited to roughly two to four feet, this subtle change can be quite effective, especially at close quarters. (See figure 6–11.) The pedestal movement can be thought of as a vertical equivalent to the truck. If the camera head is held stationary during a pedestal, then the picture subject will change as the camera is moved vertically. If the camera head is tilted during the pedestal movement, however (in a vertical analog to the arc shot), then the same subject can be kept in the frame while the angle and perspective will change.

In larger studios where the crane mounts or **crab dollies** are used, other movements are also possible. These movements are also possible, of course, with larger field cranes and booms.

Craning, or **booming** (up or down), involves raising or lowering the crane or boom arm. The effect is similar to a pedestal movement, except that much greater vertical distances can be covered. A **crab** shot (left or right) is similar to a trucking shot, with the entire crane or crab dolly being moved sideways. One different kind of motion is the **tongue** move. With a large crane, the boom arm or crane can be tongued left or right in a lateral motion (while the base remains stationary).

Hand-Held Cameras   For out-of-studio production work, increasing use is being made of hand-held cameras. The shoulder-supported professional units (see figures 15–4 and 15–5), as well as the consumer-oriented palm-sized camcorders, have popularized an informal and candid approach to production.

Needless to say, such hand-held camera work often results in poorly framed pictures, unsteady shots, and jerky camera movements (wobbly pans and shaky tilts). Such a spontaneous look may be appropriate for news cov-

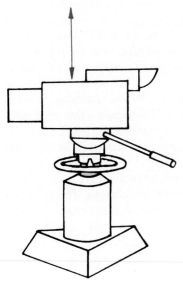

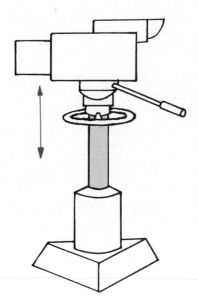

Figure 6–11
Camera pedestaling.

In a pedestal movement, the entire camera and mounting head are moved straight up or down by means of a system of counterweights or compressed air.

erage, rock concerts, or some public affairs footage—or for submission to *America's Funniest Home Videos.* However, it generally should not be considered acceptable for planned productions—except as an adjunct when its use is carefully thought through in advance.

Although sophisticated counter-weighted or gyroscopically balanced systems are often used to steady hand-held cameras for ambitious professional EFP programs or film shoots, they may not be available for smaller-scale productions. Therefore, an attempt should generally be made to use some sort of tripod for even the simplest location shoot.

6.2 Camera Perspectives

Before getting into specific camera operations, the beginning camera operator should be aware of the different ways that cameras can be employed in a television production.

The Viewpoint of the Camera

Generally speaking, the television camera can be used to represent one of three different perspectives: *reportorial* (or presentational), *objective,* or *subjective.*

Reportorial (Presentational) Perspective

This type of viewpoint is used to denote those uses of television when a presenter or reporter is speaking directly to the audience through the camera. The speaker establishes eye contact with the camera and talks directly to the lens. This approach is most often seen in newscasts, corporate training programs, instructional TV lessons, sermons, some variety acts (for example, stand-up comedians), some political talks, demonstration programs, and so forth. Camera work in this kind of situation usually calls for a relatively close shot of the speaker—unless he or she has something to display or demonstrate for the camera. Basically, the camera work is simply to give the viewer a reasonably comfortable look at the person speaking.

Objective Perspective   The easiest way to visualize this use of television is to imagine the camera as an eavesdropper. The camera is standing back, taking an objective look at what is going on. No one is addressing the camera directly; the camera is just an observer of the action. This type of camera work constitutes the bulk of what we see on television: it includes virtually all drama, most variety and musical performances, talk shows and game shows (except when the host or announcer is directly addressing the audience through the camera), sporting events, and similar productions. Camera techniques vary tremendously for objective production. A wide variety of panoramic shots, quick reaction shots, leisurely camera movement, and rapid camera transitions are required for differing formats. Virtually all of the techniques discussed in the rest of this text are applicable to objective camera work.

Subjective Perspective   This particular camera use takes on special meaning when applied to dramatic productions. It refers to those occasional moments when the playwright-director wants to place the viewer in the position of an actor. The camera actually becomes (usually for only a scene) a participant in the drama. It interacts with other players, and it views the world from the individual perspective of the character it is representing. The camera, as the actor's eyes, is in the front seat of the car for the chase sequence; it is in the boxing ring, squaring off against the champion; it is trapped in the burning building, flames licking at the lens; it is drowning, with the waves lapping over the top of the camera-actor.

These obvious filmic applications can also be applied—in a less sensational manner—in many types of studio television drama: the haggard hero looking in the mirror, the defocused glaze of the alcoholic lapsing into a coma, the scattered glances of the paranoid in a strange room, the intimate gaze of a lover seducing the camera, and so on. The subjective camera is a specialized technique, one that can have substantial impact when used judiciously. It also is a technique that requires the utmost in precision and concentration from the camera operator.

These three perspectives are intermingled in many television productions. The newscast mixes reportorial and objective perspectives as the newscaster turns from the camera to interview an in-studio guest. The drama mixes objective with subjective techniques, and a touch of the reportorial-presentational is thrown in as an actor turns to make a comment directly to the audience.[1] The talk show jumps back and forth as the host and guests turn from their conversation with each other to talk directly to the viewer. As the camera operator is aware of these varying perspectives—and the production effects appropriate for each one—it is easier to achieve good camera work.

Field of View

At this point, the camera operator should be familiar with the various terms designating the size of the shot desired, or the **field of view.** Generally, most television shots can be related to three basic categories.

The Long Shot (LS)   The long shot is far enough away from a person that the entire body and quite a bit of the surroundings are included in the shot. Often, the face of the

---

1. The impact of mixing various camera perspectives can be quite striking and original, as in "It's Garry Shandling's Show" where the host/actor frequently breaks the proscenium arch to talk directly to the audience.

EXTREME CLOSE-UP
(XCU)

CLOSE-UP
(CU)

MEDIUM SHOT
(MS)

LONG SHOT
(LS)

In addition to these basic shots, many other designations and modifications are possible, such as the "extreme long shot," the "medium long shot," the "medium close-up," and so forth.

Figure 6–12
Basic television shots.

person is indistinguishable at this distance. The label *wide shot* is used to denote a picture that encompasses the larger, external aspects of the program at a particular point in time. This **establishing shot** relates those people involved in a program not only to each other but also to the setting and circumstances of that program. The establishing shot is frequently used at the beginning of a program to establish the general locale or setting for the program or scene to follow. It also is often used as a closing shot to signal to the audience that we are pulling back from the action, out of the drama, as it comes to a close. Thus, the wide shot is generally used to communicate the broader elements that make up a program. Figure 6–12 illustrates the various fields of view.

The Medium Shot (MS) All of the shot designations are, of course, relative. What is a long shot for one dramatic segment may be considered a medium shot in another situation. Generally, a medium shot of a person includes most of the body, perhaps cutting the talent off slightly above or below the waist. The medium shot is probably the basic shot in standard television production. It is used to convey much of the dialogue in a drama and most of the action in talk shows, game shows, variety programs, and many other studio productions.

The Close-Up (CU) On the other hand, the close-up shot—with its sense of physical intimacy—can probe the individual and personal aspects of what a program is communicating. The eyes and facial expressions provide an important insight into the full meaning of a person's words. In many dramatic situations—as well as in many reportorial-presentational circumstances—the close-up is reserved for moments of high intensity and deep emotion. The close-up is usually defined as a shot consisting of the head and top of the shoulders of a subject. Of course, a close-up shot may be of objects other than a person; it may be a close-up of some item being demonstrated or of some picture being examined. Again, the term is relative.

Many programs obviously call for a wider range of shots, or fields of view, than these three categories. Many times a director will want to establish a panoramic scene or cover the sweep of action with a very wide shot. If characters are so far away that they are hardly identifiable as specific individuals, the shot can be labeled an **extreme long shot** (ELS or XLS).

At the other extreme, there may be times when the emotions are so intense, the suspense so unbearable, that you simply must get much closer to the individual. When the situation calls for a shot closer than a close-up—say of just the eyes or of the eyes, nose, and mouth of an individual—the shot is labeled an **extreme close-up** (ECU or XCU).

The process of alternating between the long shot and close-up aspects of a program is possibly the most important element in the communicative language of both film and television. This basic principle was discovered by pioneers such as Edwin Porter and D. W. Griffith during the early days of the motion picture. They realized that by moving the camera into a closer position they could accomplish what is automatically done by the eye and the mind. While the scope of human vision is almost 180 degrees, we immediately isolate and particularize the focus of our attention to a single person or object when the brain is motivated by a stimulus such as motion or sound. Cutting from a wide-angle to a close-up camera shot is much the same process, except that the distance factor is greatly reduced by lens magnification.

6.3 Picture Composition

Much has been written on the subject of picture composition and the related concepts that deal with the cumulative effect of a series of picture images. As in the motion picture, the main concern of television is usually the human element. Sets, props, and graphic arts have an important auxiliary function, but it is people we watch—the movements of their bodies and the expressions on their faces. When one considers the viewer sitting at some distance from a 19-inch or 25-inch screen, the positioning of those faces and bodies assumes a critical importance.

As we discuss the following elements of framing, headroom, lead room, depth composition, angle of elevation, and balance, keep in mind that these various "rules" that have evolved as part of the grammar of the medium should be considered *guidelines*—not federal regulations. Once the rules have been mastered, they exist to be modified or broken with proper justification and basis—dramatic motivations, artistic considerations, and so forth.

Framing

Television directors (borrowing somewhat from their older film cousins) have developed a simple terminology to describe to the camera operator the basic dimension of a shot. The scope of a shot is described in terms of that portion of the body that is to be cut off by the bottom edge of the picture. Thus a *full shot, thigh shot,* or *chest shot* quickly communicates the desired *framing* of a person in the picture. Generally speaking, try to frame shots so they do not cut a person off right at an obvious body segment (knee, waist, or neck), which results in more of an awkward or ungraceful frame.

Equally useful are the terms **single, two-shot,** or **three-shot,** which describe the number of people to be included in the shot. For closer face shots ("eyes-and-mouth shot," "eyes only"), the precise terminology may vary somewhat with the individual director.

Other descriptive labels have evolved to specify certain kinds of desired shots. For example, an **over-the-shoulder shot (O/S),** as illustrated in figure 6–17, might be called for in a situation when two people are facing each other in a conversation (such as a dramatic scene or an interview program). This is a shot favoring one person (who generally is facing the camera) framed by the back of the head and shoulder of the person with his or her back to the camera.

Headroom

An important discipline for all camera operators is that of consistently maintaining an adequate amount of **headroom.** This term refers to the space between the top of a subject's head and the top of the frame. When this distance

Camera Operations and Production Techniques

Figure 6–13
Correct headroom framing.

WRONG   WRONG

CORRECT

Although it is largely a matter of subjective judgment and artistic "feel," it is important that the camera operator *always be aware* of the headroom on every shot. Too much headroom is as bad as too little.

As a general rule—with many exceptions—the longer a shot is, the more headroom it should have.

Figure 6–14
Correct headroom on different-sized shots.

is not observed, the results can be somewhat distracting. (See figure 6–13.)

It is especially important that headroom distance be uniform among all of the cameras on any production. A helpful guide for shot consistency is to place the eyes of subjects at the point of an imaginary line approximately one-third of the way down from the top of the picture. In close-up shots, the framing is best with the eyes slightly below the line; in wider shots, they should be slightly above the line. (See figure 6–14.)

There is a very good technical reason why headroom distance is carefully watched by camera operators and directors. Due to several factors, most home television sets lose up to 10 or 15 percent of the picture area at the outer edge. As a result, framing that would appear to be adequate on the studio monitor will actually result in a **cropping** of heads or graphic arts lettering on the home receiver.

Lead Room

When speakers or performers directly address the camera (reportorial perspective), they generally are centered in the frame, unless there is some foreground object or over-the-shoulder visual effect to be included in the frame. When subjects are speaking to one another, however, as in a dramatic presentation or a public affairs panel discussion (objective

Figure 6–15
Proper lead room or "talk
space."

BAD   BETTER   BEST

The camera operator should always intuitively give
talent additional space in the direction in which he
or she is looking.

Figure 6–16
Proper lead room for a
moving subject.

BAD   CORRECT

Whenever a person is moving across the screen,
the camera operator should anticipate the flow of
movement, always giving the talent additional lead
room to move into.

perspective), the framing is much more attractive if there is an added amount of **lead
room** or *talk space* in the side of the frame to
which they are speaking. By the same token,
a distracting, crowded effect is created if the
framing is such that the face of the subject is
placed too close to the frame edge. (See figure
6–15.)

The concept of lead room applies even
more strongly to moving subjects. If a person
is moving laterally across the screen, it is important to allow lead space in front of the
person. Lead the talent; do not follow. (See
figure 6–16.)

Depth Composition

Television is a two-dimensional medium. In
order to simulate some feeling of depth, the
director and camera operator can manipulate
certain elements in pictorial composition. The
feeling of depth is enhanced if some familiar
background is used; it helps give a feeling of
scale or perspective. If a plain or abstract
background is used, the viewer has no yard-
stick against which to gauge the distance from
the subject to background.

Foreground objects can add significantly
to the feeling of depth. By framing some

Camera Operations and Production Techniques

Figure 6–17
Depth staging.

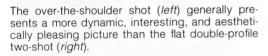

The over-the-shoulder shot (*left*) generally presents a more dynamic, interesting, and aesthetically pleasing picture than the flat double-profile two-shot (*right*).

By shooting the person behind the desk from an angle (*left*), a more inviting and vigorous effect can be achieved than with a formal head-on flat shot (*right*).

nearby objects off to one side of the picture or along the bottom of the picture, the subject in the background is placed in greater relief. Care must be taken, however, not to force an unnatural effect for its own sake as this will undoubtedly appear contrived to the viewer.

Whenever possible, depth composition can be achieved with the arrangement, or **blocking,** of talent. If several people appear in a scene, try to arrange them so that some are closer to the camera than others. Nothing is deadlier than three or four people stretched out in a straight line, all equidistant from the camera. Even with only two persons, an over-the-shoulder shot as a rule is preferred to a flat two-shot of a double profile. (See figure 6–17.)

A feeling of depth can also be achieved by careful use of angles. If a shot calls for someone to be sitting behind a desk, the camera can get a much more interesting shot by trucking right or left and shooting the desk and subject from an angle. (Of course, the dramatic context might call for a formal head-on shot of a judge or stern employer.)

Angle of Elevation

For most conventional composition, you want the camera to be shooting at a relatively level angle to the subject. Generally speaking, try to place the camera lens at eye level with the talent. This is fairly normal when the talent is standing. With seated talent, however, this means that you must pedestal down so that the camera is as low as the talent. In order to achieve this level angle, most "talk sets" (news programs, interviews, discussion shows, talk shows) will be staged on a raised platform or *riser* or low stage (figure 6–18). Without such raised staging, we would be training a whole generation of bent-back camera operators.

If you cannot avoid shooting down into an interview or discussion set, the steep angle can be minimized somewhat by using a longer lens setting and dollying back away from the set. The farther back you can get, the less steep the angle will be. Of course, you pay for this by demanding more studio space and by settling for potentially shakier camera work—the longer the lens, the more any camera unsteadiness is magnified (section 6.1).

There are times, however, when—for dramatic effect—you will not want to be shooting the talent at a level angle. To portray an actor as being overwhelmed, submissive, or downtrodden, you will shoot the actor from a higher elevation. Shooting from a high angle implies control and dominance over the individual. On the other hand, if you want to give a character

Figure 6–18
This modern news set is staged on a platform to bring the newscasters up to camera eye level. (Photo courtesy of KNBC, Los Angeles)

Figure 6–19
Asymmetrical balance and the rule of thirds.

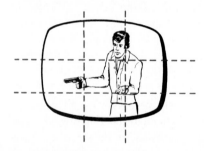

Note how the two main focal points—the face and the hand holding the gun—are located at the intersections of the thirds.

power and authority, you should shoot that actor from a low angle. By placing the viewer in the lowered position, you endow the character with force and strength.

Balance and Other Considerations

There are many artistic elements to be considered in composing an aesthetically pleasing picture: balance, tone, unity, rhythm, proportion, line, mass, and others. It is beyond the scope of our discussion to try to treat these factors in this book.

A few words about **balance,** however, would be in order. Many beginning camera operators try to achieve a pleasing composition by striving for **symmetrical balance.** They try to place the most important element directly in the center of the picture and/or try to balance picture components with equal elements equidistant from the center. This kind of mechanical or symmetrical balancing can lead to very stiff, dull, formal pictures.

A more dynamic kind of composition is **asymmetrical balance,** wherein a lightweight object some distance from the center of the picture can balance a heavier object closer to the center (similar to a seesaw with a light person at the end of the board balancing a heavier person seated close to the center; see section 10.1).

Another way to avoid centralization of picture elements is to think in terms of the **rule of thirds.** Imagine the television screen divided horizontally and vertically into thirds. If major pictorial elements are placed at the points where the lines intersect, the result is a more pleasing balance than if perfect symmetry is achieved. (See figure 6–19.)

Camera Operations and Production Techniques

Movement

A final consideration of picture composition is the temporal and fluid quality of the medium. Since an important element of television is *movement* of one kind or another, pictures rarely remain static for any period of time. Even in a discussion program, the guests will turn their heads as the conversation shifts to another person. In large musical or dramatic productions, the set and other background elements must be taken into consideration. For these reasons, proper composition involves a constant process of adjustment and an exercise of discretion in matters of balance and proportion.

Some aesthetic considerations involved in editing moving images are discussed in chapters 13 and 14.

6.4 Operating Techniques

At this point, the beginning camera operator should feel ready to start working with the cameras. A few words about some operating procedures—especially some safety precautions—should, however, be mentioned first.

Safety Procedures

There are several basic standard rules that every camera operator should always follow.

1. Put on your headset; make sure you are in contact with the control room before doing anything else.
2. If your camera is equipped with a **lens cap,** check with the video engineer before removing it. Always ask for "permission to uncap." Unless you get this permission from the director or someone else in control, assume you are not yet authorized to use the camera.

3. Virtually every studio camera has provisions on the camera mounting head to lock the pan and tilt mechanisms. The pan and tilt locks should always be securely engaged whenever the camera is not in use. Release the locks, making certain you have a firm grip on the panning handle. Although all mounting heads should be balanced so that the camera head will not lurch forward or fall backward when unlocked, it is conceivable that something could go wrong and the camera could be damaged. Once you have the pan and tilt heads unlocked, *never let go of the panning handle* without first locking the mounting head!
4. In all camera operations, always be alert to the possibility of an accident, which could result in the camera falling over or off its mount. Check all tripod leg adjustments; make sure the camera mounting head is securely fastened. Be especially careful, with lightweight tripods, of the possibility of tipping over the whole camera mount (for example, by stumbling over a camera cable).
5. Never stand on the camera cable. The **coaxial cable** consists of numerous individual strands of wire. Any unnecessary pressure on the cable can break some of these fragile wires.
6. Always take care to make sure you never inadvertently tilt the camera up and shoot into the lights. Camera pickup tubes are quite sensitive and can be permanently damaged by shooting a bright source of illumination. On remote shoots, make sure you never allow the camera to be pointed at the sun. With CCD cameras, this is no longer a major concern; never-

theless, it is a good practice to never point *any* camera directly at a bright light.

7. After the production, reverse the procedures you followed in setting up the camera. Lock your pan and tilt heads before doing anything else. Cap your lens and remove your headset.

8. Return your camera to its storage area and coil your cable in a figure-eight pattern.

Operating Hints

Aside from these rules, there are several operational techniques that will help you in most studio situations. Check to see exactly what procedures are followed in your studio.

Camera Setup (Prerehearsal) Even before you are ready to set up your camera, see if you can help with other studio preparations. Can you be of assistance during the early stages of lighting and staging setup? In union studios, of course, this is not allowed; but in many university, corporate, and educational closed-circuit operations, all crew members are expected to assist in all positions. Always be ready to help out wherever needed. This is part of the *discipline* of a successful team member.

With the consent and assistance of the video engineer, check out all connections, locks, adjustments, and controls on your camera. Make sure everything is in working order. Do not try to adjust the specific camera controls on the back of the camera (except for viewfinder adjustments) without explicit guidance or permission from the supervising engineer. (See section 5.5.) Check your f-stop, but do not change or adjust it without higher authority.

Most camera mounting heads have adjustments that will apply a variable amount of drag or resistance to the pan and tilt controls.

Depending upon the explicit production requirements, you may want your pan and tilt controls rather loose and free or you may want them tightened up. Adjust them accordingly.

Rehearsals In general, do not abuse the P.L. intercom (section 3.5). Quite a few production positions will be using the same line. Use it for speaking only when absolutely necessary. Use it for *listening* all the time. You can never be sure when the director or an engineer will have to get you to react instantaneously.

During the early technical or blocking rehearsal, familiarize yourself as thoroughly as possible with the production and your role in it. Make certain you have floor assistance wherever and whenever you need it—someone to handle any graphics, someone to pull your cable in a difficult move. If you are working a boom or crane camera, make sure you coordinate all moves with your camera assistants. Practice all transitions and difficult moves; practice starting and stopping your pedestal and trucking moves; go over your different dollies.

If you are using a zoom lens, make sure you know what all of your on-the-air zooms will be. Preset your focus for your various zoom movements. (Depending upon your position and the camera-to-subject distance, each zoom will have its focus preset differently.) Make sure you have plenty of cable to handle every move you may need to execute on the air.

On-the-Air Production In general, be extra alert. Be prepared for anything. Anticipate the worst. (Your camera cable may tangle; your zoom lens may jam; your camera may get caught in a microphone cable.) Assume nothing. Again, this kind of alertness and sense of anticipation is what separates the disciplined professional from the "I'll get by" dilettante.

Camera Operations and Production Techniques

Prepare and anticipate all of your moves. Preset your zoom lens every time you get on a new long shot (and you should then be ready to zoom in, staying in focus, if called upon to do so). Make certain you are zoomed out all the way (to a wide-angle position) before attempting any camera moves (such as dolly, truck, arc, pedestal). If you are using a free-wheeling tripod, be certain your casters are set, all pointing in the correct position, before trying any camera-mount moves.

Always be ready for your next shot. Use your **shot sheet** (section 13.4) if the director is working from one; otherwise, anticipate your next shot based upon the rehearsal. Every camera should be equipped with **tally lights** on the front of the camera (for the talent) and the viewfinder (for the camera operator); these indicator lights tell you when the camera is actually on the air. Watch your tally light; break to your next shot as soon as you are off the air—but not before.

If you are shooting an **ad-lib** or a semi-scripted program, do all you can to help the director. Anticipate shots the director may want. If you have the director's prior permission (or command), "fish" for good shots. Do not, however, try to dictate to the director what shot to take. In many panel or interview programs, the director will not want you to move from your basic shot; do not presume to know more about the program than the director; stay with your assigned shot until you receive other orders. Watch the talent for signs that will telegraph any moves on his or her part. When the talent leans forward, shifts feet, looks toward the next set element, be ready to move with the first step or the rise from the chair. Again, anticipate; be alert.

At this point, you should be ready for your first camera assignment.

Summary

Camera movement can be divided into four classes: (1) movement of the lens (*zooming*); (2) movement of the camera mounting head (*panning, tilting*); (3) elevation and lateral movement of the camera mount (*pedestaling, tonguing, craning* or *booming*); and (4) movement of the entire mount—tripod, pedestal, or crane (*dollying, trucking, arcing, crabbing*). A zoom resembles a dolly except that when dollying, the viewer is physically moved while the viewing angle does not change; when zooming, the viewing angle is narrowed and there is not the same feeling of movement.

There are three different camera perspectives that can be employed: *reportorial-presentational* (the camera is addressed directly); *objective* (the camera is an eavesdropper); and *subjective* (the camera is an actor). The field of view of a camera can be thought of as consisting of long shots, medium shots, and close-ups—with quite a few variations and combinations.

In determining picture composition, *shots are labeled descriptively*—such as full shot, thigh shot, chest shot, single, two-shot, three-shot, and over-the-shoulder shot. *Headroom* and *lead room* (talk space) are two important framing considerations. The illusion of *depth* in a television picture can be enhanced with proper background considerations, foreground objects, blocking of talent, and use of staging angles. Generally, the camera lens should be at *eye level* with the talent. *Asymmetrical balance,* which is generally more interesting than symmetrical balance, can be partially achieved by using the *rule of thirds*. Picture composition also has to be achieved in *movement*—as television is a temporal medium, constantly changing.

Before operating a camera, there are several *safety procedures* the camera operator should follow. There also are a number of *operating hints* the camera operator should be aware of during the setup period, during the rehearsals, and during the actual production.

Once the production crew member has mastered camera operation, the next step is to tackle the video switcher. Chapter 7 deals with the way camera outputs are selected and/or mixed to become the program video.

6.5 Training Exercises

1. Write a two-page analysis of how picture composition and camera movement were used during a 30-second or 1-minute television commercial that exhibited more than the usual slick or banal application of these disciplines. Choose one you have already seen several times.

2. Set up a class practice session during which every member of the class has an opportunity to practice all of the lens and camera movements outlined in this chapter: lens movement (zooming); panning and tilting; pedestaling (if your studio has studio pedestals); and camera-mount moves (dollying, trucking, arcing); plus crane movements if your studio is so equipped.

3. Stage five or seven class members in a manner similar to figure 6–8. Practice both a dolly in and a zoom in. Carefully note the differences. What are the emotional effects or subjective feelings of each movement? For what purposes would you use a dolly? A zoom?

Camera Operations and Production Techniques

The Switcher: Disciplines of the Technical Director

● ● ● ● ● ● ● ● ● ● ● ● ● ● ● ● ● ● ●

A number of complex and impressive components are to be found in the modern video production center. One piece of equipment, the **switcher,** goes back to the very beginnings of television. It remains the *sine qua non* of multiple-camera video production.

This video switcher, much like the audio console, has three primary functions. First and foremost, it is an *editing device,* developed to facilitate the time-ordered *sequencing of inputs* within a live, or live-to-tape, video production. To do this, the switcher serves a *channeling,* or routing, function—selecting a video source from all of the available inputs such as cameras, videotape machines, remote feeds, character generators, and still-store units.

Second, the switcher functions as a *mixing component* that can combine two or more picture sources by means of **superimpositions, key effects, wipe transitions,** and other **special effects.**

Third, to accomplish some of these other special effects, the switcher also functions as a *shaping device* that can alter not only the color and luminance quality of a picture but also its physical design and shape—for example, in executing various specialized transition effects.

During the process of channeling, mixing, and shaping, the switcher must at all times be able to maintain the waveform and synchronization information of these various signals, so that its final *program output,* whether broadcast or recorded, can ultimately produce a picture on the cathode-ray tube of the receiving TV set. As we shall see, there are various other components that aid in this process.

At the networks and top production houses, switchers are in use that carry these traditional functions to new levels of electronic wizardry. More and more during the past decade, traditional switcher operations and effects have been greatly augmented through the use of **digital video effects** (**DVE**) equipment

● ● ● ● ● ● ● ● ● ● ● ● ● ● ●

Figure 7–1
Entertainment Tonight
Technical Director Wayne
Parsons working on the
Grass Valley 300 SEG/
Switcher. (Photo courtesy
of *Entertainment Tonight*)

that converts the basic analog video signal into a series of digital signal pulses. (See section 7.4.) It is this digital processing that enables us to achieve the eye-dazzling computer effects that have become common in the past few years—the enhanced graphic designs and continuous-motion animation that generally surpass similar film-based visuals.

When these digital capabilities are added to the more traditional switcher functions, the unit is usually referred to as a **special effects generator (SEG).** (See figure 7–1.) Used in conjunction with a number of specific function modules, the unit can create and execute a wide range of video displays and transitions. Many of the *folding, zooming,* and *sliding* effects that serve as elaborate transitions from one picture to the next are built into the sort of SEG that is typically used in the production of sports events and game shows.

Even more elaborate effects are accomplished with switcher/SEG units that are designed to work within the disciplines of the **postproduction editing** process. Here, great amounts of time and talent (and money) are lavished upon special animated effects. The graphics one sees on television today are seldom the work of an artist with pen and brush; they are increasingly the electronic product of a creative artist-technician working with a character generator and/or an SEG computer-graphics package. (See sections 10.6 and 10.7.)

The "smart switcher" allows the operator to preprogram effects such as dissolves, wipes, tumbling cubes, flipping pages, and shrinking inserts. Effects that include timed transitions—such as an exact 2½-second (75-frame) wipe—can be similarly programmed into the switcher's microprocessor for later precise ex-

The Switcher: Disciplines of the Technical Director

ecution. The digital technology that makes this possible is discussed in section 7.4.

Many educational institutions find that budgetary restrictions make it difficult to keep up with such state-of-the-art equipment. Schools and small-scale video operations are more likely to have basic switchers such as the one pictured in figure 7–2. It is therefore important to keep in mind that with the switcher, as with many other components, there are a few basic principles of design, function, and operation common to all units—no matter how simple or complex the construction. Once these essential principles are understood, you can more confidently approach the task of operating the impressive switcher units found in professional studios. Once you know what you are looking for, the process of understanding machine function is greatly simplified.

For example, the concept of video signal flow, as presented in section 5.1, is integral to understanding how the switcher serves as a channeling device. It is suggested that, before proceeding, you review both section 5.1 and section 5.2, which provide a background for understanding the nature of the color signal that our switchers will be controlling.

7.1 The Principle of the Switcher

The switcher in a network television studio is indeed an impressive instrument. With its multiple rows of buttons, switches, levers, and lights, it is quite a formidable piece of machinery. Despite all of its complexity, however, it operates on exactly the same fundamental

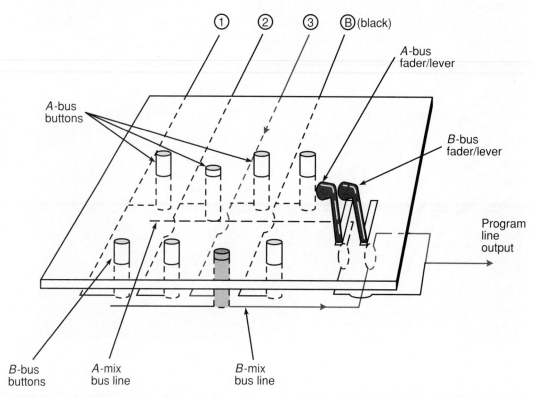

Camera/Source inputs

① ② ③ Ⓑ (black)

A-bus fader/lever

A-bus buttons

B-bus fader/lever

Program line output

B-bus buttons

A-mix bus line

B-mix bus line

Figure 7–3
Cutaway schematic drawing of a two-bus switcher.

On the *A* bus, camera 2 is punched into the mix-bus line. On the *B* bus, camera 3 is punched into the mix-bus line. Thus, with the fader arms in the down position (activating the *B* bus), camera 3 is providing the program line output. If the fader arms were to be moved into the up position (activating the *A* bus), camera 2 would then provide the program line output.

principles found in the simplest units. Basically, the switcher can be thought of as a sophisticated *connection panel*—an electronic "box" where all of the camera signals and other inputs come into one side of the box and the edited program is sent out of the other side. All of the various buttons, levers, and knobs are just a means of taking video signals from several sources (cameras, film chains, video recorders, remote feeds) and selecting those to be sent out as the *program signal,* or "program line out."

The basic elements of any switching device are represented in figure 7–3. A group of buttons (which can be depressed or "punched up") is arranged in simpler switchers in two rows or **banks.**[1] The top row is designated as the *A* bank or **bus,** and the lower row is the *B* bank or bus.

1. Technically speaking, the mixing bar that connects the buttons under the switcher panel is the *bus* and the row of buttons above the bus is the *bank.* However, in common usage, the two terms are used interchangeably.

The Switcher: Disciplines of the Technical Director

Each button is, in effect, the temporary termination point of a video cable leading back to a picture source (camera, video recorder, or so forth). The two rows are, in that way, identical. In figure 7–3, there is a position for each of three cameras and also a button for the **black** picture signal; the black picture is a fully synchronized signal with the luminance (brightness) information set at the lowest possible point. This is used whenever you want to send out a blank (or black) picture.

When pushed down, a button makes contact with a separate video line running beneath the row of buttons correspondingly labeled *A bus* (usually upper) and *B bus*. The signal from the camera (or other source) connected to that button, for example, camera 3 on the *B* bus in figure 7–3, is then connected to the bus line. Only one signal source can be connected to a given bus at a time; the buttons are mutually canceling so that when a button is pushed, that action releases the previously depressed button. Therefore, each bus can have just one camera signal punched into it at any given moment.

The incoming picture source is thereby sent on "downstream" (try to envision the signal flow as flowing downstream from the original video source, merging with other tributaries and inputs along the way, to its terminus in a completed picture) to a **fader lever,** which is designed to control the strength of the signal output from each bank. Each bus has its own corresponding fader arm or lever. The fader functions just like a fader on the audio console, with each lever controlling the strength of the video signal flowing through its respective bus. Therefore, when the *A*-bank fader is activated, the signal from the *A* bus is sent out on the program line. When the *B*-fader arm is activated, the signal punched up on the *B* bank becomes the program output.

Although the early switchers had two separate fader bars as seen in figure 7–3, all units

today are more like those seen in figure 7–4. They are usually locked together. In this manner when one fader is activated, the other will automatically be deactivated. Thus, when both fader arms are pushed up toward the *A*-bank position, the *A* bus will be activated and the *B* bus will be dead. By keeping the two fader arms locked together—moving them up and down simultaneously—we will always have one bus activated (sending out the program signal) while the other bus is dead. (Although, as we shall see, there are occasions when they are separated).

Therefore, as in figure 7–3, if both fader arms are placed in the *B*-bank position, the *B* bus will be sending out its signal as the program feed and the *A* bus will be inactive. Thus, the full video signal is being sent out from whatever picture is punched up on the *B* bank—in this case, camera 3. If you press a button on the *A* bank (for example, camera 2), there is no effect upon the line output because the *A*-bus fader is in its deactivated position. With camera 3 pressed on the *B* bank, you will see the picture from that camera on your line monitor. If you want to replace that picture with the picture from another camera (for example, if you want to go from camera 3 to camera 1), you would perform a camera **cut** (a **take**) by pressing the camera 1 button on the same *B* bank. With no loss of synchronization, you will see an instantaneous change of picture on the program line monitor—cutting from camera 3 to camera 1.

7.2 Fades, Dissolves, and Superimpositions

From its earliest film beginnings, the moving picture art has always made use of the gradual transition between pictures known as the **dissolve.** Related techniques include **fades** to and from black, as well as **superimpositions.**

Figure 7–4
Simple television switcher.

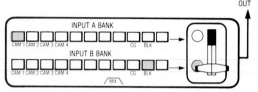

This figure shows how the two mix banks on a simple switcher would be set up to execute a dissolve from black (or fade-up from black) to camera 1. The red tinted buttons indicate which input selector buttons would be pressed. "Black" is punched up on the *B* bank, and camera 1 is punched up on the *A* bank. The small red light just to the left of the fader lever in the *B*-bank position serves as a reminder of which bus is feeding the program line. As the fader arms are raised from the *B* bank to the *A* bank, the *A* bus will be activated and camera 1 will gradually be faded in and appear on the line monitor.

Figure 7–5
A dissolve on a two-bank switcher.

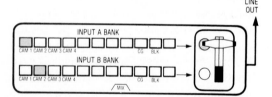

As a continuation of the switching sequence started in figure 7–4, the switcher is shown here as it would be set up for the next transition—a dissolve to camera 2. The camera 1 selector button is still punched up on the *A* bank (from the fade-in executed in figure 7–4) and is feeding camera 1 as the line output—since the fader arms have activated the *A* bank at this point. Punch up camera 2 on the deactivated *B* bank ("black" was previously punched up for the initial fade-in) and you are ready for your dissolve from camera 1 to camera 2. Simply pull the fader arms down from the *A*-bank position to the *B*-bank position and you have dissolved from camera 1 to camera 2.

Most video programs are begun with a one- to two-second "fade-up" from black to the first picture. (An instantaneous *take* from black to picture would seem very abrupt.) Figure 7–4 shows how the **technical director** prepares a simple two-bank switcher for an

initial fade-in.[2] This follows the director's command, "Prepare to fade from black to camera 1." (See section 7.5 for a discussion of commands of preparation and execution.) With both faders locked together in the lower *B*-bank position, the "black" button is pressed on the *B* bank and camera 1 is pressed on the *A* bank. Your program line monitor would at this point show a "blank" screen. At the command, "Fade from black to camera 1," or "Fade in camera 1," the technical director gradually moves the interlocked fader arms from the lower to the upper position (gradually reducing the strength of the *B*-bus signal and simultaneously increasing the *A*-bus signal with camera 1 punched up on it). On the monitor you will see the camera 1 picture gradually fade in and come up to full strength.

At this point, if the director asks for an instantaneous cut (take) to camera 2 or camera 3, it is accomplished by pressing the designated button on the *A* bank.

Dissolves   If, for any one of a number of dramatic or aesthetic reasons, the director wants to get to the next shot by momentarily blending the images of two cameras in a transition, you can utilize a *dissolve*. Assuming you have the switcher set up as shown in figure 7–5 (with camera 1 punched up on the *A* bank), camera 1 is on the line because both levers (locked together) are in the *up* position, so all the video signal is coming through the *A* bus (camera 1). When the director gives the preparatory command, "Prepare a dissolve to camera 2," you, as the technical director, will

2. Throughout this chapter, the term *technical director* (T.D.) will be used to denote the person who operates the switching unit. The term is derived from professional situations where the person given that title has a much larger engineering responsibility for supervising the entire technical staff and operates the switcher/SEG only at the latter part of the production effort. There are circumstances when a person may function only as the SEG operator and is usually then known simply as the *switcher*.

The Switcher: Disciplines of the Technical Director

prepare the switcher by punching up camera 2 on the *B* bank; there is, of course, no change in the picture on the line monitor because all the signal is coming through the *A* bus (where camera 1 is punched up).

When the director gives the command, "Dissolve to camera 2," you move the interlocked fader levers downward, which activates the *B* bus while deactivating the *A* bus—thus decreasing the video signal from camera 1 on the *A* bank at the same rate that you are adding power to the picture (camera 2) on the *B* bank. When both faders are at the bottom position—fully activating the *B* bus and cutting out the *A* bus—you see only camera 2. But for a brief period, you had the two camera pictures overlapping during the *dissolve* transition.

It should be noted that for years motion picture directors, working in the dramatic idiom only, used what was termed the *lap-dissolve* to denote the passage of time or a change in physical location from one scene to the next. With the advent of television as a medium for many idioms, such as music, news, sports, the dissolve is more often used in these program formats as a way of aesthetically *connecting* two visual ideas.

Superimpositions   If the director wishes to blend two images together and hold them in combination for a specific period of time, the result is termed a **superimposition** or, more often, a **super.** A superimposition is really nothing more than a dissolve that has been halted at midpoint. With both the *A*- and *B*-bank levers locked together at the halfway point—and different cameras punched up on the two banks—the switcher is simultaneously feeding 50 percent of the picture from the *A* bank and 50 percent from the *B* bank. The result is a "blended" picture with two half-strength ghostlike images seen at the same time.

A good example of when to use such a super may be in a musical production—for example, a vocalist accompanying herself on the guitar. At a point dictated by the nature and tempo of the music, the director will have a wide shot on camera 1; then, telling the camera 1 operator to slowly pan left (moving the performer to the right half of the frame), a close-up shot of the singer's face, from camera 3, is supered in the left half of the frame.

If one or both of the camera shots in a super seems to be relatively weak in terms of brightness, it is possible to press a release button on the handle of the faders and separate the *A* and *B* levers. Each fader can then be adjusted individually to enhance its brightness level. This process is called *splitting the faders.* Since both pictures are only at half-strength when two pictures are *in super,* an obvious question might be, Why not split the faders on all supers—activating both buses all the way—and have the full value of both pictures? The best answer is that the resulting two-picture video level will often exceed what the video control system can handle. The effect is usually a *blooming* (or white domination) of the brightness scale of the picture. (See color plate D.) In order to achieve the best balance of the two pictures, ideally, the T.D. should have a chance to note the needed levels during a rehearsal period. However, because this is not always possible in live programs, we begin to see the inadequacy of our simple two-bank switching system.

There is one other transitional effect that our basic two-bank switcher is able to accomplish *after* the **superimposition** has been set up as the output of the switcher. Called an **undercut,** it is a matter of *retaining* one of the picture sources making up the super and *changing* the second picture by means of a simple **camera cut** procedure. As an example, let's say that we have started a program with the lettering of the opening title originating from the **character generator** (position #5 on the *B* bank) *in super* with a still picture being shot by **camera 1** (on the *A* bank). After our initial fade-in from black to camera 1 (on the *A* bank), you would then super the character generator (on the *B* bank) over the camera 1 shot by pulling the fader arms down to the halfway point. Next the director wants to replace the still picture (on camera 1) with a wide shot of the studio (which is on **camera 2**) but still leave the title supered. To accomplish this **undercut,** you would simply push the camera 2 button on the *A* bank—without moving the fader arms—and the studio shot (on camera 2) replaces the camera 1 shot *in super* with the title.

Fades to Black   At the end of the program—or at the end of a major segment—the usual transition is a fade to black. The normal method of fading out is to use the black position on the inactivated bus as another camera source and dissolve to it. For instance, in figure 7–5, if the director called for a fade to black, you would first have to punch up "black" on the *B* bus. Then, on command, you would move both faders down to the *B*-bus position. In actuality, you would be fading out the *A* bus with camera 1 on it while you are simultaneously fading in the *B* bus with black (a synchronized signal with no picture) punched up on it.

An alternative method of fading to black is to *split the faders*. This involves unlocking the two fader arms so that they can be operated independently of each other. The *A* fader lever is then moved *down* to the *B*-bus position, and the *B* fader arm is moved *up* to the *A* bank. In effect, both buses have now been inactivated—no program signal is coming through on either bank—and we have black on the screen. This method of fading to black is generally used only when you are fading out of a super (see the previous discussion). You have two buses supered on the screen, so you cannot move the fader arms in tandem either

up or down without bringing in one picture or the other full strength. But by splitting the levers, you can fade out both pictures simultaneously.

7.3 Operation of the Special Effects Generator

The visual transitions previously described are exactly those that were available to directors during television's formative years in the 1950s. The top network shows from what is often called "The Golden Age of Television" did not have their creativity limited by what would today be considered a rather primitive switcher.

Evolution of the Modern SEG/Switcher
This is not to say that directors and technical directors did not wish for more flexibility. Supered titles always looked washed out. And even if you wanted to split the faders for added video strength, there was no way to *preview* a super in advance to set up the desired camera strength from each bus. There was no way to combine two solid pictures with any kind of a split screen. There was no way to combine more than two pictures at once.

However, as the age of color TV became a reality, the engineers who had done such wonders in getting television developed this far went to work and not only solved these limitations, they began to build switchers with an enormous range of control over the picture sources—and added a bewildering number of special effects capabilities along the way.

Today's "state-of-the-art" switcher is often termed a **special effects generator (SEG),** because this label more accurately describes the functions and capabilities of modern units. Along with the basic cuts, dissolves, and supers, the simplest SEG can create, for example, **two- and three-source keys, chroma key effects,** and **pattern wipes** that are very impressive—

The Switcher: Disciplines of the Technical Director

Figure 7–6
The Grass Valley Model 100 switcher introduces considerable flexibility with its deceptively simple design. (Photo courtesy of Grass Valley Group)

although somewhat complicated from an operational standpoint for the beginning student.

If, however, one approaches the SEG/ switcher in a manner that seeks to understand the *functional logic* that goes into the creation of each of the individual effects, then the unit is not nearly so intimidating. Always try to picture the underlying video signal flow, and the basic operations should be much easier to follow. In other words, one should look for certain *patterns of operation* that apply to a number of different production functions. For example, whether you are doing a camera cut, dissolve, or wipe, you must first make certain that the correct camera or other picture source has been selected on the proper switcher bank. Only then can you proceed with the specific operations that will accomplish the desired effect.

The Grass Valley Group Model 100 Production switcher, as shown in figure 7–6, is in use in over 5,000 production facilities throughout the world. With a price range and functional complexity designed for the medium-sized operation, it is perhaps the best known of all switchers used in industrial and educational institutions. With its impressive special effects capability and other electronic components relating to picture control, it has many of the features found in larger and more expensive units. Therefore, we shall use the GVG Model 100 as an example to show the sort of operational techniques that students will be using as they move into professional video activity of all types.

Specific Operational Techniques for Basic Transitions

Having previously outlined some of the general switcher operations in terms of fader bars, which always correspond to a specific *A* bank or *B* bank, we must now modify that generalization because on many of the newer switchers, such as the GVG Models 100 and 110, this is not the case. In the following example of the dissolve, the fader arms could be placed in either the upper or lower position prior to the beginning of the move. It would

Figure 7–7
Operating buses of the
GVG 100 switcher. The
"transition control section"
is comprised of the
individual buttons on each
bank for input selection
and the fader arms for
dissolves and effects.

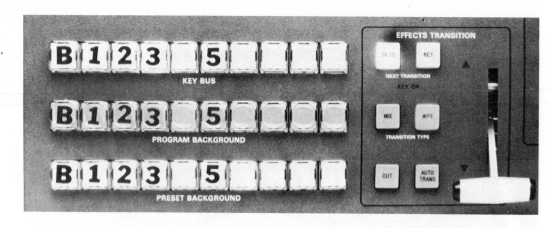

not matter at that point—as long as other buttons were preset properly.

A careful look at figure 7–7 shows that there are two lower switching buses (sometimes called *crosspoint buses*). These are labeled **program** and **preset.** (We shall for the moment ignore the additional *background* aspect of their function. We shall also for the moment ignore the **key bus** directly above.)

The key concept in this arrangement is that the upper **program** bank (the middle of the three buses) is *always* the bank that provides the source of the picture that is the *line output of the switcher.* And it follows, then, that the **preset** bank is where you press the button for the camera picture that will be the *next line output* following the completed transition.

Using the GVG 100 model, let us follow an example of a simple fade from camera 1 to camera 2. We would first press the **background (bkgd)** button above the *next transition* section of the effects transition group of controls and the **mix** button just above *transition type.* (We will look at these in more detail later.) Next, with the fader lever in the **upper** position, the **camera 1** button is pressed on the upper **program** bank and the **camera 2** button is pressed on the lower **preset bank.** The camera 1 button on the program bank will glow brightly with what is called *high tally;* this reinforces what

our program monitor tells us—that we are feeding a camera 1 signal on the program line. The camera 2 button on the preset bank glows with a softer intensity called a *low tally;* this indicates that camera 2 is selected to be the next camera on the air.

As we begin to move the fader downward, we will see a *green arrow* begin to glow at the place where the fader arm will be when we have completed the dissolve to camera 2. (This reinforcement of the direction of our lever move is important in more complex operations.) As we continue the fader movement downward, both the camera 1 and the camera 2 buttons will glow brightly as both cameras are seen briefly on the program monitor (a momentary superimposition) during the dissolve.

As the dissolve is completed and the fader lever makes contact at the lower position, we have put camera 2 on the air, and we see camera 2 on the program line monitor. But the surprising thing is what has happened to the two banks. The upper **program** bank now shows its *camera 2* button glowing brightly (high tally); and on the lower **preset bank,** the *camera 1* button (the camera from which we have just dissolved) is now glowing dimly (low tally). As we completed our dissolve, the two cameras switched positions on the buses, executing what is called a **flip-flop** because their positions as

line feed and **off-line feed** cameras have just been reversed. Looking again at the switcher, we see that even though our fader is in the **lower position,** the line feed camera (camera 2) is shown on the **upper** bank, indicating it is on the **program** bus. It is the brightly glowing tally that reminds us which camera is our line feed and *not* of the position of the fader—as with older switchers.

Automatic Transitions If we had wanted a dissolve lasting exactly two seconds, we could have used the **Automatic Transition** feature of the GVG 100 and not even used the fader levers at all (since the position of the fader arms no longer indicates which bus is on the air). We would start out by having the program and preset buses set up exactly as in the beginning of the previous example—with the fader arms in the upper position (although we could just as well have started with them in the lower position). We would then have used the **Auto Transition Rate** controls at the upper right-hand corner of the unit (see figure 7–8). Keeping in mind the 30-frames-per-second rate explained in chapter 5, we would use the **set** controls to put the transition rate at sixty frames.

In this same group of controls, we would use the **select** button to move the red indicator light to the **Auto Trans** position. The *Mix* button for the "transition type" and the *Bkgd* button for the "next transition" are still pressed (figure 7–7). By pressing the *Auto Trans* button, we will achieve a perfect two-second dissolve from camera 1 to camera 2. The "flip-flop" will occur as before. The faders are not moved—although they can be used to *override* the automatic dissolve at any time.

For an instantaneous **cut** between cameras 1 and 2, we would only have had to press the **cut** button (right next to the **Auto Trans** button) instead of the *Auto Trans* button itself.

Wipe Transitions Between Cameras

In making a transition between two consecutive pictures, there are times when neither the take nor the dissolve is suitable. An example might be where you want to draw special attention to a picture or series of pictures. The **wipe transition** often accomplishes this perfectly—by letting the viewer see portions of both pictures as the separation line moves through the screen. Used excessively, the wipe

● ● ● ● ● ● ● ● ● ● ● ●

calls attention to itself as a gimmick, but when used with discretion, it is an important part of a director's visual vocabulary.

Many production switcher/SEG units in use today have dozens of *patterned wipe* designs—ranging from the traditional vertical line moving horizontally across the screen (or the horizontal line moving vertically down the screen) to diagonals, diamonds, circles, and all manner of boxes, to the jagged shark tooth effect, which is the cliché of the late-night horror movie show.

Split Screens and Corner Inserts   Just as the superimposition may be thought of as a dissolve suspended in midtransition, so might the **split screen** and **corner insert** (or any one of a number of fancy inserts) be thought of as a wipe effect that has been halted in midpoint.

As a common application of a "suspended" wipe transition, the *split screen* is a means of combining two pictures with either a horizontal or vertical (and occasionally diagonal) line separating the screen into two distinct areas—with a different picture (from separate cameras or other video sources) in each part of the screen. By means of the special effects faders, relative sizes of the two pictures can be adjusted.

By manipulating the horizontal and vertical special effects faders separately, it is also possible to achieve a *corner insert*. (See figure 7–9.) This places the inserted camera picture in any quadrant of the screen. In a televised baseball game, for example, when you see the runner at first base within a small insert in the top right-hand corner of the primary "behind-the-plate" wide shot, you are actually seeing a corner wipe that has only been taken part of the way—in what could have been a full-screen wipe from one camera to another. Again, the exact size and proportion of the corner insert can be easily adjusted by the control levers.

A further technical advance is the *multiple-source split screen*. With this device, it is possible to split the screen into a number of individual sections, each with a separate picture. Again, these separate divisions can be positioned and shaped to meet a variety of artistic demands—even resembling bordered

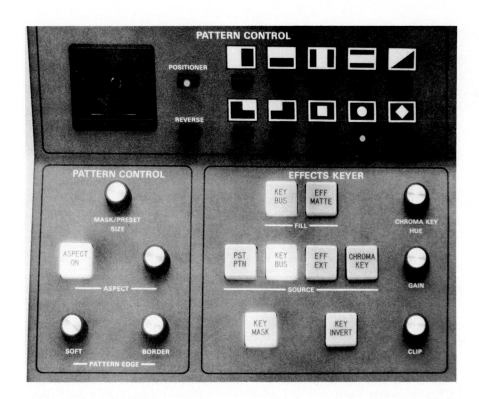

Figure 7–10
The "pattern control"
section of the GVG 100.
The pattern control buttons
allow the T.D. to select
specific patterns for wipes
and inserts. It also has
controls that can further
position and shape the
patterns.

snapshots in a photo album. The most conventional multiple-source split screen is probably the four-camera *quad split*.

Another useful special effect is the *spotlight,* which enables the operator to dim the entire screen except for one circle of light that can be shaped, changed in size, and positioned anywhere on the screen with a joystick. This effect can also be considered as a special application of the suspended wipe transition.

Execution of the Wipe Transition   The method of handling the patterned wipe transition is not too difficult once one understands the basics of the dissolve transition.

Returning to our specific example with the GVG 100, we first need to push the *wipe* button for "transition type" next to the fader arms (see figure 7–7), cancelling the *mix* transition button. On the "Pattern Control" section of the switcher (see figure 7–10), the **select button,** under the pattern with a confirming red light, determines the basic shape of the wipe. Keep in mind that the new video from the preset camera will appear in the *white* area of the pattern. With the *center circle wipe,* the new picture will emerge on the screen as the white circle in the middle of the picture; its image will be widened by the movement of the fader.

There is also a **reverse** option in which the *black area* of the pattern represents the new camera. Other controls allow for changes in *position* and *shape* of the circle or other selected design. You can also adjust how *hard* or *soft* you want the edge of the wipe to be and how wide you want to make the *border* between the two video source pictures.

The *Auto Transition* feature discussed previously can be utilized for the execution of wipes as well as for dissolves.

● ● ● ● ● ● ● ● ● ● ● ● ●

Figure 7–11
Two monitors illustrating the difference between a super and a key. The monitor on the left shows a black-and-white graphics card supered over the woman's face. The right-hand monitor shows the same card keyed over the woman's face.

Keyed Special Effects with Two and Three Sources

For all practical purposes, the superimposition has been almost totally replaced with the **key** effect, which "cuts out" and combines solid images from two or more video sources.[3] The basic principle of the key is a process by which differences in brightness and/or color are used to insert one picture into another. Often the analogy of a "cookie cutter" is used to explain how one image electronically *dominates* all or part of a second background picture to produce a **key effect,** such as white letters over a studio camera shot. Unlike a superimposition where the two images bleed through onto each other, the key cuts a clean electronic hole into

3. Occasionally the word **matte** is associated with the *key* process. The term was derived from the traditional film technique that printed or "matted" inserts within the larger film frame.

which it inserts its signal. Figure 7–11 illustrates the difference between a super and a key.

In many such effects, a **wipe pattern** is used to create the **outline shape,** and a **third source** is used as an input to fill the hole with another picture. Another version of this three-source effect, known as an **auto key** (formerly labeled the "external" key), uses one video source to establish the external shape of a letter or figure—in effect, stamping out an image much like a stencil might cut out a shape. The key effect then utilizes a third source to fill in the picture and color of the "stenciled out" part of the design.

However, for our example, we will use the least complex of these special effects—white titles keyed over a camera shot. This is what is termed a **self key** (also known as a **luminance** key or an "internal" key) because the dominant brightness level of the lettering cuts its own electronic pattern in the background

The Switcher: Disciplines of the Technical Director

picture. However, even this simple special effect should always be previewed and adjusted before it is used.

Let us say that we are going to use our key at the beginning of a program. The director's command would be to "Prepare to fade up from black to a key of titles on the C.G. over camera 1." The technical director would press **black** on the **program (background)** bank, **camera 1** on the **preset background** bank, and **button #5** (for the character generator) on the **key bus.** In this case, camera 1 is our *preset background* and the character generator will be our *key* source. Our fader arms can be in either the upper or lower position to start the exercise. (Remember, their position does *not* relate to the bank that is feeding the program line.)

The two buttons under "effects transition" allow us to select which bus (the *preset background* or the *key bus*) we will be using for the effect. In this case, we press *both* the **bkgd (background)** and **key** buttons because when we come up from black we are going to fade in the key consisting of *two* images—a video source on each bank (the "preset background" and the "key" bus); that is, we will come up on camera 1, which is now preset as our background, *and* keyed over camera 1 will be the preset lettering originating from the **character generator** on the **key bus** #5 position.

In the **effects keyer** section (see figure 7–10), we must press *both* **key bus** buttons because the **key bus** will be both the **source** *and* the **fill** of the effect. (If we were preparing a three-source key, we would punch up different sources for the source and for the fill.)

Once the selections have been punched up on the **preset background** bank (camera 1) and on the **key bus** bank (the character generator), the **preview monitor** will be displaying the key effect of those two sources (see the following discussion). Because the difference in brightness between the lettering and the background is always a matter of delicate balance, a look

at this preview monitor will now tell us just what adjustments must be made. The **clip knob** sets the *brightness* threshold for the key source video, which allows the letters to "cut" the electronic hole, and the **gain knob** sets the *sharpness* of the key effect itself. After viewing the result of these adjustments, the director gives the command, "Fade up on the key effect," and the technical director executes the fade-in to the effect by moving the fader arms from wherever they are to the opposite position. The key effect is brought up on the line, and we see the results on the **program monitor.**

On the GVG model 110, there is a feature called **Key Memory** that is built into the unit. It will remember the **clip** and **gain** settings for a source image that has been used previously and noted. When that source is used a second time, the clip and gain settings will automatically be returned to their previously established levels. Other state-of-the-art SEG/switchers have even more amazing electronic memory innovations (see section 7.4).

Monitors

At this point in our study, you will have become aware of a series of monitors in the video control room.[4] There may be up to a dozen different monitors, each performing an important individual function (see figure 7–1). Each video source will have its own monitor. Each studio camera, character generator, and video recorder will have a small individual monitor. In addition to these 7- to 10-inch units, there will be several larger monitors. The most crucial of these is the **line monitor,** which shows the

4. The video *monitor* is distinguished from the regular television *receiver* in that the monitor is usually a high-quality unit with ability to reproduce fine detail. It receives a direct unmodulated video signal, as opposed to a modulated radio frequency signal (see sections 2.2.1 and 5.1). Thus, there is no audio and no channel-selection capability.

actual picture that the switcher is sending to master control for live transmission or recording. This is the one that the director must watch constantly as a final check on the program picture content.

The other large monitor, often to the left of the program monitor, is the **preview monitor,** which is used heavily by the technical director to adjust keys and other special effects in advance of their use—and to show the director just how these effects or any upcoming shot will look.

In complicated network sports programs, this preview function may be done on separate **preset** monitors used just for effects. In some production systems, the preset monitors may be used to routinely preview the upcoming shot so that the director will always be able to see precisely what is going on the air next. There may also be a number of preview monitors for remote location feeds in addition to the basic preview monitor. In a live broadcasting situation, there also would always be an **air monitor** to show the actual broadcast picture.

7.4 Additional Special Effects Features and Digital Effects

Because this section has been written only as an *introduction* to the capabilities of SEG/switchers being used today, we have not tried to describe every option and function found on the Grass Valley Group 100 and 110 switchers and similar models. New processes and effects are constantly being developed. It is sufficient at this stage that the production student simply be aware of some of the basic effects and how they can be used; skill and refinement in using these sophisticated techniques can come at a later period in a student's professional development.

Indeed, there is a very real danger in getting too involved with elaborate special effects at an early stage. Too often they are used solely

for the sake of playing around with the equipment. The student should learn to master the basic pieces of standard equipment before jumping unprepared into the world of electronic legerdemain. A person must master the disciplines of communicating effectively with the medium of television before trying to exploit its full electronic potential. For this reason, we will not be concerned with diagrams and illustrations of how all these various effects are technically achieved. There are a few other features, however, that should be mentioned.

One important component in many systems is the **downstream keyer.** This is an additional keying device that can be added to any existing system "downstream" of the SEG/switcher; that is, it is used to add an effect to the video signal after it leaves the switcher. When viewed on a monitor, the output of the downstream keyer looks much the same as the output of the internal key component. It is designed to insert captions or other key effects into the final output of the switcher and, as such, handles sources such as a character generator or a graphics camera.

The *Key Memory* feature of the GVG Model 110 was previously described. Other state-of-the-art SEGs have even more amazing electronic memory and execution innovations. For example, the Grass Valley Group Model 300 (see figure 7–12) offers a much more sophisticated memory feature called the *E-MEM,*[5] which can combine digitally produced animated graphics along with color, brightness, and other design information in its memory unit. With the pressing of a single button, the animated effect/transition can be recalled and executed with no other preparation or commands.

Other features of today's switchers include all sorts of ways to manipulate colors and

5. *E-MEM* is a trademark of the Grass Valley Group.

The Switcher: Disciplines of the Technical Director

Figure 7–12
The Grass Valley Group
300 SEG/switcher.

shapes of backgrounds and borders. The actual **color** itself is adjusted by the **hue** control. The **chroma** knob varies the **intensity** of a color (the "bluishness" of blue). And the **luminance** control can regulate the amount of brightness in the image. All of these controls interact to a degree that can only be appreciated with hands-on experience.

Chroma Key

Now one of the most common of the electronic special effects, the **chroma key** is a matting process that has become a staple of much color production. This is a technique in which a specific color—rather than a graphic design or pattern—is used as the electronic key to cut out part of the picture. (Any color can be designated to be used as the key; however, blue or green is most often used because it is farthest from any skin tones.) Wherever the foreground or key camera detects the designated hue (or *chroma*) in its picture, that video information is discarded and background picture signals are supplied from a second—or background—camera (often from the film chain, although it can be from another studio camera, a videotape, or any other source).

For example, if camera 1 is shooting the talent standing in front of an evenly lit blue background (and not wearing any blue item of clothing), this picture can be combined with the picture from camera 2 (say, a panorama of the Israeli landscape), and the picture from camera 2 will appear only where there was blue in camera 1's picture; hence the talent is seen standing in front of the Dead Sea. Anyone can be placed in front of any background desired.

This type of chroma key application is routinely used, for example, in newscasts where the picture information for a particular news story is keyed in behind the newscaster. (See

Figure 7–13
Chroma key.

Picture from "key" camera. Subject in front of solid blue background.

Background picture from telecine or other camera.

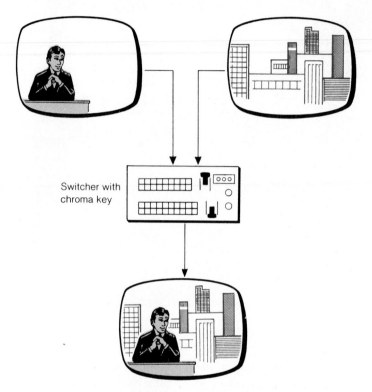

Switcher with chroma key

Composite picture. Foreground subject set against background image—wherever blue appeared on the key camera.

figure 7–13.) This matting technique also has obvious applications for dramatic formats, instructional programs, variety shows, and virtually every other type of production. News and sports would be a pretty dull place without chroma key.

Although the use of chroma key is widespread, it is not without numerous potential difficulties. The electronic equipment has to be delicately adjusted; lighting of the color background of the key camera has to be perfectly even; considerable attention must be given to selection of costumes and scenery. Slight problems in any of these areas lead to conspicuous troubles such as tearing of the foreground image, an obvious border around the foreground figure, discoloration, or indistinct contours.

Many of these drawbacks have been overcome by newer systems, such as *Ultimatte*,[6] which has supplanted or replaced chroma key in most major professional studios. In addition to conventional color matting features, Ultimatte can render not only highlights and re-

6. *Ultimatte* is a trademark of the Ultimatte Corporation.

flections off of glass, but the actual glass object itself will be visibly matted over the background image. The process is sensitive enough that it can capture every strand of a person's hair and even wisps of smoke.

Single-Camera Effects

In addition to the electronic transitions and keying and matting effects, certain other single-camera electronic effects should be briefly mentioned here. These are devices for image manipulation that do not involve the use of a second camera.

The video engineer has the ability to effect several changes through manipulation of the camera control unit (CCU). **Sweep reversals** can electronically reverse the scanning process of the camera. *Horizontal sweep reversal* reverses the left and right directions of a picture, creating a mirror image. This can be useful when shooting through a mirror for special angles (for example, shooting up at an overhead mirror to get a view of a tabletop, and then reversing the horizontal sweep in order to counteract the mirror reversal). On the other hand, *vertical sweep reversal*—turning a picture upside down—is usually only for obvious spectacular or comedic effects.

On black-and-white cameras, a negative-like image can be created with **polarity reversal.** This changes all of the blacks to white and whites to black. This has some fascinating artistic possibilities as well as some limited practical uses (for example, projecting negative film from which no positive print has been made).

High-contrast images can be achieved a couple of different ways. One is through **debeaming.** The video engineer can turn down one of the CCU controls (the intensity of the scanning beam), which reduces the image to stark white and black contrasts. A similar effect can be achieved with the internal key on the switcher. By keying a picture over black and

adjusting the *clipper,* a strong high-contrast image can be created with all of the grays removed.

Just as it is possible to get audio reverberation or an echo effect by recording and playing back almost simultaneously a given sound source (section 3.4), so is it possible to achieve a form of **video feedback.** By feeding a camera's signal into a floor monitor and then using the same camera to shoot the face of the monitor, a wide variety of bizarre video effects can be obtained. The picture in figure 1–6 was achieved by keying over black and then using video feedback.

One area where color television can be exciting is in the possibility of **colorization.** This process involves a special colorizing generator—also referred to as a *color video synthesizer*—that can add various colors to black-and-white pictures, create various abstract patterns, and even produce color images without the use of a camera at all. Such artistic applications take us out of the realm of basic communication and into the arena of video art (section 1.3).

Digital Effects

One of the most exciting frontiers of video imagery is in the area of digital manipulation or *digitalizing.* With digital technology it is possible to expand the creative and production capabilities of television far beyond what had been possible earlier.

The audio and video signals described in chapters 2 and 5 are *analog* systems; that is, variations in electrical current actually represent and define the sound and picture. The brighter the image hitting the lens, the greater the intensity of the electrical signal. With *digital* encoding, on the other hand, the video information is transformed into a series of *binary* (base-two) numbers. (See figure 7–14.) Each of the 400 picture elements that are spread across a single scanning line, for example (see

Figure 7–14
Comparison of analog and
digital encoding.

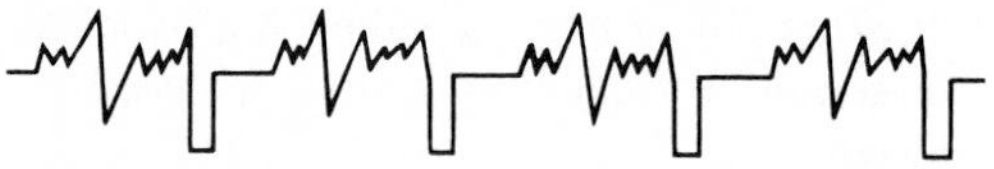

(a) Representation of an analog signal.

1-0-0-1-1-0-1-1/1-0-0-1-1-0-1-0/1-0-0-1-1-0-0-1

(b) Representation of a digital signal.

section 5.2), is reduced to a brightness level on a **luminance scale** from 1 to 256. The video signal can thus be translated into a series of binary numbers expressed as off/on blips. (A point registering at a brightness level of 155 on the luminance scale, for instance, would be encoded as 1–0–0–1–1–0–1–1 in the binary system.)[7]

Once the television signal is encoded into a binary-digital format, the system has many advantages: (1) memory or storage capacity can be significantly increased; (2) the quality of the video information does not deteriorate as it is processed, amplified, channeled, duplicated, edited, and transmitted; and (3) most importantly, the signal information can now be manipulated, rearranged, enhanced, and augmented in ways that are impossible with analog information.

Digital Video Manipulator   Several marvelous television devices, introduced in section 5.1, have emerged from the digital age so far: the **time-base corrector,** so important in restoring sync in editing and switching operations (see section 8.2); the *framestore syn-*

chronizer, used for synchronization of all major network feeds and remote pickups. None, however, offers as much excitement as the **digital video manipulator (DVM).**

Many of the electronic wonders described throughout this chapter are a result of the DVM. Other advances include *continuous image compression,* which enables the switcher operator to compress the full-frame picture down to the size of a tiny circle (at any speed, to any size) and—with a joystick—to place the shrunken image anywhere on the screen. This is what makes the squeeze zoom possible as a transition.

Image expansion allows the director to take any segment of the video frame and enlarge it up to four times its original size (beyond which point it becomes unintelligible). A combined phenomenon is *image stretching.* Any portion of the picture can be expanded or compressed in any direction; ratios can be altered; graphics can be shaped to fit the picture.

Other transitional devices—in addition to effects such as the fold-over and squeeze zoom—include the *video split,* which literally can take a picture and pull it apart in the middle to make room for a new frame, and the *push-off,* which simply shoves a whole frame off the tube sideways while replacing it with another image (as opposed to the wipe, which does not move the two stationary frames involved in the transition).

The impact of many of these advances is with postproduction editing. (See chapter 9.) Once the basic video images have been recorded, the director can sit down with an editor and decide how to time each transition, when to compress this image and bring in another, whether to electronically zoom in on a particular frame, how to shape graphics as they are added later, and so forth. The video editor now

7. Binary encoding, of course, is what forms the basis for all digital computers and microprocessing equipment. It is built on the base-two counting system, which reduces all numerical information to a two-symbol number (using *zero* and *one*). Thus, all numerical data can be handled as a series of *off* (zero) and *on* (one) electrical connections.

The Switcher: Disciplines of the Technical Director

has at his or her command more sophisticated and less expensive creative opportunities than film editors have ever enjoyed.

The switcher, the SEG, and the DVM have come a long way since the crude connection panel we started with at the beginning of section 7.1.

7.5 Commands of Preparation and Execution

In discussing audio production techniques (section 3.5), we stressed the difference between commands of *preparation* and commands of *execution.* Nowhere is this distinction more important than in giving commands to the technical director. Because the switcher operator has two entirely different physical operations to perform (straight takes and effects involving two or more buses)—depending upon which command is given—the commands of preparation must allow for sufficient lead time. Such commands, given over the intercom system, also give a warning to the operator of the upcoming camera.

One helpful rule is that the command of preparation for any straight take is "ready." The preparation for any dissolve, super, fade, or special transition or effect that involves getting something set or prepared on another bus, uses the command "prepare." (A few directors prefer to use the command "set up.") Although some directors use the term "standby" as a preparation for both takes and dissolves, this can be confusing to the crew. The use of correct terminology immediately lets the technical director know whether he or she simply has to get ready to push a button on the same bus or whether it is necessary to prepare or set up another camera or effect on another bus.

The command sequence for a direct take from camera 1 to camera 2 is stated by the director as follows:

(Preparation): "Ready camera 2" (or simply) "Ready 2"
(Execution): "Take 2"

The word *ready* lets the technical director know that he or she only has to place a finger on the camera 2 button on the activated bus.

No matter how rushed the director may be or how fast paced the program may be, the director should never skimp on the command of preparation. *Accuracy in getting the technical director properly prepared is the most important part of calling shots correctly.* If the director does not have time to give full commands, he or she should abbreviate the commands of execution, not preparation:

(Preparation): "Ready 2"
(Execution): "Take it"
(or simply) "Take"

If time is so short that even this much preparation is impossible (for example, shooting a game show, fast-paced panel discussion, or football game), the command of preparation still must be given priority:

(Preparation): "Two"
(Execution): "Take"

A dissolve requires a different-sounding command of preparation to allow the technical director time to prepare for a more complex series of actions. Assuming you already have camera 1 on line, the correct commands for a dissolve would be:

(Preparation): "Prepare a dissolve to 2" (or) "Prepare 2" (or) "Set up 2"
(Execution): "Dissolve to 2"

For a super, the actions are the same so the commands are much the same:

(Preparation): "Prepare to super 2 over 1"
(or) "Set up 2" (or) "Set up a super of 2 with 1"
(Execution): "Super camera 2" (or) "Super 2 over 1"

We depart slightly from the basic pattern whenever two cameras are to be taken together in a super. While this effect also involves a movement of the control levers, the movement is not one of program execution. In other words, the result of the lever movement is not seen, when it is being done, on the line monitor or on the air. As previously outlined, the command of execution is a "take"—calling only for the pressing of the *line mix* output button or *take bar.* For this reason, the voice procedure in this case should be as follows:

(Preparation): "Ready to take 2 and 3 in super"
(Execution): "Take 2 and 3 in super"

The "in super" at the end of the command is optional, but does reinforce the intent of the command.

Much of the discipline necessary for keeping a program under control comes from this pattern of preparation and execution. The technical director knows exactly what is coming. Of necessity, this pattern must occasionally be broken—when complicated effects are called for. Usually a key, for example, must be preset several shots before its use. In this situation, after the command of preparation, there may be several intervening commands before the execution of the key. The command of preparation must be given far enough in advance so that the technical director has a chance to do the preset at a time most convenient during the ongoing program. The director keeps an eye on the preview monitor to see when the key is ready. The commands might be as follows:

(Advance preparation): "Prepare a key of camera 2 and credits on the C.G."
(Ongoing shots in the program continue): "Ready 1, take 1, . . . etc."
(Immediate preparation): "Prepare to dissolve to the key of credits over camera 2"
(Execution of the key): "Dissolve to the credits"

Similarly, any command to preview and adjust—say, of a corner wipe or an insert—in the coverage of a live event may be given well in advance of its eventual use on the air. There may be several intervening ad-libbed shots. This can be thought of as a "non-time-specific command." For example:

(Advance preparation): "Preview a top-left corner insert, camera 3, of runner off first base, within camera 2"
(Intervening shots ad-libbed): "Ready 4, take 4, . . . etc."
(Adjustment of preparation): "Tighten the framing on camera 3 insert"

The Switcher: Disciplines of the Technical Director

(Intervening
shots
ad-libbed):   "Ready 1, take 1, . . .
etc."
(Immediate
preparation):   "Ready to take corner
insert effect"
(Execution
of the effect): "Take effect"

When the switcher technology includes the use of the *cut bar* (which interchanges a preset picture or effect and the program line feed), the term "preset" is used as a part of the command of preparation.

(Preparation): "Preset a key of C.G. lettering and camera 1"
(Execution):   "Take preset effect" (or) "Cut to the key"

Finally, fades to and from black are handled in a manner very similar to the dissolve (the fade to or from black is in essence a dissolve to or from black). Due to the fact that a sync black picture has such a definite connotation of separation and/or conclusion, most directors reserve the term "fade" for use as a command only to dissolve to black. This serves as a safeguard to protect against any inadvertent dissolve to full-screen black. At the beginning of a program, let's assume the director wants to fade in from black to lettering on the character generator. The typical commands will be something like the following:

(Preparation): "Prepare to fade from black to character generator"
(Execution):   "Fade up on C.G."

And the closing fade to black will be simply:

(Preparation): "Prepare black"

(Execution):   "Fade to black"
(or) "Fade sound and picture out"

These, then, are the basic elements of television's visual language: camera takes, dissolves, supers, cameras taken together in super, cameras preset for keys or corner inserts, and fades to black. In the creative sense, the important consideration is that the transitions be appropriate to the context of the visual idea the picture sequence is expressing. Technically, their use depends upon the operating capabilities of the switcher, which can follow only from a certain amount of hands-on practice and discipline.

Crucial to the successful operation of the switcher is the use of the proper preparatory commands: "ready" for a take; "prepare" or "set up" for a dissolve, fade, or super. This terminology is fairly standard throughout the country, and its use is essential to any good control room operation. Just the use of the word *prepare*—even before the camera is mentioned by number—starts a response pattern in the thinking process. This is an integral part of the discipline of the technical director.

Summary

The switcher is the key *channeling* and *mixing* device in the video signal flow system. In conjunction with the special effects generator (SEG) and digital video manipulator (DVM), it is also involved in *shaping* the video signal.

The switcher can be thought of as a simple connection panel, with additional *banks* and *fader arms* added to increase the flexibility of the unit. The basic camera transitions and effects used on the switcher include the *take, dissolve, fade,* and *super.*

There are several variations of more complex switchers that, in conjunction with the various video *monitors,* enable the technical director to *preview* and *preset* certain effects. Special electronic effects include *wipes* and *split screens* and numerous *key and insert* effects and the chroma key. Single-camera effects include sweep reversals, polarity reversals, debeaming, video feedback, and colorization.

Effects available through the *digital video manipulator* encompass image compression and expansion and image stretching—as well as transitions such as the fold-over, squeeze zoom, video split, push-off, and numerous others.

This chapter has been concerned with the operation of the TV switcher and the techniques of live studio editing. In chapter 8 we will look at videotape recording.

7.6   Training Exercise and Class Production Project

Class Exercise

The following written exercise is designed to help the student think about the actual operating process of the control room switcher in preparation for its use in later production exercises.

First draw a sketch of the switcher in your own control room, with the appropriate identifying terminology.

Following each of the given commands of preparation or execution, write the necessary sequence of operation, the buttons to be pressed, and the levers to be moved in order to accomplish the command request. Assume that only the *black* buttons on all buses have been pressed and that the control levers are in the *B-mix bank* position. Keep in mind that this exercise represents an ongoing series of actions, as in a program sequence. Each movement is done only in the light of what has just previously been done. A technical director must constantly ask himself or herself, Which buttons are already pressed, and what is the position of the faders?

If possible, each student should have the opportunity to run through this exercise at the switcher, with another student giving commands as the director. For contrast, title cards, as well as wide, waist, and close-up shots, can be used. If also done as a studio exercise, the sequence of commands can be altered in order to give some variety of action.

Command Sequence

Prepare a key of opening titles on the C.G. and the wide shot on camera 2

Prepare to fade from black to the key

Fade up on the key

Ready to take the C.G. out of the key

Take out the C.G.

Prepare to wipe to camera 1

Wipe to camera 1

Prepare to super camera 3 over camera 1

Super camera 3

Ready to undercut to camera 2, leaving camera 1 on the air

Undercut to camera 2

Prepare to split to black

Split to black

Class Production Project (Appendix D-2)

The first combined use of all production facilities is a rewarding but difficult step. For this reason, we have provided a live

The Switcher: Disciplines of the Technical Director

announcer and picture-card production exercise that concentrates on the development of the techniques of the use of the switcher, while at the same time affording an opportunity for an introduction to the basics of both lighting and camera work.

The photographs used in the exercise are included in appendix D. At relatively small cost, these can be photographically enlarged to a width of at least two feet to provide for some degree of camera movement. Each photo offers both long-shot and close-up aspects of the subject material. The photos present the director and camera operator with opportunities for both panning and zooming camera work, as well as some problems with proper composition.

There is no one correct way to do the exercise. Each person should study the photos and decide upon a meaningful sequence of images. The production is designed to allow for a maximum of individual input in the selection of music as well as the direction of the pace and style of the announcer and related camera work. Promotional copy also is provided in appendix D. Students should be encouraged to rewrite the script with possible changes in the order of the pictures. The concluding section offers an opportunity to intercut a montage of several pictures used earlier or to undercut them with the title card. What students are working toward is a totality and unity of production in which the end result is more than equal to the sum of its parts.

Function and Operation of the Videotape Recorder

8

••••••••••••••••••••

One of the last steps in the video signal flow is the recording (and playback) operation. This chapter deals specifically with the electronic and functional aspects of magnetic recording. We will examine the general concepts of electromagnetic videotape recording and playback—relating the various component functions to operational controls. Chapter 9 will extend the discussion of magnetic video recording with an analysis of editing equipment and procedures—especially as it relates to *postproduction editing.*

In spite of the rapid development of the television industry during its first decade, there was no satisfactory way of recording the electronic camera picture until the mid-1950s. The *kinescope* process (developed in the 1940s) was a specialized technique that used motion picture film to photograph the moving image off a receiver (kinescope) tube; the result was a blurry, washed-out picture with degraded audio quality.

A way had to be found to record the electromagnetic signals that actually generated the television picture. The subsequent development of videotape technology not only changed the nature and scope of video production, but it has shaped the whole modern telecommunications industry.

8.1 Principles of Videotape Recording

The idea of video recording is based upon several aspects of the electromagnetic phenomenon. We will be looking at two interrelated electromagnetic concepts—electronic and magnetic principles. Chapter 5 presented a simplified model of how the three-chip camera creates an ongoing sequence of signals that are translated by the receiver/display (kinescope) tube into a color video picture. Although a brief recap of that material will be presented here, it is suggested that you go back and carefully review section 5.2 before proceeding.

The Electronic Basis of Videotape Recording

Both the **CCD chip** or **image sensor** (see figure 5–6) and the display picture tube **raster** (viewing area) are organized into 525 horizontal scanning lines. Each of these lines is composed of more than 450 separate illumination points or picture elements. (This number can vary with the manufacturer.) Even though some of the top and bottom lines are used for synchronizing signals and information other than the video picture, there are still well over 250,000 separate picture elements or *pixels* that make up the mosaiclike electronic image.

As the lens focuses the incoming light from the subject onto the CCD image sensor, each one of the 250,000 pixels is individually energized in direct relationship to the specific amount of light hitting the pixel. This process produces the signals that are the electronic version of the optical image focused on the face of the lens. In tube-type cameras, a stream of electrons (the *scanning beam*) is shot at the *target* at the front of the tube—essentially a similar plate of pixels—by means of electromagnets located just forward of the *electron gun,* which is the source of the electron beam. In the CCD camera, this "scanning" function is accomplished by **vertical** and **horizontal shift registers,** which in effect, collect the sequential output of the pixels. (See the following discussion.)

This scanning process actually occurs in two phases. Starting at the top left of the picture, the odd-numbered lines are first scanned to produce a top-to-bottom picture *field.* Only one-half of the illumination points have been used to produce this picture. Once this half-picture has been scanned, the scanning beam starts at the top left of the picture again, and this time all the even-numbered lines are scanned to produce another picture field. There are sixty of these half-picture fields occurring every second. This odd-even field alternation, called *interlacing,* is designed to cut down on the unwanted "flicker" effect of the picture (sixty half-pictures a second cause less flicker than thirty full pictures per second). This interlacing of fields adds up to a theoretical figure of thirty *frames* per second—although no complete frame ever really exists as a static entity.

Horizontal and Vertical Sync Examining this process in greater detail, you will find that several additional factors are needed to ensure the stability of the picture. It is imperative that the scanning sequence in the camera, whether tube or chip type, be precisely synchronized at every stage of its journey—through the switcher, in all recording and editing equipment, during broadcast transmission, and at the home receiving set. A series of specialized pulses—generated independently of the color and luminance portion of the video signal—are utilized for this purpose. First of all, there is a **horizontal sync pulse,** which activates the video system at the beginning of each scanning line and turns it off for a brief retrace period (*blanking*) as the beam returns to the beginning of a new line on the left side of the picture tube.

At the completion of each field, there is a similar retrace period as the scanning beam returns to the top left of the picture. At this point, a **vertical sync pulse** is used to coordinate the start of each new field. While there are only two vertical sync pulses for every 525 horizontal sync pulses, they must nevertheless be considered as an extremely important part of the video sequence. Because it denotes the beginning of a new picture field, the vertical sync pulse has an important application in videotape editing.

Function and Operation of the Videotape Recorder

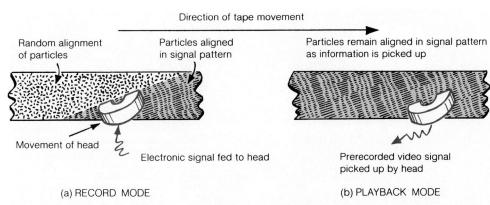

Direction of tape movement

Random alignment of particles

Particles aligned in signal pattern

Movement of head

Electronic signal fed to head

(a) RECORD MODE

Particles remain aligned in signal pattern as information is picked up

Prerecorded video signal picked up by head

(b) PLAYBACK MODE

Figure 8–1
Video recording and playback heads.

(a) **Record Mode.** The electronic video signals sent to the record head activate the magnetized head to align the iron oxide particles on the tape to retain a permanent (until erased) pattern of the recorded electronic video signal.

(b) **Playback Mode.** The prerecorded video signals on the videotape generate a small amount of electrical current in the playback head that is an exact duplicate of the original video signal.

The Magnetic Basis of Videotape Recording

Previous sections of the text discussed how sound waves (section 2.2.1) and light waves (section 5.2)—through a series of transformations (transducing)—can be put into an electromagnetic form that is suitable for broadcast. By utilizing these and other qualities of magnetism and electrical energy, this complex broadcast signal can be permanently "memorized" for later use. As youngsters, many of us demonstrated how a magnet on the underside of a piece of paper can align iron filings into a magnetic pattern. The principle involved in that simple demonstration provides the basis for all audiotape and videotape recording.

The record-playback **head** on any tape machine is actually a magnet, and the tape is a polyester strip coated on one side with iron oxide particles. (On some of the newer high-resolution formats, metal particles are used.) If electrical energy—organized into a video signal—is fed into the head, the iron oxide or metal particles in the tape passing in contact

with the head will be aligned into a continuing series of magnetic patterns. Thus, in the *record mode,* the resulting magnetic patterns are themselves a memory of the television signal. (The patterns are physically visible only if the oxide is treated with certain chemicals.)

In the *playback mode,* no electrical energy is sent to the magnetic head. Instead, as the tape moves across the head, the interaction of patterned iron oxide or metal particles in the tape and the magnetic head produces an electronic signal in the playback head that is a duplicate of the original input. This is how the "memorized" pattern on the tape produces the electrical signal that is transduced back into pictures and sound. (See figure 8–1.)

Occasionally, even with the best of equipment, there can be some loss of quality. The tape itself may have imperfections that cause momentary *glitches.* The very process of having the tape pass through the transport system makes it vulnerable to small but destructive changes in speed. If any one of a number of setup adjustments are done incorrectly, quality can be seriously impaired. Eventually the iron oxide or metal particles are

Figure 8–2
Quadruplex high-band
videotape recorder. (Photo
courtesy of Ampex
Corporation)

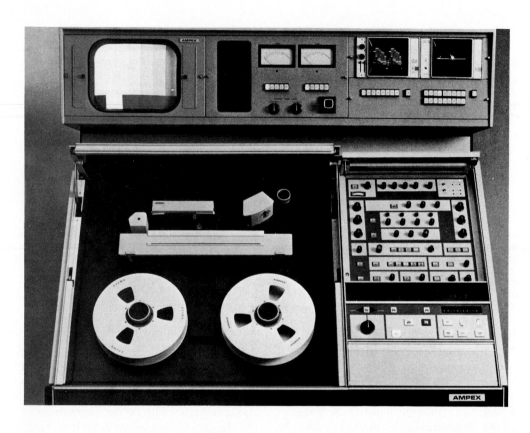

rubbed off and the tape physically deteriorates. But for the most part, state-of-the-art video recording equipment is very impressive. It is reliable, with a high degree of fidelity to the original signal. With equipment like a **frame synchronizer,** a recorded image can even have its quality enhanced. Such was not always the case. For those who were present at the beginnings of video recording, it has been a minor miracle.

Development of the Quadruplex Videotape Recorders

In the fall of 1956, CBS first used a videotape machine to delay the broadcast of its early evening newscast to the West Coast. It originated from an Ampex machine that utilized a **quadruplex** video head assembly. The *quad-head* recorder was named for the four rotating

video heads that vertically came into contact with a 2–inch videotape. (See figure 8–2.)

Some very impressive control signals and editing equipment were developed for the quad machines, and these recorders became the industry standard for many years. Some are still in use at a few television stations.

It became apparent, however, that this format had some very definite limitations. Because of the basic elements of its design, it could not produce a recognizable picture at tape speeds other than precisely fifteen inches per second (ips)—or, with modifications, at 7½ ips. Slow motion as well as faster-than-normal search speeds were not possible. Also, the tape could not be stopped in order to produce a **freeze-frame.** Not only did this make the editing process difficult, it also ruled out the production use of any stop-motion special effects.

Function and Operation of the Videotape Recorder

Additionally, the quad-head recorders were very bulky and quite expensive—advanced models costing well in excess of $100,000 by the mid-1970s. A final drawback was that the machines were costly to maintain; they were electronically delicate and involved considerable engineering attention to keep the four heads aligned.

8.2 Helical-Scan Videotape Recorders

The answer to many of these problems was to be found in the **helical-scan** (*slant-track*) videotape recorders (VTRs) developed in the late 1960s. Introduced originally as low-cost alternatives to the quadruplex machines, these helical-scan video recorders were rapidly adopted for nonbroadcast applications—school TV projects, hospitals, industrial training, and television production curriculums.

Evolution of the Slant-Track Machines

With the helical-scan (slant-track) recorders, equipment costs were much lower, videotape was cheaper, there was less machine setup time. Despite the fact that the technical quality of early helical-scan VTR machines did not generally match the broadcast quality of quad-head machines, many closed-circuit systems and educational institutions chose to rely upon the helical-scan formats—for reasons of economy, reliability, and ease of operation.

During the late 1960s numerous manufacturers brought out competing formats and standards—utilizing tape widths from one-quarter inch to two inches. Altogether there were close to forty different, noncompatible standards. Then, under the leadership of the SMPTE (Society of Motion Picture and Television Engineers), the industry adopted a ½-inch format that was picked up by most educational and training institutions.

The U-Matic Format In 1970 the ¾-inch U-matic videocassette system was introduced. Although there were earlier attempts to establish a standard cassette or cartridge system, the U-matic format was the first to become solidly accepted by educational and industrial users. With its many refinements and editing innovations, it became the workhorse of the closed-circuit television field. And it eventually became the ENG standard for broadcast stations. (See figure 8–3.)

Betamax and VHS After several abortive attempts to establish a consumer market with a home cartridge or cassette system, Sony finally succeeded with its Betamax format—followed closely by other manufacturers with the VHS system. Although the VHS format still dominates the home entertainment field, several competing formats are vying both for the consumer market and for the professional field. The greatly improved *Super-VHS* (S-VHS) format has technical specifications that equal broadcast and cable TV quality.

The 8mm Formats The S-VHS system is in turn being challenged by Sony's 8mm format. After several different competing 8mm (and ¼-inch) systems were introduced, a superior format, the *Hi8* system, emerged and is moving into both educational and professional applications. Many practitioners are waiting until the various competing formats are winnowed down and one clear-cut superior format emerges as the standard. If past experience is any indication, however, this may never happen.

Betacam and M-II In the meantime, the ½-inch Sony Betacam system (similar to Betamax, but with faster moving tape) and the ½-inch RCA/Panasonic M-format emerged to impress video professionals. Their updated formats, the Betacam SP and the Panasonic

Figure 8–3
Helical-scan head
assembly of a
U-matic ¾-inch VTR as
seen from above.

M-II, have been adopted by hundreds of stations and network news operations. (See section 15.1.)

The improved video quality of these two competing (and incompatible) systems is based, in part, on their design, which splits the video into two separate feeds, the *luminance (Y)* and *chrominance (C)* signals. This is *component video* (as introduced in section 5.2) as opposed to *composite video* where the two signals are part of one combined feed. (It should be noted that while S-VHS does separate the luminance and chrominance signals, it is still not considered as a true component video system.) Both the Betacam SP and M-II systems produce picture quality that far surpasses the much older ¾-inch U-matic format.

(See figure 8–4.) In an attempt to save the ¾-inch format, Sony has successfully marketed a U-Matic SP format with greatly improved linear resolution.

Formats are increasingly intermixed in the interests of economy. For example, it is not uncommon to find S-VHS camcorders used as the recording or *acquisition format*. Then during editing, the playback machine is an S-VHS unit but the edit/recorder may be a ¾-inch U-matic SP unit. This produces a high-quality master that can be used to dub back into any distribution format. Corporate or educational operations, for example, may elect to distribute multiple copies of their training programs on a Hi8 format or some other 8mm system.

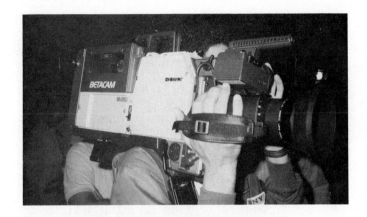

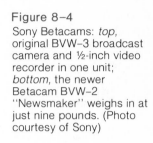

Figure 8–4
Sony Betacams: *top,* original BVW–3 broadcast camera and ½-inch video recorder in one unit; *bottom,* the newer Betacam BVW–2 "Newsmaker" weighs in at just nine pounds. (Photo courtesy of Sony)

The C-Format Through most of the 1980s, the analog 1-inch C-format remained the video editing and delivery system of choice at the network level for prime-time programming. This was the format that had, in effect, supplanted the older 2-inch quad format for broadcast purposes. Programs shot on 35mm film and even 16mm film were immediately transferred to the C-format for editing, adding special effects, and broadcasting. Betacam and M-II, which started out primarily for sports and news ENG and EFP operations, have begun to be used in other programming applications at the local station and cable network level.

Digital Recording and the D-2 Format
As interest in the benefits of digital video increased, it was inevitable that digital recording machines would be developed. The D-2 format was developed by Ampex to replace the C-format as a network-level videotape system. Whereas the earlier D-1 format would have forced production facilities into buying totally digital equipment, D-2 is compatible with existing composite analog video equipment. The Ampex-VPR 300 tape machine, shown in figure 8–5, has a number of impressive control features as well as improved picture and sound quality. Digital recorders are especially valued for editing

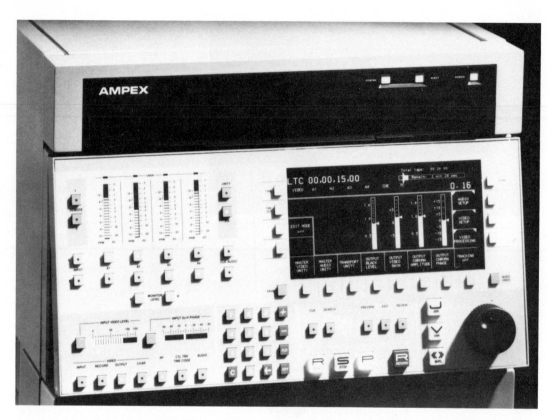

Figure 8–5
The Ampex VPR-300 is a
D-2 studio format video
recorder that can digitally
process a composite video
signal.

purposes, as successive generations of a recording can be made and worked with without any deterioration of the recorded image.

The Helical Idea

Many of these improvements in machine capacity were made possible by the innovative design of the helical-scan video head assembly. Each of the angled parallel lines shown in figure 8–6 represents one continuous scanning of the tape by one of the several video heads mounted on the circular drum (as shown in figure 8–7). Each single scan contains exactly the video information needed to record one complete 262.5-line picture field (section 8.1).

As the tape is pulled around the head drum, successive parallel angled (helical) tracks are scanned. In the *record* mode (as shown in figure 8–1), the heads are leaving a magnetized memory of the picture signal from the camera.

In the *playback* mode, a still picture can be produced if the tape movement is stopped while the video heads are still revolving; the heads will scan and reproduce the same picture over and over again. If the tape is moved at a slower-than-normal speed, a slow-motion effect is achieved. As long as the revolving head speed remains constant, the video sync of the picture is maintained—no matter how fast or slowly the tape is pulled around the head drum.[1]

---

1. In the quadruplex 2-inch machines, the tape speed must remain constant (slow motion is not feasible) because each of the 1½-inch vertical scans provides only enough information for *one-sixth* of a picture field. By contrast, the simplicity of the helical-scan recorder is that it is a *continuous field* format, with each scan providing one complete field.

Start of scan

End of scan   Each slanted recording track contains one complete picture field

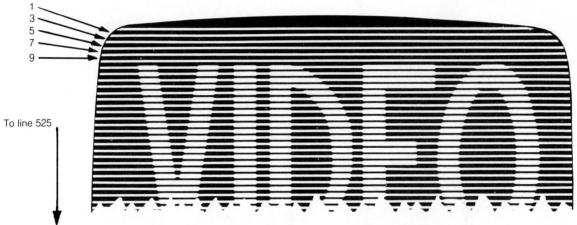

1
3
5
7
9

To line 525

The 262.5 odd-numbered scanning lines equal one picture field (½ frame).

The continuous video signal from one slanted video track contains enough information to record 262.5 odd-numbered scanning lines (one complete field) and to play back the field on the picture tube raster.

Figure 8–6
Helical-scan slanted track.

Figure 8–7
Helical-scan videocassette drum assembly.

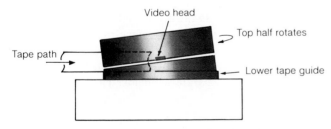

Video head

Top half rotates

Tape path

Lower tape guide

The playback/record heads are attached to the rotating top half of the tilted head assembly.

It must be remembered, however, that this 262.5-line picture *field* is the basis of the picture used to produce the *freeze-frame* or *slow-motion* special effect. However, it contains only one-half of the video information necessary to reproduce a full 525-line picture *frame*. This problem is solved on broadcast-quality 1-inch type-C and other units by means of some electronic wizardry. One of the five video heads on this machine has a special function that allows

Figure 8–8
Transport mechanism of
the RCA TH–900 type-C
video recorder.

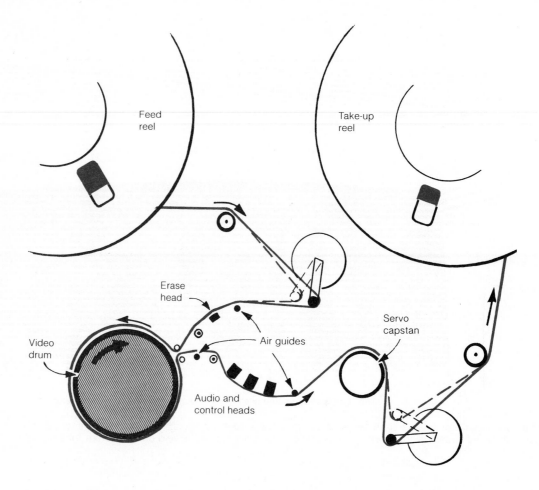

Feed
reel

Take-up
reel

Erase
head

Servo
capstan

Video
drum

Air guides

Audio and
control heads

the unit to "borrow" part of a stored video signal from an earlier frame. This is used to fill out the rest of the 525-line "slo-mo" picture.

The Helical-Scan Head Assembly The slanted track on the tape is achieved by one of two slightly different methods—one for the 1-inch reel-to-reel type-C machines and one for the enclosed cassette formats. On the reel-to-reel models, the tape is angled as it wraps around the circular video drum. With cassette formats, the tape cannot be angled (since it travels in the same plane from feed reel to take-

up reel), so the drum itself is tilted (as shown in figure 8–7) to achieve the angled, helical effect.

In either case, the video drum is made up of two separate segments. The bottom half is a part of the base on which it rests; this does not move. The top half, called the *head wheel,* has two or more very small video heads placed at equidistant points around the drum—with the heads protruding just slightly from the lower circumference of the movable wheel.

With the head wheel rotating rapidly in one direction and the tape moving in the opposite direction, a ¾-inch U-matic cassette

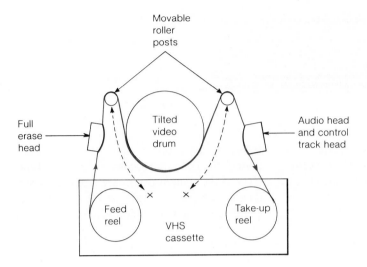

Figure 8–9
VHS cassette engaged by
transport system for play/
record mode.

Movable roller posts

Tilted video drum

Full erase head

Audio head and control track head

Feed reel

Take-up reel

VHS cassette

format, for example, will achieve a *writing speed* of 400 inches per second—even though the tape itself is moving through the unit at only 3¾ ips. (Note that there are many more scanning lines on the tape—roughly sixteen per inch—than could be indicated in figure 8–6.)

Transport Mechanism   The various mechanisms that move the tape from the feed reel to the take-up reel are called the **transport system**—as shown in figure 8–8. Note that the tape wraps almost completely around the drum in the type-C format. This gives the picture more stability, better resolution, and more sophisticated special effects capabilities.

With sophisticated broadcast machines, extreme care is taken to protect the tape from stretching or scratching. Some of the round tape guides are actually lubricated by compressed air. The *servo capstan,* the main drive mechanism that pulls the tape through the unit, keeps its firm grip on the tape by means of a vacuum pressure rather than with the usual pinch roller—thus protecting the tape from any potential abuse at that point. The capstan function is extremely important in that

it must maintain a constant tape speed. It does this by means of a feedback signal from the *control track* on the tape itself.

The video drum is but one of several magnetically activated heads within the transport section of a tape machine. In some of the new professional equipment, there may be six or more heads that perform various video, audio, control cueing, and erase functions. The configuration will vary with the complexity of the recorder. One can get an idea of this basic structure, however, from figure 8–9, which shows the arrangement of a VHS cassette unit.

"Upstream" of the video drum (before the moving tape reaches the drum), there is a full erase head. "Downstream" there is a unit that contains two separate heads—one for the control track and one for audio. Figure 8–9 also shows the way in which the two movable rollers engage the tape and pull it out of the cassette into the play/record position. They move along two grooved metal tracks (dotted lines) to put the tape into contact with the heads. (There are several other guides and rollers not shown in this figure.) The ¾-inch U-matic cassette machines operate in a similar fashion (al-

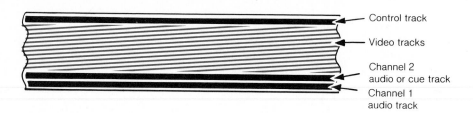

Figure 8–10
Configuration of ¾-inch
U-matic videotape format
(not to scale).

Control track

Video tracks

Channel 2
audio or cue track

Channel 1
audio track

though they are much more complicated)—a large loop of tape is pulled out of the cassette, wound around the drum, and put into contact with the other heads.[2]

8.3 Videotape Track Functions

As discussed previously, the videotape contains more information than just picture signals. Figure 8–10, for example, is a representation of the four tracks that are used by the U-matic format. Other VTR formats will use slightly different configurations to handle similar functions.

The Video Track   The portion of the videotape that carries the series of slanted video scanning lines is known as the *video track;* this occupies roughly 80 percent of the tape area in helical-scan formats. It is here that the information dealing with the picture signal, color, and brightness is carried. As mentioned previously, with the ¾-inch U-matic format (figure 8–10), the tape moves through the

transport assembly at the rate of approximately 3¾ inches per second. During this time, sixty of the slanted tracks are scanned to produce sixty fields—resulting in the rate of thirty completely scanned picture frames every second.

The 1-inch (type-C) and ½-inch VHS formats pack even more video information on the tape by means of the *Azimuth* system. With this process, the distance between the parallel lines is reduced even further by having alternate "A" and "B" video heads (two of each) touch the tape at slightly different angles.

Sony's Betacam recording system (figure 8–11) uses the A/B concept in a slightly different way. One video track carries the *luminance* (brightness) information, and the next track carries the *chrominance* (color) information. As described in section 8.2, this is the **component video** format with its separate Y and C video signals. Each of the tracks has two designated video heads. And there are also two "flying" erase heads—one for each track—revolving around the drum head (as opposed to stationary erase heads), needed to erase specific fields prior to editing in new information. The concept of keeping color and brightness information separate has many advantages in terms of picture control.

As shown in figure 8–11, in addition to the video tracks, there are several tracks on the videotape for other information—on the Betacam format as well as in all other formats. There are two *audio* tracks, a *control* track and a separate "address" or *cue* track at the bottom of the tape.

2. As with self-contained audio sources, the term *cassette* refers to a two-reeled unit in a semiclosed case; the videotape is not exposed to human handling. Once the cassette is inserted into its loading deck, the player mechanism automatically engages the tape around the recording head assembly. A *cartridge,* on the other hand, refers to a single-reel container that is, in effect, a sealed supply reel; the take-up reel is enclosed in the player mechanism. When the cartridge is inserted into the player, it is automatically threaded; again, human hands do not become involved in the loading and threading operation.

Function and Operation of the Videotape Recorder

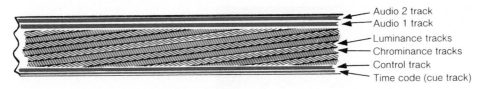

Figure 8–11
Configuration of ½-inch
Betacam format (not to
scale).

- Audio 2 track
- Audio 1 track
- Luminance tracks
- Chrominance tracks
- Control track
- Time code (cue track)

Note that alternate video tracks carry the luminance information while every other video track carries the chrominance signal.

The Control Track   In sections 5.2 and 8.1, we described how the continuous display of the picture on a monitor is synchronized with the original camera picture by means of *vertical* and *horizontal synchronization* pulses. For every 262.5 horizontal pulses, there is one vertical pulse that initiates the scanning of either the odd- or even-lined picture field. When a broadcast picture is received, it is these sync pulses that "lock together" the TV set with the camera signal.

When the television picture information is recorded, these sync pulses—and some related information—are separated from the color and brightness signals and recorded on an individual band or **control track** of the tape. During the playback of recorded videotape programs, the sync pulse serves an additional important purpose. The playback machine reads the signals and uses them to regulate the speed at which the *capstan* pulls the tape through the transport system—as well as the speed at which the video head wheel turns. This **servo control** system, in effect, tells the playback VTR exactly how fast the tape was moving when it was originally recorded.

The Cue Track (Optional Second Audio Track)   On older video recorders, a second audio track or **cue track** can be used either for an auxiliary audio track (for stereo broadcasting or for a second language audio track) or as a *cueing* track—so named because it was

originally used to record either verbal cues or high-frequency tones as cues for early editing systems.

This track is often used to lay down the signal for an editing location system called the **SMPTE time code.**[3] This location system produces a digital clocklike numerical readout or *address* for each hour, minute, second, and frame recorded on the videotape. It can reflect the "real time" at which the tape was being recorded, or it can be added later, showing time elapsed from the beginning of a production or from some other reference point on the tape. The readout, as illustrated in figure 8–12, can be displayed on the picture monitor by a process similar to the way titles are matted over any picture source.

For some editing applications, the *window* display becomes a part of a "workprint" tape dub and is seen as a permanent part of the picture. Also, during the editing process, the time code can be viewed by means of LED (light-emitting diode) readouts located at the control panel and on the machines themselves (as seen in figure 8–13).

In advanced editing systems (see section 9.5), a computer can "read" the unseen time code to locate predetermined edit points for the

3. This editing system was so named because the technical standards were established by the Society of Motion Picture and Television Engineers.

Figure 8–12
Display of time-code
information. The SMPTE
time code (hours, minutes,
seconds, and frames) is
displayed at the touch of a
button.

Figure 8–13
LED readout of the time
code on an EECO TCR–65.
In addition to the time code
showing directly on the
monitor, it can also be
displayed on editing
peripherals designed as
rack-mounted components.
(Photo courtesy of EECO
Incorporated)

execution of cuts, dissolves, and special effects. The system is used on most productions
at the network level—except for news. Time-
code referencing is especially important for
programs such as *Wide World of Sports*—or
the Olympics—where tapes from a number of
recorders in many different locations must later
be edited together in precise chronological
synchronization. Most contemporary tape
formats—such as the type-C standard—have
two *or more* audio tracks *plus* the cue track,
so that the time code can be utilized in conjunction with a stereo production or a dual-
language sound track.

It should be noted that newer ¾-inch
U-matic equipment has been developed that
allows the time code to be incorporated in an
unused portion of the video signal or placed on
a separate horizontal address track that over-
lays the slant video track. This frees the cue
track for use as a second audio track.

A form of SMPTE time code has been incorporated into the Sony Hi8 system, which
permits interaction with ¾-inch U-Matic and
other machines for editing purposes. It should
also be noted that there is a different type of
address system that utilizes the *control track
signal*. It is most commonly used for editing
on VHS systems. It works on the basis of a zero
point from which hours, minutes, seconds, and
frames on any piece of tape are determined.
This information, however, is not a permanent
part of the tape track itself, and the zero point
can be moved as necessary.

Function and Operation of the Videotape Recorder

The Audio Track   The audio track hardly needs further explanation. The technology involved is exactly that of conventional sound recording. It must be noted, however, that the quality is somewhat less than that of professional audio equipment used in recording studios. The television industry is just beginning to take advantage of its capacity for stereo and high-fidelity sound—up to the 15,000-Hertz level now heard on FM radio. As more home receivers are sold with this *MTS* (multi-channel television sound) capacity, more stations and cable systems will begin to make the necessary modifications for increased audio fidelity. Most VTR machines designed for educational and industrial use formerly had a 5,000-Hertz limitation, but newer equipment—including some of the Sony Hi8 line—have high-quality *PCM (pulse code modulation)* and stereo audio.

8.4 Video Recorder Operations and Controls

The setup and operation of any VTR machine involves the use of components that generally fall under three headings: *connectors, control mechanisms,* and *visual indicators.* The arrangement, appearance, and even terminology may vary with the manufacturer—but once one knows what to look for, these basic components can be identified on any video recorder.

First, since videotape machines work in conjunction with other electronic units (cameras, switchers, microphones, other recorders, speakers, receivers, editing equipment, and so forth), you must be able to make such hookups as a primary step. Second, you must learn how to manipulate the collection of knobs, switches, levers, and push buttons that are used to start, stop, or change the basic audio and video func-

tions of record, playback, and editing. Third, you must be able to monitor and understand those things that tell whether or not the machine is operating the way you want it to—feedback provided by items such as lights and meters.

Connections

Of these three concerns, it is often the area of *connections* that demands the most care and attention. In a studio situation where equipment and its related cables are permanently in place, the connection process takes place primarily at the patch bays where labeled receptacles indicate the sources and termination points of feeds.

However, much of the small-format video for educational and industrial purposes—and much of the semi-EFP production for training purposes—involves a temporary "lash-up" of video recorders, cameras, mikes, monitors, and associated gear in out-of-studio, *field* locations (see chapter 15). In either case—whether in the studio or not—the operational linking of components is most efficiently accomplished when three interacting factors are kept in mind:

1. The nature and purpose of all signal feeds
2. The direction and pathway of all signal flow
3. The structure of the connective hardware

If you know *what* your signal is supposed to do, it is easier to know *where* it should be going and *how* you are going to have to connect it to get it there.

Figure 8–14 is a composite drawing of the sort of receptacles you would find on half-inch home recorders and industrial-level VCR machines. This illustration indicates the variety of different connections that handle audio and

Figure 8–14
Video recorder connection area (composite illustration).

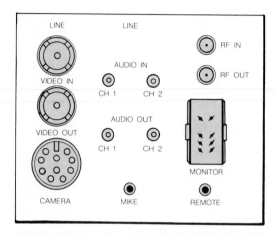

video signals. This apparent duplication of inputs is due to the fact that the elements of picture and sound are processed in differing strengths and formats during various stages of both recording and playback. Most machines are designed to accommodate a number of recording, playback, and editing situations.

Signal Flow   The first thing to keep in mind when making any connection is simply whether you are dealing with an *input* or an *output*. You should first look at a wiring diagram. If one is not available, the very act of making a sketch of the probable *sequence of signal flow* will bring some order to the process. Does the receptacle into which you are putting one end of a cable represent the signal output of a component? If so, with that connection made, the other end of the cable obviously becomes the new output of the signal—and as a result goes into an input receptacle to continue the movement of the signal. It must be emphasized that incorrect connections not only cause operational delay, they can cause serious damage to equipment by overloading circuits.

Signal Levels   One of the main principles involved in the connection process is that of understanding the different types of signals

that one deals with in making those hookups. In addition to knowing audio from video feeds, one must realize that signals vary in amplification and that some signals are combined to become *composite* signals. The basic concept of amplification differences was introduced in discussing audio patching—both amplification considerations (section 2.2.4) and impedance levels (section 3.1).

The same principle applies to the way in which the video recorder handles audio and video. The recorder has a provision for the input of an external microphone ("mike in"). This low-level signal is then amplified to *line level* within the machine before being recorded on tape. However, previously amplified signals (an audio recorder, for example) are only to be plugged into "line" audio inputs. If these are plugged into a "mike" input, you will get a distortion from the double amplification.[4]

The traditional television signal, which is broadcast to the home, is an example of a *composite signal*. Audio and video from the studio have been *modulated* into an **RF** (*radio frequency*) signal; that is, the audio and video information have been superimposed on a radio-frequency carrier wave in order to be broadcast through space as part of the electromagnetic spectrum (section 2.2.1).[5] This signal picked up by your TV antenna is then

4. Recall our discussion regarding impedance levels (section 3.1). In the studio, where the distance from the mike to the audio console may be up to fifty feet, a *low-impedance* (low-line resistance) cable and microphone are used. However, home VCRs and many industrial-level recorders are designed to work with less expensive *high-impedance* (greater resistance) mikes and lines—designed to carry not more than six to eight feet. If you mismatch these two elements, you will cause intolerable audio distortion.

5. A pure unmodulated audio or video *line* signal can be distributed only over a cable or closed circuit. Generally this video signal is of higher quality than an RF signal. However, in order to broadcast a signal, it must be encoded or modulated onto the carrier wave and then decoded (demodulated) by your home receiver.

Function and Operation of the Videotape Recorder

carried on a twin-lead (2-wired) 300-ohm line to your set. If the signal is transformed to be carried on a 75-ohm coaxial shielded cable, it is then the same type of signal that comes from your local cable TV company. All home and industrial VCRs have provisions for both input and output of the RF signal. They also have line-level inputs (and outputs) so that they can receive and record pure unmodulated video and audio (line) feeds from a camera or other VCR. Recall that line video signals can be either *composite* or *component* (section 8.2).

Connecting Hardware Connective hardware for audio and video equipment involves a wide variety of receptacles and matching plugs. For example, *line video* may utilize a BNC, UHF, or RCA phono plug. *Audio* is usually handled by a phone plug, Sony mini-plug, or RCA plug. With low-impedance mike lines, a three-pin Cannon Connector is quite common. See figure 8–15 for an idea of the most commonly used connecting hardware.

Temporary setups for audio mixing, video editing, and camera work often mean borrowing components from various sources and lashing together pieces that were not designed by the same manufacturer—much less at a similar point in video development. Figure 8–16 shows the rear connection panel for the Sony VO 4800 video recorder. Its variety of receptacles is still typical of many smaller portable recorders.

Manufacturers are well aware of the numerous pieces of equipment that both professional and consumer video users will have to tie together. They try to provide for as many alternatives as possible. A good example of the sort of redundancy that is built into even consumer-level products is found in the number of options that exist for getting signals from a camcorder into either a standard video recorder or an S-VHS model for dubbing and editing.

The Magnavox Escort C-format model, for instance, has two multiple-pin receptacles on the side of the camcorder. One receptacle is an output for the four-pin S-VHS video signal, and its cable connects to a similar input at the rear of the recorder. The other receptacle takes one of two plugs. One connects to an RF transformer that has a two-way switch for feeding either the camcorder output or an antenna feed to the recorder. (This is an RF, not an S-VHS, signal.) The second option splits its output into ordinary line-level audio and video signals. There may seem to be an overlap of function here, but thinking carefully about the consumer's needs, the manufacturer has provided for every eventuality.

Adapters, Splitters, and Terminators
Because of all of the differences in plugs and receptacles, the connecting process is greatly aided if one has a good supply of **adapter plugs** on hand (see figure 8–17). It should also be noted that a variety of cables are available with different connectors at the two ends. Such cables often make the most convenient types of adapter. With a variety of these on hand, one can quickly connect a number of components from different manufacturers with some degree of confidence. However, caution and common sense should always be exercised when making such connections. One simply cannot make a high-impedance mike function with a low-impedance cable by trying to use an adapter.

Attempting to connect two or more audio or video monitors to a single feed calls for the use of another type of specialized connector—a **splitter.** For instance, "Y" and "T" plugs allow you to tap into a line and send the signal to two different points—feeding one monitor while sending a signal on to another. The effect is much the same as using an *RF splitter* on your home system to send an incoming cable TV signal to more than one receiver. However, splitting a signal does weaken its strength, and

Figure 8-15
Commonly used audio and
video plugs and
connectors.

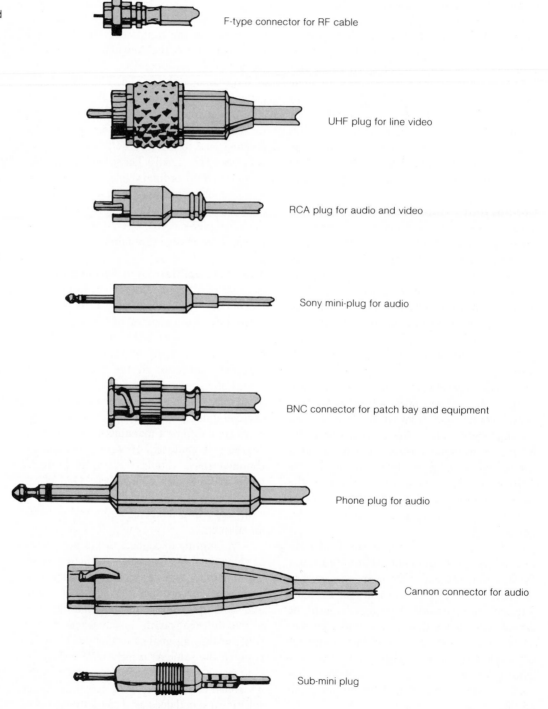

F-type connector for RF cable

UHF plug for line video

RCA plug for audio and video

Sony mini-plug for audio

BNC connector for patch bay and equipment

Phone plug for audio

Cannon connector for audio

Sub-mini plug

Function and Operation of the Videotape Recorder

AUDIO OUT jacks
(phono)

DC IN 12V connector

EARPHONE JACK

EARPHONE LEVEL
control

VIDEO OUT
connector
(BNC)

RF OUT connector

TRACKING control

MIC/LINE select
switches

AUDIO IN jacks (mini)

Battery compartment
(closed)

VIDEO IN connector
(BNC)

CAMERA/TV
connector
(Q type)

INPUT SELECT
switch

Figure 8–16
Sony VO 4800 rear panel connections. The input-output panel is designed to provide compatibility with equipment found in professional studios. (Photo courtesy of Sony Corporation)

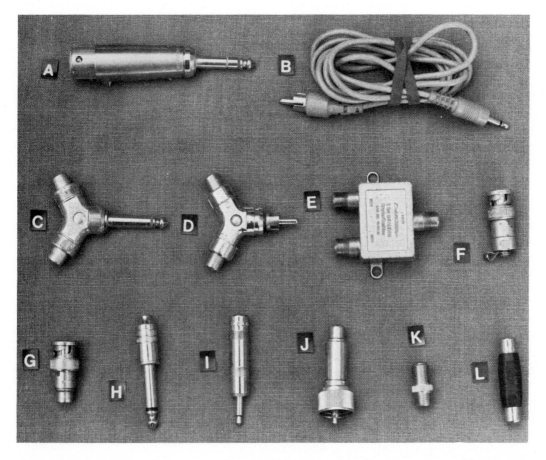

Figure 8–17
Some of the more common adapters, splitters, and terminators found in typical video and audio hookups: (A) convertor plug, female cannon to phone jack; (B) RCA to mini-plug convertor line; (C) phone jack to female RCA splitter; (D) RCA male to RCA female splitter; (E) RF (75-ohm) splitter; (F) BNC terminator; (G) RCA female to BNC convertor; (H) mini-plug to phone jack convertor; (I) phone jack to mini-plug convertor; (J) RCA to UHF convertor; (K) RF barrel plug; (L) RCA barrel plug.

Function and Operation of the Videotape Recorder

thus additional amplification may be needed. Most industrial video monitors can easily be set up in series so that the "video out" receptacle from one monitor can feed the same signal on to the next set. However, in this case, the final monitor in the chain must **terminate** the signal flow—either by means of a termination switch or with a video termination plug. (See figure 8–17.)

Power Sources   Another type of connection to be considered is the AC power and/or battery source. The internal battery in the Sony VO 4800, for example, can power the recorder and camera for up to an hour of continuous use when fully charged. Over a period of time, however, batteries lose the ability to hold a charge, and battery time is always precious. For that reason, most portable recorders have an AC power adapter/charger for use wherever AC power is available. This unit is also used to recharge the battery as needed.

It is not uncommon to find an AC power outlet located alongside the input/output connections on the recorder. Most manuals will list a 500-watt limit when this outlet is to be used to power lighting equipment or some other component. It is important to note that the provision for the third rounded prong is an important grounding device. Do not try to defeat this safety feature. It also helps to ensure that the other two prongs go into the proper power outlets. If a two-prong adapter is used to go into a two-pronged wall receptacle, the ground wire on the adapter should be connected to the screw that fastens the wall socket plate to its wall box, or to some other suitable ground.

Again, in thinking through the connections to be made with any system—regardless of how simple or how sophisticated the recorder and its components may be—it is important to think ahead and carefully plot out the types of connections to be made. Try to visualize all of the related signal flows—as emphasized at the beginning of section 2.2.2.

What is the signal supposed to do? *Where* must it be directed? And *how* must it be properly connected?

Controls

Regardless of the age or simplicity of design, the transport (tape movement) functions on all video recorders will have eight to ten basic controls. Normal-speed playback is accomplished by activating the control (pressing a button on most models) labeled either *play* or *forward*. The recording mode is initiated by pressing *play/forward* simultaneously with the *record* button; this activates the record head while the tape is moving forward in the play mode. (Because there is the possibility of accidentally pressing the record button at the wrong time and inadvertently erasing information on the tape, the record control is usually interlocked with the play button so that it can be activated only when they are both pressed at the same time.)

On most cassette machines, the *stop* control not only stops the tape movement, but it also causes the tape to unwind from the video drum and be retracted into the cassette. This allows the *eject* control to be used to remove the cassette from the machine. "Stop" should not be confused with the *pause* control that halts forward tape movement but leaves the tape in contact with the heads that are still revolving. In this "pause" mode, the heads continue to scan the same slant-track over and over again. This produces, on some machines, the "freeze-frame" effect. However, the machine should not be left in this mode for more than a minute or so at one time as the heads are continually wearing away at the oxide on one specific track; tape damage and/or head clog can occur—especially when old or inexpensive tape is being used.[6]

6. On professional editing machines, such as the Sony BVU 800 and 820, the *stop* button actually puts the machine into the "freeze-frame" *pause* mode. Head movement stops only when the *eject* button is pressed.

To get the tape quickly from one point to another, *fast-forward* and *rewind* controls are used. On some units, these two modes will produce a somewhat recognizable picture for "search" purposes. Many VTRs—especially those designed for editing—also will have *variable-speed* controls that facilitate slow or speeded-up motion, either forward or backward.

The *audio dub* (audio edit) control puts the audio record head into the record mode—without activating the video record heads. This enables you to make audio-only edits or to lay in a whole new audio track.

There is one other control that is important to accurate tape transport. The path of the tape around the video drum is crucial to the playback of a proper picture. Bands of picture distortion sometimes result when a tape recorded on one machine is played back on another VTR with a slightly different horizontal alignment. This problem can usually be corrected by an adjustment of the *tracking* control. The normal operating setting as determined by the factory is located at the top point (12 o'clock position) on the dial. The slight click one feels when passing this point is known as a "detent" position. After any tracking adjustment is made, the knob should be returned to this position for each new recording or playback.

On studio-based recorders designed for production playback and/or editing purposes, the controls (and their related meters and indicators) become more numerous and at first seem quite complex to the uninitiated operator. It helps to keep in mind that each control has been created to help make the job easier or to maintain the best possible picture quality.

For example, on most professional units, there is an additional control for the tape transport called *skew*. When the top third of the picture appears to bend to the left or the right, it is usually caused by an incorrect amount of tension on the tape as it passes around the video drum. This is adjusted by means of the skew control knob. Keep in mind that this is a problem on the playback machine, not on the machine to which you are editing or dubbing. As with the tracking control, the knob should always be returned to the detent position before that same machine can be used for a subsequent recording or playback.

Selector Switches   As discussed previously, most video recorders are designed to function with a variety of different types of inputs such as a *camera,* the tuner in a *receiver/monitor,* or a studio *line* feed. There must, therefore, be an *input selector switch* that differentiates among the various levels and/or sync sources of these inputs. The advice of a studio technician may be needed to determine proper switch position. Whereas a camera signal from the studio switcher would feed through the line input, a single camera might utilize some other selector position.

On some machines there is another switch that separately controls the use of internal or external *sync sources.* (On several VTR makes, the alternative to the external position is labeled "defeat.") This *internal sync* position allows the recorder to "strip off" any incoming sync signal and utilize the synchronization pulse from the machine itself during the recording process.

Visual Indicators and Meters

Our final area of concern is with visual monitoring and feedback indicators. Although these will vary from machine to machine, there are a number of controls that group together in operational units and directly relate to a visual readout—starting with the *pilot light* that indicates when the *power on/off* switch is activated.

One important indicator on most VTR machines is the *VU meter.* Some machines have multiple meters—perhaps one for each

Figure 8–18

The control panel on the
Sony VO 4800 shows how
a single control system (VU
meter) can be used for
multiple functions
(monitoring video level,
battery condition, audio
channel 1, and audio
channel 2). (Courtesy of
Sony Corporation)

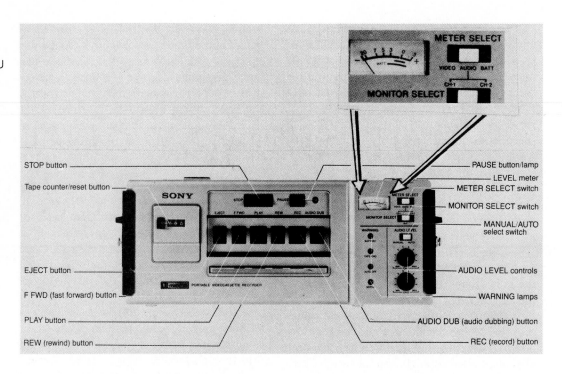

STOP button — PAUSE button/lamp

LEVEL meter

Tape counter/reset button — METER SELECT switch

MONITOR SELECT switch

MANUAL/AUTO
select switch

EJECT button — AUDIO LEVEL controls

F FWD (fast forward) button — WARNING lamps

PLAY button — AUDIO DUB (audio dubbing) button

REW (rewind) button — REC (record) button

audio channel and one for the level of the video
signal. However, the number of meters does not
necessarily correlate with the sophistication of
the machine. As an example of effective
economy of design, the Sony VO 4800 (figure
8–18) has only one VU meter. By means of
monitor and selector switches, this one meter
can show the video level, either or both audio
channels, or the battery strength. There is, of
course, a separate *potentiometer* for each of
the two audio channels. (Video gain is adjusted at the camera control.)

Although the VO 4800 is an older model,
it is included here because it is typical of the
sort of portable recorders that have remained
in use in spite of the popularity of camcorders.
While ENG applications find camcorders ideal
for their ease of operation in fast-moving situations, many producers who do location shoots
for longer periods of time prefer to establish
temporary "lash-ups" with portable recorders,
monitors, and a camera with tripod or pedestal.

In answer to these overlapping needs, the
industry has responded with the design of a
camera and recorder having a "dockability"
option. When docked together, you have a sophisticated camcorder. With the components
disconnected, you have both an individual
camera and a separate video recorder. If the
camcorder shown in figure 8–19 seems to have
an elaborate control panel, it is because the rear
of the unit is actually a removable video recorder—the Sony Hi8 EVV-9000. The front
is a separate camera, the DXC-325. As a
"stand-alone" camera, it can feed video to Betacam or U-matic portable recorders through
an adapter unit.

Automatic Gain Control   Most portable
recorders have an *automatic gain control*
(AGC) option for audio. When this is switched
on, the AGC serves as a limiter (section 2.2.5)
that keeps incoming audio feeds within a range
that does not exceed the capabilities of the re-

Figure 8–19
The Sony EVV-9000. What would appear to be a camcorder is actually a "dockable" Sony EVV-9000 video recorder mounted with a Sony DXC-325 camera. The camera can operate as a "stand-alone" unit or it can be connected by cable to a separate portable video recorder.

corder. However, the AGC often will automatically boost the "noise" of the line signal when there is momentarily no other incoming signal (a pause in the voice or music source), thereby recording an amplified hiss. The AGC selector switch allows you to defeat this feature.

Most machines will reflect their recording and editing functions with additional video control switches and indicators. There will be a *video control* knob that adjusts the level of incoming video—as well as a related *AGC off-on* switch that allows for automatic gain control of the video signal. These are usually grouped with the video VU meter.

An increasing number of portable recorders are including a number of warning lights and status indicators that provide several types of important feedback to the operator. On some machines there is a *pause mode* light that serves as a reminder that the heads are continuing to scan the tape. There are also lights that indicate the condition of the *battery,* the presence of moisture that is dangerous to the circuitry (*auto off hr.*), a *tape supply* warning light, and a *servo* lamp that warns of improper tape transport.

Counters and Location Indicators

Virtually all recorders have some sort of *counter* or other component that allows an operator to locate predetermined points on a recorded tape. On portable machines and older studio models, there is simply a three- or four-digit readout that counts the revolutions of the take-up reel. Since the circumference of the

Figure 8–20
The Panasonic video recorder AG 7500 is a high-resolution Super-VHS (S-VHS) industrial-quality editing VCR designed to interface with the AG 750 edit controller. Note that the conventional revolutions counter has been replaced by a time-code display (right side of the central panel) in hours, minutes, seconds, and frames. (Photo courtesy of Panasonic Industrial Company)

tape on each reel will change as the reels unwind and wind, the operator must keep in mind that a given number of revolutions will indicate differing amounts of tape footage—depending upon how far into the program one is.

There is also a counter *reset* button that allows the operator to set the counter at zero at the beginning of the tape—or to designate an arbitrary "zero point" anywhere on the reel.

Advanced industrial models, such as the Panasonic AG 7500 (figure 8–20), have an LED readout in hours, minutes, and seconds based on the control track signal. An important adjunct to these search controls is the *memory on* switch that allows the operator to mark any new point on the tape as a new zero point. When put into rewind or fast forward, the machine will return to this point and come to a stop.

Units such as the Ampex VPR-300 have an electronic readout panel that can be used to display a variety of status functions—depending upon what diagnostic, recording, playback, or editing information the operator needs (see figure 8–21).

Recorders that have the hours-minutes-seconds electronic readout operate on the basis of signal information derived from the control track on the tape—as differentiated from the SMPTE time code (used on much broadcast-quality editing equipment), which comes from the cue track (section 8.3). Both of these electronic digital readouts are designed to work with *variable-speed* control dials. They are engineered to allow the operator to "feel" the speed and direction of tape movement. At the straight-up detent position, the tape is in "pause." The more you twist the dial to the right (clockwise), the faster the tape moves forward. As you turn the dial to the left (counterclockwise), the tape moves in reverse (rewind)—again with the speed determined by the extent you turn the dial. On most machines, speeds range from slow motion one-frame-at-a-time to five or more times normal speed.

Successful Performance and Maintenance The key to successful operation of the videotape recorder—whether a complex broadcast-quality machine or a simple

Function and Operation of the Videotape Recorder

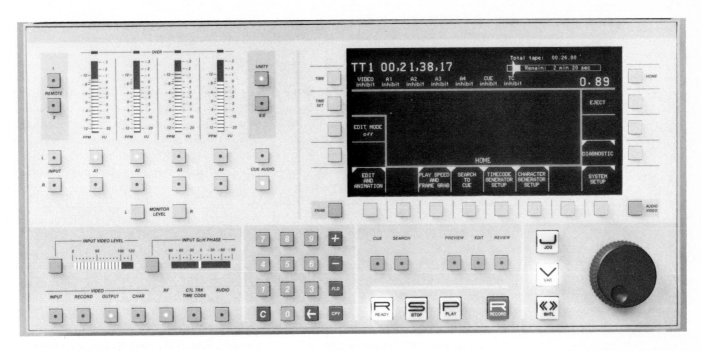

backpack for basic location recordings—is *familiarity* and *practice*. Instructions and specific controls will, of course, vary significantly from machine to machine. Become familiar with the ones you have access to. Make certain you have taken full advantage of the instructions and directions for the particular models you will be working with. Especially, follow the recommended care and maintenance instructions; this is particularly important for routine cleaning of the video heads. And then practice. Become familiar with the recorder. Under the guidance of a trained technician or instructor, work with the machine; experiment with it. Find out what it will and will not do. And then you should have the confidence and discipline to handle any video recording and playback assignment given to you.

A major part of your professional discipline will be care and respect for all production equipment; and the video recorder is one of the most expensive and delicate machines you will handle. Everyone will benefit if you follow a few common rules of preventative maintenance.

1. Videotape recorders require a constantly renewed supply of clean, cool, dry air. Heat, moisture, and cigarette smoke are damaging to all electronic equipment—especially VTR machines. Never place books, cassette cases, or papers on top of the recorder; it seriously inhibits the flow of air. Liquid containers and ashtrays—anywhere adjacent to video recorders—are simply a disaster in the making.

2. Place a dust cover on the machine when it is not in use—but only after the unit has had time to cool off.

3. When a video recorder is moved, be extremely careful not to bump or jar the unit. Delicate components are easily damaged by slight shocks. Do not attempt to operate a recorder immediately after it has been moved from a cold to a warm environment.

Figure 8–21
The control panel of the Ampex VPR-300 features an extensive array of electronic readouts for operator convenience.

4. Videotape should not be left in the recorder when the unit is not in use. Tapes should be rewound and properly stored in a cool, dry place.
5. Keep the recorder and tapes at a distance from other equipment that may be generating strong magnetic fields.
6. Do not tinker with various controls and functions without a clear purpose and idea of what you are doing. Do not fool around, for example, with the color lock control and other critical mechanisms. Maintenance personnel who are unaware of the misadjustments may spend hours trying to find and correct the resulting problems.
7. As the videotape operator, always allow yourself time to carefully think through all connecting and patching procedures—as well as the basic disciplines of machine operation. The time spent always pays off later in time saved.

Summary

The video recording process involves an understanding of the entire electromagnetic concept. For our purposes, we have looked at two aspects of the electromagnetic phenomenon—*electronic principles* (such as the horizontal and vertical sync pulses) and *magnetic principles* (the electromagnetic properties of an electrical current rearranging iron oxide or metal particles) to record a video signal on videotape.

The first VTR machine, introduced in the late 1950s, was the *quadruplex videotape recorder,* which utilized four revolving video heads to record video information transversely to the path of the 2-inch tape. The bulky and expensive quad-head machines have largely been supplanted by the *helical-scan video recorder,* which wraps its narrower tape around a cylindrical head drum in a slant-track pattern.

Both *reel-to-reel recorders* (such as the broadcast-quality 1-inch C-format machines) and the *cassette recorders* (like the professional ¾-inch U-matic, the ½-inch Betamax and VHS home formats, and the combination camera-recorder [*camcorder*] such as the Sony Betacam) have videotape configurations that include space for picture information, control track, cue signals, and audio track(s).

Operational functions for VTR machines include three considerations: *connections* (with cameras, switcher, line feeds, microphones, other recorders, speakers, monitors, editing facilities, and so forth); *controls* (for all operating modes such as play, record, fast forward, rewind, stop, pause, variable speed, dubbing and editing, input and sync selection, tracking and skewing adjustments); and *indicators* (lights, VU meters, counter, and so forth).

In chapter 9, we continue looking at the video recording process as it applies specifically to electronic editing.

8.5 Training Exercise

Ideally, each student should be able to go through the following exercise individually. If time or facilities do not permit, students may be assigned in pairs.

On the videotape recorder(s) available in your facility, go through every step mentioned in the chapter. Thread the VTR machine and work with it in every function: play, fast forward, rewind. Record some sample programming from the studio. Use the pause-hold modes; experiment with any variable-speed controls. Carefully, with engineering supervision, familiarize yourself with other adjustments such as tracking and skewing.

Function and Operation of the Videotape Recorder

Videotape Editing Equipment and Techniques

●●●●●●●●●●●●●●●●

Previous chapters have dealt primarily with video production that is for the most part accomplished by means of **real-time editing.** This multiple-camera technique requires considerable preproduction planning and rehearsal of camera shot assignments. Program elements must be carefully timed and organized into their projected sequence. During a live broadcast, the task of the director is largely that of making a series of precise editing decisions.

The technical director uses the switcher to connect the succeeding elements of the program by means of takes, dissolves, and special effects such as wipes and mattes. Prerecorded segments on disc, tape, and film are combined with the live camera inputs—all within the time disciplines of the continuous production operation. The spontaneous aspect of real-time production gives sports, news, and even game shows an important sense of immediacy and realism.

These benefits notwithstanding, there are also some serious difficulties that arise from working within the time constraints of the live or live-on-tape technique. The director, working in a moment-by-moment decision process, must also be constantly alert for unforeseen production difficulties. When the director is forced to solve production problems while on the air, there is a good chance that the overall quality of the production will suffer. Many types of programs simply do not fit well into this studio concept of television production because they are composed of individual segments often shot out of sequence and frequently shot in different locations. A different type of assembly or editing process, similar to that used in film, can be more effective.

In this chapter we will look at the production options that have been made possible by electronic editing and explore the equipment, processes, aesthetics, and procedures involved with editing.

9.1 Reasons for Videotape Editing

Editing is used for a wide variety of purposes. Probably the most obvious reason is to cover mistakes. Someone may muff a line; a piece of scenery may fall down; a camera may be out of focus; a careless onlooker might slam the studio door. Rather than redoing the whole program, the small segment with the mistake can be reshot correctly and inserted to cover the error. Or if the error is caught in time, the production can be stopped, and the remainder of the program can be completed from a spot immediately prior to the mistake.

Sometimes it is not actual mistakes that lead to editing but rather a desire to improve or **sweeten** a program. For example, the pace of a game show may drag at some point so part of it will be removed. Or—involving a more controversial technique—the audience reaction may not be as lively as desired, so a laugh track is added.

One of the earliest uses of videotape editing revolved around the desire to tape elements of a program out of order—particularly prevalent in variety shows. Because of availability of talent or complicated production changes, acts could be taped in some order other than that of the final show. Or the production could be interrupted while complicated scenery or costume changes were effected; then the segments would be assembled in the proper order.

Also, sometimes a number of sequences would be taped at one time for inclusion in several shows. This is often done for soap operas as well as for variety shows. A guest star who is to appear in four or five programs may only be available for taping on one day, so all of his or her segments are recorded on that one day and inserted in programs as they are later assembled.

Even when programs are edited through the switcher and taped straight through from beginning to end, one or more of the individual cameras may be separately *slaved* to a videotape recorder. This means that although the camera's output is going to the switcher, it is also going to a separate videotape recorder that is recording everything the camera shoots, even when it is not "on the air." The director can look at the separate recordings later and change decisions made at the time of the taping. For example, the director may have switched to camera 2 for a close-up during taping and then later decided that the reaction shot on camera 3 would be better. This reaction shot from the *slaved* camera, also known as the **isolated camera,** can then be substituted in the editing process. This method is frequently used, for example, with situation comedies.

In fact, sometimes the shows are shot with multiple isolated, slaved cameras and no "live" switching at all during the taping. The program is edited together later when the director can look at all shots leisurely and decide which are best in which situation. Figure 9–1 shows the signal feed configuration of a commonly used **iso** setup with each camera slaved to a separate video recorder.

Editing also is used when material shot outside the studio is incorporated within a studio production. News programs are an excellent example of this. The news anchor in the studio may lead off with a story about a fire. Various edited shots of the fire are then rolled into the program.

Of course, some programs are shot entirely out of the studio and edited at a later time. Numerous variations of this approach exist. Sometimes the programs are shot and edited on film; other programs are shot on film, transferred to tape, and edited on tape; and, of course, many location productions are shot on

Videotape Editing Equipment and Techniques

tape and edited on tape. This type of shooting-editing is common for documentaries and dramas shot mostly on location.

So for a variety of reasons, out-of-studio editing has become very prevalent in television production. Although there are still some programs that are live or live-on-tape, most productions today involve some type of **postproduction** editing.

9.2 Methods of Editing

Early editing of videotape was performed much the same as film editing in that the tape was physically cut and then spliced together. This was a very tedious and inaccurate process because pictures on tape are not visible to the eye as they are on film. A microscope-like device (see figure 9–2) was used to see where frames ended, but it was time-consuming, was cumbersome, and often yielded unacceptable edits. Even edits that were spliced correctly tended to cause picture breakup. This type of physical editing did not last long.

Crash Editing   Physical editing of videotape was replaced by what later became known as *crash editing.* A special edit button forced a VTR into the record mode. The operator would get two machines up to speed and essentially dub from one to the other whenever the edit button was activated. This kind of editing was dependent on the speed of the human hand and the speed at which the recorder's electronics could react. While this was an improvement over physical editing, it was still unsatisfactory because precise edits seldom could be made and the edits often had **glitches**—rolling frames or momentary picture breakup—when the edit did not take place precisely in synchronization.

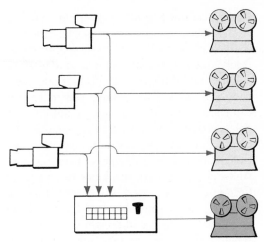

Figure 9–1
Studio cameras feeding signals to individual "isolated" tape recorders.

While the switcher is used to feed the "live" edited program to a master VTR, each camera is also feeding its individual signal directly to its own VTR for later postproduction editing and fine cutting.

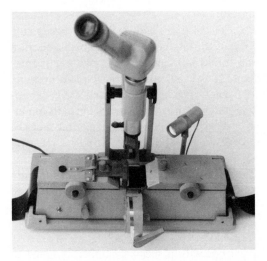

Figure 9–2
Early Ampex VR-1000 tape splicer.

This piece of equipment was used to make physical edits on 2-inch videotape. The editor would chemically treat the tape to make the actual blanking intervals visible and then use the microscope to look at the impulses on the videotape to determine where a frame ended so that the tape could be physically cut and spliced. (Equipment courtesy of John Streets, Merlin Engineering Works)

Control-Track Editing   A more sophisticated type of editing involves using the videotape's control track. The sync pulse of this track (sections 5.1 and 8.1) is used to produce a numerical location that reads in frames, seconds, and minutes. An editing controller that can count pulses to both edit-in and edit-out points is connected to VCRs that can play and record material. An operator uses the controller to mark editing points. Then the controller backs up both machines to give them time to get up to speed, starts them forward in sync, counts control pulses to the edit-in points, and starts the edit—which is again basically a dub from the machine with the information on it to the one recording the material. If the edit-out point has been electronically marked, the controller will also terminate the edit. The operator also has the option of pushing a special button that will stop the edit.

Control-track editing is an acceptable form of editing, but it has drawbacks because the frame location numbers are not permanent. They exist only in relation to a movable "0" point, which can be changed by the operator at any time. Sometimes the edits are inaccurate because edit points slip after they are previewed.

Time-Code Editing   SMPTE time-code editing was developed by a special committee of the Society of Motion Picture and Television Engineers. It was the original professional frame-location system. Each frame of video is identified with a specific number assigned to it. As mentioned in section 8.3, this system produces a digital clocklike numerical readout or address for each hour, minute, second, and frame recorded on the videotape.

This form of editing requires a time-code generator that writes the code on the tape, a reader that reads it from the tape, and an editing controller that can respond to time code. This makes time-code editing more expensive than control-track editing, which uses the sync pulses that are already part of any videotape configuration. Because of the added expense, many colleges and low-budget industrial producers use control-track editing rather than time-code editing.

The time code can be added to the tape in one of two places. Sometimes it utilizes one of the audio tracks and, as such, is referred to as *longitudinal time code*. This, of course, means that one of the audio tracks is lost as far as the recording of a second audio track is concerned. The other place where time code can be applied is in the section of the tape known as the vertical interval. This is the *retrace* area where the scanning process stops at the bottom of the frame and returns to the top of the frame. Because it uses the *vertical blanking interval,* this type of time code is known as **VITC (vertical interval time code).**

Time-code editing is very accurate because each frame always has the same address. If an edit is to be made at 1:20:46:10 (1 hour, 20 minutes, 46 seconds, and 10 frames into the program), the edit will occur precisely at that frame—there will be no slippage. Also, decisions can be made with the computer-controlled editing equipment and changed before the actual editing takes place. Once the edit address is entered into the electronic editor's memory, that exact spot can always be found again to undertake the edit.

9.3 Editing Equipment

In its simplest form, editing requires three basic pieces of equipment. However, it can also utilize a full complement of control room and studio equipment. The three basic pieces of equipment are the *source* or playback videotape deck, the *edit* or recording deck, and the **controller** or editor. Usually, both the source and edit decks will have monitors so their outputs can be viewed. However, with some of the

Videotape Editing Equipment and Techniques

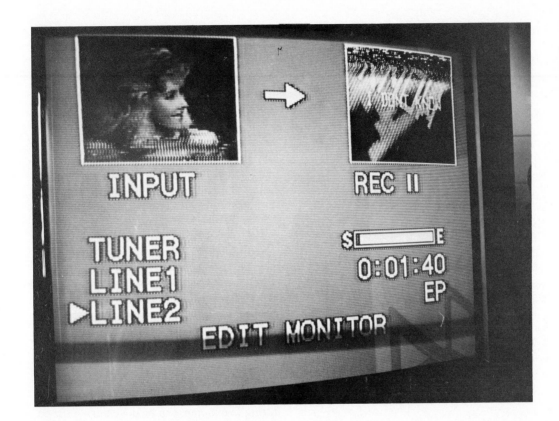

Figure 9–3
A regular TV set can be used to display both the source and edit outputs for this Sony VHS consumer-grade editing system.

newer editing systems, both the source and edit outputs can be seen on one screen at the same time. Such a configuration is shown in figure 9–3.

The Source Deck   The source deck (also referred to as the *playback* deck) is the video recorder that contains the material that will be edited—the segments shot in the studio and material recorded in the field. The source deck is basically like any other videocassette recorder, having the usual functions—fast forward, play, rewind, and so forth. One control that is particularly important to the editing function is the *tracking knob*. (See section 8.4.) If tracking is not adjusted so as to match the setting on the original recording machine, a *banding* effect will occur—a severe picture breakup where a horizontal strip of the picture

will lose its sync. With some equipment, there often is also a related *skewing* adjustment that must be checked.

The Edit Deck   The edit deck (also referred to as the *record* deck or the *master* deck) is the one onto which the selected material is edited. On the edit deck you would load a blank tape or the program that needs to have a segment corrected. This machine resembles a regular VCR but contains extra electronics and function controls that allow it to accept signals that select and execute the editing procedure.

The Edit Controller   The edit controller is the brains of the editing setup. Usually it is possible to use this unit to execute the normal functions of both the source and edit decks (fast forward, stop, rewind, play, and so on).

Figure 9–4
The Panasonic AG 750 edit controller is designed to interface with both VHS and S-VHS edit decks. Most editing systems feature simultaneous display of picture information from both the original source and edit VCR decks. When both machines are in pause at the edit points, you can see clearly how your edit will look. This can help prevent continuity problems.

Other Equipment   This basic setup of two VCRs and a controller can be used for edits that use only straight cuts. If the editing is to include dissolves, special effects, audio mixing, or other more complicated functions, other equipment must be brought into play—additional source VCRs, the switcher, the audio board, the character generator. In these editing situations, the output of each source VCR must be fed through a time-base corrector so as to coordinate the differing sync signals of the VCR units with those of the switcher used for the dissolve. (See section 5.1.)

Incorporating control room equipment into the editing process means that the director can do anything that would be part of a live taping situation—and then some. The edits that are made can utilize all the dissolves, fades, keys, wipes, and other special effects that the technical director could execute during taping. However, they can be programmed and made with more care so that they occur at precisely the right moment. Also, some effects, such as the *still frame,* which cannot be accomplished during live taping, can be done during the editing process.

Many productions that utilize extensive *postproduction editing* will contract this job out to specialized companies. As pictured in figure 9–5, these companies feature the latest in editing equipment as well as appealing "creature comforts" for the clients.

Studio equipment can also be used in the editing process. A shot from a camera can be routed through the switcher and edited into a tape. This is not done very often because it ties up a whole studio for one simple editing insertion. Also, more control is possible if the shot to be inserted comes from the source VTR—because the tape can be stopped at any point, precise edit points can be determined, and the edit can be previewed.

The type of edit—insert, assemble, audio-only (see sections 9.4 and 9.6)—is also selected on the controller. In addition, it has a search dial (or **joystick** on older models) that enables the operator to move the tape of either machine at varying fast and slow speeds, seeing it on the monitor at all times. It also has buttons that provide the operator with a means of setting the points where edits are to begin and end. Usually there is a **trim** function so that edit points can be moved several frames without having to reset them totally. And the edit controller (see figure 9–4) has provisions that enable the operator to preview an edit to make sure it will look right, then to automatically execute the edit, and finally to review the edit to make sure it was successful.

Videotape Editing Equipment and Techniques

Figure 9-5
Two modern editing facilities. *Top*, this postproduction editing studio has been designed with "human engineering" factors in mind. Easy access to equipment, soft lighting, and comfortable working stations are important when editing sessions may last twelve hours or longer. (Photo courtesy of Pacific Video) *Bottom*, this Editel editing facility is designed primarily for film-to-video transfer and editing; virtually all productions shot on film for broadcast on television are transferred to videotape for all editing and effects work. The Da Vinci color correction unit beneath the main monitor is the central component in this editing setup. (Photo courtesy of Editel)

However, editing is used frequently in conjunction with studio equipment when a mistake is made during a taping. The production can be stopped, and an edit point can be set on the record tape slightly before the mistake occurred. When the tape hits the edit point, the production in the studio can resume and proceed to the end of the program. The spot where the mistake occurred will be covered by a clean edit. This type of on-the-spot studio edit is referred to as a **pickup.**

Most editing, however, involves material that has been prerecorded and is transferred from the source deck to the record deck.

9.4 Basic Editing Distinctions

There are a number of different ways of editing material. They all involve laying down individual segments of recorded material from a source deck (or decks) to an edit deck. Often the end result is the same, regardless of which method is used—but the terms and distinctions discussed in this section are important during the actual editing process itself.

There are two major concepts we want to introduce here: (1) the distinction between **assemble** and **insert** editing, and (2) the difference between **on-line** and **off-line** editing.

Assemble Editing

Both assemble and insert editing can be used to lay down segments of material sequentially—one after the other. The viewer cannot tell which mode has been used, and in fact, any given program may use both methods. The main difference is in the laying down of the control track.

In assemble editing, the control track to be used is the one from the material on the source deck. As the first edit/transfer is made,

audio, video, and *control track* are transferred to the edit tape deck. At the point where the edit/transfer ends, the picture will break up and snow will appear because the control track has ended.

When the second edit/transfer is to be made, both the source and edit tapes are precisely backed up (usually five seconds) from the edit point (the end of the first transfer). The edit controller "reads" the sync pulse on the control tracks from both the source tape and the edit tape (which was laid down during the first transfer). In this way, the edit controller makes sure that the two control tracks match when the second edit is made—the edit controller picks up on the control track of the first edited segment and continues the same sync pulse pattern under the second edit.

The first edit will now be glitch-free because of the continuing control track; but a picture breakup will occur where the second edited piece of material ends (as the control track ends there also). However, when the third edit/transfer is laid down, it will synchronize itself to the control track of the second segment to produce a second glitchless edit; this, in essence, transfers the end-of-edit picture breakup to the end of the third segment.

Continuing this way, successive edits can be *assembled* with each edit latching onto the preceding control track to produce a continuous synchronized control track. (See figure 9–6.) This all works fine as long as the final segment fades to black at the end (to avoid the picture breakup that results from the abrupt end of the control track).

Assemble editing is relatively quick and easy because it can be started without any special preparation of the master (or edit) tape. It is used when the editing job is fairly simple and straightforward—for example, when segments of a program taped out of sequence need to be assembled into the proper program order.

Videotape Editing Equipment and Techniques

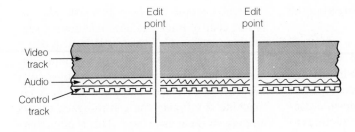

Edit point   Edit point

Video track

Audio

Control track

As each segment is assemble-edited, a new section of control track is laid down along with the video and audio signals.

Figure 9–6
Assemble editing.

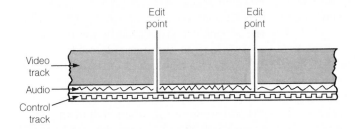

Edit point   Edit point

Video track

Audio

Control track

After a continuous control track has been laid down, each insert edit attaches the video and audio signals to this existing control track.

Figure 9–7
Insert editing.

Insert Editing

Once a program has been recorded, or once a program has been assemble-edited, other program segments can be inserted into the completed program—in essence, replacing some material already in the recorded tape. The crucial editing process here is that the material being inserted from the source deck (video only, video and audio, or audio only) has its control track stripped off as it is being transferred from the source tape, and this inserted segment is electronically mated to the existing control track (and sync pulse) already laid down on the master tape. This ensures a glitch-free edit at both the beginning and *the end* of the insert edit.

In other words, when editing is executed in the insert mode, the control track from the source deck is not utilized; only the video and audio signals are transferred. The control track used is the existing track that already has been laid down on the master tape. Therefore, as each edit is made, there are no glitches or picture breakups because the control track is continuous. (See figure 9–7.)

For example, suppose you have assembled a rather long speech by one person and you want to cut away to a reaction or *cutaway* shot (section 9.7) in the middle of the speech—say, a picture of the automobile being discussed by the speaker. You can insert this picture by going into the insert mode and editing in a shot of the car for, say, five seconds; by using a video-only insert edit, you do not interrupt the audio track of the speaker.

This is one main advantage of insert editing; audio and video can be edited separately. Whereas with assemble editing, both the video and audio must be laid down at the same time. If, for example, you want to lay down a continuous piece of music and then cut pictures to it, you must use the insert mode. The same is true if you want to use a specific piece of video footage—say, a continuous shot of a train wreck—and then edit audio-only narration to fit the picture. In this way, you may use video from one spot in the source tape and audio from another place on the source tape.

Assembling in the Insert Mode　The terms *assemble* and *insert* can be somewhat confusing because the word "assemble" means to place one thing after another and the word "insert" means to place something in between two other things. This is essentially what happens with videotape editing—the assemble mode is used to transfer one scene (with its control track) after another in consecutive order, and the insert mode is used to drop a particular segment (without its control track) into a program that has already been completed.

However, it is also possible to "assemble" segments in the *insert* mode. This concept can be utilized when a videotape has had a sync pulse laid down with a "black" control track prior to the start of the editing session. The tape that is to become the edited master is put on the record/edit deck and rolled through to the end with the VCR in the *record* mode—but feeding no signal other than "black." With no camera picture source, the machine provides the recorded sync pulse. This process is usually referred to as "laying down black" or *blacking*. "Black," of course, is not the crucial component; anything with a control track and sync pulse can be used—color bars, the output of a de-focused camera, and so forth.

Once a tape has been blacked—that is, once a control track has been laid down—segments can now be transferred in sequential order as with the assemble-edit technique; but you are actually doing a series of *insert* edits because, as each new edit is made, the VTR machine is utilizing the control track that is already on the master tape. This is often done because you may want to split audio and video as you are editing. Also, insert edits tend to be a little more stable due to the fact that you are working with a control track that has been laid down all at once.

(It is not possible, of course, to "insert" in the *assemble* mode. This is because when you are working in the assemble mode you are laying down a new section of the control track with each edit. Therefore, if you tried to insert a segment in the assemble mode, the end of the edit would result in a glitch as the newly transferred control track ended at the end of the edit; the sync pulse of the "inserted" segment would not connect in sync to the previously laid down control track.)

Off-Line and On-Line Editing

The other distinction that should be introduced at this point is the difference between **on-line** and **off-line** editing. These labels have come to be used to describe two distinctly different phases in the editing process.

"On-line editing" is the term applied to the sequence of work that goes into the final assembly of the **edited master tape.** It refers to the last step in editing the master tape. (As indicated below, in some situations it may refer to the *only* step in editing the master tape.)

In the case of a network prime-time variety, magazine, or awards program, on-line editing could involve the director, the producer, an assistant director, an editor, an assistant editor, plus any number of other production assistants. The session might call for five or six source VTR machines, a production switcher/SEG, digital video effects equipment, as well as editing facilities that can interface with a computer.

Most working professionals would also apply the term "on-line" to the efforts of a reporter/producer and an editor working with two VTR machines to beat a deadline on a breaking news story. In this case, the on-line finished program consists of a "cuts-only" hurriedly assembled product. The key to the *on-line* definition is that in both situations a final master tape is prepared for distribution.

In the network productions described above, this final assembly can occur only after a large amount of preliminary work has been done to prepare for the on-line edit session. This earlier work is the *off-line* phase of production; its purpose is to construct one or more intermediate *work print* versions of the program. Off-line editing takes place prior to assembling the final master tape; it does not involve any actually editing of the master tape.

Such off-line "work print" versions of program material are usually the responsibility of the director, although often the A.D. is delegated to do much of the work. Using notes taken during the production phase, the A.D. sorts out which of the several scene "takes" is actually to be used, inserts pickup shots of additional close-ups, adds titles, credits and any special effects, and is generally responsible for cleaning up ("sweetening") these first trial runs of the program.

On some low-budget productions (as in the early days of video editing), this off-line work is simply noted on paper in terms of SMPTE time-code listings of in- and out-edit points. On most major productions today, however, the A.D.'s work is usually in the form of a computer disk that carries a complete coded description of everything needed to construct one or more work print versions of the program. Not only are the in- and out-edit points noted, but there is a complete coded description of transition types such as takes, dissolves or wipes and their duration times, numbers for the source tape reel and playback machine, and other information such as the source of any special digital video effects.

During the on-line editing session, this information is displayed on a video terminal in clear view so that the director and the editor can make the final corrections and changes. It is the digital information on the disk that drives the final assembly of the master video tape.

The type of program being produced has much to do with the nature of the on-line session. In episodic programming such as situation comedies, the editing decisions are made almost completely in the off-line phase with the director and/or producer present. The on-line assembly may then be entirely an **auto edit** session, where an operator simply puts the computer disk into the machine and equipment such as a CMX EDITOR automatically executes the directions and assembles the entire program.

9.5 Fundamental Editing Procedures

When the earliest crude attempts at physical editing of tapes was attempted (section 9.2), the idea of editing as a production technique was a process directors originally tried to avoid—rather than utilize.

However, producers and engineers recognized the need for a reliable and an efficient system of handling electronic editing. Leaders in the engineering field gradually developed today's technologies whereby segments taken from one (or more) original recorded videotapes are electronically transferred to a second tape machine, where they are re-recorded in the desired edited sequence. The two factors that are crucial to the process are *picture stability* and the *precision of operator control* over the edit points. The improvements of the past decade concerning both of these factors have produced a truly impressive technology.

Figure 9–8
Recorded segments on the
original master.

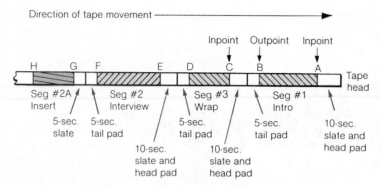

In this example, there are three segments of program material plus one insert segment to be edited
in later. These are to be "assembled" in the order
of the segment numbers, that is, *A-B* first, followed
by *E-F,* then *C-D.* The editing task is to remove the
unwanted pads and slates between the segments
and to rearrange the segments as indicated.

The Basic Process

In presenting the basic procedures and terminology of on-line assemble editing, we will
utilize a simple editing situation such as one
would find in field production or news work.
Figure 9–8 indicates how four separate camera
segments might be recorded in the field on the
original master reel. (In studying these illustrations, keep in mind that the direction of the
videotape is left to right; therefore it is necessary that you follow the action from the head
of the tape, on the *right,* to the end of the tape,
on the *left.*)

Shot Order   Like single-camera film
production, the individual shots are not necessarily recorded in the order in which they will
be edited together. In figure 9–8, the segment
numbers (1, 3, 2, and 2A) refer to the eventual
editing sequence—not the shooting order.
Segment #1 is the host introducing the program. Segment #3 is the solo host conclusion
or wrap-up; this would actually be videotaped
as the second shot (while the host is still in position and before the guest has arrived). Program segment #2 is the host interviewing a

guest (actually shot as the third recorded segment). Segment #2A (the fourth segment to
be shot) is some picture information that will
be used later as a *video-only insert* over some
of the interview audio.

Ahead of each segment, you would have
at least five seconds of picture and sound identification of the upcoming segment. Known as
the **slate** (see section 9.8), this material consists of the camera pointed at a chalkboard or
card with printed words such as "Segment 2,
Take 1, Interview." The words should also be
read aloud to confirm the audio level. With the
tape still rolling, the slate is pulled away to
reveal the host and subject for a period of about
five more seconds prior to their cue to begin.
This short sequence and a similar continuation
of picture at the conclusion of the interview are
known as **head pad** and **tail pad.** The function
of these pads is to provide an adequate margin
of picture signal, which, as we shall see, is necessary to the editing process.

Figure 9–9 indicates how the segments
from the original master, located on the *source
deck* or *playback* VTR machine, will be transferred so as to be edited in program sequence
onto the *edited master reel* located on the *edit*

Videotape Editing Equipment and Techniques

deck or *record* VTR machine. As stated earlier, the numbers given the various segments do not reflect the sequence in which the segments were recorded in the field, but rather, the numbers indicate their eventual program sequence. In many circumstances, the slate reflects the structure of the script—with prenumbered segments. (This underscores the importance of thorough preplanning before ever packing production gear in a box and heading for the field.)

Determining Edit Points   Prior to the actual assembly process, there is usually a viewing session involving the director, editor, and others responsible for the creative aspects of the program. This is called the **pre-edit session.** Its purpose is to carefully check the tape in order to determine not only what material will be selected for final editing, but also to designate the precise **inpoint** and **outpoint** of each segment that is to be edited into the finished program.

In the example (figures 9–8 and 9–9), let us say that segment #1 consists of the host/interviewer talking directly to the camera. Outpoint *B* is roughly the end of a sentence introducing a second person who will appear with the interviewer at the beginning of segment #2. Our edit must allow for a normal time lapse between the end of this final sentence and the beginning audio of the next (interview) segment. A pause that is too long or too short would be unnatural and would distract the viewer. Our **edit decision** (sometimes called the *edit event*) in this case is relatively simple. Outpoint *B* will be established at a point that will allow for one more second of picture to follow the final word spoken. Inpoint *E* of the segment #2 interview will be set to allow one additional second of establishing video ahead of the first audio.

The tape editor must look carefully for small but important visual elements that may have gone unnoticed at the time of the recording. For example, if the host was making

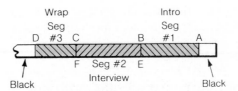

As the program segments (from figure 9–8) are assembled, the outpoint of segment #1 (*B*) is butted against the inpoint of segment #2 (*E*); the outpoint of segment #2 (*F*) is butted against the inpoint of segment #3 (*C*); and the outpoint of segment #3 (*D*) is edited to the final segment of black.

a small hand gesture at the end of segment #1, then that gesture should be seen as it is being completed before the edit is made. Similarly, if there was any movement at the beginning of segment #2, that movement should be seen from its beginning, or entirely eliminated. To edit from or to a movement that is in progress produces a distracting edit, similar to the jolting effect of a *jump cut* or *position jump*. (See sections 9.7 and 13.1.) Instead, the edit can be made by adding a little of the nonaudio tail pad at the end of segment #1 and *trimming* a bit of what was to have been one second of head pad at the beginning of segment #2. The idea is to have enough flexibility to achieve a perfectly matched picture before and after the edit decision. This situation illustrates how head and tail pads can give the editor a margin to play with when determining the precise edit point.

As each edit point is determined, its position on the reel must be noted in terms of some sort of numerical location or *address* system. Ideally, both *off-line* and *on-line* editing would be done on VTR machines equipped for SMPTE time code (section 8.3). However, under tight deadlines (with news and *actuality* production), on-line editing may be executed on equipment that utilizes only a control track-based counter unit. Some of these systems provide minute, second, and frame number readouts, while others may only provide a minute and second readout. (See figure

Figure 9–9
Program segments transferred to the edited master.

8–13.) In either case, pre-edit notes are of limited value if they are not expressed in terms of specific numerical addresses or locations of edit points.

Operation of the Edit Controller

The process described earlier, whereby exact edit points can be precisely adjusted, is relatively simple for the operator/editor as long as he or she is working with equipment that has the capacity to control the movement of the playback and record machines. This intermediate unit—or *edit controller* (section 9.3)—is designed to perform several important functions. First, there must be a component such as a dial or joystick that allows the operator to move the tape on either machine at varying fast and slow search speeds (figure 9–4). This same control must also be able to put the machines into the *pause* (freeze-frame) mode.

Second, the editing system must have the capacity to "remember" designated inpoints and outpoints on both the playback and record tape machines. Also, in the final stage, the editing system must be able to provide a **preview** of the edit, showing exactly what the moving edit will look like—but without executing any actual signal transfer. In other words, the edit monitor will change pictures at the edit point to show what the edit will look like, but the master deck will not actually record the edit. Then, on command, the editing unit is capable of progressing through the programmed series of mechanical and electromagnetic operations that accomplish the transfer edit.

Because of the constant upgrading of editing technology, state-of-the-art equipment will vary widely. A complete understanding of operating techniques must ultimately revolve around a detailed study of the operator's manual of each individual editing system. There are, however, a number of general operational concepts that can be applied to all such equipment. It is hoped that the general operational examples that follow will provide students with a basic approach to the facilities in their own studios.

Making the First Edit   Referring again to figure 9–8, the first step in the editing session is the transfer of segment #1. You realize you must set up the tape so that the transfer begins at approximately one second before the host's first word. This strips away the slate and most of the *head pad*. You will, however, want to record three to four seconds of *tail pad* after the host's last audio—this provides plenty of sync picture for the editing manipulations that were discussed.

Using the variable-speed control knob (or joystick) and keeping your eye on the *playback* machine monitor, move the playback tape to inpoint *A* of segment #1 one second ahead of the host's first word. Using the designated control, you enter this as the first inpoint into the editing system's memory. On most equipment, you can also set the outpoint where you want the edit to end. However, you can also edit without an outpoint and end the edit manually by *punching out* (pushing a button that ends the edit). If you punch out a little later than where you actually want the edit to end, no harm will be done because you can set your next inpoint wherever you wish.

After setting the inpoint (and possibly the outpoint), you will begin the actual edit. The control unit will return both the playback and record tapes to a spot five seconds before the point where the edit/transfer is eventually to take place. This sets up the *pre-roll* period, which is designed to make certain that the video heads and tape transport are up to speed at the time the edit occurs.

Your next step is to transfer segment #1. Roll the two machines and execute the edit at your predetermined point. Make sure you have recorded four to five seconds of tail pad. After making the edit/transfer, check the entire segment on the record machine, verifying that there is a stable picture throughout. Now put

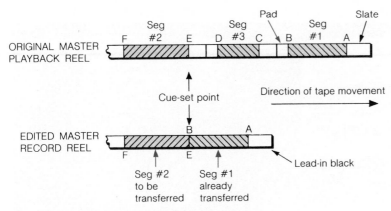

Figure 9–10
Playback and record tapes as they would be positioned relative to the cue-set point.

With segment #1 (*A-B*) already transferred from the original master (playback reel) to the edited master (record reel), the cue-set point is selected to determine the precise spot for the next edit (assembling segment #2).

the *record machine* into the *stop mode* (to save head and tape wear) and turn your attention to the *playback machine*. You are now approaching your first complete *edit event* (figure 9–9).[1]

Making the Second Edit During the pre-edit session, you noticed that the outpoint of segment #1 should occur at the conclusion of a slight hand movement by the host roughly one-and-a-half seconds after his last word. Considering that an audio pause of more than two seconds between the end of the introduction (segment #1) and the beginning of the interview (segment #2) would be too long, you decide to make the inpoint *E* of segment #2 just a half second before the host's first word in the interview segment. Maneuvering the

1. In some circumstances, the operator might be able to leave the record machine in the *pause mode,* providing for a quicker relocation of the outpoint. Much of the newer equipment has a feature that will automatically advance the tape one frame every sixty seconds while the machine is in *pause*. This permits you to have a monitor picture of the tape location at all times. Check with your operator's manual, instructor, and/or supervising engineer to determine the best operating procedure for your equipment.

search control to locate this point can be relatively simple if you are working with a counter system that provides a readout that includes individual frames. On less sophisticated systems, a bit of guesswork may be involved.

With inpoint *E* located on the playback machine (and the machine left in *pause*), you turn your attention to locating a precise outpoint *B* of segment #1 on the record machine. (This machine is also left in *pause* once the endpoint is found.) We now have the two tapes whose position relative to each other is shown in figure 9–10. It may help to visualize the status of the tapes at this point and during subsequent procedural descriptions if you think of the video heads as being at a constant point in both time and space relative to tape movement. This is reinforced by the fact that freeze-frame pictures are available on both the playback and record monitors, as pictured in figure 9–11.

If the edit/transition point is satisfactory, your next step is to activate some sort of **cue-set** control (the terminology and exact functioning of this component will vary with the editing system). This process programs the memory part of the editing unit, telling it that

Figure 9–11

Simultaneous display of picture information from both the playback (original source) and record (edited master) machines.

Playback   Record

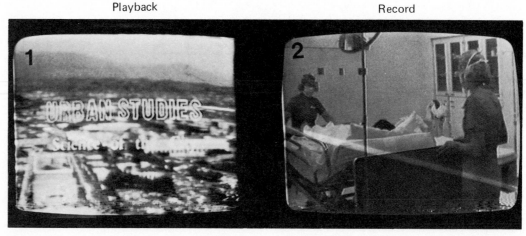

The operator watches the picture on the playback machine (*left*) while searching for the starting point of the next segment to be recorded. When located, the machine is put into the pause mode as seen here. During this search, the last frame of the previously recorded segment can be viewed on the monitor (*right*). The operator can easily compare these two pictures while making the edit decision.

Figure 9–12

Tapes on the playback and record machines in position for the pre-edit roll period.

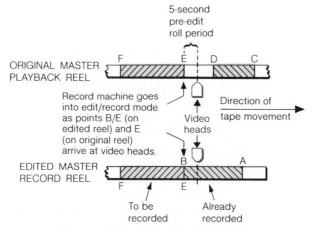

In this example, segment #1 (*A-B*) has already been transferred to the "edited master record reel" on the record machine. The next step is to transfer segment #2 (*E-F*) from the original master on the playback machine to the record machine at point *B*. Thus, the edit point (the cue-set point) will be *B/E* on the record machine. Therefore, both recorders are rolled back exactly five seconds before point *E* (on the playback machine) and point *B* (on the record machine). Both recorders are started simultaneously, and precisely five seconds later (when the playback machine reaches point *E* and the record machine reaches point *B/E*) the record machine is automatically switched into the "edit" mode. The butt edit of segments #1 and #2 is accomplished at point *B/E*.

Videotape Editing Equipment and Techniques

the positions now in *pause* on both machines are the locations for the next *edit event*. With many control units, the act of entering the cue-set command also activates both machines to roll the tape in reverse and come to a stop at a point that sets up the 5-second pre-edit roll period necessary for proper tape speed. This new position of the tapes relative to the video heads is shown in figure 9–12.

The machines are now set up to perform an edit. At this point, however, most editors prefer to *preview* the point at which the sound and picture transition between the two segments will take place. This can be done without any actual transfer of the signal to the record tape. On command, both machines are put in motion. As the tapes reach the edit points *B* and *E*, the record monitor (showing the tail of segment #1) automatically switches over and shows segment #2 from point *E* on. On some editing systems, this preview period may run only five seconds; at this point the unit automatically stops both machines and reverses them to the pre-roll setup points. On other systems, the operator has manual control and can terminate the preview at his or her discretion.

If the sound or picture transition points do not seem quite right, the operator can repeat the preview process as necessary and make **trimming** adjustments in the relative position of either of the tapes. On equipment that has the *trim* control for a frame-by-frame adjustment, you can easily add or subtract individual frames to or from either segment. On less sophisticated systems, adjustments made with the control knob or joystick are done with somewhat less certainty.

Whatever the complexity of the editing system, the process of adjusting the edit point between segments is an important one—but not a concept that is difficult to understand. For example, figure 9–13 shows segment #1 as transferred along with its 5-second tail pad. Had the edit shown in figure 9–14 been made without preview, it would have been discov-

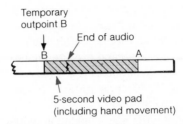

Figure 9–13
Segment as transferred from playback to record machine.

In this example, segment #1 has been transferred with a 5-second video pad, which includes the completion of a hand movement by the host.

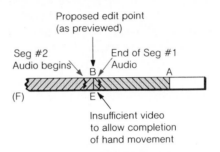

Figure 9–14
Preview of tight edit with insufficient video.

A preview of the proposed edit shows that the edit point cut off too much of the video pad; the edit was placed in the middle of the hand movement.

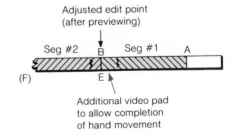

Figure 9–15
Adjusted edit point with sufficient video.

The completed edit has added two seconds more to the video pad at the end of segment #1 in order to allow for completion of the hand movement.

ered that there was not sufficient separation to allow for the completion of the hand movement. But by previewing the edit, the operator can see the need for added video pad at the end of the segment and adjust accordingly—as shown in figure 9–15.

Once you are confident that the edit point has been properly established, the actual edit itself becomes a rather routine matter of telling the machine to go ahead and execute the programmed transfer. What takes your time is the decision-making and preparation process leading up to the edit event.

Immediately after the completion of the edit, the entire transfer must be carefully reviewed for both technical and operator errors. You must rewind back to a point at least ten seconds ahead of the just-completed edit and roll through the whole segment—checking not only the edit point itself, but also the remainder of the segment for any deviation of picture quality. To shortcut this process is to invite trouble. Immediately redoing an assemble edit is much simpler than trying to fix it once the subsequent segments have been added on.

Inserting a Segment

With segment #2 transferred, you now have two options as to what the next step should be. You can either continue with the assemble editing and add segment #3, or you can put in the video insert (segment #2A) that is to be included within segment #2. In the simplified example, it really would not make much difference which is done next. In a more complex editing situation, the decision would be based upon time and efficiency factors as well as upon creative considerations. In one situation, the editor might decide to work in terms of whatever segment materials happened to be placed most conveniently on the playback reel. In another situation, the editor might wish to assemble-edit all of the dialogue segments first—getting them in proper sequence with ideal timing—and then review them before doing any of the video-only insert work.

For purposes of our example, let us assume you will do the insert editing (of segment #2A) next. This process must be based upon deci-

sions made only after the segment has been carefully screened. You must determine the most logical times for the inpoint and outpoint of the inserted video information. In the interview example, for instance, you must listen for audio cues—specific oral references to some visual information—that signal the spot where the video insert should be placed.

For purposes of the illustration, the interview segment #2 runs a total of thirty seconds—this is the previously transferred segment from inpoint E to outpoint F. During this segment the host and guest are discussing a large piece of equipment that has thus far been seen only in the background of the two-shot (segment #2). During the original location *shoot*, at the end of the reel, the director has taken an *anticipated insert shot* of the equipment (segment #2A) for later editing purposes as a *cutaway* shot (section 9.7). At eight seconds into segment #2, the guest says the words, ". . . this machine." This provides the obvious cue for the picture transition point.

Choosing a suitable outpoint might be a somewhat more subtle matter. What you are looking and listening for is that point where the insert picture has provided the viewer with the maximum amount of information before becoming redundant—distractingly boring. In this case, assume that the shot to be inserted has an "information life" of ten seconds. Exact timing might depend upon the location of the end of a sentence or phrase so as to provide a neat cue for the outpoint.

Figure 9–16 shows how, with these considerations in mind, the tapes would be set up in relationship to each other. Note the allowance for at least five seconds of picture head pad on the playback machine. This is necessary in order to assure proper picture sync at the time of the inpoint edit. As stated previously, the insert will begin eight seconds past the previously transferred edit point B/E and run for ten seconds.

Videotape Editing Equipment and Techniques

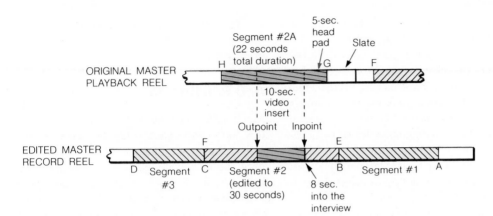

Figure 9–16
Playback and record machines set up for an insert edit.

The shot to be inserted (ten seconds from segment #2A) is to be edited into segment #2 (E-F) eight seconds after point B/E (the beginning of segment #2). The two VTR machines are rolled simultaneously from points at least five seconds ahead of the anticipated edit, and the "edit" (insert in) and "edit out" (insert out) commands are executed either manually or by the preprogrammed microprocessor.

The operational techniques used in setting up and completing the insert edit will, of course, vary with the type of editing system used and the desires of the person doing the editing. On some equipment, the operator must listen for word cues and manually *punch out* of the edit. On other machines, the out-cue might be programmed just like the in-cue was.

Insert editing is by no means limited to just video. The insert can obviously be video and audio combined. And most equipment is designed so that either one or both audio tracks can be edited or re-recorded while the original video remains untouched.

Completing the Editing   In order to complete this editing exercise, all that remains is to assemble-edit segment #3, the host's conclusion and wrap-up, to the end of segment #2. Determine the precise outpoint *F* of segment #2 and inpoint *C* of segment #3 and proceed with the assemble-edit process. If segment #3 does not fade to black at the end of the host's close, the final assemble-edit step is to attach some black at the end of segment #3 (endpoint *D*).

9.6 Additional Editing Concepts

Much postproduction editing involves more sophisticated procedures than the basic assemble and insert practices described up to this point.

Audio-Only and Video-Only Editing

Usually an editing controller will have four buttons labeled "assemble," "video," "audio 1," and "audio 2." Obviously, *assemble* is activated when assemble editing is desired. Under this configuration, the other three buttons are inoperable because video and audio cannot be edited separately.

When insert editing is desired, the other three buttons (*video, audio 1,* and *audio 2*) can be activated simultaneously or independently. If all three buttons are activated, edits will include all elements. If, however, only video is desired, as in the case of a cutaway, the two audio buttons can be deactivated. Likewise, if you wish to add an audio track (perhaps nar-

Videotape Editing Equipment and Techniques

ration) to an already edited video segment, you can do so by deactivating the video.

In the case of audio editing, you can choose which audio track you want to edit—either audio 1 or audio 2. Or you can record the audio on both tracks simultaneously by activating both *audio 1* and *audio 2*. Thus, if you wish to add a foreign language translation to an existing program, you can activate only the *audio 2* button and add the second language without disturbing either the picture or original sound track.

(If, however, you are working with three sound tracks—say a music-and-sound-effects track, an English dialogue, and a Spanish translation—you must go through an initial audio editing session at an audio console, adding the music and sound effects to both the English and Spanish versions independently. Then you would add the two composite audio tracks to the two videotape audio tracks separately.)

This two-track configuration is not possible with video, however. You do not have two video tracks so you cannot simply add visual labels over a pre-existing picture. Some students mistakenly believe they can edit their whole program and then insert keyed labels with name identifications. If you try to do this, you will erase the picture and wind up with only the label identifications. It is possible to add keyed titles to an existing picture only if you go to another generation of the tape and add the keyed labels (for example, from the character generator) as you are making the second-generation edited tape.

Something you must always remember to do is to reset the buttons after you complete one form of editing—before you start another editing job. Similarly, whenever you sit down to an editing session, always make sure that the buttons are configured for your particular task. Many hours of student editing have been ruined because an editor thought that he or she was adding background music to a program as

a final touch, but inadvertently the video button was activated and, as a result, the program video was totally erased.

A/B Roll Editing

Machine-to-machine edits as described up to this point can be used when the desired effect is that of an instantaneous *take*. Cuts-only editing can be accomplished with nothing more than two VCRs and a controller. However, when dissolves or special effects are desired, the levers, buttons, and mix banks buttons of a switcher or SEG must be utilized. As in any dissolve or effect, this means that there must be two simultaneous sources of video signal. Also, when mixing various video sources, the time-base corrector (section 8.2) is used to guarantee that all video signals will lock up with no picture breakup.

If you want to dissolve between two segments, you need to set up separate tape feeds on *A* and *B* source machines for playback. The technique is somewhat the same as in traditional *A* and *B* roll editing for film, where the final composite film is automatically printed from two specially edited film rolls. In television this system can either be set up for automatic computer control or be done manually at the switcher during the edit session. The basic principles involved in setting up the tapes are roughly the same in either situation.

When a dissolve (or wipe or other effect) between segments is planned, it is imperative to allow considerably more video pad (compared to editing a straight cut) following the outpoint of the first segment and preceding the inpoint of the second. For example, in the diagram shown in figure 9–17, the edit point E/B is the midpoint of a 2-second dissolve between segment #1 and segment #2. However, both playback machines must feed a video signal to the record machine throughout the duration of the dissolve. Although only two seconds of pad from each segment are actually

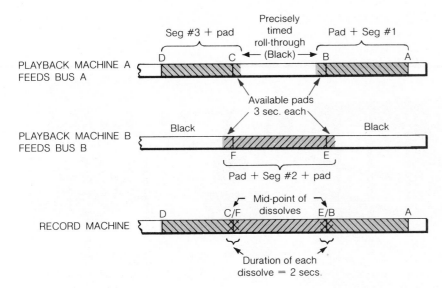

Figure 9-17
Three VTR machines set
up for a dissolve edit.

In preparing the *A* and *B* playback videotapes, care must be taken to ensure that every segment and each "roll-through" (black space between segments) is precisely timed—including the exact pads that are wanted. As the two playback tapes are fed into the switcher, the actual dissolve edits (on non-preprogrammed editing units) are accomplished simply by using the fader arms.

needed for the 2-second dissolve overlap, it is always advisable to have extra-protection source video available. Most professional directors would not feel comfortable without a working margin of at least an additional three seconds added to each segment.

A sequence in which all of the segments are to be connected by dissolves must be planned in order to be recorded from beginning to end. For all practical purposes, there is no way in which the record machine can be stopped to set up the next dissolve without doing some sort of cuts-only edit.

The three-segment sequence shown in figure 9-17 calls for two dissolves. Setting up the pre-edit roll periods on the *A* and *B* playback machines for the E/B dissolve edit poses no real problem. Note, however, that segment #2 is of such short duration that there is not enough time for the operator to stop and re-cue the *A* roll to get segment #3 in position. The solution to the problem is to have prere-corded segment #3 on the *A* roll in a precisely timed position so that—allowing the *A* machine to keep rolling—segment #3 will be available just prior to the end of segment #2. After the dissolve to segment #2, the *A* tape continues to roll and segment #3 is available for the next dissolve.

If the segments would have been at least two minutes in length, there would have been time for the operator to locate each upcoming segment and set up the pre-edit roll period. In this situation, markings on the tape or audio beep tones on the cue track are important to the operator. In any case, the use of *A* and *B* rolls for dissolve edits must of necessity involve careful planning just for the preparation of the playback/source tapes.

More sophisticated (and expensive) equipment (such as the CMX editing system) allows for almost infinite dissolves of any length by using multiple-source decks. Two or more source machines can be computer pro-

Figure 9–18
The Ediflex editing system consists of twelve ½-inch VCR players, a computer, and a ¾-inch VCR. Usually each of the twelve ½-inch VCRs contain all the material for the program being edited. The machine that is cued up closest to the segment that is to be edited next goes to that segment and displays it on one of the monitors in the center. In this way, the twelve machines are able to race to edit points and show how an entire edited program will look without actually recording anything. The computer is used to mark and change time-coded edit points. If an edit point in the middle of a production is changed, all the edit points after that edit will change automatically. The ¾-inch VCR is used to make a copy of how the final program will look after all the edit points have been determined.

grammed to "leapfrog" ahead and set each machine for a series of dissolves or cuts.

At its cheapest, A/B rolling is more expensive than cuts-only editing because it involves more equipment, including at least one time-base corrector. For this reason, many colleges do not have the facilities for A/B rolling or, at best, may have only one system with this capability.

Off-Line and On-Line Applications

Under ideal circumstances, both off-line and on-line editing are used in putting together a polished production. Raw footage is shot (often on 1-inch tape or Betacam SP or M-II for professional work—although it may be ¾-inch, ½-inch S-VHS, or Hi8) and immediately dubbed to a work print—usually a ¾-inch or ½-inch cassette. This work print is used to make all the editing decisions, saving the orig-

inal footage from the wear and tear of shuttling back and forth to determine edit points. If both the original and work print have SMPTE time code, the exact edit points can be determined on the work print. If control track editing is being used, approximate edit points can be determined on the work print, but the master tape will undergo shuttling to arrive at the exact desired edit points.

With sophisticated editing systems (see figure 9–18), a computerized edit list can be generated if the time code is used. This list keeps track of all edit points as they are marked on the work print. Then the master tapes can be edited using this same edit list. Sometimes this final editing is done virtually without the intervention of human button-pushers. Computers find the edit points and assemble the appropriate segments, one after the other, following the preprogrammed instructions.

Videotape Editing Equipment and Techniques

In many editing situations, something close to the final program is edited on an off-line, cuts-only system so that the director or producer can see how the program will look—minus any dissolves or special effects. Sometimes, the off-line work print can show dissolves and effects if the off-line ¾-inch or ½-inch equipment includes a switcher and other necessary gear. Then the original material is used to edit the final program on the more expensive (often 1-inch) on-line system. On-line editing can be cuts-only, if that is all that is needed, but generally the on-line final version of the program involves A/B roll, titles, multiple sound tracks, and other features.

Using off-line editing before going to the final on-line version takes a little more time overall, but it saves wear and tear on original footage; and it usually saves money because you do more editing on the less expensive off-line equipment and less editing on the more expensive on-line system. Sometimes, however, time is of the essence and material is edited on-line only. This is common, for example, for news broadcasts where footage shot at 4 o'clock must be edited and on the air at 6 o'clock.

It should be noted that the term *A and B roll* has a somewhat different application when used in a purely news-oriented operation such as CNN (Cable News Network). In a straight news production, the *A* roll contains all of the interviews and the individual quotations or *sound bites* to be inserted into the program. In a first phase, these are all edited together in sequence to get the informational content organized. Then all of the related picture information on what are called the *B* rolls is insert-edited over selected segments of the prepared *A*-roll material. For example, there may be footage of a reporter interviewing a fire captain. After five seconds of the *A*-roll interview shot, the *B*-roll footage of the fire would be shown while the audio still continued from the *A* roll with the discussion of the fire. You would edit out of the *B*-roll material in time for the reporter to be seen ending the interview.

A common variety of semi-off-line editing used by many students involves making a dub of original footage to a ½-inch VHS cassette and taking this ½-inch cassette home to view on a standard consumer VHS machine. Although editing cannot be done with one machine at home, you can make your editing decisions. And once again this semi-off-line procedure saves wear and tear on the original tape, and it saves precious time on the on-line editing machines at school.

9.7 Aesthetics of Editing

Editing is both a mechanical and an artistic function. The stringing together of video and audio information in a logical order can be quite mechanical. But doing it in a way that is aesthetically pleasing and understandable requires special talent and skill. The end result of all television production, remember, is *communication*—producing and delivering a message as clearly as possible with a minimum of interference or communication *noise*. The essence of good editing is simply clear communication.

A number of aesthetic principles for editing have been developed over the years, primarily in the film industry. None of these are federal "rules." They are primarily conventions that have developed to give filmic elements their own "language."

These principles and conventions are common to both single-camera field production and multiple-camera studio production. From the perspective of the viewer, the grammar of editing is the same whether the drama was shot in the studio in one sequential "real-time" production or shot completely out of sequence in twenty locations over a period of six months. The shot relationships are the same. Pacing is pacing. Continuity is continuity. Therefore, much of the material introduced in this section is treated also—frequently in more depth—in chapter 13, "Directing Your First Studio Production."

Orientation and Shot Size

When you are shooting in the field, you must be constantly aware of how you are going to edit together the various shots back in the editing bay. One crucial consideration is the relationship of shot sizes. This is sometimes referred to as the *LS-MS-CU Principle*. In section 13.1, we examine the effect of combining *collective* or long shots and *particularized* or close-up shots.

For example, an editing sequence that starts with a long shot (LS) establishes for the audience the locale and often the mood. If the second shot is a medium shot (MS), the audience still recognizes the locale but now can direct its attention to a specific item or person. A close-up (CU) then reveals a particular emotion or image that is understood because the audience knows its relationship to the overall picture. Through the years, this LS-MS-CU organization of editing has become the established pattern for orienting the audience. (See figure 9–19.)

This does not mean, however, that all films or tapes must start with a long shot. Many reasons exist for breaking the LS-MS-CU pattern. Starting with a CU of a smashed wristwatch lying on a road map, for example, can build suspense.

Nonetheless, beginning editors wishing to orient an audience would be well advised to start new scenes with a long shot and progress to medium and close shots in order to enhance audience understanding.

When shooting in the field, you might also want to consider the advisability of using the extreme long shot (XLS) for occasional effect—the sweeping panorama and grand vistas. Although not as effective as it is on the theater screen, the occasional XLS, nevertheless, might have some justification.

Keeping in mind that television has traditionally been the medium of the small intimate image (although bigger sets and sharper projection systems are gradually changing that image), it might also be appropriate—even for location shooting—to take advantage of the occasional extreme close-up (XCU) for heightened impact.

Continuity and Shot Transitions

Continuity is a broad term that refers to keeping things the same throughout an entire scene or program. Much of this refers to how material is recorded and later edited. For example, if a scene of a man holding flowers and opening a door is shot on Monday, and the scene of that man entering the room is shot on Wednesday, the man should still be holding the flowers. If he does not have them, editing cannot create them.

However, if he has the flowers behind his back as he opens the door and then brings them out as he enters the room, the edit point should be while he still has the flowers behind his back. Similarly, if a two-shot shows an interviewer with her hand raised, an edit that cuts to a close-up of her should show her hand similarly raised. Shots must be properly matched so they appear to flow from one to another.

Violations of this principle of continuity can also lead to **position jumps** (see figure 9–20) where a person or an object appears to instantaneously jump from one position to another in the frame. (See section 13.1.)

Sometimes editing to a shot from a distinctly different angle will minimize continuity problems. For example, if an edit from a close-up of a person's profile to a MS of the person head-on is made, slight changes in body position will not be as noticeable as they would be if both the close-up and MS were head-on.

Videotape Editing Equipment and Techniques

Figure 9–19
Long shot, medium shot, and close-up.

If a cut were made from the long shot to the close-up, the viewer would be quite disoriented; it is possible the viewer would not even connect the two shots as being in the same locale.

Figure 9–20
Examples of right and
wrong continuity.

(a)

(b)

(c)

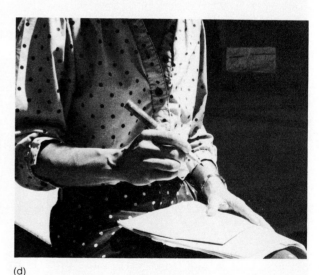
(d)

(*Upper photos*) If the close-up (b) followed the long shot (a), the pen would appear to jump from the raised position to the paper.
(*Bottom photos*) On the other hand, if you were to cut from the long shot (c) to the close-up (d), the pen would appear to jump from the paper to the raised position. A correct edit could be made by cutting from (a) to (d) or from (c) to (b).

Videotape Editing Equipment and Techniques

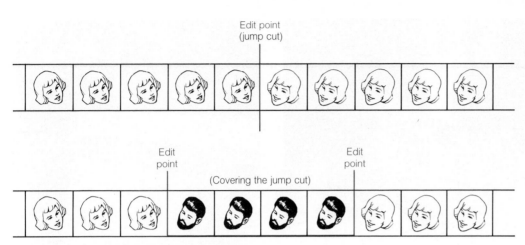

Figure 9–21
Covering a jump cut.

Edit point
(jump cut)

Edit
point

Edit
point

(Covering the jump cut)

In the top example, the edit results in a jump cut as the woman's head suddenly shifts position. If a reaction shot of the man is insert-edited over the spot where the woman's head moves (lower example), her head movement will not be noticeable.

Jump Cuts   Continuity errors quite frequently lead to **jump cuts** (section 13.1)—movements on the screen that are not natural. Jump cuts present a frequent problem in news interviews when something that a person says is condensed. For example, a hospital spokeswoman may begin a statement about someone's condition, then be distracted or lose her place; after a momentary lapse she collects her thoughts and continues her explanation. Her head may have been in the right-hand portion of the screen when she became distracted and in the left-hand portion when she regained her composure and finished. If the part where she was distracted is edited out, her head will jump unnaturally from one side of the screen to another.

One way to solve this problem is to put in a video-only cutaway of something else at the edit point. If, for example, a picture of the person being discussed is shown right before

and right after the edit, the change in the head position will go unnoticed. Of course, the cutaway should make sense within the context of what is being said. The most common type of cutaway, especially in news, is a reaction shot of the interviewer listening to what a person is saying. (See figure 9–21.)

Jump cuts used to be considered unacceptable in all forms of editing. However, with the advent of music videos, they have become acceptable as part of a new grammar. Because of the unrealistic effect they convey, jump cuts are recognized as a specific stylized kind of artistic statement. This again reinforces the point that editing principles are not inviolable rules.

Axis of Action/Conversation   Another potential editing trap is crossing the imaginary line that places the viewer on one side of all action that is taking place (the **axis of**

Figure 9–22

A person leaving the frame at one location and entering another. This is one way to denote the passage of time.

action) or crossing the line that connects two people in a conversation (the **axis of conversation**). (See figures 13–5 and 13–6.) When shooting in the field, it is imperative that the director keep in mind the *screen direction* at all times. Camera positions have to be carefully planned in order to avoid editing problems later.

These related principles of continuity and shot transitions apply to studio productions as well as to single-camera productions. However, the principles are much easier to apply and control in the studio than in the field. When you are looking at three camera monitors side by side in the control room, it should be a simple matter to make sure that successive shots will not result in a jump cut, position jump, or violation of the axis of action/conversation. In the field, however, with a single camera, you do not have the luxury of comparing shots side by side. You must shoot your pictures one at a time—recalling what the previous shot looked like. It is much easier to make a mistake and shoot several successive

shots that when edited together later will violate these principles. This underscores the importance of very careful preplanning (section 15.2) for all single-camera productions.

Pacing and Movement

Passage of time is another filmic element that has evolved its own grammar. Various visual transitions (the cut, the dissolve, the fade) each reflect a distinct sense of movement of time. (See section 13.2.) Probably the most obvious is the fade to black that is used much like the lowering of a curtain in the theater. It signifies that one element has ended and another is about to begin.

Time and distance are also handled by placement of people within a frame. Two people walking down a long street for an extended time is a very boring shot, so their walk is foreshortened by editing—showing them at only a few places along the street. The audience will accept this foreshortening as realistic if the editing occurs in such a way that the

Figure 9–23
Seamless editing.

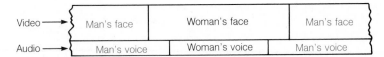

Video →	Man's face	Woman's face	Man's face
Audio →	Man's voice	Woman's voice	Man's voice

Note that the picture and sound are cut at different places. We cut to a shot of the woman's face while we are still listening to the man's words, and then the woman's face remains on the screen for a couple seconds after the man starts to speak again.

people leave the frame at the end of each shot and enter it at the beginning of the next shot. (See figure 9–22.) As a general rule, whenever people leave a certain location, they should exit the frame. This gives the illusion that enough time has passed for them to enter the next frame at a new location. Of course, the shots must be recorded with the talent leaving and entering each shot before the scene can be edited properly.

Pacing   Closely related to the passage of time is the aesthetics of pacing. The way that people interact must look realistic when the editing is completed. If, for example, one camera is used to tape a man and a woman arguing, the camera will first record a two-shot of the whole scene and then record a close-up of the man saying his lines followed by a close-up of the woman saying her lines. When all of this is edited together, the *beats* or pauses between their lines must have a realistically effective pace.

This is where the **trim** function on the edit controller is particularly effective. It can be used to add or subtract one frame at a time from edit-in or edit-out points. After subtle frame changes have been made, the edit can be previewed to see if the pacing is realistic.

Pacing is also important in showing the audience what it wants to see—when it wants to see it. If a chef is talking about a particular way he is stuffing a duck and the editor stays on a close-up of the chef's face, the audience

will be frustrated. At that point in the demonstration, an edit should be made to show a close-up of the chef's hands stuffing the duck.

Seamless Editing   The manner in which audio and video are edited in relation to each other can also give an illusion of pacing. It is not always desirable to cut to the speaker exactly when he or she starts to speak. If the argument between the man and woman is cut in such a way that both a CU of the man's face and his voice are cut at the same time and similarly you cut to a CU of the woman whenever her voice is heard, the effect will be one of abruptness and fast pace. If that is the effect you want, then that is the way to edit.

If you want to soften the effect, however, a better technique is **"seamless editing."** To accomplish this, the audio is cut at a slightly different place than the video. In other words, the picture of the woman can begin slightly before the man has stopped talking or the voice of the man can begin slightly before his picture is shown—as illustrated in figure 9–23.

Because picture and voice are not cut at the same point, the abruptness is mitigated, and a smooth effect is given. Of course sometimes (particularly in an argument) a brusque pace may be desired. Also, seamless editing is more time-consuming than straight-cut editing, so straight takes that are not obviously obtrusive are often advisable—in order to keep editing time under control.

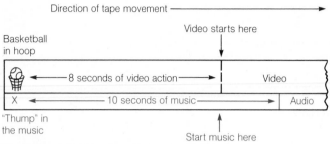

Figure 9–24
Back timing.

Direction of tape movement ⟶

Video starts here

Basketball
in hoop

←— 8 seconds of video action —→ Video

X ←————— 10 seconds of music —————→ Audio

"Thump" in
the music

Start music here

The 8-second video clip and the 10-second music
segment are lined up at their crucial points (where
the basketball hits the hoop and the music goes
"thump"), and then both tracks are back-timed
eight seconds so they will reach the climactic point
at the same time.

Timing and Motion   Other crucial factors in editing relate to the timing of camera transitions—takes and dissolves—in relation to the program content and movement. Generally speaking, cuts should be made on action, with camera movement, on the beat in music presentations, on dialogue changes (except as previously noted), and on reaction. (See section 13.2.)

Many of the principles involved in cutting on motion have also been violated effectively in music videos. But, in most instances, these "language" concepts still hold. For example, if movement is occurring within a shot, that movement should be seen in its entirety before the edit is made. Or conversely, a cut may be made immediately before the action begins. But to edit from or to a movement that is in progress produces a distracting edit similar to a jump cut.

Similarly, camera movement such as panning, zooming, or tilting should start after an edit is made, and the movement should stop before a new edit is made. If an edit is made during camera movement, it should be to another similar movement. For example, if a camera is panning right, an edit can be made to another camera that is also panning right at the same pace. Cutting to a camera panning left or zooming in would be very jarring. But

of course, there are situations where this abrupt effect is desired.

Cutting to Music   Cutting to music has its own set of principles—and problems. (See sections 13.2 and 14.2.) If the music is already composed, then the video should be laid down (insert-edited) after the audio so that the pictures work in conjunction with the music. Aesthetic satisfaction is usually enhanced if the visual editing is executed at the beginnings of distinct musical phrases—usually four or eight measures in length. This means the video has to be shot so its length is commensurate with the section of music it will accompany. Camera movement must be well planned so pans and zooms are the right length.

In fact, timing is probably the most crucial consideration in cutting to music. Sometimes **back timing** is involved. For example, if you are cutting a series of sports shots to fast-paced music, you may want a basketball to fly into a basket on a particular note. In order to accomplish this, you have to match the basket with the note and then move both the music and picture backwards so that the basketball action starts at a point that will conclude with the basket being made on precisely the right beat. (See figure 9–24.)

Videotape Editing Equipment and Techniques

One useful audio timing procedure is the *dead pot* technique that involves rolling music (or other effects) at a predetermined point with the pot down—and then bringing up the audio as the visual calls for it. Few recorded audio tracks will ever fit the time slot for which they are needed.

Another practice—when specific openings and closings are needed—is to make a second recording of the music track. Back-time one music tape to end with the visual segment. Start the beginning of the other music tape with the opening of the video segment; and then find a place to make an unobtrusive audio segue to the tape with the back-timed close.

Whenever you are working with music, you should dub it to videotape so you can edit it accurately. You will find it easier to mark edit points for the entrance of music than to try to bring it in at precisely the right place through an audio board.

Editing Narration and Video   Cutting to narration involves procedures similar to cutting to music. If certain picture elements are crucial, you may wish to lay down the video first and then have your announcer add narration to describe the pictures. On the other hand, if the exact text of the narration is more important, the audio should be recorded first and then the pictures can be cut to fit the narration.

There are other principles of editing grammar (some to be covered in chapter 13) that have built up over the years, but the ones discussed in this section represent the major ones. And as stated previously, virtually all of these "rules" can be violated with excellent, and sometimes startling, results—once you understand the language, once you can demonstrate that you can follow these principles, and when you know specifically what aberrant effects you are after.

9.8   A Sample Editing Procedure

What follows is a method for editing a short piece that consists of four segments:

1. A 30-second opening by a studio host introducing a popular new singer.
2. A one-minute interview, shot at an airport, between a reporter and the singer. Within this interview will be four cutaways of album covers and a keyed name identification (from the character generator) of the singer.
3. Thirty seconds of audio of a current hit by the singer that is accompanied by a montage of still photographs of her in concert.
4. A 15-second closing by the studio host.

The editing method described in figure 9–25 is certainly not the only one possible, but it will demonstrate many of the principles discussed in this chapter.

Shooting Order

As discussed previously, the individual shots would not be recorded in the order in which they will eventually be edited together. In this example, the interview would probably be shot first because, in all probability, the piece is not worth doing without the interview—and what the host says in the opening will be dependent upon what the singer says in the interview. The second segment taped would probably be the host's introduction followed by the host's closing.

The album covers and photographs could be shot in a corner of the studio using a card stand and one camera. Each shot should be taped for about thirty seconds. Whether or not there is camera movement will depend upon

Figure 9-25
Edited segments.

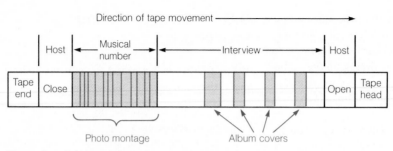

Direction of tape movement →

| Host | ← Musical number → | ← Interview → | Host |

| Tape end | Close | | | Open | Tape head |

Photo montage

Album covers

The order of the segments in our editing exercise
as they would appear in the final edited version.
(All inserted video is tinted red.)

your creative conception of what you want the montage to be—so the music should be auditioned before the photos are actually taped. In this way you can control the length of any camera movement to make it coincide with the length of musical sections.

The order in which you will record the material then would be as follows:

Segment 2, interview at the airport

Segment 1, host introduction

Segment 4, host closing

Segments 2A–2D, album covers

Segments 3A–3F, photographs

Ahead of each segment you would have at least five seconds of picture and sound identification of the upcoming segment—the **slate.** (See section 9.5.) Make sure you also record enough *head pad* and *tail pad* to provide an adequate margin of picture coverage for your editing process.

Logging

Once the material is all recorded on tape, it should be dubbed onto a *work print* and then viewed carefully by the people responsible for the final product. If a **log sheet** was made during taping, it should be checked. If one was not made, it should be at this point. The log

sheet includes at least the beginning and end point of each take (including the slate for each take), a description of the shot, and comments. It might look something like this:

Tape 1:

0:00:00–0:00:30—color bars and tone

0:00:30–0:05:40—interview

0:05:40–0:08:50—reporter questions, too much airplane noise

0:08:50–0:12:05—reporter questions . . . good take

0:12:05–0:13:30—reporter reaction shots, one at 13:05 is best

0:13:30–0:15:14—outside of airport

Tape 2:

0:00:00–0:00:30—color bars and tone

0:00:30–0:01:50—host's introduction

0:01:50–0:02:15—closing (muffed lines)

0:02:15–0:02:55—closing

0:02:55–0:08:30—album covers, did second one twice

0:08:30–0:23:10—photographs

Although there are no plans at this stage to use either the reporter reaction shots or the shot of the outside of the airport, these were taped—just in case cutaways are needed.

Videotape Editing Equipment and Techniques

The Edit Decision Sheet

From this log sheet, an **edit decision sheet** should be made that lists all shots in the order they will be used. Some editors and directors like to write descriptions of each shot on 3-by-5-inch cards and then arrange and rearrange the shots. This form of editing on paper saves time and tape wear and tear.

The edit decision list might look something like this:

Tape 2, 1:05–1:35—Introduction. Start with "welcome to" and end with "spoke to her."

Tape 1, 9:00–9:04—Question about latest hits. Start with "why" and end before "and a."

Tape 1, 1:07–1:27—Singer's answer. Include the little laugh at beginning and end with smile.

Tape 2, 3:10–3:13—Green cover. Insert over previous edit where she says "Forever."

Tape 2, 3:17–3:20—Blue cover. Insert where she says "Keep the faith."

Tape 1, 11:50–11:55—Question about newspaper. Start with "when" and end with "think."

Tape 1, 5:10–5:25—Answer about publicity. Start with "Now you're" and end with "soon."

Tape 2, 5:14–5:18—Yellow cover. Insert in previous edit where she says "In a kind."

Tape 1, 10:13–10:15—Question about concert. Start with "Why" and end with "concert."

Tape 1, 3:02–3:16—Answer about concert. Start with "Monday" and end with "Friday."

Tape 2, 8:00–8:04—Red cover. Insert in previous edit where she says "Thinkin' Again."

Tape 2, 9:01–9:04—Long hair. Take to first major beat.

Tape 2, 11:15–11:23—Blue dress. Get whole zoom.

Tape 2, 21:14–21:18—Large group. To loud drum.

Tape 2, 12:16–12:19—Back view. Take to major beat.

Tape 2, 18:10–18:18—Auditorium. Get whole pan.

Tape 2, 19:04–19:08—Close-up. To music's end.

Tape 1, 2:33–2:48—Closing. Start with "That" and end with "Good afternoon."

Not all edit sheets necessarily have to look exactly like this. Such detailed instructions might not be needed if SMPTE time code is used accurately. But sometimes even more detail is listed—especially if the person doing the physical editing is not the producer or director who made the actual decisions.

The Editing Process

This edit decision sheet can then be used to edit *off-line* to make sure that all edits are exactly what was wanted. If time is short, the program may have to be edited *on-line*.

Beginning Tape Material　　In either case (off-line or on-line), the tape should start with at least thirty seconds of color bars and tone, twenty seconds of slate, and a countdown. *Color bars* usually come from a color bar generator routed through the switcher; they are used to calibrate colors when the tape is played back. *Tone* comes from the audio board and should be set at 100 percent on the VU meters on all machines so that the audio level of all sound segments will have a reference point. Either the character generator or a card can be used to record the slate. This should normally include the title, the director's name, the

Figure 9–26
Placement of the
preprogram identification
material on a videotape—
color bars and tone, slate
and countdown.

Direction of tape movement ⟶

Program video	Black	Countdown	Slate	Color bars	Tape head
Program audio		"2-3-4-5-6-7-8"	(Read the slate)	Tone	

segment number ("scene 3"), the length, the date, and the number of the "take" (in the event that several takes of the same scene have to be recorded because of airpane noise, some *muffled* lines, or other problems—and you are not sure which take you will want to use until you get back to the editing booth and look at each one carefully). The *countdown* ("8–7–6–5–4–3–2") is usually from a preproduced tape.

The entire tape could be *blacked* and everything—including color bars, tone, slate, and countdown—could be insert-edited. But for purposes of this exercise, we will primarily use assemble editing with some insert editing.

Therefore, bars, tone, slate, and countdown can be recorded all at once just as they would be for a studio shoot, or they can be assemble-edited one at a time. In either case, about ten seconds of black should be recorded after the "2" of the countdown so that a steady control track is established. (See figure 9–26.)

The First Edit   Now you can begin the editing of the actual material. Using the source deck variable-speed control knob or joystick, and keeping your eye on the source machine monitor, move tape 2 until it is cued right before the host's introduction starts. If you are using SMPTE time code and have done your edit sheet correctly, this should be at 00:01:05. If you are using control track editing, set up the tape right before the beginning words, "welcome to." With the machine in *pause,* enter this as the source deck entry point or inpoint on the edit controller.

Then set up the master tape on the edit deck in the *pause* position at two seconds after the countdown "2" and mark that as your edit deck entry point. You can mark an exit point for the source tape that is several seconds after your outpoint ("spoke to her"), or you can wait and make your exit point while you are doing the edit. You want several seconds after the final words to guarantee that you have adequate control track for the next edit and also so that you have the freedom to manipulate the inpoint of the next edit. If you ended the edit precisely after the word "her," you would have no room to establish the *beats* needed before the next edit.

Regardless of how you exit the edit, you will want to preview it—especially because this is your first edit. By using the *preview edit* function, you will not actually record the edit, but the edit monitor will simply show you exactly how the edit would look if you were actually recording it. This is the time to make sure all audio and video levels are coming through properly.

If you are totally unsatisfied with the edit, you can start over and reset your inpoints and outpoints from scratch. If you just need to tighten or loosen the edit a bit, you can use the *trim* function to add or subtract a few frames before and/or after the edit points.

If you are satisfied with the preview, you can go ahead and execute the edit. Both machines will back up five seconds to get up to speed and to establish a strong control track. This is why the pads are so important. If there

Figure 9–27
Hi8 to U-matic editing system. This editing system uses the Hi8 format as the source and the U-matic SP format as the master. The Hi8 deck is positioned above the U-matic deck. It can also accommodate Video-8 and the regular U-matic formats. Such editing arrangements facilitate the use of smaller gear (such as the Hi8 camcorder) for the "acquisition format" while relying on an industry standard (such as the U-matic) for the mastering format.

is no control track laid down on the tape more than five seconds before any edit point, the machines will not edit. After backing up, the machines will automatically roll forward five seconds and, at your predetermined inpoints, the material on the source deck will be recorded onto the tape on the edit deck. (It will also be displayed on the edit deck monitor.) The edit will stop when the preselected outpoint is reached or when you push the *edit stop* button. You should then play back the edit (most controllers have a review function) to make sure it recorded properly. (See figure 9–27.)

Additional Assemble Edits If the edit was executed properly, you are ready to start your second edit. Remove tape 2 from the source deck and replace it with tape 1. Cue

this tape to the reporter's question that starts with "why," and cue the edit deck up to the desired end of the first edit ("spoke to her"). Mark the edit points and execute the edit. Be particularly careful with audio here because there may be an abrupt level change between the studio introduction and the field interview. Preview the edit carefully because you may find you do not have proper beats between the two segments and you may need to use the trim function to lengthen or shorten the edit points.

In the same manner continue editing the interviewee's answer, the second question, the second answer, the third question, and the third answer. You will not be able to do *seamless editing* because you cannot edit audio and video separately while in the assemble mode. That is one important consideration as to why you might decide to use insert editing for a production that has extensive interview editing involved.

You will need to be particularly careful of continuity. The interview will be shortened so there may be jump-cut problems. If the interviewer was moving a microphone back and forth, you must make sure the microphone does not jump from one edit to the next. If the talent made a funny face or the camera was out of focus at some crucial point, you may want to use one of the reaction shots that were taped "just in case."

You will also need to bring in the character generator identification during one of the edits where the guest is on the screen.

Insert Edits   The four record album covers need to be shown at the points where they are mentioned. The best way to do this is to use the insert-edit mode. Because a control track has been laid down throughout the assemble editing, you can now go back and do insert editing over what has been recorded.

The controller has been in the assemble-edit mode throughout your editing so far, but now you change it to the *video-only* insert mode. You must be very careful not to insert edit *audio* or you will erase the audio (what the guest was saying about the album covers). Set the source deck to the first album cover—3:10 on tape 2. Mark the entry inpoint. Set the edit deck to the place where the singer talks about that album. Mark both an inpoint and *precise outpoint* on this deck because you do not want the edit to carry over into the rest of the interview. In other words, make your edit tight; do not set an exit point several seconds past what you actually want.

After previewing and executing this album-cover insert edit, follow the same procedure for the other three album covers.

Editing the photographs to the music presents a new situation. You must lay down the music track in one continuous segment and then go back and edit in the pictures to the music. This means video and audio must be done separately, so you have to be in the insert mode. However, you cannot just set the controller to the insert mode because there is no control track beyond the interview. The montage could be edited on a separate tape and then assemble-edited, but this would deteriorate the production by one generation. A better method might be to assemble-edit black beyond the end of the interview (*blacking* the remainder of the tape) and then the tape would be prepared for your insert editing. In fact, black could be laid through the switcher while the music (on record or tape) comes through the audio board.

Whichever method you use, you are now faced with the situation of editing pictures to music. This is a creative process that in all likelihood would be accomplished in different ways by different editors.

If dissolves or special effects are desired, the material must be A/B rolled. This means that some of the photographs need to be dubbed to another tape. A better arrangement would have been to record the photos originally on two different tapes. This means you need to have an idea of how all the edits will be arranged before you tape the photos; you need to be able to envision your finished product before you start any studio shooting. Again, the importance of the *discipline of preplanning* must be stressed.

Some directors may choose to fade the music up under the interview and fade it out under the closing. This can be done if the audio for the interview is on one channel (probably channel 2) and the music is on the other channel (channel 1). The music can be faded up and out through the audio board or by raising and lowering audio pots on the VCR—the "dead pot" technique. Once again, care must be taken to make sure the proper combination of audio and video edit buttons are activated on the edit controller. If the audio has been transferred to a videotape, it can be cued more accurately than if it comes directly from the audio board.

Generally, it is not a good idea to prepare a finished tape with different audio tracks on channel 1 and channel 2 (say, voices on channel 2 and music on channel 1) because it is difficult to judge the relative volume of the two channels. The music recorded on channel 1 might drown out the dialogue recorded on channel 2. Also, some playback facilities air only channel 2. One reason they do this is because they occasionally receive tapes with time code placed on channel 1, and if this is played back, it makes a terrible noise. Another reason for favoring channel 2 is that on many videotape formats, channel 1 is on the outside track of the tape and is therefore more likely to be subjected to any tape wear or abuse. (See section 15.7.)

Therefore, if you have music on channel 1 and inadvertently only channel 2 is played back, the audience will not hear your music. To avoid this, you can make a **mix-down** on your final tape that could be either channel 2 only (with the dialogue and music properly mixed) or the same identical mixed audio tracks on both channels 1 and 2.

The closing can be a straightforward assemble edit, but it should be followed by black from the switcher or an assemble edit of black. This is to prevent ending the production with a picture breakup.

The simple exercise presented here certainly does not cover all aspects of editing. Editing is a complicated and fascinating process that involves both considerable technique and quite a bit of discipline, a process in which you improve both technically and aesthetically with practice and experience. Many students learning editing spend over an hour laying down their first edit. But as confidence and knowledge build, some of the process becomes fairly routine—with increasing room for creativity.

Summary

Editing is one of the more recent developments in television production, but even so, it has evolved through several stages that include *physically cutting* the tape, *crash* editing, *control-track* editing, and use of *SMPTE time code*.

Originally, editing was used primarily to stitch together program segments that had been recorded out of order. Now it is used for a multitude of purposes: *correcting* mistakes; *sweetening;* allowing for *sequences all shot on one day* to be included in programs that will air different days; *slaving* of cameras so that a polished production can be put together, including field pieces within a studio shoot; and total editing of material that has all been shot in the field (*single-camera filmic techniques*).

Editing equipment always includes at least an *edit controller* or *control deck* and two videotape recorder/monitor setups—the *source deck* and the *edit deck*. More complicated editing procedures can also involve just about all the equipment normally used in studios and control rooms—switchers, SEGs, character generators, audio consoles, and so forth.

Material can be either *assemble-edited* or *insert-edited*. Assemble editing uses the *control track* of the source material and is generally the faster way to edit if the editing is simple. For insert editing, either a completed program must exist on the tape or the tape must first be *blacked,* and the control track from this synchronized black signal is used to execute the edits.

On-line editing involves editing the final program directly on the master tape with or without an intermediate *work print* stage. If material can be edited *off-line* before it is edited on-line, a great deal of money can be saved because time spent determining *edit points* uses fairly inexpensive equipment. Off-line editing also saves wear and tear on the master tapes because a dub is used as a work print.

Insert editing makes it possible to use either *video-only* or *audio-only* edits—techniques that are not possible with assemble editing. If dissolves or other special effects and transitions are desired, *A/B rolling* is necessary with material prepared on two different source tapes.

A number of principles have evolved over the years that relate to the aesthetics of editing. The *LS-MS-CU* sequence orients the audience well. *Fades* (and, to a lesser extent, *dissolves*) denote passage of time, and people leaving and coming into frames can denote changes in both time and location. Proper *beats* are important when editing material shot single-camera style. One way to achieve a smooth effect is to use *seamless editing* of audio and video. Problems with *continuity* must be watched carefully in order to avoid *position jumps, jump cuts,* and *crossing the axis of action/conversation.* Edits generally should not be made on movement; but if they are, the movement should be going in the *same direction.* Cutting to music should be done *on the beat* and must be carefully timed.

When actually involved in editing, the editor should first *log* any material that has been shot and then make an *edit decision sheet* that designates what shots will be used in what order. The tape should start with *color bars, tone, slate,* and *countdown.* Editing the actual material involves finding and marking the edit *inpoints* and *outpoints, previewing, executing* the edits, and *reviewing.*

In chapter 10, we will be concerned with important scenic and graphics elements that apply to both single-camera and multiple-camera studio production.

9.9 Training Exercises

The first exercise is an individual assignment that should be carried out by each member of the class. The second exercise is a team project that could be done in groups of three or four students to a team.

1. Tape one of your favorite comedy or drama shows. Play it back making frequent use of *pause* and *slow scan,* and write down what you consider to be the major editing techniques and principles used. Pay particular attention to such aesthetic principles as where video edits were made in relation to audio edits; how long shots, medium shots, and close-ups are used; how passage of time is indicated; and what elements are used to establish pace. See if you can spot any continuity errors. Try to determine if the program was assemble-edited or insert-edited. Were there segments where A/B rolling probably had to be used? Assume you have been given the assignment of cutting three minutes out of this program. Write down what you would cut out.

2. Select a favorite piece of music that has a definite beat. Lay it down on videotape along with black. Then find (or shoot) some random footage. Edit some of it to the music. Try for creativity and unique effects. After several teams have edited similar projects (perhaps some of them using the same music and same footage), discuss the similarities and differences between the various approaches and the end results.

Videotape Editing Equipment and Techniques

Pictorial Elements: Sets and Graphics

10

In this chapter, we will examine some of the scenic and pictorial elements that make up the visual aspects of the television production. What are the principles of design that should be applied to the use of sets and the construction of graphics? Persons trained in the older tradition of hand-produced artwork for slides and physical graphic cards have been quick to realize that the same basic principles of composition are now applied to the contemporary world of computer-generated graphics and electronic animation.

Although the student of production is initially concerned with the technical aspects of reproducing sound and picture—the hardware of microphones, cameras, lights, switchers, and recorders—you must also concentrate on the pictorial elements of what the cameras are looking at. Without a decent setting and without intelligible graphics, the best mechanical reproduction of video components can result only in a technically sharp program with no meaningful visual content.

10.1 The Concept of Pictorial Design

There are several elements of pictorial design that apply both to sets and to graphics. Although these two topics will be discussed separately in the remainder of this chapter, it may be helpful to consider some of the common elements first.

Functions of Design Elements

In discussing audio production and lighting techniques, we mentioned that there was both a *technical consideration* and a *creative aspect* to the use of these elements. There is, to some extent, a parallel consideration when examining pictorial elements. Here, however, instead of thinking in terms of technical and creative criteria, it is more applicable to consider the differences between *informational* functions of design and *emotional* or *psychological* functions of design.

First, the *informational aspects of pictorial design* must be considered. They are concerned with conveying appropriate information cues to the audience as accurately and efficiently as possible. In the case of a dramatic setting, you ordinarily want to tell the audience as much as possible about the time and locale of the action. Where is the scene taking place? What is the historical period? What time of day is it? You may also want to give other pictorial cues. What is the status of the main character? Where does he or she live? (Of course, there are many dramatic programs where this type of information is deliberately concealed from the audience for purposes of suspense or dramatic surprise.)

Nondramatic programs also need to convey this kind of information data. Are we in a newsroom? A classroom? A corporate office? Are we on a stage in front of a live audience? Are we in a pulpit? How much do we need to tell the viewers about where they are and what they should know about their surroundings? All television staging considerations should start out with these types of questions.

With graphics, the informational considerations are even more important. The overwhelming use of graphics—especially for simpler productions and basic formats—is to convey information. What is the name of the program (title card)? What is the name of the person talking (key or super card)? How much of our tax dollar goes to education (pie chart)? What does the race course look like (diagram)? How does the piston work (animated graphic)? How bad was the accident (photo)? In designing graphics, the need for clarity is paramount. The director and graphic artist must always be asking, How can I get this in-

formation across as clearly and efficiently as possible? Most of the discussion in sections 10.4 and 10.5 is concerned with this question.

Second, the *emotional* or *psychological functions of pictorial design* must be considered. There are many subtle messages that the total production design can convey. All of the scenic elements—sets, props, graphics, furniture—combine to give a "feel" or "image" to the program. In a news program, do you want the image of an advanced technological communications center, of an abstract setting (figure 10–1), or of a working newsroom (figure 10–2)? In an instructional TV program, do you want the image of a typical academic setting or of a research lab? In a religious program, do you want the image of a traditional church service or of an avant-garde contemporary movement? In a variety program, do you want the image of a conventional stage presentation or the electronic collage of a music video? Again, it is important that the director and designer begin with these types of questions before any decisions are made regarding the design or assembling of set pieces or graphics.

In dramatic programs, of course, the overall *atmosphere* or *mood* is very important. Staging elements—combined with lighting—will tell us much about the mystery of an event, the state of mind of the hero, the lurking tragedy, the atmosphere of a family gathering, the majesty of an accomplishment, the power behind a particular move, the potential danger behind a closed door, the emptiness of a certain thought. The designer should always be concerned with maintaining or building the mood or feeling of every particular scene.

The emotional function of design also includes creating a given *style* or *continuity* to a program—helping to maintain a unity throughout the entire production. In the use of graphics, for instance, it would be jarring to establish a pattern of cartoons to illustrate a

Pictorial Elements: Sets and Graphics

Figure 10–1
Abstract news set for local news program. (Photo courtesy of KABC-TV, Los Angeles)

Figure 10–2
Two views of a working newsroom used as actual on-the-air background for news set. (Photo courtesy of KCBS-TV, Los Angeles)

Pictorial Elements: Sets and Graphics

certain process and then suddenly switch to a series of detailed photographs. Several years ago, a church group produced a syndicated variety program dealing with the broad theme of the family. It was a composite of serious vignettes, vocal numbers, comedy sketches, talks, and dances and featured many different performers and guest stars.[1] The production very easily could have fallen apart into many mini-programs; however, the entire program was held together by its scenic design. Every segment of the program was staged on and around one scenic unit—a large, white, abstract open set combining several different levels, platforms, and stairs. Because it had a scenic unity, the production had a continuity that it otherwise could have lost.

Thus, every pictorial design should serve both an *informational* function and an *emotional* function. The set should not only tell us what time of day it is, but also give us a hint as to what is going to happen this day. The chart should not only tell us the information but emphasize how important the information is.

One word of warning should be mentioned at this point—to be emphasized later in this chapter. Directors and artists must guard against the temptation to go overboard in their artistic embellishments. This is an especial danger with computer graphics; it is so easy to generate numerous flashy pictures and dancing images that the television production can easily be overwhelmed with a glittering display that ultimately detracts from the content of the program. Just because numerous pictures can be created by pushing a few buttons and waving a magic wand, this does not mean that you should do so. Think carefully about what your informational requirements are and what your emotional/artistic goals are.

1. *The Family and Other Living Things,* produced by the Church of Latter-day Saints, 1976.

Elements of Pictorial Design

Artists and critics discourse long and eloquently about the many different factors that constitute aesthetic criteria—unity, harmony, texture, color, rhythm, proportion, and so forth. It is beyond the scope of this book to get into any detailed treatise on aesthetics of the still and moving picture. The beginning production student should be aware, however, of at least three fundamental elements of pictorial design: (1) balance and mass; (2) lines and angles; and (3) tone and color.

Balance and Mass   The concept of balance was introduced in section 6.3 in connection with camera work. Asymmetrical balance is generally preferred over formal symmetrical balance. The larger a mass, the nearer it must be to the center of the scene in order to preserve a sense of balance with a smaller mass (figure 10–3). In addition, the placement of mass within a scenic element will tend to affect the stability of the picture. A heavy mass in the bottom part of the picture implies firmness, solidarity, support, importance. A heavier mass in the top part of the picture projects more instability, suspense, impermanence (figure 10–4). These considerations of balance and placement have strong implications for the design of sets and graphics as well as for camera composition. A title card with lettering in the bottom of the frame projects a solid, strong opening. A scenic unit with heavy ornamentation near the top implies a feeling of uneasiness and suspense.

Lines and Angles   The use of dominant lines is one of the strongest elements available to the scenic designer. Straight lines suggest firmness, rigidity, directness, strength. Curved or rounded lines imply softness, elegance, movement. The direction of the dominant lines in a picture will carry strong connotations. Horizontal lines represent serenity, inactivity, openness; vertical lines are dignified, important, strong; diagonals imply action, imbalance, instability, insecurity. (See figure 10–5.)

Lines and angles can also be used to reinforce or exaggerate perspective, giving more of an illusion of depth. Painted on the studio floor, *forced perspective* lines can reinforce a great feeling of depth. *False perspective* lines can also be worked into other scenic elements. This kind of false perspective is limiting, however, in that the illusion works from only one specific camera location. (See figure 10–6.)

Tone and Color   The predominant tones determine, to a great extent, the overall emotional image of a production. Light tones result in a delicate, cheerful, happy, trivial feeling, whereas dark tones result in a feeling that is heavy, somber, serious, forceful. Tone also affects balance. A dark tone carries more mass, weighs more, and can be used to balance a larger mass that is light in color or tone.

The position of various tones or blocks of dark and light mass in a picture also affects its stability and emotional quality. A dark mass at the top of a picture tends to induce a heavy, unnatural feeling of entrapment and depression; heavier tones in the bottom of a picture give it more of a stable base. (See figure 10–7.)

Color is usually discussed in terms of three characteristics. **Hue** is the actual color base itself (red, green, purple, orange, and so forth). **Saturation** refers to the strength or intensity of a color, how far removed it is from a neutral or gray shade. **Brightness** (or *lightness*) indicates where the color would fall on a scale from light (white) to dark (black). The considerations mentioned for tone apply to color; for example, highly saturated colors (a vivid red) appear heavier—for purposes of balance—than unsaturated colors (a grayish red).

Various hues are also subjectively classified as *warm* (yellows and reds) or *cool* (blues

Figure 10–3
Symmetrical and
asymmetrical balance.

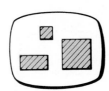

(a) Symmetrical balance usually results in a rigidity and precision that is usually not desired—except for certain formal settings.

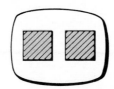
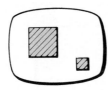

(b) Asymmetrical balance usually is more interesting and dynamic—resulting in a more fluid and creative mood—and just as well balanced aesthetically.

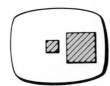
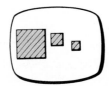

(c) An unbalanced picture can result, however, if care is not taken to position the asymmetrical elements with respect to their weight and mass. Temporarily, this may be desired.

and greens). Warm colors appear to be "heavier" than cool colors. Much of the secret of achieving good color balance is the art of mixing various hues that are compatible, balancing highly saturated colors with grayer shades, and selecting the right brightness of a particular hue (for example, baby blue rather than navy blue). (See section 5.2.)

All of these elements of design—balance, line, tone—must be kept in mind as you look specifically at the elements of set design and graphics composition.

Figure 10–4
Location of mass in the picture.

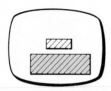

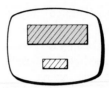

(a) Heavy weight in the bottom of the frame tends to give an impression of stability and security.

(b) If the top of the picture contains more mass than the bottom, the result is a feeling of uneasiness and suspense.

Figure 10–5
The effect of straight and curved lines.

(a) Horizontal lines are restful, inactive, stable. Vertical lines suggest solemnity, dignity, dominance. Diagonal lines represent action, movement, impermanence.

(b) Curved lines generally imply change, beauty, grace, flowing movement. With an upward open curve there is a feeling of freedom and openness. A downward open curve has more of a feeling of pressure and restriction.

Figure 10–6
Lines and perspective.

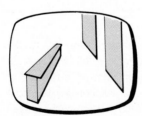
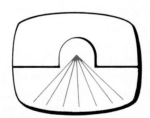

A forced perspective can be created by careful use of scenic elements and even by painting false perspective lines on the studio floor.

Pictorial Elements: Sets and Graphics

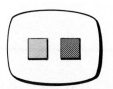

Figure 10–7
Tone and balance.

(a) A darker tone tends to imply more mass; thus the darker tone will overbalance the lighter mass (*left*). A smaller dark mass can be used to balance a lighter mass that is larger (*right*).

(b) A darker tone or darker color at the top of the picture or scenic element will tend to imply a top-heavy feeling of depression (*left*). The lighter tone or brighter color at the top gives a feeling of more solidarity and normalcy (*right*).

10.2 The Staging Design

As you begin to plan for scenery and staging, there are several different aspects that need to be considered: staging styles, scenery elements, and staging requirements and considerations.

Staging Styles

One of the first decisions to be made by the director and designer concerns the style of staging that would be right for a particular program. Neutral, decorative, and realistic settings are three options.

Neutral Settings   One basic approach that is appropriate for many different production purposes is the **neutral** or *nonrepresentational* style. This is a **nonassociative** approach—the setting does not attempt to represent anything at all; there is no identifiable locale; all of the action takes place in **limbo,** and there is no attempt to establish any location. *Cameo* staging (section 4.3) is an example of a neutral setting, as are some types of *silhouette* staging (although the latter usually is used only for a fragment of a larger scene). Most limbo settings, however, are staged simply in front of a gray cyclorama or other neutral-colored plain background. In terms of overall production effect, the neutral staging might be used with the reportorial

camera perspective (section 6.2)—for segments of a variety show, newscast, instructional TV lesson, and so forth.

Decorative Settings   If some elements are added to the neutral setting—purely for the sake of artistic gratification—then it slips into a **decorative** (or even a *fantasy*) style. In an *abstract* setting, some elements have been added, but there still is no attempt to suggest any kind of realistic location or identifiable elements. (See figure 10–8.) Lighting effects and colors might be used; different scenic elements—platforms, steps, a podium—might be incorporated; but there still is no endeavor to represent anything recognizable. The various shapes, textures, colors, levels, and other scenic elements are used purely for their own artistic impact.

Again, many reportorial uses of television would be appropriate for this abstract kind of decorative setting, such as newscasts, talk shows, educational programs, and so forth. The biggest programming format to use this kind of staging, however, would be variety shows—dance numbers, musical performances, concerts, stand-up comedians, rock groups, singers, magicians, and others.

Realistic Settings   In dramatic programs, almost all staging is realistic to one extent or another. There are several levels of realism in stage and television setting. *Repli-*

Pictorial Elements: Sets and Graphics

Figure 10–8
Example of decorative or abstract setting.

Figure 10–9
This set for the CBS series *Uncle Buck* is typical of a realistic set, with flats, set pieces, and detailed set dressing all contributing to a generalized atmospheric realism.

Pictorial Elements: Sets and Graphics

cated realism refers to the actual replication of a real locale—the Oval Office of the White House or the interior of Grand Central Station. Accurate down to tiny details, this style corresponds to the *naturalism* of the stage. For the most part, the approach is too detailed and cluttered for successful television production.

Much more common is *atmospheric realism,* where the set conveys a certain type of place—a western saloon, an elegant drawing room, a busy office. (See figure 10–9.)[2] With this modified form of realism, you can use selected details and highlight certain elements that help strengthen the drama. It is certainly realistic enough for virtually all dramatic purposes.

Another type of realism that is often employed is *symbolic realism.* In this staging style, an open set is used. Rather than have a solid-walled closed set, the background is discontinuous—relying upon the viewer to fill in the missing pieces with *psychological closure.* In this staging style, selected symbols and props are used to represent the idea of the real thing—a table and two chairs comprise the kitchen, a tree trunk and tent make up the campsite, a desk and filing cabinet symbolize an office. There is no attempt to create an illusion of reality—just to suggest it.

Symbolic realism is often employed for brief comedy skits and slapstick sketches that are incorporated into a larger variety program, for example. Some abstract dramas may be staged entirely in symbolic realism. Nondramatic formats also make use of symbolic realism—the talk show with its desk and sofa, the homemaker program with a few kitchen appliances, and the illustrated lecture in front of a freestanding bookcase.

The open set gives the director much more freedom and flexibility in staging and shooting

patterns. Blocking, camera movement, lighting, and microphone placement are all much easier to handle in the open set.

Scenery Elements

Regardless of the staging style, the director and the crew will probably find it convenient to think in terms of three broad categories of scenery and staging elements for purposes of ordering different items, constructing needed units, and considering storage and construction.

Settings   The term **setting** is usually used to refer to all of the major scenic pieces that make up the background and surrounding environment of the scene. This category would, in turn, include about three different kinds of scenic elements: **standard set units,** such as flats, two-folds, and other standing background pieces; **hanging units,** including various cloth drops, hanging drapes, and the cyclorama (or cyc), that might cover two or three walls with a flat, neutral surface; and **set pieces,** which include pillars, steps and stairways, arches, platforms, wagons (platforms on casters), fences, lampposts, and so forth. The term *staff* is used in many professional studios to refer to three-dimensional constructions of plaster or other fibrous materials that are utilized for building facades and other ornamental elements.

Many of the set or staff pieces can be incorporated into realistic settings; others can be used in various artistic configurations in decorative or fantasy settings. Discussion of the construction and use of some of the setting components follows.

Set Dressings and Furniture   These terms, along with the label *stage props,* are used by different practitioners to mean slightly different things. Basically this category includes all of those major items that are involved in *dressing* a set, filling out the naked

2. Subject matter for all photographs in figures 10–9 through 10–20 is by courtesy of Universal Studios, Universal City, California.

Pictorial Elements: Sets and Graphics   **259**

setting represented by the flats and major set pieces. This includes all of the major items of furniture (desk, lectern, chairs, tables, appliances, and so forth) and large exterior stage props (bicycles, cannons, trees, and other natural or man-made objects). The term **set dressing** is often used to refer even more specifically to those smaller items that are used to make the set look lived in—lamps, ashtrays, pictures, books and magazines, household plants, vases, and other furnishings. Set dressings and stage props come from different sources, depending upon one's ingenuity and budget: a station's prop storage, the drama department, secondhand stores, or one's own living room.

Hand Props   A specialized, but extremely important, category is that of hand **properties**—those items that are actually handled and manipulated as part of the television production. They include all those props needed for a dramatic production (telephones, bottles, kitchen tools, food, books, glasses, weapons), or for a commercial in a talk show (the box of cereal or can of dog food), or for an instructional program (globes, models, chemistry apparatus). Obviously some of these items overlap with other set dressings, the distinction being that hand props are actually *used* in the program, rather than being planted as *decoration*.

Staging Requirements and Considerations

At this point, before the director proceeds any further, there are several other considerations that must be given some thought. All of the staging and scenery elements will have to fit in with a total production design. Staging concerns have to meet other criteria also.

Camera Movement   No matter what staging style is used, there must be provision for adequate camera movement. Several cameras will have to be free to have access from different angles in the setting. This usually poses no problems with neutral or limbo sets; it generally is no major problem with decorative settings or the open set; but it could be a problem with some elaborate realistic settings. For this reason, sets are usually constructed as just two-walled or three-walled sets. The open wall (the missing side of the set) is used for camera access. In three-walled sets, the walls do not have to be set at exactly ninety degrees; they can be left open at oblique angles so that the camera can have even more access. In some sets (occasionally a four-walled set may have to be used), it is possible to position cameras behind the flats or other scenic elements and shoot through a window, doorway, hole in the bookcase or fireplace, and other camouflaged openings.

Microphone Placement   The setting also has to have provision for adequate microphone placement and, if on a boom, movement. Although the wireless microphone (section 3.2) is increasingly used in studio dramas—soap operas and situation comedies—the beginning audio operator must learn how to cope with staging concerns involved with wired microphones. For most *dramatic* productions (since lavalieres usually are not worn, hanging mikes result in bad audio, and hidden microphones are not encouraged), some sort of boom or giraffe or fishpole is used. This can lead to two kinds of problems.

First, if the set is small and the boom is large, there will be movement and coordination troubles; cameras will also have to maneuver around the boom and microphone cables; adequate room has to be left open. Second, the mike boom can cause bad boom shadows. If the lighting has not been carefully worked out with the precise boom placement in mind, there will be a strong possibility of unwanted shadows from the horizontal boom or fishpole. Ironically, this could be more of a problem in a neutral setting, with its plain

Pictorial Elements: Sets and Graphics

background, than in a busy realistic set that may make a shadow less noticeable. In most cases, however, either the mike boom or the lighting instrument will have to be repositioned somewhat or the light will have to be *"barn doored"* off the boom (section 4.6).

Lighting Instruments   Other lighting problems can be caused by certain kinds of setting arrangements. Occasionally, pillars or other foreground set pieces may be blocking crucial front lighting from a certain angle. Sometimes a strong key light may throw a very distracting shadow on a close-up shot of some small object; or if the talent is lighted too close to the set (flat or cyc), the key light may throw too much illumination on the set. One of the most common problems, however, is the blocking of the back light by a flat. If the flat is too high for the studio (a 10–foot flat might be high if the studio has a low ceiling), or if the flat is out too far into the studio from the back light, or if the talent is standing too close to the flat, it is going to be difficult to hit the talent with the back light. (See figure 10–10.) In this case, something—the back light or the flat or the talent—will have to be moved.

Talent Movement   Finally, the setting has to take into consideration all anticipated movement by the talent. How much action is required? Will several people be moving in the same direction simultaneously? How much space is needed for certain movement (a dance step or tumbling demonstrations)? Is there plenty of room for all entrances and exits? Will the talent be forced to maneuver so close to the set walls that part of their lighting will be cut off? Or, if the performers work too close to the set, will they cast unwanted shadows of the flat or cyc? Once the director is satisfied that there is enough room for talent movement, lighting instruments, microphone placement, and camera movement, he or she is ready to look at the functional aspect of using scenery.

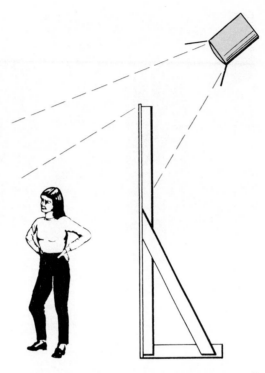

Figure 10–10
Back-lighting problems with scenic flat.

In this kind of situation, either the back light will have to be mounted higher, the light will have to be repositioned closer to the flat, the flat will have to be moved back (closer to the back light), or the talent will have to move forward, farther away from the flat.

10.3 Using Sets and Scenic Elements

Having considered several of the principles of staging design, we turn now to some of the practical factors connected with handling scenic elements and specific studio production techniques.

Handling Scenery

The physical manipulation and handling of all scenery units—construction, assembling, and storage—is a major study by itself. Television scenery is closely related to stage and film scenery; anyone who has ever worked in tech-

Figure 10–11
The rear of this window flat shows typical construction of 1″ × 3″ rails and stiles with a luan covering.

Figure 10–12
Construction of an ordinary flat.

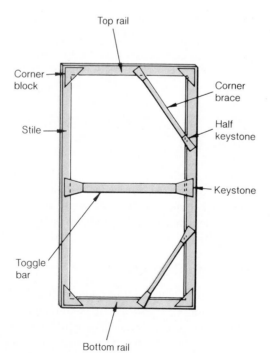

Top rail

Corner block

Corner brace

Stile

Half keystone

Keystone

Toggle bar

Bottom rail

Standard construction of a simple wooden flat consists of a frame made of 1″ × 3″ pine with ¼″ plywood for the corner blocks and keystones. The front of the frame is typically covered with canvas or with plywood (or pressed hardboard). If a solid wooden front covering is used, then the corner braces will not be needed.

nical theater or visited the back lot of a major motion picture studio has a feel for the scope of the scenery and props department. All we can do in this text is touch upon some of the basic elements involved in making scenery units, assembling them for studio use, and storing them for repeated use.[3]

Construction   The basic scenic unit for television, like that for the stage, is the **flat**— a cross-braced wooden frame faced with either canvas (which is lightweight, but too flimsy for repeated heavy use) or thin pressed board or plywood (which will take more abuse, al-

3. For a full discussion of scenery construction and use, consult any good theater stagecraft text or manual, such as Willard F. Bellman, *Scene Design, Stage Lighting, Sound, Costume and Makeup* (New York: Harper & Row, 1983) or Jay Michael Gillette, *Theatrical Design and Production* (Mountain View, CA: Mayfield Publishing Co., 1987).

Pictorial Elements: Sets and Graphics

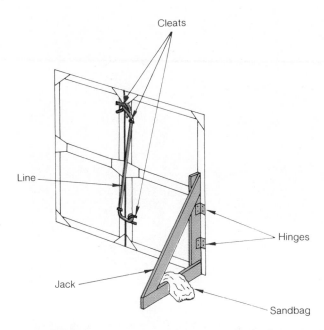

Cleats

Line

Jack

Hinges

Sandbag

Figure 10–13
Connecting and bracing
flats.

Cleats on both flats allow the units to be lashed
together by means of the line, which is permanently tied onto one of the flats. The jack is a hinged
stage brace that, when weighted, forms a good
self-supporting unit.

though it is heavier to work with). Typical
construction consists of 1″ × 3″ studs on
2–foot centers, with a 1/4″ luan covering (see
figure 10–11). More often than not, the flat will
simply be stapled together.

The layout for a standard flat is shown in
figure 10–12. Flats can be made in any size,
but common heights are ten feet for larger studios and eight feet for studios with lower ceil-
ings. Widths also will vary, although they are
seldom broader than five feet (the width that
one person can comfortably handle with arms
outstretched).

Whenever wider widths are needed, flats
can be hinged together semipermanently. Two
flats hinged together are known as a **two-fold.**
Three flats similarly connected (seldom will
you see more than three) are known as a *three-*

fold. When a wider span needs to be covered,
the flat units are temporarily lashed or connected together. (See figure 10–13.)

In addition to standard wooden construction, studios are increasingly turning to other
rigid but lightweight materials, such as foam-
board and corrugated feather board, for
making flats and other scenic elements.

Construction of other set pieces (stairways, platforms, and so forth) is more complicated, requiring heavy bracing and sturdy
framing for the amount of abuse and wear they
will be subjected to. (See figure 10–14.)

Cycs can be either a permanent solid cyc
(faced with plywood or some other hard surface, which may tend to give audio problems)
or a *cyc cloth* (canvas, duck, or gauze, depending upon the desired texture and reflec-

Figure 10–14
A section of an airplane fuselage shows construction that is typical of specialized set pieces.

tance quality desired). Cycs as a rule are designed to be used while stretched taut, giving a smooth limbo background, although they may be hung loosely in pleats to give the appearance of opened drapes. Canvas cycs can also be painted and used as the backdrop for a set, as illustrated in figure 10–15.

Drapes, which are usually of a heavier material and often darker, can be either pulled taut or pleated, depending upon the desired effect. Darker, low-reflectance drapes are effective backing for cameo lighting. Drapes are usually used in smaller widths than a cyc and can ordinarily be easily rigged or hung for specific applications. A cyc, on the other hand, often is permanently mounted, covering two or even three walls of a studio.

Staff pieces can be constructed out of a variety of plasticized and rubberized materials. However, due to environmental considerations (the gases given off in various chemical reactions are environmentally dele-

terious), there is decreasing use made of fiberglass, plaster, and numerous sprayed plastics.

Increasing use is being made of styrene plastic shaped in vacuum-formed molds. These vacuum-form machines can mold the thin layers of styrene in virtually any shape and texture desired. The plastic is placed on top of any given object, heated, pressed, and formed to the desired object, and then the excess air is sucked out. When cooled, the resulting styrene copy is amazingly true to the original object. Figure 10–16 shows several different vacuum-formed styrene staff pieces.

Vacuum-formed pieces are relatively thin and flimsy—suitable usually just for gluing or stapling onto the front of a solid unit. When a heavy set piece is needed—a freestanding piece or something that will hold up under some amount of handling—fiberglass often has to be used. Realistic units can be cast from wooden or plaster molds that will withstand

Pictorial Elements: Sets and Graphics

Figure 10–15
Canvas backdrop painted
to serve as a street-front
scene.

quite a bit of abuse. Figure 10–17 shows the process used to mold a series of fiberglass columns.

Natural-looking ground covers also pose a problem for studio productions—if any amount of action or camera work is going to focus on the ground. How do you create a realistic plot of dirt or a sandy beach on a studio floor? Figure 10–18 shows one answer—the use of a *dirt skin* to simulate a patch of natural earth. Similarly, natural vertical surfaces—cliff faces, rocks, mine walls—must be carefully constructed to simulate the real thing. These upright pieces, however, must be constructed from fairly rigid material. Again, fiberglass can be used effectively (see figure 10–19).

Assembling   Most flats are built with special hardware that facilitates easy temporary joining of two or more units. The stiles of the flats can be fitted with cleats so that a line can be used to lash two flats together quickly. (See figure 10–13.)

Other methods of joining flats include the use of various metal fasteners (such as *L-plates*, which have drop-in fasteners and loose pin-hinges) and the use of large *quick-fix* clamps, which can be used to clamp the stiles of two adjoining flats together.

Most flats also have some sort of bracing or supporting unit so that they can be completely freestanding as a self-supporting unit. Several different types of stage braces are used. One of the most common is the **jack** or hinged wooden brace. (See figure 10–13.) When the flat is in place, the jack is swung out behind the flat at right angles to the front of the flat and held in place with stage weights or sandbags.

When flats are assembled for a set that is likely to remain in place for a prolonged period, they often are permanently secured with a stage screw. Figure 10–20 illustrates the use of a metal brace screwed into the floor for a set that is part of a long-running situation comedy.

Figure 10–16
The vacuum-form process uses thin styrene plastic to form three-dimensional "staff" pieces.

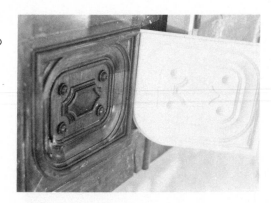

(a) An ornate door panel and its styrene copy.

(b) Detailed vacuum-formed decorative pieces.

(c) A stack of styrene brick panels.

(d) A variety of vacuum-formed styrene rock facades.

Most set pieces are solid and freestanding units that need no special bracing when assembled for use in the studio. However, many of them—such as stairway units—do need to be fastened to other units or flats to make them as secure and immobile as possible. Door flats also need to be securely fastened to other set units to guarantee that the doorway will function properly without sticking or falling down when used. Some set pieces, such as *parallels* (collapsible platforms), can be partially disassembled and folded for storage. They must be carefully put together and securely set up before being used.

Pictorial Elements: Sets and Graphics

(a) A master mold must be constructed of plaster or some similar material.

(b) Individual fiberglass pieces are cast from the mold.

Figure 10–17
Fabricating fiberglass pieces is a multistage process.

(c) The fiberglass columns can then be painted or finished to suit the set requirements.

Storage   In many small stations and educational institutions, scenery storage can be a serious problem. There is never enough room to house everything that is needed, and scenery storage always seems to be one area that suffers the most. This can be a particularly critical problem because so many of the flats and special set pieces can be reused over and over in a variety of ways—with different set dressings—in a number of configurations. Yet, they have to be stored somewhere and catalogued for easy retrieval.

Flats and other narrow units are usually stored in racks, which are simple frames designed to hold a number of flats in an upright position. Each rack can be designed and labeled to hold similarly matched scenic units (for example, living room flats, office flats, green-speckled flats, log cabin flats, and so forth).

Props and other small items can be stored on deep shelves in the storage area. Again, it is important that each shelf and/or cubicle be clearly labeled: "telephones," "dishes," "bottles," and so on. Even furniture and other large

Figure 10–18
Fiberglass "dirt skins" are made from burlap impregnated with fiberglass mixed with dirt or any other desired soil texture.

Figure 10–19
Rigid fiberglass pieces can be used to simulate the texture of mine walls or other rough surfaces.

Pictorial Elements: Sets and Graphics

stage props can be stored in multitiered shelves. Large overstuffed chairs, sofas, and heavy tables can be stored on the floor level; medium-sized chairs and tables can be stored on another level (four to five feet off the floor); and lightweight chairs and stools and small appliances can be stored on a third level (perhaps seven to eight feet above the floor).

Studio Techniques

In moving into actual studio usage, there are several other factors that the director and staging director need to be aware of.

Floor Plan   First of all, as we have stressed throughout this text, the success of any television production is dependent to a great extent upon the discipline exercised in pre-production planning. As with the considerations of the lighting director, much valuable studio time and frustration can be saved by careful planning and plotting by the staging coordinator (section 4.6).

A good floor plan allows the director to make the most economical use of all studio and staging space. Sets can be planned efficiently; equipment can be placed with precision. The director can plan how best to take advantage, for example, of the *corner set*—a two-walled setting positioned in a corner of the studio—that provides good set backing for many types of productions (better than a flat backdrop), while allowing great depth and freedom of camera movement (more so than with a three-walled set).

A typical studio staging floor plan will include the placement of all flats and other set pieces and the exact location of all stage props and furniture. Other prominent studio facilities should also be included, as they are important to the production setting. It is important that all flats and furniture be drawn to exact scale; otherwise the director's shooting angles, the talent's movement, and the lighting design will all be off. Figure 10–21 shows a

Figure 10–20
A metal brace used for semipermanent support of a flat.

typical plot plan, drawn to the scale of one-eighth inch to one foot. Once the accurate floor plan is drawn, it will be used by the director, staging director, staging assistants, floor manager, audio engineer, talent, and even the lighting director (to confirm and complement the lighting plot). It is therefore essential that the plan be prepared with as much detail and precision as possible.

Lighting Effects   In addition to the regular lighting required for illumination of the production area, there are other special lighting effects that should be considered as part of the overall staging design. We have already mentioned the use of the cucalorus, or cookie, pattern (section 4.4) to cast various shadow patterns (venetian blinds, prison bars, Moorish latticework, and so forth) on the set wall. (See figure 10–22.)

Colored gels can be used to throw colored lights on a plain cyc or other surface. Subtle lighting changes (with the dimmer) can be

Figure 10–21
Sample staging floor plan.

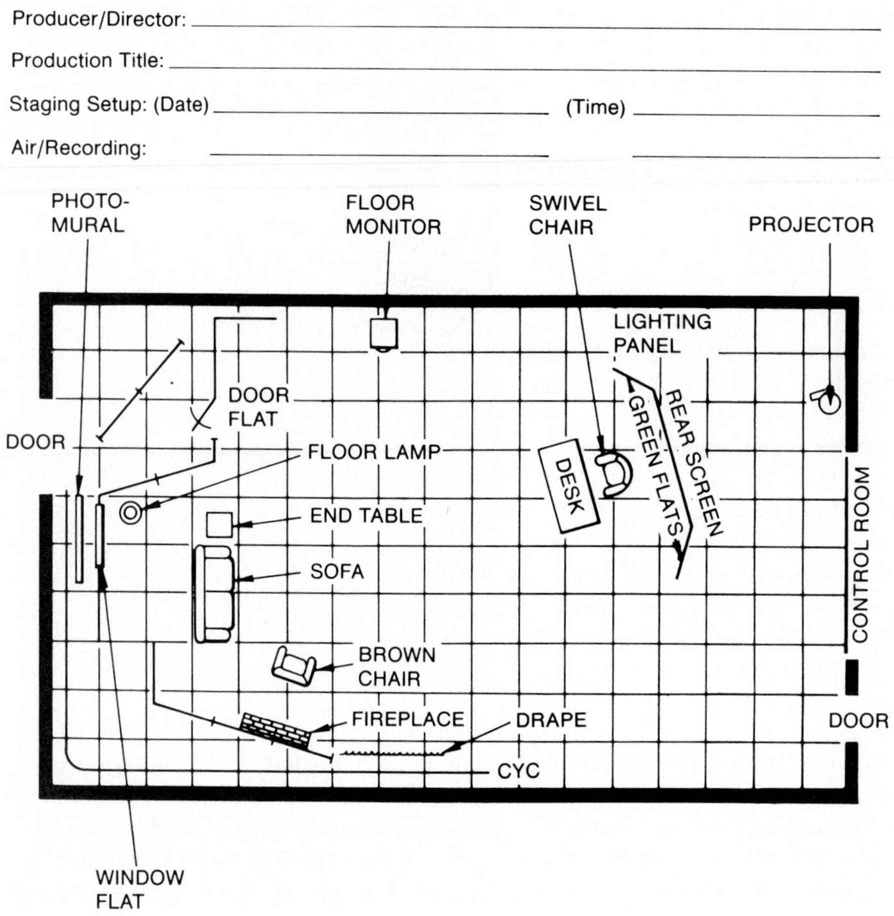

Producer/Director: _____

Production Title: _____

Staging Setup: (Date) _____ (Time) _____

Air/Recording: _____   _____

In this particular floor plan, the squares on the floor correspond to 3-foot tiles actually laid on the studio floor. In other floor plans, a lighting grid or pipe battens might be superimposed over the studio layout.

employed to change color or shadowing as dramatic action unfolds. Other creative lighting effects (determining shape and texture, modifying reality, and establishing mood) were discussed in section 4.3. Staging and lighting must be considered as one integral production element; they cannot be looked at as isolated independent components.

Special Staging Effects   There are several different kinds of mechanical and optical **staging effects** that can be used. Although some of the effects depend upon expensive equipment and elaborate arrangements, others can be adapted to most studio situations.

Large electric fans can create *wind* effects. Dry ice plunged into a tub of hot water

Pictorial Elements: Sets and Graphics

Figure 10–22
Use of a cucalorus pattern
to project a shadow on the
back wall of a set.

creates *fog*. (Both of these effects cause studio noise that can be compensated for in a number of ways, including sound effects records.) *Lightning* and *explosions* are best suggested by lighting effects (off set) coupled with sound effects.

To produce a *fire* effect, shake silk strips on a stick in front of a spotlight to create flickering shadows or super film footage of a flame over the set (since flame is translucent, the super effect works well). Again, use sound effects to present a total contextual effect. *Smoke* can be added by carefully pouring mineral oil in a container on a hot plate.

Rain can be simulated by preparing a rain **drum** graphic—a continuous loop of black paper with white streaks splashed on it, attached to a studio crawl (section 10.5)—and rotating the drum; super a slightly defocused shot of the drum over the scene (with the actors in wet clothing). Again, add sound for a total effect.

There are several different kinds of optical effects that also can be incorporated into many kinds of productions. **Rear screen projection** can be used in many dramatic and reportorial settings. Ranging in size from four or five feet wide up to twelve feet across, rear screens can be used with regular slide projectors or, preferably, with special high-powered 4″ × 5″ projectors. They can be placed behind talent for newscasts or corporate videos, or they can be incorporated into a dramatic setting for outdoor locations or window backing. Special lighting and studio problems can occur, however. The use of the rear screen takes up quite a bit of floor space behind the set. Lighting is critical because no spill light (from the front or rear) can be allowed to fall upon the screen; lighting has to be from the sides or from very high, steep angles.

Mirrors can be used in a variety of ways. For example, a large mirror suspended from a lighting grid can be used to get a shot looking straight down onto a demonstration table or into a cooking pot. Mirrors can also be used in musical productions. High and low shots—for example, dancers' feet on a bandstand program—can be obtained by using a double-mirrored periscope.

Gobos are another handy staging device that enable a camera to frame a shot through some special foreground design. The gobo is a cutout (for instance, a simulated gunsight or keyhole) that is positioned several feet in front of the camera; it is an obvious stylistic effect that can be used judiciously to good advantage. Other optical devices using special filters and prisms also can be utilized in more sophisticated situations.

Production Problems   Finally, mention should be made of several common troubles that periodically plague even the best-planned staging plan. One is the difficulty of obtaining a consistent background from all angles. Whether a person is using a lighted cyc or a realistic set of flats, care must be taken to make certain that the set is evenly lit so that each camera, shooting from its particular angle, will be getting the same background shot. Also, care must be taken to ensure that the sets are wide enough—that there is enough cover at each end of the set—so that a camera shooting from outside angles will not be shooting off the set.

Troubles frequently occur with functional furniture. Chairs, stools, and sofas must be appropriately matched with talent. There are some common furniture problems: the *swinging swivel chair,* in which guests vent their nervous energy by rotating back and forth; the *precarious perch,* which involves sitting uncomfortably on top of a high, hard stool; and the *talent swallower,* overstuffed chairs and sofas that are so plush and soft that the person sinks down so far the director is left with nothing but a shot of knees. Make sure you use solid furniture that is comfortable but firm.

One last production problem that has ruined many a final take is the *forgotten prop.* In any kind of production that relies on hand props (dramas, variety acts, demonstration shows, training programs), there is always the danger of failing to return a given prop to its starting point after a rehearsal. The gun must be returned to the bedside table; the magician's paraphernalia must be repacked and checked; a new set of vegetables must be prepared for the cooking demonstration; the toys must be put back in the clown's sack; and so forth. Both the talent and the stage manager should double-check, after the dress rehearsal, to determine that everything is in place for the final production.

10.4 Principles of Graphics Design

In this section we turn from the large picture of the entire setting to the area of television **graphics**—those two-dimensional visuals specifically prepared for television presentation. This definition includes physical items—such as title cards, charts, drawings, cartoons, diagrams, photographs, maps, super (key) cards, slides, and chalkboards—as well as computer graphics.

In today's well-equipped production centers, we must become increasingly involved with electronic graphics and computer-generated animation. In professional studios, the character generator and computer graphic have almost totally replaced the physical card.

Ideally, the skills of the traditional pen-and-brush artist are still to be desired as a basic requisite for successful electronic graphics. The computer cannot substitute for the color and composition sensitivity of the artist. Although any reasonably bright computer-literate individual can learn how to assemble fancy electronic images with a moderately priced computer-graphics program, it still takes the training and creativity of an artist to create art. As a general rule, you will have more success by training a good artist in computer graphics than by trying to turn a computer whiz into an artist.

For example, using the *capture* capability of many character generators (section 10.6), a specialized camera is used to take a shot of a conventionally prepared piece of physical artwork on a card; this image can then be electronically shaped, colored, and combined with other electronic effects. But the original artwork still must be prepared by a graphic artist.

Nevertheless, many low-budget television operations will be able to utilize the talents of a reasonably astute computer technician in preparing attractive visuals. Just as an amateur camcorder and at-home VCR editing system or complex stereo system can help train the neophyte video/audio enthusiast with certain production and editing skills, so can home computer-graphics programs help to acquaint the budding TV artist with an introduction to the videographics industry.

But moderation is called for. The ease of image manipulation with electronic graphics is both a blessing and a curse. It facilitates the creation and utilization of a lot of unnecessary and overdone video graphics. As discussed later under "Simplicity and Style," picture complexity should not overpower the content. Too many fancy images can corrupt the information. You do not want to litter your program with unwarranted dazzling images that do not carry forth the purpose of your production.

As we move into a discussion of television graphics, keep in mind that many principles of graphics design that evolved with physical graphic cards—aspect ratio, essential areas, quantity of information that can be conveyed, symbol size, simplicity, and color contrast—apply to computer graphics as they did to physical cards.

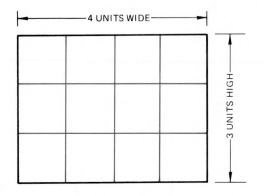

Figure 10–23
Regardless of the size of the television graphic—whether it is four centimeters wide or eight feet wide—it must always be in the three-to-four aspect ratio if it is designed to be used full frame.

Aspect Ratio

The first rule of graphics preparation is that all physical and electronically generated visual material must be prepared with a *three-to-four aspect ratio*—the television screen is three units high and four units wide. Nothing can be done to change that ratio: regardless of the size of a graphic, it still has to fit into that three-to-four ratio. (See figure 10–23.) This is approximately the same ratio as a horizontal 35mm slide. Most slides, therefore, can be used *horizontally* in the television format.

Vertical slides, of course, cannot as a rule be used successfully on the television screen.

However, there are some exceptions when a physical graphic card that is not in the three-to-four ratio can be used. A long horizontal card can be used as a **pan card**—that is, the camera can pan across the card, revealing part of the information at a time. Similarly, a tall narrow graphic can be used as a **tilt card**—with the camera tilting down (or up) the card, revealing only a portion of it at a time.

Also, it is possible to use a tall card or a vertical slide as part of a split screen (section 7.4), with the remainder of the screen filled by the talent or some other subject. Similarly, it would be possible to use a vertical slide if it is projected on a rear screen, and the rest of the television picture is filled with something else

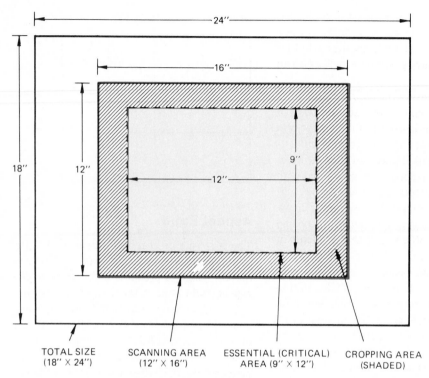

Figure 10–24
Relationship of scanning area to essential area.

TOTAL SIZE (18" × 24")   SCANNING AREA (12" × 16")   ESSENTIAL (CRITICAL) AREA (9" × 12")   CROPPING AREA (SHADED)

In this particular example, suppose you are working with a card that is actually 18" × 24". The scanning area is two-thirds of the total card size, or 12" × 16" (which includes the shaded area). The essential (or critical) area is three-fourths of the scanning area (or half of the total card size); that is, 9" × 12" (indicated by the area in color). The cropping area (shaded) is the portion of the scanning area that may be seen by the television camera, but that may or may not be seen on the home television receiver.

(like the talent standing next to the screen). In general, however, all television material must be prepared to fit on the television screen with that three-to-four aspect ratio.

Scanning and Essential Areas

All material that is prepared on a physical graphic card will not necessarily be seen on the home receiver. There has to be some room around the border of the card for numbering and identification of the graphic, handling, smudge prints, and so forth. Let us call this the *border area* and assume that it will not be used for any information at all. The camera will never intend to shoot this area. To give ourselves plenty of room, let us assume that this margin should be about one-sixth of the total card: that is, if the card is twenty-four inches wide, we will take off one-sixth, or four inches, from each edge. This leaves us with a total usable width of sixteen inches. (See figure 10–24.)

The remaining area that we have left is called the **scanning area.** This is the area actually to be scanned by the television camera. If we started out with a card that measured 18" × 24" and reduced that with a border one-sixth the dimension of the card on all sides, we would now have a scanning area of 12" × 16"—still in the three-to-four ratio. (See figure 10–24.)

Pictorial Elements: Sets and Graphics

Still, not everything in the scanning area will be transmitted through the entire system to reach the home TV set. The scanning system of the camera monitor may be slightly misaligned, so the camera operator will inadvertently cut off part of the graphic. The home TV set may clip off, or *crop,* some of the picture. To be safe, you should decrease the total width of the usable scanning area by taking off about one-eighth on all sides. Starting with our original card twenty-four inches wide, we would now have a remaining width of about twelve inches. (See figure 10–24.)

The remaining area is known as the **essential area,** or the **critical area.** All of the essential information that we want to transmit through the system must be placed in this critical zone. This amounts to about one-half of the original card size. It is still a three-to-four ratio.

The information that is outside of the essential area but still within the scanning area (the shaded area in figure 10–24) may or may not be seen on the home receiver. Depending upon the various components in the total transmission system, some of this information may reach the home set; some of it will be cropped. This information, therefore, must be part of the total graphic design, but it cannot be essential. Anything outside of the scanning area—on the border of the card—is technically known as *garbage,* and it is assumed that the camera will not try to transmit any of it.

With computer-generated graphics, you will not have to be concerned with physical borders and the precise extent of the scanning or essential areas. However, you should still be concerned with leaving an adequate aesthetic border on all electronic graphics you design. Do not run your lettering all the way to the edge of the screen; leave some room for artistic balance and visual space; and allow for the home receiver that still may be cropping some of the transmitted video signal.

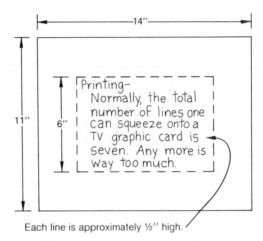

Figure 10–25
Quantity of information on a graphic card.

Printing—
Normally, the total number of lines one can squeeze onto a TV graphic card is seven. Any more is way too much.

Each line is approximately ½″ high.

On a typical 11″ × 14″ graphic card, the essential area will be about 6″ high. This means that each individual letter will be about ½″ tall. The information on the card above represents the maximum amount that should be put on one card.

Quantity of Information

The amount of information that can be communicated on television obviously is limited. The quantity of printed characters that can be successfully included in one TV picture is determined basically by three factors: the size of the symbols (lettering); the style of printing; and color and tonal contrast. Each of the three factors is discussed in the next three sections.

Symbol Size   As a general rule of thumb, lettering on television should be *no smaller than one-fifteenth of the screen height.* If the critical area of a physical graphic card is fifteen inches high, that would mean that lettering could be no smaller than one inch. If the critical area is two inches high, individual letters would have to be a little over one-eighth inch high. Figure 10–25 indicates the amount of material that should be considered maximum for a typical TV graphic. If no line is less than one-fifteenth of the height of the critical area (and assuming some space is left between each line of letters), this would mean

Tehran ●

IRAN

Baghdad ●

IRAQ

SAUDI
ARABIA

KUWAIT

that normally *no more than seven lines of information* should be included on a TV graphic card.

Of course, artistic considerations—balance and arrangement of mass—might dictate that much less material be used. And it is recognized, on the other hand, that there are specialized exceptions to this rule; print information stored on videodiscs, teletext printing, computer displays, and other high-resolution formats may include more than twenty lines on the screen. Given the ease of creating bountiful clean, crisp lettering with a character generator, the temptation is to flood the screen with information.

But seven lines should generally be considered the maximum number of lines for a normal TV graphic. Think not of the high-quality monitor directly in front of you in the control room; rather think of the myopic viewer at home sitting across the room from his or her slightly fuzzy old TV receiver.

Simplicity and Style   If there is one primary rule about the preparation of TV graphics, electronic or physical, it is simply this: *Keep it simple*—all lettering, all design elements, all artwork. The screen is too small and the scanning lines are too blurry to permit any fine detail work.

This is particularly true with lettering styles. Letters should be bold, thick, well-defined, with sharp, firm contour. Elegant lettering with fancy serifs and swirls must be avoided (except possibly for large stylized two- or three-word titles). Letters should be of even thickness throughout—both horizontal and vertical lines should be the same. (Thin horizontal lines, for example, can be obliterated in the scanning lines.) Choose electronic fonts that are basic and uniform, such as *Gothic, Helvetica,* or *Futura.* (See figure 10–29.)

Any other artwork on a graphic card with lettering should also be kept simple. If it is too detailed, the audience will not get a chance to comprehend it; if it is too confusing and domineering, the audience will be distracted from the lettering.

All nonverbal graphics—pictures, cartoons, drawings, slides—must also be kept as simple as possible. Drawings or photographs showing a certain component or step in a process must show only what is absolutely necessary. One of the main troubles in trying to use visuals prepared for other media (for example, charts from a book or photos from a magazine) is that they invariably contain too much detail. They are designed for a medium without the pressing temporal limitations of television. Usually they are visuals designed to convey as much information as possible in a single picture; they are designed for detailed study and comparison. Television, by contrast, may have to use three or four graphics sequentially to get the same information across. Do not try to crowd everything into one picture.

This admonition is particularly true with *maps.* It is safe to say that no prepared maps (designed for nontelevision application) can safely be used on television. Any television graphic that tries to squeeze in more than twenty-five words is really too cramped and the information is too small. (See figure 10–25.) How many words are there on a typical map section that you might want to use? Maps have to be redone for TV. (See figure 10–26.) Use only outlines of countries or natural geographical bodies and a few key labels or key locations. Use a series of maps if movement or detail is needed.

Color Contrast   A third factor that can help determine the readability of either a physical or computer-generated graphic is color contrast. Working with color graphics, it is important to use hues that contrast and complement each other without actually clashing. (See color plate B.) Artistic judgment and experience will help determine which hues go well together. It is often very effective to combine different saturation levels of the same or closely related hues. Contrast in brightness levels also is effective in making certain segments of a graphic stand out.

With most basic character generators, thousands or even millions of colors are possible. Take time to experiment with your system and see what combinations of hues, saturation, and brightness work best for your purposes.

Video engineers like to have just a little white and a little black in a picture for reference points. Thus, a good graphic would be one that has two or three shades of brightness plus a little white and black for sparkle and interest. Avoid graphics that are all black and white (except for super and key cards, which have to be white letters on a black card) or that consist entirely of high-contrast colors.

One problem to be avoided is the use of colors of the same brightness or saturation in preparing graphics. Two different hues (say, red and blue) will contrast best if you also consider differing levels of saturation and brightness. A dark brownish red will contrast better against a brilliant royal blue than against a dark navy blue.

In fact, contrasting saturations of the same hue (for example, a vivid chartreuse and a grayish olive green) provide considerable contrast. And even contrasting brightness or lightness of the same hue and saturation (for example, a light pink and a dark rose) provides essential contrast and legibility.

Having considered these basic principles of designing television graphics, and keeping in mind some of the basic concepts of balance and line discussed in section 10.1, let us now look at some of the functional aspects of how TV graphics can be used in the studio—whether working with physical cards or computer graphics.

10.5 Construction and Use of Physical Graphics

The character generator has replaced the physical graphic card for most titling and labeling purposes. And computer animation has taken the place of much conventional TV artwork. However, there still are occasions when traditional two-dimensional TV graphic cards are used—for large maps, on-set graphics, pan and tilt cards, artwork integrated into demonstrations, and so forth. Therefore, it is helpful to review some of the techniques and considerations concerned with physical graphics—especially as they may apply to small-format productions and many training situations.

In the actual preparation and use of graphics, several questions need to be answered about the way in which they are to be displayed, the ideal size for graphics, how they are to be constructed, and specific production applications.

Location and Display

Perhaps the first question to be asked about the use of a particular graphic is where and how it is to be displayed. There is one basic distinction that must be made. Is the graphic to be used on the set? Or is it to be an off-set graphic?

On-set graphics are meant to be displayed in front of the audience. Usually, a shooting pattern will be worked out that includes some shots of the talent and graphic(s) in the same shot. On-set graphics can be used on a floor easel or on a desk easel. They can be hanging as a decoration in the middle of the studio; they may be attached to freestanding poles. They may be mounted on a wall of the set; or they can be used on a rear projection screen with the talent in front of the screen. One of the most common examples is the news scene electronically matted in behind the reporter in a typical news set (section 7.4). In one way or another, however, they are designed to be used as an integral part of the set. The audience sees where and how they are used.

Off-set graphics, on the other hand, are never seen as an integrated part of the set. They appear out of nowhere. The audience has no reference point for them; for example, the audience would never know the actual size of the graphic. In pre-computer production, physical off-set graphics were employed in a variety of ways, but most often they were used on a graphics stand or floor easel. They may also be mounted on a drum or **crawl**—a large revolving drum that can be turned at varying speeds (either by hand or by an electric motor) with a long flexible graphic card attached to it.

Computer-generated visuals, of course, are considered off-set graphics—unless they are projected behind the talent. Off-set graphics may also be used as slides from telecine or the master control room film chain. This is often much easier and more convenient in that (a) the graphics are already framed and readily accessible without the chance of a slipup on the floor, and (b) a camera can be freed for other studio work. The graphics may also be prepared ahead of time and recorded on videotape; they can then be edited into the studio program—either live during the production or later during postproduction editing.

One reason that the distinction between on-set and off-set graphics is important is that you may design a graphic differently if it is to be an on-set graphic. For instance, conceivably you could use a vertical ratio—if you knew that the talent would always be standing in the same shot with the graphic. Or you may design a graphic with more information than is otherwise recommended—if the talent will be talking at considerable length (perhaps with the aid of a pointer) about different parts of the graphic. In addition, color coordination and the use of mass and balance may be different if it is an on-set graphic, designed to be seen in the same shot with something else.

Whether a graphic is to be used on set or off set, if it is not firmly attached or stapled to some other scenic unit (such as a wall or a studio crawl), it must be firmly mounted. All graphics for easel stands must be either constructed directly on heavy poster board or firmly attached (glued) to heavy board.

Size of Graphics

To the viewer at home, it does not matter what size the physical graphic card actually is as long as it is attractive and legible. For production purposes, however, size makes a difference. (With computer-generated visuals, of course, all graphics are the same size; they exist only on the screen.)

On-set graphics have to be a reasonable size that balances with the talent and/or with other set elements. Size depends upon the purpose and the setting. A good average on-set size is probably the full 22″ × 28″ poster board size; for simpler desktop graphics, 11″ × 14″ is probably adequate. Seldom will on-set graphics be any smaller than that. At the other extreme, on-set graphics could be quite large—taking up an entire wall or, as has been done, covering half the studio floor with a painted map. One recent example was a series of ABC News specials that had a giant map of the

Pictorial Elements: Sets and Graphics

Middle East painted on the floor and blended into the rear wall; Peter Jennings was able to step from one country to another as he explained the geography of the Gulf War.

Off-set physical graphics could vary considerably in size, again depending upon the exact use to which they are put. For most purposes, the ubiquitous 11″ × 14″ would be a good size—it is convenient, readily available, and easy to handle. When necessary, much smaller sizes can be used. Many cameras can focus in on a 3″ × 4″ card without too much trouble. The smaller a graphic is, however, the more time and difficulty it takes for the camera operator to adjust focus. It is possible, with many camera and tube complements, to get tight enough on a small area to use type-written material on camera.

One general consideration to keep in mind is that the smaller a physical graphic card is, the more every little camera movement is going to be magnified on the screen. With a 3″ × 4″ card, the slightest camera jiggle will turn out to be a major movement on a 25–inch screen. Also, every little blemish on the graphic itself and every minor letter imperfection will be magnified. For these reasons, directors usually like to stay away from undersized graphics. In addition, if a camera is going to have to execute any movement on a graphic—panning or tilting, moving around on a map—the bigger the graphic is, the smoother the movement will be. For these purposes, the 22″ × 28″ size is often utilized.

Graphics Preparation

There are quite a few methods for lettering on graphic cards. Depending upon one's artistic abilities, budget, and access to equipment, any one of the following might be appropriate. *Hand lettering* can be done with quite a variety of media and tools: pen, pencil, paint (poster paints, tempera), charcoal, chalk. Felt-tip marking pens may be one of the fastest and easiest (for rough lettering). There are a number of ready-made, *ready-to-apply letters* that can be purchased: wax rub-on letters come in a variety of styles; large cutout, paste-on letters in various formats are available. Different types of *mechanical lettering aids,* stencils, and lettering sets can be effectively used in some applications. Specific *printing machines,* such as the hot press and other mechanical cold-press machines that use ribbon or tape acetate, can be very useful, if available.

The *typewriter,* as mentioned, can be considered for some jobs—under some conditions. In particular, if large primary type is available, with good sharp carbon ribbon, the typewriter can prepare simple textual material. But as a rule, ordinary typewriter print, when magnified by the camera, does not look very satisfactory. Also, the camera runs into extensive production problems when trying to work with something as small as ordinary type. Many newer lenses, however, have a close-up **macro-lens** setting designed to make it easier to get tight shots of small objects.

In working with these various media and materials, take care to avoid—or work very carefully with—any highly reflective matter. Some of the cold-press acetate tape, for instance, makes letters that are very shiny. Be careful working with glossy photos, too. Matte finishes are to be preferred, if you have a choice. Otherwise, lighting is critical in order to avoid reflected glare.

One advantage to hand lettering and some of the ready-to-apply rub-on and paste-on letters is that you can optically space the letters. With most of the machine-generated letters, such as the typewriter and some printing machines, each letter is mechanically spaced from the ones next to it—with a rigidity that is more convenient than artistic. (See figure 10–27.) Most computer-graphics programs allow for *kerning*—which lets the operator/artist determine exact spacing between individual letters.

SP|A|CI|N|G SP|A|CI|NG

(METHODICAL)   (OPTICAL)

Left, in methodical spacing, each letter is spaced exactly the same distance from the one on either side of it. This results in an uneven appearance because letters with vertical lines (such as the "I" and the "N") appear very close together, while those with open spaces at the top or bottom (such as the "P" and the "A") appear too far apart when next to each other. *Right,* with optical spacing, variations can be taken into consideration as each letter is spaced visually according to its shape.

One other hint for successful physical graphics preparation is to assemble your graphics in segments. Prepare your lettering—by whatever method—on appropriate shades of colored paper; and then cut the segments out in blocks and glue them onto your different colored basic board for the graphic. This accomplishes three things for you. First, it allows you to work more easily with blocks and masses. You can better control the balance and layout of each graphic. Second, the approach gives you more of an opportunity to work with varying textures and shades on one graphic. If you print black letters on a light green paper and then cut out the blocks of paper and paste them onto darker green poster board, you have introduced another tone in a rather pleasing and easy-to-handle manner. Third, it allows you to compensate more easily for any mistakes you make. If you ruin the lettering on one small segment or block, you do not have to throw out the whole graphic and start from scratch.

As a transition to computer-generated graphics, it should be noted that the **character generator** (figure 10–28) is a very handy, always available source for the quickest jobs of all. The character generator allows the operator to electronically type right on the screen.

Most models allow for quick retrieval of previously prepared material and flexible positioning and movement on the screen. Advanced character generators today can produce an amazing array of varied alphanumeric data and background artwork.

10.6 Computer-Generated Graphics

All major production studios, networks, and virtually all stations and corporate video operations have added the computer to their art departments. Commercial networks and ambitious cable operations such as CNN (Cable News Network) will have thirty to forty graphic workstations available—with up to a dozen workstations in operation at any one time. Even a medium-sized television station or studio facility will have upwards of $50,000 to $250,000 invested in computer-graphics capabilities.

But as the costs of microcomputers and simple software programs have come down, many schools and audiovisual operations have also been able to utilize the computer for graphics work. It is possible to get into some simple computer-generated graphics production with equipment costing as little as $500.

Computer graphics are used for a variety of training programs, titles and credits, illustrated lectures, weather charts, news graphics, cartoons and animation, commercials, and numerous other applications. It is essential that tomorrow's video professionals become as familiar and comfortable with the computer as they are with the TV camera and switcher.

Computer graphics can be defined in terms of increasing complexity—ranging from simple lettering programs to complex "paint" and animation operations. One way of examining computer graphics is to consider the various

Pictorial Elements: Sets and Graphics

Figure 10–28
Chyron RGU character
generator.

sources of visual material and the complexity of treatment of such material. In the next two sections, we will be introducing you to the following concepts:

1. Character generation—using equipment designed to allow you to generate and manipulate alphanumeric symbols electronically.
2. Frozen-frame retrieval—capturing a still frame of video information from any existing videotape or disc.
3. Camera capture of an existing still picture—using a dedicated camera (usually mounted on a camera stand in a graphics workstation) to take a picture of any visual (original artwork, magazine photo, glossy print).
4. Creation of freehand art—using a graphics pad or tablet to draw original artwork.

5. *Paint* programs—allowing the artist to modify shapes, colors, textures, edging effects, embossing, and so forth.
6. Digital effects—altering the picture by stretching, shrinking, squeezing, twisting, and otherwise distorting the original.
7. Animation—adding movement by rotating, spinning, inverting, key framing, ray tracing, and other effects.

Character Generator   First, it should be recognized that the humble character generator (C.G.) of a decade ago has evolved into a major graphics facility. Today's C.G. is actually an extremely refined stand-alone word processor—a computer dedicated to the generation and manipulation of text and back-

Figure 10-29
Lettering variations
available with character
generator.

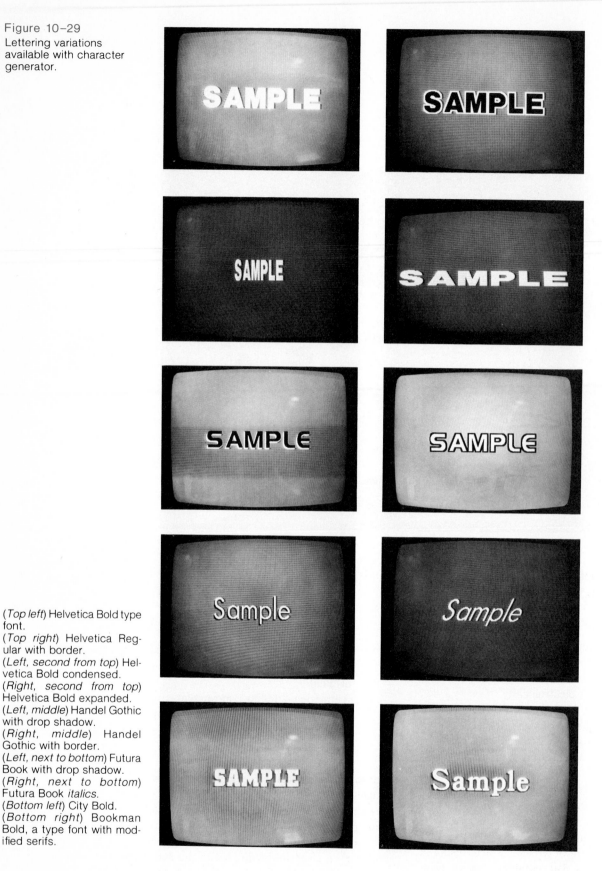

(*Top left*) Helvetica Bold type
font.
(*Top right*) Helvetica Reg-
ular with border.
(*Left, second from top*) Hel-
vetica Bold condensed.
(*Right, second from top*)
Helvetica Bold expanded.
(*Left, middle*) Handel Gothic
with drop shadow.
(*Right, middle*) Handel
Gothic with border.
(*Left, next to bottom*) Futura
Book with drop shadow.
(*Right, next to bottom*)
Futura Book *italics.*
(*Bottom left*) City Bold.
(*Bottom right*) Bookman
Bold, a type font with mod-
ified serifs.

Pictorial Elements: Sets and Graphics

Figure 10–30
Most character generators allow the operator to mix type fonts and styles and repeat type images in a variety of sizes and colors.

(*Left*) A single word can be entered and then repeated using different colors and sizes as part of a logo or title card.

(*Right*) An electronic slate, consisting of three different type fonts, generated for a studio production.

ground material. Anyone who is comfortable composing text on a word processor will find it a manageable transition to the advanced C.G. (Conversely, any production student who has mastered all of the ins and outs of a complicated studio C.G. will have no trouble working with a computer-based word processing program.)

The earliest character generators enabled an operator to type electronically directly onto the TV screen. Today's C.G.'s allow you to select from dozens of font types; alter the height and width of the characters; select any desired color (from millions of options) for the characters and for the background; choose boldface, italic, and other modifications of the type; and add edges and borders of any desired width and of any desired color. (See figure 10–29.)

Dozens (with some systems, hundreds) of pages of information can be stored and pulled from memory at any time. Pages can be sequenced in any order. A variety of movements can be used—variations on the basic *crawl* (moving horizontally across the page) and the *roll* (moving vertically up the screen). Pop-up animation can be used that allows you to matte

any pre-designed text onto the screen at the push of a button.

Features such as "Font-Flex"[4] allow you to mix character sizes and styles so that several different types of images can be generated simultaneously and arranged on the screen in a variety of patterns. (See figure 10–30.)

Another feature on many C.G. units is the *camera capture,* which enables you to shoot and "capture" any high-contrast black-and-white graphic design and store it. This design can be digitalized and cleaned up, colorized, and then integrated with other graphic elements. All of these features are available on units that are priced within the $10,000 range.

The keyboards and operating controls for these C.G. units vary widely from one manufacturer to another, and different terminology will often be used. The keyboard configurations can be as formidable as complicated SEG units. (See figure 10–31.) However, if you carefully study the instruction manual (often in excess of 100 pages or so), and logically think through the signal flow concepts stressed

4. *Font-Flex* is a registered trademark of the Quanta Corporation.

Figure 10–31
Keyboard of the
Quantafont QCG-500
Teleproduction Graphic
Titler (copyright by the
Quanta Corporation). Note
the many functions similar
to a word processor.

earlier, you should be able to master advanced character generators as easily as you can operate your home computer.

Computer Hardware   Moving into the arena of original computer-generated artwork, there are several essential pieces of hardware that are common to all computer-graphics operations. First, there is the **CPU** or **central processing unit.** This is the microprocessing heart of the computer that does all of the actual "computing." For most small-scale graphics operations, the familiar personal computers or PCs are used (Apples, IBM PCs, Macintoshes, Amigas, Ataris, Radio Shack TRS models, Commodores, and so forth).

Second, there is the **keyboard,** an integral part of any simple computer. This is used both for typing instructions to the CPU and for typing text directly onto the screen—as with the character generator. As we stressed in section 1.5, the typewriter is the first and most basic tool used in any TV production. As key-boarding/typing skills are transferred to the

computer keyboard, it must be stressed that any student who is not familiar and comfortable with a C.G. or computer keyboard—who is, in effect, not computer literate—is seriously handicapped in the professional world.

A third component would have to be **input memory devices**—like the **disc drives, cassettes,** or **cartridges.** Most "professional" computers and C.G.'s use a combination of disk drives—input drives utilizing removable disks (either the familiar 5¼–inch, the 3½–inch, or the 8–inch floppy discs) and internal hard disc drives with memories up to forty or eighty megabytes of information. Sophisticated systems increasingly make use of other input devices—videodiscs, CD-ROMs (compact disc/read-only memory), and newer optical disc formats.

A fourth element of the computer-graphics system—the first item that relates directly to graphics generation—is the **graphics tablet,** also called a "data tablet" or "bit pad." This tablet is used with a special electronic pen to enter digitalized coordinates. In essence, it

Figure 10–32
A graphics pad and
digitalizing pen are basic
tools for any electronic
artist.

converts the pen's touch on the pad or tablet
to a precise position (defined by X and Y coordinates) on the computer monitor. Therefore, it allows direct artist input to the
computer by using the electronic pen. It takes
but a few hours for the graphic artist to get
used to creating artwork by looking at the TV
screen while "drawing" on a tablet located
below the screen. (See figure 10–32.) Other
similar types of input devices include game
paddles, joysticks, light pens (that write directly on the screen), hand-held cursors, and
the fanciful "mouse" made popular by Apple.

A fifth component obviously is the **computer monitor.** Higher quality systems usually
will feature an **RGB** (red-green-blue) monitor.
Because this high-quality monitor does not
break the picture information down into the
chrominance and luminance channels used for
broadcast signals, the resulting "noncomposite" picture is not an NTSC (National
Television System Committee) broadcast
signal. With an RGB signal, both the color
rendition and resolution are sharper than in a
broadcast monitor or TV set. As noted in a
later discussion, however, several medium-
priced devices are being introduced that will
convert the RGB signal into a composite
NTSC signal for television purposes. Often, a
computer-graphics workstation will also include a black-and-white monitor for text information.

In more sophisticated computer systems,
another component is a **digitalizing camera**—
one that picks up picture information, either
graphics materials or a live scene, and im-

mediately converts it to a digitalized format. In its simplest application, this corresponds to the "camera capture" of the character generator. Then the image can be manipulated by computer instructions—rotating images, squeezing and elongating the picture, changing colors, and so forth. (See section 7.4.)

10.7 Computer-Graphics Applications

As we examine some of the considerations involved in making and using computer-generated graphics, we will look at three related areas: computer programs, computer-graphics features, and procedures connected with generating electronic graphics.

Computer-Graphics Programs

It takes more than just the hardware, of course, to use a computer system. The programming instructions or software package comprise the other half of the operation. Graphics software—often referred to generically as "paint systems" programs—can be considered in roughly three levels of sophistication (and corresponding price categories).

The simplest level typically will cost from $40 to $100. Sample programs include *Higher Graphics II* (Synergistic Software), *Special Effects* (Penguin Software), *Graph It* (designed for Atari), *Apple World* (United Software of America), *Dazzle Draw* (Broderbund), and *The Art Gallery* and *Micro Painter* (both from Radio Shack).

Generally these simple programs will allow you to create a variety of shapes and enable you to draw basic original designs. They also give you most of the text-creation features of a much more expensive character generator. They will provide fair resolution—the best going up to about 256 by 192 **pixels.** A pixel (a computer term derived from "picture

element") roughly corresponds to one dot on a scanning line on a TV set (section 5.2). It is the smallest definable unit or dot that one can manipulate and work with. So a resolution of 256 (horizontal) by 192 (vertical) pixels is considerably less than the capacity of a typical TV set—however, it is quite good for defining a bar graph or pie chart or lettering for a super card.

Once you add a graphics tablet to the system and incorporate a slightly more sophisticated "paint box" program, you are talking about the middle-priced systems— about $200 to $700 or $800: *Super Chartman II* (Graphics Software, Inc.), *Creative Graphics* (Accupipe Corporation), *Graphwriter* (Graphic Communications, Inc.), and *Bizgraph* (Micro-Labs), among many others. These systems, often used in conjunction with spreadsheet computer programs, offer considerable flexibility and detail. They are designed to be used with computers at the IBM PC or Macintosh level. They typically include quite a few sophisticated features and advanced applications. (See figure 10–33.) Not all systems at this level, however, will meet the color graphics standard for the next generation of PCs—the IBM PS/2 and the Apple Macintosh II. These standards include a resolution of 640 by 480 pixels.

The resolution figures being used in the previous discussion are dependent upon the type of *graphics card* or *board* included with the particular computer. Within the IBM format, for instance, the lowest standard is the CGA card. This will allow the computer to display a maximum of sixteen colors with a resolution of 320 × 200 pixels. However, there is always the possibility of a trade-off; if you are willing to settle for fewer colors, you can adapt the card to achieve a higher resolution. The next level is the EGA card. This card will typically give you thirty-two colors with a resolution of 600 × 400. Again, depending upon the number of colors you desire, it will display

Pictorial Elements: Sets and Graphics

varying degrees of resolution. The highest quality card available for most IBM PCs is the VGA board. It will display, for example, 256 colors with a resolution of 640 × 480 pixels. Other brands of computers have their idiosyncratic graphics boards, and some, like the Atari, are hard-wired so that you cannot change your graphics capabilities.

Moving up to the professional level, more sophisticated graphics boards are available that greatly increase both the color capabilities and the resolution. In this realm, prices for a system may range from a few thousand dollars to well above $100,000. These systems incorporate features that were undreamed of just a few years ago. The *Aurora/100 Digital Video-graphics System*, developed in 1973, was the first to be used by network television; it includes three different levels of animation. *Aurora*, like many other firms, also offers **three-dimensional** systems. These packages cannot, of course, project actual three-dimensional pictures, but they do render simulated three-dimensional images that can be manipulated in space. This technology was originally used by manufacturers for *CAD* (computer-aided design) applications—but it has become a popular, although high-priced, tool for TV animation.

IMAGES, developed by the New York Institute of Technology, is a high-level animation system that features one of the most advanced **key-framing** programs available, "Tween." This enables the artist to draw one pattern, give the computer a second drawing, and then instruct the CPU to fill in all of the intermediate frames to metamorphose (or "interpolate") from one image to the other (at any desired speed or number of frames).

The 3M Model *BFA Paint System,* like several others, offers the artist a theoretical total of 16.8 million colors to choose from; the working palette can display 256 colors at any one time.

The Dubner *CBG-2 Video Graphics Generator* combines the features of a character generator, background generator, animation system, electronic paint box, and three-dimensional solid modeling system; its very high resolution of 1,024 by 525 pixels is illustrative of the most sophisticated systems.

The Quantel *Paint Box* probably does the best job of emulating fine-art characteristics—allowing the artist to simulate oil paints, watercolors, chalk, crayon, and other media—with colors actually "mixed" on the artist's electronic palette. Many other high-priced systems offer similar features and flexibilities.

Computer-Graphics Features

In addition to the specific attractions just outlined, numerous other top-of-the-line systems are available that offer a variety of other features. Once the artist designates where certain reflections are placed on a still object, *ray tracing* automatically places highlights and reflections in the correct location as the object is rotated. *Motion choreography* is an extension of "key framing," allowing the artist to designate key still frames, and then instructing the computer to fill in the motion required to get from one position to the next. And *texture mapping* is used to create any desired surface texture that the artist may wish to portray.

The *AutoPaint* system offered by Cubicomp, for instance, allows the video artist to take any still video picture and alter its texture to look like an oil painting, a watercolor, a charcoal sketch, a refractive-glass picture, or a modernistic reflective-chrome art piece. A counterpart to texture mapping would be *solarization,* which can be accomplished with equipment such as the Ampex ADO 3000 ("Ampex Digital Optics") simply by altering the electronic signals (see figure 10–34).[5]

5. Subject matter for photographs in figures 10–34, 10–36, and 10–38 is by courtesy of Paramount Studios, Los Angeles, California.

(a)

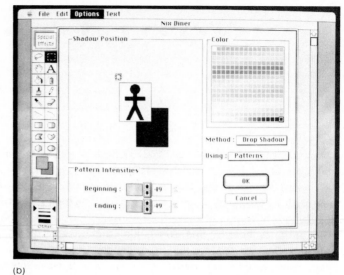

(b)

(c)

(d)

Figure 10–33
Moderately priced
computer graphics
programs can provide a
wide variety of visual
capabilities.

(a) All graphics programs are "menu-driven," which
enables artist/operators to select many options
(color, perspective, and shadowing effects in this
example) from an on-screen menu.
(b) In this example from *Pixel Paint* the artist positions the symbolic "sun" (located above and to
the left of the stick figure) to determine exactly
where the shadow effect (the large black rect-
angle) will appear on the finished art.
(c) Original artwork can be created, usually using
a mouse. In this *Adobe Illustrator* example, any individual detail—such as the bamboo leaves—can
be repeated with a simple command.
(d) Many variations of shading, texture, and color
can be added to any original or "captured" artwork.
(e) Starting with a conventional map, the artist can
add any lettering, colors, special effects, and—in
this case—distorted perspective desired.

(f) The artist can work with magnified insets to
change detail on any part of the artwork.
(g) Using a series of grids and layout rectangles,
the artist can size and position artwork in any desired configuration.
(h) The *MAC 3-D* program allows the artist to create
simulated 3-dimensional models and rotate them
to any desired perspective.
(i) Simple animation effects can be created with
modestly priced programs. In this *Videoworks II*
sequence for example, the football (located below
the "I" in "Chicago") is tumbling through the air.
(j) In this finished piece of art, the original drawing
of the puffin was created on *Adobe Illustrator* and
the lettering was created, colored, shaded, and
rotated into the circle by *Pixel Paint*.

Pictorial Elements: Sets and Graphics

(e)

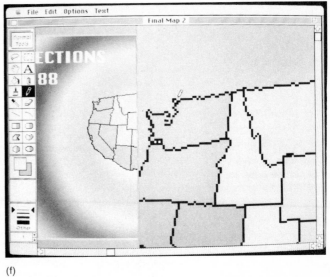

(f)

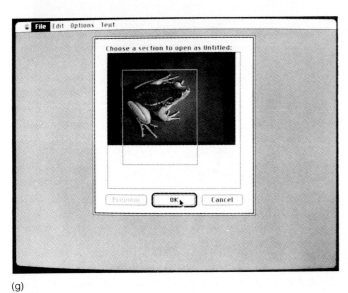

(g)

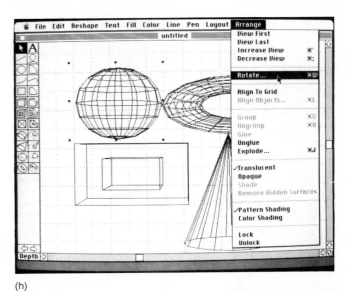

(h)

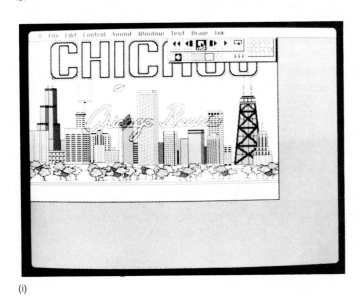

(i)

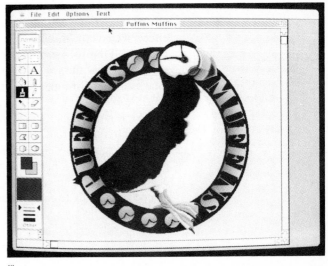

(j)

Pictorial Elements: Sets and Graphics

Figure 10–34
Solarization is a process that can be used for stylized effects.

At the highest end of the sophistication spectrum are systems such as the $250,000 *DF/X Composium* that combine graphics functions and editing capabilities into one digital workstation. Among other capabilities, the Composium handles switcher mixing and keying, key-frame editing, a variety of digital effects, video typography, multilevel paint capacity, and multiscreen pasteup, as well as incorporating a library of stored electronic images for still-frame retrieval (see figure 10–35).

At a most realistic price, many units are being introduced that incorporate features previously found only on much more expensive gear. Some features are specific to certain types or brands of computers. Two systems are designed specifically to convert computer output

directly into TV signals. Magni Systems has introduced its "VGA Producer" that enables you to encode your VGA graphic into an NTSC composite signal; this facilitates some fairly sophisticated special effects.

Similarly, NewTek has introduced its "Video Toaster" that plugs into a Commodore Amiga to create NTSC-based electronic effects. These two items—both available for under $2,000—are representative of the emerging technologies that enable relatively low-cost systems to emulate much more expensive operations. These products also are indicative of the ongoing phenomenon of blurring the line between computer technologies and video systems.

Many other midpriced systems are offering increasingly sophisticated features. The

Pictorial Elements: Sets and Graphics

Figure 10–35
The DF/X Composium edit suite combines digital keying and mixing of four live sources, keyframe editing of five video recorders, character generation, real-time digital effects, graphics/paint capabilities, and a digital library. (Photo courtesy of Digital F/X)

following are just a few examples of items offered on systems under $1,000. Computer Support Corporation's *Arts & Letters "Graphics Editor"* includes a "blend" feature that emulates a key-framing approach. Corel Systems' *CorelDRAW!* has a "Bind to Shape" command that snaps text into any desired geometric pattern (spreading text around the perimeter of a circle, for example). *Artline* from Digital Research has a large number of drawing commands that enable the user to copy, move, rotate, scale, mirror, color, shade, group and ungroup various elements. ZSoft Corporation's *PC Paintbrush IV Plus* includes a powerful image retoucher and finisher for working with scanned or "captured" video images. *ColoRIX VGA Paint* from RIX Soft-

works includes two zoom windows that can enlarge an image up to eight times for detailed pixel-by-pixel editing (its extended VGA capability provides 256 colors at an 800×600 resolution).

The list goes on and on. It should also be noted that while these few programs have been highlighted by pointing out a single attraction, most of these and many other moderately priced programs contain several or almost all of these itemized features. And as PC-to-NTSC boards—such as NewTek's *Video Toaster*—become more popular, even more television adaptations will follow.

Regardless of the sophistication of the system, there are a number of standard features and capabilities that are common to most computer-graphics arrangements. With most graphics-tablet setups, for example, the following operations are possible:

1. Using the electronic pen to select from a **menu** (an on-screen display of various options available) the type of drawing medium to be used—brush, pen, airbrush, and so forth.
2. Selecting a color by touching the desired color on a menu display. Sophisticated systems allow you to mix colors (hues) and to change saturation and brightness.
3. Drawing on the graphics tablet or using a mouse while watching the monitor.
4. Giving directions for specific lines and geometric shapes. Plot two points, and the computer will draw in the line connecting them. Specify centers and radii for circles and ellipses, coordinates for rectangles and cubes; the computer will draw them in.
5. Typing text directly onto the screen. Select from any number of type fonts, styles, sizes, or make up your own. Add shadows and dimension to the lettering.
6. Using special effects. Create mirror images, rotate designs, enlarge and shrink artwork, tilt, skew, warp, change widths and shapes. Replicate small images all over the screen. Execute any kind of "cut-and-paste" job.
7. Filling in all areas (drawings and text) with colors and textures.

The flexibility and sophistication of these systems continue to increase at an astounding rate. And it is entirely likely that some of these more expensive systems will someday be mass-produced for costs that the average small station or basic studio will be able to afford.

Computer-Graphics Procedures

Regardless of what level of sophistication you are working at in your computer-graphics applications, there are several common procedures or considerations that should be part of your planning.

1. *General design and artistic planning.* Your first step must be to create an overall concept of the artistic look or feel that you want your production to convey. Sets, titles, lighting, graphics, and costumes should all be part of a unified scheme. This is where the designer or art director will be working closely with the graphic artist to maintain a consistent visual theme for the entire program (see figure 10–36).

2. *Workstation planning.* However simple or elaborate your setup may be, you need to plan carefully your graphics environment. Think deliberately before you just plunk down your first graphics computer and monitor somewhere in a corner of your master control room. How close to the studio and/or control room must your graphics area be? Do you need access to common video control equipment—character generator, SEG, editing bay? Do you need space to train graphic artists or technicians? Will you need room for impromptu planning sessions of two or three people at a time? How much space do you need to allocate for future computer growth? Will the graphics workstation be shared by several production units—different studios or sound stages?

3. *Facilities for storage and retrieval of video sources.* Tied in with workstation considerations, you must think ahead about how you are to integrate various sources of video pictures and hard copy. As indicated at the beginning of section 10.6, there are four general

Pictorial Elements: Sets and Graphics

Figure 10–36
Graphic artist and art
director working on
Entertainment Tonight
visuals.

sources of images for any computer-graphics
system (see figure 10–37):

    a. *Character generation.* You will want
keyboard capability to create electronically any combination of letters,
numbers, and other symbols—with as
much flexibility in manipulating and
adapting these characters as your
budget will allow.

    b. *Frozen-frame retrieval.* You will want
to be able to pull in to your workstation still-frame video pictures from a
wide variety of sources—any existing
videotape, still-frame storage devices

(such as the Ampex ESS, Quantel
6033, et al.), various disc formats, and
so forth.[6] In this category, you may
also include the thousands and thousands of *clip art* pictures (a data base
of generic drawings, symbols, and
cartoons) that are supplied with many
graphics and drawing programs.

    c. *Camera capture.* Most systems will
incorporate a video camera, usually
mounted on a camera stand (see figure
10–38), to take pictures of any existing flat artwork—magazine photos,
cutouts from any source, glossy prints,
and any original hand-drawn artwork.

    d. *Freehand electronic art*—using a
graphics pad or tablet and stylus to
create original artwork right on the
screen.

    4. *Facilities for manipulating video
images.* Here is where you will be thinking
about the various software that you will need—
the wide variety of graphics programs previously described. What kinds of "painting"

6. As an example of still-frame storage and
retrieval capabilities, the series *Entertainment Tonight*
relies primarily upon two main sources: Ampex's
ADDA system, which holds 900 still pictures—each
one taking four seconds of space—on a 60–minute
1–inch tape (the series currently has over 35,000 still
images stored on thirty-nine reels); and an "RSD"
(removable storage disc) system that holds about one
megabyte of digital information per disc (with twenty-
six RSD discs, the series has over 2,000 frequently
accessed images in this system).

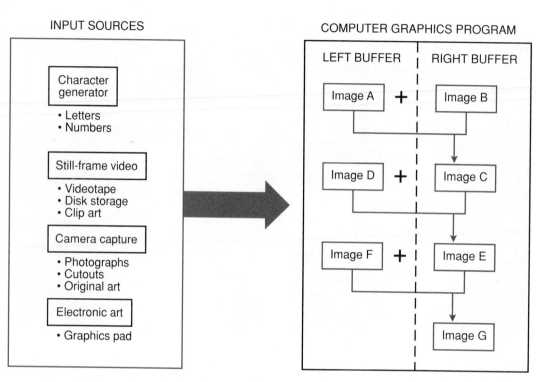

Figure 10-37
Multiple-buffer layering of computer visuals. Images from different input sources (on the left) can be combined with existing images in the right buffer to create new composite images.

features do you want to incorporate—texture mapping, color modification, rotating, mirror imaging, shading, three-dimensional effects, sizing, and image shaping? What will you need in the way of digital effects at your workstation? How much animation capability will you want?

5. *Multiple buffers.* One important consideration is the capacity for working with multiple windows or buffers (see figure 10-37). Many systems will allow you to work, for example, with three buffers simultaneously—"old" and "new" (or left and right) buffers and a "cutout buffer" on the tip of your light pen or stylus. A *restore* function allows you to take an image from either an old or new buffer file and bring it to the screen—into your current work buffer. You can work back and forth between these two buffers—painting, sizing, positioning, and redrawing images in either buffer as you wish. You can then add the image from

one buffer to the other—building and combining two separate images into a new composite picture. When satisfied with what you have created, you can save this newly synthesized image in one buffer and bring up some new material to work with in the other buffer—layering it into the previous buffer at any point. In this manner, you can continually build layer upon layer of graphic images (see figure 10-38).

For example (see figure 10-37), you work with image A in the left buffer and image B in the right buffer; when you get the pictures modified as you wish, you can edit them together and form image C. This new picture is stored in the right buffer while you work on a completely different visual, image D (pulled in from any of the available input sources), in the left buffer; when you get that picture modified as you want it, you layer it into image C (in the right buffer), and you have a newly com-

Pictorial Elements: Sets and Graphics

(a) A still photo of Madonna is retrieved from the video library. The first step is to use the graphics pad and pen to outline her head and block out all of the distracting background so that only the desired portrait remains.

(b) After a similar library shot of Roseanne Barr is retrieved and treated to remove the background, the two portraits are positioned for one of the planned on-air shots.

Figure 10–38
Many steps are involved in creating a series of graphics for a highly visual production such as *Entertainment Tonight*.

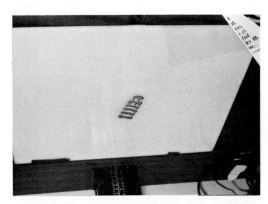

(c) In order to convey the atmosphere of Italy (the locale for the Madonna/Roseanne story), a small picture of the Leaning Tower of Pisa is pulled from the "flat art" file and placed on the copy stand.

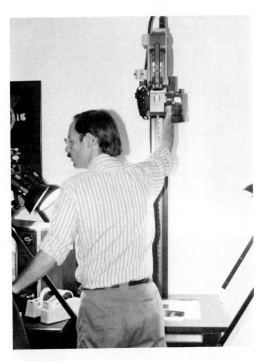

(d) This picture of the tower is shot with the video "capture camera," and the image can then be integrated into the other electronic graphics.

Pictorial Elements: Sets and Graphics

(e) The tower is positioned and layered into an existing *Entertainment Tonight* mosaic.

(f) For one segment of the story, Roseanne's image is layered (matted) over the tower. The degree of blending and transparency of the images is controlled with the light pen and "paint" program options.

(g) For another segment of the story, a "Madonna" logo is retrieved from still art and shot with the "capture camera."

(h) The black-and-white "Madonna" logo is reversed, a drop shadow is added, and it is positioned over the tower.

(i) and (j) Two of the on-the-air results with the electronic graphics keyed in behind the host.

Pictorial Elements: Sets and Graphics

posited picture, image E. This new picture is stored in the right buffer while you work on an altogether different picture, image F, in the left buffer. When you are ready, you layer together images E and F to form image G—and so forth.

6. *Storage and retrieval capabilities.* In addition to storage of your video sources as previously mentioned, you must also devise a system for the labeling and storing of the new pictures you have just created. How will these images be held in temporary storage until the director or editor is ready to incorporate them into the current production? Videotape? Computer diskettes? What images might you want to save for future use in some other program? In many news, documentary, corporate, and educational operations, this process of labeling and storing newly created pictures for future retrieval and utilization becomes a major consideration. You will soon find yourself cataloging and storing thousands of different-sized photographs, freehand art, cutouts, posters, and other pictures.

Various computer-graphics programs and systems will differ tremendously in the way you respond to these several factors. No one generic manual or textbook can detail for you the precise manner in which you will organize and utilize your particular graphics facilities. However, the factors outlined in this section should give you some guidelines for utilizing your individual electronic graphics situation.

10.8 Production Uses of Graphics

Finally, we want to mention different ways that graphics—both computer visuals and physical cards—can actually be incorporated into a production. The innovative director will do much more with graphics than simply parade a number of static images before the camera.

Sequencing   There are many times, of course, when a *sequence* of graphics will have to be used. (See figure 10–38.) Because TV graphics have to be simple, it often takes a number of them to get across the same information that could be incorporated into one detailed visual in a print medium.

With sophisticated computer systems, of course, a number of graphics can be created and stored on videotape or diskettes. Then as you want to sequence them in the production, each one is called up from the electronic memory and inserted into the program with no studio interruption or setup at all.

If you are working with actual physical photos, the most satisfactory technique would probably be to put the photos on *slides.* Then by simply alternating between two different slide drums, the director and technical director have accurate control of the sequencing with fewer chances for a mishap—once the slides are set up properly.

If you have the time and access to postproduction facilities, the most polished finished product can be obtained by shooting each graphic individually, with one camera—taking time to frame each shot, plan any movement, check the lighting—and recording the series of shots on videotape. Then in postproduction, edit the sequence together, working to get precisely the timing you want. (See section 15.6.) Computer graphics, obviously, can also be (and usually are) edited into the finished production in the postproduction process.

Graphics Movement   Some specialized training or corporate production uses of graphics may involve *panning* and *tilting* large on-set or off-set graphic cards—for instance, to simulate an outdoor panoramic shot. Ideally, if such moves are to be effective, the physical cards should be large enough so that the camera can get back some distance and still use a wide-angle lens for smooth movement. If the graphic is so small that the camera has to be too close, it will be hard to keep all areas of the card in focus as the camera lens moves closer and then farther away from the card during a pan. On the other hand, if the camera operator has to use a narrow-angle long lens on a small card, it is difficult to execute a smooth move without the magnification of every little shaky camera movement. With a good pedestal mount, *trucking* and/or *pedestaling* moves can be smoother and remain in sharper focus than panning and tilting.

Most character generators can also provide moving text to create graphics movement. Text can be *rolled* or scrolled up or down the screen; hundreds of pages can be programmed for a rolling text; rolls can be handled at various speeds; a static title may be positioned at the top of the screen with the rolling portion of the text disappearing as it rolls up to the static title. Text can also be *crawled* along the screen—moved horizontally from either side of the screen to the other (usually text is crawled from right to left, simulating eye movement reading from left to right).

More sophisticated computer systems can create other types of graphics movement. Through digitalization of the pictures, visuals can be stretched, squeezed, flipped over, and turned inside out.

Animation   In many situations, *animated graphics* can get a particular message across best. Traditionally, animation has been accomplished on film—composing and shooting one frame of celluloid at a time. With sophisticated videotape editing facilities, it is now possible to achieve the same kind of animated movement with postproduction editing. The popularity of techniques such as "claymation" that enable you to use actual clay figures (or other types of models) to subtly alter movement or position from one frame to an-

other is a relatively inexpensive (although still time-consuming) process for achieving animation effects.

With a computer-based graphics system, of course, fairly sophisticated animation sequences can be achieved—once you have put in the time to create the needed key graphics and instructions for the computer. The "pop-on" feature of many character generators enables you to create a simple form of textual animation.

Related to the animated graphic is what might be termed the *buildup* sequence. This is a production technique whereby additional information is sequentially added to a basic graphic. For example, a map with only one city indicated on it is shown first; the next graphic shows a second city added without any change in the basic map; then a third city is added; then dotted lines are added to show relationships; then a county outline is added; and so on. Both figures 10–37 and 10–38 illustrate this type of buildup process.

Although this kind of buildup sequence has been achieved in the past by physically using slides, alternating between two slide drums on the air, most production centers today would achieve this type of buildup animation with either electronic graphics or with postproduction editing.

Many other uses of graphics will be explored by the inventive director. Generally, basic productions do not take full advantage of the potential of good graphics. There are limitless possibilities in the use of graphics— electronic and physical—to reinforce and augment both verbal and nonverbal messages.

Summary

Good pictorial design—for sets and graphics— starts with consideration of both *informational* functions and *emotional* functions of the

Pictorial Elements: Sets and Graphics

picture. Emotional aspects include establishing an *image* for a program, creating *atmosphere,* and sustaining a *continuity* throughout the production. Basic elements of design that should be considered in every production include *balance and mass, dominant lines,* and *tone and color.* Color components include *hue, saturation,* and *brightness.*

In working on staging design, there are three basic staging styles that can be used—*neutral* setting, *decorative* or fantasy setting, and variations of a *realistic* setting. Scenery elements include *settings* (standard set units, hanging units, staff and set pieces), *set dressings and furniture,* and *hand props.* In designing a studio setting, consider also *camera movement, microphone placement, lighting instruments,* and *talent movement.*

In handling pieces in the studio, you should know the basic *construction of a flat,* how flats can be *joined,* and the best way of *storing* flats, set pieces, and properties. Some other studio techniques involve the preparation of a staging *floor plan,* use of *lighting effects,* other special *staging effects,* and dealing with *basic problems* of backgrounds, furniture, and props.

Some of the important principles of graphics design are the *three-to-four aspect ratio,* the relationship of the *scanning area* and *essential area,* how much *information* can be included on a card, the *simplicity* needed and the basic *style of lettering,* plus the correct use of *color* and *tonal contrast.*

In constructing graphics, the first distinction to be made is whether the graphic is to be used *on set* or *off set.* The application will help determine the best *size* for the graphic. Graphics preparation, *lettering,* can be handled with a wide variety of tools and techniques, including hand lettering, ready-to-apply letters, lettering aids, printing machines, the typewriter, and the character generator.

Computer-generated graphics are now used extensively in all types of network productions, station operations, production centers, and corporate video programming. The character generator has long outgrown its original assignment of "typing on the screen." Sophisticated systems utilizing a *graphics tablet* and *digitalizing camera* offer a bewildering assortment of drawing, text, and animation possibilities.

Sources of video input for computer graphics include the character generator, still-frame images, camera capture, and original electronic art. Working with *multiple buffers* allows the graphic artist to build up a composite picture by layering one image on top of another.

There are many different creative production possibilities involving *sequencing* graphics, *graphics movement,* and *animated graphics*—including postproduction editing and computer-based animation.

This chapter has been concerned with the nonhuman aspects of the television picture. Chapter 11 discusses the human element of the picture—the actors and performers.

10.9 Training Exercises

The following exercises should be carried out individually by each student in the class.

1. Using the dimensions and layout of your studio, design a basic staging plot for a standard dramatic scene. Be as realistic as you can in terms of the set elements, furniture, and set dressings that are available to you. Make sure that everything is accurately done to scale, and include as much detail as you can.

2. If your facilities do not yet include electronic graphics capabilities, prepare a sample graphic card that combines five or six lines of lettering with some original artwork—some sort of diagram or chart with a written explanation or heading. Make sure you carefully follow the principles spelled out in section 10.4.

3. Using your studio's character generator, prepare a sample roll for the credits of a TV program. Experiment with different colors for the lettering and for the background. Try different type fonts. Also, prepare a fancy title card using the character generator. Use larger fonts. Experiment with digitalization (stretching and squeezing the title card). If your system has "camera capture" capabilities, try different designs for the background of the title card.

Pictorial Elements: Sets and Graphics

On-Camera Talent: The Performer and Actor

In television, anyone who appears in front of a camera is referred to as *talent*. This is a traditional use of the term whether the person is giving a cooking demonstration, reciting Tennyson, interviewing the mayor, running for mayor, singing a ballad, acting in *Hamlet,* teaching long division, or giving a weather report. In this chapter we are concerned about working with talent from several different points of view.

11.1 Working with Talent

What does the director have to know in order to direct actors? How do you control a rambling interviewer? How should the crew react to a nervous guest? How do you instruct talent to use notes or cue cards? How can you get the talent to relate to the audience? These are the questions that you, as a crew member and budding director, have to answer one way or another.

In this text *we are not concerned with training television performers and actors.* We cannot attempt to teach students how to become accomplished announcers, stand-up comedians, singers and dancers, dynamic interviewers, controversial reporters, or award-winning actors. What we *are* concerned with is how to work with these people.

One effective way to train people how to *work with talent* is to look at the topic from the perspective *of the talent.* This chapter, therefore, will be examining various performance and acting requirements the talent must face. By gaining some insight into the talent's position, the director and crew members should better be able to cope with the talent's problems in various production situations.

At the same time, however, we are aware of the fact that many production personnel and station executives do have their turn in front of the camera. Numerous professional positions—especially in smaller stations—combine off-camera work (writing, producing, selling, managing) with some on-camera work (reporting, hosting, selling, interviewing, delivering editorials). Therefore, it is helpful at this stage to have some insight into the world of on-camera talent.

Also, realistically, in many types of production classes, the students will be performing the various on-camera roles. Production classes revolve around lab exercises in which all of the class members take their turns as newscasters, interviewers, TV lecturers, and actors. This chapter should be of direct assistance in helping you cope with these assignments.

The bulk of this chapter is directed toward working with talent in studio productions. Although much of what is covered, especially as it relates to actors, certainly applies to location shooting, the basic orientation—especially in the following section on "performers"—is centered on *live* or *live-on-tape* productions in the studio.

In discussing on-camera activities, the distinction is often made between two groups: (1) those presentational or reportorial roles in which the talent is serving essentially as a communicator, portraying no role except as a host or reporter; and (2) dramatic roles in which the talent is portraying some theatrical character. The first category is referred to as *performers* while the second group is referred to as *actors*. Although the two groups share many characteristics and concerns, it may be helpful to look at them separately.

11.2 The Television Performer

The category of performer includes announcers, emcees, hosts, narrators, reporters, interviewers, demonstrators, TV lecturers, panel participants, and the like—talent who are communicating personally with the audience, usually addressing them directly. In examining the performer, it may be helpful to look at his or her role as it relates to others. Specifically, let us look at performers as they relate to the *audience,* to the *production crew,* and to *other performers*.

Audience Relationships

The primary responsibility of the performer is, of course, to the audience. In addition, the performer-audience relationship is crucial to the success of any television program.

Audience Concept   Television is an intimate medium. It usually is received on a small screen, in the privacy of the home, as a rule by an audience of just a few people. The television performer is most successful when he or she conceives of the audience in that manner—three or four people sitting just a few feet away. The TV director must help the performer think of the television camera as one close acquaintance. In the mind of the individual TV viewer, the aggregate audience of thousands or millions of people does not exist. It is basically a one-to-one relationship.

There are occasions, of course, when the TV camera is recording a performer who is playing to a large audience—the singer before a theater audience, the politician addressing his supporters, the minister preaching to a church congregation. In these situations, however, television is just an *objective* eavesdropper, covering an actual event. If the singer, politician, or minister is using television as a *reportorial* medium, addressing the audience directly and personally, then the director must help the performer adapt his or her style to a different audience relationship—more intimate, subdued, with direct eye contact, using a conversational tone of voice.

The director must also help the talent learn how to concentrate while on camera—how to focus on the material, the message that

On-Camera Talent: The Performer and Actor

the talent is trying to get across; how to ignore the technicians and assistants running around in circles; how to maintain that one-to-one relationship with the audience—not to be distracted by the lights, cameras, and mike boom. Concentrate on the audience at home, not the people in the control room.

Speaking Voice The natural conversational speaking voice is one of the most elusive qualities the performer has to try to attain. The performer who can project the feeling of spontaneity and intimacy in his or her speaking style is on the way to capturing one of the most sought-after qualities of any television performer—*sincerity*. (As one comedian wisecracked, "If you can fake sincerity, you got it made.")

This is not to argue that the performer should not exhibit enthusiasm or animation or exuberance (if that is the person's natural style). It is only to point out that the speaker's *desire* to communicate with three or four people on the other side of the camera is, perhaps, the single most important ingredient in successful performing. If the host/announcer/reporter/teacher *sincerely* and earnestly *wants* to communicate (without an obvious artificial eagerness), then he or she should succeed in that communication process.

Eye Contact Just as important as vocal directness is the intimacy of specific visual directness—eye contact with the TV camera. In reportorial program formats when the performer (newscaster, TV lecturer, host, commentator) is speaking directly to the audience, the talent must attempt to maintain a direct and personal eye contact with the camera lens at all times, looking straight into the heart of the lens. A couple decades ago, working with a camera with a lens turret, the performer had to know which of the four or five lenses facing him or her was the *taking lens*. Today, it is

somewhat easier—just focus on that one big zoom lens.

This direct eye contact is the secret of maintaining the illusion of an exclusive relationship with each individual member of the audience. By looking directly into the lens, the performer is directly and personally addressing everyone who is in contact with the television receiver. A third-grade pupil was once asked why she was so enthusiastic about her television teacher, and the child replied, "Why, because he is always talking directly *to me*." The child's own live classroom teacher, of course, had to share her attention with thirty students at one time, but the TV teacher was talking directly to that one child—and to every individual viewer.

In maintaining the illusion of direct eye contact, the performer must become skilled, of course, in some of the artifice and techniques of the medium. The director must help in teaching some of these skills to the performer. In many productions the director will cut from one camera shot of the performer to another. The performer will have to reestablish eye contact with the new camera immediately. Whenever possible, the performer should be aided by the floor director's waving the talent to look at the new camera a split second before the camera cut is made. In some situations, the performer can make the transition look as natural as possible by momentarily glancing downward (or upward)—as if glancing at some notes or trying to collect his or her thoughts—and then immediately establishing eye contact with the new camera.

With the help of the director and stage manager, the performer should also be aware of what camera might be used exclusively for close-ups of some object he or she is demonstrating or discussing. If it is clearly explained to you (as talent) that camera 3 will always be getting just a close-up of, for instance, the globe, then you need not worry about looking at camera 3 every time the tally lights change

Figure 11-1

Camera pattern for
shooting a close-up.

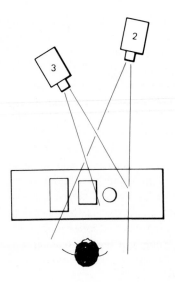

If the talent knows that camera 3 will be used only
for close-ups of the objects on the table—and that
camera 2 will always be getting the basic shot of
the talent—then he or she will not have to worry
about establishing eye contact with camera 3 every
time the tally lights change. The talent can keep
solid eye contact with camera 2.

on the cameras. You can maintain continual
eye contact with the camera that has the
medium shot of you. (See figure 11-1.)

Distracting Mannerisms   Because television is such an intimate, close-up medium,
the talent should also be aware that any visually or vocally distracting mannerism will
certainly be captured with full impact. Some
nervous mannerisms, such as a facial twitch or
the unconscious habit of licking lips, may be
hard to control. On the other hand, some
fidgety distractions—such as playing with a
pencil or pulling an earlobe—can be corrected
if the director or floor manager discreetly calls
it to the performer's attention. Many an audio
engineer has had a few hairs turn gray because a performer thumped his or her fingers
on the table next to the desk mike or idly
tapped his or her lavaliere while pondering a
weighty question.

Vocal habits and mannerisms can also be
distracting. The use of vocalized pauses (saying
"um" or "ah") every time there is a second of
dead air is a problem many of us share. The
ubiquitous "I see" somehow always becomes
part of the interviewer's basic vocabulary.
(Why is it that in day-by-day conversation we
seldom feel the need to say "I see" every time
somebody makes a point to us, but as soon as
we get on the air, it becomes part of the interviewer's response pattern?) The talent should
also be made aware of the tendency to state
the obvious for the audience. While com-
menting on a series of slides with voice-over
narration, there is no need to repeat, "Here we
are looking at . . ." and "Here we see. . . ."
Just explain simply, "This castle is one
of. . . ."

Handling Scripted Material   Depending
upon the specific function of the performer, he
or she may be working from a *full script,*
speaking extemporaneously from a *semi-script*
or full outline, or speaking spontaneously or
ad lib with no preparation at all.

Actually, aside from dramatic programs,
there are only about three types of productions
that call for working from a full script:
(1) *political talks* and other critical presentations or speeches (such as editorials), when
it is extremely important to get every fact
completely accurate, phrasing every comment
on controversial issues precisely; (2) *commercials,* when the time element is so crucial
that every second must be carefully accounted
for with exact scripting; and (3) *news and
sports reporting* (as opposed to ad-lib, on-the-
spot news coverage or play-by-play announcing), when—again—accuracy demands
that every fact reported be carefully checked
and worded and all elements be delivered in a
precise sequence.

When working with a fully scripted program, you have a choice of several different
means of handling the material. *Memoriza-*

On-Camera Talent: The Performer and Actor

Figure 11–2
Listec A-2000 prompting
system. Like many other
prompting systems, this
on-camera display unit
reflects copy from a 15-
inch monitor (bottom of
picture) onto a mirror
positioned in front of the
camera lens. The camera
simultaneously shoots
through the mirror to pick
up the talent's image.

tion usually is required only for dramatic works and is best left to the professionals. Seldom can typical television performers—unless they are exceptionally talented—deliver memorized copy without sounding too artificial and stiff. You are better off reading your copy—from a physical *script* in your hands, from **cue cards** held next to the camera, or from a prompting device such as the **teleprompter.**[1]

Reading directly from a script is satisfactory if you are somewhat familiar with the material and do not have to keep your eyes glued to the script. Some people can handle a script very well, glancing down only occasionally. Others, because of insecurity or nervousness, get completely buried in the script and never establish eye contact. If the talent has a tendency to fall into the latter category and read too much word for word, then the director would be better off using cue cards or, if it is available, a prompting device. (See figure 11–2.) If you, as director, choose to use a script, make sure you have the talent unstaple the script before going on the air and see that all of the pages are in order before starting the actual take.

If you decide to avoid the problems of working with a script, it will take some amount of extra coordination to use cue cards properly. Either the performer or some crew member will have to transfer the entire script onto large cue sheets (heavy oak tag paper or similar stiff stock). The cue-card holder also has to be trained to do a good job—holding the cards right next to the lens, reading along

---

1. *TelePrompTer*™ is a registered trademark of the Teleprompter Corporation. It is a mechanical prompting device that attaches to the front of a camera. The prepared copy, on a long sheet of continuous paper, is projected into a glass plate directly in front of the camera lens. Thus, the performer can read the copy while staring directly at the lens; and the lettering is too close to the lens to come into focus from the camera's perspective.

with the talent and raising each card to keep the exact line being read next to the lens, dropping each card silently, and positioning the next one. With a hefty stack of cue cards, holding them can become a very wearisome and demanding assignment.

If you enjoy the luxury of using a teleprompter, these tasks are taken care of with a minimum amount of trouble—and the exact spot on the script is always positioned directly in front of the lens (by means of mirrors) so that the reader's eyes cannot wander away from the lens. (The astute viewer will probably catch the eyes scanning back and forth, however, if you are using either cue cards or a teleprompter.)

Many performers think they have to work from a full script—when they probably would be better off working from an outline or a semi-scripted format. This enables the talent to have enough of a solid outline to speak with confidence; yet, by composing the exact words on the spot—*extemporaneously*—one can add vitality and sincerity that is difficult to achieve with a prepared text. When speaking extemporaneously, it is easier to use cue cards, because only one or two cards might be needed for the program outline. Many experienced performers prefer, however, to work from small note cards that they carry with them. It is a convenient and relatively unobtrusive way to handle material with confidence and ease. The talent can glance down at his or her notes when necessary but should not try to hide them from the audience. The talent can speak primarily and sincerely directly to the camera lens.

Many times the performer will be called upon to serve in specialized roles such as that of announcer, game show host, voice-over narrator, and so forth. Some of the functions come close to dramatic talent needed as an actor—interpreting lines and/or assuming a certain type of role. We will just reinforce the general advice that talent should try to handle any such role with as much naturalness as possible and avoid the temptation to try to sound like what one thinks an announcer or narrator should sound like.

Crew Relationships

After examining the primary relationship the performer has with the audience, you should think about the relationship of the performer and the production crew. As talent, you will be working closely with many people who directly can affect your performance—helping you look good and do your best job. If you inadvertently cause them trouble, however, they will not be able to do their best job; consequently, you will wind up walking out of camera range, speaking off mike, missing important cues, or finding yourself with nothing left to say and two minutes to fill. You should be thinking specifically about what you—as a performer—need to do in conjunction with the director and A.D., the camera operators, the audio engineer, and the stage manager.

The Director and A.D. Up to the beginning of the actual on-the-air studio production, your closest relationship will be with the director and the **associate director (A.D.).** In virtually every kind of performance assignment, the director and talent must work closely on the preparation of the program—arranging segments, developing material, finding resources, designing graphics, working out cues, and so forth.

As a performer, you will find that the A.D. is probably your best friend as far as timing is concerned. In many formats—variety shows, interview programs, newscasts, corporate training videos—the program will be broken down into a number of timed segments. During the actual production, you will be receiving cues relayed from the A.D. to let you know how the timing on each segment is working out, when you need to speed up, and when you should slow down.

On-Camera Talent: The Performer and Actor

Figure 11–3
Talent signaling his
intention to rise by
"leaning into" the move.

During the program, you will find that there are many times when you can help the director with some indirect signals. This is especially important on rather standardized nonscripted shows when you have not had an opportunity for a full rehearsal. You can aid the director with such cues as, "Now if we look at this through the microscope . . ." (setting up the first slide), or "Three elements are necessary for this demonstration . . ." (getting ready to walk to another area). The performer should avoid giving direct instructions to the crew, however: "Now, if I could just get a shot of this wristwatch!"

Camera Operators   As a polished performer, you will eventually find that you can put yourself in the place of the camera operator—perceiving yourself from the camera's perspective. You develop a "feel" for how you should move, for instance. You know that you cannot make any big or sweeping gestures; the chances are that the camera has you on a fairly tight medium shot. You must be careful with facial grimaces; there is a likelihood that the camera has a close-up of you.

When you are ready to make a big move, lean into it gradually, because you want to give the camera operator ample warning. For example, you may be sitting in an easy chair and are ready to stand, turn, and walk over to the demonstration area. There are several telltale cues that you give to the camera operator. For example, you place both feet firmly on the floor, you lean forward, you put your hands on the sides of the chair, you now *slowly* lift yourself out of the chair. (See figure 11–3.) The camera is able to follow you smoothly as you prepare

Figure 11–4
Talent holding an object close to her face for a close-up (when no second close-up camera is available).

the operator for your moves. The warnings are also of value to other members of the production crew, the boom operator, for one, who must follow the move with you. You also develop a habit of moving slowly as you go from one area of the set to another. Again, this gives the camera operator a good chance of moving with you gracefully. (And it always looks fast enough to the viewer.)

It does not take long before you also begin to get a feel for holding up objects to the correct camera for a close-up. In figure 11–1, the cameras are positioned correctly for a right-handed person to demonstrate something on a close-up shot. As you pick up or point to the object, it is automatically angled for a good close-up on camera 3. You intuitively position any object or graphic on your right side, aimed off to your left (camera right) for the close-up shot.

Most of the time, in the situation in figure 11–1, you would not pick the object up off the

table. You would be certain the camera had a clear, unobstructed shot of the object on the tabletop; it is much steadier and more stable to leave it on the solid table. If you must pick up the object, move it slowly; move it as little as possible; rest your elbow on the table or steady the object with your other hand. You do not ask the close-up camera to hold a shot of the object while you are gesturing with it.

Intuitively, if you see that the director does not have a second camera free for close-ups and you want to get a good tight shot of the object, you pick it up and hold it next to your face, pointing it straight at your camera, holding your arm tightly against your body to steady the hand, as shown in figure 11–4. Now the director can get a good tight shot of your face and the object, using the single camera available.

Audio Engineer   You will also develop a feel for the positions and problems of other

On-Camera Talent: The Performer and Actor

members of the crew. We mentioned consideration for the boom operator. You also help the audio engineer by making certain you do not abuse any of the mikes. Do not handle any of the microphones except hand or stand mikes. Avoid playing with the mike cords. Know the position of all microphones and avoid any sudden or explosive noises in their vicinity.

In addition, be sure you are consistent in giving the audio engineer your audio level when he or she is setting up the mikes and establishing proper mike levels. The audio person will ask you for a **level**; you are to speak into the mike so that the fader/pot levels can be determined. Some performers will mumble a relatively weak audio check and then boom out on the air with their best basso profundo. A few will do just the opposite—give a good strong audio test to set the level and then start out rather weakly on the air.

Stage Manager   Finally, you will come to know your floor manager or stage manager rather well. Once the studio doors are closed and the production is underway, the floor manager is the one person assigned to be of general assistance. One of the stage manager's prime jobs is giving you different cues (to speed up, slow down, move in this direction, speak louder, and so forth). Generally, you do not have to acknowledge the cues that call for some sort of immediate action on your part; you just do as instructed. The floor manager, however, will also be giving you time-remaining cues (time left in this segment, minutes remaining until the end of the program). Occasionally you will want to acknowledge these cues to reassure the floor manager that you have received the message. One covert way of doing this (a nod of the head is too obvious for the audience) is with a prolonged blink. The audience will scarcely notice the blink, but it will be picked up by the floor director. (See appendix C for illustrations of the various cues and floor manager's hand signals.)

As talent, you will not have to worry about where the floor director is. If you do not see him or her, it is because you do not *have* to see the floor manager at that moment. It is the job of the floor manager to be where you will definitely see him or her when you need to.

In some productions, however, the floor manager may get positioned so that he or she is always fully visible to the talent. For many performers, it is helpful to have the floor manager standing right next to the camera on the air, eagerly hanging on every word of the speaker—nodding encouragement, responding (silently), and reacting to the performer. This provides a sense of feedback and stimulation that many performers need. On the other hand, feedback can be distracting to some performers. One of the authors of this text recalls a production where the talent was so desperate for any live appreciation that every floor crew member had either to hide behind set pieces and cameras or, in the case of the floor manager, turn his back on the talent—in order to get the talent to look at the camera. If the performer could find one pair of eyes in the studio, he would address that single individual rather than the camera lens.

Relationships will vary tremendously among performers and those in crew positions. Both the performer and the crew should try to be as sensitive as possible to the feelings and working patterns of others. This is all part of the *discipline* of the production crew.

Relationships with Other Talent

Finally, some mention must be made about the relationship that you—as talent—will have with other performers in the studio. As host, panel moderator, or interviewer, you may often find yourself in a position of organizing and controlling others. As a host/moderator/interviewer, one of your concerns will have to be with the comfort and emotional security of others, particularly guests at the television studio and inexperienced performers who may not feel at ease. One tangible aspect of this concern will be professional courtesy while you are off camera. For the sake of the talent in front of the lens, you will be as quiet, attentive, and unobtrusive as possible.

You will get used to the idea of close physical proximity to other talent. For the sake of good camera shots, performers have to work very close together, especially in two-person interviews. You may feel uncomfortably intimate (and you may want to keep a good supply of breath fresheners handy), but to the audience, the staging looks natural. One old television adage is, "If you ain't touching, you ain't close enough."

Interviewing Techniques   One prominent situation in which you, as the performer, will frequently find yourself is the basic interview format. This may take many forms: the celebrity interview, the unprepared person-on-the-street interview, the factual interview (basically trying to present information to the audience), the controversial interview (with some outspoken public figure), and so forth. There are a few basic points to be aware of in preparing for a studio interview.

1. *Preparation.* Find out as much as you can about the guest. Research the background of the subject you will be discussing. Be familiar with what the guest has written, produced, or said about the topic. Go to other sources for outside opinions.

2. *Hospitality.* Be on hand to welcome the guest to the studio well before airtime. Make the guest comfortable. Explain all of the studio procedures, the nature of the program, and the intended audience.

3. *Organization.* Determine with the guest what main points the interview will cover. Arrange the points in a well-organized pattern, keeping some material for the middle and end of the interview.

4. *Focus.* Remember that the spotlight should be on the guest. He or she is the one the audience wants to learn more about—not you. Avoid the temptation to dominate the session by explaining all of your viewpoints and ideas on the topic.

5. *Questioning.* Ask questions requiring some solid comments and explanation (avoid *yes* or *no* answers). Ask only one question at a time (avoid double-barreled questions). With a controversial guest, do not compromise the integrity of the interview by avoiding awkward topics or hard issues; press on, courteously but tenaciously, for honest answers to honest questions.

6. *Transitions.* Keep the interview moving. Follow up on interesting answers, but do not get bogged down. Use answers as a transition to the next point. Summarize and clarify if necessary, but keep transitions short.

7. *Control.* Remember that, as host, you are in control. Do not allow yourself to be overwhelmed in the presence of a powerful personality. Be ready to take over entirely for the last thirty seconds or so—to summarize, thank the guest, and bring the interview to a smooth close, right on time.

These are a few guidelines for the interviewer. As director you will be helping the talent establish similar hints for other on-camera assignments—as lecturer, newscaster, demonstrator, and so forth.

11.3   The Television Actor

Although we cannot begin to present a separate treatise on television acting, there are a few points that should be made. Assuming that you, as a director, will be working with skilled or trained actors, we do not need to get into the basics of acting methodology in this book. Anyone seriously interested in television drama will, of course, be pursuing additional class

On-Camera Talent: The Performer and Actor

work in acting and dramatic directing. Many actors who have been trained on the stage and may have some film experience, however, are not prepared for the adaptations they will have to make to the television studio.

Many of the observations made in section 11.2, "The Television Performer," apply equally to the television actor. Actors, too, must be concerned with their relationship with the *audience* (television is an intimate medium compared to the stage, or even to film); with the *production crew* (where everyone is immediately involved in the execution of the dramatic scene); and with *other talent* (all dramatic blocking is more compact and precise in the TV studio).

Television acting invariably is compared with other media, and actors must make adaptions as they move from one medium to another. The theatre, film, and television stages all have their unique requirements and frustrations.

Theatrical acting is, of course, the ancestor of all other media. Furthermore, the stage is where most actors begin. Early television resembled the theatrical stage in that a continuous performance was presented. Actors would have to create and sustain a characterization for a full sixty or ninety minutes—but the similarity to the theatre stage stopped there.

Film acting is, like television, a medium of the recording camera, and like television, there is no proscenium arch. But there also are many differences.

In discussing television acting, one must keep in mind the wide variety of TV formats, recording techniques, and editing considerations used in different situations. Of course, "live" television acting (where the action is broadcast at the very moment it is being performed) has virtually completely disappeared. For the most part, we are discussing acting recorded either for the electronic camera (on videotape) or for the film camera.

Today, most television acting consists of recording short scenes, seldom running more than five minutes in length. Some situation comedies use a multiple-camera technique (pioneered by *I Love Lucy* and continuing on through *Happy Days* and many contemporary sitcoms), using three or four cameras—either electronic or film—recording the output of each camera separately, then splicing together the best shots in postproduction editing. Some sitcoms, on the other hand (*All in the Family* was one of the first), will use a "live-on-tape" format. The production will run straight through a 3- to 5-minute segment, with the director making live editing decisions and switching during the final "take" (with the knowledge that postproduction editing—for example, splicing in shots from a recorded dress rehearsal—can tidy up a final tape). Both of these formats are suited to shooting in front of a live audience. Daytime serials (*soap operas*) use electronic cameras, run scenes straight through, but shoot the scenes out of order, and edit the show together in postproduction.

However, most television dramas, nighttime soaps, "TV movies," miniseries, and many other sitcoms are usually recorded on film in single shots, using variations of the basic single-camera filmic techniques that have dominated the motion picture industry since the turn of the century.

Nevertheless, in discussing the requirements for television acting, there are several broad observations that can be made. Some of these points apply only to certain categories of TV acting as previously outlined; but the director must be ready to work with actors in making all of these adaptations.

The Missing Proscenium   First, and most obvious, there is *no proscenium arch*; there is no firm boundary separating the audience from the actors. The audience perspective is switched every time the camera is

Figure 11–5
Differences in the scope of gesturing. *Left,* a large sweeping gesture appropriate for the theatre; *right,* a more subdued, intimate version of the same gesture appropriate for television.

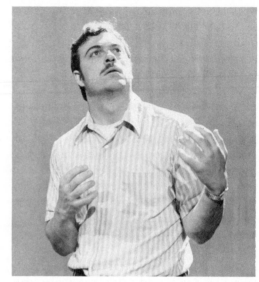

changed. The director can move the audience ninety degrees with the push of a button. Even in a theatre-in-the-round, or arena theatre, each individual viewer is in one spot for the entire production; the viewer's perspective cannot be changed. In television, the viewer can be transported sideways, in or out, or (with the use of the subjective camera) into the mind of the actor. (Even when a live audience is in the TV studio watching the taping of a situation comedy, the action is staged for the cameras and the television audience; the live audience is just watching the production of a program.) Actors must learn to adjust to this concept of moving audience perspective.

Limited Projection   Second, actors must adjust to a *smaller scope of projection.* Instead of the exaggerated movements and sweeping gestures that must be seen in the back row of the theatre, the TV actor has to restrict all actions and movement to the camera only ten feet away. (See figure 11–5.) Instead of projecting his or her voice so that every line is heard clearly sixty or seventy feet from the stage, the actor must restrict voice volume

level—without losing emotion or intensity—for a pickup point only three or four feet away. Television is a close-up medium, and actors must adjust to this intimacy.

Blocking Precision   Third, actors must learn to work with a *physical precision* in television. Compared to the stage, television blocking is very precise; every move and tiny gesture has to be carefully planned and controlled. On the stage, each movement may be accurate to within a few feet. In television, the action must be measured by inches. If the actor's head is tilted at the wrong angle, the framing for a given shot may be off. This is a discipline that many actors find difficult to adapt to.

One aspect of this precision is "cheating to camera." Frequently an actor, in a two-shot for instance, will be directed to turn his or her face slightly toward the camera—rather than looking directly at the other actor straight on. Such *cheating* is not perceived by the viewer, but it does result in more of a head-on shot into the camera.

On-Camera Talent: The Performer and Actor

Pacing Precision Fourth, television exists generally in a demanding and *nonflexible time frame*. Except for some programming on public television, all dramatic programs have to be squeezed (or stretched) into given time slots—multiples of a half hour, minus requisite time for commercials. This means that an actor may have to adjust pacing, speeding up or slowing down delivery of lines or action. This is especially a major concern with soap operas and situation comedies where there can be little flexibility in timing. It is less of a concern for filmed dramas, however, where the exact timing can be worked out in the editing process (either on the film editor's bench or by electronic editing) by cutting or augmenting silent footage, action shots, panoramic long shots, and chase sequences.

Out-of-Sequence Shooting Filmed or single-camera videotaped dramas are almost always shot *out of sequence*. There is no continuity of drama from the actor's standpoint. All of the scenes in a given location are shot during the same setup. For example, once the camera, audio, and lights are set up for the drugstore exterior, every bit of action that takes place in that locale will be filmed—from the opening boy-meets-girl shot to the final boy-dies-in-gutter shot. This demands a great deal of concentration and training on the part of the actor.

A Quick Study Finally, compared to the stage and to theatrical motion pictures, television drama (both filmed and "live-on-tape") is a *quick study* medium. Whether working with single-camera or multiple-camera techniques, regular actors in a continuing series must learn up to an hour-long script every week—the equivalent of two feature-length motion pictures every month. For the actor in the hour-long daytime soap opera, the pace is even more demanding—up to a half hour of dialogue every day!

Thus, from a variety of viewpoints, the task of the television actor is quite demanding and complicated. Your job, as a television director, is to make the transition as easy as possible for the inexperienced TV actor. The stage actor and motion picture actor will need guidance to help them adapt to the television medium.

11.4 Clothing and Costumes

Some attention also must be given to what the performers and actors will wear. There are a few general observations that are appropriate for a book of this scope.

Design Considerations

Many of the design criteria discussed in chapter 10 apply here also. In any color production, for example, the clothing and costumes of the performers have to be considered in conjunction with the color scheme of the entire setting. All designers certainly would consider costuming an integral part of the overall production design. Even in small-station and educational closed-circuit operations, color has to be a major consideration. The hostess for a local talk show normally would not wear a red ensemble on her predominantly green set (unless it was for her Christmas program).

The same color factors that were discussed in section 10.1 (*hue, saturation,* and *brightness*) apply to clothing and costume design. Unless a spectacular, deliberately colorful, dazzling effect is advised, performers generally should be encouraged to stick to clothing of a dull saturation—choose muted aqua rather than chartreuse, tan rather than brilliant yellow. Brightness and tonal balance also should be considered in terms of the overall emotional effect that is desired. Would dark, somber grays and browns be more or less appropriate than lighter shades and pastels?

Figure 11–6
The fine design on a blouse such as this would be substantially lost once it is translated into scanning lines.

Line also is an important design consideration. Vertical lines tend to emphasize tall and slender proportions; horizontal stripes tend to exaggerate weight and mass. Performers who are concerned about appearing too heavy (and television has a tendency to make people appear a little heavier) should stick to vertical lines.

One other word of advice to the performer in street clothing: be natural. Do not try to emulate the latest fashions in order to make a striking television appearance. Avoid fads, extreme styles, and flashy finery, unless that is your natural inclination. If you step out of character for the sake of making a striking appearance, the chances are that you will wind up looking more foolish than fashionable.

Production Considerations

In addition to color, line, and style, there are some other practical considerations and potential problems that you should be aware of. Try to avoid high contrast and extremes in color brightness. Remember that the television camera has a relatively limited contrast ratio (section 4.2), which makes it difficult to handle white shirts against a dark suit. Try also to avoid high contrasts with skin tones. Dark clothes will make a pale person look even more pale; light-colored clothes next to a tanned complexion will make the skin appear darker. Blacks and other dark-skinned performers, on the other hand, should be careful of light-colored clothing that would tend to heighten the tonal contrast and wash out facial details in the dark areas.

Generally, finely detailed patterns should be avoided. Whereas clothing with a rich thick texture will photograph well on television, clothing with a fine pattern usually will not. The pattern often is too busy and distracting—fighting with other picture elements, including the talent, for the viewer's attention. (See figure 11–6.) Thin stripes, herringbones, and small checks can also create the

On-Camera Talent: The Performer and Actor

moiré effect—a distracting visual vibration caused by the interference of the clothing pattern and the TV scanning lines.

Highly reflective jewelry can also cause trouble. Too much flashy jewelry—even if it does not cause glare problems as a result of its high-reflectance qualities—still can be distracting and needlessly gaudy.

There is one other minor production consideration with color TV. Be careful of the *key color* (usually blue or green)—even a tie—if any chroma key effects are to be used in the production (section 7.4). Any blue or green shade worn by the performer (depending upon the chroma key setting) will form part of the keying pattern, and the background picture will appear wherever the chroma key color clothing is otherwise visible to the camera. Imagine the effect when the newscaster has a scene from the battlefield keyed in behind him—and we see bricks and rubble appearing where his tie should be.

Dramatic Costumes

Again, all the points made for performer clothing (color harmony, line, tonal contrast, details, and jewelry) apply to theatrical costuming as well. In many respects, the use of color and style in a dramatic production is even more important.

Virtually all costuming considerations that apply to theatrical costumes apply equally to television: authenticity, historical accuracy, color, durability, and so forth. One aspect that needs to be emphasized more strongly for television than for the stage is *detail*. Although you may be able to get away with a few loose threads and a modern patch on the stage—where the nearest spectator is fifteen feet away—you cannot afford to try to fool the television camera, which brings the viewer only a few inches away. This is especially critical in costuming around the neck, shoulders, and chest areas, where the close-up picks up costume details with microscopic clarity.

11.5 Television Makeup

The field of television makeup is a specialized area that most production personnel seldom get into. The student should be aware, however, of some of the basic principles and major considerations. All television makeup is used for one of three functions: (1) to *enhance* appearance (improving the performer's basic physiognomy with color correction or emphasis on highlights); (2) to *correct* appearance (creating the effect of pulling back protruding ears or straightening a broken nose); or (3) to *create* appearance (building a new character such as Frankenstein's monster or Mr. Hyde). Ordinary television production situations rarely go beyond the first function; the last two areas are left for the specialist.

Principles of Basic Makeup

The object of television makeup is to have the performer or actor look as natural as possible. A good, basic, unobtrusive makeup job should help enhance normal colors (evening up flesh tones); minimize any blemishes or distortions (covering up birthmarks, bags under the eyes); compensate for flat television lighting (which may tend to wash out facial characteristics); and emphasize good points. However, with the close-up lens any exaggerated makeup certainly would be perceived as unnatural. This is opposed to theatre use, where exaggerated makeup is necessary in order to highlight facial features for the last row of the audience.

In many kinds of situations, a minimum amount of makeup will be necessary. If a performer looks basically good *on camera,* there is no reason to consider any heavy makeup job. For many female performers, ordinary street makeup *may* be all that is needed. However, television lighting and color technology often will distort street makeup; so its use should be carefully checked out on camera before deciding to go with it. For many male performers, a little powder to control perspiration or to reduce the shine on a bald head may be all that is necessary. Even in dramatic situations, little makeup may be called for. However, it must be recognized that in many situations—especially in educational or industrial applications (where the performers are nonprofessionals and the equipment may not give the best color rendition)—makeup may definitely be called for.

For minor skin problems or blotchiness, a base or foundation may be all that is needed. It should cover uneven skin coloring, surface blemishes, beard shadow, and so forth. The foundation can be further used, if needed, to cover lip lines, eyebrows, and other features before a new formation is drawn in.

Appearance can often be improved or enhanced by careful use of highlighting and darkening. Within prudent limits, localized highlighting will tend to enlarge the evident size and prominence of a facial feature. Darkening a feature with shadows will tend to de-emphasize its size for the camera. Thus, it is possible to strengthen the cheekbones, the forehead, or the jaw with highlights. Shadows are often used to emphasize facial hollows—under the cheekbones or behind the temple. Features can be subtly altered; highlight a thin nose to make it look broader; use shadow on either side of a broad nose to make it look thinner.

Color Correction   Some improvement in appearance can often be achieved by color correction. Depending upon lighting conditions, facial colors may need to be touched up in order to give a truer color rendition. Generally, cooler colors (those hues with a slight bluish tint) tend to emphasize facial shadows and dark areas. For this reason, warmer colors (those with a reddish tendency) generally are preferred for the basic foundation.

Care must be taken, however, that the Caucasian or Oriental skin tone is not tinted too pink and that the Black or Latin skin color is not turned too reddish. Although makeup companies will furnish detailed instructions and charts with their products (suggesting proper colors to use for different races and skin types), every individual skin tone will react differently under various lighting conditions and with diverse camera adjustments. Only by experimenting with each individual under actual lighting and camera conditions can the best color combination be determined.

Be especially careful in selecting colors for lipstick, rouge, and eye shadow. Color TV equipment may tend to distort colors that are in the blue-green range. Reds that are rich in blue or orange also may tend to be exaggerated.

Makeup personnel should also work closely with the lighting director for any production. The lighting director may be using colored gels, for instance, that could tremendously distort the effect desired by the makeup person. A green gel on a dark or black skin, for example, will completely wash out any color distinctions on the face. Generally—since most foundation color is in the reddish range—backgrounds should tend more toward blues and greens. But these subtleties must be coordinated with the lighting director.

Basic Makeup Procedures and Materials

Regardless of the extent of the makeup job to be performed, basic procedures should follow a fairly well-established pattern.

1. *Preparation.* All makeup materials should be collected and organized in one specific area of the studio complex. Ideally, there should be plenty of working space, a well-lighted mirror, and a chair of adequate (preferably adjustable) height.

A basic makeup complement should include foundation or base colors, translucent and tinted powders, creme or powder rouges,

On-Camera Talent: The Performer and Actor

a variety of lipsticks, eye shadows, eyeliners, mascara, and eyebrow pencils. Other materials should include a variety of natural and rubber sponges, various small brushes, powder puffs, tissues, towels, cleansing cream, and soap.

Before applying any makeup, the face should be cleaned and either a moisturizer, for dry skin, or an astringent (such as alcohol or witch hazel), for oily skin, may be applied.[2]

2. *Foundation or base.* The primary makeup element is the base, or **foundation.** This is the initial covering that is usually applied to the entire face or exposed area being treated (arms and hands and other parts of the body often need makeup treatment). This base is to provide the color foundation upon which all the rest of the makeup will be built. The foundation comes in several different media. *Pancake* is a water-based covering that is applied with a moist sponge; it is convenient to use and is preferred by many stations as the basic makeup treatment. *Cream-based* foundation is usually dabbed onto small areas and spread by the fingers; left unpowdered, it results in a noticeable sheen. *Greasepaint,* an oil-based theatrical standard for many years, is easily worked and occasionally used for major jobs. *Panstick* is a combination of pancake and greasepaint that, like the other bases, comes in a wide variety of colors. *Powder bases,* supplied in compacts, provide suitable covering for small areas and touch-up jobs.

3. *Powder.* Powder is usually applied next in order to *set* the base, dull any sheen or gloss, and help keep the base from smearing. Generally, more powder is needed with cream- or oil-based foundation than with pancake (which goes on with more of a matte finish). More powder may also be used on oily skin. Usually, powder that is a little lighter than the base color is applied.

4. *Highlights, shadows, and rouge.* Highlights and shadows are used to emphasize or minimize facial features. The forehead, nose, cheekbone, and jaw can all be highlighted with lighter shades or de-emphasized with darker tones. Normally, rouge is next applied to the cheeks, nose, forehead, and chin as needed to give a healthy complexion and to counteract the flatness of both the foundation color and the evenness of the lighting.

5. *Eyes and lips.* Finally, special attention is given to those most expressive features of the face—the eyes and the lips. Specific drawing tools and accessory items are applied as necessary: lipstick (avoiding colors with blues or oranges), eye shadow (preferably the dry or cake type), eyeliner (to give needed accent), eyebrow pencil, mascara, and possibly false eyelashes. (See figure 11–7.) The extent of the use of these accent items depends upon the need for remodeling and the individual taste of the performer.

Final Considerations

In addition to the basic makeup job, hairstyling and treatment need to be considered. Hairstyles with a definite shape or firm silhouette usually compliment the performer more than wispy, fluffy hairdos. Hair should be carefully combed because back light will tend to make loose strands stand out.

The performer should strive for as natural an appearance as possible. For this reason, fancy hair treatments and fresh permanents should be avoided. The performer should wear glasses if he or she ordinarily wears them; they should not be removed simply for cosmetic reasons.

For dramatic purposes, of course, much more makeup treatment is needed—getting into the third function of *creating* an appear-

2. Four of the major makeup companies that offer a wide range of supplies and more detailed instructions include the following: Max Factor & Co. (1655 North McCadden Place, Hollywood, CA 90028); Bob Kelly Cosmetics (152 West 46th Street, New York, NY 10036); Syd Simon Studios (2 East Oak Street, Chicago, IL 60611); and Ben Nye, Inc. (11571 Santa Monica Blvd., Los Angeles, CA 90025).

Figure 11–7
Makeup artist applying final touches with a fine brush. (Photo courtesy of KABC-TV, Los Angeles)

ance for certain characterizations. This includes hairpieces and wigs, *collodion* scars, nose putty, surface molding by plasticine and special waxes, and larger rebuilding jobs using latex prosthetics and face masks.

Aside from these extreme theatrical applications, the aim of good television makeup, like that of good costuming, is simply one of accentuating the natural appearance of the performer for purposes of more accurate rendering by the electronic camera. For this reason, no makeup job can be considered complete until it has been checked out on camera—under studio lighting conditions. The television monitor, not the naked eye, must be the final judge in determining whether or not the makeup has succeeded in merely making the talent appear natural looking.

Summary

Although the production student may not aspire to be a great television performer, he or she should nevertheless be familiar with the problems of on-camera performers and actors. Otherwise, it will be difficult to work with *talent* with any real understanding. Some on-camera experience and training is important for everyone connected with the production of programs. Generally, television talent is divided into two categories—*performers* (reportorial communicators such as lecturers, newscasters, hosts, announcers, interviewers) and *actors.*

The performer must be concerned with three kinds of relationships. The first is *audience relationships,* which include a sense of intimacy with the audience and a feeling for

On-Camera Talent: The Performer and Actor

sincerity as expressed by the *speaking voice* and *eye contact*. The performer must also be aware of the need to control certain distracting mannerisms. Problems in handling *scripted material* and *extemporaneous material* can be worked out for individual performers depending upon their own delivery styles and the requirements of particular production formats. The second area is *crew relationships,* which include the *director* and *A.D.* (preparation of the program and on-the-air timing); the *camera operators* (how to move on camera, how to handle a close-up of an object); the *audio engineer* (treatment of equipment, establishing audio levels); and the *floor manager* (accepting directions and cues). The third area is *relationships with other talent,* which include playing host to other performers, moderating panel discussions, and handling interview situations. Conducting an *interview* involves several basic factors—preparation, hospitality, organization, focus, questioning, transitions, and control.

The *television actor* usually has been trained for other media—the theatrical stage and/or film. There are quite a few differences between television acting and other media. The TV actor must be helped to adapt to these differences: lack of the proscenium arch; a smaller scope of projection (both gesturing and vocal); physical precision in blocking; the nonflexible time frame; shooting out of sequence (in filmed TV drama); and quick study methods of preparation.

Clothing and makeup considerations are primarily to help present as natural an appearance as possible without creating any production problems. Clothing should adhere to the fundamental design considerations of *color* and *line*. High *contrasts* should be avoided, and *small patterns* should not be worn. Other problems can be caused by jewelry and by *blue clothing* (for chroma keying). Dramatic costumes must pay special attention to *detail* for the close-up medium of television.

For most television applications, makeup consists of a few basic steps for the purpose of *enhancing natural appearance*—including covering skin blemishes and color correction. Fundamental procedures include proper *preparation*; applying a *foundation* or *base*; applying a *powder set*; using *highlights, shadows,* and *rouge*; and accenting *eyes* and *lips*. Theatrical uses of makeup for *corrective purposes* and for *creating characterizations* are seldom employed in most station operations.

This chapter has been concerned with the people in front of the cameras. Chapter 12 explores in more detail the responsibilities and attitudes of those behind the cameras.

11.6 Training Exercises

The first exercise should be conducted for the entire class. The other two exercises may be considered optional, depending upon how much emphasis the class wants to put on costuming and makeup.

1. Set up three role-playing interview situations. For each one, assign one student to play the role of the interviewer; he or she is to do as good a job as possible. For each interview, another student is assigned as the guest; unknown to the interviewer each guest is instructed to manifest some particular negative trait that should give the interviewer considerable trouble in handling the situation. Each 5–minute interview is conducted in front of the class. After each interview, the class should critique the situation and discuss what could have been done to handle that particular troublesome guest.

2. Select four or five class members and set up a camera demonstration to see how their street clothes look on television. Select those who are wearing clothing and accessories that may present specific problems—wide stripes, small patterns, high contrast, jewelry, and so forth.

3. Select one female student as a model. Have her remove all makeup. On camera, using a close-up, have her apply ordinary street makeup in sequence. Have her continue to apply what would be considered more than the usual amounts of accent items (lipstick, eye shadow, and so forth). Critique the results. If theatrical makeup supplies are available to the class, select a male model—one with a heavy 5 o'clock shadow—and go through the same process on camera, emphasizing a good foundation base.

On-Camera Talent: The Performer and Actor

The Production Crew

Throughout this text, we have touched on some of the duties and *techniques* of specific crew members as well as the development of a professional *discipline* among all members of the production team. At this point we want to look a little more carefully at some considerations and task responsibilities of various crew positions. We will be concerned with the lighting and staging personnel, audio engineer, camera operators, technical director, recording engineer, graphic artists, grips or floor assistants, and production assistants or script assistants. We will also be introducing the position of the unit manager.

In particular, however, we will be discussing the jobs of the two key crew members that we have not had an opportunity to cover previously—the associate director (A.D.) and the stage manager (or floor manager or floor director). We have saved these positions for discussion at this point because their jobs are primarily people oriented; and up to this point, we have been looking at the various crew positions that are equipment oriented.

12.1 The Associate Director

If one were to think of the television director as the captain of the production team (with the producer, executive producer, sponsors, and network executives as the higher officers), then the two lieutenants would be the assistant director or *associate director* (A.D.) and the *stage manager.* The latter is in charge of virtually everything that takes place on the studio floor, while the A.D. is the director's right-hand person and surrogate in all other matters.

General Duties of the A.D.

In almost all respects, the A.D. is considered the director's top assistant—ready to handle virtually any task that the director may request. Depending on the actual production setup and the traditional organization of the studio/station, the A.D. may be labeled either the "assistant director" or the "associate director."[1] The position often carries quite a bit of responsibility for the production, independent of the director's orders. In some network situations, the A.D. will be responsible for setting up all of the camera shots on the air.

In virtually every kind of studio operation, however, the A.D.'s primary job will be that of timing the production. The A.D. will time individual segments during rehearsals, get an overall timing of the program, if possible, and then be in charge of the pacing of the program—speeding up or stretching as required—during the actual recording.

In any extensive production that involves postproduction editing, the A.D. will also be intimately involved at that stage. The A.D. will be making editing notes before and during the production and then, with or without the director's direct supervision, be in charge of much of the later editing process. Other duties of the A.D. can be outlined in terms of time periods before the studio rehearsal, during the rehearsal period, during the actual program, and after the production.

Before the Studio Rehearsal   In any major production undertaking, the A.D. will work with the director well in advance of the actual production period—attending production conferences, working during **pre-studio rehearsals** with talent, and assembling props and other materials. During this pre-studio period, the A.D. may also be able to start getting some rough timings of the program.

Additionally, the A.D. will begin to assemble notes on what postproduction editing may have to be done. Some editing can be anticipated—especially in dramas and some

1. The Directors' Guild of America officially refers to the position as *associate director,* because the *assistant director* title is traditionally used in the film industry.

public affairs formats (reaction shots in interviews, for example). In other types of productions (game shows, sports documentaries), one cannot anticipate what editing may have to be done later.

Once the production moves into the studio, the A.D. often has several tasks before the rehearsals actually start. The A.D. may be in charge of the rest of the crew—checking to make certain that everyone is present and reporting this to the director. This is especially true on small-format productions and in training situations. The A.D. may well be in charge of arranging substitute assignments, thus ensuring that every position is covered.

The A.D. obtains all copies of the scripts and other production instructions from the producer and/or director and distributes them to members of the crew. If any slides or physical graphic cards are to be used, the A.D. might also be in charge of distributing slides to the projectionist in telecine, graphics and props to the floor manager, and other materials to the proper crew positions.

If timing arrangements have not yet been worked out with the talent, the A.D. at this point determines exactly what kind of time cues the talent would prefer (in other words, how many minutes warning the talent would want before the end of the program or before the end of each segment of the program). If there is nothing else to be done, the A.D. will remain at the director's side, ready for any requests the director may have.

During the Rehearsal Period   The A.D. will time as much of the program as possible during the various rehearsals (technical rehearsal, walk-through rehearsal, dress rehearsal, and so forth), including individual segments, film inserts, and opening and closing elements.

During the rehearsals, the director will mention various production items that need attention before the actual take: the back lighting is weak in area 2; the talent doesn't know the roll cue to the third film segment; the graphics are out of order during the map sequence; the guest's hair needs to be combed; and similar items to be cleaned up after the rehearsals. The A.D. will be jotting down the production notes, or "critique notes," as the director spots them. Additionally, the A.D. should be making notes of similar items that might have escaped the attention of the director. If the A.D. notices a major item, it should be called to the attention of the director before the rehearsal proceeds. Minor items are simply written down to be cleaned up later (note that it is the A.D. who has to make the distinction between minor items and those that are important enough to warrant interrupting the rehearsal). The A.D. will be especially concerned with noting all of the script changes that are made.

Depending upon the production techniques of the individual director, the A.D. may or may not get involved with actually making production decisions. In some situations, the A.D. will be helping to compose shots for the director, giving direct orders to the camera operators. The A.D. also may be making other suggestions regarding talent moves, graphics, script revision, lighting problems, or whatever else needs attention. In other situations, the A.D. traditionally stays out of these kinds of directorial/aesthetic decisions and sticks closely to the note-keeping and timing functions.

After the rehearsal and before the actual take, the A.D. will want to do several things. First, he or she must make certain that the director follows through on all production notes that were jotted down (fixing the back light, taking care of the talent's hair, and so forth—for minor corrections, the A.D. may take care of them without even bothering the director). Next, the A.D. must make sure that everybody involved has all of the script changes

marked down. As surely as one person did not get a crucial script change, that omission will lead to an on-the-air mistake.

Finally, the A.D. must remind the director of how much time is remaining before videotaping is scheduled to start or before the live program goes on the air.

During the Program   Just prior to production, the A.D. will "read down" the clock, letting the director know how many seconds until air. Once on the air, the A.D. should remain alert to any and all potential problems—ready to take any action needed or to call major troubles to the attention of the director; the A.D. must show initiative in this regard.

The A.D. should be following the director's marked script at all times, ready to give any assistance necessary. The A.D. will be alerting camera operators, audio personnel, character generator (C.G.) operators, and other crew positions to any special cues coming up in the script. Depending, again, upon the production complexity and studio philosophy, the A.D. may help get the camera shots lined up. In some network and station production situations, the A.D. will be giving the crew—including the camera operators—virtually all their instructions, based upon the director's script and rehearsals. The A.D. may even be giving "readies" and "prepares" to the technical director. This gives the director freedom to handle last-minute adjustments, make final artistic decisions, and call the actual takes on the air.

In many instances, the A.D. will at least be calling out shot numbers to the cameras. (In a thoroughly rehearsed production, the director will have every shot numbered in his or her script, and the camera operators will have a list of their shots by number. As the A.D. calls out the shot number on the air, all camera operators know exactly where they are in relation to the actual on-the-air shot.)

Figure 12–1
A.D. checking script timing
with a stop clock.

The primary job of the A.D., of course, is giving all time signals to the talent. The A.D. will have his or her script marked with all of the time cues and, either directly or through the director, will tell the floor manager when to give each time signal to the talent. (See figure 12–1.) Sometimes individual program segments will be timed. At the very minimum, time signals indicating the amount of time remaining in the program must be relayed to the talent. The A.D. will also be determining when the talent needs to be signaled to speed up or slow down (stretch).

Also, the A.D. will be taking notes for postproduction editing—both those items that the director points out that need to be taken care of in the later editing session (a missed shot, timing that was off a little, an opportunity to insert a reaction shot) and the items that the A.D. himself or herself notices that need to be corrected.

Finally, the associate director will be ready to take over at any time. The A.D. is literally the standby director. Should the director be unable to complete the program, the A.D. will assume responsibility for the calling of shots, and the production will continue. (Once on a network program, the director had a heart attack at the beginning of a production, and the A.D. continued to direct the program on the air. The ambulance arrived before the program was finished. The director recuperated.)

After the Production   Once the production is completed, the A.D. still has a couple obligations—especially in a training situation. The student A.D. should remind the director to thank the cast and crew; help clean up the control room of extra scripts, notes, and other materials; and debrief the director on any errors that occurred during the program, looking forward to the next day's program.

A crucial postproduction job of the A.D. in many situations is the final editing session. The associate director may need to set up a schedule with the director for any planned editing (especially on dramatic programs—daytime serials and situation comedies), **sweetening** of the program (adding audience reactions and recorded laugh tracks), or cor-

SEGMENT (Description)	IDEAL (Unit)	Cum.	REHEARSAL (Unit)	Cum.	DRESS (Unit)	Cum.	AIR (Unit)	Cum.
1. TEASER	(:20)	0:20		:25		:25		:25
2. OPENING TITLES	(:30)	0:50		:40		1:05		1:10
3. INTRO	(1:05)	1:55		1:30		2:15		2:20
4. CHART	(2:00)	3:55		1:50		4:00		4:10
5. DEMO.	(4:00)	7:55		4:45	(4:15)	8:15	(4:20)	8:30
6. INTERVIEW	(5:30)	13:25		6:00		13:45	(5:00)	13:30
7. WRAP-UP	(:30)	13:55		:20		14:05		13:55
8. CLOSE	(:35)	14:30		:45		14:50		14:30
				16:15				
				(+1:45 over)				

Figure 12–2
Sample segment timing sheet.

In this particular example, we have a demonstration/interview program with several segments, which include a teaser, the opening titles, an introduction by the host, a 2-minute chart talk, a demonstration, an interview, the host's summary, and the closing credits. The ideal times are entered in the first column. During the stop-and-go rehearsal, various unit or segment times are obtained. By totaling these times in the "Rehearsal" column, we can see that the program is likely to run 1:45 (1 minute and 45 seconds) long. Adjustments are made—the interview segment is cut short—and the actual cumulative times are entered during the "dress" rehearsal and the actual "air" recording.

recting unanticipated production problems that need to be cleaned up. The A.D. may simply continue as the director's right-hand assistant in these assignments or, depending upon the nature of the production arrangements, the A.D. may be substantially in charge of the postproduction editing session—following the director's instructions, of course.

Timing the Program

As previously discussed, the A.D.'s primary job is timing the program—ensuring that the entire production ends on time. Timing all of the segments to be electronically glued together in the editing session is also an important consideration here. In carrying out this function, there are specific hints that the beginning A.D. may want to use.

Segment Timing Sheets The fundamental tool of the A.D. is, of course, the stopwatch. The A.D. also needs some way, however, of keeping track of the various timing notes and reminders. The stopwatch is not of much use if the A.D. does not have some organized way of writing down the timing information. One way is the use of a **segment timing sheet.** It may take several forms and be used in different ways.

One sample format is shown in figure 12–2. In this particular example, there are five columns for the A.D. to use. The first column is for a brief description of each segment in the program. The next four columns are for timing notations of one kind or another. "Unit" means the actual *length of the individual segment or unit.* "Cum." is for the *cumulative time* of the program up to that point; it is the time in the program that each particular segment should (or did) end.

The "Ideal" column is the estimated time that each segment *should* run; both the ideal unit-segment times and the ideal cumulative time should be figured out in advance of setting foot in the studio. The "Rehearsal" column is for jotting down the unit times as various segments are worked through in a technical or stop-and-go rehearsal. It is difficult to get an accurate picture of the actual cumulative times at this point, but the total of the unit times should give the A.D. a rough picture of how long or how short the program is likely to be.

The "Dress" rehearsal column should give the A.D. a clear picture of how the actual cumulative times compare to the ideal times. The "Air" column is filled in as the program progresses. It lets the A.D. know how much to tell the talent to *stretch* or, in figure 12–2, how much to *cut* in order to come out on time. In this program, for example, we can see that several segments ran long, so the interview segment had to be cut short (from an ideal of five and a half minutes to an actual five minutes).

There are many variations of timing sheets. Some will include *time in* and *time out* cumulative columns. Some will work with only one or two columns. This sample, however, should give the beginning A.D. an idea of what is needed to get the program times accurately on the air.

Program Time and Body Time   Time signals are given to the talent in terms of *time remaining.* Thus, as we approach the end of a program, the A.D. will have the stage man-

ager signal the performer that there are "five minutes remaining," "three minutes remaining," "one minute to go," "thirty seconds left," and so forth (depending upon exactly what time cues the talent and A.D. had previously agreed would be used).

In many programs, such as the one illustrated in figure 12–2, the talent would need time-remaining cues in specific segments. Thus—working from the *ideal* times—the host would get, for example, a "thirty seconds remaining" cue at 3:25 into the program (as a reminder that there are thirty seconds left in the chart talk) and at 7:25 (thirty seconds left in the demonstration). The talent might want time cues to get out of the interview segment on time (that is, a 30–second cue at 12:55) or simply time cues to get through with the wrap-up summary on time (that is, a 30–second cue at 13:25). Care must be taken that the talent clearly understands what these intermediate segment cues are so that they will not be confused with time remaining in the body of the program.

This brings up one other point of potential confusion. The A.D. must be concerned both with *getting the talent wrapped up on time* and with *getting the program off the air on time.* In figure 12–2 the talent needs a 30–second cue at 13:25 because he or she has to be completely wrapped up and finished at 13:55 (leaving the director thirty-five seconds for the closing credits). Also, the director has to have a 30–second cue at 14:00 in order to get the program off the air and into black at precisely 14:30. Thus, the A.D. has to work with both **body time,** the actual *length of the program content* including the host's closing summary but not the show's closing credits, and with **program time,** the *total length of the show* from fade-in to fade-out. Figure 12–3 illustrates this. Throughout the production, the A.D. has to be very careful to distinguish between *body-time cues to the talent* and *program-time cues to the director.* As can be

The Production Crew

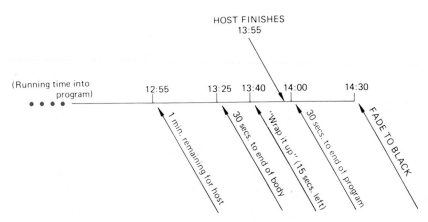

Figure 12–3
Body time and program
time.

If the host is to be completely finished by 13:55, the "time remaining" *body-time* cues to the host are "1 minute" (at 12:55), "30 seconds" (at 13:25), and "wrap it up" (at 13:40). The *program-time* cue to the director would be "30 seconds" (at 14:00).

imagined—solely from the standpoint of giving time cues—the A.D. has a very confusing and crucial role to play in any production.

12.2 The Stage Manager

The other right hand of the director is the stage manager (floor manager or floor director).[2] The stage manager is the director's surrogate to handle everything that happens on the studio floor. Actually, the stage manager's duties can be broken down into two very distinct areas: *handling the talent* and *managing all production activities* in the studio.

Working with Talent

On most major professional productions, the floor manager's primary job will probably be that of talent liaison. The floor manager will have to be a combination counselor, PR person, sympathizer, interpreter, and pillar of strength.

2. The official Directors' Guild of America designation is *stage manager*, but all three terms are used in various stations and studio operations.

Ideally, the floor director will have taken part in production conferences preceding the date of studio production. He or she has probably already met the principal talent and can anticipate the kind of problems that may exist. Once the production moves into the studio, the floor director is the primary contact the talent has with the rest of the world: the studio door is shut; the director is huddled with producers and technicians; all lights are focused upon the talent who is left isolated, facing the cameras alone—except for the support of the floor director.

There are two different kinds of talent needs that the floor director should be aware of and ready to minister to. First, there are *emotional-physical needs*—with inexperienced or exceptionally nervous talent, the floor director has to be especially sensitive in this area. Is the talent physically comfortable? Can you offer him or her a glass of water? Can you get the talent out of the lights for a few minutes? Does the talent need to talk to someone? Would he or she be better off left alone for a few moments of quiet reflection? What production mysteries should be explained to the talent?

The Production Crew

This last point is important. Because the talent is not tied into the P.L. intercom, he or she is not aware of what is going on most of the time. Explain to the talent why there is a delay (a result of the audio recorder malfunction); explain why all the crew is laughing (at the A.D.'s story—not at the talent's clothing). Try to put yourself in the position of the talent—isolated, in the spotlight, being stared at by the crew, and receiving no feedback as to what is going on.

With more experienced talent, this function becomes less of a priority. The routine production—with the continuing host/actor/teacher/newscaster—can be done fairly smoothly without having to cater to the emotional needs of the skilled performer. A few wisecracks, a slap on the back, and the experienced talent is ready to proceed.

The other kind of talent needs are more tangible *technical-production* requirements. The floor director must work these out with the talent on a program-by-program basis. What props must be available and where? How will this movement be handled? Where is the talent to stand for this demonstration? What kinds of special cues might be needed? The details of each production must be worked out so that the talent is always sure of exactly what to do and the floor director is always sure of what specific tasks and cues he or she needs to execute to get the talent's job done. These types of production details are unique to each program; it is imperative that both the talent and floor manager are completely aware of what the other is doing.

One inevitable production requirement, common to every program, is the communication of information to the talent through various hand signals and/or flip cards. (See figure 12–4.) The floor director—usually upon instructions from the director or A.D.—has to be concerned with relaying quite a bit of material to the talent: standby to start, begin talking, talk to this camera, get closer to the

mike, speed up, slow down (stretch), get closer together, get farther apart, move in this direction, everything is O.K., such and such number of minutes remain, thirty seconds to go, wrap it up (about fifteen seconds), cut, and so forth. (See appendix C for examples of the various hand signals.)

Production Management

In addition to handling talent, the other main job of the stage manager is that of handling all production details on the studio floor or stage. This may become the most important responsibility of the stage manager in small-format and training situations. In these low-budget operations, you are less likely to have electronic graphics and sophisticated lighting setups. Therefore, the stage manager is going to have to handle more physical paraphernalia. (Also, there will be fewer assistants or specialized union positions to take care of specific lighting, staging, graphics, and camera details.)

Production management includes a variety of concerns: broadly supervising staging and lighting setups and handling all staging and lighting changes during the program; coordinating all audio, camera, and other facilities; directing all studio traffic; taking care of any graphics changes and movement (where electronic graphics are not used); managing all talent movement; executing special effects; and every other production detail that might possibly occur.

The stage manager is ultimately in charge of virtually everything that happens on the studio floor, exercising dominion over all things technical—except the actual selection of shots for each camera. (In union situations, however, the stage manager may be restrained from crossing jurisdictional lines, such as giving orders to the lighting crew.) He or she must have a great deal of authority because virtually every other floor position is concerned with the production from only one spe-

The Production Crew

Figure 12–4
Stage manager using hand cards to relay time signals to the talent. (Photo courtesy of KABC-TV, Los Angeles)

cific viewpoint; for example, the camera operator, the audio engineer, and the lighting director all have their particular perspectives to take care of. Perhaps each of these three will have selected the same spot on the floor to position a camera, a mike boom, and a light stand. It is up to the stage manager to coordinate these needs and decide what goes where.

The stage manager does not work alone, of course. He or she will have a crew of floor assistants or grips, graphics handlers, cable pullers, rear screen projectionists, special effects operators, stagehands, lighting assistants, camera assistants, and so on. In a small-scale production, all of these positions and assistants may be combined in just one or two persons. In elaborate dramatic productions, the stage manager may have an assistant stage manager to coordinate the production activi-

ties of a floor crew of a dozen or so while the stage manager is occupied primarily with the job of talent managing.

As with the A.D., it may be convenient to think of the stage manager's responsibilities in terms of specific production periods: before the rehearsal period, during the rehearsals, and during the actual production.

Before the Studio Rehearsal Ideally, the floor manager will have been working with the director ahead of the production date, attending production conferences and contributing ideas to the production process. On the day of production, before the actual rehearsals start, the floor manager has several immediate tasks. Again, the smaller the scope of the production (corporate or instructional setups, small-format, and training situations), the more crucial the stage manager's job will be.

The Production Crew

He or she should obtain copies of the script and other specific instructions for various crew members and distribute them to everyone involved. The floor manager will assist the staging and lighting personnel however possible, assigning other floor people to help in the initial stages, coordinating set and light placements with the technical requirements for cameras, microphones, and so forth. The floor manager will obtain all physical (nonelectronic) graphics and props to be used in the production—making certain they are set up and arranged according to the script and the director's instructions. The floor manager, of course, will meet with the talent, cater to their comfort, and discuss any special requests.

Just as the primary tool of the A.D. was the stopwatch, the main tool of the floor manager is the clipboard. At this point in the production, the floor manager will have a good idea of all that must be done before and during the program. He or she will have started to organize lists of key tasks and requirements—people to contact, props to secure, specific instructions to pass out, special effects to develop, talent needs, specialized crew problems, staging considerations, and so forth. The clipboard will hold the master checklist that the floor manager will be working from during the rehearsal and production. This checklist will include all of the various action items that he or she must check on, supervise, or initiate during the production—arranging props, checking the sequence of all floor card graphics, securing water for the talent, checking the slides for the rear screen, closing the studio door, supervising the tricky camera move, setting up the lighting effect, ringing the buzzer, cueing the talent, changing the set piece, and so forth.

During the Rehearsal Period　　The floor manager must remain alert to the entire production process. He or she must try to anticipate problems before they escalate into crises and constantly ask, What can I do to help the production? In addition, the floor manager must be especially sensitive to coordination problems among lighting, audio, special effects, staging, graphics, cameras, and other elements.

The floor manager will plan and coordinate all movement. What set elements have to be moved during the production? What props are to be placed where? What special effects will have to be cued? All physical graphics activity—moves, flips, pulls—will have to be planned and executed. Grips and floor assistants should be assigned to these various tasks so that each will know his or her cues and what to move when.

Working with cameras and audio on any special problems—camera and boom movements, for example—is also the responsibility of the floor manager. Does the camera operator need an assistant for one particular trucking shot? Will the placement of camera and microphone cables affect other moving elements? The floor manager should always be looking two minutes ahead to see what problems might be averted by action now.

In addition, the floor manager gives the talent his or her undivided attention—always being in a position to be spotted easily by the performers. The talent should never have to turn his or her head to find the floor manager. All verbal instructions that come over the P.L. intercom from the director to the talent should be relayed clearly and tactfully, and all hand signal cues given promptly and forcefully. The floor manager will coordinate cue cards to ensure they are handled properly.

After the rehearsals and before the final take, there are several things the floor manager needs to check. All sets, props, physical graphics (and anything that is used during the body of the program) should be in place, ready for the beginning of the production; all consumables need to be replenished—water glasses, special effects, canisters. The chalk-

The Production Crew

board should be erased, and so forth. The stage manager should generally console and reassure the talent that everything is fine and that they are doing great; assemble the crew; and make certain that everyone is ready and standing by for the beginning of the program.

During the Production   The stage manager must remain extra alert for any problems and double-check to ensure that all crew and talent are in their places, handling their moves, executing their cues. The stage manager will supervise all of the rehearsed moves and effects and make certain that all cues are clear and unambiguous. In general, he or she must guarantee that everything that was worked out during the rehearsal period is executed.

After the production, the stage manager supervises the strike, helps collect the graphics and props, assists the staging and lighting crew in getting their elements properly stored and taken care of, and generally polices the studio to see that everything is returned to where it belongs, ready for the next production.

In summary, the floor manager must think of himself or herself as *the* pivotal individual in charge of the studio—the person in complete control of all production elements. He or she must take the initiative in getting things done. *The floor manager gives orders; the floor manager does not stand around waiting for someone else to tell him or her what to do.*

12.3 Other Crew Positions

Throughout the text, we have had occasion to mention various duties of several crew members as we discussed equipment items. It may be helpful at this point to summarize some of these tasks and procedures of the key crew members. There are also some other non-equipment-oriented positions that need to be introduced.

The Unit Manager

Every television production involves not only the creative talents of numerous people, but it also demands the disciplines and techniques of persons who can handle the budgets for the program. Controlling the costs of a TV production is a crucial and demanding position. In most professional situations, this becomes the job of the *unit manager*.

Most major commercial television production work is handled under contracts. The typical pattern is that the *producing agency* (say, an independent producer, a program packager, or an advertising agency) will contract with a *production facility* (network studio, station, or independent production house) to do the actual production.

In these contractual arrangements, a detailed budget is drawn up, based upon the **rate card** of the production facility. This rate card usually consists of three components: the technical personnel chart, the facilities rates chart, and the personnel hourly rate chart. (See appendix E for a detailed illustration of the rate card structure and a sample exercise.) In essence, the rate card includes all of the below-the-line costs—the equipment and personnel furnished by the production facility. (See section 1.6.)

In some instances, of course, a network or production house serves both as the producing agency and as the production facility. Such "in-house" productions do not necessitate outside contracts. However, strict budgets must still be established and tight cost-control procedures must be followed.

It is the unit manager (sometimes referred to as the *production manager*) who has primary responsibility for seeing that the production costs do not go over the contracted budget figures. Usually the unit manager is a staff member of the production facility (network, production house), and it is his or her main job to protect the production facility by

ensuring that below-the-line production costs (equipment used, graphics, studio rehearsal time, and so forth) do not exceed the contracted amount. The unit manager serves as the crucial liaison between the production facility and the producing agency.

As the A.D. lives by the stopwatch, and the floor director the clipboard, so the unit manager's main tool is the rate card. In many cases, the unit manager has been an integral party in the contractual negotiations from the start; in all cases, the unit manager is intimately involved with every detail of the complex budget process. (See figure 12–5.)

It is also essential that the unit manager be thoroughly schooled and experienced in all aspects of the production process. Although he or she may never touch a camera or adjust a microphone, the unit manager must be knowledgeable about everything going on in the studio process. As the chief fiscal overseer of

all matters dealing with the production, the unit manager must be able to make intelligent decisions about equipment needed, utilization of personnel, rehearsal procedures, master control problems, and anything else that might come up in the studio or control room.

Lighting and Staging

Depending upon the scope of a production, all lighting and staging activity may be handled by one lighting and staging supervisor, or there may be a separate lighting director and also a staging director. In any case, they will work closely together.

Lighting and staging personnel are usually the first to tackle their assignments in the studio. (See figure 12–6.) Copies of the lighting and staging plots should be given to key crew members. Tools—hammers and screwdrivers, heat-absorbing gloves and wrenches—should be distributed as needed. All major scenic units

The Production Crew

should be erected first—hanging units, flats, large set pieces. Then furniture and set dressings can be positioned as the lighting is being set up.

All lighting patches should be made with the current *turned off* for the particular line being used. Instruments should be patched into the dimmer or nondim circuits as called for on the lighting plot and detailed lighting worksheet. Lights should be trimmed—aimed and focused—using talent or stand-ins of the same size and complexion. The finished lighting effect must be checked with both a light meter and control room monitors. A note of any malfunctioning equipment must be made and reported to the technical director, instructor, or supervising engineer.

After the lights are set and all ladders are put away, the set dressing and positioning of hand props should be completed. Someone should be assigned to work with the stage manager to execute any staging changes or lighting effects that are to take place during the program. After the production, lighting and staging personnel strike all set elements, return all furniture and props to their proper storage areas, unpatch all lighting instruments, and return the studio and control areas to their original condition.

Audio

The audio engineer (and any assistant) should select the proper microphones, plug them into the studio inputs, position them on stands or booms as required, and handle all patching in the audio control booth. All other sound sources (records, audiotapes, CDs, VTR audio, cartridges) should be properly patched and threaded and checked out. Any equipment malfunction should be reported to the proper person. (See figure 12–7.)

The audio operator should then obtain a level from the various talents, testing each one and setting a correct balance. If a musical production is involved, determining the best audio

Figure 12–6
Lighting director giving instructions to the lighting crew during production setup. (Photo courtesy of KCET and Hollywood Television Theater)

balance could demand quite a bit of time. All special cues are checked out with the director or A.D. During the production, the audio director must watch the VU meter, ride levels carefully, and listen closely for all audio cues from the director. Generally, microphones should be turned off except when they are actually in use. The audio director must also anticipate cues for VTR and audiotape inserts.

After the production, the patch bay should be cleared, all switches and pots (faders) returned to off or neutral positions, and all microphones, stands, and cables returned to their proper storage areas.

Cameras

The camera operator should attach the shot sheet (if they are being used) to the camera. After staging and lighting have generally cleared the area, the camera operator can pull the camera into its approximate position,

Figure 12–7
Audio engineer monitoring
microphone levels. (Photo
courtesy of Amy Phillips)

making certain to uncoil enough cable for estimated moves. He or she should then go through the uncapping and unlocking safety procedures as outlined in section 6.4 and report any apparent camera malfunction to the proper person. The pan and tilt drag should be loose enough for smooth camera movement, but not so loose that the operator's arm carries all the weight. (See figure 12–8.)

The camera person should be attentive to all directions from the control room while working through the shot sheet. The zoom lens should be preset so that it maintains focus on major zooms. An operator should not leave a camera without permission and should lock the pan and tilt head whenever letting go of the pan handle.

Composition is part of the camera operator's responsibility. If the picture has odd amputations, incongruous juxtapositions, confusing information, poor framing, and so forth,

the operator is responsible. These things should be corrected before going on the air. If the shot is put on the air with bad composition, the operator may try to *cheat* (make slow minor adjustments that the audience will not perceive), but this is a tricky maneuver that many directors will not want to encourage. The camera operator must always notice from the tally lights when the camera is on the air and not move unless ordered to do so by the director.

It is the camera person's responsibility after the production to cap up and lock up the camera, returning it to its studio storage area, and to wind the cable in a figure-eight pattern.

Technical Director

In an actual professional situation, the technical director is just what the name implies—the chief technical person on the production team. He or she usually will be initially involved in physically checking out all of the crew

Figure 12–8
Camera operator working
with studio camera.

positions working with electronic facilities—cameras, audio, video recorders, and so forth. Prior to the beginning of the technical rehearsal, then, the T.D. will assume his or her position at the SEG/switcher.

In some training situations, the position of T.D. is used in this context to designate the person in charge of coordinating all technical operations. In other educational situations, however, the label of "technical director" is used to refer solely to the switcher operator. In either case, the student T.D. should report early to the switcher and put on the P.L. headset. While all other personnel are working around the studio in other capacities—setting up equipment, working with talent, and so forth—the T.D. is the one person who can be in intercom communication with everyone else. The audio engineer, master control room, vid-

eotape operators, camera operators, and even the director can reach the T.D. from any other point to ask a question or to relay a message (simply by putting on a headset). Thus, until other positions are settled and the director gets into the control room, the T.D. can function as the director of all production operations.

In a major studio or network production, separate P.L. hookups will be used by the production and engineering staffs (section 3.5). Thus, the T.D. will be in intercom contact only with all of the union engineering positions.

If the program is complicated or tricky from the switching standpoint, the director may want to have the T.D. go over the script and rehearse any complex transitions. (See figure 12–9.) Otherwise, the T.D. should need no special rehearsal. The T.D. should make certain, however, to check with the director

The Production Crew

Figure 12–9
Technical director operating a complicated production switcher. (Photo courtesy of KABC-TV, Los Angeles)

about the speed of dissolves, fades, wipes, and so forth. During the production, clarification of the director's commands of preparation ("readies" and "prepares") can serve as an aid to the T.D., to camera operators, and to the video engineer. The T.D. should respond as accurately and quickly as possible to the director's commands but should not anticipate the director's orders and should not try to direct from the T.D.'s chair.

Another function of the T.D. is to participate in any remote survey for any on-location shooting session. (See also section 15.3.) Prior to any out-of-studio production, the T.D. must accompany the producer and director and other key personnel to survey the site of the proposed program origination—especially for multi-camera productions. It is the T.D.'s job to scout camera positions, check for adequate power supply, anticipate lighting problems, look for potential audio interference sources, set up studio microwave links or recording facilities, decide what backup equipment should be taken, and so forth.

Recording Engineer

As with other positions, procedures will vary tremendously from one production center to another, but there are several steps that recording engineers (also referred to as *videotape operators*) generally will have to follow. The recording engineer must determine that the correct recording tape and correct machine are being used. (If the facility has more than one of the same model, the instructor or supervising engineer may have some reason why a particular video recorder should or should not be used.) The recording engineer sets up all master control room patching and checks out all lines to verify that both the audio and video signals are getting into the recording machine properly. The audio engineer should send to telecine an audio tone or some other signal at 100 percent of the audio board output so that the recording engineer can set the VU meter on the recording machine. (See figure 12–10.)

If the program also has a video insert—to be played back on some other VTR machine—the videotape operator must make sure it is patched up properly for a transfer. He or she should play back a segment to the studio control room to verify that it is patched correctly and clarify the exact cue points with the director so that the insert can roll properly.

In the past, the task of handling live film and slide projection on the air was the job of a *projectionist*. However, this position has all but totally disappeared. Most major productions today transfer any film that is to be used in a program to videotape prior to the production. The reasons for this are several: color levels can be carefully monitored and adjusted ahead of time; the videotape can be more accurately cued up than film; during any rehearsal or editing operation, video recorders can be fast-forwarded, reversed, run at variable speeds, and held in pause mode whereas film projectors cannot; and videotape playback is generally safer and more reliable than

The Production Crew

film projection (fewer mechanical break-downs, elimination of broken film, and so forth).

For similar reasons, any photographic slides to be used in a program are also usually transferred to videotape or special videodiscs ahead of the production. In effect, this becomes a preproduction editing session in which the specific editing sequence, length of program time for each slide, and so forth, are determined before the actual program is recorded.

This job of making the film-to-tape transfer has been consigned to the videotape operator or recording engineer. The projectors usually will be clustered in a film island, with two or more projectors feeding into a single camera through a system of mirrors and prisms. One or more of the film chains will be found either in the telecine area or in the master control room. The engineers must be completely familiar with threading and loading procedures for all film and slide projectors.

Once the film and slides are loaded, the recording engineer should check them out and then double-check to make certain that everything is set up right—that the film has the correct-sized loops and the right tension and that all of the slides are loaded right side up in the correct order. The engineer must make sure that all projection bulbs and exciter lamps are working and that all switches are turned on and prisms are set.

After the film has been properly transferred to videotape, the playback process is identical to any other videotape playback operation. During the production—if the videotape machines are not controlled remotely from the studio control room—the videotape operator must listen carefully for cues.

At the onset of the actual production recording, the recording engineer must make sure he or she *pushes the record button.* Many a student program has been lost because one button was not pushed! After the production, the recording engineer is responsible for

The Production Crew

turning off all equipment, removing all the patches, labeling the videotape, and returning it to its assigned spot.

Grips and Floor Assistants

Stagehands, floor assistants, grips, cable pullers, and camera assistants are the people who actually get the work done. Although often relegated to the lowest position in the production pecking order, these people are crucial because they actually *do things* on the air. If their jobs are not handled well, the whole production looks and sounds bad. In fact, on the professional level, if you do not do well in these beginning positions, you are not likely to have an opportunity to show how well you can do at the higher echelons.

As the descriptive labels suggest, there are many different functions to be performed, under the supervision of the stage manager, by the grips or floor assistants. In some studios, depending upon union jurisdictions, some of these tasks might be engineering assignments, some might be labeled staging, and some might come under the jurisdiction of the Directors' Guild.

Cable pullers and camera assistants are concerned with helping camera operators make their moves as smoothly and effortlessly as possible. This includes manipulating camera booms and dollies; occasionally assisting in pulling the pedestal camera sideways for a trucking shot; or simply pulling cable so that the camera operator does not have to worry about running out of cable on a long dolly-in or stumbling over his or her own cable during a dolly-back.

If any physical graphics are to be used in a program—say, a series of still photographs that were not obtained in time to transfer them to videotape—the job of coordinating the studio graphics and handling them on the air would fall to a floor assistant. During a fast graphics sequence, the coordination between cameras and their respective graphics flippers can be quite close. It is very easy to get out of sequence and throw a whole graphics segment out of order. Graphics handlers need to be sure-fingered and confident. After a rehearsal, the graphics handlers should check to ensure that the graphics on their particular stands or easels are all set up and in order for the beginning of the program.

In rare situations, floor assistants might also be involved as projectionists for rear screen (and occasionally front screen) projection in the studio. However, electronic matting and chroma keying have made this production technique virtually obsolete. In this situation, standard film or slide projectors are used, with a live studio camera shooting the image off the screen. Locations of the screen and projector have to be carefully coordinated with the floor manager and camera operators. This can be a very critical setup from the standpoint of staging and lighting—especially with rear screen projection. Any light falling on the face of the screen can easily wash out most of the image. In many studio slide applications (for corporate or instructional TV programs), the talent—using a long, remote control cord—will be the one to advance the slides on the air.

Other assignments for the floor assistants might include assisting with the assembly of scenic flats; changing staging elements during a scene; handling special effects such as fog or wind or shaking a fire-shadow stick; assisting talent in fast costume changes; any other special assignments; and the traditional **gopher** assignments (go for a cup of coffee, go for some paper towels). (See figure 12–11.)

In addition to being quick of feet, nimble of hand, and humble of heart, grips must possess two qualities of anonymity—they are not to be seen on camera nor heard on microphone. To meet the first requirement, they must always be careful never to cross in front of any camera or get their hands in a graphics shot. To meet the requirement of silence, grips

Figure 12–11
Grip setting up a scenery
flat with a stage weight.

must remember that almost anything can be done loudly if done carelessly. In addition to the obvious, such as talking on the air and knocking over set pieces, they must control the slightest noise associated with a particular assignment—even pulling cable or flipping graphics can be done noisily. One final hint: grips should wear sneakers; the studio floor is no place for hard-heeled shoes.

Regardless of the assignment, if a grip is really concerned about the success of the communication act and serious about his or her intentions in the field, he or she will carry out the assignment efficiently and conscientiously.

Graphics Operator

For most of the first three decades of television, the position of graphic artist was peripheral to the actual production crew. The TV artist was a creative loner who had a graphics studio or a corner of the scene shop and turned out various graphics, title cards, super cards, instructional diagrams, cartoons, charts, weather maps, or whatever else was needed in the way of physical cards. But seldom was the artist ever associated with the actual studio production (except occasionally when a graphic needed to be redone or repaired at the last minute).

With the advent of computer-generated graphics in the 1970s, however—initially with sports and election coverage—the role of the electronic artist began to emerge. As these flashy and dramatic electronic graphics evolved in the 1980s, spectacular animation effects also became part of the graphics repertoire. These computer-based graphics could be made to spin, flip, turn inside out, and change shapes;

The Production Crew

Figure 12–12
Frequently the graphic artist and computer specialist will work as a team at the keyboard.

still pictures could be squeezed and stretched, swirled about in loops, and then turned into live footage. But the manipulation of these images demanded an actual graphics *operator* who would become part of the studio production team. One or more graphics specialists/operators were needed as part of the production crew to manipulate the keyboards, joysticks, and other computer paraphernalia to make the graphics come to life during the program.

Graphics people today are very much a part of the production team. Their role is indispensable. Today no producer or director can hope to have a successful grasp of the medium without a thorough knowledge of the capabilities of the entire range of computer-based electronic effects and graphics.

Often two or three graphics specialists will find themselves working together as part of a team effort. (See figure 12–12.) On major sports remotes, there often is an entire truck devoted exclusively to special effects and visuals. On heavily visualized programs such as *Entertainment Tonight,* a team of three or more graphic artists will work close to an eight-hour shift for each half-hour program.

As the speciality is emerging, the role and job description of the artist is being defined and redefined. The top artists must combine several differing disciplines—as graphics designer, as planner, as computer operator, and as electronic visionary. The graphic artist must be able to work quickly under great amounts of pressure, especially when engaged in sports and news programming.

Because this is still an emerging speciality, commonly accepted labels for this graphic/computer/electronic artist/spe-

Figure 12–13
The production assistant (script assistant) often works side by side with the director and/or A.D.

cialist/operator have yet to be agreed upon. Most stations and production houses simply refer to their graphic artists by equipment-specific labels—the "Quantel Operator," the "Adda Operator," or the "Chyron Operator," depending upon the specific system in use at that facility. Perhaps the most commonly used generic title would simply be the *C.G. (character-generator) operator.*

Often, where there is a team of two or more "operators" working on a given production, they will be headed by a *graphics effects supervisor.* In many major studio dramatic and musical productions, the graphic artists will be part of a team working under an *art director.* This position will not only be in charge of graphics, but will be concerned with staging and scenery, lighting, and even costumes— every visual aspect of the production.

Production Assistants

One other classification of special people must be included in any major television production. The label of "production assistant" is used to cover a multitude of varying tasks. The easiest way to categorize the position is to think of it as an adjunct to the A.D. on any large complicated production (just as the floor assistant may be considered an adjunct to the stage manager).

Like the A.D., the production assistant is concerned not with hardware but with organizational details, script changes, critique notes, administrative messages, front office liaison, urgent communications, talent arrangements, and anything else that a junior-level administrative assistant may be called upon to handle. Some studios see the production assistant basically as a nontechnical gopher.

In many situations, the terms **script assistant** or **production secretary** may be used to describe essentially the same position— especially if the assignment is concerned primarily with keeping track of scripting details and changes. (See figure 12–13.) Sometimes the production or script assistant will be assigned to the director and may even be a DGA (Directors' Guild) position. In other cases, the production assistant may be assigned directly to the producer—serving in a variety of secretarial tasks.

In many small-scale productions, there would be no need for a script assistant. However, on large studio or network programs, a variety of production assistants and secretaries may be involved. (Often the label, "Assistant to Mr./Mrs. _____ " is used.) In these major production centers, the job of production/script assistant is often an entry-level position that can lead to more responsible production assignments. Any aspiring professional who has typing skills, enthusiasm, a quick mind, and a grasp of production disciplines will find the lowly production assistant job a valuable stepping stone.

Summary

The *associate director* (A.D.) is one of the director's chief lieutenants and may get involved in almost every aspect of program design and execution from program planning to helping set up shots on the air. The major responsibility of the A.D., however, is that of *timing* the entire program—getting the director started on time, giving time signals to the talent throughout the program, and getting the director off the air on time.

The *stage manager (floor manager, floor director)* is the other chief lieutenant of the director. The stage/floor manager is directly in charge of everything on the studio floor. The duties generally can be divided into two areas: *working with talent* (attending to emotional-physical needs and to technical-production needs) and *production management* (supervising all audio, camera, staging, lighting, graphics, special effects, props, and projection elements).

The *unit manager* is a crucial position in most contract production situations— handling all cost-control responsibilities and overseeing all production budget matters.

In addition to these key positions, every other assignment of the production crew has its own set of *techniques* and *disciplines* to master: those of the lighting and staging personnel, audio engineers, camera operators, technical director, recording engineer, grips and floor assistants, graphics operators, and production/script assistants and secretaries.

In the final three chapters we will look at the one position that pulls it all together—the director's job.

12.4 Training Exercises

1. Using a stopwatch, time every segment of some talk show that you can watch at home. Start with a timing sheet similar to the one in figure 12–2. You will use three columns—"Segment," "Unit Time," and "Cumulative Time." You will need quite a few blank lines, however, as there will be a large number of individual segments. As the show progresses, write down every separate segment of the program—every commercial, every monologue, every demonstration, every station break, every musical number or variety act, every interview or discussion segment, and the like. Time each segment with a stopwatch, returning the watch to zero between every program unit; enter these times in the "Unit Time" column. Using your wristwatch or a clock with a second hand, keep track of the cumulative time in the third column. When you are through, you should be able to total up the unit times and arrive at the total elapsed time as indicated in your "Cumulative Time" column.

2. If you have the opportunity, visit a recording session of some studio television program. Pay particular attention to the job of the stage manager. Before, during, and after the production, notice every task and responsibility of the floor manager. Keep a list of every specific job that he or she had to perform. What additional production and talent-liaison items might the stage manager have gotten involved with if the need had arisen?

Directing Your First Studio Production

● ● ● ● ● ● ● ● ● ● ● ● ● ● ● ● ● ●

13

This chapter and chapter 14 are designed to introduce the student to some of the concepts and techniques that are needed in directing one's first television studio productions—principles of picture continuity, use of camera transitions, simple camera patterns, scripting formats, preproduction planning, rehearsal techniques, and control room disciplines. This is not designed as a complete text on television directing. It would take a much more voluminous work to present the student with an understanding of the many facets of directing different kinds of television productions. It is recognized, however, that many introductory production courses will involve the student in directing some basic programs. These two chapters, therefore, present several production exercises and examples of different kinds of studio production formats.

Although written from the perspective of studio production, most of the pictorial and editing concepts discussed in this chapter apply both to multicamera studio programs and to single-camera productions, as explained in more detail in chapter 15. Whether one is cutting between multiple cameras "live" (editing on the switcher in real time) or shooting with a single camera in the field (planning on editing during the postproduction process), the principles of picture continuity (section 13.1) and transitions (section 13.2) are virtually the same.

13.1 Principles of Picture Continuity

Early filmmakers quickly came to the conclusion that when one picture is immediately replaced by another, an interaction occurs in the mind of the viewer that communicates something more than if each picture were viewed separately. This intriguing concept obviously can have direct bearing on the process of shot

Figure 13–1
Comparison of wide shot
and close-up. Whether in a
variety show, drama, or
panel discussion, the same
need exists to balance
wide shots (*left*) with close-
ups (*right*).

selection for any television program. Each shot must be thought of as being part of a flow of images, each with a relationship to the one that precedes it and the one that follows it.

Wide Shots and Close-Ups

The succession of pictures should be motivated by the basic tenet, "Give the viewers what they need to see when they need to see it." To a great extent, this is determined by a juxtaposition of establishing **collective** shots showing the whole picture—the relationship of all elements in the scene—and intimate **particularized** shots—giving the viewers the closer details they want. The generalities of a scene or program situation are established by the *wide shot* or collective *cover shot*. Then the director cuts or dissolves to a series of medium or particularized *close-up shots* to examine the specific facets of that situation. (See figure 13–1.) As the events of the program progress, the director again establishes the broader aspects of the program (with wide shots), followed by another series of detailed particulars (with close-ups). This follows the basic LS-MS-CU principle introduced in section 9.7.

Even with the opportunity to preplan or *block out* the camera work in live television programming, the ongoing production technique forces the director to make some rather quick, on-the-air editing decisions. A basic

problem is that of always having the proper camera ready for a shot at the exact moment the situation calls for it. On the part of the director, this requires an ability to be able to think simultaneously on at least two levels—what is on the air right now and what is going to be on the air next.

With a three-camera structure, the thinking process might work something like this: Camera 1 is on the air. You, as director, have the choice of using camera 2 or 3 for the next shot. Camera 3, however, has just been used on the previous shot. Camera 2, therefore, has more time to make a framing adjustment or even a change of position. (See figure 13–2.)

By using the commands of preparation and execution properly (section 7.6), the director can select the next camera to be used, allowing sufficient lead time to set the next shot.

It is accepted studio procedure in a three-camera setup to place camera 1 on the left, camera 2 in the middle, and camera 3 on the right. This setup allows the director to keep track easily of the relative positions of cameras on the floor and the angle of shots available to them.

Obviously, cameras usually are not employed in a repeated 1–2–3–1–2–3 rotation. In order to observe the wide-shot and close-up shot requirements of any program, at least one

Directing Your First Studio Production

Figure 13–2
Sequence of camera shots.

CAMERA 1
on the air

CAMERA 2
ready for next shot

CAMERA 3
has time to adjust
for its next shot

In this illustration, the director has just used camera 3 (before taking camera 1); therefore, camera 2 will probably have more time to get the next shot lined up.

of the three cameras at any given time will usually be designated as a wide-angle *cover shot* camera. This is especially important in shooting unrehearsed programs such as panel discussions where there are sudden changes of the individuals speaking. The technique on such a program is to cut to a wide shot on the change of voice if a close-up of the new person is not immediately available. The director then has a chance to ascertain who is talking and call for the close-up. The most glaring error on any kind of television is for an unprepared director to be caught with a speaker or performer still on camera when that person is no longer speaking or performing.

In a rehearsed program, when the camera blocking has been worked out in advance, the director can temporarily commit all cameras to close-up shots, having planned to return to a cover shot at a later specific time. Generally, however, the wide-angle and close-up shot balance requirements are such that at least one camera is always kept on a cover shot.

Shot Relationships

When changing from one shot to another, the two pictures should relate to each other in both an informational and aesthetic setting. For example, the subject in two successive shots should be readily recognizable. You would not want to cut to such a different angle that the viewer would not immediately recognize the subject from the previous shot.

Jump Cuts   On the one hand, for aesthetic reasons, you should avoid taking or dissolving between cameras that have almost exactly the same or matching shots. The result would be that the scene remains essentially the same, but the picture jumps slightly within the frame. On unrehearsed shows, the camera operators may inadvertently come up with almost identical shots; therefore, it is up to the director to watch carefully for this **jump cutting** on the control room monitors.

Directing Your First Studio Production

Figure 13–3
Three-to-one cutting ratio.

Top: In this example, the cut from the long shot to the tight close-up is jarring to the viewer. For a normal transition, the director should cut to a shot that is no more than three times the size (larger or smaller) of the preceding shot. *Bottom:* In this instance, the director has cut to an intermediate medium shot before going in for the close-up. The transition is much easier for the viewer to accept.

Figure 13–4
Subject jumping positions.

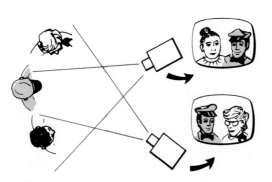

With both cameras shooting a standard two-shot, the central talent (Mr. "B") appears to jump from one side of the screen to the other as we take between shots.

Cutting Ratio   On the other hand, avoid going from one shot to another where there is too much difference in size between views of the same subject. Taking from a long shot to a tight close-up can be quite jarring to the viewer. (See figure 13–3.) One good rule to follow is that you should always keep your camera cuts within a three-to-one **cutting ratio**; that is, do not take to a shot that is three times larger or three times smaller than the preceding shot. (See figure 9–19.)

Position Jumps   Another problem to avoid is that of having a primary subject jump from one spot on the screen to another position in the next shot. This can occur, for example, if three people are lined up facing two cameras and each camera is getting a two-shot of two adjacent persons. The center person will be on the left of one picture and on the right side of the other camera's picture. (See figure 13–4.) This position jump can be avoided by having one camera go to a three-shot before cutting or, conversely, by cutting to a close-up single shot.

These related principles of shot relationships apply to single-camera productions as well as to studio productions. (See section 9.7.) However, the principles are much easier to apply and control in the studio than in the field. When you are looking at three camera monitors side by side in the control room, it should be a simple matter to make sure that successive shots will not result in a jump cut, exaggerated cutting ratio, or position jump. In the field, however, with a single camera, you do not have the luxury of comparing shots side by side. You must shoot your pictures one at a time—recalling what the previous shot looked like. With the single camera, it is much easier

Directing Your First Studio Production

Figure 13–5
Axis of action.

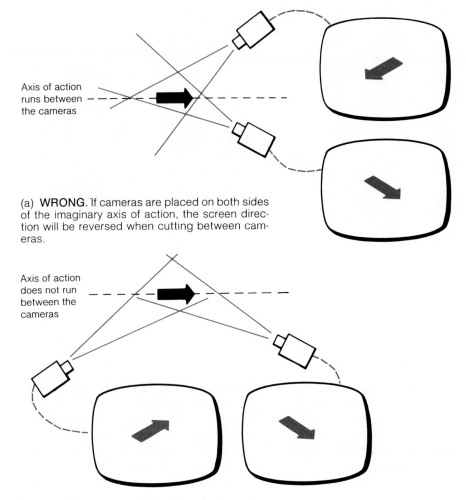

(a) **WRONG.** If cameras are placed on both sides of the imaginary axis of action, the screen direction will be reversed when cutting between cameras.

(b) **CORRECT.** When both cameras are on the same side of the axis of action, they will both perceive the action moving in the same direction.

to make a mistake and shoot several successive shots that, when edited together later, will result in jump cuts, an extreme cutting ratio, or position jumps. This underscores the importance of very careful preplanning (section 15.2) for all single-camera productions.

Axis of Action/Conversation

Another basic principle of continuity involves *screen direction*. In successive shots we want to make certain that all action is flowing in the same direction and that each screen character is facing in one consistent direction. If an imaginary line is drawn extending the path in which a character is moving, we can call this the **axis of action.** As long as all cameras are placed on the same side of this axis, the action will continue to flow in the same direction. If cameras are placed on both sides of this axis of action, however, the apparent screen direction will be reversed when cutting between the cameras. (See figure 13–5.) Directors, there-

Directing Your First Studio Production

Figure 13–6
Axis of conversation.

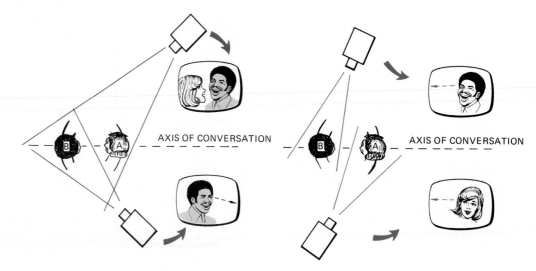

AXIS OF CONVERSATION

AXIS OF CONVERSATION

In the *left* illustration, Actor B changes screen direction as we cut from one camera to the other. In the *right* illustration, both actors appear to be looking in the same direction, making it difficult for the viewer to establish the relationship between the two.

fore, always try to avoid having cameras crossing the line. It is for this reason that all cameras covering a football game or basketball game are placed on the same side of the field of action (except when a deliberate "reverse angle" shot is specifically wanted).

Closely related to the axis of action is the **axis of conversation.** If the imaginary axis is drawn through two persons facing each other, all cameras should be kept on the same side of this line. Otherwise the screen direction (the direction in which a person is looking) will be reversed when you cut to the other side of the line. This imaginary line—the axis of conversation—will shift, of course, as performers move. Figure 13–6 shows two common errors in crossing the axis of conversation.

As with the discussion of shot relationships, these principles of "not crossing the axis" apply to single-camera productions as well as to studio productions. And, again, in a

multiple-camera studio production, it is a fairly routine job to make sure that all action is flowing in the same direction or that two persons in a conversation are looking at each other. You physically keep all cameras on the same side of the axis. However, when shooting on location, it is much easier to inadvertently "cross the axis" when you have just one camera operator moving around and setting up for each individual shot. Again, this emphasizes the necessity of thorough preproduction planning.

Other Principles of Continuity

All of these generalizations and principles have to be interpreted with flexibility. There are occasions when the experienced director will deliberately break some of the principles in order to create a certain effect—to disorient the audience intentionally, for aesthetic shock value, or for exceptional dramatic impact. Keep in mind, however, that before departing from any

Directing Your First Studio Production

such guidelines, one should have first gained a good understanding of the reason for the rule. The same can be said for the following four additional principles in planning picture continuity. (And, again, keep in mind that these rules apply to single-camera productions as well as to multiple-camera programs.)

1. *Plan the camera sequence as a whole.* Every program or sequence within a program has a beginning, a middle, and an end. Design the image flow to capture the structural form of the performance or event, utilizing the collective and particularized perspectives.

2. *Follow the action.* Be sure that motivating action or movement is picked up by the camera as it occurs. Nothing destroys the flow of ideas and images more than late camera work. The thought process of the entire crew must be such that it anticipates the progression of events in the program.

3. *Choose the camera work appropriate to the program situation.* Match the shot to the performance or action. A close-up shot denotes intimacy and personal expression. Extreme wide shots express a quality of "bigness" or importance. A superimposition serves to intensify further whatever is being expressed by the component images.

4. *Observe a consistency of style and pace.* Different types of programs require differing camera work, ranging from the subjective artistic to the reportorial pragmatic. Similarly, there is often a pattern to the frequency of camera change that stems from the program sequence itself. An effective series of fast camera cuts can lose its intensity if, for no motivated reason, a dissolve is suddenly used.

The essence of all television is movement, either physical or psychological or both. Pictorial composition and sequence flow must be designed to interact in such a way that they not only capture accurately but also enhance further the events of the production sequence. The skill necessary for effective camera work requires both study and practice as well as a great amount of judgment on the part of both the camera operator and the director.

13.2 Continuity and Transitions

Picture continuity refers to the sequential relationship of successive screen images. The mechanics of continuity are carried out by the actual camera transitions—the manner in which we change from one picture to another. This can be effected in several different ways, and we need to be aware of the how, when, and why of camera transitions.

Types of Camera Transitions

Without getting into computer-based SEG devices, there are essentially five different transitional methods for going from one camera to another. The director must be aware of the psychological and grammatical impact of each—when to use one and when to use another. These transitions can be accomplished in postproduction editing as well as with the switcher during a multicamera studio production.

The Take   The instantaneous *cut* or straight take replaces one picture immediately with another. It implies that there is no change in time or locale. It happens right now. The audience is not moved anywhere, except to a different perspective of the same scene. The shots relate directly to each other as far as time and space are concerned. It is the basic transition. It is the device that the audience has accepted since the beginning of the motion picture film for changing a point of view without making any major dramatic change. In terms of grammar, it is the end of a sentence—a period—and the beginning of a new sentence.

The Dissolve   The dissolve, simultaneous fading out of one picture and fading in of another picture, creates a temporary overlapping of images. Dramatically, this implies a change of *place* or a change in *time* (usually a lapse of time). It shows a relationship with the previous shot, but there has been a change; the audience has been moved somewhere else or somewhere later in time. Grammatically, the dissolve corresponds to the end of a paragraph or possibly even to the end of a major section of a chapter.

In nondramatic television, the dissolve is often used purely for aesthetic reasons—a slow dissolve of a singer from a medium to a tight close-up profile, or a close-up of the dancer's feet dissolving to a long shot of the dancer. No change in time or locale is implied in this case—just a pleasant visual effect. In musical productions, the dissolve can be used as an artistic connecting or relating transition, whereas it has the opposite effect in dramas.

The Fade   A fade from a camera to black or a fade up from black implies a very strong separation. It is used in going from one segment of a program to another—from the juggling act to the used-car commercial. Dramatically, the fade is the curtain falling—the end of a scene or an act. Grammatically, it would be the visual counterpart of the end of a chapter—or of the story.

The Defocus   One specialized transition that can be used with no fancy electronic effects is the **defocus**; the camera on the air defocuses and dissolves to a similarly defocused shot on another camera, which then comes back into focus. This is a specialized form of dissolve that has very strong overtones. It usually implies either a deranged state of mind or a transition *backward* in time. As with other specialized transitions, it tends to call attention to itself and must be used very sparingly.

The Wipe   Wiping one picture off the face of the screen and replacing it with another also calls attention to itself. It is a highly stylized method of going from one camera to another. As with other electronic transitions—the circle wipe, the starbursts—the straight-edged wipe has to be used very cautiously. It has no special grammatical significance except to say, "Isn't this a fancy transition!"

Timing of the Transition

Understanding the different types of transitions helps to explain the *how* and *why* of changing cameras, but a word needs to be said about the *when*. Generally, camera changes must be adequately motivated; there has to be some reason for cutting at a particular point. The audience should want to see something else. ("Give the viewers what they need to see when they need to see it.") Unless the viewer feels the need for a change of camera, there probably is no reason to cut. Without proper motivation, you should avoid the temptation to change the picture just for the sake of change.

All of the following discussion on the timing of camera transitions applies equally to the timing of editing shots together in the postproduction process for single-camera production.

Cutting on Action   One of the strongest motivations for cutting is to capture action. When the action starts, you need a wider view. When the talent walks to a new area, you need an establishing shot. When cutting on action, you should always try to cut *just prior to the action*—not too long before it nor immediately after it. Ideally, as soon as the action starts, the audience needs to see the wider shot.

Cutting on Dialogue   During an interview or panel program, the strongest motivation for cutting is when a speaker *starts to talk*. The audience wants to see who is talking. The ideal timing of the take is precisely between the two speakers—not three seconds after the

Directing Your First Studio Production

second speaker has started. As a practical matter, cutting during an ad-lib discussion program will usually involve a delay of a second or so. To counteract this, the director has to be sensitive to the body language and facial expressions of all the participants (watching the off-the-air camera monitors). Who has his mouth open? Who has her eyebrows raised? Who just leaned forward? Who just took a deep breath? Anticipate who the next speaker is going to be.

Cutting on Reaction   Include appropriate—judiciously spaced—reaction shots also. How are the listeners reacting? Which listener is especially animated? In timing reaction shots, *do not* cut at the end of an obvious statement or during a break in the speaking; it will look too much like a cut to the wrong participant. Reaction shots are most effective in the middle of a speech.

Cutting on the Beat   During musical numbers, time your cuts to fit the music. (In slower tempos, purely for an aesthetic "feel," dissolves may be a better transition.) The cuts should be crisp and clean, following a regular rhythmical pattern—cutting every four bars or eight bars—as the music dictates. See section 14.2 for an extended demonstration of camera usage during a musical number.

Cutting with Movement   Generally, do not cut from a moving camera to a stationary camera. If the camera is panning a shot or zooming in or out, wait until it stops to take to another stationary camera, and vice versa—do not cut from a static shot to a moving camera. The effect is somewhat jolting to the viewer. It can be effective, however, to take or dissolve from a moving camera to another camera panning or zooming in the same direction—assuming there is a continuity in subject and tempo.

As with the rules given under section 13.1, "Principles of Picture Continuity," these guidelines can be interpreted in a flexible manner if you know what effect you are after. Exceptions can be made to the basic rules once the rules are mastered.

13.3 Basic Camera Patterns

In setting up the **camera pattern** for a studio production or blocking (positioning) the cameras for a scene, there are several principles to keep in mind. As contrasted with the several considerations discussed so far in this chapter, these following principles apply only to multiple-camera productions—situations where you have to be concerned with the placement and movement of several cameras simultaneously.

1. *Cross your camera angles.* In most staging setups, the natural pattern will have two people facing each other—or a person facing a graphic or demonstrating an object. Shooting this situation with two cameras you can get the best head-on shots by having the cameras shoot across each other's angles; that is, each camera should be shooting the person or object farthest away from the camera. The camera on the right should be getting the shot of the person on the camera left, and vice versa. (See figures 11–1 and 13–7.)

2. *Start blocking in the center of the program.* Pick the most crucial or difficult part of the production and figure out your camera pattern for that segment first. Once you know how that segment has to be blocked, you can figure backward to see how you will want to work your way up to that position. Continuing to work backward, you will be able to determine how you want to set up your cameras for the beginning of the program.

Figure 13–7
Camera pattern for simple
interview.

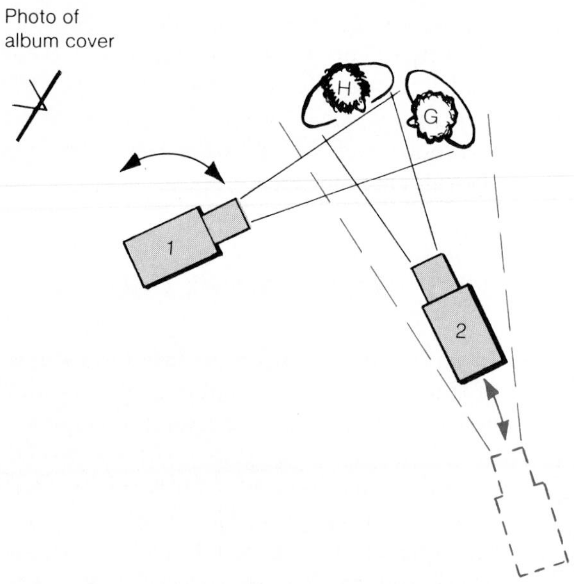

Photo of
album cover

Camera 1: Photo of album cover (on easel).
Camera 2: Single-shot of host (MS or CU). Dolly
 back or zoom back to two-shot as
 guest is mentioned.
Camera 1: CU of guest (for the introduction) and
 CU of guest and two-shots favoring
 guest (during interview).
Camera 2: CU of host and two-shots favoring host
 (during interview). Dolly in or zoom in
 to single shot of host at the end of interview.
Camera 1: Photo of album cover for closing.

3. *Select positions for demonstration objects or graphics last.* As a corollary to principle 2, you should not figure out where you will place any objects that are to be taken for a close-up until all of the crucial camera blocking has been taken care of. Once you know how the whole production is set up, you can best figure out the most convenient spot to place any off-set objects or graphics. Too many beginning directors start by positioning the objects to be shot first and then work their way into a bind from there.

Starting with these basic principles, let us see how some simple camera patterns could be worked out for a few fundamental formats.

Simple Interview

Following the principles outlined previously, a two-person interview could be staged as indicated in figure 13–7. With the host seated on the left and the guest on the right, cameras 1 and 2 would cross angles so that camera 2 would get the basic shot of the host (and an over-the-shoulder two-shot favoring the host) and camera 1 would get the basic shots favoring the guest. Assuming that camera 2, on the host, would be the first camera shot in the body of the program, this means that camera 1 is free to get an opening shot of the album cover of the guest's latest release (before breaking to the basic shot of the guest). We

Directing Your First Studio Production

did not know, however, which camera would be free to get the album cover until after we decided on the camera pattern in the body of the interview.

Simple Demonstration

The same basic pattern would hold true for a simple demonstration program. In this case, let us assume that the host/instructor is going to be demonstrating how a carburetor works; he also is going to be referring to an off-set schematic diagram of the carburetor. Figure 13–8 indicates how this demonstration-and-graphic sequence might be set up. In this case, working from the body of the program, we might determine that the host, being right-handed, wants to work with the object to be demonstrated (the carburetor) on his left side so that he can hold it in his left hand and point to various parts and manipulate them with his right hand.

Crossing angles, you see that camera 2, therefore, would get the basic head-on shot of the talent (and a two-shot of the host and carburetor), while camera 1 would get the close-ups of the carburetor. (Note the similarity to figure 11–1.) This means that camera 1 would be the one that would be free for the shot of the drawing of the carburetor in the middle of the program. (Camera 2 is always ready with a shot of the host/instructor.)

Interview and Demonstration

Following the same basic principles, let us see how a slightly more complicated camera pattern might be worked out. The host is going to start by talking directly to the camera with nothing else in the shot (position A). He then walks over to his left to interview a guest—a noted actor (position B)—about theatrical costumes. He next crosses back to his right to a costumed mannequin (position C). The opening titles are from the character generator (C.G.), but they are to be keyed over an

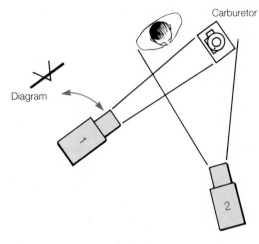

Figure 13–8
Camera pattern for simple demonstration.

Camera 2: Single-shot (MS or CU) of talent. Dolly back or zoom to include carburetor.
Camera 1: CU of carburetor.
Camera 2: Two-shot of talent and carburetor.
Camera 1: Drawing of diagram of carburetor.
Camera 2: Two-shot of talent and carburetor. Optional dolly or zoom in to single shot of talent.

opening shot of the mannequin. Closing C.G. credits will also be keyed over a shot of the mannequin.

Where do we begin to block out the camera pattern? (See figure 13–9.) The most crucial position probably would be at the interview spot (position B); let us begin there. We will want camera 2 getting the head-on shots of the host (two-shots favoring the host and close-ups of the host), with camera 1 crossing angles to get the close-ups and two-shots of the guest. This means that camera 2 will probably be the camera to pan across with the talent on his move from position A to B. (Camera 2 is the best camera for the walking shot because it is a stronger move to have the talent walking toward the camera; he is walking away from camera 1.) As the host walks toward the guest (position B), camera 2 can dolly back and pan right to keep a wide shot and show the host walking into the interview area where the guest is waiting.

Directing Your First Studio Production

Figure 13–9
Camera pattern for
interview and
demonstration.

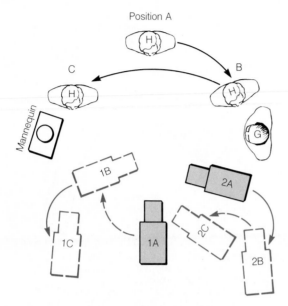

Camera 2: MS of mannequin, position A.
C.G.: Title, keyed over camera 2.
Camera 1: Single of host, position A.
Camera 2: Wide shot of host, pans with host on walk-over shot. Dollies back to position B on the walk-over.
Camera 1: Single of guest and two-shot favoring guest, position B.
Camera 2: Single and O/S of host, position B.
Camera 1: Wide shot of host, pans with host on walk-over shot to position C. Dollies back to position C on the walk-over.
Camera 2: Dollies in for tighter shot of the mannequin, position C.
Camera 1: Singles of host and two-shot with mannequin.
Camera 2: Holds on CU of mannequin.
C.G.: Closing credits keyed over camera 2. (The solid red lines indicate on-the-air camera moves. The dotted camera lines indicate repositioning off the air.)

Therefore, at the beginning of the program, we want camera 1 on the basic head-on shot of the talent at position *A*—so that camera 2 can be getting set for a wide shot in preparation for the walk-over move (from position *A* to position *B*). This also means that camera 2 is in the ideal location (position *A*) for the opening shot of the mannequin (which will consist of the opening C.G. titles keyed over the mannequin).

Once we are settled in at position *B*, each camera will then be getting the appropriate cross-angled shots of the host and guest. As the guest wraps up the interview segment, he will be on camera 2. As the host prepares to walk to position *C* (next to the mannequin), camera 1 will be located perfectly for the walk-over shot from position *B* to *C* because, as mentioned previously, it is stronger to have the talent walking toward the camera—in this case the host will be walking toward camera 1. Therefore, after he thanks the guest on camera 2, he will turn to his right, and camera 1 will be ready with a wide-angle shot. As he walks to position *C,* camera 1 will be able to pan and dolly back to keep him in frame and also to reveal him walking into a two-shot with the mannequin. Simultaneously, this gives camera 2 time to get prepared for the head-on close-ups of the mannequin (position *C*).

Once the host is located in area *C,* camera 1 will be getting close-ups and two-shots favoring the host; and camera 2 will be positioned for appropriate close-ups of the costume on the mannequin. Again, note that the two cameras are crossing angles in position *C*—so that each is getting a head-on shot of its subject. Also, camera 2 is in position for a closing shot of the mannequin so that the C.G. credits can be keyed over the mannequin shot.

Although the explanation may seem complicated at first, if you read through it carefully, checking the illustration in figure 13–9, you should be able to see how all of the principles mentioned at the beginning of this section apply.

13.4 The Television Script

The television script is the basic working document of the TV director. Everything starts with the script, and the beginning director

Directing Your First Studio Production

must learn how to interpret it and break it down, as well as how to mark it for use during the actual production.

Scripting Formats

Basically, there are three different script forms that the director may have to work with: the *fully scripted program*; the *outline,* or *semi-scripted program*; and the *show format,* or *rundown sheet.*

The Fully Scripted Program

Programs that are likely to be fully scripted include dramatic programs, newscasts, documentaries, commercials, station breaks, editorials, some talk programs such as political broadcasts, and similar productions where it is important that every single word and picture element be precisely controlled. Section 14.3 is an example of one kind of dramatic script format (appendix D-4). Section 14.4 is an example of the fully scripted station break and promotional copy (appendix D-5).

Although there are exceptions, scripts generally are constructed in vertical columns, with one column (usually the right-hand side) for audio and another column for video. On some scripts, the video column will be written in (section 13.5 and appendix D-3), and in other formats the video column will be left blank for the director to fill in. Some formats (see figures 13–10 and 13–12) will have both the audio and video integrated into one column, with the other column left open for the director to use for markings.

The Outline, or Semi-scripted Program

Many kinds of programs do not have every word written out in advance. Among them are variety shows, corporate training programs, lectures/educational lessons, interview programs, and other formats where there is a good deal of ad-libbing and extemporaneous discussion.

Section 13.5 (appendix D-3) is an example of a semi-scripted outline for a discussion program in which both columns are written out. Figure 13–10 is an example of an abbreviated script outline for a discussion program in which the audio and video elements have all been integrated into the right-hand column so that the left-hand (blank) column can be used for more extensive director's notes.

In figures 13–11 and 13–12, we have two different versions of the same program content. In figure 13–11, the ITV script outline utilizes both columns. In figure 13–12, exactly the same content is incorporated into the outline, but all the material is included in the right-hand column.

One technique that is used in some scripts, as in the previous examples, is to use upper-case and lowercase letters for everything that is actually to be heard on the air. Note that all of the announcer copy in figure 13–10 is written out, which is done in many semi-scripted formats, and the summary of the host's remarks are also in uppercase and lowercase. All other material (video instructions, audio cues) is put in uppercase letters only. This makes it easy to identify which text is copy to be heard on the air and which text is instructions for video and audio.

In addition to writing out the announcer copy in full, most outline scripts also will write out exact roll cues to be used in facilitating correct timing into videotape inserts. The semi-scripted format also will include a somewhat detailed outline of the content, together with fairly complete video information.

The Show Format, or Rundown Sheet

Many routine programs that are produced on a daily or weekly basis by a station will not even work from a complete semi-scripted outline. The daily homemaker show, ITV lectures, regular interview programs, game shows, weekly panel discussions, and other programs—where the same talent uses the same

Figure 13-10
Sample semi-scripted
outline.

(This column is left blank
for the director's notes.)

GRAPHIC: STREET SCENE

MUSIC: THEME, ESTABLISH, AND UNDER

ANNC (OFF CAMERA): Good morning, and welcome to . . .

SUPER CARD (OVER "STREET SCENE"): "LIVE"

ANNC: "Live," . . . a penetrating look at some

   of the issues and controversies surrounding the

   American scene. This fast-paced discussion

   is brought to you, live, . . .

DISCUSSION SET, IN SILHOUETTE

ANNC: . . . from the studios at KCSN-TV.

   Today's topic is "The Tax Squeeze on Middle

   America."   Your host is . . .

   _____.

HOST: Welcome, etc.   Introduces each guest.

    BODY OF DISCUSSION

   (Points to be covered:

     Federal income tax

     State income and sales taxes

     Local property taxes)

HOST: Summarizes.   Thanks guests.

DISCUSSION SET IN SILHOUETTE

MUSIC: THEME, SNEAK IN, ESTABLISH, AND UNDER

ANNC: For the past fifteen minutes, you have

   been watching another stimulating program

   in the series, . . .

SUPER CARD (OVER SET): "LIVE"

ANNC: . . . "Live," from KCSN-TV.

MUSIC: OUT

BLACK

Directing Your First Studio Production

Figure 13–11
Sample semi-scripted ITV
lesson: two columns.

VIDEO	AUDIO
	Concept of green leaves as food factories:
CHART: DIAGRAM OF CYCLE	1. Oxygen-CO_2 cycle
	2. Water and Nourishment up from roots
SLIDE #1: CHLOROPHYLL PROCESS	3. Manufacture of chlorophyll
	Role of chlorophyll in growth of vegetation
VTR: 1´20˝	VTR ROLL CUE: Now suppose we take a look at the inside of a green leaf and see for ourselves ....

Figure 13–12
Sample semi-scripted ITV
lesson: single column.

AUDIO/VIDEO

Concept of green leaves as food factories:

1. Oxygen-CO_2 cycle

    CHART: DIAGRAM OF CYCLE

2. Water and Nourishment up from roots

3. Manufacture of chlorophyll

    SLIDE #1: CHLOROPHYLL PROCESS

Role of chlorophyll in growth of vegetation

VTR ROLL CUE: Now suppose we take a look at the inside of a green leaf and see for ourselves . . .

VIDEOTAPE: 1´20˝

Figure 13–13
Sample show format.

```
              "MOLLIE'S MORNING"  (NO: 90-0314)

                          FAX:

                          VTR:
_____

          VIDEO                              AUDIO

  1. TEASER: MOLLIE AND DOG    STUDIO: MOLLIE LIVE            ( :30)

  2. OPENING VIDEOTAPE         THEME MUSIC UP: TAPE           ( :45)

  3. MOLLIE: MONOLOGUE         STUDIO: MOLLIE LIVE            (2:00)

  4. INTERVIEW SET             INTERVIEW: JOY LOOMIS          (5:00)

       LOOMIS SLIDES (6 OR 7)  VOICE-OVER DESCRIPTION

  5. MOLLIE, TO CAMERA         (ROLL CUE): One of the most enchanting

                                  things about interior decoration is

                                  the impact that simple ideas can have

                                  when done creatively.      ( :10)

  6. VTR: THE WORLD OF         VTR: AUDIO                     (2:25)

       MARIE VAYO             . . . living with such a man.

  7. MOLLIE, TO CAMERA         BOOM #2: INTRO TO JEAN HAMILTON ( :30)

       WALK TO LIVING ROOM SET

  8. LIVING ROOM SET:          INTERVIEW: JEAN HAMILTON       (6:30)

       DEMO: FABRICS

       7 OR 8 GRAPHICS

  9. MOLLIE, TO CAMERA         TRANSITION TO ZOO SEGMENT      ( :40)
```

format continually—may use only a **show format,** or **rundown sheet.** This lists just the order of the basic segments. Perhaps exact **roll cues** for VTR inserts may be included—along with times for inserted elements. Figure 13–13 illustrates a typical rundown sheet for a local variety show.

Once you, as director, have the script in hand, your job is ready to begin. Your task now is to break down the script, decide how each

element is to be handled, block camera movement, prepare instructions for the key crew members and engineering staff, and mark the script for your own directing use.

Marking the Script

Almost all script formats are at least double-spaced. This not only makes it easier for the talent and others to read, but also facilitates

Directing Your First Studio Production

the numerous notes and markings the director will have to make on the script. It is the director's task to decide what cameras will have to be used where, what instructions the technical director and engineers must have, where the audio cues will have to be, what cues the talent will need, and so forth. Preparing and marking the script is one of the most critical tasks the director has. On a major studio drama, it could involve numerous detailed drawings and hundreds of abbreviated cues and instructions and notes; with a fairly routine ongoing program (such as *Mollie's Morning*), script preparation may take no more than a few penciled reminders of unusual cues.

Standard Symbols   In preparing their scripts for production, most directors will use a system of shorthand symbols. Experienced directors have worked out their own set of symbols; each one is a very personalized system and does not have to make sense to anyone but the director. The symbols work if they are clear, easy to read, unambiguous, and do not take up much space.

There are some standardized symbols, however, that form the basis for most of the personalized systems various directors adopt. Some of these universal markings are indicated in figure 13–14. In using these symbols to mark your script, you generally should use pencil. Once you get into rehearsal, there are script changes, camera positions that do not work, graphics that did not turn out, and many other production modifications—some major and many minor—that will necessitate your changing your script markings. Therefore, it is always safer to start with pencil.

Generally, the script markings should remind you of every preplanned command you will have to give—to cameras, T.D., talent, audio, C.G. operators, floor crew, VTR engineers, lighting, and everyone else. The marked script may indicate not only the necessary commands of execution but also the important

③	Camera number three
⟨ or F.I.	Fade in
SUP or S	Super(impose)
T	Take
⟩⟨ or D	Dissolve
SD	Slow dissolve
⟩ or F.O.	Fade out
Q	Cue
⌐	At this point, cut, dissolve, or cue
D.I.	Dolly in
D.B. or D.O.	Dolly back or dolly out
PREP ②	Prepare camera 2
TC	Title card
③ TO___	Camera 3, get ready for . . .
2-sh	Shot of two persons
3-sh	Shot of three persons
O/S	Over-the-shoulder shot
CU	Close-up shot
MS	Medium shot
LS	Long shot
ECU or XCU	Extreme close-up
MLS	Medium long shot
MCU	Medium close-up

Figure 13–14
Standard script-marking symbols.

commands of preparation ("readies" and "prepares") and other off-air directions. Figure 13–15 illustrates what a thoroughly marked script might look like. As directors become more experienced and comfortable with the medium, their scripts will not be marked this heavily. For the purposes of illustration, figure 13–15 shows virtually every command and preparation for the open and close of a discussion program.

Experienced directors will work with a less detailed marked script in order to concentrate on the camera monitors. Directors must be able to watch everything that is going on; they cannot be content just to keep their eyes glued on the prepared script, reading off all instructions in order.

Figure 13–15
Sample marked script.

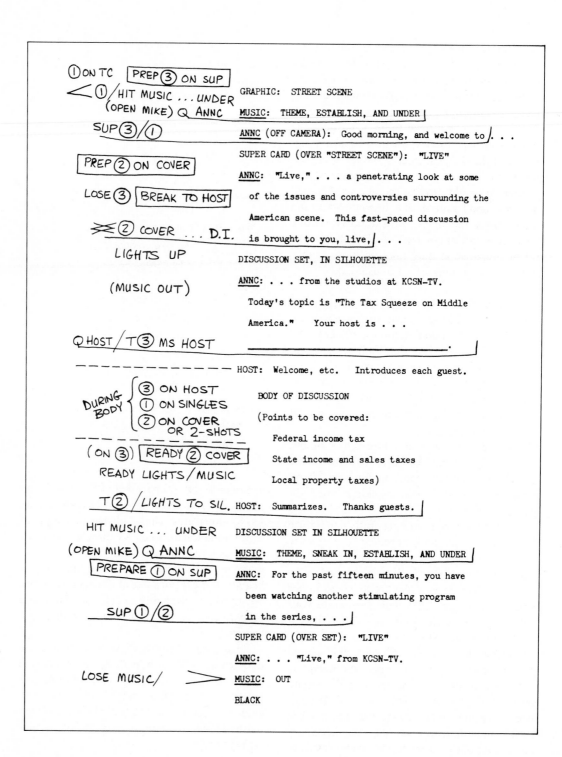

Directing Your First Studio Production

Figure 13–16
Representative shot
sheets.

CAMERA 1	CAMERA 2	CAMERA 3
2. GR #2	4. Wide Sh., Kitchen, hi-angle boom down.	1. TC (GR #1)
6. LS, Mary in doorway	7. MS Mary. Follow her	3. Sup cards (A, B, C, D)
8. LS, David in doorway	15. 2-sh., Pan L as David crosses behind Mary	5. CU coffee cup, pan to ash tray
10. MS David (he walks into O/S)	18. MS David. D.B. as he comes to her. Open to 2-sh.	9. MS Mary (she rises)
12. O/S David	20. CU Mary	11. O/S Mary
14. CU David	22. 2-sh. (tight)	13. CU Mary
17. MS Mary (she sits)	24. (Crane up) Hi angle 2-sh. D.I. & crane down to single of David	16. MS David
23. Loose 2-sh. (Mary rises)	28. Single David (wide). D.B., follow as he walks to Mary. Open to 2-sh.	19. MCU David (bust-shot)
25. O/S Mary (in doorway). She walks toward David. David turns to camera.	30. CU Mary's hands	21. CU David
27. CU David	34. MS Alice	26. 2-sh. as Mary turns
31. 2-sh. Mary walks past camera. Hold on David	37. MS David (he sits)	29. (Hook wheels) 2-sh. D.I. to ECU Mary
33. MS David. Pan to door as Alice enters	40. ECU David	32. MS Mary
36. 3-sh., favoring Alice	43. (Crane down) Loose MS Alice. Follow her to table. Follow action w/cup. Crane up & D.I.	35. Loose 2-sh. (Mary, David)
39. CU Alice		38. Loose CU, Mary
42. CU Alice		41. ECU Mary
45. Wide 3-sh., follow action		44. ECU Mary
		46. CU of knife

Shot Sheets   Once the director has the script completely marked, he or she can prepare detailed instructions for other crew members—for the floor director, audio, the technical director, the recording engineer, the graphics operators, lighting and staging, and anyone else who might be handling a complex assignment. Some of these forms have already been discussed (lighting and staging plot plans). The prepared written instructions can save considerable studio time once the director is ready to set up and start rehearsals.

The most common form of these specialized instructions is the *shot sheet* for the camera operators—an abbreviated description of every shot that a particular camera has to get. It is compact enough to be attached to the rear of the camera where the operator can quickly refer to it. Shot sheets are particularly valuable for complex, fully scripted programs, such as dramas, where every shot has been carefully worked out by the director—and where the cameras will have to be moving quite a bit to get various shots as requested. In preparing the marked script for a drama, for example, once the blocking is firmed up and the director has every shot planned, each shot will be numbered; the shot sheets then list each camera's shot by number.

Figure 13–16 shows the three shot sheets for a three-camera drama. In the illustration, all three camera shot sheets are indicated on one page. In practice these three sheets would be cut out separately, and each camera operator would have his or her own shot sheet taped or clipped by the viewfinder.

Actual Sample Rundown Sheets   The preceding discussion has presented some basic formats and principles that are fairly standard throughout the television industry. However, in actuality, it is recognized that many major studios, stations, educational and corporate organizations, independent production houses, network centers, and other operations will use a wide variety of script formats. Figures 13–17 and 13–18 are two examples from actual productions that reflect variations on the basic styles previously described.

Figure 13–17
Sample show format or rundown sheet from Easter Seal Telethon.

PAGE 1   1989 Easter Seal Telethon   *SAT*   1.

HOUR 1A

Seg. Starts at: 8:00:00-PM   Seg. Ends at :   8:15:00-PM

SPREAD -- UNDER 2:07

ITEM	ELEMENT	SEG TIME	RUN TIME	PROD REQUIREMENTS
1	OPEN/BB (Robb Weller)	:30	:30	TOTE=AMWAY VTPB: EXT. AQUARIUS VTPB: ANIMATION CART: TYMP MUSIC: THEME LOC: AI Q CARDS
2	FAT BOONE SONG "POWER TO OVERCOME" *Sideline* (Pat, Joy)	2:24	2:54	LOC: CS W/ORCH LIVE/VTPB/LIVE MUSIC: VTPB
3	PAT & JOY	:15	3:09	LOC: CS
4	INTRO MARY (Pat)	:10	3:19	LOC: CS MUSIC: MARY PLAYON
5	PAT/MARY/ROBB	1:15	4:34	LOC: CS
6	TAMMY WYNETTE SONG "ANOTHER CHANCE"	2:19	6:53	VTPB
7	PAT	:15	7:08	LOC: HOMEBASE MUSIC: RASPYNI PLAYON
8	RASPYNI BROTHERS PERFORMANCE *Ralph ...*	5:00	12:08	LOC: CS *2 WIRELESS LAVS
9	PAT/MARY ROBB – TOTE/BB	:45	12:53	LOC: CS W/ORCH MUSIC: THEME CART: TYMP

Directing Your First Studio Production

Figure 13–18
Sample show format/
rundown sheet for
Entertainment Tonight.

ENTERTAINMENT TONIGHT

5141

SHOW 2300   PAGE ___1___

DATE FRIDAY JULY 6, 1990

NO.	TITLE	AUDIO	VIDEO	NOTES
				CH/C3-BR /ADD A
1	:10 PROMO (Mary)	LIVE	LIVE	
				BLACK UT
2	MAIN TITLES/COLD TEASE (Mary)	SOT	VTR	
				X C3/ADDA 3/4
3	LEAD MITCH SNYDER (Mary)	LIVE	LIVE	CL-ADD-11 /C3-BR /ADDA
				11
4	MITCH SNYDER VTR (Mary)	SOT	VTR	
				C3 /ADDA
5	TAG (Mary)	LIVE	LIVE	
				CL-ADD /CI-E
6	LEAD UNMARRIED WITH CHILDREN (John)	LIVE	LIVE	
				TO
7	UNMARRIED WITH CHILDREN VTR (John)	SOT	VTR	

● ● ● ● ● ● ● ● ● ● ● ● ● ● ●

Summary

The successful television director must keep in mind the principles of picture continuity: the balance of *wide shots* and *close-ups;* correct use of *shot relationships* (avoiding jump cuts, extreme cutting ratios, and position jumps); observing the *axis of action* (and *conversation*); and other principles of continuity.

He or she must also use different *types of transitions* knowledgeably and be careful with the *timing of transitions.* These principles apply both to multiple-camera studio productions and to single-camera field shooting.

In blocking cameras for a multi-camera production, the director should *cross the camera angles,* start *blocking in the center of the program,* and position objects to be shot *after the camera pattern has been set.*

The director must be familiar with *three types of scripting formats*—the full script; the outline or semi-scripted program; and the show format or rundown sheet. In preparing for the production, there are standard symbols that most directors use in *marking the script.* Directors should also prepare other production instructions such as *camera shot sheets.*

In chapter 14, we will summarize the scope of the director's job and look at the production requirements for a couple of specialized formats.

13.5 Production Project: The Discussion Program

While no single phase of production could be considered as the *sine qua non* of any successful television program, the process whereby the director plans the staging and camera blocking of a show is, for most programs, one of critical importance. Although most directors refer to it as their homework, this series of interrelated decisions usually continues beyond the final rehearsal.

In some programs—such as drama—this effort may entail plotting every performer movement and camera shot. For programs of a more spontaneous nature, the director usually sets up a flexible shooting plan designed to cover all the various program contingencies.

Planning the Discussion Program

That sometimes maligned but nevertheless ubiquitous stalwart of television programming, the *talk show,* provides an excellent format for understanding the fundamental principles involved in staging and camera blocking. The absence of performer movement on such programs allows for concentration upon picture composition and clarity.

Staging   The majority of talk shows utilize some variation of either one of two basic staging configurations: an *L-shaped grouping* that places the host on the end facing down a row of other participants (figure 13–19); or a *semicircle,* in which the host is generally placed in the center. This conformity of staging is not as much a lack of originality on the part of the directors as it is their recognition that these seating plans provide an arrangement whereby the guests can best relate to each other and the host and, at the same time, provide the director with the best camera angles of the participants.

Figure 13–20 shows an open semicircular seating arrangement similar to that used on several syndicated talk shows.

On these programs, four cameras are generally utilized. One of the center cameras holds a wide shot of the entire group at all times. The other center camera holds a shot of the host for use at all times in the program. On a three-camera show, one center camera will have to alternate between these two shots. Note the extreme angle of the set of the two outside cameras. Although both can provide shots of the entire group from these positions, their

Figure 13–19
Typical setup for an *L*-shaped staging arrangement for a discussion program.

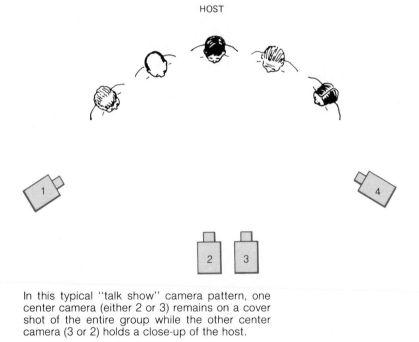

HOST

Figure 13–20
Camera pattern for semicircular staging.

In this typical "talk show" camera pattern, one center camera (either 2 or 3) remains on a cover shot of the entire group while the other center camera (3 or 2) holds a close-up of the host.

primary assignment is that of providing close-up shots of those persons facing their direction—by crossing their angles (section 13.3).

On a musical or comedy-variety type of production, the performers generally face toward a stage-front camera and audience area as they would in a conventional stage show. In a discussion program, the participants relate not to the audience but to each other and, as a result, face not to the front but in the direction of the persons to their right and left. Depending upon the role of the host/moderator, the other participants will tend to face in his or her direction during much of the program.

Lighting Two suggested lighting plans for an *L-shaped* seating configuration have been presented as sample lighting plots in figures 4–22 and 4–23 (section 4.5). A review of that section of material will be of value in the preparation of lighting plots for any of the several main seating configurations.

On a discussion program, care must be taken to ensure that the face, especially the eyes, is properly lit from all potential camera angles. The locations of the cameras provide a good guide to the location of the main lights in relation to the subjects. The amount of light reflected back from each subject to the camera must be individually balanced occasionally for equal intensity. Differences in hair, clothing, and complexion can produce unsuitably dark or light close-up shots. When taken in succession, such shots are noticeably objectionable.

Shot Continuity In section 13.1, reference was made to *wide-angle* and *close-up* shots in terms of their respective abilities to communicate collective or particularized program information. Wide-angle *cover* shots are used within a program sequence to reestablish the relationship of program participants to each other and to the elements of the set. It is

the *collectivizing* view of all those production values that contributes to the program as a whole.

By contrast, the close-up shot is a *particularized* view of a person or object at a precisely appropriate point in the program sequence. As such, the information it conveys is selective and personal, even to the point of being intimate. The eyes and facial muscles add an important dimension to the total meaning of what a person is expressing in words. This is especially true of actors or other personalities who often speak in public or on television. For this reason, the most effective close-up shots are those in which the camera angle is not more than forty-five degrees from a head-on position. (See figure 13–21.) Close-up shots from profile angles, while extremely valuable on many types of productions, should be used with caution on discussion programs.

Transitions The most important production value on a discussion program is the precision with which the camera shots follow the spontaneous flow of the conversation. Each time a new person begins to speak, the camera on the air—whether a cover shot or a close-up—should include that person. To linger for more than a split second on someone who has just stopped talking or to cut to the wrong person is very distracting to the audience.

Ideally, each change of voice should be accompanied by a change of cameras to a close-up shot or one that predominately features the person talking. On a three-camera show that features four guests and a moderator, this is not always possible. By carefully watching the panel for clues as to who may be speaking next (section 13.2), the director may somewhat improve the chances of having the shot ready.

Most directors solve the problem by having a cover shot of the entire group available for use at all times. When a close-up shot of a new

Directing Your First Studio Production

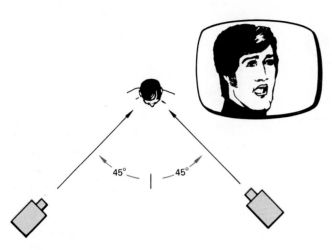

Figure 13–21
Optimum angles for close-ups.

Any camera getting a close-up shot should be as perpendicular to the talent as possible. The camera should not be more than 45 degrees from a head-on shot for a good close-up.

speaker is not readily available, a take to the cover shot performs several important functions. Primarily, it gives the director a chance to be certain of who is speaking before assigning a camera to the shot. In a fast-paced discussion, this alternative is the only way the director can stay with the quickly changing flow of the conversation. Once the cover shot has been taken, the close-up need not be used immediately. The director can let the wide shot reestablish the collective aspect of the group while waiting for the end of a sentence as a convenient point to cut to the close-up.

During a discussion program, the situation often calls for shots other than a close-up of one participant in the total group. Shots including two or three persons not only add pictorial variety but are quite useful when several people begin a rapid interchange of short statements or questions and answers. Smaller group shots have an added dimension, showing the silent but often revealing expression on the faces of persons other than the speaker. A brief close-up shot of someone moving his or her head in agreement or disagreement—a reac-

tion shot—is especially useful when one person has been speaking for an extended period of time.

On the other hand, the director must be alert to group shots in which those persons who are not talking are looking away from the speaker. Whether or not intended, the visual effect is one of boredom and, as such, has a negative impact on the program as a whole.

Camera Blocking   The range of shots available to each camera in a program situation is dependent upon the two interrelated variables of camera and subject position. These factors must be considered together when plans for shot coverage are made. On a discussion program, where the staging options are somewhat limited, the director generally uses the seating arrangement as a starting point in the camera blocking process. Primary camera positions can then be selected on the basis of the best angles for the close-up shots and the important requirement of wide-angle cover shots.

All of the shot possibilities for each camera should be plotted so that each camera oper-

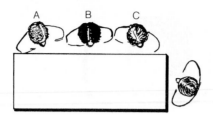

Figure 13–22
Camera patterns for
L-shaped staging.

Plan A: *Camera 1* remains on a wide-angle cover shot. *Camera 2* gets close-ups of panelists as they face camera right and two-shots or three-shots of panelists. *Camera 3* gets singles of panelists as they face camera right and over-the-shoulder shots (with host in foreground).

Plan B: *Camera 1* gets close-ups of moderator/host, two-shots of host and panelist C, and singles and two-shots as panelists turn to camera left. *Camera 2* gets close-ups of panelists as they face camera right and two-shots or three-shots of panelists. *Camera 3* remains on a wide-angle cover shot.

ator can work within the parameters of established shot assignments. Off-set visuals should be positioned for easy accessibility to camera positions—after the basic camera pattern has been established (section 13.3).

The use of a definite shooting plan aids in having critical shots available when they are needed and, at the same time, helps in holding down the talk on the P.L. intercommunication system.

The direction of conversational flow may vary at different times during a program. For this reason, directors usually develop several shooting plans to cover all contingencies. Figure 13–22 shows two such plans that could be used in the coverage of an *L-shaped* arrangement. Plan A is designed to provide

maximum close-up coverage of the three panel members, with the moderator being seen only on the wide shot on camera 1. Plan B is set up for situations in which the moderator takes a very active role in the program and, as a result, needs a close-up shot ready at all times, or for a period during which conversations develop between two guests.

Plan A has obvious limitations but has a basic utility in predictable situations such as a period in the program during which the host is bringing out individual responses from each participant. The beginning and ending of discussion programs usually assume this structure.

A director would probably quickly shift over to Plan B during the more active phases

Directing Your First Studio Production

of the conversation. By holding camera 3 on a cover shot, camera 1 is able to get a close-up shot of the moderator. Camera 1 also has the option of getting close-up shots of those who turn camera left for a two-person conversation. In this situation, camera 2 then has the option of a close-up of the other person or a two-shot of both speakers. The reverse structure is also possible with camera 1 on the two-shot and camera 2 on the single of the person facing camera right.

Even taken together, these two shooting plans by no means exhaust the possibilities available within an L-*shaped* seating configuration. The use of camera 2 as a cover camera from either a left-side or right-side studio position opens up another series of coverage patterns. The suggestion of cameras 1 or 3 for cover shots stems from the fact that their angle to the set allows for a more interesting grouping of all participants in the frame. Each person's face occupies a larger proportion of the frame than in a wide shot from the center— which also results in empty space at the top and bottom of the frame.

In the press of a fast-moving program, the director often is tempted to give up the cover shot and use that camera temporarily for smaller group shots and close-ups. It is an option that even the most experienced directors use with considerable care. Invariably, when all cameras are committed to the three people who are dominating the conversation, the fourth (off-camera) voice suddenly starts speaking. It takes quick thinking to avoid several seconds of nontalking faces being aired or, worse, a wrong shot taken in haste.

Shooting in the Round   Many directors of discussion programs have had considerable success in staging program participants in a full circle and shooting from all points outside that circle. There are several benefits to be derived from this camera arrangement and a goodly number of problems as well. Because of the varying angles involved, it is difficult to get "clean" close-ups or two-shots. Backs of heads, hands, and whole bodies seem always to be in the way of the shot that is needed. It also is very difficult to position cameras to avoid seeing other cameras in the shot, unless the set is specially designed.

Depending upon the intended nature of the program, however, it is sometimes possible deliberately to use these crowded, poorly framed shots, taken from unusual angles, in an effective manner. The very roughness of the shooting technique is visually compatible with the sense of conflict created by varying points of view. The resulting *cinema verité* quality would be suitable for a program confrontation between activist and establishment representatives. Even the presence of cameras in some of the shots would communicate something of the reality of the total program situation.

Calling Shots   In a discussion program, it is essential that preparatory commands always be used in conjunction with the commands of execution (section 7.5). An inexperienced director might be tempted to think that a needed shot could be put on the air instantaneously if only the command of execution were given. To do so, however, would be to increase appreciably the possibilities for error. The spontaneous nature of talk programs makes the command of preparation doubly important. The technical director needs this lead time to be certain that the right shot is readied. Of equal importance is the possibility that the camera operators need this time for final adjustment of the framing or as a warning to hold a shot they might otherwise be in the process of changing.

A good procedure for the director on a fast-moving talk show is to give a "ready" for a probable next shot as soon as possible after the previous shot is on the line. This does not remove any option for a subsequent change in the upcoming shot; it simply aids the director in staying ahead of the action. An example of how the director can inform the crew of several probable courses of action would be as follows (referring to the pattern in figure 13–22).

> "Ready camera 3 . . . take 3" (cover shot). "Ready camera 2 on a close-up of guest C . . . camera 1, hold the moderator close-up, but be ready to move over to guest B."

In this situation, guest C has just interrupted the moderator. The director can afford to wait on the cover shot to see whether guest C will continue talking or whether the moderator will start talking again. At the same time, the director has noticed that guest B also is trying to break into the conversation.

Discussion Program Production Project (Appendix D-3)

The somewhat simplified opening and closing format in appendix D-3 is presented as an aid to an all-class production exercise. This discussion format can be used for a repeated number of production exercises within the class. Practical experience in the utilization of cameras in a spontaneous program situation is valuable not only in itself but also it serves as an important background to camera blocking procedures in more complex productions, such as music and drama. (See chapter 14.)

A minimum running time of five minutes for each exercise is suggested so that each director has an opportunity to become familiar with the pattern of the conversational flow and the related continuity of camera shots. A realistic element can be added by having the A.D. and the stage manager feed the moderator countdown cues for time remaining in the exercise. Directors should be prepared for the fact that the transition from the body of a program to the closing segment can be difficult unless cues and other instructions are given well in advance.

Discussion topics should be carefully selected so that the conversation does not lag. One way to ensure an active interchange of comments is to have the panel members role-play assigned roles such as judge, police officer, and taxpayer. It often is easier to verbalize the supposed opinions of generalized cultural types than to express one's own point of view.

Directing Your First Studio Production

Directing Techniques for Various Formats

14

In this chapter, we want to summarize some of the elements that beginning directors should keep uppermost in their minds. We also want to present some specific considerations for directing particular formats—a musical production and a dramatic sequence. Finally, we will introduce a concluding production project—in the form of an extended station break—that involves the beginning director in integrating a number of production elements (studio host, slide, studio card, and videotape) in one short production segment. The scripted production model appears in appendix D-5.

14.1 From Planning to Postproduction

At this stage, it may be helpful for the student director to take a *chronological* look at the entire operation of putting a program together. Throughout the text, we have touched on many individual elements in the production process. In this section, we want to pull the ingredients together and add a few other considerations in creating a total introduction to the directing process.

Preproduction Planning

The discipline of thorough preproduction planning cannot be emphasized strongly enough. The success of every production is determined—to a very great extent—by the quality of the preproduction planning that the director has undertaken. For the purposes of organizing our thinking, it may be helpful to consider preproduction planning in five areas: *script familiarization, facilities and equipment, cast and crew, production requirements,* and *script preparation.*

Script Familiarization   In many academic and closed-circuit settings, the director will also function as the producer/writer and, thus, will have shaped the script from the beginning. In many other situations you, as director, will have the script handed to you and you will take the production from there.

Your first concern should be to determine the *specific purpose* of the script. Ask yourself several questions: What is the objective of the program? What should happen as a result of this production? How do you want the audience to be different when this program is over? Then you can begin to think in terms of the overall "feel" and image of the program. What kinds of settings, lighting, and graphics would be most effective in this particular *communication* process?

Next, there may be several immediate steps that need to be taken. Check the script for rough timing; read through it and get an idea of how long it might run. Is the length all right? Does it need to be cut? Does it need to be lengthened? The script should be put in its final television production format and duplicated for all personnel involved. Is any rewriting necessary? How many copies do you need? The script must be checked for any necessary copyright clearances. Can it be used as it stands? In a professional situation, this is the point at which you must be working out a specific budget. How much money do you have for the production?

Facilities and Equipment   Once you are completely comfortable with the script, you should be able to start specific *facilities planning*. In the case of a remote coverage of some event, you have to scout the location, of course. You must make arrangements for mobile equipment. In other professional situations, you may have to make arrangements for the rental of actual studio facilities. How large a studio do you need? What size sets will you be using? How long will you need the studio? This, obviously, is one of the largest items in your budget.

In most academic and training situations, the studio will be assigned to you for a definite period of time. In many institutions—even for training purposes—you will still have to fill out a facilities request form, reserving a specific studio and control room(s), cameras, microphones, video recorders, lights, sets, graphics, and other requirements. The items are requested for a particular production date and time. Failure to attend to such paperwork carefully at this stage can result in costly problems and misunderstandings later.

Cast and Crew   Again, in most academic situations, you may not have to be concerned with securing personnel. The technical crew may be assigned from your class or from some other participating class. There still may be some occasions, however, when you will be involved in selecting specific individuals for particular crew assignments. You should be familiar with the process of making out crew sheets to fill the positions you need for your production.

Casting for actors or other performers may also be done on an informal basis in the academic setting. You may work through the drama or the theatre arts departments, or you may prevail upon your personal friends. In securing such volunteer help, make certain that you have a firm commitment; many a student production has been ruined because some friend or casual acquaintance backed out of a production at the last moment. In professional situations, of course, casting is quite an involved process. The producer will probably line up the major talent and the rest of the casting will be handled by a specialized casting director.

Production Requirements   Production requirements are what the bulk of this text has been concerned with. Now comes the job of pulling it all together. In any kind of major

Figure 14–1
Production conference with
director, A.D., stage
manager, T.D., and staging
and lighting director.

production, the director should plan on holding one or more production conferences involving the chief production heads—set designer, art director, lighting chief, engineering supervisor, other key production persons, and of course, the A.D. and floor manager. (See figure 14–1.) Depending upon the nature and complexity of the program, there may be several different kinds of conferences: *script conferences* (involving writers and the producer), *art conferences, engineering conferences,* and so forth.

You must now make sure that all of the preproduction elements are properly requested and constructed. The *lighting and staging plans* are developed at this stage. If any special *costumes* or *props* have to be ordered or fabricated, they are initiated now. All *graphics* have to be ordered and produced; if you have access to an art department, graphics request forms will be turned in. What computer graphics can be prepared in advance? Any *film* or *still photography* has to be

planned well in advance. Are station photographers available? How much will you do yourself? Will you have slides made of some of your graphics? Will you be shooting any *videotaped sequences* ahead of time? Any *special effects* will have to be arranged. *Music* and *other special audio* selections must be chosen and/or ordered.

During all of this preproduction process, you have to be working within a very tight interlocking schedule of *checkpoints* and *deadlines.* Many production elements cannot proceed until other items are taken care of first. Everything, therefore, must be scheduled days and weeks in advance. The exterior videotape cannot be shot until the costumes arrive. Costumes cannot be designed until the overall color scheme of the setting is determined. Set pieces cannot be constructed until the setting design is completed. Slides cannot be shot until the graphic cards are made. And the electronic graphics cannot be made until the talent decides what he or she wants to do.

Directing Techniques for Various Formats

To protect yourself, you will put in *pads* or *cushions*—a few extra days protection here and there throughout the schedule. In major productions, the intertwining complexities of the production schedule can become quite awesome. You cannot wait until the last minute to get things started.

Script Preparation   During all of this activity, you also must be concerned with your script breakdown and specific preparations for the day of production. You start with the basics—reminding yourself that your primary job is that of delivering a clear communicative *message* in an effective, interesting, and artistically pleasing manner. How are you going to use your cameras? What balance of wide *collective* shots and close-up *particularized* shots will you strive for (section 13.1)? What kinds of transitions will best move the program forward without ambiguity? What will be the pacing you want to achieve? In short, what images and sounds do you want to create to achieve your purpose?

This process, of course, takes into consideration all of the elements of picture continuity and transitions and camera patterns discussed in chapter 13. You prepare your script with specific markings and instructions, and you prepare other written instructions for key positions on the production crew—camera shot sheets, audio instructions, and so forth.

Rehearsals

By now, you should have moved into rehearsals in one form or another. You should think in terms of several different kinds of rehearsals: *pre-studio* rehearsals, *floor* rehearsals, and *control room* rehearsals.

Pre-Studio Rehearsals   For many extensive productions—especially dramas—you will want to have some rehearsals prior to coming into the studio. Studio time is too precious to start from scratch with basic blocking.

Using a rehearsal hall, an empty studio, a warehouse, or a living room, you can begin working with actors. Specific areas can be measured off and marked with masking tape or furniture to represent major staging areas, and much of your blocking of action can take place—as well as quite a bit of the dramatic interpretation and working on lines.

For nondramatic productions, there are also many good reasons for pre-studio rehearsals. Documentaries, educational programs, political broadcasts, and the like, can benefit from having an early **dry-run** session where the director and talent can work together.

Studio Floor Rehearsals   When the director and the production crew start to work in the studio, the director usually will spend some amount of time on the studio floor before assuming the director's chair in the control room. There are a couple of different ways that you might profitably spend this rehearsal period (figure 14–2). Depending on the type of production, either the talent or the technical crew might benefit most from your presence on the studio floor. If the talent is particularly insecure or if the technical coordination of a production is really complicated, you might spend quite a bit of your time on the studio floor. On the other hand, if the talent is in control of the situation and the technical elements are no special problem, you probably would benefit from getting into the control room as early as you can.

One of the first rehearsal techniques you will conduct from the studio floor will be a *walk-through rehearsal*. This might be either a *talent* walk-through (if they are not really sure of their positions and movements) or a *technical* walk-through (to explain major camera moves, audio placement, scene changes, and special effects). In many instances, the walk-through is a combination, taking both the talent and crew through an abbreviated version of the production.

Directing Techniques for Various Formats

Figure 14–2
Director (facing camera) working out production problems with stage manager during a walk-through rehearsal on the studio floor.

Control Room Rehearsals   The full rehearsals are usually conducted with the director calling shots from the control room. If time is critical or if technical problems exist, however, the director may elect to work longer on the studio floor. The initial type of full-facilities rehearsal is called a *camera* rehearsal. For the first time, the camera operators are behind the cameras and all other technical personnel are at their positions.

This first camera rehearsal usually is a *start-and-stop,* or *stop-start,* rehearsal. In this approach, you interrupt the rehearsal every time there is a major problem. You correct the trouble and then continue the rehearsal. This type of rehearsal procedure *may* be conducted from the floor if the director feels the potential problems need his or her immediate and direct supervision. It is quite a time-consuming process—although it can be effective if you have the luxury of enough studio time.

Another approach to the first camera rehearsal is the *uninterrupted run-through.* This should almost always be conducted from the control room. In this approach, the director attempts to get through the entire production with a minimum of interruptions. If time is short—and if problems are minor—you keep on plowing through the rehearsal regardless of what happens (assuming that your A.D. is keeping thorough production notes about what needs to be corrected after you are through the rehearsal).

Finally, there is the *dress rehearsal.* Theoretically, this is the final rehearsal—a complete, uninterrupted, full-scale rehearsal after all of the problems have been straightened out. In practice, this stage is rarely reached. Realities of the medium are such that there simply is never enough studio time to do as polished a job as you would want. In many instances, the director will wind up with a combination start-and-stop and dress rehearsal, stumbling through as fast as possible to try to complete at least one full camera rehearsal of some description before airtime.

When time is short, you must economize and try to make the most efficient use of the time available. Do not stand around waiting for others to finish their jobs before starting your rehearsal; you can rehearse even while the lighting crew is still trimming the lights and while the audio engineer is establishing levels. In an abbreviated walk-through rehearsal, at least make certain you get through all of the rough spots in the production; *rehearse the open and the close* and *the crucial transitions* that call for coordination of several kinds of movement. Pick your priorities; do not get hung up on small details (such as worrying about the possibility of a boom shadow) when you have only a few minutes to work out major problems (the talent doesn't know where he or she should move next). Before you know it, the A.D. will be telling you, "Forty-five seconds to air."

Production and Postproduction

Finally, you are ready to start calling shots on your first production. As we pointed out in section 1.6, the director has three main functions—*planner, artist,* and *executor.* You have done all you can in the first two areas—as planner and as creative artist—and you now are ready to execute the program.

First, try to control your physical anxieties. Regardless of what might be churning inside, try not to let it show. Force yourself to sit down and present a calm facade. During the final minute before you go on the air, make a point of quietly and calmly assuring everybody that all will go well. Force yourself to sit back and take a deep breath; let it out slowly; and coolly tell all of the crew and the talent that everything will proceed confidently. Remember that the composure or anxiety you communicate to the crew will surely be returned to you in the same, or even an exaggerated, manner.

Give all of your commands and directions as clearly as you can. Refer to talent (when talking to the floor director) by name—"Cue Dr. Morgan," not "Cue him"—to avoid misunderstandings. Refer to camera operators, on the other hand, by numbers; you are less likely to slip up and get confused. Make sure you use correct and precise commands of preparation to the technical director (section 7.5) and to all other production positions; the commands of preparation are at least as important as the commands of execution.

Keeping the lag time of various equipment and personnel in mind, give your cues in a sequence designed to get things happening when you want them to. In opening your program, say "Hit music" and then "Fade in camera 2." It always takes a second or so before the music will be heard (if it is properly cued up), but the camera is there with the push of a lever. Similarly, always cue talent before putting his or her camera on the air. "Open-mike-cue-talent-dissolve-to-two" is often given as one command of execution. By the time the stage manager reacts and throws the cue and the talent takes a breath and starts to talk, the camera will be on the air.

Watch and listen to your monitors. Always be aware of exactly what is going on over the air—as far as picture and sound are concerned. If a picture is not what you want ("what the viewer needs"), then change it. The viewer watching his or her home receiver could care less about your sinus headache or your incompetent T.D. or your fight with the talent or the camera cable with the bad connection; all he or she knows is what comes out over the receiver, and if it is bad, it is bad.

Also, always check your camera and preview monitors before calling a shot to be put on the air. Make sure the camera you want to dissolve to or the special effects you want next are prepared and ready to be put on the air. You cannot afford to get buried in your beau-

Directing Techniques for Various Formats

Figure 14–3
Director (center) calling
shots during a production,
flanked by the T.D. and his
A.D.

tifully marked script while ignoring the realities of the picture and sound you are sending out. (See figure 14–3.)

During the course of your program, always be looking ahead two or three minutes. What possible problems lie ahead? What about the close-up we didn't get a chance to rehearse? Did the mike boom get repositioned all right? Is everything set for the lighting change? Are the dancers prepared for their entrance?

If something should go drastically wrong, tell yourself you are going to remain in control and salvage what you can. Camera 2 just went dead? Get a wide shot on camera 1 and keep going. The dancers just walked on the set ahead of their cue? The talent will have to explain the best he or she can. The C.G. operator just hit the wrong button and lost your next two graphics? You will continue without them.

Whatever happens, it is your job to keep going. Do not give up until the producer or instructor tells you to throw in the towel.

Finally, no matter what else happens, television—especially live TV and live-on-tape—is a time-bound medium. Everything has to fit into scheduled slots. If you are directing a program that is supposed to be exactly 7:30 long, that means exactly seven minutes and thirty seconds—not one second more or less. Listen to your A.D., and when you are told you have five seconds to black, that means you fade it out and sneak out the music; you have no choice—unless of course, you know you are working with a flexible time slot.

Once the program is off the air, use the studio address (talkback) to thank the crew and talent. Assure them that everything went well. Keep your composure until you have a chance to collapse in private. Supervise the strike and make certain you clear the control room of all scripts, notes, props, and everything else.

If there is any postproduction editing to be accomplished, your job is far from done (chapters 9 and 15). If it is a simple matter of inserting a clean shot to cover the one bad blunder on the air, you may be able to get it done right away. If it is a major postproduction editing job of assembling video pieces from several different sources, it will take quite a bit of scheduling and lonely master control room sessions.

In the next two sections, we want to look at two specialized production formats—the musical and the drama—and examine camera blocking and other considerations for these production types. The student should read through and study the sections carefully—whether or not they are used as class production projects—to become familiar with these specialized situations.

14.2 Production of the Musical Number

The techniques used for shooting instrumental groups are, for the most part, based upon the same collective and particularized considerations previously outlined. Musical productions, especially jazz and rock, offer the director an opportunity to explore the use of extreme wide and close-up shots. Shots that include portions of an audience can be used very effectively. At the other extreme, tight close-up shots of the face of a performer can be used to a degree that would be unsuitable in another program context.

Camera Blocking   The primary consideration in any musical production is that of consistently matching the visual aspect of the performance to the sound being heard. A "big"

sound with the entire group playing and/or singing calls for an equally "big" look from a visual standpoint. The director should seek to achieve visual contrast and a sense of movement by tight and loosely framed group shots from various angles. Vocal and instrumental solos require a more intimate use of the camera. The director can explore the more particularized elements of the performance by means of close-up shots of the face, the hands, and the instrument itself. The close-ups could be interspersed with re-establishing full and waist shots to capture performer movement and to show the relation of the performer to his or her instrument.

The director must at all times seek to capture visually the intensity and mood of the performance. If, for example, the entire group is playing at a low sound level, the intent may be a mood of sadness or alienation. To produce a matching visual effect, the group could be shot in such a way as to produce a sense of isolation. This could be achieved by shooting the group in tight profile or extremely low-angle shots.

At the other extreme, there are those numbers that create a certain degree of excitement with high sound levels and a great deal of performer movement. The director can capture and even enhance the action by dolly and trucking movements of the cameras themselves. Two camera shots can be superimposed to further enhance the intensity of a performance. A close-up shot of the lead singer supered over a wide shot of the group might capture both the particularized and collective aspects of the "high point" of a big production number.

The musical structure of the number serves as the basis for the sequence of camera shots. In an ad-lib concert performance, the director is forced to attempt to predict the sequence of the action. In a rehearsed studio production, the director would have the leader provide a breakdown of each number. This

Directing Techniques for Various Formats

usually is given in terms of the number of measures (bars) within four-, eight-, or sixteen-measure phrases. If the number is pre-recorded and the musicians are going to mime and lip-sync their performance, then the phrase groupings can be expressed in seconds. Remember that the exact timing of camera cuts or other transitions should always be on the beat (section 13.2).

Production Example

An illustration of both of these methods is given in the production script example (figure 14–4) showing the camera blocking for the first three minutes of "Beginnings" as recorded by the group Chicago.[1] The sequence of camera shots for the production model is based on the staging configuration and camera positions as shown in figure 14–5. The camera work has been planned to include a crane mount for camera 2. Cameras 1 and 3 have been kept in relatively static positions to be ready for a quick succession of shots.

This scripted production model has been designed to be used in two ways. By playing the record and envisioning the sequence of shots, the student is provided an opportunity to understand how the individual shots are made to fit together into a production whole. The script can also be used as the basis for a full-class exercise. Class members can be placed in the indicated staging positions (using real instruments if possible), and the number can be shot as a production sequence. In this case, the script should be used only as a guide. Each individual director should be encouraged to attempt some degree of variation in both staging and shot selection.

In an actual production, the director, assistant director, technical director, and possibly the audio operator work with a copy of

1. Columbia Records XSM-139684-CS 9809, side 1, cut 3.

the blocking script. Quite frequently—depending upon the type of musical production—the director and/or A.D. will be using the actual musical score as the working script. Each camera operator is given either a copy of the full script or a shot sheet, which lists only the shots for that particular camera.

14.3 Production of the Dramatic Sequence

Contemporary directors of television programming have developed a diversity of shooting techniques for both film and electronic cameras. Some have gone so far as to reverse traditional patterns and use multiple-film cameras, while others have explored the use of the single electronic camera. During the 1980s, a whole new generation of technology began to emerge based on improved electronic cameras and computer-based editing equipment. It is possible that several differently designed cameras will emerge, each suited to a particular type of production. This is already apparent with the development of the mini-cameras and the camcorder, the introduction of the CCD camera, and the promise of high-definition (HDTV) technology.[2]

While the 60–minute or 90–minute live dramatic production is probably a thing of the past, the return to the use of multiple electronic cameras on dramatic programs has been important. Soap operas, situation comedies,

2. The CBS-TV movie *Innocent Victims* in 1988 was the first American network drama shot on an HDTV system. Prior to that, HDTV technology had been used to shoot several feature films, the Canadian series *Chasing Rainbows,* and several music videos, including Mick Jagger's *Let's Work.* All of these had to be reduced to the 525-line NTSC system before they could be released on television, however. It is likely that HDTV programming will find its way into cable, cassette, and satellite distribution before open-circuit broadcasting is able to adapt to the advanced standards.

Figure 14–4

Sample musical production
script. Columns provide
the time at beginning of
each shot segment, the
number of musical bars for
each segment, the camera
use, and the shot
description for each
segment.

Musical Production Script Example

"Beginnings" Chicago Transit Authority Approx. First Three Minutes

Time	Bars	Camera	Shot
00:00	6	1	1. XCU Guitar/hand zoom out to tight waist
06	2	2	2. Drummer solo
09	4		Zoom out to include Guitarist
13	4		Pan to include Bass
17	7	1	3. Group profile Brass foreground
24	1	2	4. Drummer
26	8		Zoom out to Group wide
34	8	3	5. CU Singer low 45° angle
43	6	1	6. Bust Singer zoom in CU profile
49	4	2	7. Group high angle 45° from left
54	8		Arm across to right dropping
1:02	8		to low 45° from right
1:11	4	3	8. CU Singer profile from right
1:15	4	1	9. Tight 45° Group
1:19	4	2	10. CU Singer 45° angle
1:24	4	1	11. Tight 45° Group
1:28	4	2	12. Waist Singer and arc across
1:37	8		to left
1:45	8	1	13. Profile Group
1:54	6	3	14. Low 45° Singer Drums Bass
2:00	4	2	15. MCU head on high angle zoom out wide
2:05	8	2 slow diss.	16. High wide
2:13	8	3	17. Super CU low 45° singles
2:22	4		Dissolve thru and zoom in
2:26	4	1	18. Group profile
2:30	4	3	19. MCU
2:34	4	1	20. Group profile
2:39	16	2	21. Low angle—bust
2:55	8	1,2, and 3 ad lib takes	22. Drum solo
3:05	8	1	23. Vocal to conclusion
			Etc.

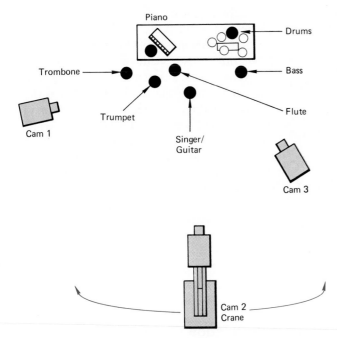

Figure 14–5
Camera pattern for musical
number.

This represents typical camera blocking with cameras 1 and 3 fairly stationary and camera 2, on a crane, available for major moves.

and even serious dramatic productions are using this production technique increasingly.[3]

Camera Blocking   The process whereby a television director plans the staging of actors borrows somewhat from both stage and single-camera motion picture techniques. The main difference between the older methods and those used for an ongoing television sequence lies in the fact that for television the director must continually relate the staging to three or more camera angles. The previously mentioned concept of the collective and particularized eye of

the camera again serves as the basis for shot framing and selection.

The wide-angle shot encompasses the totality of the scene at given points in the action. With this shot, the director establishes and, at later points, re-establishes the relationships of the actors to each other and to the elements of the set. The wide-angle shot shows the choreography of the characters within the set.

The more important dramatic elements of the story line are, however, more often portrayed by tighter shots involving two people or single close-up shots. The eyes and facial expressions may be as important in the actor's communication process as the dialogue. In the use of the close-up, the director must be careful to position the camera and lights to reveal the expression of the face fully. The profile angle, unless specifically called for, usually is avoided.

3. In 1984, the director of production system analysis for CBS pointed out that almost 90 percent of all situation comedies and variety shows were being produced not on film, but on videotape (*Broadcasting*, October 8, 1984, p. 54).

A typical pattern of shots for a short, two-person sequence at the beginning of a longer scene could be as follows:

1. Camera 2. Wide-angle cover shot. Locates the actors within the set and establishes the set itself.
2. Camera 1. Closer two-shot, possibly over the shoulder of actor A into the face of actor B.
3. Camera 3. Close-up shot of actor A.
4. Camera 1. Close-up shot of actor B.
5. Camera 2. Medium two-shot.
6. Camera 3. Tight close-up of actor A.
7. Camera 1. Waist shot of actor B.
8. Camera 2. Medium wide shot. One or both actors move to new positions within the set.

Notice that this pattern does not violate the three-to-one cutting ratio (section 13.1); it never goes from a LS to a CU. The pattern starts with a wide cover shot, gradually works into a couple tight close-ups, then works back out to a wider two-shot.

The sequence of shots within a coherent scene usually is accomplished by means of an instantaneous camera cut or take. The director's decision to take to another camera and the framing of that subsequent shot is based on the structure of the dialogue and the related movements of the actors. A close-up shot points up the importance of any line or series of lines from an actor. A two-shot alerts the audience for some sort of verbal or even physical interaction between the actors.

A wider shot allows for larger movements and can be used to permit the actors to physically express an emotional intensity. A widely framed two-shot can also be used to express an emotional separation or isolation. Cover shots also typically signal a change in the scene—watch for a door to open, an exit, a major piece of physical action or movement, or a third person to enter.

The frequency of camera cuts in a scene is related to the sense of *pacing,* or intensity of action communicated by that scene. To cut too often and without motivation can, however, create a cluttered look in a scene and actually disturb the continuity of the performance. A director often will avoid changing cameras and will instead have the performers move within the continuing frame of the camera. A side-by-side two-shot can flow into a close-up of one foreground actor as that person moves toward the camera. That actor can then turn his or her back to the camera for an over-the-shoulder two-shot. The actor can then walk away from the camera, past the first actor, for what becomes a wide shot. The director has accomplished three differently framed shots—all on the same camera—just with purposeful blocking of the actors.

Production Example

The short situation comedy script in appendix D-4 ("It's a Date?") has been designed to present the kind of camera blocking problems common to most dramatic productions. The blank space under "Video" should be used to write in the director's notes—camera numbers and shot descriptions.

For beginning directors, it is an especially good exercise to work with a **storyboard** to plot out all of your blocking—even on a simple dramatic scene. (See section 15.2.) Figure 14–6 shows a typical storyboard for the "It's a Date?" script.

The main difficulties are those that involve the handling of three or four performers. The staging of four people standing side by side should be avoided at all times. Whenever possible, actors should move both upstage and downstage, as well as in a line perpendicular to the camera.

The script can be used as the basis of a single class production exercise or as a series of individual student productions. If the latter

Directing Techniques for Various Formats

Figure 14–6
Storyboard for "It's a
Date?"

CAMERA ①	CAMERA ②	CAMERA ①	CAMERA ③	CAMERA ①	CAMERA ①	CAMERA ③
LONG SHOT	CLOSE UP	CLOSEUP	MEDIUM SHOT	LONG SHOT	CLOSE UP	TWO SHOT
HARRY ON COUCH, NANCY ENTERING	HARRY ON COUCH	NANCY AT FIREPLACE	HARRY ON COUCH, NANCY WALKING UP BESIDE HIM	KIM ENTERING ROOM	KIM	KIM AND NANCY

CAMERA ②	CAMERA ③	CAMERA ①	CAMERA ③	CAMERA ①	CAMERA ②	CAMERA ①
WIDE SHOT	MED. SHOT	MED. SHOT	TWO SHOT	MED. CLOSEUP	WIDE SHOT	MED. SHOT
HARRY, NANCY & KIM	HARRY & NANCY AT DOOR	DEREK JUMPING ON COUCH	HARRY & NANCY ON COUCH	DEREK ON COUCH	HARRY, NANCY & DEREK KIM ENTERING	DEREK JUMPING OVER COUCH

CAMERA ③	CAMERA ①	CAMERA ②	CAMERA ③	CAMERA ①	CAMERA ②	VTR CREDITS
CLOSEUP	MED. TWO SHOT	WIDE SHOT	MED. SHOT	CLOSEUP	TIGHT TWO SHOT	
NANCY	KIM & DEREK	HARRY, NANCY, KIM & DEREK EXIT	NANCY AT DOOR	HARRY	HARRY & NANCY	

This sample storyboard from "It's a Date?" illustrates only the key shots. It is presumed that repeated close-ups and reaction shots would be inserted among these key visualized moments. Thus, note that pictures five and six (counting from the left, top row) are both for camera 1; presumably, reaction shots from camera 2 or 3 would be inserted between these two pictures. The artwork reproduced for this storyboard illustrates the details, perspectives, and angles that a good storyboard should represent; however—depending upon the artistic ability of the director drawing the storyboard—any rendering of the desired pictures (even stick figures) could be used.

method is followed, each student should be encouraged to rewrite the lines to provide a variety of characterizations and actions. Various interpretations can lead to entirely different production treatments of the same basic script. (See figure 14–7.)

14.4 Full-Facilities Production Project

Most television productions include a wide range of program inputs in addition to those provided by studio microphones and cameras.

A so-called live newscast, for instance, consists of a number of production elements that have been previously recorded in one form or another. Film and videotape segments, commercials, live remote *feeds,* computer graphics, slides, music, and even announcer copy on cartridge may constitute more than half of a news program's content.

The scripted production model in appendix D-5 (full-facilities exercise) has been designed to provide an introduction to the process of combining a series of short live and recorded production elements into an ongoing

Directing Techniques for Various Formats

Figure 14–7
Rehearsal for a production
of the script, "It's a Date?"

sequence. The format is that of an extra long station break similar to one that would be viewed in the late afternoon hours. The techniques of production are much the same as those that apply to newscasts.

The coordination of roll cues for videotape inserts is one of the most difficult aspects of such a sequence. On network program feeds, a standard 10–second rolling period was originally used to ensure that tape machines had achieved stabilization of the electronic signal. Newer equipment has been developed that allows for an almost instant start. Although film is seldom rolled directly into a program any more (it generally has been transferred to tape in advance of the production), a 5–second advance rolling time for tape is the standard at most stations' commercials. News inserts are usually set up for a 1–second roll.

The 5–second delay between the roll cue and the precise moment at which the picture and sound must be put on the program line means that the command to roll tape must be given at an exact moment in the program con-

tinuum. That "five seconds to conclusion" point can be determined only by means of accurate timing of the preceding segment. If the preceding segment is copy done by a live announcer, the problem is somewhat easier. The usual procedure is for the director to time the announcer on the reading of the last eleven or twelve words of the copy. The timing generally will run a little under four seconds. By allowing for a 1–second margin of time to separate the announcer's words from the videotape audio, an accurate 5–second roll cue can be established.

Figure 14–8 shows the sequence of commands for the first part of the appendix D-5 exercise. Note the suggestion that the director reinforce the later VTR roll with an extra standby command prior to the beginning of the station break.

In preparation for the *full-facilities* station break production, each student should carefully plan a complete set of director's instructions (section 13.4) and write the commands in an abbreviated form on the left-hand

Directing Techniques for Various Formats

• • • • • • • • • • • • • • •

| DIRECTOR'S COMMANDS | | D-5 SCRIPT FOR FULL FACILITIES | Figure 14–8 |

Sequence of commands.

"READY TO FADE IN SLIDE" –:10
"STANDBY MUSIC AND ANNOUNCER"
"PREPARE VTR-2 WITH SOUND"

		VIDEO	AUDIO

"CUE MUSIC, FADE IN SLIDE" :00 SLIDE, "FRAME MUSIC: ESTABLISH, FIVE SECONDS AND
"STANDBY TO TAKE MUSIC UNDER" OF REFERENCE"

"MUSIC UNDER, CUE ANNOUNCER" :05 BOOTH ANNC (OFF CAMERA): Should the
"STANDBY TO ROLL TAPE" Government ban the sale and manufac
"STANDBY TO TAKE MUSIC OUT" Kenneth Anderson is joined by exper

"ROLL VTR-2" :10 sides of this important question on

"MUSIC OUT" Reference," Saturday afternoon at f

"DISSOLVE TO VTR-2, SOUND UP" :15 VIDEOTAPE SOUND ON TAPE
"STANDBY NEWS ANNOUNCER ON ONE" PUBLIC SERVICE
"PREPARE A DISSOLVE TO CAMERA ONE" :30

"CUE NEWS ANNOUNCER, DISSOLVE TO ONE" :45 STUDIO NEWS NEWS ANNC: Tonight on the six o'cl
 PROMO the latest statement by the Preside

 availability of Middle Eastern oil.

 from Washington that the plumbing i

The verbal commands printed in the left-hand column are what might actually be said by the director for the "full-facilities" production exercise (appendix D–5). In practice, the director would probably mark his or her script with the symbols discussed in section 13–4 (see figure 13–15).

side of the script, as in figure 14–8. The student should then mentally rehearse the whole sequence, using a watch or stopwatch to approximate the pressures of the actual time frame. During class production of the exercise, it is suggested that the sequence of materials in the script be rearranged to provide a variety of production experience.

Note: Artwork that can be used to produce the *Frame of Reference* slide is available at the end of appendix D. As an alternative, create your own title graphic on your studio's character generator. Videotaped PSAs (public-service announcements) for the demonstration

videotape inserts are available in most localities at no cost; television stations receive numerous public-service and promotional spots that they, in turn, often make available to teaching facilities.

Summary

This chapter has been concerned with various types of studio productions. In all television production, the director must be involved with several major activities during *preproduction planning*: script familiarization; facilities and equipment requests; assembling cast and crew; planning for specific production requirements (conferences, lighting and staging plots, costumes and props, graphics and videotape segments, drawing up a schedule); and script preparation (including shot sheets and other instructions).

Several different stages of *rehearsals* should be considered: pre-studio rehearsals; studio floor rehearsals (walk-through and technical); and control room rehearsals (start-and-stop, run-through, and dress rehearsals).

During the *production* phase, the director is ultimately the one in charge of the execution of the program. He or she must control his or her own physical anxieties; must give all commands clearly; must be aware of all control room monitors; and must adhere to all timing requirements.

After the production, the director is in charge of supervising the striking of the set and proper storage of all facilities. And if there is any postproduction editing to be taken care of, the director has several hours of work ahead.

In analyzing specific production requirements for the *musical number,* the *dramatic scene,* and the "full-facilities" *extended station break,* several points were emphasized: *camera blocking, staging, pacing,* and the importance of *preproduction planning.*

In the final chapter, we will take an extended look at the directing and technical considerations for single-camera field production.

Directing Techniques for Various Formats

Field Production

● ● ● ● ● ● ● ● ● ● ● ● ● ● ● ● ● ● ●

15

Most of what we have discussed in previous chapters has dealt with *live* or *live-on-tape* productions shot in a studio environment. This multiple-camera technique requires considerable preproduction planning and rehearsal of camera shot assignments. Program segments must be carefully timed and organized into their projected sequence. During the production, the task of the director is largely that of making a series of precise editing decisions. The technical director uses the switcher to connect the ongoing segments of the program by means of takes, dissolves, and special effects such as wipes and mattes. Prerecorded segments on disk, tape, and film are combined with the live camera inputs—all within the time disciplines of the continuous production operation. The spontaneous aspect of all of this gives an important sense of immediacy and realism.

However, many productions are not shot with a live multiple-camera studio technique. They are, instead, shot totally or partially in out-of-studio locations with one camera. This technique is often called "film style" because most motion pictures are shot with one camera that takes shots one by one from all the various angles employed in multiple-camera shoots. It is also referred to as **field production** because it takes place in the field rather than in a studio. Sometimes it is also called *remote* or *location* production.

There are numerous similarities between studio production and field production—mainly because much of the same equipment is used. A microphone is a microphone whether it is in a studio or at the scene of a fire. Pictures should be focused and well composed, and talent should maintain eye contact, whether in the studio or in the field. And yet there are many differences caused, to some degree, by the lack of control that exists outside of the studio. Many extraneous noises cannot be

Figure 15–1
Temporary network editing and operations control center. Hastily constructed in a hotel room, such temporary hookups are often the basis for covering fast-breaking stories in foreign countries. Note clocks and monitors for incoming feeds. (Photo courtesy of ABC News)

stopped; the sun and clouds cannot be controlled; rain cannot be held back; crowds often cannot be maneuvered to remain outside of the camera's shot. In addition, postproduction editing takes on a much greater role because the single-camera technique obviously does not utilize the switcher during the production; all editing is handled in the postproduction assemble and insert processes.

Another form of remote production is that which involves a van or remote mobile unit. This is a cross between studio production and field production in that multiple cameras and live switching are employed. The cameras are run through the switcher in the same way as they are in a studio, so the production techniques are very similar to those of studio shoots. In many instances, however, ambitious location productions far exceed the complexities of a studio program. In covering the 1988 Superbowl, for example, ABC used thirty-two

cameras—hand-held cameras on the sidelines, remote-controlled cameras mounted on the goal posts, one camera in the blimp, and so forth.

Some remote productions can be carefully planned and set up in advance. Others—especially when dealing with fast-breaking news coverage of international events, major catastrophes, or hostage situations—are quite extemporaneous, free-for-all experiences. Cameras and other pieces of equipment are hastily flown in or borrowed in foreign locales; power sources are tenuously patched together; personnel are pulled from other assignments; facilities have to be adapted to differing electrical and television standards; and space and air-conditioning and sanity are at a premium. Figure 15–1 is an actual improvised network setup, quickly lashed together in a crowded German hotel room to cover a terrorist attack.

Field Production

Figure 15–2
A Cinema Products 16-mm
film camera.

Cameras of this type were the workhorses for news coverage for many years. These cameras were capable of filming silent footage or recording sound on film.

Most multiple-camera remote shoots, however, are much more manageable affairs—three or four cameras at a political rally, a civic ceremony, a religious pickup, and similar occasions. Nevertheless, many of the elements—weather, lighting, extraneous noises—cannot be controlled; so the inconveniences of the outside world are much the same as for single-camera location production.

This chapter will concentrate on single-camera field production, looking at the similarities and differences between it and studio production. In that way this chapter will serve as a review of the rest of the book while, at the same time, introducing concepts that are crucial to this increasingly popular form of production—for news and public affairs, dramatic programs, music videos, documentaries, corporate videos, instructional programs, and so forth.

15.1 The Growth of Field Production

The importance of field production has been understood since the first days of television. In fact, as early as 1939, RCA had a mobile unit that consisted of two huge buses jammed with video equipment. But the main reason remote shooting did not occur to any great extent during the early days of television was because of the bulky equipment. It was simply unrealistic to transport the huge cameras and tripods and portable van-to-studio microwave links to the scene of a fire. Even with the advent of 2-inch tape recorders in the mid-1950s, the equipment was excessively cumbersome and often unreliable in the field.

Use of Film   Therefore, for the first two or three decades of television's history, film was used whenever something needed to be shot in the field. Film cameras and audiotape recorders were small in comparison to video equipment; the gear could be maneuvered to the site of an accident for a news story or into the back seat of a car for a chase scene in a drama. (See figure 15–2.) Film quality was adequate and, if you were in a rush, the film could be specially processed within a couple hours.

The Beginning of ENG/EFP   The first practical downsized and portable television equipment was developed in the early 1970s

Figure 15–3
A typical early ¾-inch
U-matic video recorder and
camera configuration.

and soon became known as *ENG* (electronic news gathering) equipment. It had this label because its quality did not match that of studio equipment, and therefore, it was used only for news that could get away with a grainier, less professional look. As the minicameras and portable recorders improved, the equipment became known as *EFP* (electronic field production) equipment. It was soon being used in segments of soap operas, documentaries, industrial productions, commercials, on-location interviews, and occasional dramas. The film-style technique of lighting and shooting individual shots began to take hold in video production.

Competing Formats   This ENG/EFP equipment has gone through a number of format changes. The first ENG equipment utilized ¾-inch videocassette recorders and cameras that were about half the size of common studio cameras but still employed the same three-tube configuration as conventional cameras. (See figure 15–3.) The units were lightweight enough that one strong person could carry a camera on the shoulder and wear

the VCR as a backpack. Another common configuration used two operators; one person would carry the camera and a second, walking in tandem, would operate the VCR. All the ¾-inch VCRs manufactured were of the same interchangeable format called *U-matic*. (See section 8.2.)

Competition for the ¾-inch format developed in the 1980s when the ½-inch format *camcorder* was introduced. This consisted of a minicamera and a ½-inch videocassette recorder built as one integrated unit. It had a technical quality considered at least equal to the ¾-inch U-matic format because the signal could go directly from the camera to tape without having to go through a wire connecting the two. In this way the camcorder was similar to a film camera that contained optics and recording medium (film instead of videotape) in one piece of equipment.

The two primary ½-inch systems developed for the broadcast industry are *Betacam* manufactured by Sony (not to be confused with the Sony home-VCR format, Betamax) and *M-format* offered by Panasonic and JVC. These systems are not compatible with each

Figure 15–4
Two ½-inch component cameras used extensively for ENG purposes in the industry today. *Top,* Sony's BVW 505 Betacam SP camcorder uses ½-inch metal particle tape (photo courtesy of Sony Corporation of America); *bottom,* Panasonic's M-II camcorder was used extensively in the 1988 Summer Olympics. (Photo courtesy of Panasonic Corporation)

other, although both are *CAV* (component analog video) recording formats (see sections 8.1 and 8.3).[1]

In the late 1980s, two new improvements on the ½-inch formats were introduced—the *Betacam SP,* which is compatible with the older Betacam, and the *M-II,* which is *not* compatible with the older M-format (see figure 15–4). The Betacam SP has four audio channels (plus control track and time code)—enabling someone, for example, to produce stereo audio in two different languages.

Adding to the profusion are the two older ½-inch formats that were originally developed for the consumer market—as opposed to the broadcast market—*Betamax* (shortened to "Beta") introduced by Sony, and *VHS* ("video home system") introduced by JVC. In this

1. The *component analog video* format records the luminance and chrominance signals separately, as opposed to the traditional *composite* recording system that combines them into one signal. This results in a much sharper picture on a relatively narrow (½-inch or 8mm) videotape format.

Figure 15–5
Panasonic's 3-chip color
camera, Model WV-F250, is
part of its S-VHS
camcorder.

Figure 15–6
Sony's Hi-Band 8mm
("Hi8") format camcorder,
the EVO-9100.

case, the Beta format eventually faltered in the marketplace and the VHS format survived.

As a result of the success of the consumer VHS system, JVC and Panasonic introduced *S-VHS* ("Super-VHS") (see figure 15–5), which they have promoted as being good enough to meet broadcasting quality. It, of course, is not compatible with anything else—except to a partial extent with the older consumer VHS format. Tapes recorded on regular VHS can be played back on Super-VHS recorders, but tapes recorded in the S-VHS format cannot be played on VHS recorders.

In the 1980s, several companies introduced new formats using a smaller 8mm or ¼-inch cassette. None of these succeeded until Sony introduced a whole new 8mm format called *Video-8*. An improved version of this, *Hi-Band 8mm*—soon known as "Hi8"—was introduced shortly thereafter. (See figure 15–6.) Not only are these units smaller and

Figure 15–7
Sony U-matic SP BVU-950
videocassette recorder.

more portable than any of the previous camcorder formats, they also provide a high-quality video signal.

Not to be outdone, the ¾-inch proponents introduced *U-matic SP* (figure 15–7), which is an improved version of the U-matic format—and is compatible with it.

If you are confused by all of this, so is your local TV station operator, corporate video producer, and school system. At this point, it is impossible to predict how the format wars will turn out. You should find out which format your local stations, local industries, and area schools are using for field production.

CCD Cameras　　Field cameras were quick to incorporate the *CCD* (chip) pickup devices (section 5.2), so that now most professional field cameras have CCDs and just about all consumer camcorders use them. Without the bulky tubes, the CCD cameras have become increasingly smaller and more lightweight. At the same time, they have become more dependable, easier to use, and more durable

under a variety of adverse field conditions (extreme lighting shifts, bad weather, and rough handling).

All in all, single-camera field production has experienced a tumultuous and prolific growth—an electronic explosion that cannot help but accelerate into the future.

15.2　Conceptualization and Preproduction Planning

Before a program or segment of a program is taped on location, it should be conceived in its entirety. How each individual shot is planned and executed is dependent upon how it will be utilized in the final edited program. In other words, both planning and camera work must be carried out with the eventual editing process constantly in mind.

Principal camera work on a project should only be started after completion of a script or at least after a detailed outline of shot continuity is carefully planned. More than one student production team has found that all of those great ideas they thought of back in the studio just seemed to disappear into thin air once they arrived at the shooting location. The very act of putting things down on paper is an important test of the feasibility of the operational plan.

Fundamental Elements

The 3– to 5–minute mini-documentary is a staple of both local and network newscasts; it serves well to illustrate how the remote shoot should be conceptualized. Other types of program material—fast-breaking news stories or soap opera scenes—have slight variations in structure, but they demand the same kind of preproduction discipline and careful forethought.

With the *mini-doc,* the production disciplines are those of background research, balanced presentations, and thorough preproduction planning. Even with a scheduled air date, there is lead time to put together all of the essential ingredients. This format borrows much from educational and industrial films and tapes as well as from the traditional film documentaries of the past sixty years. In rather general terms, the following are the main production elements.

Host/Reporter/Narrator There is usually a central figure who is used both on- and off-camera to accomplish several important things. This person sets up the basic background information. The audience must initially be made aware of what the presentation is all about and what they can expect to learn. When the information is complex or has negative connotations, the host/reporter/narrator must be viewed by the audience in an authoritative yet neutral perspective. He or she introduces new segments of information and gives them meaning in terms of what is to come. Ultimately there must be a summary of material presented and a conclusion as to its overall meaning to the audience. This is usually done in the form of a verbal and visual recapitulation of the highlights of material presented. Used properly, the host/reporter/narrator figure lends an important personal element that can give both credibility and continuity to the content.

The Actuality News people refer to material that comes directly from an event or a situation as an *actuality.* Few news stories are complete without at least one of two essential ingredients of the actuality: the *scene* itself (the fire in progress, the site of a plane crash, or even the lobby of the bank long after the robbers have fled) and the *interview* (with the citizen eyewitness or some authority figure such as a fire chief or corporate officer). As the very name implies, a documentary—whether for broadcast, industrial training, or classroom presentation—needs the same sort of device to establish the credibility of the information. Productions designed for instructional purposes often will have the authority figure assume a dominant role. The actuality may be the operator of a certain piece of equipment on location in the factory itself. In medical productions, the doctors and nurses may provide the bulk of the information presented.

Titles and Graphics It is often important that a production and its subsequent segments be carefully titled. A few well-chosen words that can be quickly read by the audience can be very efficient in establishing the main concept of the production, its location and position in time, and its basic subdivisions. Name and title identifications by *lower-third* keys (in the lower third of the screen) are crucial. A good deal of other important information can be presented by means of graphic displays—either full frame or keyed over portions of the video. Numerical relationships are very difficult to grasp if they are only heard.

They can have a very strong impact when presented on a bar graph or pie chart in which the drawings become a visual analog of the relative value of the numbers. Special effects animation and computer-generated graphics have reduced the time-cost factor that previously limited the use of artwork visuals.

Stock Footage   When there is no cost-effective way of shooting footage that is essential to a presentation, most professional producers turn to commercial sources. The price is high (a minimum fee of $300 is not uncommon), but those companies that supply stock footage have a large supply of videotape and film to cover a wide variety of situations. News departments that used to discard their old news stories now carefully index them on computers and file everything they shoot for possible later use. Students who cannot afford professional help should first examine the resources of their own university. Large companies that turn out numerous public relations films will often allow use of portions of footage if credits are given. The copyright laws that govern the use of all stock footage are rather strict and should always be observed.

Musical Score   Music, carefully used, can add an important dimension to almost every kind of visual presentation. Here, also, there are commercial libraries where one can pay for the use of copyrighted material.[2] The scoring of most professional films and tapes is usually done by production houses that specialize in the selection and editing of a complete musical background for a project. Students, however, can take advantage of the fact that after a specified period, musical recordings and compositions become part of the public domain and can be used without charge

in most cases. Television students at universities also may have easy access to music students who are often willing to compose and record original music in return for a credit.

The Scripting Process

Taking all of the main production elements into consideration—the host, the actuality scene and interview(s), the needed graphics, the availability of stock footage, the music, and so forth—the producer/director/writer must think in terms of the entire scripting process. Depending upon the complexity and sophistication of the production, several steps may be followed in preparing the final shooting script.

Outlining   A rough draft or an outline of the content should certainly be drawn up at the outset. This should include a detailed statement of general and specific objectives for the program. Try to answer the questions: What do I really want to accomplish in this production? What content elements do I have to include to meet those objectives?

Storyboard   Perhaps a storyboard may be essential to your production. Lay out in cartoon or visual outline form what every shot should look like. This will force you to think pictorially and establish visual continuity for the entire shoot. These rough sketches, no matter how crude your artistic ability, will help immeasurably in setting up your shots once you are out in the field. It also facilitates determination of precise inpoints and outpoints for your later editing. (See figure 15–8.)

The Final Script   Depending upon the nature of the remote shoot, your actual script may take any one of several forms. (See section 13.4.) It may be a *fully scripted* dramatic scene. It may be a *semi-scripted* demonstration at the factory. Or it may be a *rundown sheet* for an interview. The important thing is

2. Many commercial sources—such as APM's Broadcast One of Hollywood, Media General of Memphis, and Sound Ideas of Toronto—all have extensive production music libraries available on CDs.

Figure 15–8
Sample of simple
storyboard.

TITLE CARD
V.O. ANNC:
... *Brian Ham*

LS: CALABASAS
ROCKET CO.
V.O. HOST:
... *in this city*

MS: HOST IN
PARKING LOT
... *Today's
concerns*

MS: VICE-PRES
IN OFFICE
V.O. HOST:
... *Top policy*

CU: LOOMIS
(INTERVIEW
SEGMENT)

CU. HOST
(INTERVIEW
SEGMENT)

MS: MISSILE
INSERT SHOT
... *in this case*

MS: HOST IN
CORRIDOR
(GIVES CLOSE)

TITLE CARD
AND CREDITS

A series of rough sketches, plotting every camera
shot, will serve as a guide for both recording and
editing.

that you do come up with something on paper
that indicates all the important audio and video
elements. Every word of an interview segment
obviously cannot be written out in advance, but
it should be outlined. Important introductions
and transitions should be scripted before ar-
riving to set up equipment.

Breakdown Sheets   One important aid
you may find helpful is the breakdown sheet.
If you are planning to shoot a complex production that involves a number of individual
scenes shot in different locations, breakdown
sheets are indispensable. They list—for each
scene to be shot—a synopsis of the scene, the
location, the people who will be needed, the
props, and any special considerations. (See
figure 15–9.)

Program material in extensive remotes is
almost always shot out of order, so you use your
breakdown sheets to juggle your production
shooting and determine the order in which
scenes will be shot. Usually the primary ele-

Figure 15–9
The breakdown sheet lists
all of the talent, crew,
facilities, and other
elements needed for every
scene.

BREAKDOWN SHEET

Program: PARK MINI-DOC

Location: Park with a slide & swing

Segment Number: 3

Synopsis: Mary Ellen talks of the need for greater

safety standards for playground equipment

Cast	Props	Equipment
Mary Ellen Thomas	Jump rope	½" portable VCR & camera
Jason	Tricycle	Reflector
Tiffany		Mike & Cable

Crew	Special Needs	Comments
Tom	Mike cable must be able to reach the slide	Should be shot at a time when children are there
Susan		
Tasha		

Field Production

ment for determining shooting order is location; all scenes occurring in the park will be shot at one time, even though they will be interspersed at various points throughout the program. However, sometimes the primary element for determining shooting order is the talent; if someone who is crucial to the production can only work one day, all of the shots involving that person will have to be shot on that one day, even though this means traveling all over town. On rare occasions, shooting order may be determined by a prop; if you need to rent a vintage automobile, you might want to shoot all scenes with it on one day so that you can cut down on rental fees.

Shooting Schedule   Once the breakdown sheets have been made and assembled in order, a shooting schedule can be developed. This lists everything that is to be shot during each day, giving the description, the cast, and the location. It is used throughout the shooting and, of course, must be revised when production gets behind schedule. (See figure 15–10.)

You can devise your own lists, forms, schedules, or pictures to help yourself organize your material. Like the major multiple-camera studio production, every hour spent in preproduction planning and scripting will save countless hours of valuable crew time on the shoot. Careful script preparation and preproduction planning are perhaps the most crucial *disciplines* involved in single-camera field production.

15.3   Producing and Directing

Producing a remote shoot is similar to producing a studio program in that all elements must be in the right place at the right time. However, this is usually much more complex for a remote shoot because everything is out of its usual habitat. Equipment logistics, travel arrangements, power supplies, coordination of props and talent—all involve extraordinary consideration. One of the crucial initial steps you must undertake is the preproduction location survey.

SHOOTING SCHEDULE

Program: ___PARK MINI-DOC_____

Date	Time	Description	Cast	Location
4/20	1:00	Mary Ellen discusses playground equipment and safety needs (seg # 3)	Mary Ellen Thomas Jason Sorkin Tiffany Barr	Alcove Park
4/20	2:30	Mary Ellen discusses need for flowers (seg # 7)	Mary Ellen Thomas Mr. Hamilton	Patterson Park
4/22	11:00	Interview with park supervisor (seg # 2)	Mary Ellen Thomas Dr. Belling	Dr. Belling's office, Park building
4/22	1:00	Interview with park planners (seg #9)	Mary Ellen Thomas Mr. Loomis Mrs. Robbins	Planning offices, Park Building

Figure 15–10
The shooting schedule is indispensable for coordinating location shoots on a major production.

Location Surveys

The shooting-day production schedule should be drawn up only after you, as the producer (preferably accompanied by the director and camera operator), have made a personal inspection of all shooting sites. If you shoot in a studio regularly, you are aware of the location of power outlets, the positions of the cameras, the types of curtains and set pieces available, the location of lighting instruments, and other similar information. With each remote shoot, these elements are different.

It may not be possible, of course, to check out the location for all fast-breaking news stories. However, some places where news is likely to occur, such as the city council chambers or the police station, can be "cased" ahead of time and notes made so that crews that need to go there have some idea of what they will face.

But for productions planned in advance, thorough preproduction will pay big dividends at production time. Usually you know approximately where you will be doing the shoot, and you go mainly to see the lay of the land. If, for example, you are interviewing a doctor about a new medical breakthrough, you will want to shoot at the hospital where the instruments used for the procedure will be available. Sometimes, however, you will need to scout locations to find the most ideal spot for your purposes. If you are shooting a piece about the need for more parks, for example, you might have to go to several parks before you find one similar to the type being advocated.

One of the first things you should do as part of a remote survey is obtain the name of a person who is in charge—someone who gives you the permission to shoot at any particular facility and someone you can contact when you arrive with equipment, someone to turn to fast when any unexpected problems crop up. Who has the keys? Whom do you contact when you trip a circuit breaker?

You may wish to draw up a floor plan of the location. Take Polaroid shots of the scene to share with other crew members and to remind you of important details as you plan specific shots. What about transportation and parking?

Determine ahead of time where you will position your camera, VCR, mike, and lights. Find out how much power is available, what plugs operate on which circuits, whether or not you will need extension cords. One broadcaster tells the story of plugging in his equipment at a live remote sports coverage; but unknown to him the only outlets conveniently available were on the same circuit as the popcorn popper. Sure enough, every time the popcorn popper kicked on, his cameras, recorder, and mike went dead. All the outlets had been checked out ahead of time—but no one had thought to try them out with the popcorn poppers operating.

If you are shooting outdoors, or if you are shooting indoors with any natural light, you will want to scout the location at the same time of day that you will be doing the shoot so that you can see exactly what you will have to deal with in terms of sunlight, shadows, and windows.

What about possible interruptions and conflicts? Do scheduled events at the location conflict with the shoot? Heavy equipment starting up? Airplanes taking off? If you are shooting on campus, for example, will the end of a class period send large numbers of people walking through the shot? What about those campus chimes? Make note of these items so you are not in the middle of a take when any of these noises occur. Listen for continuous extraneous noises such as an air conditioner or telephones ringing that will interfere with your audio. Try to obtain permission to turn them off while you are shooting. If you cannot, plan to work with more directional and less sensitive mikes closer to the talent.

Make a comprehensive checklist of everything to be taken care of on the shoot day: an inventory of all equipment; all props and costumes; all necessary permissions and clearances; and so forth. Do you need to arrange for field maintenance? What backup gear should be taken?

Production Procedures

While many production and directing principles are common to both studio programs and location shoots, there are special considerations for the field production.

Rehearsals   Rehearsing for a remote shoot should involve the same procedures as rehearsing for a studio program (section 14.1). However, you often do not have the luxury of rehearsal on a remote—which suggests that you substitute other creative alternatives. Can you at least have a walk-through with the primary talent—to familiarize him or her with the actual location? How about rehearsing in a substitute location? Rehearsal hall? Your living room?

The Production Shoot   On the day of production, many events occur that have nothing in common with studio production. First of all, the equipment must be packed and taken somewhere. For this, it is essential to double-check that everything you need is packed and is in working order. If you get to a location site without any videotape, you are in big trouble. Likewise, if you have a faulty cable, you cannot go into the back room and find another one.

Slating and Taping   The taping procedure, itself, is quite different from that in a studio. If a camera has a color bar generator, at least thirty seconds of color bars should be recorded on the tape before anything else. This is to allow you or your engineer time to adjust controls that will enable the tape to be played back with proper color balance at your later editing sessions.

Each shot needs to be *slated*. As soon as the VCR is up to speed, one of the crew members should hold a cardboard sign, small chalkboard, or professionally prepared slate in front of the camera. This should indicate the scene number, take number, director's name, and description of the shot (section 9.5). While this written slate is being taped, the person holding it should read the information into an open mike so that both a video and audio slate are recorded. (See figure 15–11.) Then, with the camera still rolling, the director should say "Action," and after waiting several beats, the talent should begin.

After the segment is taped, all talent on camera should hold their positions for at least five seconds while the camera continues to roll. These beginning and ending procedures are crucial for the editing function in that they provide both the necessary sync information and adequate pads for maintaining proper pace. (See chapter 9.)

Someone, usually the production assistant or script supervisor, should keep a careful *production log* of every shot; this should include the scene number, take number, description, length of shot, and any special comments. (See figure 15–12.)

Shot Variety

Probably the most important production technique associated with field shooting is that of making sure enough varied shots are taken—mainly so that they can be used, if necessary, as cutaways during editing (to avoid jump cuts). If, for example, the taping involves an interview, the single camera will be on the guest throughout the interview. After the interview is over, the interviewer should be taped asking the questions over again. Reaction shots of both

Figure 15–11
The slate should contain all of the pertinent identifying information that will be needed for later editing.

Figure 15–12
Excerpt from sample production log.

PRODUCTION _Campus Parking_
SHOOTING DATE _8 Nov_

PAGE _2_
PRODUCER _Evans_

Slate	Count In	Count Out
Univ. Sec. Off. Seg 3 Shot 4 Take 3	Lt. Jones. 253 "My Job	270... this problem."
Sec. Off. Intro. Meyer Seg 3 Shot 1 Tk 1	275 "Lt. Jones ...	287... no parking."
——————— Cassette #2 ———————		
Parking Lot student #1 Seg 4 Shot 1 Tk 1	025 "Well everyday....	037... no spaces."
Parking lot student #1 Seg 4 Shot 1 Tk 2	045 "Everday....	051... really mad."
Parking lot student #2 Seg 4 Shot 2 Tk 1	059 "I don't see	071 ... parking ticket."

the interviewer and guest listening should also be taped. And close-ups of anything the guest talked about should be recorded. Take a long shot of the location with the two people appearing to be talking. Tape some over-the-shoulder shots and zoom-in reaction shots. In general, record as many different shots as you think you might conceivably be able to use in editing.

Dramatic scenes almost always include at least a cover shot of everyone involved, close-ups of each person delivering his or her lines, and reaction shots of each person.

Of course, this formalized procedure is not always possible—especially with fast-breaking news. If a production crew has an opportunity to record a criminal being apprehended, you certainly would not want to take a chance on missing the crucial action while you prepare a proper slate.

Aesthetics and Continuity   Most of the aesthetic principles regarding studio camera shots (sections 6.2, 9.7, and 13.1) certainly apply in remote shoots. However, some of them take on an even increased importance. For example, the concepts of *continuity* and *axis of action* must be watched even more closely in a remote because so many shots are taped out of order.

The producer and director must be able to envision shots that will be edited together even though they may not be taped immediately after each other. For example, if a long shot of someone running is recorded before lunch and a close-up of the person running is shot after lunch, the camera must not cross the long shot's 180–degree line when it is used for the close-up. Otherwise, when the two shots are cut together, the person will appear to change direction.

In a complicated shoot, such as a drama, a production assistant or script supervisor has the full-time job of making notes about each scene—what the actors were wearing, where certain props were set, in which direction the action was flowing, how heads were tilted, and which hand actors used to make certain gestures. Then when scenes that are to be intercut are shot several days later, all elements can be matched.

Postproduction

The directorial role during postproduction is obviously greater for remote shoots than for studio productions. In fact, if a program is truly live or live-on-tape, there *is* no postproduction. But material shot single-camera film style must be edited. In fact, the actual show is made in the editing room. Because of the generally uncontrolled conditions during shooting, post-production can be quite a tedious prospect. It can also be quite rewarding, however, if pre-production and production have been carried out effectively—and the potential for a successful program is apparent.

All of these items make producing and directing a remote more difficult than a live-on-tape studio production. But there are several obvious compensating advantages of the remote shoot. A much more realistic production can be obtained from shooting on location. If preproduction is properly executed, more care can be taken on the remote; each shot can be set up individually and taped a number of times. And editing decisions are not made instantly; therefore, the finished product can be edited much more carefully and creatively.

15.4 The Production Crew

Fewer people are usually needed for a remote production than for a studio production. There is, for example, only one camera operator and there are no technical directors or projectionists. Stage managers and A.D.'s do not exist, as such, for location shoots. However, many remotes require someone to handle continuity, the slate, and the log. In a way, this person—often a production assistant or script supervisor—functions as a combination stage manager/A.D. with slightly different responsibilities.

There may be considerable variation in what is actually expected of a person who is functioning within a given job title. Sometimes the jobs of producer and director are handled by one person. That person is the producer for the preproduction part of the show and then becomes the director for production and postproduction. The director's job is different because he or she cannot give commands (zoom in, pan left) during taping—they would be picked up on the mike. Shot composition must be worked out ahead of time by the director and camera operator.

The crew structure for single-camera field productions may range anywhere from two to ten or more people—depending upon the budget, union restrictions, and scope of the assignment. Most production groups divide their areas of responsibility into something like the following job descriptions. (See also chapter 12.)

1. *Producer:* Overall financial and creative responsibility. In charge of pulling the total production together. The person who makes it possible for everyone else to do their job at the highest level of efficiency.
2. *Writer/Researcher:* Basic source of background information for scripting and graphics. Pulls final script together.
3. *Director:* In charge of field production from a creative standpoint. In charge of on-air talent directions and all camera instructions. Usually responsible for edited version of project.
4. *Production assistant:* Works directly with either director or producer or both. Keeps production notes, log shots, script changes, continuity notes, and other paperwork. May also serve as technical assistant if needed.
5. *Camera operator:* Chief technical person. Usually involved in all technical decisions. In charge of lighting. Functions as video recording engineer.
6. *Sound operator:* Handles all audio recording. Serves as technical backup. May help out with lighting.
7. *Editor:* Responsible for final assembly of the finished program, including a strong creative input. Actually controls the editing process.

With larger budgets the crew structure will increase. Assistants are added to some of the described positions. Lighting will often require a separate person in any of the more complicated types of production. On the other hand, when the organization is small, each person may wear several hats. A small-format or student production group (figure 15–13) might have the following configuration.

1. *Producer,* also writer/researcher.
2. *Director,* also editor.
3. *Camera operator,* also editing assistant, maybe lighting.
4. *Production assistant,* also sound operator, maybe lighting.

Other crew positions are doubled up sometimes for lack of budget or for lack of space. For example, one person may handle audio and VCR. The producer/director may also serve as camera operator. Starting in the late 1980s, some professional ENG operations started using one-person news crews because the camcorder could be operated by one person.

As with most task-oriented working groups, an efficient operation must have a clearly established plan for areas of responsibility and authority. Whatever the size of the crew, each individual member of the shoot should have a clear idea of his or her responsibilities—but with the understanding that flexible working arrangements may find each one helping out with other jobs.

One of the absolute essentials that all crew members on a field shoot must handle carefully is cleanup. If a crew member carelessly leaves a mike cable on the floor of the studio, someone else will probably find it later and put it away. But if a mike cable is left in the middle of a park, it will quickly disappear. Everything must be conscientiously disassembled, coiled, cleaned up, stowed away, and neatly packed—in part as a courtesy to the next people who use the equipment and, in part, because such care adds to the life of the equipment.

Figure 15–13
This field production student crew worked out its own configuration of assignments under the leadership of the producer. (Photo courtesy of Amy Phillips)

Remote shoots are often more fun than studio programs simply because they are in unusual locations and they offer interesting challenges. But nevertheless, the professional discipline needed on a remote production probably exceeds the discipline needed in a studio situation.

15.5 Talent on Location

Most of what applies to talent in a studio production also is true for a remote shoot. Sincerity, eye contact, and proper clothing are important to any television performer. Constantly scratching an ear will be as distracting in front of the local courthouse as it will be in front of a studio talk show set. (See chapter 11.)

However, in many ways performing at a remote site is more difficult than being on camera in a studio. For starters, there will be no teleprompter and probably no one to hold cue cards—which means talent must handle their own notes or script and they must know their lines and material well. There also are fewer crew members, which means fewer people to help out with talent requests.

Nonsequential Shooting

One of the hardest parts of remote shooting, though, is that scenes are shot out of order. This can create continuity problems and difficulties for performers.

Dramatic Continuity Sometimes it is necessary for an actor to switch emotions on and off for the convenience of a shooting

Figure 15–14
Reporters and interviewers often have to tape reaction shots after the interviewed guest has departed.

(*Left*) During the interview the single camera would have been behind the male interviewer, focusing on the female guest answering questions.

(*Right*) After the guest has departed, the camera should be repositioned to shoot the interviewer repeating the same questions for later editing.

schedule. Often two scenes will be shot back to back because they are at the same location, but the emotional content of two shots may be diametrically opposed. An actor might be called upon to portray the emotion felt about the tragic death of a friend two days before the death of the friend has been acted out.

Even within one scene, lines are sometimes shot out of order. When actors' close-ups are shot, they deliver their lines often without benefit of cues and other lines in the rest of the scene. Frequently the characters they are supposedly talking to are not even on the set. Imagine professing mad passionate love—to a camera.

Of course, there are many professional actors (chiefly those who are experienced in film) who have learned to perform in this way. But crew members must let them have their "space" so that they can build up to the required emotions. This is part of the reason that stand-ins are used for camera rehearsals. The stand-in can concentrate on changing positions to meet technical and lighting requirements while the actor is off the set concentrating on getting into character and building emotion.

Nondramatic Productions   Taping out of order is a problem for talent in nondramatic shoots also. Because the camera is on the guest during an interview, the interviewer's face will not be seen. This means that after the interview has been completed, reverse-angle shots must be taped of the interviewer asking the questions over again. This is often very difficult for the interviewer. He or she must sit there and earnestly ask questions of a camera lens—because the person being interviewed has already departed. (See figure 15–14.)

This brings up a related ethical problem. How much can the wording of the questions change between what was asked during the actual interview and what is asked on the reverse-angle shots taped later? The answer should be, "Not much." If the question is changed significantly, the guest's answer may take on an entirely different meaning. Networks have policies regarding the need to keep the questions the same. Because of this, a continuity person should listen to the original interview and jot down the exact wording of the questions that are asked. An audiotape recorder, of course, can serve the same purpose. Then the interviewer can review the questions before the reverse-angle shots are taped.

Field Production

Sometimes even more difficult than asking questions after the fact is the need to react after the fact. In almost all single-camera remote interviews, shots of the interviewer listening and reacting need to be recorded—usually after the guest has departed—so that they can be edited into the interview to prevent jump cuts. (See section 9.7.) This requires the interviewer/reporter to just sit there looking at an empty chair and smiling or frowning every once in awhile; this is a difficult acting job—especially for novices. People tend to break up into laughter or to exaggerate movements such as nods of the head.

Equally awkward can be just standing doing nothing for the five seconds or so needed at the beginning and end of each take. Inexperienced talent will often lose composure during that time and ruin the take.

Uncooperative Talent

A common problem in many *actuality* programs are people who do not want to be on television. Usually these are people who are in the news in a negative or controversial way and, as a result, try to avoid being interviewed. The degree to which these people should be pursued depends on the nature of the assignment, the context and reputation of the program, and the personalities of all involved.

Some people do not want to be on TV because they know they come across poorly. If these people are not crucial to obtaining the message, they should not be used—they may be self-fulfilling prophecies. And certainly, there is little justification for pursuing an interview with the grieving relative of a person who has just been killed in a tragedy.

Unwanted Talent   At the other end of the spectrum is the common problem of unwanted talent. Random people do not wander into a studio very often, but when a shoot is being conducted on a city street, the curious

are bound to appear. If a drama is being taped, crew members (or off-duty law officers) are often hired for crowd control purposes—placed at the edges of the scene to keep onlookers out of the shot.

But there is no guaranteed way to keep people out of shots that involve fast-breaking news stories. Egomaniacs and self-proclaimed clowns who strut around in the background and make faces (or obscene gestures) at the camera can be a real nuisance. If the director deals with these folks in a firm but pleasant manner, such behavior can sometimes be modified.

15.6   Sets and Graphics

Graphics are essentially nonexistent in actual remote shooting. Some consumer cameras have built-in character generators so that graphics can be included during taping, but these are generally used only for slating/identification purposes. Occasionally, an on-set wall chart may be shot as a cutaway, but it is not likely to be designed for television, so the camera operator must frame it as well as possible under the circumstances.

If actual physical charts or illustrations are to be included in a program, they are better shot in a studio where lighting can be controlled. Most graphics, of course, are computer-generated (see sections 10.6 and 10.7)—graphs, charts, titles and lower-third keys (for name identification). All of these will be incorporated into the program during the postproduction editing.

Sets, as such, do not usually exist either. The main reason you go on a location shoot is to obtain realistic scenery and settings that are not possible with constructed sets in a studio. However, when you are scouting to find proper locations, keep in mind the pictorial design elements discussed in sections 10.1 and 10.2. For example, yellows and reds are always warm colors, and greens and blues are always

Figure 15–15
Hallway to be considered
for a location shoot.

How many problems can you spot as you plan on using this hallway for a remote production? How will the mixture of indoor and outdoor light affect color temperature and white balance settings? What can be done about the potential glare? How will the automatic iris function as the talent works along the corridor—moving in and out of extremely bright spots? What will be the safest angles to use?

cool colors—whether they are in a studio or out in the country. Whether you are shooting indoors or out, the principles of balance and mass, lines and angles, always apply.

Unless you find some very cooperative people or you are willing to pay a great deal of money, you cannot usually change much in a location setting. You can clean up someone's desk so that the clutter will not be visually distracting; but you cannot readily change the color of the walls, the location of trees, the intensity of the fire burning a building, or the placement of windows.

When shooting interior scenes, windows do present particular problems in that they cause glare and interfere with proper lighting. The best advice is to avoid shooting into windows. This, of course, is one reason to scout a location ahead of time. However, it may not always be possible to avoid a passing shot of a window; perhaps it is absolutely necessary to pan with the talent while he or she walks across

a room, passing in front of a window. In such a situation, you should consider disabling the automatic iris control; set the *f*-stop manually for the best interior (nonwindow) lighting and keep it consistent as the talent passes in front of the window. This will result in an overexposed background through the window, but the alternative (if the automatic iris is left on) is to allow the talent to turn to a silhouette when passing in front of the window.

In one sense, the setting is much easier (and less expensive) to deal with in a remote location than in a studio because very little, if anything, needs to be constructed. However, an improper setting can totally destroy the concept and atmosphere of your program. (See figure 15–15.) You can wind up with the wrong colors, architecture, period furnishings, traffic flow, backgrounds, and so forth. Therefore, you may have to spend many hours scouting and searching for just the right setting.

Field Production

Figure 15–16
Network news crew
covering a still very active
forest fire. Notice the wind
shield on the shotgun mike
in the foreground. (Photo
courtesy of ABC news)

Real locations are invariably much "busier" than studio sets; they will have a lot of elements that are extraneous to what you will be taping—furniture, props, wall coverings, table objects, appliances, and so forth. As a result, you must pay particular attention to make sure you do not wind up with shots that have light switches or flower pots that look like they are growing out of someone's head.

15.7 Field Audio

As with other technical components, many of the elements of field production audio are the same as those for studio audio; any differences are caused primarily by the uncontrollable elements of the outside world. As a starting point, ask the same questions concerning frequency, pickup pattern, impedance, and usage categories for both studio and remote productions (sections 3.1 and 3.2).

Mike Characteristics Sometimes the answers are different, however. Generally, microphones need to be more directional for remote locations because of all the extraneous noise. By the same token, mikes that are less sensitive (and therefore need to be located closer to the talent) are desired because they will pick up less of the background noise.

Also, because of the transportation jolts and rough handling that field equipment is subjected to, mikes for remote shoots usually are of a more rugged design—*dynamic* rather than *condenser*. Quality and frequency response often have to be sacrificed for dependability and ruggedness.

Mike Location In the category of "limited-movement mikes," fishpole, wireless, and shotgun microphones tend to be used more frequently in the field than boom mikes; huge perambulator booms simply are not practical outside of the studio. If mikes need to be hidden for some reason, difficulties can arise because no "set" has been constructed with the provision for hiding mikes. Foam or sponge wind shields also will often have to be used in windy or noisy areas (see figure 15–16).

Field Production

At times you may want to attach the microphone to the camera in order to eliminate the need for someone holding it. This is usually not a good idea, however, because the camera, of necessity, is located at some distance from the person talking. Thus, the mike will have to be of a more sensitive design and will therefore pick up noises close to the camera much more efficiently than it picks up the person talking. As a general rule, in the field, microphones should always be as close as possible to the people talking—closer than in studio production—because of all the background and extraneous noise.

Control Equipment   The sophisticated control room equipment that produces clean, well-balanced sound is not available at a remote site. There are no patch bays, equalizers, or separate audiotape recorders. Usually there is not even a board—just a "ballpark" meter and some cheap headphones. Audio on a remote is only transduced and recorded—and usually monitored. Channeling, mixing, amplifying, and shaping (section 2.2) are all accomplished in postproduction. And yet great care must be taken to keep recording levels within a consistent range so that they can be matched when edited.

Automatic Gain Control   Use of *automatic gain control* (AGC) is not always the solution to this problem of keeping audio levels within a consistent range. This is because AGC can be the cause of another serious sound problem encountered with outdoor audio. The AGC equipment automatically amplifies whatever sound is picked up by the mike; therefore, when no one is speaking, the level of the background noise is automatically amplified—producing a hissing or roaring effect.

Because there is a built-in delay factor of one second or so, the effect is most noticeable at the beginning of segments or during long pauses. Attempts to erase this unwanted sound involve the risk of upcutting program audio. One solution may be to have the announcer say a few words right up to a second or so prior to the beginning of your program audio.

Audio balance is particularly difficult if two people are talking and one has a very soft voice while the other has a booming projection. AGC cannot completely compensate. Sometimes the better solution is to record each person through his or her individual mike onto a separate track and then try to match the volumes in postproduction.

Audio Tracks   Most ¾-inch videotape recorders include two *linear* audio tracks, usually identified as *channel 1* and *channel 2*. Channel 2 is generally the better one to use for recording because on most common formats it is located as an inside track on the videotape. Channel 1 is at the edge of the tape, so it is more subject to any distortion if the tape wrinkles even slightly. Also, as noted in section 9.8, channel 1 is often used to record a separate time code, so many facilities routinely use only channel 2 for audio. However, if separate audio sources (such as loud and weak voices) need to be recorded in the field separately but simultaneously, to be mixed later, the two channels should be used.

Many of the ½-inch and 8mm formats are capable of recording sound diagonally, in the same manner that the picture is recorded. One method of recording sound this way is referred to as *hi-fi* and the other is called *PCM* (pulse code modulation). Both of these methods allow for high-quality stereo recording and playback. With hi-fi recording, the sound is recorded with the picture and cannot be separated from it during editing. With PCM, the sound is recorded on its own real estate and can be separated for editing purposes (see figure 15–17).

Sometimes you will be able to choose whether you want to record linear, hi-fi, PCM, or some combination of them. When you have

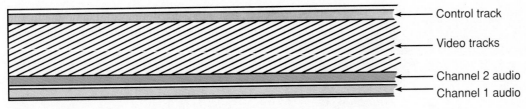

— Control track

— Video tracks

— Channel 2 audio
— Channel 1 audio

(a) two linear tracks are available on the U-matic format;

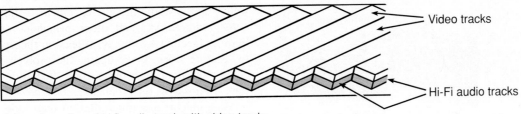

— Video tracks

— Hi-Fi audio tracks

(b) configuration of hi-fi audio track with video track;

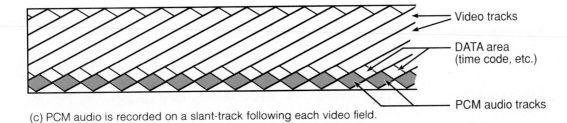

— Video tracks

— DATA area
(time code, etc.)

— PCM audio tracks

(c) PCM audio is recorded on a slant-track following each video field.

Figure 15–17
Three different ways that audio is recorded on field systems.

options, you should note how the audio was recorded because this information will be needed when editing begins.

If you have a large number of different audio sources that need to be recorded at the same time, you will need to take a portable audio board on location with you. You can then feed several mikes through the board, their levels can be set individually, and this mixdown can be recorded on the videotape on one of the linear channels or on the hi-fi or PCM track. However, setting up such an audio board takes additional space and time, both of which are often unavailable on a remote shoot.

Wildtrack   Audio operators on location should always make sure they record some separate *wildtrack* sound—background sound from the location recorded with no voices. Sometimes this is for a specific purpose. For example, a narrator may be standing next to a machine that is important to the story line but the machine has a distinctive sound. In the final edited program, shots that include the machine are to have a voice-over narration, which is to be recorded later in the studio. If the director wants to have the sound of the machine as a part of the background under the narration, then a wildtrack of that sound must be recorded for a later audio mix.

At other times the wildtrack sound is just general background noise that can be used to cover abrupt transitions during postproduction editing. Good sound operators will make

Figure 15–18
This Lowel portable lighting kit contains the lights and supporting equipment needed for effective field production. (Photo courtesy of Lowel-Light)

a practice of recording numerous pieces of wildtrack sound as protection against unforeseen editing problems.

Extraneous Noise   The audio operator must also listen carefully to the sound that is occurring and being recorded while a take is being shot. The human brain subconsciously filters out unwanted sound in ordinary live conditions. The noise of an airplane flying overhead often goes unnoticed by two people engaged in conversation; they effectively hear only each other. But this *selective attention* principle does not work with videotaped presentations. An unnoticed airplane recorded on an audio track will come through loud and clear on playback. For that reason, the audio person must listen intently and stop production if an unwanted noise is too evident. Any differences in the levels of background noise will become very obvious when different shots are assembled together in the editing process.

In many ways, a person operating audio on a remote shoot must have a disciplined "feel" for audio. He or she must have enough experience to know how something will sound

in the final edited program even though it is next to impossible to envision that sound during the taping.

15.8   Field Lighting

The basic *three-point lighting* approach (section 4.5) is appropriate for remote shoots as well as in the studio. Likewise, *contrast ratio, color temperature,* and other principles of lighting (section 4.2) apply, at least in theory, to location work. Once again, the problems come in dealing with the uncontrolled situations. In this case, the problems associated with lighting indoors are quite different than those found outside.

Indoor Location Lighting

Since lighting grids are far from common in city halls, university classrooms, corporate offices, hospitals, and other locations, portable lighting apparatus must be brought to the remote shoot by the production crew. Portable lights (see figure 15–18) usually are mounted on stands that can then be placed in positions roughly approximating those of the basic key, fill, and back lights.

Often this is difficult or impossible to accomplish because of lack of space or because the light stands will show in the camera's picture. The back light is particularly tricky because it is essentially impossible to position it correctly without having the stand visible in a long shot. Occasionally, clip-on *internal reflectors* can be clamped onto a door or tall piece of furniture to serve as a back light. However, many remotes are shot with only key and fill lights.

In fact, many news shoots utilize only one light; it is mounted on the camera and is used only for basic illumination. The result is a very flat, nonaesthetic, washed-out effect—which is, nevertheless, better than shooting a silhouette.

The lighting instruments taken on a remote shoot are usually limited, too. Scoops, ellipsoidal spots, and even Fresnels (section 4.4) are too bulky to lug along. And certainly the vast array of lights available in the studio cannot be taken. The main portable lights used are broads (see figure 4–12), but their beams are somewhat difficult to control.

Lighting Control   Lack of a dimmer board adds to the control problems. In order to increase or decrease the intensity of a light, the stand must be moved in accordance with the principles of the *Inverse Square Law* (section 4.6). However, space limitations may hinder this. Space and time limitations also hinder the use of scrims, barn doors, flags, and other devices that could help diffuse or shape the light.

Power   Another big problem is securing adequate electrical power. A studio is specially wired in anticipation of the power that will be needed to meet extensive lighting demands. People's homes and offices are not. Lighting properly with key, fill, and back lights all plugged into one circuit is almost guaranteed to blow the circuit breaker.

This is why it is particularly important to learn where the circuit breakers are, how many amps each circuit is rated for, and which outlets are on which circuit. You should also become familiar with the basic formula: *watts = volts × amps.* (This is often referred to as the "West Virginia" formula, *W = VA.*) The watts will be written somewhere on the lamp of your lighting instrument—usually 500, 1,000, or 2,000 watts. Amperes should be indicated on the circuit breaker—usually 10, 15, or 20 amps. Voltage is regulated by the power company and in most ordinary circumstances will be 110 volts. (In industrial settings, it may be 220 volts.) Therefore, if the circuit breaker is rated for 10 amps and the voltage is 110, you can plug in lights totaling 1,100 watts on

that circuit. To be on the safe side, use a figure of 100 for the voltage (this also makes the arithmetic easier). So a 20–amp circuit could handle 2,000 watts.

However, you cannot assume your lights can use the whole circuit. The total wattage of all appliances and devices on the circuit must be taken into consideration. The office copier or the home refrigerator may be using the same circuit that you want to plug into. One group of students were taping a remote shoot at a factory; they had been recording without problems for an hour or so when suddenly the lights went out. Lunchtime had arrived and the employees began using the company microwave oven that was on the same circuit as the lights.

Usually you must plug in lights on at least two separate circuits, and generally, this means using plugs in two different areas. In many homes and offices, outlets in one room are all on the same circuit, and you may have to go several rooms down the hall to use a different circuit. This means you must take along extension cords. As you can begin to appreciate, all of these factors reinforce the necessity for scouting the location ahead of time.

Safety   The use of extension cords raises another question—the problem of safety. First of all, make sure that the extension cords you plan on using are rated for the electrical load you expect to plug into them. Using cords that are not heavy-duty will result in tripping the circuit breaker—or worse yet, overheating and starting a fire.

Also, electrical cable strung all over the floor is likely to cause people to trip—often unplugging the light and/or bringing down the light stand (as well as causing bodily injury). Where cords must be laid along the floor, covering them with a wide tape will help ensure that they will not be tripped over. Ideally, you should run the cords along the walls and up

• • • • • • • • • • • • • • •

Figure 15–19
Crew member taping power cord above a doorway to ensure that no one will trip over it during the recording.

turn off all regular lights and just use the quartz lights from your remote lighting kit. However, sometimes available lights can be used for general illumination—if they are of a color temperature close to 3,200 degrees Kelvin (section 4.2). Regular incandescent light bulbs can usually be used, but fluorescents should definitely be turned off. Not only will they result in a recording with a definite blue tint, they may also create a hum or buzz on the sound track.

Outdoor light coming through windows should also be avoided, if at all possible, because it is about 5,500 degrees K—far bluer than the 3,200-degree K quartz lights. The problem is not with the outdoor light itself, but with the fact that you are mixing types of light—daylight and quartz. If you set the camera's filter for quartz light and some of your light source is from daylight, your footage will look blue. If you set the filter for daylight, the footage will be orange because you are using some quartz light. (Any still photographer who has used *daylight* film when shooting indoors with normal incandescent lighting is familiar with the orange tint that results.) Gels are made to place on windows to change the color temperature of the outdoor light, but they are expensive and difficult to install. A simpler solution is to avoid mixing the types of light.

Outdoor Location Lighting

If you are shooting outside, your main source of light is the sun. This has both advantages and disadvantages. You do not need to worry about light stands or power requirements. However, you have no control over the sun. It changes position; it can be overly intense; it darts behind passing clouds. Its color temperature changes as the day progresses (ranging from 4,500 to 12,000 degrees K)—so that scenes shot at noon will not match scenes shot at 5:00 P.M. Not only will these scenes have a color switch, but they are likely to show different lengths of shadows, different molding of

over door jambs. (See figure 15–19.) For these taping purposes, you must bring along heavy-duty tape—preferably something like *duct tape* that is a very strong adhesive. Where cords must be taped to painted surfaces, it is best to use *masking tape* that will not peel off paint when it is removed.

Lights also create a safety problem because of their heat. They should not be placed where someone is likely to bump into them accidentally. Also, they should not be placed where they are touching curtains or paper and could thereby start a smoldering fire. At the end of a shoot, they should be turned off *first* and packed away *last*. This gives them time to cool before crew members must handle them.

Available Light   One other problem associated with shooting indoors comes from available light. If at all possible, you should

Field Production

facial features, and different amounts of glare. This is a particular problem if long shots are taped at noon and close-ups, which are to be intercut, are not shot until 5:00 P.M.

Second Light Sources   Sometimes the sun is so bright that you need extra lights. This seeming contradiction is caused by the fact that a bright sun can wash out facial features. It acts, in essence, like a very bright key light. In order to counteract this, artificial lights can be added to create the effect of a fill. Of course, these lights have to be the same color temperature as daylight.

One way to do this is to cover the quartz lights used indoors with special *filter* gels that convert the 3,200-degree K light to 5,500-plus degrees K. However, the filters cut down on the efficiency of the light, so more lights are needed than normal. Another way is to use *HMI* (hydrogen medium-arc-length iodine) lights that are made to produce 5,500-degree K light (figure 15–20). These lights have a separate *ballast* that protects the lamp from power surges.

In order to minimize problems from the sun passing behind clouds and changing color temperature as the day wears on, large HMI floods can actually be used to create an artificial source of sunlight (see figure 15–21)—even for interior scenes.

If auxiliary lights are needed, getting power to them can be a problem. Powerful battery-operated lights do exist, but they are not commonly or inexpensively available.

A more feasible alternative for obtaining a second light from a different direction is to use a reflector. A commercially available *foil reflector* can be used to bounce sunlight onto a subject's face from almost any direction. (See figure 4–30.) And if the sun is behind the subject (functioning as a back light), the reflector placed in front of the subject can be used to provide a satisfactory key light. Even if a professional reflector is not available, any large

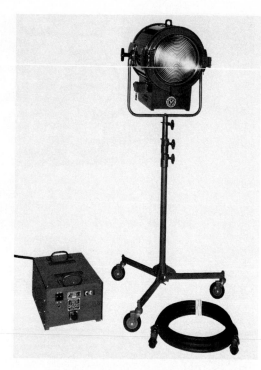

Figure 15–20
Fresnel *Mole Solarspot.*

This 2,500-watt HMI (hydrogen medium-arc-length iodine) light is used in field production where it is necessary to match the color temperature of sunlight. The control unit known as a *ballast* protects the lamp from sudden surges of power and provides for longer bulb life. (Photo courtesy of Mole Richardson)

Figure 15–21
As an example of the new techniques being used in portable lighting, these four 12,000-watt HMI instruments were focused through a scrim to produce a soft, flat illumination for an interior scene.

Figure 15-22
In this setup, reflectors are being used to bounce the sunlight onto the two actors sitting on the sand, providing both fill and back light.

piece of white material (a white poster board, for example) can be used in an emergency to provide some fill light from a complementary direction. Obviously, the more highly polished or reflective the surface of the reflector is, the more efficient it will be. (See figure 15–22.)

Lighting Individual Shots   Overall, lighting can be one of the biggest headaches of field production. However, there is one very distinct advantage that location lighting has over live-on-tape lighting—location lighting allows each shot to be lit individually. When a studio program is shot with three cameras simultaneously, lighting must be general enough that it will provide acceptable illumination for any camera shot that is to be used. Often in multiple-camera shooting, compromises have to be made in setting the lights, and few shots

are really properly lit. With location shooting, however, the camera is stopped after each shot, and the lights can be reset to light the next shot optimally.

15.9 The Camera on Location

Most of the aesthetic principles of picture composition (sections 6.2 and 6.3) apply in the field as well as in the studio. So do the general principles dealing with f-stops, depth of field, lens ratio, focusing, and filters (sections 5.3 and 5.4).

Camera Controls

However, in a studio, once cameras are set, the characteristics under which they shoot remain fairly constant. Controls and levels, once they are established, do not need to be continually readjusted. White balance set at the beginning of a studio program, for instance, can be depended upon to give accurate color throughout a taping.

White Balancing   Such is not the case with field production. *White balance* must be reset frequently as lighting conditions change—because the white balance control adjusts the strength of the basic video level to suit the composition of the light that is available for an individual shot. It "reads" a designated item as *white* and then readjusts the electronics associated with the other colors so that they will render true color. (See section 5.5.)

As the sun peeks in and out of clouds, the light source changes and you need to readjust the white balance. The changes in the sun's color temperature over the course of a day also require changing white balance. Going from outdoors to indoors definitely requires repeating the white balance procedure.

Fortunately, white balancing is easy—just the push of a button on most cameras. In fact, some cameras automatically white balance as changes in color temperature occur. If the camera you are using does not automatically redo white balancing, however, your main white-balancing problem may simply be remembering to do it. Sometimes this problem is exacerbated because no one remembered to bring to the remote shoot a white card that can be used to determine your *reference white.*

Filters   A related item that is very easy to forget in the process of field shooting is the changing of the camera filter (section 5.4). Most cameras have four filters—for instance, one for indoor quartz light (which also works for outdoor sunrise and sunset), one for sunny daylight, one for cloudy outdoor shooting, and one that acts as a cap. (See figure 5–18.)

When you move from outdoors to indoors, or vice versa, you must change the filter, or your footage will have a decided orange or blue cast. The outdoor filters are orange to compensate for the fact that quartz light is "orangish" and daylight is "bluish." The main difference between the *sunny daylight* and *cloudy outdoor* filters is the amount of *neutral density* in the filter. *Neutral density* lessens the intensity of the light; therefore, the *sunny* filter has more neutral density.

DB Gain   Many remote cameras have *db* (decibel) gain switches to use in instances of low light. This boosts the electronics so that the camera "sees" better in the dark. However, using this switch makes the picture grainier and also shifts the color somewhat. It should be used only when it is absolutely impossible to add light—generally in the covering of a news story.[3]

Power   Another problem in the field is the power source for the camera. Most cameras can be operated either on regular AC (household alternating current) or on batteries. Whenever possible, AC should be used because it is more reliable. However, cameras do add wattage to electrical circuits that may already be taxed from your portable lights. For this reason, you should find out how many watts your camera-VCR setup uses—so that you do not exceed the capacity of a circuit.

Batteries have a disadvantage in that they do run out of charge—usually when you are in the middle of shooting your most important scene! If you do use batteries, make sure the battery is fully charged before you are scheduled to take the camera on location.

3. Some new CCD surveillance cameras have internal circuitry and *db* gain that allows them to operate with less than one lux of illumination; that is less than one-tenth of a footcandle! These are so sensitive they are generally not in use for normal field production, however.

Secondly, while in the field, make sure you are not unintentionally discharging the battery when you are not shooting. By all means, disconnect the battery while you transport equipment from one location to another. Some cameras have a *standby* position that keeps the electronics operational but cuts down on battery use. This should be used while shots are being set up and rehearsed. Cameras differ as to how they conserve on battery power, so be sure to find out when the battery is and is not engaged on your particular camera.

Camera Mounts and Movement

Keeping a picture steady on a remote camera can be a problem. You usually do not have the luxury of the sturdy pedestals and cranes available in a studio (section 6.1). What you are more likely to have is a three-legged tripod and/or a strong shoulder.

The Tripod   Whenever possible, the tripod should be used; it is steadier than the strongest of shoulders. Many student shots have been ruined because the camera operator or director did not want to take the time to put the camera on the tripod—thus fulfilling the axiom, "There's never time to do it right, but there's always time to do it over."

Pans, tilts, and zooms can all be executed very effectively on a tripod mount. However, assuming you do not have the benefit of a field crane (see figure 6–6), movements such as trucks and dollies do require the human body to simulate wheeled movement—combining the strength of a gymnast, the agility of a ballet dancer, and the balance of a tightrope walker. Improvised dollies and trucks can sometimes be achieved with wheeled conveyances such as a child's wagon or a grocery cart.

Achieving smooth movement can be difficult, especially in a crowd. Shakiness in news footage is accepted by the audience because the camera is being used *subjectively*. It is the

audience eye, showing people what they would see were they there—including the bumping and jostling. But, even so, camera operators should try to keep the picture as steady as possible at all times.

Camera operators and directors must also be willing to reposition the camera frequently for both aesthetic and informational purposes. This requires effort and muscle on the part of the person operating the camera, but it is needed for everything from reaction shots of the reporter re-asking questions (after the guest has left) to low-angle shots to convey a sense of power.

Camera Care and Maintenance

Care of the camera must also be a high-priority item for the camera operator. The high level of activity and unanticipated problems on any location production occasionally mean that some of the usual equipment precautions may be temporarily forgotten. Cameras are very vulnerable to the careless treatment they may be given on a field shoot. The camera operator must take special pains that no one points an open lens of a tube-type camera toward the sun or other hot light source, for example.

The lens should be capped between scenes and whenever the camera is moved—because that is a time when light can accidentally strike a camera. The camera should also be put on automatic iris so that if the lens cap is off and light strikes it, the lens will automatically close down to minimize the damage. Even the CCD camera—which will not be damaged from exposure to an intense light source—should be capped so that stray elements such as pebbles or moisture do not damage the lens. Shock, water, dust, and extremes of heat and cold can cause considerable damage to all equipment.

Many types of professional location productions pose enormous engineering challenges for the optimum functioning and protection of cameras and other equipment.

Field Production

Special housings and mountings have to be used for many adverse situations: dust protection in arid country, heaters for arctic conditions, shock-resistant mountings for rough terrain chase sequences, gyroscopic mountings for helicopter shots, and underwater housings for perhaps the most adverse environment of all. (See figure 15–23.)

In all probability, you will not be shooting in any of these extreme conditions for class projects, but whoever is operating the camera should realize that he or she is in charge of an expensive piece of rather delicate equipment that must remain operational for many future projects.

15.10 Videotape Recorders

Field videotape recorders employ the same processes and same controls as do studio tape recorders. In fact, sometimes ½-inch recorders used in the studio are the same machines taken on location shoots. However, in the ¾-inch format, the field tape recorder is likely to be a smaller version that can handle only 20–minute tapes. With the ½-inch or 8mm camcorders, of course, the VCR is part of the single integrated unit.

Setup and Connections

In a studio setting, all of the video equipment is more or less permanently connected. Cameras and video recorders are all routinely cabled to their associated pieces of equipment—the power supplies, camera control units, time-base corrector, switcher, monitors, scopes, and so forth.

Such is not the case in the field. It is up to crew members to know how to attach both video and audio to the VCR. For this reason, you must be very familiar with the traditional routing processes. Generally, *video out* on the camera must be connected to *video in* on the

VCR—usually by means of a UHF or BNC connector. (See section 8.4 and figures 8–14 and 8–15.)

Sometimes, however, a multi-pin connector is used. This contains, within one cable, wires for various functions—*video; audio* (in case a microphone attached to the camera is used); *power* (so that the VCR can operate from the camera's power source); *remote control* (so that the VCR can be operated by a switch on the camera); and *return* (so that the camera viewfinder can function as a monitor to view tapes after they are shot). Having a multi-pin connector gives a great deal more versatility to a production situation, but multi-pin connectors are expensive and not all cameras and VCRs can accommodate them.

Because of the several connections between the camera and VCR, these two pieces of equipment should be located physically close together. The VCR can be on the ground next to the camera, or it can be on the camera operator's back. The camcorder provides the ultimate in closeness.

As with the camera, the VCR should operate on AC rather than battery whenever possible. All video recorders intended for remote shoots have provisions for battery operation—but you will operate a bit more securely if you are able to use AC power.

Audio is usually routed separately—even if a multi-pin connector is used—because, as discussed previously, in order to get the microphone as close as possible to the talent, an external mike should be used (as opposed to the mike attached to the camera). The VCR input for a microphone may be a *Cannon* connector, a *phone* plug, an *RCA,* or a *mini-plug.* (Review figure 8–15.) Make sure you check before you leave the studio/control room to confirm that the connector on the end of the microphone cable is the same as that required by the VCR. If it is not, change the microphone plug or get an adapter that will convert from one type of connector to the other.

A multi-pin connector will enable you to use the camera viewfinder to make sure you did, indeed, tape what you intended to—and that is generally sufficient for video monitoring. However, you may want to attach a monitor to *video out* so that the director and crew members can also see what the camera is taping; this involves extra cabling and an extra monitor, however, and generally is not done.

You will want to connect headsets into the earphone output of the VCR (if one is available) or into the earphone jack on the camcorder.

As a general rule, always double-check to make sure you have all the proper cables and connectors for the VCR before you leave the studio; this is a *must* because you will waste valuable production time if you have to return to the control room for one little cable. One good approach to the discipline of field production is to lay out all of the cables and connectors you will need for your particular assignment—and then plug everything together before you leave just to make sure you have it all.

Taping Procedures

The VCR operator should set the audio level and check all controls before taping begins. The operator should make sure the machine has been up to speed at least five seconds before anything crucial is taped and, likewise, keep the machine running for about ten seconds after the shot is completed.

During taping, the person in charge of the VCR will always be watching all the "vital signs"—monitoring the video level, audio level, end-of-tape warning, battery condition, and so forth. Monitoring is usually accomplished through one or several meters or warning lights located on the front of the VCR or in the viewfinder of the camcorder.

The machine should not be left in *pause* for long periods of time because this will wear the oxide off the tape and clog the video heads (section 8.4).

One of the problems connected with operating the VCR in the field is that the recording operator is usually given other duties—audio, log keeper, camera, lights. In fact if a camcorder is used, the videotape operator and camera operator are one in the same. This means the camera operator has to be extra careful to make sure the recorder part of the camcorder is operating properly. The best of shots will be useless if they are not recorded properly and ready to be edited.

15.11 Editing

The term *postproduction* is usually used to refer to all those production efforts that take place after the field and/or studio camera work has been completed. This editing process is the culmination of the single-camera field shoot. Although most of this postproduction process will take place after the program material has been shot, some important "post" work can be dovetailed with the final phase of camera work. It makes a lot of sense, for example, to at least start working on such things as setting up titles and credits on the character generator. Other graphics, along with stock (file) footage, can be obtained and organized for the editing process. Much important audio editing can be profitably accomplished before postproduction is totally underway.

The Editing Process

As all professional producers know, this process of "getting into" the final phase of postproduction is a crucial time. Much of the strength—and discipline—of a good producer is an ability to generate the sense of momentum and enthusiasm that is needed to complete a production. In live television, the relentless clock focuses everyone's attention; in single-camera postproduction, the constant pressure of a knowledgeable guiding hand is needed.

It may be difficult to understand the time frame that is necessary for the editing process; an inexperienced crew may initially waste a considerable amount of energy and effort. Usually, this phase passes as crew members become more efficient at their assigned responsibilities and the leadership and organization become more evident—just as they did during the shooting process.

Although many professional editing sessions involve only the producer or the director working in conjunction with the editor (or even the editor working alone with only a detailed set of notes), student postproduction sessions should, as much as possible, become a learning process for the entire team. Without proper organization, however, this process can drift into noisy chaos. The important thing is that there has to be someone who is acknowledged as being definitely "in charge." This may be the producer, the director, or the editor; but it should be the same person who has initiated and established the basic structure of the project.

Editing sessions, which can last for hours, should be set up so that while the person operating the edit control unit is executing each transfer/edit, a second person or team is finalizing the next edit decision—locating the precise reel number, footage/revolution counter number, and exact word cue for the inpoint and outpoint. (See figure 15–24.) Of course, much of the efficiency of the editing session will depend upon how much preparation—viewing and planning—has gone into the pre-editing process.

Audio Editing

High-quality audio work in a video production all too often goes unappreciated. We are diverted by the flow of the picture images; but

Figure 15–24
For students, a two-person editing team can be a very efficient way to work. Many professionals, however, prefer to work alone whenever possible.

poor audio can quickly destroy the impact of a well-executed visual sequence. A good sound track is the result of the all-important *mixing* process (section 2.2.3). The average TV commercial, documentary, or topflight industrial production has a final sound track that is the result of the skilled mixing of anywhere from sixteen to thirty-two separate sound tracks together onto the final **mix track.**[4]

Audio training facilities for most colleges and universities do not approach this level of sophistication—although inexpensive audio software that operates with off-the-shelf computers is enabling some universities to have at least semi-sophisticated audio mixing capability. Additionally, many TV production stu-

dents have not had the opportunity for a substantial course in audio production. Therefore, it is all the more important that the preparation for the sound track must start with the very first planning of the shape of the project. The director and producer should question each other continually as to the exact details of how each sound or combination of sounds (announcer, on-camera narrator, voice-over studio narrator, background noise, music, special sound effects, and so forth) is to be achieved. One often hears the phrase, "We'll fix it in post. . . ." This is an invitation to audio disaster. If you have not thoroughly thought out the procedure during preproduction planning, it is often too late to fix it in postproduction.

Generally, what you should aim for is a finished videotape with a completed, mixed audio track on one channel (or two if it is stereo). This is the standard that should be accepted for a finished product—except for a few situations such as news footage that is going

4. Some professional music recording sessions will use in excess of 100 different tracks. Quincy Jones, for example, has used over 200 in some sessions! This involves several *slave* tapes (up to twenty-four tracks each) that are premixed before the final mixing session. Some audio consoles, however, can handle more than fifty inputs for a single mixing session.

to be rolled into a live newscast. For this type of situation, sometimes the sound from the field is on one channel and a narration is on the other channel. When the material is aired, the audio operator can mix it properly.

Audio Preplanning   In order to facilitate successful postproduction editing, careful preproduction planning is a must. For example, the following cautionary suggestions are offered:

1. Avoid a production concept that calls for the mixing of music and/or sound effects with the words of an *on-camera* announcer. Once the voice track has been recorded in sync with the picture, it is difficult to mix it with additional sound unless some specialized equipment can be utilized. Instead, the benefits of music and sound effects can be mixed with *off-camera* narrative sequences—which can be more easily handled.

2. Avoid staging an on-camera announcer segment when background sound (traffic, equipment, music) will also be picked up on the sound track. As the various segments are edited into the program sequence, the disruption of the original continuity of the sound produces a "choppy" interrupted effect. If background sound is unavoidable (and, indeed, may even be desirable for authenticity), one solution—if you have the audio equipment—is to utilize a *wildtrack* mixing procedure. Have the announcer work as closely to the microphone as practical (thus cutting out as much background sound as possible); then record a long sequence of the background sound or music on a separate track. In postproduction, you can mix this continuous sound from the wildtrack with the announcer's voice at a level that will adequately mask the discontinuous background audio picked up by the announcer's mike. (This process works best when mixing machine or traffic noise, rather than music.)

3. Avoid the "two-track" solution in solving the problems of achieving a final audio mix. More than one student production has ended up with all spoken dialogue on one audio track and all music and sound effects on another track. The plan usually calls for one more *dubbing* (duplicating) session during which the two tracks will be mixed into one final master track. Unfortunately, this means an additional generation loss of the video information.

There are situations, however, in which the two audio tracks of the videotape can be utilized without going through an additional video generation. Let us use the example of the wildtrack sound of a piece of machinery that is to be combined with the studio-recorded voice of the off-camera narrator. Using the studio facilities, these two sources are put together in an audio *mix track* on a separate videotape work cassette. Now the editor has two working options. He or she can first assemble-edit the video for the sequence and then later do an audio-only dub to match it; or the mixed audio track can be transferred to the master tape as an audio-only track with the video added afterwards, edited to match the finished audio track. Laying down an audio track and then editing video to it (the second approach) is often used when a picture montage is being matched to a particular piece of music. With this method, video shots can be edited to cut precisely with the rhythm of the music.

Once these and similar techniques have been worked out, the editing can proceed with maximum efficiency. Even after sufficient testing to check machine operation, the first few edits should be carefully checked. Audio, video, and control track levels should be continually monitored in order to provide consistent levels throughout the editing process. This is of special importance when editing takes place over a period of several days.

Preplanning and Interaction

We cannot stress too strongly the importance of preplanning—for both video and audio—as it relates to the postproduction process. Everything must be recorded correctly, both technically and aesthetically, or you are not going to have a successful editing session. All of the processes involved in assemble editing, insert editing, A/B roll, audio-only, and video-only cannot make a successful program out of something that has been shot poorly.

Finally, as stressed in the opening chapter (section 1.2), in all types of team-oriented video production, it is the "people" part of the work that is at once the most rewarding and at the same time the most difficult phase of putting a program together. As with professional situations, each new project with each new crew means a whole new process of each member fitting into the team. This personal interaction is never easy because individual needs and ego trips seem to keep getting in the way of the larger group project. But the discipline required and the ability to cope with these difficulties are the signs of the true professional.

Summary

Most of the differences between studio production and field production arise because of the *uncontrollable nature* of the outside environment and the fact that material is recorded in a filmic *single-camera* technique.

Field production is also much more recent than studio production—progressing through *ENG/EFP* concepts: ¾-inch *U-matic* and *U-matic SP*; ½-inch *Betacam* and *Betacam SP*; ½-inch *M-format* and *M-II*; *VHS* and *S-VHS*; *Video-8* and *Hi-Band 8mm*; and *CCD* cameras.

Field material must be conceptualized in a manner similar to studio-produced material, but the process of editing must be more closely considered throughout. The *mini-doc* and other field forms consist of elements that include: *host/reporter/narrator*; the *actuality*; *titles and graphics*; *stock footage*; and *musical score*. Scripting aids that are likely to be used for remotes are the *outline, storyboard, final script, breakdown sheet*, and *shooting schedule*.

The producer/director should scout potential locations to find out such information as the name of the *person in charge*, the best *places to locate equipment*, the *power* possibilities, the effects of the *sun*, and possible *extraneous noises*. On the day of the shoot, all the equipment to be taken should be double-checked, *color bars* should be laid on the tape, all shots should be *slated*, and *head and tail pads* should be included. During shooting, *continuity* and *axis of action* must be carefully watched.

In general, fewer people are needed for a remote than for studio shoots, but someone is needed to handle *continuity* and *logging*. All crew members should help with cleanup.

Performing can be difficult because shots are taped out of order. This often means the *emotional continuity* must be artificially created by the actors. *Reacting to "nothing"* is awkward, especially for untrained performers. *Would-be stars* who wander into the location and *people who do not want to be interviewed* also present problems.

Graphics are rarely used in the field, and *sets* are the result of what exists naturally—with minor modifications. Windows can present particular problems.

Directional, rugged mikes work best in remote situations. Although camera mikes are used, they are not recommended. *AGC* sometimes creates more problems than it solves, especially if two people talk at different volumes or if there are silent pauses. The channel on which sound is recorded and/or the type of sound (*linear, hi-fi, PCM*) should be carefully noted. Audio operators should make sure they record *wildtrack* sound and should listen carefully for *extraneous noises* that may ruin takes.

Indoor lighting is hampered by *lack of grids,* a *dimmer board,* and *space.* Portable lighting demands great amounts of *power,* so attention needs to be paid to the *load on circuits. Safety* is a problem because of *extension cords* and the *heat* of the lights. Light coming from *fluorescents* and *windows* also creates problems. Careful attention must be paid to *color temperature.* Outdoor lighting uses primarily the *sun,* but this creates problems as the sun moves across the sky and darts behind clouds. *HMI* lights, *reflectors,* and *filters* on quartz lights are often used to supplement sunlight.

Cameras need to be *white balanced* frequently, especially when moving from outdoors to indoors, or vice versa. These moves call for the changing of *filters* also. Cameras can be powered either by *AC* or by *batteries.* The latter must be used sparingly so they do not run out of charge. *Tripods* should be used whenever possible, but *hand-held* cameras are also common. Cameras should be *capped* when not in use.

The *videotape recorder* is the main piece of equipment to which other equipment is connected. *Connectors* must match both *inputs* and *outputs.* The VCR should be placed near the camera, and its *"vital signs"* should be monitored before and during shooting. Tape should not be left in *pause* for long periods.

Some of the *postproduction* procedures such as developing *titles* and *editing audio* can begin before taping has ended. If more than one person is involved with editing, *group cooperation* is essential. Special care must be given to audio because it usually involves a combination of sources.

Despite all the problems facing remote shooting, it can be a very rewarding form of production because care can be given to each individual element.

15.12 Training Exercises

The first exercise is an individual assignment that should be carried out by each member of the class. The second exercise is a class project that should involve everyone in the decision-making steps required.

1. Plan a simple, single-camera location production. Start with a precise statement of objectives, outline the content, write a final shooting script, draw a simple storyboard, make a breakdown sheet, and prepare a shooting schedule. Prepare a checklist of the items that you would want to include when you survey the location(s).

2. As a class, record the segments necessary for editing a simple, single-camera location actuality. Keep in mind that such material is seldom shot in the order in which it will eventually be edited. Most remote productions follow established filmic tradition in that all shots in a particular setting, using the same talent, are recorded at one time—almost always out of sequence with respect to the final edited program. In this exercise assume that you want to shoot the interview segment first; then the opening and closing statements by the host/narrator are to be recorded (once we know what the interview consists of); and finally the silent insert segment of the item being discussed will be shot. Thus, the four segments should be shot in the following order:

   a. A field interview with a simulated expert on any subject chosen—

furniture making, automotive repair, pottery, or any other topic (segment #2).

b. An opening statement or introduction by a host/narrator (segment #1).

c. A summary by the host/narrator (segment #3).

d. An insert shot (silent) of the item being discussed in the interview— table, carburetor, vase, etc. (segment #2A).

Assemble-edit the first three segments together, in the proper sequence, following all due considerations of visual and audio continuity. *Insert-edit* the insert shot into the appropriate spot in the interview.

15.13   A Wrap-Up and Summary

The traditional **wrap-up** is given to a performer about fifteen seconds before he or she has to get off the air. It means that there is very little time left to wrap things up, quickly summarize, and say good-bye. Perhaps it is appropriate that we wrap up quickly at this point.

This text has been concerned with the production *techniques* of handling audio, lighting, camera, switcher, recorder, editor, staging, graphics, talent, floor crew positions, and directing—both for studio productions and for field production. If it has been successful, it has also gotten into the *disciplines* of handling these various elements. Discipline has been defined in several ways throughout this text. As much as anything, it can be considered a matter of attitude.

Attitude toward learning and improving is one major ingredient of discipline. If you truly want to learn as much as you can about the business of television, you will gain quite a bit from this course. You will observe intently. You will try conscientiously. One of the most important secrets of learning in a course such as this is the ability to admit areas of temporary ignorance and then ask questions or seek experiences to fill in those areas. If you are unsure about audio patching, ask to have it explained to you. If you are insecure with the switcher, get all the experience you can as technical director. Do not try to bluff your way through; no one gets very far in that manner.

Attitude toward communication is important. Unless you have a strong feeling for the pursuit of communication—unless you really have a deep desire to want to succeed in communicating a message—then you are in the wrong field. Television is not just a business of glamour or money or excitement. It is the business of communication. For example, every program starts with a specific purpose— a clear-cut idea of what is to be attained in the production. Until you begin program planning with this attitude, your productions may be slick and polished, but they most certainly will turn out to be meaningless and devoid of any substance.

Finally, *attitude toward a professional obligation* must be considered. The terms *professional attitude* and *professionalism* are bandied about with little thought as to their implications. We use the terms here to imply more than just a means of earning a livelihood. We challenge the student to think of professionalism in the original sense of the three learned professions (law, medicine, and theology), which carried a strong societal obligation. The true professional is one who is dedicated to high principles and a sense of community benefit. If you are committed to this kind of self-giving professionalism, you certainly will be more likely to leave your mark upon the field of broadcasting.

Field Production

Electromagnetic Waves

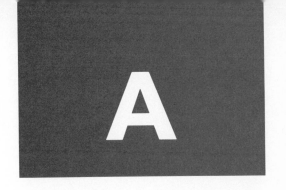

A

*T*he principles employed in the transmission of television picture and sound are extensions of several important discoveries made more than 100 years ago involving the related phenomena of electricity and magnetism. In 1856 James Clerk Maxwell further developed Faraday's concept of magnetic lines of force and expressed the theory that electrical energy existed within the universe in the form of oscillating waves. He further suggested that not only did these electrical waves travel at the same speed as light but also that the waves were physically related to light itself.

By 1887 Heinrich Hertz was able to prove the existence of waves of electrical force by developing the equipment with which to generate them. His experiments revealed that the waves had varying lengths and differing rates of oscillation. It was further seen that these two factors interact with each other in a mathematical relationship also involving the wave velocity.

Before proceeding, it should be pointed out that while the vibrations that constitute natural sound in some ways resemble the qualities of the waves of the **electromagnetic spectrum,** present-day scientific thinking considers each of these to be a separate phenomenon, existing side by side within the physical laws of the universe. (See chapter 2 and appendix B.) Pressure sound waves can be transmitted only through the media of the atoms and molecules of solids, liquids, and gases; whereas electromagnetic waves can move also through the vacuum of space.

The analogy to water waves has developed as a convenient way of expressing the very complex properties of both of these forms of energy transmission. While sound pressure waves are relatively well understood, most scientists confess an inability to comprehend totally the nature of electromagnetic energy.

In any case, let us use the water wave analogy as a means of understanding the properties of both types of oscillations. Think of a series of ocean waves as seen from a cutaway

Figure A–1

Relationship of wavelength, frequency, amplitude, and velocity.

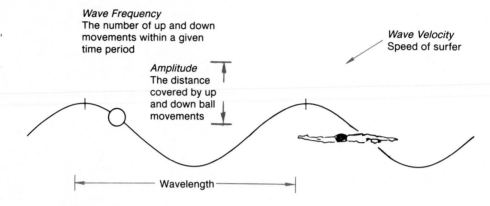

Wave Frequency
The number of up and down movements within a given time period

Amplitude
The distance covered by up and down ball movements

Wave Velocity
Speed of surfer

Wavelength

Figure A–2

AM and FM modulation of a carrier wave.

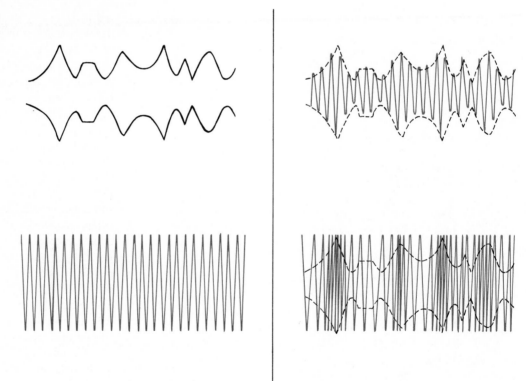

Top, the electronic signal coming from the microphone or recorder consists of electrical information that carries the original sound waves. *Bottom*, the unmodulated carrier wave is generated at a specific frequency in the electromagnetic spectrum.

Top, **AM Broadcasting.** The electronic signal can be superimposed onto the carrier wave by changing or *modulating the amplitude* of the carrier wave. (The dotted line indicates the original electronic signal.) *Bottom*, **FM Broadcasting.** The electronic information also can be combined with the electromagnetic wave by varying or *modulating the frequency* of the carrier wave. Where the original electronic signal is strongest (indicated by the pattern of the dotted lines), the frequencies are relatively compressed.

Appendix A

side view. In the water there is a rubber ball that floats up and down with the crests and troughs of the passing waves but remains stationary in relation to a fixed point on the sand beneath. Riding just in front of a wave crest is a body surfer. If the person moves in a straight line, he or she will indicate the speed at which the wave is traveling relative to the shoreline. In our hypothetical ocean, all of the waves come into the shore at the same speed. With this in mind, we can tell several important things by looking at the ball and the surfer. (See figure A–1.)

First, we can measure the distance from crest to crest to determine the **wavelength.** We then notice that this wavelength has a definite relationship to the number of times the ball goes up and down in a certain period of time. This crest-to-trough and back-to-crest rate of oscillation is the measure of **frequency.** If the wavelength were shorter (distance between crests), the ball would go up and down more often in the same period of time. (Do not forget that our waves move through the water at a constant velocity.) This is an important quality of waves of electrical energy—*the greater the frequency, the shorter the wavelength.*

Watching the up-and-down movements of the ball over a long period of time may give us one more important piece of information. The ball may continue its same up-and-down movement at a consistent number of oscillations per minute, but as the hours pass, we may notice that it is not going as far up and down. As in a real ocean, the height of the wave is often the result of energy expended by a storm out at sea. The height of the wave will decrease as the energy creating it decreases. In electrical energy wave theory, the *amplitude* or amount of oscillation is the result of the amount of energy applied to the wave.

The *velocity* of the wave is simply a measure of how long it takes the crest of a single wave to move from one given point to another.

In the case of electromagnetic energy, this speed is constant—the same as the speed of light, roughly 186,000 miles per second. As with light, the direction follows that of a straight line. The complex exceptions to this general rule are such that they need not draw our attention.

The basic wave cycle that measures one complete oscillation from crest to trough and back to crest again is usually called a *hertz* in honor of Heinrich Hertz, who did so much of the preliminary research in this scientific area. Because the number of cycles per second is so large in most scientific measurements, figures are usually expressed in *kilohertz,* or thousands of cycles, and *megahertz,* or millions of cycles.

Looking at the AM radio, we see that the carrier frequencies utilized for transmission are those of 540 kilohertz (540,000 cps) to 1,600 kilohertz. Each AM station occupies a band of frequencies ten kilohertz wide. The station's call letters are identified with the midpoint of these frequencies. For example, KNX in Los Angeles, 1070 on the dial, actually utilizes 1,065 to 1,075 kilohertz for broadcast purposes.

In AM (amplitude modulation) radio, the broadcast signal is, in effect, added onto the carrier frequency and, in the process, variously alters the amplitude of the signal. It is this modulation of the amplitude that the receiver translates back into sound. (See figure A–2.)

FM (frequency modulation) radio uses much higher carrier frequencies, from 88 to 108 megahertz. Here, it is the frequency of the carrier signal that is changed by the modulation process and, in turn, translated or demodulated back into sound. (See figure A–2.)

As shown in figure A–3, radio and television occupy but a small part of the immense range of the known electromagnetic spectrum.

Figure A–3
Electromagnetic spectrum.

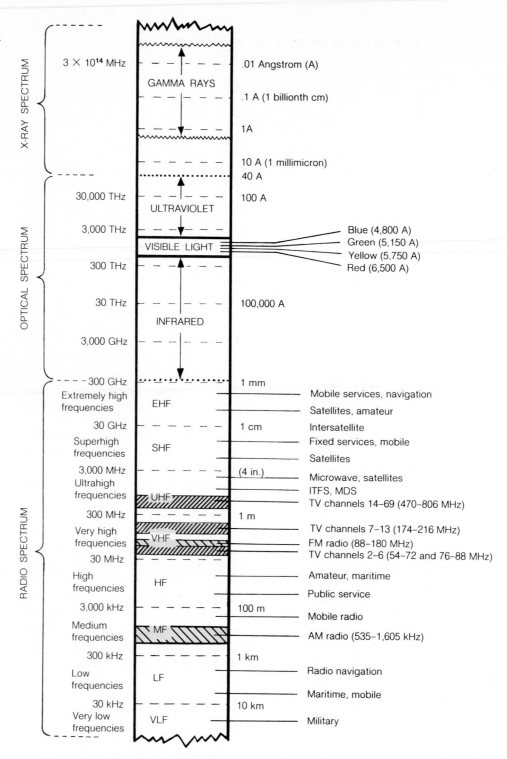

Frequency Designations

1 Hertz	(Hz)	= 1 "cycle" per second
1 kiloHertz	(kHz)	= 1,000 Hz
1 megaHertz	(mHz)	= 1,000 kHz
1 gigaHertz	(gHz)	= 1,000 mHz
1 teraHertz	(tHz)	= 1,000 gHz

The entire electromagnetic spectrum includes waves that range from infinitesimally short X rays to light waves measured in *angstroms* (1 angstrom equals 1 ten-millionth of a millimeter) to radio waves that vary in length from 1 millimeter to sev- eral miles. Radio and television broadcast services occupy only a very small portion of the radio spectrum. Most of the electromagnetic space is assigned to hundreds of various services—military, navigational, satellite services; data transmissions, cellular radio, amateur (ham radio), public service, cable TV distribution; fire, police, emergency services; mobile radio (taxis, businesses), maritime, CB radio, aircraft, microwaves, remote telephones; forest services; medical, government, industrial, mobile paging; highway maintenance; short wave; civil air patrol; power utilities; transportation; and on and on.

The Overtone Series

*I*n the early chapters of this text, we explained in rather simple terms the process whereby the waveform of natural sound, known as pressure waves, is transformed for broadcasting purposes into the very different electromagnetic energy wave. The production use of microphones, speakers, and other audio equipment depends largely upon a good understanding of the qualities of sound itself. The water wave analogy used in appendix A is of considerable help in examining these qualities.

The factor that distinguishes the tone of middle C on a piano from its higher neighbor, D, is its frequency. Whether it is the string on a violin, the reed on a clarinet, or the vocal cords of the human voice, each instrument has an element that is able to vibrate at varying rates of cycles per second. The relative size of the vibration is the measure of amplitude. If more force in terms of air pressure is applied to the reed, the vibration is bigger and the tone therefore is louder. The frequency, however, does not change. The pitch of the note stays the same—until the apparatus producing the tone (the clarinet's column of air or a violin string) is altered in shape or length to change the frequency of the vibration.

The velocity, or traveling speed, of a sound wave is relative to the density of the form of matter within which it moves. In the air, altitude and temperature can affect this speed. In fairly average conditions, the velocity of sound is 1,120 feet per second. With the increased density of water, the speed is 4,700 feet per second. In solid steel, for example, the velocity is sixteen times that which occurs in the air. Such velocities are a very minor consideration in broadcasting.

Our primary consideration is the effect of a vibrating instrument upon the molecules of the air. Let us take the example of a middle C tone struck on a piano. Actually, three middle C strings are set in motion when struck by the hammer, but let us follow just the action of one.

Figure B–1
Sound pressure waves.

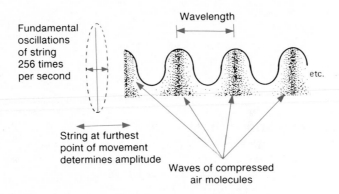

Fundamental oscillations of string 256 times per second

Wavelength

String at furthest point of movement determines amplitude

Waves of compressed air molecules

etc.

Figure B–2
Fundamental tone.

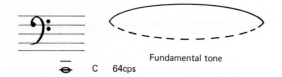

Fundamental tone

C   64cps

The string is set in motion at the rate of 256 cycles per second. Each oscillation presses against the molecules of the air and creates a moving pressure wave. When 256 of these pressure waves strike the ear every second, we hear it as middle C. (See figure B–1.)

This simple example of the back-and-forth movement of the string is not a complete description of what is happening to the agitated string. Actually, a vibrating string further subdivides itself into smaller vibrating lengths that produce additional pitches or *overtones* or *harmonics* at higher frequencies. The main tone we hear is called the *fundamental tone.* As an example, we shall move two octaves down the piano keyboard to the low C just off the musical staff. As a fundamental tone, it vibrates at a frequency of sixty-four times a second. (See figure B–2.)

Together with this main vibration of the string between its two endpoints, a series of smaller subdivisions occurs, each of which produces its own tone. The first subdivision divides the string in half and produces the first overtone. (See figure B–3.) Each subsequent subdivision separates the vibrating string into quarters, eighths, sixteenths, and so forth. (See figure B–4.)

The series of succeeding overtones are of far less intensity or loudness than the fundamental tone. Only the most discriminating ear even hears them as separate notes. Generally speaking, the lower overtones predominate, with the higher frequencies becoming almost inaudible. It is the resonating quality of each type of instrument that determines the presence or absence of overtones. The fundamental tone of A, at 440 cycles per second, on

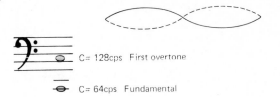

C = 128 cps First overtone

C = 64 cps Fundamental

Figure B–3
First overtone.

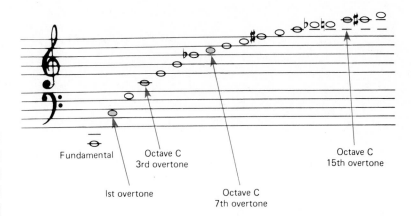

Fundamental

1st overtone

Octave C
3rd overtone

Octave C
7th overtone

Octave C
15th overtone

Figure B–4
Overtone series.

a violin will resonate and thereby reflect certain overtone frequencies better than others in the series as a result of the very design of the instrument. A metal flute playing the identical tone will resonate an entirely different series of overtones. It is this differing profile of selected overtones from among the entire series that determines the distinctive tonal quality of an instrument.[1] The electronic synthesizer artificially creates tones closely resembling real instruments by manipulating the overtone series. In the same manner, it can create tonal effects previously unattainable on conventional instruments.

1. The equal-tempered scale of the modern keyboard instruments such as the piano has made necessary some minute compromises in the tuning of such instruments. As a result, several of the overtones on the piano, notably the sixth, tenth, twelfth, and thirteenth, are at slight variance as to the exact number of cycles per second. A well-written description of the development of the modern keyboard scale is contained in the book *Science and Music*, written by Sir James Jeans (New York: Dover Publications, 1968).

Hand and Arm Signals

*I*n a production situation, the hand and arm signals of the stage manager are simply a visual extension of the director's commands. Most of these gestures were developed during the early days of radio. A few have been altered somewhat for use in television production. The following examples show the signals most generally in use today.

TELEVISION HAND SIGNALS

CUE		MEANING	DESCRIPTION
STAND BY	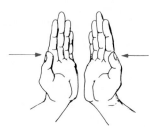	Ready to start show Ready to record Quiet on the set	Stage Manager raises hand in air, with fingers pointing upward
YOU'RE ON TAKE YOUR CUE	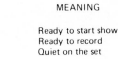	Start talking Talent is on the air	Points to performer or live camera
GET CLOSER TOGETHER		Talent, performers or reporters too far apart Get closer together Get closer to object of interest	Stage Manager plays an invisible accordian, bringing palms together repeatedly

CUE	MEANING	DESCRIPTION
GET FARTHER APART	Talent too close together	Stage Manager moves hands together, back to back, then spreads them sharply apart

| STOP THAT'S FAR ENOUGH | Close enough or far enough, stop moving together or apart | Traffic cop's signal, similar to standby signal |
| TALK TO THIS CAMERA CAMERA CHANGE | Changing cameras | Stage Manager swings hands through a wide arc from camera that is on the air to the camera that will be on the air |

| GET CLOSER TO THE MICROPHONE OR SPEAK LOUDER | Audio level too low Get closer to the mike | Stage Manager moves hands toward himself/ herself or toward the mike |

| GET FURTHER FROM MICROPHONE OR SPEAK LOWER | Opposite of above | Opposite of above |
| KEEP TALKING STRETCH | Too much time left Fill in | Extend thumb and forefinger horizontally, move them like the beak of a bird |

CUE	MEANING	DESCRIPTION
STRETCH IT OUT SLOW DOWN	Talking too fast	Move hands as if pulling taffy apart or stretching rubber bands

| SPEED IT UP | Talking too slow Running out of time | Move forefinger in circles |

| ON THE NOSE PROGRAM ON TIME | Program is running right on time, no problems | Stage Manager touches nose with forefinger |

| O.K. ALL IS WELL YOUR POSITION IS FINE | Well done Stay right there | Form an "O" with thumb and forefinger with other three fingers raised |

CUE	MEANING	DESCRIPTION
FIVE MINUTES TO GO TWO MINUTES TO GO ONE MINUTE TO GO	Time cues to end of show	Raise hand with corresponding number of fingers spread apart or raise flash cards

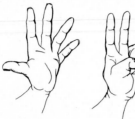

HALF A MINUTE TO GO	Time to end of segment or end of show	Cross forefingers or forearms at midpoint

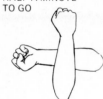

WRAP IT UP	10 seconds left Come to a conclusion	Rocking or shaking of clenched fist

CUT FINISH OFF THE AIR	Segment or show is over	Stage Manager slashes own throat with forefinger or edge of hand

STATION BREAK (I.D.)	Commercial	The motion of breaking a twig is made with clenched fists

Appendix C

Production Projects

D–1 Class Audio Production Project (Chapter 3)

COPY: "INTEGRATED SOUND CORPORATION" COMMERCIAL

MUSIC: UP FULL FOR TEN SECONDS AND UNDER

ANNC #1   THE <u>INTEGRATED SOUND CORPORATION</u> OF MANHATTAN CORDIALLY

                INVITES YOU TO A PREVIEW PRESENTATION OF THE NEWEST

                DEVELOPMENTS FROM THE <u>OLYMPIA</u> LINE OF FINE SOUND

                REPRODUCTION SYSTEMS. FOR THE NEXT WEEK, ALL TEN

                <u>INTEGRATED</u> STORES IN NEW YORK CITY AND NEW JERSEY WILL BE

                DEMONSTRATING STEREO COMPONENTS DESIGNED TO PRODUCE A

                FULL-FREQUENCY RESPONSE HERETOFORE HEARD ONLY IN

                PROFESSIONAL SOUND RECORDING STUDIOS.

MUSIC: FADE UP FULL TEN SECONDS AND UNDER

ANNC #2   <u>OLYMPIA'S</u> GREATEST ADVANCE IN THE PAST TWENTY YEARS HAS

                BEEN MADE POSSIBLE BY THE NEW HORIZONTAL FIELD EFFECT

                TRANSISTOR, WHICH PRODUCES A CLEAN, UNCOLORED SOUND POWER

                OF INCREDIBLE DIMENSION.

MUSIC: FADE UP FULL TEN SECONDS AND UNDER

(CONTINUED)

ANNC #1	THE OLYMPIA T-E-A 850 STEREO AMPLIFIER, WITH 100 WATTS PER CHANNEL, REPRODUCES FREQUENCIES AS LOW AS 20 CYCLES PER SECOND UP TO 20,000 CYCLES PER SECOND. THESE RANGE FROM TONES THAT ARE LOWER THAN THE LOWEST NOTE ON THE PIANO KEYBOARD UP TO THE HIGHEST OVERTONE FREQUENCIES THAT ARE WITHIN THE RANGE OF HUMAN HEARING. THE RESULT IS A LIFELIKE "OPEN" SOUND QUALITY PRODUCED WITH SOLID STATE HIGH STABILITY AND RELIABILITY.
MUSIC:	FADE UP FULL TEN SECONDS AND UNDER
ANNC #2	SEE ALL OF THE COMPONENTS IN THE EXCITING NEW LINE FROM OLYMPIA THIS WEEK AT ANY OF YOUR INTEGRATED STORES IN NEW YORK CITY AND NEW JERSEY.
MUSIC:	UP FULL FIVE SECONDS AND OUT

D-2 "The Magnificent Burden"

VIDEO	AUDIO

FADE UP FROM BLACK, ANNOUNCER IN NEWSROOM SETTING

ANNOUNCER: I'm speaking from the anchor desk to tell you about an important program produced by our newsroom staff. Mindful of recent events, we are going to examine the demands the office of the presidency puts upon the occupant of the White House.

PICTURE: JOHNSON

MUSIC: MARTIAL STRAINS, UP TWO SECONDS AND UNDER ANNC (V.O.): Lyndon Johnson, blamed by many for the escalation of the Vietnam War, refused to run for a second term in office.

PICTURE: NIXON

Richard Nixon's attempts to cope with growing dissension over the war were overshadowed by the startling disclosures of the Watergate Inquiry and his ultimate resignation. Paradoxically, he is still held in high esteem in many other countries.

(CONTINUED)

VIDEO	AUDIO
PICTURE: FORD AND CARTER	Plagued by controversy over his pardon of Richard Nixon, Gerald Ford saw his bid for a full term in office denied by less than one percent of the popular vote. Jimmy Carter enjoyed widespread popularity early in his term but was unable to get re-elected because of his faltering media image.
CARD, REAGAN AND GROUP	Ronald Reagan was twice elected to the presidency by overwhelming margins. He achieved significant progress in international diplomacy, but success with domestic policies was often denied him by a Congress controlled by the Democrats.
CARD, CAPITOL TITLE CARD, KEYED OVER CAPITOL	Sharing the burdens and frustrations of the nation's highest office, these men have known the peaks and valleys of triumph and defeat. Join us for an insight into the world of presidential politics from the personal standpoint on . . . "The Magnificent Burden," Sunday evenings at nine. MUSIC: UP FULL FOR FIVE SECONDS
FADE TO BLACK	MUSIC OUT

D–3 Production Project: Discussion Program (Chapter 13)

OPENING AND CLOSING FORMAT

VIDEO   AUDIO

WIDE ESTAB.
SHOT   MUSIC: ESTABLISH FIVE SECONDS AND UNDER
CAM 2
C.G.: TITLE,
KEYED OVER   ANNC: "Frame of Reference," an information service
CAM 2
program designed to explore the multifaceted issues that

affect us, both as individuals and as members of an

increasingly complex society. Here with our guests is the

"Frame of Reference" moderator, _____ .

MUSIC: OUT

MCU, CAM 1   MODERATOR: Our area of examination today is _____

_____ .

MODERATOR: (CONTINUED) To help us in gaining a greater

understanding of the problems that are involved in this

issue are three people who hold somewhat differing views

on the solutions to those problems. Seated next to me is

_____ from _____ .

(CONTINUED)

VIDEO	AUDIO

CU CAM 3   Our second guest is _____

                           who represents _____ .

CU CAM 2   Our final guest, who is from _____ ,

                           is _____ .

WIDE SHOT
CAM 1   As a way of establishing the background to today's issue,

                           I would like to address my first question to

                           _____ .

                           (BODY OF PROGRAM)

CU MODERATOR
CAM 1   <u>MODERATOR:</u> With that last point we must, for now,

                           conclude our discussion of _____ . The issue is

                           a large one and our program time is, unfortunately,

ZOOM OUT TO
TIGHT 4-SHOT   limited. I would like to thank our guests _____ ,

                           _____ , and _____ for joining us today and for

                           measurably adding to our collective knowledge of this

                           controversial issue. This is _____ .

                           Good-bye until next week.

VIDEO	AUDIO
EXTREME WIDE SHOT CAM 2	MUSIC: ESTABLISH FIVE SECONDS AND UNDER
(KEY CREDITS)	ANNC: As a program, "Frame of Reference" makes no attempt to establish any final solutions to the problems under discussion. Our goal is that of presenting well-informed opinion leaders to our viewing public so that each individual can come to his or her own conclusions. Next week our "Frame of Reference" will encompass the matter of _____ . Be sure to join us then.
	MUSIC: UP FULL TO CONCLUSION
FADE TO BLACK	MUSIC: FADE OUT

D–4 Production Exercise: "It's a Date?" (Chapter 14)

VIDEO	AUDIO	(APPROX. 4:00 MIN.)

HARRY: (TALKING TO NANCY, WHO IS OFFSTAGE) I see where old Harold Osgood is fighting with the university again.

NANCY: (ENTERING FROM CAMERA RIGHT) What, dear?

HARRY: Councilman Osgood objects to the fact that taxpayers' money is being spent on a college course called "The Crisis in Human Sexuality." He says that it's part of a plot to destroy the morals of American youth.

NANCY: Oh, it's probably just one of those courses that teach people how to get along with one another.

HARRY: (SARCASTICALLY) Yeah, I'll <u>bet</u> it is.

NANCY: Oh, Harry, it's not <u>that</u>. Those kind of classes just help people to establish their personal identity . . . you know, who they really are.

HARRY: Well, when I was in college no professor had to tell me who or what I was.

VIDEO	AUDIO

NANCY: I remember very well what kind of a guy you were. (KIDDING) You were a big <u>wolf</u>, that's what you were.

HARRY: (SMILING) Oh, come on, Nancy, I was just a normal red-blooded American boy.

NANCY: Well it just might have done <u>you</u> some good to have taken one of those courses. Things are different now with men and women, Harry. We're no longer in the Dark Ages.

HARRY: Yeah, a lot of good it's done . . . a bunch of so-called liberated females running around. . . .

NANCY: (INTERRUPTING) Harry, they don't run around. They do a lot of constructive things. Why only last week. . . .

KIM: (INTERRUPTING FROM OFFSTAGE) Daddy, what time is it? (ENTERING SOMEWHAT BREATHLESSLY) Derek will be here any minute.

(CONTINUED)

VIDEO	AUDIO

HARRY: (STERN BUT FATHERLY) It's seven twenty-five, and who's Derek?

KIM: He's only a really neat guy, that's all. And don't be so uptight, Daddy.

NANCY: Kim, you know that your father always thinks of your dates as being direct descendants of Attila the Hun.

KIM: Well he's not. He's really nice. He writes on the school newspaper and he's really into broadcasting.

HARRY: If he has somehow made you suddenly aware of the discipline of time, he can't be all bad.

KIM: Well, he's very . . . you know, intellectual. He knows all about music and things.

HARRY: Yes, I can imagine. I remember that football player friend of yours. He spoke English like a second language.

MUSIC: ROCK AND ROLL MUSIC UNDER THE CONVERSATION AS IF FROM OUTSIDE THE HOUSE.

VIDEO	AUDIO

HARRY: (CONTINUING) The only trouble was that he didn't have a first . . . say, what's that noise?

KIM: Oh, that must be Derek. Will you go to the door? I'm not ready! (EXITS)

NANCY: Well, we should be thankful that Derek at least comes to the door . . . not like the boy who sat in the driveway and honked. (SHE EXITS CAMERA RIGHT.)

(HARRY PUTS DOWN THE NEWSPAPER AND SLOWLY STANDS UP SHAKING HIS HEAD.)

NANCY: (OFFSTAGE) Hello, I'm Kim's mother. You must be Derek. Won't you come in? She will be right out.
(ENTERING FROM CAMERA RIGHT) Harry, this is Kim's friend, Derek. I'm afraid that Kim hasn't told us your last name.

DEREK: Uh, Derek's O.K. . . . or, Rick.
(THERE IS AN AWKWARD 5-SECOND PAUSE WHILE ALL TRY TO THINK OF SOMETHING TO SAY.)

(CONTINUED)

VIDEO	AUDIO

NANCY: Well, it's so nice.

HARRY: (OVER NANCY'S LINE) Is that music coming from your car?

DEREK: That's my van. It sleeps two.

(HARRY STARTS TO SAY SOMETHING, THINKS BETTER OF IT, AND QUICKLY TRIES TO COVER HIS STARTLED EXPRESSION.)

DEREK: (CONTINUING) Like, I do a lot of camping. It's really great with my tape deck out in the woods.

HARRY: (STRAIGHT BUT WITH A TOUCH OF SARCASM) Yes, I guess you could really get back to nature.

(NANCY CROSSES TO HIM, TAKES HIS ARM, AND GIVES IT A WARNING SQUEEZE.)

DEREK: That's Wretched Yellow playing "Boogie 'Til 1995." It's their big hit. Great guitar. (HE MOVES SLIGHTLY WITH THE MUSIC.)

NANCY: Kim tells us that you write for the school newspaper.

VIDEO	AUDIO

DEREK: Yeah, I write a column called "Diggin' the Discs." They wanted me to call it "Pickin' the Platters," but I thought it sounded kinda' corny.

HARRY: You're right, it just doesn't have the same ring to it.

(NANCY GIVES HARRY ANOTHER WARNING SQUEEZE.)

DEREK: What do you do, Mr. Olmstead?

HARRY: Well, I . . . uh . . . I'm a loan officer at First Federal.

DEREK: Oh yeah, Kim told me. Well, I guess everybody has to do something.

HARRY: (REACTING) It may seem sort of quaint, but in today's society. . . .

KIM: (INTERRUPTING AS SHE ENTERS FROM CAMERA LEFT) Hi, Derek. (SHE CROSSES TO HIM.)

(CONTINUED)

VIDEO	AUDIO

DEREK: Wow, you are some kind o' looker.

KIM: Rick, I just love your jacket. It's really neat.
Hey, we better go.

NANCY: Wait a minute. Where are you two going?

KIM: To the movies. We can either see a musical, "The
Monster on Lead Guitar" or "My Secret Swedish Summer."
They say it's a beautiful, artistic movie about this
couple in love. . . .

HARRY: I don't think I want to hear . . . I can already
guess.

NANCY: Isn't there something else playing?

DEREK: Yeah, but they're just like what's on television.
Kim, let's go to the monster movie. They say that Lulu
Bash is fantastic in the death scenes. She does karate
moves while playing the love theme from the movie on her
guitar.

VIDEO	AUDIO

KIM: Super. Well, we better go. See you later. (EXITING)
Everybody at school has seen it by now. We just have to
go.

NANCY: Don't be too late, dear.

KIM: I won't. (OFFSTAGE) Bye-bye.

(WHEN THEY ARE GONE, THERE IS A PAUSE AS NANCY AND HARRY
LOOK AT EACH OTHER.)

HARRY: (LAUGHING RUEFULLY) Where did we go wrong?

NANCY: Oh, he's a nice boy, Harry. He's just at that
age.

HARRY: I guess you're right. I hope so anyway. Say . . .
how would you like to sneak off and see "My Secret
Swedish Summer?"

NANCY: (LAUGHING) Let me think about it.

MUSIC: BRIEFLY FADE ROCK MUSIC UP FULL AND OUT.

D–5 Script for Full-Facilities Production Exercise (Chapter 14)

VIDEO	AUDIO
C.G., "FRAME OF REFERENCE"	<u>MUSIC</u>: ESTABLISH, FIVE SECONDS AND UNDER <u>BOOTH ANNC</u> (OFF CAMERA): Should the United States government ban the sale and manufacture of DMSO? Kenneth Anderson is joined by experts on both sides of this important question on "Frame of Reference," Saturday afternoon at four.
VIDEOTAPE PUBLIC SERVICE :30	<u>SOUND ON TAPE</u>
STUDIO NEWS PROMO :30	<u>NEWS ANNC</u>: Tonight on the six o'clock news we have the latest statement by the President on the availability of Middle Eastern oil. . . . A report from Washington that the plumbing in the Watergate Hotel has sprung its own leak. . . News from Detroit that thousands of new cars have been recalled before they ever got off the assembly line . . . and sportscaster Stan Dilbeck has a report on the Matadors and their chance for a winning season.

• • • • • • • • • • • • •

VIDEO	AUDIO
STUDIO HOST	HOST (ON CAMERA): Tonight at nine our program series "The Magnificent Burden" presents an account of the triumphs
CARD: JOHNSON C.G.: MATTE "THE MAGNIFICENT BURDEN"	and defeats of Lyndon B. Johnson. As a man forced to assume power in a time of crisis, he was often admired for the way in which he took over the responsibilities of leadership. Many of his proposed social reforms were, however, sacrificed to the demands of a war that seemingly could not be ended. "The Magnificent Burden" tonight at nine.
STUDIO	HOST (ON CAMERA): Coming up in just a moment we have something in a lighter vein on "Campus Rock." Host Charlie "Red" Stewart presents The Grass Valley Boys singing "Pure Pleasure," Bonnie Street does her version of "The Sadness of My Life," and that new group, The Electric Car, performs their hit, "Turn on the Lights."
STATION I.D.	They get it all together, next on _____ TV.
VTR	SOUND ON TAPE

The five photographs and one key card included in this appendix are to be photographically enlarged and used in the class production projects for sections 7.6 and 14.4.

Production Projects

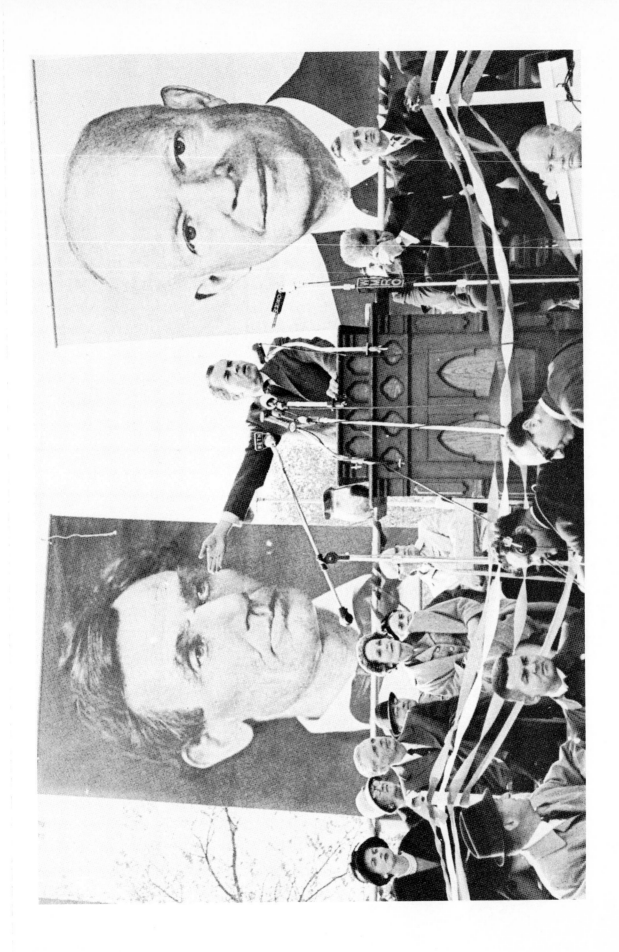

Production Projects

THE MAGNIFICENT BURDEN

Sundays, 9:00 pm

The Rate Card

_A_s introduced in chapter 12 (section 12.3), the unit manager (or production manager) is usually the chief budget supervisor on any professional production. It is his or her job to oversee all fiscal aspects of the production contract. To help you understand some of the details and concerns of the unit manager's position, the rate cards and associated materials in this appendix have been prepared for examination and utilization in production courses.[1]

It is suggested that these materials be removed (at the perforations) and used for actual studio productions. Students should be given the experience of working through these sheets and estimating actual production costs as part of their curricular training. These forms may be used as they are, or instructors may want to revise the figures in order to reflect actual dollar costs in a given locality.

Below-the-Line Costs

Each production house or network has a set of rates that it charges for its services. Essentially, these are the below-the-line costs as introduced in section 1.6. These rates are listed on the **rate card,** which is updated each year to reflect economic realities. As union contracts are negotiated periodically—increasing the salaries of those personnel assigned to the production—so the rate charged to the producer must be increased.

The charges listed on the rate card do not reflect the actual money paid to the listed engineer or production person. In fact, the salary of that person may be as little as one-third of the charge for that position levied against the show producer. The production studios and networks must maintain large staffs—management, clerical, maintenance, legal,

1. Most of this appendix is based upon materials developed by Jay Roper, Director, NBC News West Coast, for use in production courses. The authors gratefully thank Mr. Roper for his permission to use the materials in this text.

janitorial, budget and personnel officers, support staff, technical operations schedulers, and so forth—to support those production positions. Fringe benefits, medical insurance, taxes, and other deductions are all covered by the charges on the rate card; these costs must all be passed along to the contracting/producing agency.

Generally, the rate card can be broken down into three separate components: (1) *Technical Personnel Chart;* (2) *Facilities Rates Chart;* and (3) *Personnel Hourly Rate Chart.*

Technical Personnel Chart   The size and complexity of any given production will obviously determine the staff needed for that show. Additionally, sometimes the contractual obligations will dictate the needs for a production. For example, some equipment—such as a crane—may require, according to the engineering contract, a certain number of people to operate it.

All engineering positions cost the same on the rate card—even though some individuals will actually receive more pay than others (due to seniority, expertise, responsibility, and so forth). The Technical Personnel Chart (table E.1) reflects costs on a quarter-hour basis, adjusted to a 3-hour production period for training situations.

Engineers usually will be assigned to a production in 8-hour blocks—the standard workday defined by the union. (Of that eight hours, one is set aside for a meal. And if you, as a producer, are shooting on location at some distance from a restaurant, you will want to have the meals catered; otherwise the union contract states that travel time to the nearest restaurant is "on the clock.")

In case of overtime, the producer will have to pay an additional rate. Also, charges are less per hour after a certain amount of time; this is done to discourage producers from renting facilities in short blocks of time. Therefore, it is most cost-efficient to plan your production within 8-hour periods.

Facilities Rates Chart   At most networks and production facilities, the charges for studio rental might vary from perhaps $300 per hour to as much as $700 an hour for a large stage (for a 6-hour minimum). This charge includes basically an empty studio with cyclorama, lighting instruments and controls, normal camera complement, and control rooms—no sets, no special electronic effects, no special lights, and of course, no personnel.

The charge indicated on the Facilities Rates Chart (table E.2) for videotape facilities are for playback only. Charges for editing time usually would be much higher since editing would demand much more sophisticated equipment. Costs for 2-inch (quad) and 1-inch (type C) playback machines are higher than for ¾-inch format players because of both (a) higher initial costs and maintenance and (b) longer setup time.

The rental of the film chain includes the full facilities of the chain (slides, 16mm and 35mm film projectors) as well as the video control panel for that telecine chain and the patching necessary to deliver the feed to the studio control room or other destination.

A production may require additional engineering equipment and special effects such as frame storers, character generators, advanced SEG switchers, editing facilities, and so forth. These costs would have to be added to the basic Facilities Rates Chart.

Although the additional production costs would appear to be quite steep for these added extras, it may be that the increased expenditures are worth the cost because of the time that can be saved; computer graphics capabilities or editing facilities may save you hours of preproduction, production, or postproduction work that you would otherwise be paying for in other ways. Therefore, the thorough producer must carefully "cost out" all possible production options.

Personnel Hourly Rate Chart Many different categories of non-engineering production personnel must also be considered. Depending upon the needs of the producer, many of these costs will be below-the-line expenses. These personnel also can be provided by the network or the production house. Again, the fees charged on the Personnel Hourly Rate Chart (table E.3) are not indicative of actual pay scales—as overhead costs must be covered by the production house or network.

Before the Show Before the production moves near the studio, much work must be accomplished. Design, construction, acquisition, transportation, and placement of sets, set pieces, props, artwork, costumes, drapes, and lights call for the "renting" (from the production house) of many different types of personnel—carpenters, set designers, wardrobe staff, graphic artists, stagehands, grips, prop handlers, drape constructionists, electricians, and so forth.

During the Production The chief below-the-line positions would probably be the associate director and the stage manager(s). Other specialized positions may have to be considered—pages (to handle the studio audience), security guards (to stand over the game show prizes), makeup, production assistants, and so forth.

After the Production Somebody must clean up. Sets must be struck. Props and costumes have to be returned. In effect, the studio must be returned to the condition it was in prior to the production. Personnel must be retained to handle all this.

In summary, it should be realized that the rate card is a *guide* and that while these charges reflect an honest, competitive position, there is always room for negotiation—especially if you are planning on producing a number of productions at the same production facility. Nevertheless, the rate card is a basis for that negotiation and you, as a producer, must learn to use it in planning and determining your below-the-line costs.

Above-the-Line Costs

In addition to the below-the-line expenses, you must also plan on budgeting for above-the-line costs. These are the expenses that are incurred by the producer outside of the production house or network studio charges (section 1.6).

Many of the above-the-line budget items are for personnel, and most of these are *negotiated fees*. The American Federation of Television and Radio Artists (AFTRA), the Writers Guild of America (WGA), the Directors Guild of America (DGA), and the American Federation of Musicians (AFM) all have contracts that specify the fee that the creative talent involved is to receive. In addition to these stated minimum guild and union (federation) fees, many artists of "star" caliber will, of course, negotiate much higher salaries. Special *perquisites* may also have to be provided—limousine service, personalized travel arrangements, private hairdressers, personal secretaries, and so forth.

In addition to the salaries paid to the talent and creative personnel, consideration must be given to other salaries (of production associates, secretaries, typists) and to other business expenses (rental of offices, telephones, office supplies, and similar items).

In the case of remotes or *location shoots,* other costs may involve housing, catering, transportation, telephone lines, microwave links, and possibly satellite time and uplink facilities. Other special services may involve standby firefighters (for any explosive or incendiary effects), ambulance and medical contingencies (for difficult stunt work), off-duty police officers (for security and traffic control), teachers (tutors for child actors), helicopter services, and any other extraordinary services the production may require.

The two contract forms (tables E.4 and E.5) are variations of basic contracts that can be used for directors and for performing talent, respectively. (As with the three preceding below-the-line charts, these forms may be torn out and used as they are or may be modified to reflect specific university training situations.)

The final four pages of this appendix comprise a Production Cost Report, which can be used as a realistic exercise in working out detailed budget projections for a typical television production. It is suggested that student producers and/or unit managers be required to turn in an accurate budget estimate, following these forms. The first form is a summary cover sheet. The remaining forms are below-the-line and above-the-line worksheets.

This appendix has been but a cursory simplification of the business end of producing a television program. We have only briefly touched upon some of the complexities with which producers and networks must be involved—negotiating studio costs, union contracts, personnel services; scheduling crews; booking transportation; renting outside facilities; arranging for special police and medical services, communication utilities and hookups; and so forth. However, this should serve to familiarize the beginning student with some of the budget considerations that producers and unit managers must learn to juggle in managing any kind of production enterprise.

Table E.1 Technical Personnel Chart

Number of Engineers

Rate	Hour	1	2	3	4	5	6	7	8	9	10
$20	¼	20	40	60	80	100	120	140	160	180	200
$20	½	220	240	260	280	300	320	340	360	380	400
$20	¾	415	430	445	460	475	490	505	520	535	550
$20	1	565	580	595	610	625	640	655	670	685	700
$20	1¼	725	750	775	800	825	850	875	900	925	950
$20	1½	975	1000	1025	1050	1075	1100	1125	1150	1175	1200
$20	1¾	1230	1260	1290	1320	1350	1380	1410	1440	1470	1500
$20	2	1530	1560	1590	1620	1650	1680	1710	1740	1770	1800
$20	2¼	1830	1860	1890	1920	1950	1980	2010	2040	2070	2100
$20	2½	2130	2160	2190	2220	2250	2280	2310	2340	2370	2400
$20	2¾	2435	2470	2505	2540	2575	2610	2645	2680	2715	2750
$20	3	2790	2830	2870	2910	2950	2990	3030	3070	3110	3150

College Engineering Contract Provisions

1. In the event the engineers are scheduled for fifteen minutes or less, the following provisions do not apply.
2. Engineers will be given a 5-minute break each half hour. These break times may be accumulative.
3. Engineers may be given their accumulated break time (up to fifteen minutes of accumulated time) prior to their beginning work.
4. Engineers will be given a break of at least five minutes no later than 1½ hours into the schedule regardless of the accumulated time.

Table E.2 Facilities Rates Chart

1. Minimum rental of studio is a half hour with the charges being assessed at the rate of $50.00 per 15-minute period. This means a minimum rental of $100.00.
2. The rental of a film chain will be $15.00 per 15-minute period. Minimum rental is fifteen minutes.
3. Videotape facilities will be $20.00 per 15-minute period with a half hour being the minimum rental.
4. The following are miscellaneous studio costs:
   a. Graphics easels .... $10.00 per day each
   b. Slides* .... $ 5.00 per day each
   c. Matte cards* .... $ 5.00 per day each
   d. Full pictures* .... $ 5.00 per day each
   e. Film* .... $20.00 per thirty seconds
   f. Flats .... $10.00 per day each
   g. Desks .... $ 5.00 per day each
   h. Chairs .... $ 5.00 per day each
   i. Risers .... $10.00 per day each
   j. Any furniture brought from outside .... $20.00 transportation each item
   k. House piano .... $20.00 per day
   l. Musical instrument brought in .... $15.00 per day transportation

*Remember that if you had been working with a production house or a network, you would either have had to "farm out" services for matte cards and full pictures to the graphic arts department or you would have had to hire a photographer for your film. These are costs that you would have had to pick up. So you, as a student, must be billed for these services even though you may have done the graphics or the films yourself.

Table E.3 Personnel Hourly Rate Chart

One-Hour Call Minimum

Associate Director	$25.00
Stage Manager	$25.00
Stagehands/Electricians	$20.00
Wardrobe[1]	$18.00
Makeup/Hair Stylist[2]	$18.00
Graphic Artist[3]	$22.00
Scenic Designer[4]	$25.00
Costume Handler[5]	$18.00
Prop Handler	$19.00
Scenic Carpenter[6]	$19.00
Scenic Artist[7]	$22.00
Drape Constructionist[8]	$25.00

1. If the performers use any clothes other than street clothes, even though it is their clothing, this charge must be assessed.
2. If the performers require any makeup, even though they may apply it themselves, this charge must be assessed.
3. If any full pictures or matte cards are used, this charge must be assessed.
4. If a set of any kind is used, this charge must be assessed.
5. If the performer uses any clothing that would be considered a costume (i.e., period clothing), this charge must be assessed.
6. If any of the flats or risers are used, this charge must be assessed.
7. If any artwork other than matte or full cards are used, this charge must be assessed.
8. If drapes other than the cyclorama are used, this charge must be assessed.

Realize—due to the structure of this class—that some of these costs will be "dummy" costs; that is, there will not be a person fulfilling each one of these tasks—unlike the assignment of a person to a camera. Nevertheless, if you were producing at a production house or a network, these would be real costs, and in order to familiarize you (as a student) with the real world, these costs should be figured into your production.

Table E.4 Directors Contract

Directors working on production projects will be paid the following rates:

News and Documentary

0–5 min.	5–10 min.	10–15 min.	15–30 min.
$150.00	$175.00	$200.00	$400.00

Dramas

0–15 min.	15–30 min.
$400.00	$750.00

Musicals

0–5 min.	5–15 min.	15–30 min.
$350.00	$500.00	$750.00

Each director may negotiate his or her own agreement but the above are the minimum salary rates that must be met. In the event a personal services contract is negotiated, a copy of the following must be attached to the Production Cost Report by the unit manager:

The minimum salary for a personal services contract will be 150% of the rate shown above.

- Tear here -

Date: _____

To: Business Affairs

From: _____ (Unit Manager)

    This constitutes an agreement between the below-signed producer and the below-signed director that the director shall receive as compensation for services the figure shown below.

AMOUNT: $ _____

Director: _____ Producer: _____

Appendix E

• • • • • • • • • • • • •

Table E.5 Artists Contract

Performers working on production projects will be paid the following rates:

Principle Performers (dramatic, nondramatic)

0–5 min.	5–10 min.	10–15 min.	15–30 min.
$100.00	$150.00	$200.00	$300.00

Performers—five lines or less

0–5 min.	5–10 min.	10–15 min.	15–30 min.
$50.00	$75.00	$100.00	$130.00

Off Camera—five lines or less (includes announcers)

0–5 min.	5–10 min.	10–15 min.	15–30 min.
$25.00	$37.00	$50.00	$65.00

Off Camera—six lines or more (includes announcers)

0–5 min.	5–10 min.	10–15 min.	15–30 min.
$50.00	$75.00	$100.00	$125.00

Groups/Chorus (includes musicians but not lead singers)

Three to Seven People (each)

0–15 min.	15–30 min.
$25.00	$45.00

Eight or More People (each)

0–15 min.	15–30 min.
$15.00	$30.00

Additional payment for stepping out as soloist or part of chorus for eight bars or more but less than sixteen bars:

150% of above rate

Additional payment for sixteen bars or more:

200% of above rate

Sportscaster:

Each sportscaster shall receive $200 per event.

This fee is only for sports events—if in a news segment, the principle performer rate shall apply.

Extras/Walk-ons

0–5 min.	5–10 min.	10–15 min.	15–30 min.
$10.00	$15.00	$20.00	$30.00

Production Cost Report

Show Name: _____

Producer: _____

Unit Manager: _____

Description	Estimate	Actual	Notes
Below-the-Line Costs			
Above-the-Line Costs			

Total Estimate: _____

Total Actual: _____

Comments:

_____

• • • • • • • • • • • • •

Below-the-Line Costs Worksheet

Show Name: _____

Producer: _____

Unit Manager: _____

Description	Estimate	Actual	Notes
Scenic, Graphic, and Prop Charges Piano			
Flats			
Risers			
Desks			
Chairs			
Matte cards			
Full pictures			
Graphics easels			
Transportation			
Slides			
Film			
Personnel Costs Engineers			
Associate director			
Stage manager			
Stagehands			

(CONTINUED)

Electricians

Wardrobe

Makeup/Hair stylist

Graphic artist

Scenic designer

Costume handlers

Scenic carpenter

Scenic artist

Drape constructionist

_____

_____

_____

_____

Studio Facilities
Film chain

Videotape

Studio rental

_____

_____

_____

Estimated Total: _____

Actual Total: _____

Comments: _____

Above-the-Line Costs Worksheet

Show Name: _____

Producer: _____

Unit Manager: _____

Description	Estimate	Actual	Notes
Personnel			
Talent			
Talent			
Talent			
Talent			
Talent			
Talent			
Talent			
Talent			
Director			
Musician			
Musician			
Musician			
Musician			
Musician			
Musician			
Musician			

Estimate Total: _____

Actual Total: _____

Comments: _____

Glossary

above-the-line costs Expenditures for creative and performing personnel (such as the producer, associate producers, writers, artists, musicians, actors, and others) and other administrative elements (such as office space, rehearsal halls, studio space, and so forth).

A/B roll editing An editing process that involves preparing two source tapes with alternate segments to be assembled, carefully spaced so that dissolves and other two-tape effects can be executed through the SEG during the editing procedure.

actuality The part of a news story that features the actual event or the person involved in the story.

A.D. (associate director, assistant director) A key production assistant—usually responsible for timing of the program—who may be delegated any other key responsibilities by the director.

address system Those editing components with their numerical readout—based either upon the SMPTE time code or upon the vertical sync pulse on the control track—that allow for the precise location of each recorded picture frame on a given reel of videotape.

ad-lib Dialogue or action that is completely spontaneous and unrehearsed.

ampere (amp) A measure of the rate of flow of electrons.

amplifier A device that can magnify an electrical signal—either audio or video—for mixing, distribution, and transducing purposes.

amplitude Measurement of the intensity of an electromagnetic wave.

aperture The opening in the camera lens that determines how much light will pass through.

arcing A combination trucking, panning, and dollying movement, in which the camera is moved in an arc around a subject while the camera head is always pointed toward the same subject.

aspect ratio The ratio of the height of the television screen (three units high) to its width (four units wide).

assemble editing Creation of a television production by adding various segments sequentially in the final program order.

asymmetrical balance An informal arrangement in which an important object placed close to the center of the picture is balanced by a lightweight object some distance from the center.

attenuator *See* Potentiometer.

audio The sound portion of a television production.

audio booth (audio control room) The room where all audio signals are controlled and mixed; all audio inputs (microphones, prerecorded tapes and records, and the like) are centrally controlled and then sent on to a master control room, video recorder, or transmitter.

audio compressor An electronic device used to bring weak audio levels up to an averaged volume.

audio signal flow The theoretical schematic model that sequentially traces every step of the audio path from the microphone (or other audio source) to the home radio or TV receiver.

auto key *See* External Key.

automatic gain control (AGC) An internal control device, for either audio or video signals, that automatically increases and decreases (as needed) the strength of the incoming sound or picture in order to maintain optimum signal strength for recording, playback, editing and other production purposes.

axis of action/conversation An imaginary line that (1) extends the path in which a character is moving or (2) connects two persons talking to each other; all cameras should remain on the same side of this line.

back focus *See* Tube Focus.

background light *See* Set Light.

back light A highly directional light coming from above and behind a subject, adding highlights, shape, and separation from the background.

backpack VTR *See* Portapak.

back timing The process of timing a piece of music or other audio track so that it can be started at a precise point with the video—in order to make the sound and picture end at the same time.

balance 1. In audio, the achievement of the correct ratio among several sound sources. 2. Visually, the relative composition and stability among elements in a picture.

ballast A unit used with an HMI light that protects the lamp from surges in power and allows the bulb to last longer.

banding Severe breakup of a picture where a horizontal strip of the video signal has lost its sync.

bank *See* Bus, definition 2.

barn doors Movable metal shutters, attached to the front of a lighting instrument, that are used to limit the area of the projected light.

base light The basic lighting needed for adequate illumination to achieve a technically acceptable television picture.

beam splitter The optical device in a color camera, consisting of a prism and mirrors, that separates the incoming visual image into the primary colors of blue, red, and green.

below-the-line costs The technical and production personnel (such as the engineers, camera and audio operators, stagehands, and others) and other production equipment, facilities, and services.

Betacam A broadcast-quality camcorder manufactured by Sony.

Betamax A consumer-quality 1/2-inch videocassette system developed by Sony.

black Technically, a synchronized video signal that contains no picture information—a blank screen.

blacking (laying down black) The process of preparing a master videotape for editing by recording black on the tape—in actuality, recording the control track so that a continuous sync pulse is available for editing.

blanking The process of momentarily turning off the scanning beam while it retraces its path before starting to scan another line.

blocking Careful planning and coordinating of all movement and positioning of talent and production equipment.

body time Time remaining in the body of the program—not including closing credits and titles—indicating the time signals that must be given to the talent.

boom (mike boom) Any device consisting of a movable base, an adjustable stand, and a long arm for suspending a microphone above and in front of a performer.

booming (craning) Moving the boom arm or tongue of a camera crane up or down. (*See* Crane, definition 2.)

breakdown sheet A production outline of the script, breaking down each scene in terms of location, cast and crew needed, props, equipment, etc.; it is helpful in planning remote productions so that all scenes in one location or all scenes involving a certain actor can be shot at the same time—regardless of the actual sequence of the final program.

brightness (lightness, value) 1. The intensity of the picture on a television tube. 2. An indication of where a color would fall on a scale from light (white) to dark (black); corresponds to the gray scale for monochrome television.

broad A floodlight with a large rectangular, panlike reflector.

broadcasting *See* Open-Circuit Broadcasting.

buffer A section of the memory part of a computer's CPU that is set aside for a specific work task, e.g., to temporarily store a file you have been working on while you call up another file or buffer on your screen.

burn-in *See* Image Retention.

bus 1. A common audio circuit that collects signals from several audio sources and feeds them into one source (for example, a mix bus feeds the combined audio signal to the master potentiometer). 2. The row of buttons representing various video sources on the switcher (also called a *bank*).

butt edit The editing of two segments together so that the end of the first is immediately followed by the beginning of the second.

camcorder An integrated unit that contains both a camera and videotape recorder in one housing.

cameo lighting Lighting the foreground subject with carefully controlled, directional light; the background is kept dark.

camera capture An electronic graphics feature that enables the artist to take the input of a black-and-white camera (block lettering or some flat art) and then manipulate that "captured" image and integrate it into a more elaborate graphics display.

camera chain The electronic camera plus associated equipment such as the sync generator, camera control unit, and so forth.

camera control unit (CCU) Electronic control equipment, usually located in the master control area, that regulates all of the engineering functions of each camera.

camera head (camera) The electronic picture pickup device, which includes the lens (or lenses), pickup tube (or tubes), and viewfinder; the camera serves as a video transducer that converts incoming light energy (pictures) into electrical signals.

camera mount The support arrangement that holds the camera mounting head and the camera itself—usually a movable tripod, pedestal, or crane.

camera mounting head (pan head) The mechanism that connects the camera itself to the camera mount; it allows the camera head to be tilted vertically and to be panned horizontally.

camera pattern The basic positioning and blocking of studio cameras and subsequent movement of the cameras for a particular program sequence.

cardioid pattern *See* Unidirectional.

carrier frequency A specific portion of the electromagnetic spectrum assigned, by the Federal Communications Commission, to a radio or television station for transmission of its modulated broadcast signal.

cartridge An audiotape or videotape recording and/or playback unit that uses a self-contained single-reel case that can be cued up automatically.

cassette An audiotape or videotape recording and/or playback unit that contains both a supply reel and take-up reel in a self-contained case.

catwalk A walkway, one in a system of walkways suspended below the studio ceiling, that allows lighting personnel easy access to lighting instruments.

CAV *See* Component Analog Video.

CCD (charge-coupled device) A microchip—consisting of a photodiode and transistor—that is used to pick up picture information, replacing the conventional picture pickup tube.

C-clamp A metal clamp with a pivot adjustment for attaching lighting instruments to a lighting grid.

CCU *See* Camera Control Unit.

CD *See* Compact Disc.

central processing unit *See* CPU.

channel The specific pathway used to get a signal from source to destination. In audio, it may refer to one of a number of available lines (input channels) within an audio console where various control functions such as volume, equalization, and routing take place for that specific line.

channel selector key An audio channeling switch, usually located adjacent to a pot, that can send the audio signal out through either of two or more line-out channels.

character generator (C.G.) A special electronic effects device with a typewriterlike keyboard that can produce letters and numerals directly on the television screen.

cheat Make minor on-the-air adjustments that the audience will not notice: (1) adjust camera composition; (2) angle a performer toward a camera.

chip *See* Silicon Chip.

chroma key A special effects color matte whereby a specific color (usually green or blue) is used as a key to determine what picture information is to be cut out of the picture with the foreground image.

chrominance channel The color portion of a video signal that contains hue and saturation information, as opposed to luminance information.

clip art A collection of generic art pieces (cartoons and line drawings of a wide assortment of figures, buildings, vehicles, symbols, utensils, and the like) purchased from a commercial source—either as actual artwork on sheets of paper or as computer data that can be electronically inserted into any computer graphic.

clipper knob An SEG adjustment that can set a threshold level for a particular video variable—hue, chrominance, or luminance—for keying.

closed-circuit (CCTV) Television distribution between points connected by cable—anything from a simple two-room hookup to a multichannel state-wide interconnection.

close-up (CU) View of a subject from a relatively short distance.

coaxial cable (coax) Standard camera and video cable with a central insulated conducting wire and a concentrically arranged outer wire.

collective shot A wide shot showing the collective effect or relationship of various elements—an establishing shot.

color bars An electronically generated pattern of vertical color strips, which when sent through the switcher can be used to standardize and calibrate the color values on all cameras, monitors, etc.

color burst A part of the composite video signal produced by a camera (or reproduced by a VTR) that serves as a reference point for the receiving tube. This pulse synchronizes the three incoming color signals.

colorization The use of a special color video synthesizer to produce abstract color effects.

color temperature The relative reddish or bluish quality of a light source, as measured in degrees Kelvin.

comet-tailing *See* Lag.

compact disc (CD) A popular audio recording medium in which the audio signal is recorded in a digital format on a 4¾-inch disc in microscopic "pits" and is read by a laser beam so there is never any physical contact with the disc.

component analog video recording (CAV) A high-quality video recording system that records luminance and chrominance signals separately.

composite signal Also known as composite analog video. Video signal that contains both chrominance and luminance picture information as a single feed.

condenser microphone A high-quality microphone whose transducer consists of a vibrating condenser plate and a fixed backplate.

console (audio board) The control panel or *mixing board* where all audio signals can be amplified, combined, shaped, and channeled.

continuity *See* Picture Continuity.

contrast ratio The ratio of the brightest area to the darkest area in a given camera shot, as determined by reflected light readings.

controller (edit controller) The electronic editing control console that actually controls both the source deck and edit deck and executes the edit.

control room (video booth, studio control room) The room where all video signals are mixed; the director and T.D. control all program elements from this location; sometimes audio and lighting control will also be incorporated into the same area.

control track Portion of a videotape that is used to record the synchronizing pulse.

corner insert A split screen with one camera inserted into a specific quadrant of the picture.

countdown A series of numbers, visual and audible, counted backward (usually from ten to two) indicating the number of seconds on a videotape before program material starts.

cover shot *See* Establishing Shot.

CPU Central processing unit, the actual microprocessor that is the heart of any computer-based equipment (for graphics generation, editing, special effects) that does the actual "computing" or processing of digitalized information.

crabbing Moving the crane or crab dolly base sideways, similar to a *trucking* shot.

crab dolly A small studio crane, first developed for film camera movement.

crane (studio crane) 1. Large camera mount with an extended boom arm or tongue for the camera, with everything—including a seat for the camera operator—placed on a large, four-wheeled dolly or crane base. 2. To move the boom arm up or down.

crash editing An earlier method of editing in which a videotape operator would get two machines up to speed and then transfer a signal from one to the other—without any precise synchronization of the control tracks.

crawl 1. The horizontal movement of electronic text across a screen. 2. *See* Drum.

critical area *See* Essential Area.

cropping Cutting off the edges or border of a picture.

cross-fade 1. An audio transition in which one sound is faded out while another is simultaneously faded in (similar to a video dissolve). 2. A video transition in which one picture is faded out and another picture is immediately faded in from black (similar to an audio segue).

cucalorus (cookie, kook) 1. A special metal cutout pattern that can be inserted into an ellipsoidal spotlight to achieve definite shadow effects. 2. A cardboard or wooden cutout pattern that is placed in front of a spotlight to produce a shadow effect on a scenic background.

cue 1. To give a signal to a talent to start or to perform a certain action. 2. To prepare an audio source (record or audiotape) for a precise start at some predetermined point.

cue cards (idiot sheets) Large, lightweight cards, containing either script material or content outline, held next to the camera for the talent to read.

cue position (audition position) A position on most audio pots and faders that connects the audio source to a separate nonprogram *cue* amplifier and speaker to enable the audio operator to listen to the source without interfering with the program audio.

cue-set The editing function that allows the edit controller to "remember" a specific edit event on both the source and master tapes, thereby enabling the operator to preview and execute the actual edit.

cue track Portion of a videotape that is used to record electronic or audio cues, the SMPTE time code, or similar information.

cut 1. To eliminate some program material, leave out part of the script. 2. To interrupt a rehearsal. 3. *See* Take, definition 1.

cutaway A reaction shot or informational shot that can be insert-edited into a program to cover a jump cut, to explain a point being made, or simply to provide visual interest.

cut button (take bar) A switcher feature that enables the operator to instantaneously alternate the preview and program banks—putting the preview effect on the air and converting the program bank to the preview bank.

cutting ratio The relationship between the size of an object in two successive shots; ordinarily this ratio should not be more than three to one.

cyc (cyclorama) A large, continuous, smooth backing—usually made of cloth—that may cover two or three walls of a studio.

cycles per second (cps) *See* Hertz.

D-1 The earliest internationally recognized digital recording system; it utilized a further encoding of the component video signal into a digital format. The term is often used to refer to all component digital video systems.

D-2 The digital recording system that is based on a composite video signal. It was designed to be compatible with existing composite analog equipment found in most studio facilities.

dailies The videotape or film footage shot during a day's production sessions.

DCC (digital compact cassette) A digital audio tape format introduced by Phillips aimed primarily at the consumer market, housed in a cassette that is physically comparable to the standard audio cassette, and can be played back in a dual-function unit that will play both the DCC format and the standard audio cassette.

dead pot An audio technique, usually used in conjunction with back timing, whereby a piece of music or other audio track is started at a predetermined point with the pot closed; the pot is then opened when the audio is wanted.

debeaming Turning down the intensity of the scanning beam, resulting in a high-contrast picture that gradually deteriorates into a faded gray image.

decibel (db) A unit of measurement of sound that compares the relative intensity of different sound sources.

decorative setting An abstract style of staging with nonrealistic elements added purely for artistic effect.

deflection magnets The wire coils at the rear of the video tube. They produce a constantly changing magnetic field that "pulls" the stream of electrons across and down the inside face of the tube. This sequentially energizes the individual pixels that make up the 525 lines of the two alternating picture fields.

defocus dissolve A camera transition in which the on-the-air camera defocuses and the switcher then dissolves to a similarly defocused camera, which then focuses after it is on the air.

depth of field The distance between the nearest point at which objects are in focus and the farthest point at which objects are in focus.

depth staging The use of foreground and background elements in order to give a feeling of depth to the television picture.

diaphragm 1. The vibrating element in a dynamic microphone that responds to the compressed air molecules of sound waves. 2. The adjustable mechanism that controls the size of the lens aperture.

digital recording An advanced form of video and/or audio electromagnetic recording wherein picture and/or sound information is converted into computerlike off-and-on bits of data.

digital video manipulator (DVM) An electronic control device that can manipulate video signals—once they have been converted into digital information—to achieve a wide variety of pictorial effects.

dimmer board A lighting control unit, operated on the same principle as a rheostat, that determines the intensity of a light by controlling the amount of electric current flowing to the instrument.

director The person in charge of actual production and editing operations—everything that takes place in the studio or on a remote—directing all picture and sound elements to create a final program.

disciplines Those learned and acquired attitudes and habits, developed over a period of time, that comprise an internalized system of professional behavior—such as responsibility, self-control, respect, and initiative.

disk drive The input memory device, which may be either a "floppy disk" or a much larger (in terms of storage) hard disk, for a computer system that stores the programs or data for various tasks—generating graphics, manipulating images, editing, producing special effects, and so forth.

dissolve A simultaneous fading out of one picture while fading in another picture, thus effecting a gradual transition between shots with a momentary overlapping or *superimposition* of images as one strengthens while the other weakens.

dollying Moving the entire camera mount closer to (dollying in) or farther from (dollying out) the subject.

downcut During either production or editing, the loss of a small amount of audio and/or video material at the end of a segment—usually occurring at the point of transition between program elements from two different sources.

downstream A term used to describe any process that occurs beyond a given point in terms of signal flow. (Think of the analogy to water flowing downstream.) For example, the audio console is downstream of the patch bay; a downstream keyer manipulates the signal after it has left the switcher.

dress rehearsal Final, full rehearsal before the actual production take—using all sets, props, and costumes—designed to be conducted straight through without interruption.

drum (crawl) Large cylindrical graphics-mounting device (similar in appearance to a bass drum) that can roll a long vertical graphic up a television screen.

dry-run rehearsal Rehearsal—either in a rehearsal hall or in the studio—without any technical facilities.

dubbing The electronic duplication of a videotape onto a second tape.

dynamic microphone A rugged microphone whose transducer consists of a diaphragm connected to a movable coil.

edit decision (edit event) The exact point on both the source and master tapes where an edit is to be made.

edit decision sheet A log of all recorded segments as they will be assembled during the postproduction editing process.

edit deck (master deck, record deck) In electronic editing, the VTR that records the edited program being put together.

editing Putting together pieces of program either by physically splicing film or tape or by arranging program elements by means of electronic transfer.

effects *See* Special Effects *and* Staging Effects.

effects bus The switcher bus that is used for special electronic effects such as inserts, keys, and wipes.

EFP (electronic field production) The use of a single video camera to record any kind of program in the field (on location) for later editing in the postproduction process.

electromagnetic spectrum The entire range of electromagnetic energy wavelengths (and frequencies), which includes everything from cosmic rays and visible light to broadcast waves.

electron gun The device, in the rear of the camera pickup tube and/or the kinescope picture tube, that shoots out the electron scanning beam.

electronic editing Joining together program elements on videotape by sequential signal transfer from an original (playback) tape to a second (record) tape.

ellipsoidal spotlight (leko) A specialized spotlight with a highly defined beam that can be further shaped by means of metal shutters and the insertion of a cucalorus pattern.

ENG (electronic news gathering) The use of a high-quality, portable broadcast camera to record news events and other actualities; it is a single-camera technique (replacing a film camera with an electronic camera), resulting in a fast and mobile professional operation.

equalizer An electronic device used to increase or decrease the levels of different audio frequencies. It can alter the quality of a tone by augmenting or diminishing specific frequencies related to its overtone structure.

essential area (critical area) That center portion of the *scanning area* of a graphic card that contains all of the critical or essential information that probably will be seen on the receiving set.

establishing shot (cover shot) An all-inclusive long shot that, by its collective nature, establishes the relationships of performers and other elements in a given scene.

extemporaneous Speaking from a semi-scripted format or outline—broadly prepared but not written out word for word.

external key An electronic keying effect whereby a third camera furnishes the keying (or stenciling) image used in combining two other video signals.

fade 1. The gradual bringing in or taking out of an audio source. 2. The gradual transition from black to a picture (fade-in) or from a picture to black (fade-out).

fader (slide-fader) *See* Potentiometer.

fader arm On the switcher, a small lever—operating on the same principle as a rheostat—that controls the amount of video signal flowing to a specific bus.

feed A program signal, audio and/or video, brought into a mixer (audio console or switcher) from some outside (nonstudio) source; e.g., a remote location, a satellite, or a network line.

feedback 1. In audio, a high-pitched squeal that results from accidentally feeding a program monitor into a live microphone, causing an instantaneous overamplification of the system. 2. A video effect caused by re-entry of a video signal into the switcher with subsequent overamplification.

fidelity The ability to reproduce a given tone, with all of its overtones, accurately.

field One-half of a television picture, consisting of alternate scanning lines, lasting one-sixtieth of a second.

field of view Size or scope of a shot, indicating how much is encompassed.

field production (location production) Television production, usually consisting of single-camera recording and postproduction editing, that takes place outside of the studio. (*See also* Remote Production.)

field synchronizer *See* Frame Synchronizer.

fill light An unfocused and diffused (nondirectional) light used to complement the key light, coming from the side opposite the key, filling in dark areas and softening the shadows.

film chain (telecine) A film island where various picture sources (16mm film,

8mm film, slides) can be mixed through a multiplexer and fed into a television pickup camera.

filter 1. An audio device that can be used to eliminate selected low-frequency or high-frequency overtones. 2. A glass or gelatin element mounted in front of a lighting instrument that changes light characteristics such as color temperature.

fishpole A small, lightweight pole to which a microphone is attached, to be hand held by an audio assistant outside of the picture frame.

fixed-focal-length lens A simple lens that is one specific focal length.

flag A rectangular cloth-covered frame placed in front of a lighting instrument to produce a precise shadow on one side of the light beam.

flat A standard staging unit, constructed of a wooden frame covered with cloth or hardboard, often used to represent walls of a room or the exterior of a building.

"flip flop" A slang term to denote the action of certain switchers (with program and preset buses) that, at the conclusion of a dissolve, automatically switch the illuminated buttons on the buses to indicate that the camera on the preset bus has now become the program feed.

floodlight A lighting instrument that produces a highly diffused, nondirectional source of light.

floor manager (floor director) *See* Stage Manager.

floor plan A scaled plan of the studio floor indicating where all scenery and staging units are to be placed.

focal length The distance from the optical center point of a lens, when it is set at infinity, to a point where the image is in focus (that is, the front surface of the camera pickup tube).

fold-over A digital-based electronic transition in which one picture is squeezed and apparently flipped over (revealing a second picture) to simulate a turning page.

font A complete set of type of one style and size.

footcandle (ftc) A unit of light measurement equivalent to the amount of light falling upon a surface one foot away from a standard candle.

foundation makeup The makeup base upon which more detailed accent items are constructed.

frame 1. One complete television picture, consisting of two fields, lasting one-thirtieth of a second. 2. To compose a picture artistically within the frame of the television screen.

frame store A unit that uses a computer disk drive to hold hundreds of still-frame visuals in a digital format—for the origination of sports and news graphics.

frame (field) synchronizer The electronic component that takes outside video sources (satellite, microwave, and other feeds), analyzes their sync pulses as compared with studio sync, converts the signals to a digital format, adjusts the differences, and thereby can route all signals through the same switcher.

freeze-frame *See* Pause Mode.

frequency 1. The number of cycles per second of a given tone—which determines the basic pitch of that tone (the greater the frequency, the higher the pitch). 2. Measurement of the number of oscillations per second (hertz) of an electromagnetic wave of a given wavelength (the greater the frequency, the smaller the wavelength).

frequency range The total of frequencies or pitches (and overtones) that a microphone, an ear, a loudspeaker, or a transmitter is able to discriminate and/or reproduce.

Fresnel lens A lightweight spotlight lens developed by Augustin-Jean Fresnel that uses a system of concentric ring-shaped steps to achieve its focusing effect.

f-stop A notation that indicates the size of the lens aperture; the higher the *f*-stop number, the smaller the opening; the lower the *f*-stop number, the larger the opening.

gain control *See* Potentiometer.

gel (gelatin) A thin, translucent, colored material such as gelatin or plastic that can be mounted in front of lighting instruments to produce specific color effects.

giraffe A medium-sized mike boom, consisting of a tripod base and a telescoping arm.

glitch A brief picture breakup caused by momentary loss of a continuous sync pulse, usually as a result of a faulty editing procedure.

gobo A scenic cutout unit that is positioned several feet in front of a camera to provide foreground design, depth, and framing interest.

gopher An assistant who is asked to "go for" specific items—coffee, scripts, tape, paper, and so forth.

graphics Two-dimensional visuals specifically prepared for television presentation—charts, drawings, photographs, maps, slides, and the like—including computer-generated artwork.

graphics tablet An electronic pad that contains numerous X and Y (horizontal and vertical) coordinates buried beneath its surface so that when contact is made by a special electronic pen, the precise location of the spot can be transmitted to a monitor.

gray scale A theoretical scale, representing several shades of gray from TV white to TV black, that can be readily distinguished by a camera pickup tube; most good camera systems can be relied upon to reproduce only a seven-step gray scale.

grip A floor assistant or stagehand, especially one who is concerned with scenery and set dressing.

hanging mike A microphone suspended by its cord from a lighting grid or catwalk.

hanging units Any background pieces that are hung or flown in the studio—such as drapes, cloth drops, and the cyclorama.

harmonics *See* Overtones.

HDTV *See* High-Definition Television.

head The small electromagnet—on either a video recorder or an audio recorder—that puts the electromagnetic information on the tape (records), or erases the signal from the tape, or reads (plays back) the information that is on the tape.

headroom Space between the top of a subject's head and the upper edge of the camera frame.

headset The apparatus (worn over the head and consisting of an earphone and mouthpiece) that connects all production personnel on the intercom network.

helical-scan (slant-track) VTR A videotape recording format that lays down the video information in a long, slanted, helical pattern on the tape.

hertz (Hz) Basic unit of frequency measurement for electromagnetic waves—named after Heinrich Hertz—replacing the older term of *cycles per second;* broadcast frequencies are often measured in terms of kilohertz (kHz) and megahertz (MHz).

Hi-Band 8mm An improvement on Sony's Video-8 format that uses metal particle tape and a higher luminance bandwidth.

high-band recording High-quality video recording, recorded in a high-frequency range, featured in most quality color recorders.

high-definition television (HDTV) A television system that uses 1,100 or more scanning lines, resulting in an incredibly sharp picture; such systems also usually feature a wider screen ratio.

high-key lighting Overall intense illumination, with a fully lit background.

HMI A hydrogen medium-arc-length-iodide lamp that is daylight balanced and is used outdoors to supplement natural sunlight.

horizontal sync pulse The portion of the synchronizing pulse that controls the horizontal sweep of the scanning beam.

hue The actual color base, such as red, green, orange, and so forth.

iconoscope No longer used, this was the first practical electronic camera pickup tube.

image-orthicon (I-O) A particular type of camera pickup tube, long the standard of the broadcast industry for monochrome production.

image retention (burn-in, sticking) A phenomenon, characteristic of older I-O tubes, where the tube superimposes a negative image of a shot (especially a high-contrast shot) over succeeding shots the tube picks up.

impedance Resistance to the flow of an audio signal in a microphone cable.

incandescent light The conventional lamp, housed in a glass bulb, that produces light by the glow of a heated filament.

incident light Light coming directly from the source of illumination.

inpoint The precise spot on both the source tape and master tape where an edit is to begin.

input selector switch The switch found on many audio control boards (either a toggle switch or a push-button connector) that will connect a specific patch bay input to a particular microphone position on the console.

insert editing Electronically inserting a new program segment into the middle of a previously recorded production; the new material (video and/or audio) to be inserted is locked into the existing control track.

intercom network (P.L.) A closed-circuit intercommunication audio network connecting all production personnel with headsets.

interlacing The process of combining two picture fields to produce one full frame.

internal key An electronic keying effect whereby one of the two cameras involved also furnishes the key (or stenciling) signal.

internal reflector A light with a filament in the rear and glass covering on the front, resembling a large light bulb.

Inverse Square Law A principle of physics that states that when the distance between a light (or an audio source) and its point of perception is cut in half, its intensity will be increased fourfold.

I-O tube *See* Image-Orthicon.

isolated (iso) camera A camera that is patched directly to its separate video recorder—which can be used either for instant replay (in live productions) or for postproduction editing.

jack 1. A socket or receptacle (female) for an audio connection. 2. A hinged stage brace attached to the rear of a flat.

joystick On older editors, a stick control that enables the operator to move the source deck and edit deck back and forth to locate precise editing points. (*See also* Search Dial.)

jump cut A take between two cameras— or a badly planned edit—that results in connecting two shots that have almost identical views of the same object; as a result, the object appears to jump slightly for no apparent reason.

kerning Adjusting the space individually between letters to allow for closer spacing of letters such as *O*'s and *T*'s, and more distance between letters such as *M*'s and *H*'s.

key A generic term for any number of special visual effects whereby video signals from two or more sources are electronically combined. Generally, one camera is used to cut a solid image into a background picture produced by another camera—for example, stenciling white lettering over a background picture.

key framing A computer graphics feature that enables the artist to enter two different images and then instruct the computer to create all of the intermediate frames needed to evolve from one image to the other.

key light The primary source of illumination falling upon a subject, highly directional, producing a definite modeling or shaping effect with well-defined shadows.

kicker Additional light, usually a spotlight, coming from the side and slightly to the rear of the subject.

kill To turn off equipment (such as microphones, lights).

kinescope recording The process of using a specially adapted film camera to record a television program from the face of the kinescope tube.

kinescope tube The television receiving tube.

kook (cookie) *See* Cucalorus, definition 1.

lag (smear, comet-tailing) A cometlike tail that follows a moving image across the screen, characteristic of the vidicon tube at low light levels.

laser disc A record-sized recording disc, similar in structure and operation to the compact disc (CD), which records both video and audio in a digital format— to be read by a laser beam.

lavaliere (chest mike, neck mike) A very small microphone that can be worn around the neck on a cord or clipped onto an article of clothing.

laying down black *See* Blacking.

lead room (nose room, talk space) Additional framing space in a camera picture on the side toward which a subject is looking or moving.

leko *See* Ellipsoidal Spotlight.

lens 1. The optical glass disk, usually having one or both surfaces curved, used for focusing rays of light coming from a spotlight, for example, plano-convex or Fresnel. 2. The optical elements that make it possible to focus visual (light) images onto the face of a camera tube.

lens cap Protective covering that can be placed on the front of a camera lens.

lens turret A round metal plate on the front of a camera, holding three to five lenses, that can be rotated to place any one of the lenses into position in front of the pickup tube.

level Sound volume or intensity from a specific source or talent.

lighting grid A permanent arrangement of pipes suspended below the studio ceiling, upon which lighting instruments can be hung.

light meter A photoelectric device that measures the amount of light falling upon a specific area.

light plot A floor plan that indicates the lighting requirements—location, type, and function of each instrument—for every staging area in the studio.

limbo A neutral setting, often set against a plain backdrop with no staging elements in view.

limiter An electronic device used to cut off audio levels when the volume is too strong.

linear audio recording   A format that records audio on a videotape in a straight line (as opposed to diagonal or slant tracks) near the edge of the tape.

linear key   A keying device that adds a given color to a key effect. (*See also* Chroma Key.)

line monitor   The master program monitor that displays the final program picture that is to be recorded or transmitted.

live-on-tape production   Program that is recorded on videotape in its entirety, or in long complete segments; the viewing audience watches the performance, unedited, as it actually took place earlier.

live production   Studio or remote production where the program is transmitted (either broadcast or closed-circuit) as the action takes place; the viewing audience watches the performance as it actually is happening.

location production   *See* Field Production.

log sheet   A list, usually used in conjunction with field production, of all of the shots that were taped—including time in and time out and description of the segment.

longitudinal time code   A series of reference numbers placed on an audio track of a videotape. (*See also* SMPTE Time Code.)

long lens   A long focal-length lens with a narrow viewing angle; it includes relatively little in the picture but tends to compress distance.

long shot (LS)   View of a subject from a relatively great distance.

looping   An audio technique whereby a single loop of audiotape can be repeated endlessly on either a reel-to-reel recorder or on an audio cart machine.

loosen up (loosen a shot)   To decrease the size of an object in a picture, either by dollying back or by zooming out.

lower third   A person's identifying information (name and title) superimposed or keyed on the screen, positioned in the lower third of the frame.

low-key lighting   Selective lighting, with an overall low level of intensity and a dark background.

luminance channel   A monochrome signal, in color cameras, that is derived from the three color pictures; it is used to provide the correct contrast for the color signal as well as to produce the compatible black-and-white picture for monochrome receivers.

luminance key   *See* Internal Key.

macro lens   Special wide-angle lens designed for close-ups of small objects at short distances.

master control room   Primary engineering control center where all video and audio signals are ultimately channeled; program input (both studio and network feeds), camera controls, video recording, and transmitter distribution usually are all handled from this location.

master deck   *See* Edit Deck.

matte   A special electronic effect whereby two cameras are electronically keyed together, with one furnishing a foreground image, and the other the background.

medium shot (MS)   View of a subject from a comfortable medium distance, between a long shot and a close-up.

menu   A list of choices and instructions displayed on the computer screen that enables the operator to select the next task or operation to be performed by the computer.

M-format   A broadcast-quality camcorder manufactured by Panasonic and JVC.

microchip   *See* Silicon Chip.

microphone (mike, mic)   An audio transducer that converts sound pressure waves (sound energy) into electrical signals.

MIDI (musical instrument digital interface)   An electronics or computer language (code) that communicates music performance data among electronic instruments—with one keyboard controlling synthesizers, lighting controllers, effects processors, and computers.

mini-doc   A short documentary, often included in a newscast, frequently presented in serialized form.

mix buses   The switcher buses, with fader arms, that are used for on-the-air fading and mixing of video sources such as supers and dissolves.

mix-down   An intermediate audio editing step in which two or more audio tracks are mixed onto one track and then used as submasters—added to additional audio tracks in the final editing session.

mixer   1. An electronic control unit for selecting and combining audio or video signals from more than one source and forming a new program signal—such as the audio console or the video switcher. 2. *See* Potentiometer.

mixing   1. The combining and balancing of two or more audio sources through the audio console. 2. The combining of two or more video sources through the switcher.

mix track   The final edited audio track, often consisting of numerous individual sound tracks balanced and mixed together.

modulation   The alternation of a carrier frequency—either by amplitude modulation (AM) or by frequency modulation (FM)—in order to superimpose a video and/or audio signal for broadcast purposes.

moiré effect Distracting visual vibration caused by the interaction of a narrow striped pattern and the television scanning lines.

monitor 1. An audio speaker used to check the actual sounds being mixed. 2. A video display device that features a high-quality television picture that has not been modulated to an RF signal; it is ordinarily used in studio and control room applications.

multiple-camera production Conventional television production situation—either in a studio or remote on-location origination—where several cameras are used simultaneously to pick up the action or performance; whether transmitted live or recorded, the pictures from the various cameras are edited instantaneously as the program progresses.

multiplexer A system of mirrors and prisms in the film chain designed to direct the various projected images into the television camera.

narrow-angle lens *See* Long Lens.

neutral density filter A lens filter that cuts down the intensity of incoming light without altering the color temperature.

neutral setting (nonassociative style) A setting with no identifiable elements at all.

noise 1. Any interference that distracts from the communicative act. 2. Specific audio interference (unwanted sounds or static) or video interference (electronic disturbance or snow).

nondirectional *See* Omnidirectional.

normalled Having a certain output on an audio patch bay permanently wired to a given position on the console so that a patch cord is not needed to make the temporary connection.

nose room *See* Lead Room.

NTSC National Television System Committee, an industry body that developed the basic technical specifications (525 lines, thirty frames per second, FM audio) and color standards still in use today in North and South America and Japan.

objective perspective Use of a camera as an observer or eavesdropper; no one addresses the camera directly.

off-camera Any sound or action that takes place out of the camera's view.

off-line editing A basic electronic editing process whereby original footage is edited onto an intermediate submaster tape. This may be an early step in compiling a "workprint" for a more sophisticated on-line editing session.

off-mike The audio quality resulting from a sound source that is a great distance from the microphone or out of the pickup pattern of a unidirectional mike.

off-set graphics Graphics, such as title cards and slides, that are never seen in or on the set; the audience has no idea where they are originating.

omnidirectional (nondirectional) A microphone pickup pattern in which sounds are received equally well from all directions.

on-line editing The concluding electronic editing stage in which all editing takes place on the finished master or release tape. In simple news operations and industrial programs, this may be the only editing step. In more sophisticated productions, this is the final operation in an elaborate editing process—usually working from multiple video workprints—compiling a final program from a computer-generated edit list to combine numerous VTR sources.

on-location production *See* Field Production, Remote Production.

on-set graphics Large graphics and display devices designed to be integrated into the set.

open-circuit (broadcasting) Television distribution through open space; a specific carrier frequency is modulated with video and/or audio signals and then transmitted from an antenna to receivers that are not connected by wire or cable to the origination point.

oscilloscope Engineering evaluation instrument that displays various electronic patterns on a video screen.

outline script *See* Semiscripted Outline.

outpoint The precise spot on the source tape and/or edit tape where an edit is to end.

over-the-shoulder shot (O/S) Camera shot looking at one person framed by the back of the head and shoulder of another person in the foreground.

overtones (harmonics) Acoustical or electrical frequencies that are higher than the fundamental tone.

pad 1. Extra video material that is recorded before and after a program segment to facilitate a margin of judgment during editing. 2. Extra script material that may be used if the program begins to run short. 3. An audio component that can reduce the strength of a preamplified feed so that it does not exceed the volume limits of a control channel.

pan card A long horizontal graphic designed to be panned on the air.

pan head *See* Camera Mounting Head.

panning Turning the camera horizontally by rotating the camera mounting head.

panning handle (pan handle) The handle extending toward the rear of the camera with which the camera operator controls movement of the camera.

pantograph A scissorslike spring, counterbalanced lighting mount that enables lights to be quickly pushed up or pulled down to any height.

particularized shot A close shot showing the important aspect of some specific object.

patch bay (patch board) A board with numerous terminals (inputs and outputs) through which various audio, video, or lighting signals can be connected by patch cords to other channels or circuits.

pause mode (still frame, freeze-frame) Repeated scanning of a single video frame—while holding the videotape stationary—resulting in a still frame during playback.

PCM (pulse code modulation) An audio signal that is recorded on videotape diagonally in its own area, at the end of a video slant track, so that it can be separated from video for editing.

pedestal 1. Heavy camera mount that facilitates easy raising or lowering of the camera head, usually with a counterweight system or with compressed air. 2. To move the camera head up or down with the pedestal mount.

perambulator boom A large boom on a dolly base, having a platform for the mike operator, with a long counterweighted boom arm.

performer Any talent who is addressing the audience directly, as opposed to an actor portraying a dramatic character.

perspective 1. In audio, the quality of matching visual and sound distance. 2. In scenery, the illusion of distance caused by several lines converging at one point on the horizon.

phasing The relationship of the positive and negative portions of the sine waves of two different electrical signals to determine to what extent their oscillations are synchronized.

photon The basic elemental unit of light/electromagnetic energy; it has no mass or charge but demonstrates momentum and displays characteristics of both particles and waves.

pickup edit A type of unplanned edit used in studio productions to cover a production error by going back and assemble editing at a point immediately prior to the mistake.

pickup tube The transducing element of the camera that receives the visual image and converts it into an electronic signal.

picture continuity The relationship of visual images from one shot to the next, involving flow of action, screen direction, composition, cutting ratio, type of transitions, motivation, and similar considerations.

pin Concentrating or narrowing the beam of a spotlight by moving the bulb-reflector unit away from the lens.

pixel The computer-derived term for "picture element" that designates the smallest addressable triad of phosphor dots on a picture tube that can be manipulated and illuminated for graphics display.

P.L. (private line) *See* Intercom Network.

plano-convex lens The basic, relatively heavy, spotlight lens—with one flat surface and one convex surface—from which the Fresnel lens was developed.

playback The process whereby the recorded magnetic information stored on the recording tape is picked up by the playback head to re-create the original video and/or audio electronic signals.

playback deck *See* Source Deck.

Plumbicon® A lead-oxide version of the vidicon tube, used extensively for color cameras. (The word *Plumbicon* is a registered trademark of N. V. Philips.)

polarity reversal Interchange of the black and white aspects of a picture, thus attaining a negative image.

pop filter A protective shield attached to a microphone that filters out air blasts from plosive consonants such as *P*'s and *T*'s.

portapak (backpack) Small, portable, battery-operated, lightweight video recorder—typically using 1/2-inch or 1/4-inch tape—used for small-format television.

position jump A cut between two cameras—or a poorly planned edit—in which a person or object appears to change positions or jump from one side of the screen to the other.

postproduction editing Electronic editing process that takes place after the individual program segments have been produced and recorded.

potentiometer (pot) A volume control device that is manipulated by either a rotating knob or a sliding *fader.*

preamplifier An electronic device that can magnify the low signal output of microphones and other transducers before the signal is sent to a mixing board or to other amplifiers.

pre-edit session A planning conference during which the director, editor, and others decide how a program will eventually be edited.

"prepare" (or "set up") The standard command of preparation preceding a fade, dissolve, super, or special effect that involves preparation of another bus.

preproduction editing Electronic editing process whereby individual program segments—especially in news and sports coverage—are edited in advance for later insertion or assemble editing into a finished production.

preproduction planning All of the preparation and careful planning that a director must complete before starting studio rehearsals.

pre-roll The period of time in the editing process when both the source deck and edit deck back up (usually about five seconds) and then move forward in sync to get up to speed.

presence The audio phenomenon of performing very close to a microphone, with a consequent intimate quality resulting from a lowered pitch, breathiness, and subdued tone.

preset 1. On a lighting board, to prearrange a given lighting setup so that it can be automatically executed when needed. 2. To adjust a zoom lens so that a given object is in focus at all focal lengths. 3. To use the switcher preview bus and preview monitor to set up a given effect before punching it up on the air.

pre-studio rehearsal Rehearsal with talent (e.g., actors) in a rehearsal hall or other location before coming into the studio.

preview bus The switcher bus, connected to the preview monitor, that is used for setting up any special effects or other picture before it is put on the air.

preview monitor A large monitor that can be used to look at any camera picture or video effect before putting it on the program line.

proc amp Process amplifier, the electronic component that takes the composite video signal from the switcher (chrominance, luminance, sync pulses, and blanking pulses), stabilizes the levels, and removes unwanted elements (noise).

producer The creator and originator of a television program, usually in charge of all above-the-line elements such as writing, art, music, securing actors, and financial considerations.

production assistant (production secretary, script assistant) An assistant who may be assigned to either the director or producer, concerned with a variety of details—production logs, script details, personnel problems, talent coordination, logistical arrangements, etc.

program bus The switcher bank that controls the actual picture being sent out on the air.

program time Time remaining in the overall program until the program fades to black; this determines the time-remaining signals that must be given to the director.

props (properties) 1. Hand props, which include all items actually to be handled and used in a television production. 2. Stage props (*see* Set Dressings).

proscenium arch In the theater, the arch that separates the stage from the auditorium.

pull focus (rack focus) To change the focus of a camera from one extreme to the other—using a selective focus technique—in order to shift attention from one object to another (either in the foreground or background).

PZM (pressure-zone microphone) A flat microphone that consists of a thin pickup plate that, when mounted on a flat table or large sheet of plexiglass, uses the surface it is mounted on to collect the sound waves—thus eliminating phasing problems and balancing the audio levels from a fairly widespread area.

quadruplex (transverse) VTR (quad head) An older videotape recording format that uses four rotating heads in a pattern transverse to the movement of the videotape.

quartz light A highly efficient lamp with a high-intensity tungsten-halogen filament in a quartz or silica housing.

rack focus *See* Pull Focus.

racking 1. Rotating the lens turret in order to place a different lens in front of the pickup tube. 2. On monochrome cameras, moving the pickup tube closer to or farther from the lens (*see* Tube Focus).

raster The display of scanning lines on a cathode ray tube, covering the entire face of the tube.

rate card The printed list of prices charged by a production facility for its services and equipment; the rate card usually consists of three sections—the *technical personnel chart* for engineering costs; the *facilities rate chart* for all studio usage, telecine and videotape machines, furniture, and all other facilities; and the *personnel hourly rate chart* for all nonengineering below-the-line positions.

"ready" The standard command of preparation preceding a camera take or cut.

real-time editing Assembling a multiple-camera production by using a switcher or SEG during the continuing action of an event or performance.

rear focus *See* Tube Focus.

rear screen (R.P., rear projection) A translucent screen set up in the studio; slides or film are projected from the rear and photographed from the front.

receiver The device that receives the radio broadcast signal (radio set) or television signal (TV set) and demodulates the carrier wave to reproduce the original studio electrical signals.

record deck *See* Edit Deck.

recording The process whereby the audio and/or video electronic signal is used to arrange iron-oxide particles on the magnetic recording tape to store a record of the electronic signal for later retrieval.

reel-to-reel Audiotape or videotape recording format that uses open reels (a supply reel and a take-up reel) and manual threading, as opposed to closed *cassette* or *cartridge* systems.

re-entry A switcher process that allows the operator to take a processed or mixed video signal and enter it into another processing circuit or mixing bus.

reference white Any large piece of white material used in the white-balancing process, to enable the automatic circuitry of the camera to compensate for the operating color temperature. (*See also* White Balance.)

reflected light Light bounced back from the surface of an object.

reflector A rigid flat piece of framed material—often foil or silver (but even white cardboard will work)—that can be set up on a tripod (or hand held) to reflect sunlight onto a subject on a remote shoot; the reflected light serves as either fill (with the sun as the key light) or as a key (with the sun as back light).

remote production (on-location production) A television production, usually directed from a portable control room, that takes place outside of a regular studio.

reportorial perspective Use of a camera with the talent talking directly to the audience through the camera.

resolution Sharpness and detail of a television picture.

retrace The period when the scanning beam is turned off at the bottom of a field and returns to the top of the picture.

reverberation (reverb) The process of adding an electronic echo to music or spoken sound to produce a deliberate artificial resonation.

RF (radio frequency) Modulation of a specific radio frequency carrier wave with a video and audio signal—necessary for broadcasting and most closed-circuit distribution.

RGB The designation (referring to the primary colors of red, green, and blue) used to label the uncoded (noncomposite) outputs of a color camera or computer.

rheostat A device that can control the amount of current or signal flowing to a specific control point or circuit—allowing a gradual increase or decrease in the amount of flow—such as the *pot* on the audio console, the *dimmer* handle on a lighting board, or the *fader arm* on a switcher bus.

ribbon microphone (velocity mike) A sensitive microphone whose transducing element consists of a ribbon suspended in a magnetic field.

riding gain (riding levels) Continually watching the VU meter and adjusting audio faders accordingly, in order to maintain proper volume levels throughout a program.

roll Vertical movement of electronic text up a screen.

roll cue The exact words or actions that a talent will use at the precise point when a film or videotape insert is to be rolled a few seconds before it is actually put on the air.

rule of thirds Principle of composition that divides the TV screen into thirds, horizontally and vertically, and places objects of interest at the points where the lines intersect.

rundown sheet (show format) Abbreviated scripting format that simply lists the various program segments in sequence.

run-through Usually, the first full-facilities (start-and-stop) rehearsal.

saturation (chroma) The strength or intensity of a color—how far removed it is from a neutral or gray shade.

scanning The pattern of movement of the electron beam, in both the camera tube and the TV receiver, horizontally and from top to bottom. Also refers to the scanning of the electric charges registered on the CCD chip.

scanning area The portion of a graphic card that actually can be seen by the camera pickup tube.

scanning beam The electron beam that is pulled back and forth, up and down, across the television tube to produce the scanning pattern.

scoop A rounded floodlight with a spherical diffusing reflector.

scrim A translucent filter, often made of fiberglass or fine screening, used in front of either a spotlight or floodlight to soften and diffuse the light quality.

script assistant *See* Production Assistant.

seamless editing An editing technique whereby audio and video segments are cut at slightly different spots in order to avoid an abrupt change of sound and picture simultaneously; the result is a smoother transition.

search dial The editing control that enables the operator to move the source deck and edit deck forward or backward at varying speeds to locate the precise frame for editing precision.

segment timing sheet A list of all of the segments of a production with space for unit times and cumulative times (ideal and actual) for each segment.

segue An audio transition in which one sound is completely faded out and then a second source is immediately faded in (similar to a video cross-fade).

selective focus The technique of using a shallow depth of field to deliberately keep either foreground or background objects out of focus, in order to concentrate attention on a particular object that is in focus.

semiscripted outline A summarization of a program's content—with opening and closing material (and other crucial elements such as roll cues) written out in full while the remaining content is presented in outline form.

set dressings (stage props) Major items of furniture (desks, tables), large props (bicycles, tree stumps), and minor items (ashtrays, books) used to dress up a set.

set light (background light) General lighting of the set and background behind the talent.

set pieces Three-dimensional items, usually functional, that are integrated into the set—platforms, stairways, pillars, arches, lampposts, and so forth.

setting The major pieces that comprise the background and environment of a scene—set units, hanging units, and set pieces.

set units Staging units such as flats, twofolds, and other standing background pieces.

shading (video engineering) Operating the video controls of a CCU in order to maintain the best engineering quality control of the picture.

shaping The alteration of an audio signal by controlling volume, filtering out certain frequencies, emphasizing upper or lower pitches, creating an echo effect, and so forth.

shoot 1. To record program information on either film or videotape. 2. The entire enterprise of a remote, on-location television or film recording session, including all production operations of the nonstudio, in-the-field situation.

shooting schedule A list of everything to be shot each day of a field production; usually derived from the breakdown sheet, it contains an indication of who and what is needed for each scene.

short lens (wide-angle lens) A short focal-length lens with a wide viewing angle; it includes quite a bit in the picture but tends to exaggerate distance.

shotgun microphone A highly directional microphone, used for picking up sounds from a distance.

shot sheet A small sheet or card, attached to the rear of the camera, listing a summary of all shots the camera operator is to get during the production.

show format *See* Rundown Sheet.

silhouette A lighting effect where the foreground figures are dark and the background is fully lit.

silicon chip A tiny electronic component containing microscopic electrical circuits that amplify and in other ways control the flow of electromagnetic information; the heart of every computer operation.

sine wave A graphic depiction of the oscillation of a wave of electrical energy—showing the relationship of amplitude, wavelength, and frequency—with both a positive phase (above a theoretical horizontal reference line that represents the exact assigned frequency) and a negative phase (below the line).

single Shot of just one person.

single-camera production Television production situation in which a single electronic camera is used to record all of the action—similar to the traditional film-camera technique; one camera is repositioned for each shot, and the individual shots are then electronically edited together in the postproduction editing process.

skewing The phenomenon of a picture bending or turning in at the corners.

slant-track recorder *See* Helical-Scan.

slate An identification procedure whereby date, scene, segment, and other information necessary to tape and film editing are recorded at the beginning of a designated camera sequence.

slave To send the output of a camera being used in a multicamera production to its own separate videotape recorder. (*See also* Isolated Camera.)

small-format television (video) Inexpensive, small, lightweight television gear (camera, microphone, and video recorder)—usually portable—that can be used for a variety of nonbroadcast (and nonprofessional) applications.

SMPTE time code A frame-location "address" system—developed by the Society of Motion Picture and Television Engineers—that can label and find any section of a videotape by hour, minute, second, and frame.

snoot A stovepipe-like attachment that can be put on the front of a spotlight to reduce the beam to a smaller, clearly defined circle, without increasing the intensity of the spot.

SOF (sound-on-film) A designation used to denote a film sound track.

soft edge The line between two video signals (as in an insert or wipe), which can be blurred so that the two pictures dissolve or blend together.

sound bite A short "newsworthy" quotation from a person, usually someone involved in an actuality.

source deck (playback deck) In electronic editing, the VTR that contains the original raw footage that is to be edited.

speaker (loudspeaker) An electronic device, actually a transducer, that converts an electronic audio signal back into audible sound waves.

special effects Fancy electronic video transitions and methods of combining video sources, such as wipes, keys, mattes, inserts, and so forth.

special effects generator (SEG) Part of a sophisticated switcher that can produce a variety of special electronic effects.

speed up A signal to the talent to read faster or get through the script outline faster.

split screen A special effect with the screen split into two or more sections, with a picture from a different camera filling each portion of the screen.

spotlight A lighting instrument that produces a highly directional, controlled source of light.

spread To open or enlarge the beam of a spotlight by moving the bulb-reflector unit closer to the lens.

sprocket holes Small, square holes on the side of film, used to guide the film and keep it moving at a constant speed.

squeeze zoom A digital-based electronic transition in which the picture is reduced in size and squeezed down to a pinpoint before disappearing from the screen.

staff A construction of plaster or other fibrous material used for facades and ornamental work.

stage manager (floor manager, floor director) The director's key assistant in charge of all production concerns on the studio floor.

staging effects Special optical and mechanical studio effects, such as smoke, wind, fog, rain, fire, and so forth.

"standby" General command of preparation.

start-and-stop rehearsal (stop-start, stop-and-go) Usually the first full-facilities rehearsal with cameras operating—designed to be interrupted to work out problems as the production progresses.

stereophonic sound Audio that is recorded, transmitted, and played back through two separate (left and right) channels to simulate binaural sound.

still frame *See* Pause Mode.

stop-start (stop-and-go) rehearsal *See* Start-and-Stop Rehearsal.

storyboard A series of simple drawings or rough sketches that lays out visually the content of a commercial or program—showing how every scene should be staged and what each shot will look like.

stretch A signal to the talent to slow down, read slower, and stretch out the remaining script.

striking To remove specific set pieces or props; taking down and removing everything on the studio floor at the end of a production.

strip lights A series of broads (pan lights) or low-wattage bulbs mounted in a row of three to twelve lights in one housing, used as a specialized floodlight for lighting a cyclorama or other large background area.

studio The primary room devoted to television production, containing all of the paraphernalia for sets, lighting, cameras, microphones, and so forth—the space where all acting or performing takes place.

studio address (S.A., talkback) A public-address loudspeaker system, allowing the control room to talk directly to the studio floor.

subjective perspective Use of a camera as an actual participant or actor in a dramatic sequence, viewing the scene from the standpoint of a person who is involved.

super (superimposition) A picture resulting from the simultaneous display of two complete images on the screen.

super card A graphic card with white lettering on a black background, used either to *super* or to *key* the printed information over a background picture.

S-VHS (Super-VHS) A high-resolution videocassette format that is compatible with the standard VHS system.

sweep reversal Reversal of the scanning pattern of a camera (either horizontally or vertically) to attain either a mirror image or an upside-down image.

sweetening The process of augmenting an audio track during postproduction editing by adding prerecorded laughter and other audience reactions.

switcher 1. A video mixing panel, consisting of selection buttons and control levers (fader arms), that permits the selection and combining of incoming video signals to form the final program picture. 2. The person who operates the video switcher, usually the technical director.

symmetrical balance Formal arrangement with the most important element centered in the picture and other equal objects placed equidistant from the center.

sync generator The part of the video system that produces a synchronizing signal (sync pulse), based on the basic 60-cycle alternating current (in the U.S. and other countries using the NTSC color system), which serves as a timing pulse to coordinate the video elements of all components in the video system (cameras, switcher, recorders, and so forth).

sync pulse A complex signal (added to the picture information) consisting of electronic control information that keeps all video components synchronized.

take 1. An instantaneous change from one video source to another (cut). 2. The final production of a program as recorded or distributed live.

take bar *See* Cut Button.

talent Any person who appears in front of a camera.

talkback system *See* Studio Address.

tally lights Small red indicator lights on each camera to let the talent and camera operator(s) know which camera is on the air.

target The electronic elements that form the light-sensitive (photoemissive) front surface of the pickup tube, which is read by the scanning beam.

technical director (T.D.) Engineer or production person who operates the switcher.

techniques Those learned and acquired skills utilized in operating various pieces of equipment and in performing specific crew assignments.

telecine 1. Same as film chain. 2. The room where the film chain is located.

telephoto lens A lens with a very long focal length, used for close-ups of objects from great distances.

teleprompter® A mechanical device that projects the moving script, via mirrors, directly in front of the camera lens. (The word *TelePrompTer* is a registered trademark of the Teleprompter Corporation.)

telescope hanger A lighting mount, consisting of a system of telescoping pipes, that enables the lighting instrument to be positioned at varying heights.

three-point lighting The traditional arrangement of key, fill, and back lights.

tie lines Permanent audio lines connecting various control rooms or patch bays and engineering locations.

tighten a shot (tighten up) To increase the size of the object in a picture, either by zooming in or by dollying in.

tilt card A tall, vertical graphic card designed to be tilted on the air.

tilting Pivoting the camera vertically by pointing the camera mounting head up or down.

time-base corrector (TBC) The electronic apparatus that takes the video feed from the video recorder (which has been slightly altered by variations in the tape transport system), encodes that signal into a digital form, and then reconstructs an enhanced control track and video signal for distribution and playback.

title card A graphic card containing basic information about the program title, used at the open (and close) of a program.

tone An audio signal used to calibrate various audio facilities at a consistent 100 percent level.

tonguing Moving the tongue or boom arm of a camera crane laterally to the left or right.

tracking The VTR control that adjusts the video head to put it in the optimum position when a tape is played back.

transducer Any device (such as a microphone or camera) that receives energy in one form (sound waves or light energy) and converts it into another form of energy (electrical signals).

transfer edit The electronic re-recording (or dubbing) of video and audio information from an original videotape to a second tape for assembly in program sequence.

transmitter The broadcasting apparatus that modulates the audio and video signals onto a carrier frequency and, through an antenna, broadcasts the signals as electromagnetic waves.

transverse video recorder *See* Quadruplex VTR.

trim 1. To adjust a lighting instrument by aiming the housing and focusing (pinning or spreading) the beam. 2. That part of the editing process whereby small amounts of program information at the head and/or tail of a video segment are added or deleted as the final editing decisions are perfected.

tripod Three-legged camera mount, usually with casters to facilitate camera movement.

trucking Moving the entire camera mount laterally to the left or right.

tube focus (back focus, rear focus, rack focus) To change focus, on monochrome cameras, by physically moving the pickup tube in relation to the lens.

turret *See* Lens Turret.

two-fold Two stage flats, hinged together to form a self-standing unit.

two-shot Camera shot that includes two people or a person and one other prominent object.

U-matic The standard 3/4-inch videocassette format.

undercut To changer one video source of a two-camera super or effect instantaneously while the effect is on the air.

unidirectional (cardioid) A microphone pickup pattern in which sounds are received best from one direction, in a heart-shaped or cardioid pattern.

upcut During either production or editing, the loss of a small amount of audio and/or video material at the beginning of a segment—usually occurring at the point of transition between program elements from two different sources.

variable-focal-length lens *See* Zoom Lens.

vectorscope A specialized electronic monitor that graphically displays the saturation levels for each of the three primary colors and complementary colors.

vertical interval time code (VITC) A frame-location system where the reference numbers are placed in the vertical blanking period when the scanning beam is momentarily not used while returning to the top of the picture. (*See also* SMPTE Time Code.)

vertical sync pulse The portion of the synchronizing pulse that controls the vertical movement of the scanning beam between fields.

VHS (Video Home System) A consumer-quality 1/2-inch videocassette system introduced by JVC.

video 1. The visual portion of a television production. 2. An unmodulated electronic picture signal distributed over a closed-circuit system without converting to an RF signal, resulting in a higher quality picture. 3. *See* Small-Format Television.

video disc 1. A magnetic video recording format in which short segments can be recorded for instant playback, freeze-frame, and slow-motion production applications. 2. A distribution medium in which lengthy programs are pressed onto discs for consumer retail. (*See also* Laser disc.)

Video-8 A consumer-grade video format developed by Sony that uses tape eight millimeters wide.

video engineering *See* Shading.

video feedback Process of feeding a camera's signal into a floor monitor and then using the same camera to shoot the face of the monitor (*see* Feedback, definition 2).

video signal flow The theoretical schematic model that traces every step of the video path from the picture picked up by the camera to the home TV set.

videotape A plastic tape, coated with iron oxide, that can magnetically record various audio, video, and control track information.

videotape recorder (video recorder, VTR) A magnetic-electronic recording machine that records audio, video, and control signals on videotape.

vidicon A simple and inexpensive type of camera pickup tube used for many basic television purposes.

voice-over (V.O.) A script instruction indicating that the voice of an off-camera (unseen) narrator is to be heard over a specific picture segment.

volt A unit of measure of the force of electricity.

VU meter (volume unit meter) A display meter that shows the relative volume of an audio signal.

walk-through rehearsal An abbreviated rehearsal—conducted from the studio floor—to acquaint the talent and/or production crew with the major outline of the production.

watt A unit of measure of the power of electricity.

waveform monitor A type of oscilloscope that displays the brightness of all picture elements on a video screen and, like a VU meter, allows the operator to keep the elements with highest intensity from exceeding the capabilities of the equipment.

wavelength Measurement of the length of an electromagnetic wave from one theoretical crest to the next; since the velocity of all electromagnetic waves is constant (186,000 miles per second), the longer the wavelength, the lower the frequency.

white balance An adjustment process through which light reflected from a white card in a given lighting situation is used as a reference point. In this setup mode, the camera automatically balances the red and blue intensities with the available light.

wide-angle lens *See* Short Lens.

wildtrack A nonsynchronous audio recording made on a remote or location production to record actual background sounds, which can then be mixed with other audio (e.g., an in-studio, voice-over narration) during postproduction editing.

wipe A camera transition whereby one image is gradually pushed off the screen—horizontally, vertically, or diagonally—as another picture replaces it.

wireless mike A microphone with a self-contained miniature FM transmitter built in; the microphone-transmitter can send its signal several hundred feet to the control room, eliminating the use of mike cables.

workprint An intermediate step in on-line editing whereby an interim copy of the assembled program is edited together for previewing purposes.

wow The audible result of putting a record on the air before the turntable has reached full speed.

wrap-up (windup) A cue to the talent that there are about fifteen seconds remaining in this program segment or in the total program.

zoom in To change a zoom lens to a narrow angle (long focal-length) position.

zoom lens A variable-focal-length lens that, through a complicated optical system, can be smoothly changed from one focal length to another.

zoom out (zoom back) To change a zoom lens to a wide angle (short focal-length) position.

Bibliography

General Background

Agee, Warren K., et al. *Main Currents in Mass Communication.* New York: Harper & Row, 1986.

Eastman, Susan Tyler, et al. *Broadcast/ Cable Programming: Strategies and Practices.* 2d ed. Belmont, CA: Wadsworth Publishing Co., 1985.

Gross, Lynne S. *Telecommunications: An Introduction to Radio, Television, and Other Electronic Media.* 2d ed. Dubuque, IA: Wm. C. Brown Publishers, 1986.

Harless, James D. *Mass Communication: An Introductory Survey.* Dubuque, IA: Wm. C. Brown Publishers, 1985.

Head, Sydney W. *World Broadcasting Systems: A Comparative Analysis.* Belmont, CA: Wadsworth Publishing Co., 1985.

Head, Sydney W., and Christopher H. Sterling. *Broadcasting in America: A Survey of Electronic Media.* 5th ed. Boston: Houghton Mifflin, 1987.

McCavitt, William E., and Peter K. Pringle. *Electronic Media Management.* Woburn, MA: Focal Press, 1986.

Newcomb, Horace, ed. *Television: The Critical View.* 4th ed. New York: Oxford University Press, 1987.

Sherman, Barry L. *Telecommunications Management: The Broadcast and Cable Industries.* New York: McGraw-Hill, 1987.

Warner, Charles. *Broadcast and Cable Selling.* Belmont, CA: Wadsworth Publishing Co., 1986.

Wood, Donald N. *Mass Media and the Individual.* St. Paul, MN: West Publishing, 1983.

Production, General

Breyer, Richard, and Peter Moller. *Making Television Programs: A Professional Approach.* New York: Longman, 1984.

Carlson, Verne, and Sylvia E. Carlson. *Professional Lighting Handbook.* Woburn, MA: Focal Press, 1985.

Huber, David Miles. *Audio Production Techniques for Video.* Indianapolis, IN: Howard W. Sams & Co., 1987.

Hyde, Stuart W. *Television and Radio Announcing.* 5th ed. Boston: Houghton Mifflin, 1987.

Iezzi, Frank. *Understanding Television Production*. Englewood Cliffs, NJ: Prentice-Hall, 1984.

Kehoe, Vincent J-R. *The Technique of the Professional Make-Up Artist for Film, Television, and Stage*. Woburn, MA: Focal Press, 1985.

LeTourneau, Tom. *Lighting Techniques for Video Production: The Art of Casting Shadows*. White Plains, NY: Knowledge Industry Publications, Inc., 1987.

Mathias, Harry, and Richard Patterson. *Electronic Cinematography: Achieving Photographic Control over the Video Image*. Belmont, CA: Wadsworth Publishing Co., 1985.

McQuillin, Lon. *Computers in Video Production*. White Plains, NY: Knowledge Industry Publications, Inc., 1986.

Millerson, Gerald. *The Technique of Lighting for Television and Motion Pictures*. 2d ed. Woburn, MA: Focal Press, 1982.

Millerson, Gerald. *The Technique of Television Production*. 11th ed. Woburn, MA: Focal Press, 1985.

Millerson, Gerald. *Video Camera Techniques*. Woburn, MA: Focal Press, 1983.

O'Donnell, Lewis B., et al. *Modern Radio Production*. Belmont, CA: Wadsworth Publishing Co., 1986.

Wiegand, Ingrid. *Professional Video Production*. White Plains, NY: Knowledge Industry Publications, Inc., 1985.

Winston, Brian, and Julia Keydel. *Working with Video: A Comprehensive Handbook to the World of Video and TV Production*. New York: Amphoto, 1986.

Wurtzel, Alan. *Television Production*. 2d ed. New York: McGraw-Hill, 1986.

Zettl, Herbert. *Television Production Handbook*. 4th ed. Belmont, CA: Wadsworth Publishing Co., 1984.

Audio, Technical

Alten, Stanley R. *Audio in Media*. 2d ed. Belmont, CA: Wadsworth Publishing Co., 1986.

Bartlett, Bruce. *Introduction to Professional Recording Techniques*. Indianapolis, IN: Howard W. Sams & Co., 1987.

Davis, Gary, and Ralph Jones. *The Sound Reinforcement Handbook*. Milwaukee, WI: Leonard/Yamaha, 1987.

Jeans, James. *Science and Music*. New York: Dover Publications, 1968.

Lowery, H. *A Guide to Musical Acoustics*. New York: Dover Publications, 1966.

Nisbett, Alec. *The Use of Microphones*. 2d ed. Woburn, MA: Focal Press, 1983.

Oringel, Robert S. *Audio Control Handbook: For Radio and Television Broadcasting*. 5th ed. New York: Hastings House, 1983.

Pohlmann, Ken C. *Principles of Digital Audio*. White Plains, NY: Knowledge Industry Publications, Inc., 1985.

Video, Technical

Amos, S. W. *Dictionary of Electronics*. 2d ed. Boston: Butterworths, 1987.

Arlen, Gary H. *Tomorrow's TVs: A Review of New TV Set Technology, Related Video Equipment and Potential Market Impact, 1987–1995*. Washington, DC: National Association of Broadcasters (COM/TECH Report Series), 1987.

Bensinger, Charles. *The Video Guide*. 3d ed. Santa Fe, NM: Video-Info Publications, 1982.

Benson, K. Blair. *Television Engineering Handbook*. New York: McGraw-Hill Book Co., 1986.

Gross, Lynne S. *The New Television Technologies*. 2d ed. Dubuque, IA: Wm. C. Brown Publishers, 1986.

Hanson, Jarice. *Understanding Video: Applications, Impact, and Theory*. Newbury Park, CA: Sage Publications, 1987.

Heller, Neil. *Understanding Video Equipment: Design, Operation and Maintenance of Videotape Recorders and Cameras*. White Plains, NY: Knowledge Industry Publications, Inc., 1988.

Noll, Michael A. *Television Technology: Fundamentals and Future Prospects*. Norwood, MA: Artech House, Inc., 1988.

Smale, P. H. *Introduction to Telecommunications Systems*. Blue Ridge Summit, PA: TAB Books, 1986.

Society of Motion Picture and Television Engineers. *Components of the Future*. Scarsdale, NY: SMPTE, 1985.

Truxal, John G. *The Age of Electronic Messages*. New York: McGraw-Hill Publishing Company, 1990.

Utz, Peter. *Today's Video: Equipment, Setup, and Production*. White Plains, NY: Knowledge Industry Publications, Inc., 1987.

Directing and Aesthetics

Armer, Alan A. *Directing Television and Film*. Belmont, CA: Wadsworth Publishing Co., 1986.

Blumenthal, Howard J. *Television Producing and Directing*. New York: Harper & Row, 1987.

Kennedy, Tom. *Directing the Video Program*. White Plains, NY: Knowledge Industry Publications, Inc., 1988.

Rabiger, Michael. *Directing the Documentary*. Woburn, MA: Focal Press, 1987.

Verna, Tony. *Live TV: An Inside Look at Directing and Producing*. Woburn, MA: Focal Press, 1987.

Zettl, Herbert. *Sight-Sound-Motion: Applied Media Aesthetics*. Belmont, CA: Wadsworth Publishing Co., 1973.

Single-Camera and Small-Format Video

Compesi, Ronald J., and Ronald E. Sherriffs. *Small Format Television Production: The Technique of Single-Camera Television Field Production*. Boston: Allyn & Bacon, Inc., 1985.

Fuller, Barry J., Steve Kanaba, and Janyce Brisch-Kanaba. *Single-Camera Video Production*. Englewood Cliffs, NJ: Prentice-Hall, 1982.

Medoff, Norman J., and Tom Tanquary. *Portable Video: ENG and EFP*. White Plains, NY: Knowledge Industry Publications, Inc., 1986.

Quinn, Gerald V. *The Camcorder Handbook*. Blue Ridge Summit, PA: TAB Books, 1987.

Shook, Frederick. *The Process of Electronic News Gathering*. Englewood, CO: Morton Publishing Company, 1982.

Postproduction and Editing

Anderson, Gary H. *Electronic Post-Production: The Film-to-Video Guide.* White Plains, NY: Knowledge Industry Publications, Inc., 1988.

Anderson, Gary H. *Video Editing and Post-Production: A Professional Guide.* 2d ed. White Plains, NY: Knowledge Industry Publications, Inc., 1988.

Browne, Steven E. *The Videotape Post-Production Primer.* Burbank, CA: Wilton Place Communications, 1982.

Hubatka, Milton C., Frederick Hull, and Richard W. Sanders. *Audio Sweetening for Film and TV.* Blue Ridge Summit, PA: TAB Books, 1987.

Shetter, Michael D. *Videotape Editing: Communicating with Pictures and Sound.* Elk Grove Village, IL: Swiderski Electronics, 1982.

Weynand, Diana, ed. *The Post Production Process.* Woodland Hills, CA: Weynand Associates, 1985.

Staging, Design, and Graphics

Arnold, Richard L. *Scene Technology.* Englewood Cliffs, NJ: Prentice-Hall, 1985.

Bellman, Willard F. *Scene Design, Stage Lighting, Sound, Costume and Makeup.* New York: Harper & Row, 1983.

Blank, Ben, and Mario R. Garcia. *Professional Video Graphic Design: The Art and Technology.* White Plains, NY: Knowledge Industry Publications, Inc., 1986.

Gillette, Jay Michael. *Theatrical Design and Production.* Mountain View, CA: Mayfield Publishing Co., 1987.

Merritt, Douglas. *Television Graphics—From Pencil to Pixel.* New York: Van Nostrand Reinhold, 1987.

Millerson, Gerald. *Basic TV Staging.* 2d ed. Woburn, MA: Focal Press, 1982.

Vince, John. *Computer Graphics for Graphics Designers.* White Plains, NY: Knowledge Industry Publications, Inc., 1985.

Vince, John. *Dictionary of Computer Graphics.* White Plains, NY: Knowledge Industry Publications, Inc., 1984.

Wershing, Stephen, and Paul Singer. *Computer Graphics and Animation for Corporate Video.* White Plains, NY: Knowledge Industry Publications, Inc., 1988.

White, Tony. *The Animator's Workbook: Step-by-Step Techniques of Drawn Animation.* White Plains, NY: Knowledge Industry Publications, Inc., 1986.

Writing

Armer, Alan A. *Writing the Screenplay: TV and Film.* Belmont, CA: Wadsworth Publishing Co., 1988.

Lee, Robert, and Robert Misiorowski. *Script Models: A Handbook for the Media Writer.* New York: Hastings House, 1978.

Matrazzo, Donna. *The Corporate Scriptwriting Book: A Step-by-Step Guide to Writing Business Films, Videotapes & Slide Shows.* Portland, OR: Communicom, 1985.

Mayeux, Peter E. *Writing for the Broadcast Media.* Boston: Allyn & Bacon, 1985.

Miller, William. *Screenwriting for Narrative Film and Television.* New York: Hastings House, 1980.

Newson, Doug, and James A. Wollert. *Media Writing: Preparing Information for the Mass Media.* Belmont, CA: Wadsworth Publishing Co., 1988.

Stovall, James Glen. *Writing for the Mass Media.* Englewood Cliffs, NJ: Prentice-Hall, 1985.

Van Nostran, William. *The Nonbroadcast Television Writer's Handbook.* White Plains, NY: Knowledge Industry Publications, Inc., 1983.

Wood, Donald N. *Designing the Effective Message: Critical Thinking and Communication.* Dubuque, IA: Kendall/Hunt, 1989.

Careers in Broadcasting

Allman, Paul. *Exploring Careers in Video.* New York: Rosen Publishing Group, 1985.

Berlyn, David W. *Exploring Careers in Cable/TV.* New York: Rosen Publishing Group, 1985.

Career Associates. *Career Choices for Students of Communications and Journalism.* New York: Walker & Company, 1985.

Ellis, Elmo I. *Opportunities in Broadcasting Careers.* Lincolnwood, IL: National Textbook Co., 1986.

Elmore, Garland C. *Communication Media in Higher Education: A Directory of Academic Programs and Faculty in Radio-Television-Film and Related Media.* Annandale, VA: Association for Communication Administration, 1987.

Jurek, Ken. *Careers in Video: Getting Ahead in Professional Television.* White Plains, NY: Knowledge Industry Publications, Inc., 1988.

Martin, Pat. *How to Improve Your Career in Radio: The Major Market Method.* Milwaukee, WI: Pat Martin, 1987.

Pearlman, Donn. *Breaking into Broadcasting: Getting a Good Job in Radio or TV—Out Front or Behind the Scenes.* Chicago: Bonus Books, 1986.

Reed, Maxine K., and Robert M. Reed. *Career Opportunities in Television, Cable, and Video.* 2d ed. New York: Facts on File, 1986.

Bibliography

Index

C

N

Narration, 243
Naturalism, 259
Negative/positive selector, 138
Negotiated fees, 471
Networks, 6
Neutral settings, 257
News programs
  camera perspectives, 150
  microphone selection, 57
  on-line editing, 235
  recorded production elements, 385
  scripted material, 304
  shot variety, 402–3
  unwanted talent, 407
  videotape editing, 214
NewTek, 290
Noise, background, 400, 411–12, 423
Nonbroadcast telecommunications, 8–10, 14
Nondirectional microphone, 48–49
Nonsequential shooting, 313, 405–7
Normalled connections, 30–31

O

Objective perspective, 150
Off-camera lighting effects, 79
Off-camera microphones, 51, 53
Off-line editing, 223, 234–35, 245
Off-mike distortion, 49
Off-set graphics, 278, 279
Omnidirectional microphone, 48–49, 59
On-camera microphones, 51
On-line editing, 222–23, 225, 234–35, 245
On-set graphics, 278–79
Organization, interview, 310
Orientation, audience, 236
Original master reel, 224
Oscilloscopes, 114–16
Outline, script, 306, 357, 397
Out-of-sequence shooting, 313, 405–7
Outpoint, 225, 226, 227, 230
Output
  audio, 30, 34
  mixing, 34
Over-the-shoulder shot (O/S), 152, 155
Overtones, 38, 47, 48, 431–33

P

Pacing, 240–43, 351, 384
Pads, audio, 35, 37
Paint Box, 289
Paint programs, 281
Pan card, 273
Pan control, audio, 41
Panning, camera, 143, 157, 297
Pans. *See* Floodlights
Pantograph, 97
Parallels, 268
Particularized shots, 346, 368
Patch bay
  audio channeling, 29, 30–31, 33
  master control room, 63
Patch board, 17
PC Paintbrush IV Plus, 291
Peak, decibel, 41
Pedestal, camera, 116, 144, 148, 298
Perambulator booms, 53
Performers, 302–10. *See also* Actors; Talent
Permissions, 400
Persistence of vision (visual lag), 126
Personal recording, 10–11
Personnel, rate chart, 470, 471
Perspective
  audio, 59–60
  camera, 149–52
  false lines, 255
  lighting, 78
Phase control selector, 138
Phasing, audio, 61–63
Phonograph records, 44–45, 64–65
Photodiodes, 120
Physical needs, 327–28
Pickup editing, 220
Pickup patterns, 48–50, 59, 60
Pickup tube, 116
Picture composition, 152–57, 334
Pipe grid, 97
Pixels, 120–21, 286
Planning. *See* Preproduction planning
Playback deck, 217
Playing back
  audio, 38–39, 42–44
  video, 113
Polarity reversal, 179

Polar pattern, 48
Political talks, 304
Pop filter, 53
Porter, Edwin, 152
Position jump, 225, 236, 248, 348–49. *See also* Jump cut
Postproduction editing, 162, 218, 324, 379–80, 403. *See also* Editing
Potentiometer, 34, 64, 71
Powder, makeup, 317
Power sources, 206, 400, 413, 417–18. *See also* Batteries; Electricity
Precision, acting, 312, 313
Preedit session, 225
Preparation, interview, 310
"Prepare" command, 181, 183
Preplanning, 248, 423, 424
Preproduction planning
  directing, 22, 373–76
  discipline, 107
  field production, 395–99, 400, 421
Prerecorded sound, 42–46
Prerehearsal, 158
Presence, audio, 59–60
"Preset" command, 183
Pressure-zone microphone (PZM), 53
Preview editing, 226, 246
Preview monitor, 176
Primary colors, 117
Private line (P.L.), 69
Process amplifier, 113
Producing, 21–22, 399–403, 404
Production
  approaches, 12–14
  audio, 68–71
  camera operation on-the-air, 158–59
  clothing and costumes, 314–15
  directing techniques, 378
  graphics use, 297–98
  multiple-camera lighting, 93–95
  operations, 6, 8–12
  stage manager, 328–31
Production assistants, 341–42, 401, 403, 404
Production Cost Report, 472
Production log, 401
Production secretary, 341–42
Professionalism, 426. *See also* Attitude

Time
  associate director, 324, 325–27
  directing techniques, 379
  editing and passage of, 240–41
  transitions, 352–53
Time-base corrector, 113, 180
Time code, 199, 200, 216
Titles, 396
Tone, pictorial design, 255
Tongue move, 148
Top hat, 103
Transducing
  audio, 26–28, 42
  microphone construction, 50
  video, 111
Transitions
  interview, 310
  picture continuity, 351–53
  talk show, 368–69
Transmitter, 21
Transport system, 197–98
Trim function, 229, 241, 246
Tripod, 144, 418
Trucking, camera, 146–47, 298
Turntable, phonograph, 64–65
Two-fold flats, 263
Typewriter, 14, 279

U

Ultimatte, 178–79
U-matic videocassette system, 191, 392, 395
Undercut, 167–68
Unidirectional microphones, 49
Uninterrupted run-through, 377
Unions, labor, 338, 471
Unit manager, 331–32
Unit times, 326
Unity gain, 41
Upcut, 65
Uplinks, 17

V

Vacuum-formed molds, 264
Variable-focal-length zoom lens, 133
Variable-speed control dials, 210
Variety programs, 13, 214
Vectorscope, 114–15, 116
Velocity, 429, 431
Vertical interval time code, 216
Vertical synchronization pulse, 124, 188, 199
VHS systems, 191–92, 393–94
Vibration, 431
Video art, 11–12
Video control room, 17
Video drum, 197
Video-8, 394–95
Video engineers, 277
Video feedback, 179
Video gain, 116, 119
Video Graphics Generator, 289
Video-only editing, 231–32
Video-only insert, 224
Video output control, 138
Video split, 180
Video system. *See also* Camera
  attributes of color, 116–18
  camera image-sensing technologies, 119–21, 123–26
  control components, 113–14
  control functions, 111–12, 113
  depth of field, 131–33
  field procedures, 401
  focal length of lens, 126–29
  focusing characteristics of lens, 129–30
  f-stop aperture, 130–31
  luminance and chrominance signals, 118–19
  operator control adjustments, 136–38
  oscilloscopes, 114–16
  zoom lens, 133–36
Videotape audio tracks, 42, 201
Videotape operator. *See* Recording, engineer

Videotape recording, 13, 17, 187–91
  field audio, 410–11, 419–21
  helical-scan recorders, 191–98
  operations and controls, 201–3, 206–12
  track functions, 198–201
Vidicon tube, 119–20
Viewfinder controls, 138
Vocal commands, 70–71
Voltage, 413
Volume, audio, 34, 58. *See also* Decibel (db) scale
Volume unit (VU) meter, 39–41, 65, 71, 207–8

W

Walk-through rehearsals, 376
Warning lights, 138
Wash lighting, 95
Watts, 413, 417
Waveform monitor, 114, 115–16
Wavelength, 429
White
  balance, 137–38, 417
  color, 117
Wide-angle lens, 126, 128, 129
Wide shot, 151, 346–47, 368, 383
Wildtrack, 411–12, 423
Wind, 270, 409
Windows, 408, 414
Wipe transitions, 171–73, 174, 352
Wireless microphones, 55
Word processor, 14
Workprint, 223, 234
Workstation, computer, 292
Wow, audio, 65
Wrap-up, 426
Writer/researcher, 404

X

X-Y microphone placement, 61

Z

Zoom lens, 126, 130, 133–36, 141–42